World War One

D0082154

World War I and its aftermath witnessed a global revolution. This was reflected in the revolutionary war aims of most of the belligerents, the technological revolution that made the war so deadly, the revolutionary sentiment that grew among ordinary combatants, and the revolutionary pressures that led to the collapse of the Romanov, Habsburg, and Ottoman empires. In this revised edition of *World War One*, Lawrence Sondhaus synthesizes the latest scholarship on the war and incorporates insights from the vast body of work published during the war's centenary. He charts the political, economic, social, and cultural history of the war at home and on the front lines as well as the war's origins, ending and transformative effects on societal norms and attitudes, gender and labor relations, and international trade and finance. The accessible narrative is supported by chronologies, personal accounts, guides to key controversies and debates, and numerous maps and photographs.

Lawrence Sondhaus is Gerald and Marjorie Morgan Professor of European History at the University of Indianapolis. His publications include *German Submarine Warfare in World War I* (2017), *The Great War at Sea* (2014), *Strategic Culture and Ways of War* (2006), *Naval Warfare, 1815–1914* (2001), and *Franz Conrad von Hötzendorf: Architect of the Apocalypse* (2000).

World War One

The Global Revolution

Second edition

Lawrence Sondhaus

University of Indianapolis

CAMBRIDGE
UNIVERSITY PRESS

CAMBRIDGE
UNIVERSITY PRESS

University Printing House, Cambridge CB2 8BS, United Kingdom

One Liberty Plaza, 20th Floor, New York, NY 10006, USA

477 Williamstown Road, Port Melbourne, VIC 3207, Australia

314–321, 3rd Floor, Plot 3, Splendor Forum, Jasola District Centre, New Delhi – 110025, India

79 Anson Road, #06–04/06, Singapore 079906

Cambridge University Press is part of the University of Cambridge.

It furthers the University's mission by disseminating knowledge in the pursuit of education, learning, and research at the highest international levels of excellence.

www.cambridge.org
Information on this title: www.cambridge.org/9781108496193
DOI: 10.1017/9781108866354

© Lawrence Sondhaus 2011, 2021

This publication is in copyright. Subject to statutory exception and to the provisions of relevant collective licensing agreements, no reproduction of any part may take place without the written permission of Cambridge University Press.

First published 2011
Second edition 2021

Printed in the United Kingdom by TJ Books Ltd, Padstow Cornwall

A catalogue record for this publication is available from the British Library.

ISBN 978-1-108-49619-3 Hardback
ISBN 978-1-108-79163-2 Paperback

Cambridge University Press has no responsibility for the persistence or accuracy of URLs for external or third-party internet websites referred to in this publication and does not guarantee that any content on such websites is, or will remain, accurate or appropriate.

Contents

Illustrations

Text illustrations

Chapter opening illustrations

Online essay illustrations

Please visit www.cambridge.org/sondhaus for Online Essays to accompany the book.

Maps

Boxes

Perspectives

Online Essays

Please visit www.cambridge.org/sondhaus for Online Essays to accompany the book.

Preface

The goal of this book is to provide a global history of World War I, useful to general readers as well as to students of history. The thoroughly revised second edition aims to satisfy all readers seeking an up-to-date synthesis of the latest work on the subject. Revolution provides the unifying theme, including coverage of the revolutionary war aims of most of the combatants, the technological revolution that made the war so deadly for those in uniform, the revolutionary sentiment that grew among ordinary combatants (manifested most dramatically in wartime mutinies), and the revolutionary pressures that led to the collapse of the Romanov, Habsburg, and Ottoman empires. Beyond the military, political, and diplomatic realm, the book addresses the war's transformative effects on societal norms and attitudes, gender relations, and labor relations, especially in the urban areas of Europe and America, and on international trade and finance, with the rise of the United States to replace Britain as the center of the global economy.

Among general histories of World War I, this book is distinctive in the manner in which it reflects my insights into the Habsburg Empire and the relationship between Germany and Austria-Hungary. The alliance of the Central Powers not only made possible the start of the war, but also shaped its course and outcome more than most historians (especially those writing in the English language) have recognized or acknowledged. Most Anglophone historians of World War I have completely misunderstood Austria-Hungary and the dynamic between the Central Powers and, as a consequence, have to some extent misunderstood the war. Among the competing works, even those marketed as "global" still reflect either a strong emphasis on the Western front or a greater depth of understanding of the Western front when compared to the other theaters of the conflict (the Eastern, Italian, and Balkan fronts, and the action at sea or beyond Europe). I have endeavored to produce a superior summary account especially of these other theaters as well as the naval war.

With an eye toward making the book as useful as possible to its intended audiences, I have included features that are linked to, but can stand apart from, the main narrative of the text. More than fifty "boxes" provide excerpts of primary documents or voices of individuals, the latter including the broadest possible representation of roles, ranks, classes, and genders, as well as of combatant countries and theaters of action. Six chapters include "Perspectives" boxes providing examples of scholarly debate on the war's most controversial aspects. Each of the fifteen chapters includes a timeline and captioned illustrations, and ends with a list of suggestions for further reading. The number of chapters allows roughly one chapter per week for a course offered in a semester format. The relatively short chapters, further subdivided, should allow instructors great flexibility in assigning readings that match up with their lectures or class topics. Finally, ten topical essays offered in online format shed further light on the human experience in areas such as life in the trenches or aboard a submarine, as well as the learning curve of strategists and tacticians in their use of artillery, air power, and tanks, and the development of combined arms approaches. Such features, supplementing an engaging narrative, should make this book appealing to general readers as well.

Acknowledgments

I owe a great debt of gratitude to the mentors, colleagues, and friends who have influenced my understanding of World War I over the years, and for the countless exchanges and conversations that prompted me to articulate many of the ideas and interpretations now incorporated in this book. The first edition benefited from the helpful comments of three of my colleagues at the University of Indianapolis, Ted Frantz, Milind Thakar, and Joseph Prestia, on the sections concerning the United States, India, and Romania, respectively. The revised edition continues to bear the mark of their insights. I would like to thank my editor, Michael Watson, for his constructive suggestions and overall role in shaping the first edition, and for securing from seven anonymous readers the suggestions for improvements that are reflected in the present volume. I would also like to thank Emily Sharp, editorial assistant, for guiding me through the process of preparing the second edition for publication.

Introduction

"Thank God, it is the Great War!" General Viktor Dankl, commander designate of the Austro-Hungarian First Army, penned these words on July 31, 1914, the day it became clear that the dispute between Austria-Hungary and Serbia, stemming from the assassination of Archduke Francis Ferdinand a month earlier, would not be resolved peacefully or limited to a Balkan war. Forty-three years had passed since the last war that matched European powers against each other and, like many European military officers of his generation, Dankl, then fifty-nine, feared he would serve his entire career without experiencing such a conflict. On August 2, when Dankl in another diary entry referred to the rapidly escalating conflict as "the World War," he could not have imagined just how accurate the label would become: that the action would extend to the Far East, the South Pacific, and sub-Saharan Africa, that more than a million men from the British and French empires would see action on European battlefields, that the United States would have an army of more than 2 million men in France just four years later, or that European countries would account for a minority of the states participating in the postwar peace conference.[1]

World War I as Global Revolution

The central thesis of this book is that World War I and the peace settlement that ended it constituted a global revolution. Like Dankl and the generals, the statesmen who led Europe to war in the summer of 1914 did not envisage the worldwide revolutionary consequences of the conflict whose onset they welcomed (or, at least, did so little to discourage). Though the emergence of the Bolshevik government in Russia would serve as a reminder that the world was not yet safe for democracy, old-fashioned authoritarian governments, Hohenzollern and Habsburg as well as Romanov, had no place in a postwar Europe that featured no fewer than eleven republics on a map redrawn from the Franco-German border deep into Russia, featuring a net increase of six independent states and the elimination of one traditional great power, Dankl's own Austria-Hungary. Beyond Europe, the redistribution of former German colonies affected the map of Africa, East Asia, and the Pacific, while the demise of the Ottoman Empire brought the wholesale redrawing of boundaries in the Middle East and, in Palestine, the roots of the modern-day Arab-Israeli conflict, stemming from Britain's conflicting wartime promises to the Zionist movement and Arab nationalists.

Beyond questions of boundaries and territory, the war would also revolutionize power relationships within European societies. In the Europe of 1914, most adult males lacked truly meaningful voting rights; aside from Portugal, which had just overthrown its king, France had Europe's only republic, and among the other five European powers only Britain and Italy had fully functioning parliamentary governments. Only in Britain, and only recently, had there been a serious movement calling for the extension of women's rights to include the vote. While the war strengthened the position of organized labor and provided unprecedented employment opportunities for women, most of the latter proved to be only temporary. Nevertheless, postwar Europe west of Soviet Russia consisted of democratic republics and constitutional monarchies, few if any restrictions on adult male suffrage still existed, and in their first postwar national elections, Germany and Austria joined Britain in conceding women the right to vote (with the United States following shortly thereafter). In postwar Russia the Soviet government went so far as to grant women the right to abortion on demand.

The war had an equally dramatic impact on Europe's position in the world. White Europeans had enjoyed an unquestioned domination of the world of 1914, a world in which 40 percent of the human race was of European stock. Yet in 1919, the thorniest moral issue facing the peace conference concerned whether to include in the Covenant of the League of Nations a statement of global racial equality. Though proposed (somewhat disingenuously) by Japan, the debate reflected Europe's loss of stature, both symbolically and demographically, in the world as a whole. Indeed, as an example of European fallibility, World War I sowed the seeds of the anti-colonial movement that erupted after World War II, by which time the population explosion in the non-Western world further reduced the relative weight of a Europe that had never recovered from the demographic shock of World War I, a war in which the overwhelming majority of the millions killed had been Europeans or of European stock.

Conceptualizing the "First" World War

By the first days of August 1914 many observers and participants joined Viktor Dankl in acknowledging the onset of a "Great War" or "World War," the likes of which Europe had not seen since the end of the age of Napoleon a century earlier. The Napoleonic Wars, and the wars for empire in early modern Europe, had featured worldwide action on the high seas and in the colonies, as well as on European battlefields, but by the end of August the scope and intensity of the unfolding conflict, in which most of the belligerents already had lost more men in a single day or even a single battle than in entire wars fought during the nineteenth century or earlier, led most to recognize that they were witnessing something unprecedented. In September 1914, in remarks quoted in the American press, German biologist and philosopher Ernst Haeckel made the first recorded reference to the conflict as the "First World War," in his prediction that the emerging struggle "will become the first world war in the full sense of the word."[2] The label "First World War" or "World War I" did not gain currency until after September 1939, when *Time* magazine and a host of other publications popularized its use as a corollary of the term "Second World War" or "World War II," but as early as 1920 British officer and peacetime journalist Charles à Court Repington published his war memoirs under the title *The First World War, 1914–1918*.[3] In the interwar years a handful of cynics and pessimists used "First World War" rather than the more common "Great War" or "World War," to reflect their dismay that it had not been, as Woodrow Wilson had hoped, "the war to end all wars."

The use of the term, since 1939, reflects our conceptualization of World War I as the precursor to World War II, a belief universal enough to accommodate not only polar opposite views of the nature of the causation (e.g. that World War II occurred because Germany had not been completely crushed during World War I, or that it occurred because Germany had been needlessly antagonized at the peace table afterward), but, more so, the remarkable diversity of lessons learned and applied by the countries, leaders, and peoples involved. Whereas in Germany and Russia the Nazi and Soviet regimes proved to be far more efficient and ruthless than their predecessors of 1914 in mobilizing their countries for war and seeing it through to the bitter end, regardless of the cost in human lives, the Western European democracies, the British Dominions, and Italy showed little desire to repeat the blood sacrifice of World War I, and in various ways tailored their strategies accordingly, disastrously so for France and Italy. The United States, whose people were not yet ready to embrace the mantle of global leadership at the end of World War I, a generation later rallied to the cause with great fervor after the shock of Pearl Harbor, while their leaders benefited from the experience of 1917–18 in mobilizing American resources to fight World War II. Of the considerable resources of the United States only its manpower made a difference in World War I, as the fighting ended before American industrial might could be brought to bear;

thus, both Germany and Japan fatefully underestimated the war-making capacity and national resolve of the United States in World War II.

World War I and Modern Total War

No less than in the public and political realm, World War I produced radically different responses to the same lessons learned in military strategy, tactics, and operations. The bloody stalemate of the trenches on the Western front led Germany to develop the Blitzkrieg in order to eliminate static positional warfare, while France built the Maginot Line in an attempt to perfect static positional warfare. Thanks to the German example, which built upon the British example of the late summer of 1918, it became the norm in World War II for offensives by infantry to be supported by sufficient numbers of tanks and aircraft to avoid bogging down as they had in World War I, except in cases where the fighting was in or near a major city, or in the confined space of a Pacific island. World War II featured more lethal iterations of every weapon and battlefield tactic that had revolutionized warfare during World War I, with the notable exception of the use of poison gas.

The magnitude of death and destruction wrought by World War II far surpassed that of World War I, especially for civilian populations, yet from August 1914 onward World War I featured acts of brutality against non-combatants that presaged what would happen on a far greater scale a quarter of a century later. From the summary executions of Belgian civilians by German troops and of Serbs by Austro-Hungarians, to the persecution and, ultimately, genocidal slaughter of the Ottoman Empire's Armenians, to the aerial bombing of London and other cities by German Zeppelins, civilian populations endured atrocities the likes of which Europe and its periphery had not seen since the Thirty Years' War (1618–48) marked the end of the Catholic-Protestant wars of religion. Meanwhile, at sea the indiscriminate sinking of millions of tons of Allied shipping by German submarines cost thousands of lives and foreshadowed the unrestricted submarine warfare campaigns of both sides in World War II, while the Allied (primarily British) naval blockade of the Central Powers brought malnutrition to the home fronts of Germany and Austria and, ultimately, illness and premature death to hundreds of thousands of their most vulnerable civilians. Remarkably, the home-front populations not only endured these unprecedented hardships but, in most cases, became firmer in their resolve as the war dragged on. Indeed, while war weariness ultimately triggered the revolutionary collapses in Russia in 1917 and Germany and Austria-Hungary in 1918, for most of World War I their civilians persevered just as their counterparts in the Western Allied countries did, rejecting the notion of a compromise peace that would render meaningless not just their personal privations but, more important, the deaths of their sons, brothers, fathers, and other loved ones. Such perseverance served notice to political leaders of the risk as well as the reward in mobilizing a country for a total war effort in the era of modern nationalism: a war could not be won without such support, but once governments received it, war became an all-or-nothing proposition, for their own people would not accept compromise as the reward for such sacrifices. The infamous remark attributed to Joseph Stalin during his great purges of the 1930s, that one death is a tragedy, a million deaths a statistic, could just as easily have been applied to the bloodletting of World War I and, indeed, would have been unthinkable if that bloodletting had not come first. World War I, in so many ways a global revolution, above all else redefined what people could accept, endure, or justify, and thus stands as a milepost in the human experience for the extent to which it desensitized so much of humanity to the inhumanity of modern warfare.

NOTES

1. Dankl quoted in Holger H. Herwig, *The First World War: Germany and Austria* (London: Arnold, 1997), 55.
2. Fred R. Shapiro, *The Yale Book of Quotations* (New Haven, CT: Yale University Press, 2006), 329.
3. Charles à Court Repington, *The First World War, 1914–1918* (London: Constable, 1920).

Wedding of Archduke Charles, 1911

Among Europe's great powers of 1914 only Austria-Hungary had no dominant nationality, making the Habsburg dynasty the focal point of state unity. In this photograph, taken in 1911 at the last prewar Habsburg wedding, Emperor Francis Joseph (1830–1916), center, congratulates his great-nephew Archduke Charles (1887–1922) and his bride Princess Zita of Bourbon-Parma (1892–1989), as the bride's mother, Maria Antonia of Parma (1862–1959), looks on. Charles became Francis Joseph's successor after the emperor's nephew and heir, Archduke Francis Ferdinand (1863–1914), pictured left, looking out of frame, was assassinated on June 28, 1914, touching off the crisis that led to World War I.

1 The World in 1914 and the Origins of the War

1878	Congress of Berlin alters Balkan borders; Ottoman Empire weakened.
1882	Triple Alliance formed (Germany, Austria-Hungary, Italy).
1889–1914	Second Socialist International provides leading forum against militarism.
1892–94	France and Russia conclude military convention and treaty of alliance.
1898	German Reichstag approves "Tirpitz Plan" for naval expansion.
1898	Spanish-American War signals emergence of the United States as an imperial power.
1899–1902	Anglo-Boer War exposes Britain's isolation; Anglo-Japanese alliance (1902).
1903	Coup in Serbia installs pro-Russian Karageorgević dynasty.
1904–05	Entente Cordiale links France with Britain. Russo-Japanese War foreshadows trench warfare.
1906	HMS *Dreadnought* commissioned; Anglo-German naval race accelerates.
1907	Anglo-Russian Entente completes Triple Entente.
1908	Austria-Hungary annexes Bosnia (occupied since 1878).
1911–12	Italo-Turkish War features first combat use of airplanes.
1912–13	Balkan Wars further weaken Ottoman Empire, destabilize region.

The controversy over the origins of World War I began in the summer of 1914, as soon as the declarations of war were exchanged. The decision of the victors to include a war-guilt clause in the Treaty of Versailles reflected their conviction, unanimous as of 1919, that Germany had been responsible for the war. Their verdict was rejected by virtually all German academicians and, during the 1920s, by a broad spectrum of revisionist historians who blamed the alliance system, the great powers collectively, or one or more of the great powers other than Germany. While the experience of World War II refocused the lion's share of the responsibility on Germany, the scholarship of subsequent decades further explored the roles of all of the belligerents, their domestic politics, diplomatic alignments, and war aims as of 1914. General factors such as nationalism and other ideologies, the faith military men placed in offensive warfare, and the prewar arms races likewise received greater scrutiny.

The crisis resulting in the outbreak of World War I occurred within a system of international relations dating from the Peace of Westphalia (1648) at the end of the Thirty Years' War. Europe's four to six most powerful states made or broke alliances in pursuit of their own interests, within an overall balance of power, but rarely divided into mutually hostile armed camps in peacetime. This changed in the decade prior to the outbreak of World War I, when Britain, France, and Russia formed the Triple Entente in response to the Triple Alliance of Germany, Austria-Hungary, and Italy. The Triple Alliance, established in 1882, by 1914 ranked as the longest running multilateral peacetime alliance in European history, enduring despite the strong mutual animosity of Austria-Hungary and Italy because each considered the friendship of Germany indispensable, for the former against Russia and for the latter against France. The Triple Entente, in contrast, had been formed by three separate agreements – the Franco-Russian military convention and treaty of alliance (1892–94), the Anglo-French Entente Cordiale (1904), and the Anglo-Russian Entente (1907) – each motivated by a fear of the growing might of Germany.

The Triple Alliance: Germany, Austria-Hungary, Italy

Germany achieved political unification under Prussia thanks to the leadership of Otto von Bismarck, whose victorious wars against Denmark (1864), Austria (1866), and France (1870–71) led to the creation of the Second Reich, with Prussia's King William I as emperor. While Bismarck annexed Schleswig-Holstein from Denmark and Alsace-Lorraine from France, he made Austria (from 1867, Austria-Hungary) Germany's closest ally and a cornerstone of a post-1871 alliance system designed to keep France isolated. The constitution of Imperial Germany provided for a strong chancellor accountable to the emperor rather than to a legislative majority. Bismarck held the office from 1871 until 1890, followed by seven less capable men, most notably Bernhard von Bülow (1900–09), who served as foreign secretary before becoming chancellor (see Box 1.1), and Theobald von Bethmann Hollweg (1909–17). The Reichstag judged bills placed before it but could not initiate legislation. Balancing these authoritarian aspects, the constitution of 1871 made Germany the second European power after France to hold elections based on universal male suffrage. Between 1890 and 1913 the German population boomed from 49 million to 67 million, and urban areas doubled in size. Germany's per capita gross domestic product (GDP) ranked behind only the United States, Britain, and the British Dominions, and its industrial productivity surpassed that of Britain. Politically, these developments benefited the Social Democratic Party (SPD), favorite of the growing working class, which gained strength despite Bismarck's constitution not having provided for redistricting to account for population shifts. In the election of 1912, the SPD won 35 percent of the vote – twice as much as any other party – and 27 percent of the seats in the Reichstag. The rise of the SPD concerned Emperor William II (Figure 1.1) and conservative leaders, because it favored reforms that would make Germany a true constitutional monarchy and also

Box 1.1 **Germany's "place in the sun"**

In his first speech to the Reichstag on December 6, 1897, Bernhard von Bülow (1849–1929), foreign minister from 1897 to 1900 and chancellor from 1900 to 1909, issued a thinly veiled retort to the British boast that "the sun never sets on the British Empire." Defending the onset of German imperialism in China – the seizure of Kiaochow (Jiaozhou), in retaliation for the murder of two German Catholic missionaries in China on November 6 – he asserted that Germany, too, must have her "place in the sun":

The days when Germans granted one neighbor the earth, the other the sea, and reserved for themselves the sky, where pure doctrine reigns – those days are over. We see it as our foremost task to foster and cultivate the interests of our shipping, our trade, and our industry, particularly in the East. A division of our cruisers was dispatched to and occupied the port of Kiaochow to secure full atonement for the murder of German and Catholic

missionaries and to assure greater security against the recurrence of such events in the future.

… We must demand that German missionaries, merchants, goods, as well as the German flag and German vessels be treated with the same respect in China that other powers enjoy. We are happy to respect the interests of other powers in China, secure in the knowledge that our own interests will also receive the recognition they deserve. In short, we do not want to put anyone in our shadow, but we also demand our place in the sun.

True to the tradition of German policy, we will make every effort to protect our rights and interests in East Asia … without unnecessary harshness, but without weakness either.

Source: Bernhard von Bülow on Germany's "place in the sun" (1897), translated by Adam Blauhut for *German History in Documents and Images*, available at germanhistorydocs.ghi-dc.org/sub_document. cfm?document_id=783, from *Stenographische Berichte über die Verhandlungen des Reichstags*, vol. 1, IX LP, 5th Session (Berlin, 1898), 60.

Figure 1.1 William II

Emperor William II (1859–1941, German emperor 1888–1918) in the uniform of a Prussian field marshal. Son of an English mother (Queen Victoria's eldest daughter), William considered Britain to be Germany's primary role model as well as its greatest rival. His favorites included Admiral Alfred von Tirpitz, whom he appointed to head the Imperial Navy Office in 1897. William supported Tirpitz's fleet plan and the pursuit of German world power status (*Weltpolitik*) even though it drove Britain to form the Triple Entente with France and Russia. The volatile emperor became notorious for his gaffes, most notably the *Daily Telegraph* affair of 1908, touched off by an interview with a leading British newspaper including his opinions on foreign policy. The affair raised concerns about William's instability and led some Germans to call for his abdication. Afterward he played a less active role in the affairs of state and, during the war, acquiesced in the army's domination of the German home front.

opposed the country's aggressive foreign policy, consistently voting against funding for Europe's strongest army and second strongest navy. The fleet did more harm than good to Germany's strategic interests, pushing Britain into the camp of its traditional rivals, France and Russia, while growing to consume more than one-third of the defense outlay. Only in 1913 did the Reichstag reverse the trend, approving an 18 percent increase in the size of Germany's peacetime army, to 890,000 men.

After defeat at the hands of Prussia in 1866 ended its traditional role in German affairs, the Austrian Empire transformed itself into the Dual Monarchy of Austria-Hungary. Henceforth, Francis Joseph (emperor since 1848) reigned over a uniquely constructed state with a common foreign policy, army, and navy, but separate prime ministers, cabinets, and parliaments at Vienna and Budapest. Austria and Hungary maintained separate law codes, citizenship, and reserve military formations, and renegotiated their economic relationship every ten years. This "compromise of 1867" aimed at bringing domestic peace to the multinational Habsburg domain by elevating the ethnic Hungarians (Magyars) to co-equal status with the traditionally dominant German Austrians, but because the latter accounted for just 25 percent of Francis Joseph's subjects and the Magyars 20 percent, it excluded more than it included. For Austria-Hungary, more so than any other European power, domestic and foreign policies were inextricably linked. The Dual Monarchy's per capita GDP trailed every European power other than Russia, and half of its foreign trade was with Germany, putting it in the uncomfortable position of dependent ally. But both of the dominant nationalities supported Austria-Hungary's close ties with the Second Reich (German Austrians viewing it as the next best thing to being part of Germany, Magyars as the best insurance against a Russian invasion from the east). The Panslav movement, supported by Russia, appealed to the intelligentsia of the Slavic nationalities that made up almost half of the overall population of 52 million (as of 1913), and the millions of Italians, Romanians, and Serbs within the empire affected its relations with those neighboring states. Each half of the empire took its own approach to the nationality problem, neither providing much hope for the future. Austria gave all nationalities access to its parliament via universal male suffrage, granted in 1907, but ended up with twenty-two parties in the Reichsrat of 1911, leaving prime ministers unable to govern without frequent resort to the emperor's emergency powers. In contrast, Hungary's restricted franchise kept power in the hands of Magyars, and except for a fixed number of seats reserved for Croatians, the rest of the population went unrepresented. Francis Ferdinand, nephew and heir of the aging Francis Joseph, hoped to reduce dependence on Germany and reorganize the empire to empower the South Slavs as a third political force. Such ideas earned him the enmity of many German Austrians, virtually all Magyars, and those Slavs (the Serbs in particular) who feared a revitalization of the empire. Austria-Hungary had the smallest army, per capita, of any European power, with a peacetime strength of just under 400,000. The small but respectable navy – one of the empire's only truly integrated, multinational institutions – by 1912 received more than 20 percent of the total defense outlay.

Italy achieved national unity in the same decade as Germany, with Sardinia-Piedmont playing the role of Prussia and its monarch, Victor Emmanuel II, becoming king. The similarities ended there. Italy relied upon France in the war of 1859 to drive Austria from most of its northern Italian possessions, acquired Venetia by allying with Prussia against Austria in 1866 (despite being defeated by the Austrians on land and at sea), and secured Rome upon the demise of the pope's protector, Napoleon III, at the hands of Prussia in 1870. Afterward, Italians remained self-conscious about the less than glorious nature of their unification. Under Italy's British-style constitutional monarchy, the centrist Liberal party dominated parliament from 1870 to 1914, in part because so many conservative Catholics heeded the call of Pope Pius IX to protest the annexation of Rome by boycotting Italian politics altogether. The issue of the pope's status vis-à-vis the Italian state – unresolved until Benito Mussolini's Lateran Treaty of 1929 established Vatican City – also affected the kingdom internationally. Official visits from countries with large Catholic populations, including Italy's own allies, Germany and Austria-Hungary, had to be hosted in cities other than Rome. Italian statesmen who saw France as their country's primary rival championed the Triple Alliance and, after 1882, developed Mediterranean and African ambitions that depended upon German diplomatic support, accepting as part of the bargain alliance with the Austrians and continued Austrian possession of ethnic Italian territories in the Alps (the South Tyrol or Trentino) and on the Adriatic Sea. Italy's industrialized north boosted its per capita GDP to a level significantly higher than Austria-Hungary, but it ranked as the least of the great powers in population (35 million in 1913) and in armed might. Indeed, Italy had the smallest standing army (just over 250,000 men) of any European power except Britain, and every other great power except Austria-Hungary had a larger navy. Italy lost faith in the Triple Alliance after 1900, when the deterioration of Anglo-German relations raised the specter of war with Britain, but on the eve of World War I the Italo-Turkish War (1911–12) damaged Italy's relations with all three members of the Triple Entente and resulted in the renewal of the Triple Alliance in 1912.

The Triple Entente: Britain, France, Russia

Under the Pax Britannica of the Victorian era, Britain had functioned as global hegemon, claiming one-quarter of the world's land surface, dominating its oceans with the largest navy, and dominating its economy with an industrial sector that for years out-produced all other countries combined. Secure in its "splendid isolation," Britain also wielded a great deal of what international relations specialists call "soft power," not only because of its widely admired parliamentary system and concepts of individual rights, but also its tremendous influence over world culture on both the elite and popular levels. Internationally, these achievements sparked a complex mixture of admiration, envy, and in some cases outright hostility. The Anglo-Boer War (1899–1902) underscored the isolation of Britain and made British leaders self-conscious about it. Afterward they moved quickly to conclude an alliance with Japan (1902), the Entente Cordiale with France (1904), and rapprochement with Russia (1907), the latter two agreements laying the groundwork for the Triple Entente. In per capita GDP Britain still led Europe, but had fallen behind the United States, and its aging industrial base had been surpassed by Germany in key areas such as steel production. Nevertheless, the Royal Navy's innovative battleship *Dreadnought* (1906) (Figure 1.2) and battle cruiser designs enabled Britain to face down the German naval threat. The Liberal government of Herbert Asquith (prime minister 1908–16) paid for naval expansion and an ambitious social welfare program with unprecedented taxes on the rich, proposed in Chancellor of the Exchequer David Lloyd George's "People's Budget" of 1909. When the predominantly Conservative House of Lords vetoed the budget, the Liberals fought back with the Parliament Act of 1911, eliminating the veto power of the Lords and paving the way for the passage of Home Rule for Ireland (home to almost 5 million of Britain's prewar population of 46 million), which Liberals had long championed and Conservatives opposed. The Labour Party, an emerging third force in British politics, supported the Liberals on reform and Ireland, but none of the three parties had the courage to embrace women's suffrage, whose proponents after 1910 adopted increasingly violent tactics. On

Figure 1.2 HMS *Dreadnought*

HMS *Dreadnought* (18,110 tons, 527 ft long, ten 12-inch (30-cm) guns, 11 inches (28 cm) of armor, with a speed of 21 knots), laid down in October 1905, commissioned in December 1906. The *Dreadnought* featured the lethal combination of unprecedented size, all big-gun armament, and turbine engines. It revolutionized naval shipbuilding worldwide, rendering all existing "pre-dreadnought" battleships obsolete. By 1914 every European power had "dreadnought" battleships in service or nearing completion, as did the United States, Japan, and several second-tier naval powers. Like nuclear weapons later in the twentieth century, dreadnoughts meant that a country mattered in global or regional balances of power, and the ability to build them from one's own domestic resources became the measure of true great power status. Ironically HMS *Dreadnought* never fought a battle, as the prewar naval race gave Britain dozens of dreadnoughts larger and more formidable than the original. It was not with the Grand Fleet at Jutland in 1916, and was sold for scrap in 1921.

the eve of war Home Rule finally passed into law, effective September 1914, only to be suspended by Asquith for the war's duration, embittering Ireland's Catholic majority and strengthening the revolutionary elements within it. In order to win the naval race with Germany, Britain increased naval spending by 57 percent between 1907 and 1913; in the same years, spending on Britain's 200,000-man volunteer army rose by just 6 percent. The relative decline of Britain in Europe increased the strategic significance of its empire (see "Dominions and Colonies" section below).

As of 1914, France was arguably Europe's most vulnerable great power other than Austria-Hungary, but its deepening partnership with Britain under the Entente

Cordiale, the rapid recovery of Russia from its defeat in the Russo-Japanese War, and the Anglo-Russian rapprochement of 1907 had improved its strategic situation considerably. The isolation France had endured between the Franco-Prussian War (1870–71) and the conclusion of the Franco-Russian military convention (1892) was a thing of the past. The Third Republic, established after Napoleon III's defeat at Sedan in 1870, featured a strong legislature and a weak, indirectly elected president, sacrificing stability to spare it the fate of France's two previous republics (which gave way to Bonaparte monarchies in 1804 and 1852). Between 1871 and 1914 the premiership changed hands forty-nine times. During its isolation the Third Republic expanded the French overseas empire, and after nearly coming to blows with Britain on the Nile at Fashoda (1898) leveraged British support under the Entente to face down German designs on Morocco in two crises (1905–06 and 1911), emerging with a protectorate there. The conservative French Army was deeply shaken by the Dreyfus Affair (1894–1906), in which Captain Alfred Dreyfus, the only Jewish officer on the general staff, stood accused of passing secrets to the Germans. The affair revealed a deep political and social divide between conservative Catholics and liberal secularists; the latter, triumphant following Dreyfus' exoneration, scrapped Napoleon's Concordat of 1801, thus achieving separation of church and state, and pressed for a more egalitarian army with a two-year service term. These measures helped to provoke a conservative backlash in the legislative elections of 1910, and the second Moroccan crisis the following year ushered in a "nationalist revival." The issue of Alsace-Lorraine returned to the forefront, personified by Raymond Poincaré (president 1913–20), a son of Lorraine, for whom the fate of the lost provinces formed the foundation of a visceral anti-Germanism. Among the European powers France ranked third in per capita GDP, only narrowly trailing Germany, but demographic trends left the French in no position to fight the Germans on their own, in part because France was the first country whose population had practiced birth control on a widespread basis. By the late 1800s, France had Europe's lowest birth rate, and in 1913 its population stood at 40 million, just 2 million more than in 1890. The year before the outbreak of war France increased its peacetime army to 700,000 men (compared with Germany's 890,000), but only by resorting to a three-year service term (to Germany's two) and increasing defense spending to 36 percent of the national budget (to Germany's 20 percent). France's allies would not support an attempt to reconquer Alsace-Lorraine in an aggressive war, but once a general war broke out, neither the French nor their allies would accept a peace that left the provinces in German hands.

Tsarist Russia and republican France, ideologically the most unlikely of partners, on the eve of World War I had Europe's closest alliance. Russia entered the twentieth century with the continent's last absolute monarchy and most backward economy. The country was industrializing rapidly thanks in part to loans from France, but 40 percent of its foreign trade was with Germany, the leading importer of Russian grain. In per capita GDP Russia trailed even Austria-Hungary by a wide margin, and only 7 percent of Tsar Nicholas II's 175 million subjects lived in urban areas. Few peasants had prospered after the abolition of serfdom in 1861, and their disaffection, along with that of the country's small, overburdened working class, led to a revolution against Nicholas in 1905, during Russia's lost war against Japan. The tsar saved his throne by agreeing to a limited constitutional monarchy; the Russian prime minister (like the German chancellor) was responsible only to the monarch, and the parliament, or Duma, that opened in 1906 was elected on a restricted franchise that left most peasants and workers unrepresented. In 1907, Russia ended its long-term rivalry with Britain in an agreement that delineated their respective spheres of interest from Persia across Central Asia to the Far East. Defeat at the hands of Japan and entente with Britain left the Balkans as Russia's only outlet for future expansion. Russian Panslavism struck a chord with the emerging Slavic nations of the Balkans – Serbia, Montenegro, and Bulgaria – all of whom also shared Russia's Eastern Orthodox faith. Russia likewise had friends in Romania and Greece, which were Orthodox but not Slavic, and the entire region appreciated Russia for its historical role as the primary enemy of Ottoman Turkey. Because Russian Panslavists also encouraged revolutionary elements among the Slavs of Austria-Hungary, the Dual Monarchy provided sanctuary and support to Russian revolutionaries, including Lenin, Trotsky, Stalin, and most other Bolshevik leaders of 1917, all of whom were living in Austria-Hungary as of 1914, as well as Polish socialist Józef Piłsudski, who received command of a Polish legion serving alongside Austro-Hungarian troops on the Eastern front shortly after the war began. Russia's 1.3 million-man army, the world's largest, had been wracked by mutinies during the Russo-Japanese War, and most of the navy had been sunk. Both recovered quickly afterward, though the country still lacked the industrial base to support them adequately. By 1914, the degree to which Germany and Austria-Hungary underestimated Russia was perhaps Russia's greatest strategic asset.

The Ottoman Empire and the Balkan Wars

Ever since the Ottoman Turks seized Constantinople and overthrew the Byzantine Empire in 1453, the southeastern European lands known as the Balkans (after the Balkan Mountains of eastern Serbia and Bulgaria) had served as a bridge between Europe and the Muslim Middle East. After their apogee of power in 1683, when the sultan's armies last laid siege to Vienna, the Turks lost strength and territory on a consistent basis: to the Austrians in the western Balkans, to the Russians in the Caucasus and around the Black Sea, and eventually to local independence or autonomist movements (supported by various great powers) in the eastern and southern Balkans and in North Africa. Not without justification, the statesmen of the nineteenth century labeled the Ottoman Empire "the sick man of Europe."

During the nineteenth century the Ottoman Empire sought to modernize itself, yet with no industrial revolution of its own it became dependent upon Europe for arms, manufactured goods, and the expertise to construct its railways and exploit its raw materials. The Turks (like the Chinese and Japanese later) granted humiliating extraterritorial privileges to foreigners who managed these projects; after the Ottoman government defaulted on its loans in 1882, Europeans even administered the state debt. Sultans used their absolute powers to reorganize their armed forces, bureaucracy, schools, and legal system along European lines, but these measures only earned them the enmity of local and regional noblemen, Islamic leaders, and devout Muslims in general, foreshadowing the travails of twentieth-century Middle Eastern rulers who would attempt to establish more secular states. In particular, secularization jeopardized the loyalties of the empire's non-Turkish Muslim population – mostly Arab, mostly Sunni – because for centuries Turkish sultans had also been recognized as caliphs (successors to the Prophet Muhammad) by the Sunni majority of the world's Muslims. Ironically, the Ottomans succumbed not to the opponents of reform, but to frustrated advocates of greater reform. The Young Turks, established in 1889, sought to reduce the sultan to a figurehead and revitalize the empire as a secular, constitutional Turkish national state. They gradually infiltrated the Ottoman army officer corps and seized power in a coup in 1908, thereafter ruling as the Unionist Party (Committee of Union and Progress). Their program included legal equality for all nationalities and freedom of religion, but also established Turkish as the official language. These measures threatened the empire's Arab and Armenian populations, and especially the Slavs in the part of the Balkans still under Turkish rule.

At the time of the Young Turk coup, the Balkans had been stable since the Congress of Berlin (1878), which had left Serbia, Montenegro, and Romania independent, Bulgaria autonomous but still under Ottoman suzerainty, and Bosnia-Herzegovina still technically Ottoman but occupied by Austria-Hungary. Fearing a change for the worse under the Young Turks, in 1908 Austria-Hungary annexed Bosnia-Herzegovina and Bulgaria declared its independence. Thereafter the Turks faced the loss of their remaining Balkan territories – Albania, Macedonia, and Thrace – which were coveted in whole or in part by Bulgaria, Serbia, Montenegro, and Greece. After the Turks became embroiled in the Italo-Turkish War (1911–12), these four states formed the Balkan League and mobilized for war. In October 1912, just as the Turks made peace with the Italians by relinquishing Libya, the Balkan League declared war on the Ottoman Empire, initiating the First Balkan War. Russia supported the Balkan League and Austria-Hungary the Ottomans, and tensions between them became serious enough for each to partially mobilize its army. When the war ended in May 1913, the great powers allowed Serbia to keep Kosovo and Greece to retain Epirus, but assigned the rest of Albanian territory to a new independent state. Greece also received Crete and, with Serbia, partitioned Macedonia, limiting Bulgaria's gains to Thrace. Public outrage over the meager spoils prompted Bulgaria to go to war with Serbia and Greece just one month later, in the hope of securing a share of Macedonia. In the brief Second Balkan War the Turks resumed hostilities against the Bulgarians and Montenegro also intervened, but the entry of Romania (neutral in the First Balkan War) proved decisive as Bulgaria abandoned some of its earlier Thracian gains in order to defend itself against Romanians invading from the north. In the peace settlement of August 1913, Bulgaria retained Western Thrace and an outlet to the Aegean Sea, but returned Eastern Thrace to the Ottoman Empire and ceded Southern Dobruja to Romania. The Balkan wars left the region more volatile than ever. Ottoman territorial losses (in the Italo-Turkish War as well as the Balkan wars) had reduced the empire's population to just 21 million, down from 39 million in 1897, although the Turks still governed 6 million non-Muslims.

In January 1913, as the First Balkan War was winding down, the Young Turks established a one-party state. Leaders of this second coup included Ismail Enver Beyefendi (Enver Bey), who became war minister at age 31. His subsequent role in reconquering Eastern Thrace in the Second Balkan War earned him the title of pasha, and early in 1914 he added the role of chief of the general staff. In these capacities he worked closely with General Otto Liman von Sanders, head of a German military mission established at Constantinople in October 1913. Because the Turks (at least since the Crimean War) had relied upon Britain and France for protection against Russia, the alignment of those powers in the Triple Entente pushed the Ottoman Empire toward Germany. Meanwhile, a British naval mission continued to advise the Turkish fleet, which traditionally relied upon Britain for warships and ordnance. In 1914 the Ottoman Navy had three dreadnoughts under construction in British shipyards, and the fate of these ships weighed heavily in the calculations of the Unionist government.

Serbia and the Balkan States on the Eve of War

The Balkan wars left each of the Balkan countries larger in territory and population but also dissatisfied. The outcome alarmed Austria-Hungary in particular, as Serbia doubled in size, increasing its population to 4.5 million and its battle-tested army to 260,000, but it still coveted Bosnia-Herzegovina (where Serbs accounted for only a plurality of a heterogeneous population) and an outlet to the sea. Ever since Serbia achieved autonomy within the Ottoman Empire in 1830, its throne had alternated between the pro-Russian Karageorgević dynasty and the pro-Austrian Obrenović dynasty. The latter returned to power in 1858, accepted the Austro-Hungarian occupation of Bosnia-Herzegovina in 1878, and in general pursued a foreign policy that was not ambitious enough for Serbian nationalists. Finally, in 1903, Captain Dragutin Dimitrijević and a group of junior army officers murdered King Alexander I and installed Peter Karageorgević as king. By 1914 the volatile Dimitrijević had risen to the rank of colonel and extended his influence within the army via his roles as professor at the Serbian war academy and chief of army intelligence. At the same time, he was active in the semi-secret National Defense (*Narodna Odbrana*), founded in 1908 to undermine Austria-Hungary. Later, working under the revolutionary alias "Apis," he directed the terrorist group Union or Death (*Ujedinjenje ili Smrt*), also known as the Black Hand. With the Karageorgević dynasty back on the throne, relations with Russia warmed considerably, but the Serbs were deeply disappointed in 1908–09 when the Russians failed to support them after Austria-Hungary proclaimed the annexation of Bosnia-Herzegovina. Serbia mobilized its army, prompting Austria-Hungary to order a partial mobilization of its own, but when Germany backed Austria-Hungary, Russia backed down. Afterward, Serbia promised to cease its efforts to undermine Austria-Hungary but did nothing to stop the Black Hand from recruiting and training Bosnian Serbs for assassination attempts against Habsburg officials in the south Slav lands of Austria-Hungary. Following an unsuccessful attack against the military governor of Bosnia in 1910, the Black Hand shot and wounded a member of the Croatian government in 1912 and the governor of Croatia in 1913.

The Black Hand cast a long shadow over the domestic politics of Serbia. Nikola Pašić, five-time prime minister whose Radical Party governed the country after 1903, shared Dimitrijević's goal of a Greater Serbia including Bosnia-Herzegovina and adjacent south Slav lands, which could be achieved only by the dismemberment of Austria-Hungary. Pašić feared a backlash over the terrorist attacks, but was too intimidated to take action against Dimitrijević and his growing rogue element within the army officer corps. In the decade before 1914 the Radical Party led the way in democratizing Serbian politics, at the same time promoting and exploiting nationalist sentiments. Fatefully, in the summer of 1914 the crisis following the Black Hand's assassination of Francis Ferdinand coincided with an election campaign in Serbia, generating nationalist rhetoric that inflamed public opinion within the country and heightened the level of outrage across the border in Austria-Hungary.

Aside from Serbia, Montenegro ranked as the most anti-Austrian of the Balkan states. It coveted the small but strategically important bay of Cattaro (Kotor) at the southern tip of Dalmatia, a vital base for the Austro-Hungarian Navy, and also resented the Austrian role in bringing about the end of the First Balkan War, after which it had to turn over some of its hard-won gains to the new Albanian state. For Bulgaria, bitterness over the outcome of the Second Balkan War overrode whatever Panslav and Eastern Orthodox kinship it had once felt for the Serbs, the Montenegrins, or their Russian patrons. King Ferdinand I, born a German prince in Vienna, was leaning hard toward Germany and Austria-Hungary by 1914. Romania, whose king, Carol I, was a Hohenzollern cousin of William II, had an alliance with the Central Powers dating from 1883. After the Second Balkan War, Hungary's province of Transylvania was the only predominantly Romanian territory not under Romanian control, but Romania feared Russia more than it wanted Transylvania, and thus maintained the safer course of alignment with Germany and Austria-Hungary. The Hohenzollerns likewise enjoyed a connection with Greece, whose King Constantine I had married William II's sister. After World War I began, Constantine would struggle to keep Greece neutral in the face of rising pro-Entente sentiments among the Greek public (which grew stronger after the Ottoman Empire and Bulgaria became allies of Germany and Austria-Hungary). At the outbreak of war, no Balkan state was more vulnerable than Albania, created in 1913 in the wake of the First Balkan War, because neither Austria-Hungary nor Italy wanted Serbia to gain a foothold on the Adriatic. Early in 1914 the great powers installed an obscure German prince, William of Wied, as the country's ruler, but his Muslim subjects never accepted him. He reigned for just six months before abdicating shortly after the outbreak of war, leaving behind a country in chaos, among neighbors all too eager to plunge into the abyss in the hope of emerging with their national goals fulfilled.

The Dilemma of Europe's Smaller States

The division of the great powers of Europe between the Triple Alliance and Triple Entente made the smaller and weaker states of the rest of Europe relatively more important in their calculations. The Germans in particular never missed an opportunity to persuade these states to align with them either formally or informally. When Belgium's King Albert visited Germany in November 1913, William II made the case personally, and his chief of the general staff, Helmuth von Moltke the Younger, stated it even more bluntly to the Belgian military attaché, warning that "the *furor teutonicas* will overrun everything" once a general war began.[1] Such intimidation would work for the Third Reich, but paid few dividends for the Second. While its leaders shared the hubris of their counterparts in Nazi Germany a quarter of a century later, Imperial Germany had not amassed the same degree of power relative to the other leading states of Europe, leaving the smaller or weaker countries of 1914 with a range of viable options they would not have in the late 1930s. Beyond the great powers and beyond the Balkans, Europe's non-aligned countries of 1914 would all remain neutral throughout the war, with the exception of Belgium and Portugal.

The great powers had issued a mutual guarantee of Belgium's neutrality in 1839 upon recognizing its secession from the Netherlands, and installed the German house of Saxe-Coburg-Gotha to rule as constitutional monarchs. Roman Catholicism provided the only cultural bond for a population (7.5 million as of 1914) otherwise sharply divided between French-speaking (Walloon) and Dutch-speaking (Flemish) components. The country's territory, entirely west of the Rhine, had been annexed by France during the Napoleonic Wars, and everyone assumed that any future crisis involving Belgium would be precipitated by a French invasion. Belgium enjoyed cordial relations with Germany and as late as June 1914 its leaders still feared France more. In the prewar years the Belgian press and public criticized Britain more than any other great power, taking a pro-Boer stance during the Anglo-Boer War and rejecting British criticism over Belgium's mismanagement of its vast colonial holdings in the Congo. Belgium's assets included a prosperous industrialized economy more than strong enough to support the army of 340,000 that it could mobilize under a compulsory service law passed in 1913.

In contrast to Belgium, Portugal enjoyed only the advantage of British protection under history's longest standing bilateral alliance (dating from 1373), and a relatively safe neighborhood. It bordered only Spain, in decline for centuries and recently deprived of most of its remaining colonies by the United States in the war of 1898. The chronically impoverished country, home to just over 5 million people, ousted its monarchy in a revolution in 1910 and the following year adopted a constitution modeled on that of the French Third Republic. Portuguese republican Francophilia combined with traditional pro-British sentiment to predispose Portugal to support the Entente. As of 1914 the remnants of Portugal's overseas empire included four colonies that would be strategically significant in the upcoming world war: the future Angola and Mozambique, both adjacent to German colonial possessions in Africa, and the Atlantic islands of Madeira and the Azores.

The United States and Japan

During the two decades preceding the start of World War I, the United States and Japan achieved a great power status previously limited to European states. The construction of a modern navy (from 1883) set the United States on course to win a dramatic victory in the Spanish-American War (1898), in which it acquired the Philippines, Guam, and Puerto Rico. American military action freed Cuba from the control of Spain and, in 1903, gunboat diplomacy helped free Panama from Colombia; both became dependents of the United States, the former ceding a naval base at Guantanamo Bay, the latter the Canal Zone, where the Panama Canal was constructed (1903–14). The United States also annexed Hawaii in 1898. Meanwhile, for Japan, naval strength likewise facilitated victories in the Sino-Japanese War (1894–95) and Russo-Japanese War (1904–05), resulting in its acquisition of Taiwan, southern Sakhalin, and spheres of influence in Korea and Manchuria, including a naval base at Port Arthur. The Russo-Japanese War confirmed Japan's emergence as a great power as much as it exposed Russia's weakness. Japan annexed Korea in 1910, and four years later used its British alliance as a pretext for entering World War I. These developments soured relations between Japan and the United States. Even though the two countries would be allies in World War I, its outcome left them on a collision course in the Pacific.

The population of the United States grew from just 5 million in 1800 to 75 million in 1900, a boom fueled by European immigration. The country's decentralized political system provided few benefits to its citizens other than a degree of freedom unrivaled elsewhere, at least for Americans of white European stock. On the strength of a population that grew by another 30 percent (to 97 million) between 1900 and 1913, the United States had the world's highest per capita GDP, was the world's leading agricultural producer, generated a third of the world's manufacturing output, and milled almost as much steel as the next four producers combined. After Congress slashed tariff rates in 1913 the United States became the world's leading advocate of free trade. By the outbreak of war the United States trailed only Britain and Germany in warship tonnage, but its peacetime army remained very small; in 1914 even Italy had more than twice as many men in uniform as the United States. American politics featured a stable two-party system in which the Republicans – the party of Abraham Lincoln – had long dominated. Woodrow Wilson, elected president in 1912, was just the second Democrat to win the White House since 1856. His career as a professor of political science had taken him to Princeton, where he eventually became university president before securing election as governor of New Jersey in 1910. The self-righteous Wilson, son of a Presbyterian minister, personified the best and worst of American impulses. He sought to make the United States a better country and, after 1917, to use American power to create a better world. His convictions, though often contradictory, were passionately held nonetheless.

Japan had the distinction of being the only non-Western country targeted by Western imperialism to survive the onslaught, modernize itself, and emerge as a great power in its own right. Traditionally, Japan had operated under a feudal system in which the emperor, considered a god in the Shinto religion, had no political role, and the shogun, a hereditary warlord, served as de facto ruler of the country. The isolationist Tokugawa shogunate (1603–1868) was forced to open Japan to the outside world in 1853 when the United States sent a naval squadron to Tokyo Bay. After European powers followed suit, the humiliating concessions they extracted sparked a revolution whose leaders concluded that Japan could save itself only by modernization. In 1868, they seized power under the guise of "restoring" the authority of the emperor. The government of the Meiji Restoration abolished feudalism, established business enterprises and Western-style schools, and founded a modern army and navy on the German and British models, respectively. Japan's constitution (1889), like Bismarck's German constitution, featured a strong prime minister responsible to the emperor alone, but a very narrow franchise allowed only the wealthiest Japanese males to vote. The peasants shouldered the burden of modernization, paying heavy taxes that doomed them to an impoverished existence. Owing to its relatively large population (51 million in 1913) on the eve of World War I Japan had a per capita GDP slightly lower than Russia and a similar level of industrialization, yet it had the world's fifth largest navy and almost twice as many men in uniform as the United States. Japanese steel production stood at less than 1 percent of the American output, but by the time of their war with Russia the Japanese were manufacturing their own heavy artillery to supplement European imports. All of the larger warships deployed against Russia were built in Britain (Japan's ally as of 1902); only afterward did Japanese shipyards build their own battleships, the first dreadnought being launched in 1910. Japan transformed itself from feudal hermit state to modern great power in less than forty years, yet it had the smallest industrial base of any of the great powers and, in order to remain in their ranks, would have to devote a far greater share of its resources to its armed forces. Japan managed to do so thanks to the ability of its authoritarian government to get the most out of a patriotic population that remained willing to endure burdens in support of the nation's goals despite the conditions under which it lived. Indeed, anti-peace rallies in Tokyo at the end of the Russo-Japanese War indicated that the public not only supported an ambitious foreign policy, but would rather make greater sacrifices than accept lesser spoils than anticipated.

Dominions and Colonies

The self-governing Dominions of the British Empire – Australia, Canada, New Zealand, and South Africa – would play a unique and important role in World War I, participating as partners rather than dependents of their mother country. Taken together, they were among the most prosperous lands on earth, with a collective per capita GDP trailing only the United States and Britain. Along with the colonies of the British Empire (most notably India) and the colonies of France (in particular, those in Africa), they provided significant resources to the Entente's war effort.

The British Dominions had their own parliaments and political parties, cabinets and prime ministers, but until the Statute of Westminster (1931) their governments had only a limited ability to conduct foreign policy and did not enjoy independent war and peace powers. When Britain went to war, they, too, were at war, yet they enjoyed an important prerogative that colonies did not: they were not formally obligated to send troops overseas to fight for the mother country. Thus, their governments had a voice in how many troops they contributed, where, and when. The oldest dominion, Canada – self-governing since 1867 – had a population of 7.8 million in 1914, but just over 3,000 regulars in its Permanent Force, a subset of the otherwise part-time Active Militia consisting of volunteers aged 18–45. The Reserve Militia, in which all males aged 18–60 were liable to serve, existed only in theory. The Active Militia could be deployed overseas in case of an imperial emergency, and brought up to strength via a draft if the number of volunteers proved insufficient. In 1913 roughly 55,000 Canadians received militia training. When the war broke out, Canada would meet its commitment to Britain by sending composite units including Permanent Force and other Active Militia.

Australia, granted dominion status in 1901, implemented a system ten years later requiring boys and young men to undergo compulsory annual military training from ages 12 to 25, of whom those aged 18–25 could be mobilized for duty in case of war. The system was designed to enable Australia (a country of barely 5 million people in 1914) to mobilize eight cohorts totaling roughly 250,000 men, but the trained active duty force of 1914 included just the first three cohorts, none of whom was over 21, an "army of boys" Australia would opt not to send overseas. Instead, it established a separate volunteer army, the Australian Imperial Force (AIF), for service in Europe, and the much smaller Australian Naval and Military Expeditionary Force for service in the Pacific against Germany's colonies. New Zealand, self-governing since 1907, likewise had compulsory military training beginning with boys still in adolescence, with the Defence Act of 1909 requiring it for all males aged 14–21. In the summer of 1914, the country of 1.1 million would meet its commitment to Britain with detachments from existing units of its army.

The Union of South Africa, granted dominion status in 1910, had a population of 6 million, within which the white minority of 1.3 million enjoyed formal, legal superiority over 4 million black and 700,000 Indian and mixed-race ("colored") South Africans. The country had a military structure similar to that of Canada, with a small regular army, the Union Defence Force, supplemented by a militia in which white males aged 17–60 were liable to serve. The militia could be brought up to strength by conscription and, unlike its Canadian counterpart, included a number of draftees to compensate for the general unpopularity of the service among Afrikaners, whose independent Orange Free State and South African Republic (Transvaal) had been forcibly incorporated into British South Africa as a result of the recent Anglo-Boer War. Once the war started, South Africa would send no troops to Europe until after its forces had conquered the neighboring colony of German Southwest Africa.

In population the 20 million British subjects of the four Dominions were dwarfed by the 380 million of the British colonies, more than two-thirds of whom lived in India. The largest body of colonial troops, the 150,000-man Indian Army, was recruited on a voluntary basis and thus included disproportionate numbers from South Asian peoples with proud martial traditions, such as the Gurkhas of Nepal and the Rajputs of Rajasthan. Indian provinces sending more than their share of men into military service included Punjab (giving the army a large number of Sikhs), while southern India contributed little and heavily populated Bengal almost none at all. Ultimately, India would mobilize 1.4 million men during World War I, of whom 1 million served overseas, including 580,000 combat troops. Britain's black African colonies contributed much smaller numbers of troops, either to the Royal West African Frontier Force (RWAFF), raised from Nigeria, Sierra Leone, Gambia, and Gold Coast (Ghana), or the King's

African Rifles (KAR), raised in Kenya, Uganda, and Nyasaland (Malawi). During the war the RWAFF and KAR would not leave the continent, but played important roles in the Allied campaign against Germany's African colonies.

France's colonial empire had a population of just 60 million in 1914 and thus potentially could produce less than one-quarter the manpower of British India alone. France's Army of Africa, raised in the North African territories of Algeria, Tunisia, and Morocco, included separate units for troops from the large French settler colony in Algeria and the Arab and Berber population, although by 1914 the lines had blurred somewhat – for example, allowing some French cavalrymen into the otherwise Arab *spahis*, as well as some Arab infantrymen into the otherwise French *zouaves*. The French colonials were mostly conscripts serving under the same obligations in effect in France. The Arabs included some chosen by conscription (introduced in Algeria in 1913), but most of the 33,000 Muslim Algerians serving as of 1914 were volunteers. The Army of Africa also included the all-volunteer Foreign Legion and military convicts serving time in the African Light Infantry. Troops raised in the rest of the French empire, along with French troops serving in those colonies, were designated as "Colonial Troops" (*Troupes coloniales*). Like the soldiers of British black Africa, they were organized into rifle units, most notably the *Tirailleurs sénégalais* (raised not just from Senegal, but all of French West Africa and central Africa), the *Tirailleurs malagaches* (from Madagascar), and the *Tirailleurs indochinois* (from Indochina). Owing to the French Army's chronic shortage of manpower, its African units saw action in the mother country throughout the war.

Beyond the British and French possessions, Africa's largest colony, the Belgian Congo, also produced its largest peacetime body of troops. The Congolese "Public Force" (*Force publique*) was a typical colonial army in its modest size – just 17,000 troops in 1914, for a colony of 7 million – and terms of service, as a professional force of long-service volunteers. Like the troops of British black Africa, they would see action in World War I against Germany's African colonies. Without exception, the colonial forces of Asia and Africa were commanded by European expatriates or officers on assignment from the regular army of the mother country.

Europeans traditionally had valued overseas colonies for their economic resources, but in the industrial era their relative importance declined. While in the industrialized mother countries per capita GDP continued to rise in a time of population growth, in most overseas possessions (the British Dominions being a dramatic exception) productivity failed to improve fast enough to sustain a similar rise. In 1913, Britain had a per capita GDP more than seven times as great as its empire (minus the Dominions), while for France, the figure was more than five times as great as its colonies. With the productivity of colonies lagging farther behind that of their mother countries than ever before, they had little surplus to exploit after local demand was met. Furthermore, distance from the mother country made it difficult to bring this small surplus to bear in Europe once the war began.[2] Only the British Dominions were productive enough to compensate for their distance from Europe, and only French North Africa was close enough to Europe to compensate for its low productivity. Among the overseas possessions, they would have the greatest impact on the war.

Nationalism, Darwinism, and the Cult of the Offensive

The great powers of Europe, emerging non-European powers, peripheral states, Dominions, and colonies all shared the common denominator of having their pre-World War I behavior shaped by the nationalism that had emerged a century earlier in the French Revolution and Napoleonic Wars. During the nineteenth century the benign cultural nationalism of the Romantic era evolved into a racial nationalism further sharpened and defined by Darwinism, after Charles Darwin's fateful decision to use the imagery and language of war to articulate natural and biological concepts in his *Origin of Species* (1859) and *Descent of Man* (1871). Thereafter, basic Darwinian concepts such as the survival of the fittest and the struggle for existence provided a "scientific" underpinning for aggressive ideologies and, in a general sense, "scientific" racial nationalism supported national unity in the cause of national greatness. Such thinking infected intellectuals throughout Europe. Darwinism affected France less than the other great powers, but even there Émile Zola, hero of the French Left, in 1891 declared that "war is life itself! Nothing exists in nature or is born, grows up or multiplies other than through combat. It is necessary to eat or be eaten that the world may live. Only warrior nations have prospered; a nation dies from the time that it disarms."[3] Indeed, what some scholars have labeled "militarism" and attempted to generalize in social, economic, or political terms originated in the decades before 1914 as a distinct manifestation of Darwinian racial nationalism.

In this atmosphere, Bertha von Suttner (see Box 1.2) and other European pacifists faced an impossible task. Even the peace prize awarded annually from 1901 to recognize their work came thanks to the largesse of the inventor of dynamite, Alfred Nobel. On Europe's political landscape only the socialists overtly embraced international peace and cooperation, and within individual countries their parties tended to be either isolated because of their electoral strength (such as the German SPD) or ignored because of their electoral weakness (such as the British Labour Party). The socialist Second International (founded 1889) reflected the deep division of the movement between moderates, who subscribed to the egalitarian ideals of Karl Marx but not his revolutionary methods, and radicals, who insisted (problematically, for the pacifist cause) that genuine change must come through violent upheaval. Only in Germany were the socialists strong enough to truly concern government leaders, and even the SPD – after consistently opposing military and naval spending throughout the prewar years – would vote for war credits in the crisis atmosphere of the summer of 1914. In the midst of the July Crisis, the Second

Box 1.2 **A voice in the wilderness**

Excerpt from the Nobel lecture of Baroness Bertha von Suttner (1843–1914), Austrian peace activist and winner of the 1905 Nobel Peace Prize, delivered in Oslo, Norway, April 18, 1906:

The instinct of self-preservation in human society, acting almost subconsciously, as do all drives in the human mind, is rebelling against the constantly refined methods of annihilation and against the destruction of humanity. Complementing this subconscious striving toward an era free of war are people who are working deliberately toward this goal, who visualize the main essentials of a plan of action, who are seeking methods which will accomplish our aim as soon as possible ... When [Theodore] Roosevelt received me in the White House on October 17, 1904, he said to me, "World peace is coming, it certainly is coming, but only step by step." ... However clearly envisaged, however apparently near and within reach the goal may be, the road to it must be traversed a step at a time, and countless obstacles surmounted on the way.

... The advocates of pacifism are well aware how meager are their resources of personal influence and power. They know that they are still few in number and weak in authority, but when they realistically consider themselves and the ideal they serve, they see themselves as the servants of the greatest of all causes. On the solution of this problem depends whether our Europe will become a showpiece of ruins and failure, or whether we can avoid this danger and so enter sooner the coming era of secure peace and law in which a civilization of unimagined glory will develop.

The many aspects of this question are what the second Hague Conference [held July–October 1907] should be discussing rather than the proposed topics concerning the laws and practices of war at sea, the bombardment of ports, towns, and villages, the laying of mines, and so on. The contents of this agenda demonstrate that, although the supporters of the existing structure of society, which accepts war, come to a peace conference prepared to modify the nature of war, they are basically trying to keep the present system intact. The advocates of pacifism, inside and outside the Conference, will, however, defend their objectives and press forward another step toward their goal – the goal which, to repeat Roosevelt's words, affirms the duty of his government and of all governments "to bring nearer the time when the sword shall not be the arbiter among nations."

Source: nobelprize.org/nobel_prizes/peace/laureates/1905/suttner-lecture.html.

International saw its dream of an international general strike to stop the armies from mobilizing shattered by the sobering reality that, for the vast majority of Europe's workers, national identity mattered more than class identity.

Prewar military thought, not surprisingly, reflected the nationalist and Darwinian spirit of the times, manifested in the cult of the offensive that affected all armed forces by the turn of the century. The cult of the offensive had its roots in the Prussian-German way of war born in the military reforms Prussia adopted after it suffered a crushing defeat at the hands of Napoleon's France in 1806. Karl von Clausewitz (1770–1831) served as the prophet for this faith, his posthumous *On War* (1832) its holy scripture, and Field Marshal Helmuth von Moltke the Elder (1800–91) its delivering messiah. Following Moltke's triumphs against Austria (1866) and France (1870–71) in the Wars of German Unification, Clausewitz's *On War* was translated and studied throughout Europe, often with a Darwinian preface. Colonel F. N. Maude's preface to a prewar reprint of the original 1873 English translation of *On War* declared that "what Darwin accomplished for biology generally Clausewitz did for the life history of nations nearly half a century before him, for both have proved the existence of the same law in each case … the survival of the fittest."[4] German general and military writer Colmar von der Goltz, the leading Darwinist interpreter of Clausewitz, accelerated the trend with his international best seller, *The Nation in Arms* (1883). Paradoxically, weaker states were no less likely than the strong to embrace offensive warfare, as it offered them hope that their vitality could be proven on the battlefield. Thus, the cult of the offensive had a special relevance for two of the more vulnerable military powers of Europe, Austria-Hungary and France. Franz Conrad von Hötzendorf, instructor at the War School in Vienna (1888–92) before becoming chief of the Austro-Hungarian general staff (1906–17), and Ferdinand Foch, instructor (1895–1901) and commandant (1907–11) at the War School in Paris before becoming supreme Allied commander in 1918, both advocated offensive strategies that proved to be completely inappropriate for the situations facing their countries in World War I. The results would be fatal for Austria-Hungary and nearly so for France.

The cult of the offensive persisted despite evidence from the Anglo-Boer War, Russo-Japanese War, and Balkan wars that emerging technologies favored defensive warfare. The Anglo-Boer War was the first in which both sides deployed infantry armed primarily with magazine rifles, and infantry firepower had clearly been decisive. Quick-firing artillery and smokeless powder, which had revolutionized naval combat in the 1880s, likewise made their first appearance in land warfare. Tactically, British infantry failed at every bayonet charge they attempted, but were more successful when deploying in extended order and advancing in small groups under cover. Future commanders of World War I's British Expeditionary Force, Sir John French and Sir Douglas Haig, downplayed the fact that the cavalry they led in South Africa had been most useful fighting dismounted with rifles, like the Boer commandos.

The Manchurian campaign during the Russo-Japanese War featured unprecedented numbers of troops, the greatest employment of trenches to date, and the first extensive use of the machine gun. The decisive battle of Mukden (February–March 1905) involved roughly a quarter of a million men on each side, in continuous trench lines 90 miles (145 km) long. As in the Anglo-Boer War, infantry operated most successfully in extended order and when advancing in small groups under cover, but both armies pursued open-field bayonet charges successfully, albeit at horrific costs, invalidating (at least for many observers) the lessons from South Africa concerning the decisive nature of firepower by dispersed infantry. The Japanese demonstrated that an assault force with the morale to absorb losses of 35–40 percent could still prevail even on a battlefield where modern technology – most notably, the first generation of the machine gun – clearly favored the defender. Ultimately, the outcome supported the conventional wisdom of the cult of the offensive: the Japanese had attacked and won, while the Russians had stood on the defensive and lost.

Observers of the Balkan Wars praised the Bulgarians for their assault on the Çatalca line, which resembled the Western front of World War I more than anything in Manchuria during the Russo-Japanese War. The Turkish last line of defense just 20 miles (32 km) west of Constantinople, the Çatalca line consisted of a 15-mile (24-km) continuous front of trenches from the Black Sea to the Sea of Marmara, leaving no flanks to turn and frontal assault the only option for the attackers. Those praising the bravery of the Bulgarians and lauding the offensive spirit of their commander, General Radko Ruskov Dimitriev, did so despite their horrific casualties – 90,000 in just five days of attacks in November 1912 – and their failure to break through to Constantinople. The Bulgarian Army learned from this bloodbath that infantry assaults required robust artillery support and acted on the lesson with an innovative creeping barrage in taking Adrianople in March 1913, but few foreign commentators noticed. The Allies would not introduce the creeping barrage to the Western front until after suffering millions of casualties in infantry assaults undertaken without adequate artillery support.

Because the observers of and participants in the wars of 1899–1913 were shaped by their own national perspectives and by the prevailing wisdom of the times in which they lived, most of the lessons they applied by 1914 had clear implications for offensive warfare. While they underestimated the casualties that a future major war would generate, they expected losses to be heavy and sought to limit the damage through improvements in equipment and training. The Anglo-Boer War sealed the fate of colorful field uniforms in the British Army and accelerated a trend that led all major powers to adopt drab or camouflage colors, in all cases except France (which adopted *horizon bleu* in July 1914), in time for the opening campaigns of World War I. The British experience in the South African war, which quickly exhausted their small, regular army, also led them to upgrade their reserve formations (creating the Territorial Force in 1908, to replace the traditional yeomanry, militia, and volunteers). Most other great powers took notice and adopted similar measures to close the gap in fighting ability between their reserves and regular troops. While armies generally underestimated the significance of artillery and machine guns, in the prewar arms races most of them also attempted to secure a quantitative or qualitative superiority in those weapons.

Arms Races, Alliances, and the Security Dilemma

The years immediately preceding World War I witnessed an unprecedented increase in military and naval expenditure, with the six great powers of Europe collectively spending 50 percent more in 1913 than in 1908. The prewar arms races are history's best example of the "security dilemma" – the phenomenon of a state's actions to ensure its own security causing another state to feel insecure, thereby provoking a response that ultimately feeds a spiral of increased armaments spending and an atmosphere of suspicion that makes war more, rather than less, likely. After 1918 the role of the arms races in the origins of the war received considerable attention, and the future appeals by various statesmen for a regime of "collective security," first in the interwar period and, later, during the Cold War, aimed at avoiding a repetition of the disaster.

The Anglo-German naval race served as centerpiece to the general prewar competition in armaments. Germany's quest to rival Britain at sea began in 1897, with the appointment of Admiral Alfred von Tirpitz as state secretary in the Imperial Navy Office. The goals of Tirpitz's initial fleet program appeared modest enough, including twenty-seven battleships and twelve large cruisers, of which twenty and ten, respectively, were already in service or under construction. The Reichstag approved his plan in 1898, after hearing a speech in which he used ominous Darwinian language to characterize the expansion of the fleet as a "question of survival" for Germany.[5] Two years later a second navy law raised the targets to thirty-eight battleships and fourteen large cruisers, and supplementary laws eventually increased the number of battleships to forty-one and large cruisers to twenty. The Tirpitz plan quickly moved Germany from fifth to second place among Europe's naval powers. The debate over his navy bills focused on the new warships they required, overlooking provisions for the automatic replacement of battleships after twenty-five years and large cruisers after twenty. Fortunately for Tirpitz, the oldest of the existing battleships counted in his 1898 plan reached the end of their prescribed service lives in 1906, just as Britain introduced its two new revolutionary warship designs, the *Dreadnought* battleship and the battle cruiser. Because the new designs rendered all existing larger warships obsolete, the British negated their own considerable advantage in pre-dreadnought battleships and armored cruisers, and gave the Germans the opportunity to catch up with them in battle fleet strength. Tirpitz subsequently built all new German battleships as dreadnoughts and large cruisers as battle cruisers. In 1908 the Reichstag approved another supplementary law enabling Tirpitz to accelerate the construction of dreadnoughts and battle cruisers ("capital ships," as the two types together became known), and Germany soon had ten built or building to Britain's twelve. At that pace Tirpitz could achieve much better than the 3:2 ratio of inferiority which he felt would give the German fleet a chance of defeating the British in the North Sea, but the acceleration of German naval construction shocked Parliament into funding eight capital ships for 1909–10, supplemented by another pair paid for by Australia and New Zealand. The Germans countered these ten new British capital ships with just three of their own, and thus fell behind in the race by twenty-two to thirteen. Thereafter, the British continued to out-build the Germans on an annual basis, though not as dramatically as in 1909–10. At the end of July 1914, Britain had twenty-nine capital ships in service and thirteen under construction, while Germany had eighteen in service and eight under construction. The British advantage, slightly better than 3:2, would suffice to keep the German fleet in port for most of World War I.

The prewar competition to build Europe's first air forces hardly constituted an arms race, as few envisaged just how important the skies would be in future warfare. In 1908, five years after their first successful flight, the Wright brothers brought their aircraft to Europe for a series of public demonstrations. The French Army incorporated airplanes into the annual maneuvers of 1910, and the following year the German Navy began experimenting with airplanes but favored dirigibles instead, under the influence of Count Ferdinand von Zeppelin and other German airship pioneers. Prewar Italy likewise favored dirigibles, even though Italian pilots were the first to fly airplanes in combat missions in the 1911–12 war against Turkey. In 1912, Britain established separate army and navy air services, and Austria-Hungary established a seaplane station at Pola. In France, Italy, and Russia, the armies initially monopolized air power and the navies controlled no aircraft. In 1910–11, the US Navy became the first to launch and land airplanes from warships (in each case using temporary deck platforms) and the first to use aircraft for long-range artillery spotting. Early in 1914 the British Admiralty authorized the construction of a seaplane tender, the 7,080-ton *Ark Royal*, built on the hull of an unfinished merchantman.

For every European power except Britain, armies based on a universal service obligation remained the cornerstone of national defense. In the prewar years, most of the great powers reduced their service requirement to mirror the German model of two years of active duty (France in 1905, Austria-Hungary in 1906, and Italy in 1910) while following the British lead in upgrading the caliber of reserve formations. The French Army added back a third year only after Germany's Army Law of 1913 promised to reduce the number of men exempted or furloughed by the German Army. This Franco-German competition to improve the capabilities of the two armies, like the Anglo-German naval race, only heightened tensions and contributed to the sense that a general war was inevitable.

Conclusion

Internationally, the prewar years witnessed the creation of the conditions in which World War I began and escalated. The Anglo-Boer War underscored the isolation of Britain, made its leaders self-conscious about continuing the "splendid isolation" of the Pax Britannica, and led to its partnerships with Japan, France, and Russia. The Russo-Japanese War confirmed Japan's emergence as a great power and exposed Russia's weaknesses; in 1914 an emboldened Japan would use its British tie as a pretext for intervening in World War I, while Russia would demonstrate that it had recovered from the debacle of 1904–05 much faster than expected. Finally, the warfare of 1912–13 had rendered the Balkans more volatile than ever, as each of the Balkan countries emerged with more territory and larger populations but harbored still grander ambitions, of which none surpassed those of Serbia, which could be fulfilled only at the expense of Austria-Hungary. Ideologically, the overheated nationalism of the age, sharpened by Darwinism, established the context within which the general public in most countries, along with most political and intellectual leaders, would accept, if not welcome, the prospect of a general war. Militarily, the fighting in South Africa, Manchuria, and the Balkans provided glimpses of the horrors to come, but strategists and tacticians refused to abandon their faith in offensive warfare. They went to war in 1914 knowing it would be bloody (though underestimating just how bloody), and expecting it to be brief. Perhaps most important of all, the wars of 1899–1913 served notice that a successful modern war effort required the wholehearted support of the home front. In particular, the anti-peace riots in Tokyo that greeted the treaty ending the Russo-Japanese War in 1905, along with the Bulgarian public's rejection of the treaty ending the First Balkan War in 1913, served as reminders that when civilian populations gave such support, they would accept nothing less than total victory.

SUGGESTIONS FOR FURTHER READING

Afflerbach, Holger, and David Stevenson (eds.). *An Improbable War? The Outbreak of World War I and European Political Culture before 1914* (New York: Berghahn Books, 2007).

Broadberry, Stephen, and Mark Harrison. *The Economics of World War I* (Cambridge: Cambridge University Press, 2005).

Clark, Christopher. *The Sleepwalkers: How Europe Went to War in 1914* (New York: HarperCollins, 2012).

Fogarty, Richard S. *Race and War in France: Colonial Subjects in the French Army, 1914–1918* (Baltimore, MD: Johns Hopkins University Press, 2008).

Hamilton, Richard F., and Holger H. Herwig (eds.). *The Origins of World War I* (Cambridge: Cambridge University Press, 2003).

Kelly, Patrick J. *Tirpitz and the Imperial German Navy* (Bloomington, IN: Indiana University Press, 2011).

Mulligan, William. *The Origins of the First World War* (Cambridge: Cambridge University Press, 2010).

Rüger, Jan. *The Great Naval Game: Britain and Germany in the Age of Empire* (Cambridge: Cambridge University Press, 2007).

Stevenson, David. *Armaments and the Coming of War: Europe, 1904–1914* (Oxford: Clarendon Press, 1996).

NOTES

1. Quoted in Fritz Fischer, *War of Illusions: German Policies from 1911 to 1914* (New York: W. W. Norton, 1975), 227.
2. See Stephen Broadberry and Mark Harrison, "The Economics of World War I: An Overview," in Stephen Broadberry and Mark Harrison (eds.), *The Economics of World War I* (Cambridge: Cambridge University Press, 2005), 6–9.
3. Quoted in Daniel Pick, *War Machine: The Rationalisation of Slaughter in the Modern Age* (New Haven, CT: Yale University Press, 1993), 86.
4. Maude quoted in introduction to Karl von Clausewitz, *On War*, ed. Anatol Rapaport (New York: Penguin Books, 1968), 83.
5. Quoted in Holger H. Herwig, *The German Naval Officer Corps: A Social and Political History, 1890–1918* (Oxford: Clarendon Press, 1973), 11.

Gavrilo Princip

Francis Ferdinand's assassin Gavrilo Princip (1894–1918) photographed while awaiting trial. Born at Obljaj, Bosnia, son of a postal worker, Princip joined anti-government protests as a student and in 1912 was expelled from school for his political activity. He moved to Belgrade, where he joined the Black Hand. Because Austria-Hungary did not allow persons under 20 to receive the death penalty, Princip, one month short of his 20th birthday (July 25) when he murdered the archduke, could not be executed for his crime. He spent the war imprisoned at Theresienstadt (today Terezin, Czech Republic), where he died of tuberculosis on April 28, 1918.

2 The July Crisis, 1914

June 28	Black Hand assassinates Archduke Francis Ferdinand at Sarajevo.
July 3	Serbia makes first overture to Russia for aid.
July 5–6	"Hoyos Mission" to Germany secures "blank check" for Austria-Hungary.
July 16–29	France's Poincaré and Viviani visit Russia.
July 23	Austria-Hungary issues ultimatum to Serbia.
July 25	Serbia rejects key parts of ultimatum; Austria-Hungary declares war (July 28).
July 31	Russia mobilizes against Austria-Hungary and Germany.
August 1	Germany orders general mobilization, declares war on Russia; France orders general mobilization.
August 2	Italy declares neutrality.
August 3	Germany declares war on France.
August 4	Germany invades Belgium; Britain declares war on Germany.
August 6	Austria-Hungary declares war on Russia.

Of all the international crises in history, none has been subjected to greater scrutiny or more scholarly analysis than the July Crisis of 1914, which began with the assassination of Archduke Francis Ferdinand at Sarajevo on June 28 and culminated in the great powers of Europe exchanging declarations of war beginning on August 1. As soon as the war began, the governments of the individual countries sought to construct a record of the diplomatic machinations that defended or justified their actions and placed the blame elsewhere: Austria-Hungary against Serbia; Russia against Austria-Hungary; Germany against Russia; France and Britain against Germany. Historians likewise began to analyze the July Crisis while the war was still underway, touching off a protracted debate that would remain alive at the war's centennial (see Perspectives 2.1, 2.2). The volumes of diplomatic documents and thousands of monographs published in dozens of languages over the ensuing decades contributed to the overall understanding of the outbreak of the war but, at the same time, obscured some of the central elements of the July Crisis: that it began in the first place because Serbia, an ambitious small state to some extent held hostage by a rogue element within its own armed forces, ignited the entire continent in pursuit of its own national goals; that two of the weaker great powers, Austria-Hungary and Russia, behaved with an uncharacteristic resolve rooted in their own doubts about their future status as great powers; that Austro-Hungarian and German leaders had incompatible notions of the war they wanted, with the Germans getting their way at the expense of their ally; and, finally, that French leaders, though not desiring war in the first place, likewise saw the July Crisis unfold in a manner that gave them a war under the circumstances they considered the most favorable.

Black Hand at Sarajevo, June 28, 1914

In January 1914, when the Austro-Hungarian general staff set its schedule of army maneuvers for the year, Archduke Francis Ferdinand agreed to attend the summer exercises of the XV and XVI Corps in Bosnia. On June 26–27 the archduke observed the maneuvers in the company of the Dual Monarchy's two leading generals, Franz Conrad von Hötzendorf (Figure 2.1), chief of the general staff, and Oskar Potiorek, military governor of Bosnia, before visiting the Bosnian capital, Sarajevo, with his wife, Sophie, on Sunday, June 28. While touring Sarajevo in an open car, the archduke survived an initial assassination attempt around 10:30 a.m. and continued with his itinerary, only to be shot and killed, along with Sophie, some 30 minutes later. Police captured the assassin, 19-year-old Bosnian Serb Gavrilo Princip, at the scene of the crime, and arrested his co-conspirators later that day. Thus, the Black Hand succeeded in murdering its biggest target, after failing in its earlier attempts against

Austro-Hungarian officials in Bosnia and Croatia. Conrad, who for years had advocated a preventive war against Serbia, called "the murder in Sarajevo … the last link in a long chain. It was not the deed of an individual fanatic … it was the declaration of war of Serbia against Austria-Hungary."[1] Within days of the assassination Austro-Hungarian authorities suspected the involvement of Serbian military intelligence officers in general and Colonel Dimitrijević in particular. They ascertained that Princip and two of his co-conspirators had been recent visitors to Belgrade, where they had been given their guns and several bombs, one of which had been thrown at Francis Ferdinand's motorcade in the initial, unsuccessful assassination attempt on the morning of the 28th.

Perspectives 2.1: The July Crisis

French historian Marc Ferro (born 1924) holds Germany responsible for escalating the Balkan crisis into a general war, but also finds fault with Britain's conduct while emphasizing the relative helplessness of France:

The role of "evil genius" behind the explosion no doubt goes to the German leaders … [who] tipped the balance towards radical solution of the Serbian question, carefully stage-managed its course so as to have a kind of "perfect crime", deliberately rejected attempts at mediation when the conflict threatened to go further, and deliberately risked this when Russia threatened to intervene. On the other hand, England was "the apostle of peace", trying not to aggravate the Austro-Serbian conflict and to ensure it would not lead to war. Just the same, her policy of conciliation did as much to produce war as the Germans' "calculated risks" – the Germans, sure that whatever happened England would stay neutral, went further in their adventurous way than they would have done had they known they were wrong … French leaders were simply being dragged into the war, more worried about their alliances' solidarity than about the fate of peace. Within the narrow framework of the July crisis they had almost no role at all, neither fomenting nor arresting the explosion.

Source: Marc Ferro, *The Great War, 1914–1918*, trans. Nicole Stone
(London: Routledge, 1973), 45.

• • • •

American historian Samuel R. Williamson, Jr. (born 1935) rejects the traditional depiction of the Dual Monarchy as little more than a puppet of Germany, concluding instead that Austro-Hungarian leaders made their own fateful decisions:

In Vienna in July 1914 a set of leaders experienced in statecraft, power and crisis management consciously risked a general war to fight a local war. Battered during the Balkan Wars by Serbian expansion, Russian activism and now by the loss of Franz Ferdinand, the Habsburg leaders desperately desired to shape their future, rather than let events destroy them. The fear of domestic disintegration made war an acceptable policy option. The Habsburg decision, backed by the Germans, gave the July crisis a momentum that rendered peace an early casualty.

Source: Samuel R. Williamson, Jr., *Austria-Hungary and the Origins of the First World War* (London: Macmillan, 1991), 215. (Reproduced with permission of Palgrave Macmillan.)

Perspectives 2.2: The July Crisis

German historian Holger Afflerbach (born 1960) sees a paradox at the heart of the July Crisis: that war was considered both improbable and inevitable, and that these two competing notions interacted "in a dynamic and mobile way":

The mistake that was made by German and Austrian leaders—by Berchtold, Bethmann Hollweg, and their subordinates—was based on their assumptions both of how widespread the fear of a Great War in Europe was, and how improbable it seemed. They thought, as a result, that they could carry out the maneuver against Serbia without further consequences. The July crisis was a huge bluff on the part of the Central Powers—a bluff that ended in catastrophe, of course— which would allow them to realize a local war that they considered necessary for the political stabilization of the Habsburg monarchy. But there was an afterthought: if, against all expectations, the other powers could not be intimidated, and would break the European consensus that a Great War must be avoided, it would simply prove that they had evil designs for the future anyway, and thus a Great War was imminent and it was better to fight now rather than later.

Source: Holger Afflerbach, "The Topos of Improbable War," in *An Improbable War: The Outbreak of World War I and European Political Culture before 1914*, ed. Holger Afflerbach and David Stevenson (New York: Berghahn Books, 2007), 174–75.

• • • •

In the 1920s, scholars rejecting the Versailles Treaty and German war guilt typically blamed tsarist Russia for starting the war. Revisiting the issue of Russian responsibility, American historian Sean McMeekin (born 1974) focuses on the tsar's decision to make Russia the first of the great powers to declare a general mobilization:

The decision for European war was made by Russia on the night of 29 July 1914, when Tsar Nicholas II ... signed the order for general mobilization ... So clearly did the tsar know this that, on being moved by a telegram from Kaiser Wilhelm II, he changed his mind. 'I will not be responsible for a monstrous slaughter' is the key line of the entire July crisis, for it shows that the tsar, for all his simplicity ... knew exactly what he was doing when he did it. He knew exactly what he was doing when he did it again, sixteen hours later, after agonizing all day about it.

Source: Sean McMeekin, *July 1914: Countdown to War* (New York: Basic Books, 2013), 398. Reprinted by permission of BasicBooks, an imprint of Hachette Book Group, Inc.

Figure 2.1 Franz Conrad von Hötzendorf

Franz Conrad von Hötzendorf (1852–1925) was the most highly regarded Habsburg officer of his generation. A prolific military writer, Conrad taught at the Austro-Hungarian war school (1888–92) where his students included fifty-one future generals of World War I. As a tactician Conrad lacked the strategic vision to excel as chief of the general staff, but accepted the post in 1906 at the insistence of Francis Ferdinand. He later clashed with the archduke, who rejected his appeals for preventive wars against Serbia and Italy. Conrad, a Darwinist and agnostic, privately criticized both the emperor and his heir but (aside from a brief interlude in 1911–12) remained chief until 1917, helping push Austria-Hungary toward war in 1914. A widower by the time he became chief, he tarnished his reputation in a scandalous affair with a younger woman who eventually became his second wife (and lived with him at headquarters) during World War I. Conrad's four sons all became officers; two died in the war.

A decade later a minister in the Serbian government of 1914, Ljuba Jovanović, admitted that the plot had been discussed in cabinet meetings beforehand: "one day [prime minister] Pašić said to us … that there were people who were preparing to go to Sarajevo to kill Francis Ferdinand." Having failed to rein in Dimitrijević and other officers who supported such conspiracies, Pašić at that stage could do little other than instruct Serbia's ambassador in Vienna to "dissuade the archduke from the fatal journey" without giving an explanation that would in any way compromise the Serbian government.[2] The ambassador's overture was so vague that Austrian authorities failed to grasp its significance, and Francis Ferdinand never received the warning. After the assassination, Serbian leaders took heart in the news that Princip and the other conspirators arrested in Sarajevo all were Bosnian Serbs and thus Austro-Hungarian subjects, and hoped the Dual Monarchy would treat the crime as a domestic case rather than an international incident. Dimitrijević, the Black Hand, and other extremists may have welcomed war with Austria-Hungary in the summer of 1914, but few of their more moderate countrymen did. While the Serbian Army had won great victories and gained valuable experience in the recent Balkan Wars, it had not recovered from the 130,000 casualties it had suffered or been completely rearmed and resupplied; furthermore, the country had just doubled in size and it would take years for the newly acquired lands to be integrated into Serbia. Pašić resolved to move carefully and distance the Serbian government from the Black Hand and the assassination. On July 3 he made his first overture to the Russians. The following day the foreign minister in St. Petersburg, Sergei Sazonov, endorsed Pašić's cautious approach, advising that Serbia do nothing that might provoke Austria-Hungary. Unfortunately, this would be difficult for the prime minister and his Radical Party colleagues, as they faced elections in mid-August, and in Serbia candidates the public considered insufficiently anti-Austrian stood little chance of being elected. The less-than-conciliatory campaign speeches of Pašić and his colleagues were quoted in the Vienna press, increasing the level of outrage in Austria-Hungary.

If war had come with Francis Ferdinand still alive, the heir to the throne would have served as Austro-Hungarian commander-in-chief, with Conrad functioning as his chief-of-staff. Upon his death 26-year-old Archduke Charles, grandson of the emperor's younger brother, became heir, but he lacked the experience to inherit Francis Ferdinand's military role. Francis Joseph soon chose his cousin, Archduke Frederick, to serve as commander, an arrangement that made Conrad the de facto head of the wartime army. Even before the emperor formalized this arrangement, it became clear that Conrad's influence had increased and, with it, the likelihood that the Dual Monarchy would seek a military solution to the crisis. Back in his office in Vienna on June 29, Conrad informed his staff that war with Serbia was inevitable. That evening he met with foreign minister Count Leopold Berchtold, who suggested that Serbia should "abolish certain organizations" it had earlier promised to suppress.[3] Berchtold did not jump to the conclusion that the assassination meant war, yet he recognized that it could not be treated as a domestic crime, as Pašić had hoped. Conrad responded that only war would resolve the Serbian problem, and over the days that followed the overall exasperation with Serbia converted most Austro-Hungarian leaders to his point of view. On June 30, Berchtold began to limit his own options, accepting Conrad's argument that the army should be mobilized only if it were going to fight, and not in support of a diplomatic initiative. It marked the first step in the foreign minister's rapid transformation into an advocate of war.

Conrad's first imperial audience after the assassination came on Sunday, July 5, two days after the funeral of Francis Ferdinand and Sophie. He found Francis Joseph anxious over whether Germany would support Austria-Hungary in case of war, but the old emperor had only himself to blame. In part because he had clashed with Francis Ferdinand over many issues – most notably the archduke's insistence upon marrying Sophie, a mere countess, making their children ineligible for the Habsburg throne – he had given his nephew a funeral barely appropriate for a man of his station, and had denied requests by William II and other foreign dignitaries to attend the ceremonies. As a result, Francis Joseph and his ministers had no first-hand evidence of where German leaders stood on the question of how Austria-Hungary should deal with Serbia. During the week after the assassination the Germans sent mixed signals, prompting Berchtold to seek clarification of their position before proceeding further. By the time Conrad met with Francis Joseph, the foreign minister's chief of cabinet, Count Alexander Hoyos, was on a train to Berlin on a mission to secure a promise of support.

Germany's "Blank Check" to Austria-Hungary

Berchtold sent Hoyos to Berlin because he had no confidence that his ambassador to Germany – Ladislaus de Szögyény-Marich, an elderly Hungarian count – could deliver a clear signal that Austria-Hungary wanted war with Serbia. Nevertheless, Berchtold involved Szögyény in the overture to the German leadership, which began when Hoyos arrived in Berlin at midday on July 5. Szögyény met with William II while Hoyos met with Arthur Zimmermann, undersecretary in the German Foreign Office. Later that afternoon, William II met with Chancellor Bethmann Hollweg and his war minister, General Erich von Falkenhayn, and decided to support Austria-Hungary, accepting the risk that Russia might intervene on Serbia's behalf and plunge Europe into a general war. In further discussions with Szögyény and Hoyos on July 6, Bethmann Hollweg and Zimmermann confirmed Germany's commitment, urged that Austria-Hungary should act immediately, and recommended that they keep their understanding secret from their Triple Alliance partner, Italy, at least for the moment. The Germans thus sent Hoyos home with a specific assurance of support, enabling Austria-Hungary to use the assassination of Francis Ferdinand to justify a settling of accounts with Serbia.

Hoyos was back in Vienna by July 7 to brief the ministerial council, a body including the heads of Austria-Hungary's three common ministries – foreign minister Berchtold, war minister General Alexander Krobatin, and finance minister Leon von Bilinski – and the two prime ministers, Count Karl Stürgkh of Austria and Count István Tisza of Hungary. Hoyos was present for the entire four-hour meeting; Conrad was called in to comment on possible military operations but otherwise did not participate in the discussion. He made much of this fact after the war, claiming that he had not been a policymaker during those crucial days, "only a military expert" called in to explain war plans after the Hoyos mission. But at this stage his direct participation was unnecessary, because of his recent success in converting the civilian leadership to his views. Bilinski and Stürgkh had been members of his "war party" since the time of the First Balkan War, and Berchtold now joined them in accepting Conrad's arguments. As a fellow general officer, Krobatin shared his outlook completely. Unlike the chiefs of the other general staffs of Europe during July 1914, Conrad outlined his war plans to the civilian leaders in great detail. The army's sixteen corps were divided into three groups: *A-Staffel* included nine corps; *B-Staffel*, four; and *Minimalgruppe Balkan*, three. Plan B, for a Balkan war against Serbia, required the army to mobilize seven corps (*B-Staffel* plus *Minimalgruppe Balkan*), but if the crisis escalated into a war against Russia the entire army would be mobilized for Plan R, with thirteen corps (*A-Staffel* plus *B-Staffel*) deployed against the Russians while three corps (*Minimalgruppe Balkan*) stood on the defensive against the Serbs.

In the meeting of July 7 Conrad acknowledged the possibility of Russian intervention, but Stürgkh and Bilinski argued that domestic considerations precluded anything other than the decisive use of overwhelming force. As prime minister of Austria, Stürgkh fully appreciated the fragile nature of a multinational empire in which no nationality wanted a continuation of the status quo and some, at least covertly, favored the breakup of the empire into national states. The Czechs traditionally had been the most vocal opponents of the regime, and their leaders, most notably Tomás Masaryk, would be among the first to go into exile in Paris or London as soon as the war began. Under such circumstances Stürgkh believed that any sign of weakness on the part of the government would only embolden its internal critics. Bilinski likewise appreciated the need to move decisively. As finance minister his portfolio included the administration of Bosnia, whose rival Serb, Croat, and Muslim parties had been jousting for control of their own provincial diet since its creation in 1910. He echoed Stürgkh's fears that Austro-Hungarian rule in Bosnia could not continue unless Serbia were crushed, and also felt that a protracted crisis would bring unwanted disruption to the Dual Monarchy's economy. Tisza alone hesitated, believing no good could come from the war Conrad described: if things went well, more Slavs likely would be annexed to the empire, diluting the influence of the Magyars, and if they did not, his own Hungary eventually would bear the brunt of a Russian invasion.[4] When Tisza remained skeptical after the ministerial council of July 7, Berchtold attempted to bring him around by emphasizing that Germany now expected Austria-Hungary to go to war, and if the Dual Monarchy failed to rise to the occasion its alliance with Germany – an alliance that Tisza, like most Hungarians, valued greatly – would be in jeopardy. The foreign minister's words to the Hungarian prime minister, taken out of context, have been cited as evidence by historians who overstate the role of German expectations in shaping Austro-Hungarian behavior during July 1914. With the sole exception of Tisza, the Dual Monarchy's leaders clearly wanted war with Serbia and were willing to risk war with Russia as long as they had the support of Germany.

Waiting for War

Various factors have been cited to explain the delay of sixteen days between Hoyos' report to the ministerial council and the delivery of Austria-Hungary's ultimatum to Serbia. The more charitable accounts cite the gradual process of getting Tisza and the Hungarians behind the idea of risking war, while harsher critics allege sheer bumbling and indecision. But as early as the evening of July 6, when Hoyos returned from Berlin with the "blank check," the Austro-Hungarian general staff determined that Serbia should not be handed the ultimatum any earlier than July 22 or 23, because of the number of troops then on harvest leave. Aside from Russia, the Dual Monarchy was the most rural of Europe's great powers, with barely 9 percent of its population (as of 1913) living in cities and towns. Traditionally, troops had been released for agricultural labor during the summer, on a schedule staggered territorially by corps and tailored to meet the crop-harvesting needs of the various regions of the empire. At the time of the Hoyos mission seven of the army's sixteen corps had already been granted their leave for summer 1914; to recall them abruptly would affect the harvest and arouse suspicions abroad that Austria-Hungary intended to go to war with Serbia. For five of the furloughed corps, leaves would end on July 19, and for the remaining two, on July 25.[5] Unless the leaves ended early, an ultimatum to Belgrade could not be delivered more than a few days in advance of the latter date. On July 8, when Conrad met with Berchtold, Hoyos, and other leading foreign ministry officials, Berchtold confirmed that "we will deliver the ultimatum only after the harvest," no earlier than July 22. In coming to this decision, Austro-Hungarian leaders failed to appreciate that, with each passing day, the international outrage over Francis Ferdinand's assassination was dissipating, undercutting the moral high ground upon which they stood, or that a delay of such length might give the other great powers an opening to manipulate the crisis to the Dual Monarchy's disadvantage. Confident in the course they had set, Berchtold closed the meeting with the suggestion that Conrad and Krobatin go on holiday "to give the impression that nothing is happening."[6] And so they did, for the next eleven days.

At this stage Conrad made no effort to coordinate war plans with his German counterpart, Helmuth von Moltke the Younger, with whom he had maintained a direct channel of communication since the Bosnian crisis of 1908–09. If the present conflict

unfolded in the same manner as the Bosnian crisis, the threat of a German mobilization would suffice to back down the Russians, leaving Austria-Hungary free to attack
Serbia and consultation between the two armies unnecessary. If it escalated into a general European war, each already knew what to expect from the other. Conrad knew
the general outlines of Germany's plan for a two-front war against the combination of
France and Russia, the plan attributed to Alfred von Schlieffen, Moltke's predecessor as
chief of the German general staff. Schlieffen had retired in 1906 and died in 1913, but
his general concept of defeating France first with overwhelming force, then turning to
face a slower mobilizing Russia, survived him. Conrad was aware that, in case of a general war, seven of Germany's eight armies (thirty-five corps, including thirteen reserve
corps) would be deployed against France, leaving just one army (four corps, including
one reserve corps) in East Prussia to stand against Russia. Thus, the thirteen Austro-
Hungarian corps deployed along the Russian border (under Plan R) would have to
shoulder most of the burden in the east until Germany defeated France. In the years
before 1914 Conrad repeatedly pressed Moltke to allocate more troops to the Eastern
front, but the calculus never changed. In their last prewar meeting, on May 12, 1914,
at the Bohemian resort of Carlsbad, Moltke again reiterated the assumption of the
Schlieffen Plan (or at least his modification of it) that Germany would "be finished
with France in six weeks after the beginning of operations." He did not specifically ask
Conrad for a holding action against the Russians at the onset of war, instead clinging
to the old assumption that the tsar's army would take an inordinately long time to
mobilize, making the Austro-Hungarian Army's initial obligation in the east neither
burdensome nor risky.[7]

While Conrad made no effort to contact Moltke in the wake of the Hoyos mission,
Moltke and his own general staff likewise took no additional measures. Their elaborate mobilization timetables had already been revised to accommodate the larger
army the Reichstag had given them in the Army Law of 1913, an army they would not
be afraid to use. In December 1912, during the First Balkan War, Moltke had given
William II and Tirpitz his opinion on a general European war: "the sooner the better,"[8]
because in another five years the Franco-Russian combination would be too strong for
Germany to overcome. Tirpitz did not share his sense of urgency, for the navy's enemy
was Britain and he felt certain that, in the naval-industrial competition, time was on
Germany's side. Thereafter, the German leadership stood ready to exploit any crisis
to get its general war, provided that Russia appeared to be the aggressor and Britain
remained neutral. The emperor and his ministers felt confident that if the tsar were
the first to proclaim a general mobilization, even the Social Democrats would support
the funding for Germany to respond, but in any other scenario the Reichstag's largest
party and its millions of followers would pose a serious domestic problem. Thus, as the
July Crisis of 1914 unfolded, they took a wait-and-see approach. If Austria-Hungary's
attack on Serbia provoked Russia to mobilize, the Schlieffen Plan would be activated

and they would get the war they wanted; if it did not, they would remain on the side-lines while the Dual Monarchy pursued what would amount to a third Balkan War. Of course, even if Russia behaved the way Germany wanted it to, there was still the matter of ensuring Britain's neutrality. Toward this end, on July 6 – the day Hoyos left Berlin – the German foreign secretary, Gottlieb von Jagow, began to deliberately misinform his own ambassador in London, Prince Karl Max von Lichnowsky, that Germany's policy was to dissuade Austria-Hungary from overreacting to the assassination of Francis Ferdinand; thus, Jagow ensured that the ambassador would pass along this lie to Britain's foreign secretary, Sir Edward Grey. Believing through most of July that Germany sincerely sought to avoid war by restraining Austria-Hungary, Grey pledged Britain to do its part by restraining its Entente partner, Russia.

The desire of Germany and Austria-Hungary to keep Italy in the dark as the crisis unfolded reflected a lack of trust in their Triple Alliance partner; indeed, it appeared likely to all but the greatest optimists in Berlin and Vienna that the Italians would not remain faithful to the alliance much longer. As late as their Carlsbad meeting of May 1914, Moltke had still counted on Italy to join in a war against France, while Conrad hoped for nothing more than a genuine Italian neutrality. Instead, they faced an Italian neutrality clearly leaning toward defection to the enemy camp. On July 10, foreign minister Antonio di San Giuliano had told the German ambassador in Rome that Italy would expect to receive the entire Italian-speaking South Tyrol from Austria as compensation for any Austrian gains in the Balkans. San Giuliano considered the issue of compensation serious enough not just to wreck the Triple Alliance, but to cause war between Italy and Austria-Hungary.

As the July Crisis continued to unfold, France remained the least engaged of the six European powers, owing to the state visit of President Poincaré to Russia and the Scandinavian countries (July 16–29) with an entourage including Premier René Viviani, who also held the portfolio of foreign minister. Ever since World War I, some accounts of the July Crisis of 1914 have linked Poincaré's visit to Russia with the timing of Austria-Hungary's ultimatum to Serbia, arguing that the Dual Monarchy, on Germany's advice, deliberately sought to act when Poincaré was en route, cut off from Paris but also unable to coordinate a response to the crisis in face-to-face meetings with the Russians. But Austro-Hungarian leaders never discussed Poincaré's travel plans in any of their deliberations and, in any event, delivered their ultimatum to Serbia just before the French delegation left St. Petersburg, while Poincaré and Viviani were hosting a dinner for Nicholas II and the imperial family aboard the dreadnought *France*. For their part, Poincaré and Viviani held only the most general discussions with Russian leaders while in St. Petersburg (July 20–23), during which the French president found the tsar more concerned about Russia's relations with Sweden than with the looming crisis in the Balkans. Before departing, Poincaré assured Nicholas II of the "unshakable solidity" of their alliance.[9]

Austria-Hungary's Ultimatum to Serbia

In the days after Pašić's exchange of July 3–4 with the Russian foreign minister, Sazonov, the prime minister and other Serbian officials proved to be incapable of the sort of prudence their situation dictated. Just as Serbian politicians campaigning for their August 1914 elections gave inflammatory speeches, Serbian diplomats in various foreign capitals gave newspaper interviews laced with anti-Austrian statements. On July 14 Pašić presided over a state funeral in Belgrade for the Russian ambassador, Nikolai Hartwig, whom he eulogized not only as a great friend of Serbia but also a Panslav hero. Speaking before a huge crowd, Pašić did not miss the opportunity to praise Nicholas II as the protector of Slavic peoples. His optimism that the crisis would end peacefully continued to wane, and on the night of July 18/19 he telegraphed all Serbian posts abroad (except Vienna) alerting his diplomats that Austria-Hungary would be likely to make demands incompatible with Serbia's sovereignty, and instructing them to appeal for diplomatic support.

Back in Vienna, the ministerial council finally met on July 19 to draft the Austro-Hungarian ultimatum to Serbia and determine the precise timing of its delivery. Conrad returned from holiday to join the five ministers for the meeting, and once again reviewed the war plans. He focused on Plan B (for a Balkan war against Serbia) and treated Plan R (Russia) as a mere contingency. He played no role in formulating the ultimatum, which in any event Berchtold and the ministers had already concluded must be worded in such a way as to guarantee that Serbia would reject it. The ultimatum began with a long preamble scolding Serbia for failing to honor the commitment it had made in March 1909 at the end of the Bosnian crisis to pursue "friendly and neighborly relations" with Austria-Hungary. It went on to indict Serbia for the assassination of Francis Ferdinand:

It is clear from the statements and confessions of the criminal authors of the assassination of the twenty-eighth of June, that the murder at Sarajevo was conceived at Belgrade, that the murderers received the weapons and the bombs with which they were equipped from Serbian officers and officials … and, finally, that the dispatch of the criminals and of their weapons to Bosnia was arranged and effected under the conduct of Serbian frontier authorities.[10]

The document dictated the text of a 178-word statement of contrition that Serbia would be required to issue, then listed ten demands (see Box 2.1). Some were specific, others more general; point 2, demanding the dissolution of *Narodna Odbrana* rather than the Black Hand, revealed that Austro-Hungarian leaders did not know of the existence of the terrorist group that actually carried out the assassination. Embedded in the list were two demands that no sovereign state could accept: point 5, allowing Austro-Hungarian officials a general role in suppressing the anti-Austrian movement within Serbia; and point 6, allowing Austro-Hungarian officials a specific role in judicial proceedings against the assassination plotters within Serbia. Berchtold's ambassador in Belgrade, Baron Vladimir von Giesl, delivered the ultimatum at 6:00 p.m. on Thursday, July 23, giving the Serbian government 48 hours to respond unconditionally or face a declaration of war.

Later that evening, Pašić and his ministers met with King Peter, and resolved to reject the ultimatum. Over the next two days Britain, France, and Italy urged a conciliatory response, if not unconditional acceptance, and among the Balkan states only Montenegro pledged to support Serbia in case of war. Pašić assumed that Germany would stand behind Austria-Hungary, and thus feared the same scenario that had ended the Bosnian crisis of 1908–09, when Russia failed to support Serbia. But over the preceding five years the line-up of the tsar's council of ministers had changed almost completely, and Russia had grown stronger militarily. Russian leaders, like their Austro-Hungarian counterparts, also felt a need to show resolve on this particular occasion for the sake of their country's future status as a great power. Their humiliating defeat at the hands of the Japanese a decade earlier, followed by their retreat in the most recent Bosnian crisis, certainly left them feeling less respected internationally; this was, indeed, the case, as reflected in the latest war plans of Germany and Austria-Hungary, both of which seriously underestimated Russia's capabilities. When the Russian ministers met on July 24, Sazonov urged action on Serbia's behalf, even if it risked war with Germany as well as Austria-Hungary. While he acknowledged Germany's strengths he did not consider them insurmountable and feared the consequences of backing down again. As he had noted earlier to Russia's ambassador in London, "to feel at one's strongest and yet to go on giving way to an opponent whose superiority consists solely in his organization and discipline is not only a humiliating business but is dangerous because of the demoralization it brings in its train."[11] Of the other ministers only the finance minister, Pyotr Bark, hesitated before making it unanimous. They saw nothing but opportunity in the present crisis; indeed, for the tsar's generals, the greatest challenge came in deciding whom to attack first. While Russian military intelligence had not divined the specific details of the Schlieffen Plan, it was no secret that in the event of a two-front war the initial German focus would be on the French, creating a window of opportunity for Russia to score a victory in East Prussia. The Russians were also supremely confident in their ability to defeat Austria-Hungary, whose war plans had been passed to them by Colonel Alfred

Box 2.1 **Austria-Hungary's ultimatum to Serbia**

The Austro-Hungarian ultimatum to Serbia, delivered on July 23, 1914, made the following demands of the Serbian government:

1. to suppress any publication which incites to hatred and contempt of the Austro-Hungarian Monarchy and the general tendency of which is directed against its territorial integrity;
2. to dissolve immediately the society called Narodna Odbrana [and] all other societies and their branches in Serbia which engage in propaganda against the Austro-Hungarian Monarchy;
3. to eliminate without delay from public instruction in Serbia ... everything that serves or might serve to foment the propaganda against Austria-Hungary;
4. to remove from the military service, and from the administration in general, all officers and functionaries guilty of propaganda against the Austro-Hungarian Monarchy...
5. to accept the cooperation in Serbia of representatives of the Austro-Hungarian government in the suppression of the subversive movement directed against the integrity of the Monarchy;
6. to take judicial proceedings against accomplices in the plot of the 28th of June who are on Serbian territory; delegates of the Austro-Hungarian government will take part in the investigation relating thereto;
7. to proceed without delay to the arrest of Major Voislav Tankosic and ... Milan Ciganovic, a Serbian state employee, who have been compromised by the results of the preliminary investigation at Sarajevo;
8. to prevent ... the participation of the Serbian authorities in the illicit traffic of arms and explosives across the frontier; to dismiss and punish severely the officials of the frontier service ... guilty of having assisted the perpetrators of the Sarajevo crime by facilitating their passage across the frontiers;
9. to furnish ... explanations regarding the unjustifiable utterances of high Serbian officials, both in Serbia and abroad, who, notwithstanding their official positions, did not hesitate after the crime of the 28th of June to give ... expressions of hostility to the Austro-Hungarian Government; and finally,
10. to inform the Imperial and Royal Government without delay of the execution of the measures comprised under the preceding ...

The Austro-Hungarian Government awaits the reply of the Royal Government at the latest by 6 o'clock on Saturday evening, the 25th of July.

Source: US Naval War College, *International Law Documents 1917: Neutrality; Breaking of Diplomatic Relations*, vol. 17, ed. George G. Wilson (Washington, DC: US Government Printing Office, 1918), 40–41.

Redl, one of Conrad's general staff officers, prior to his suicide in May 1913 when his treason was discovered. On July 25 the ministers reconvened, this time with Nicholas II chairing the meeting, and reaffirmed their decision for war, after which Sazonov, through the Serbian ambassador in St. Petersburg, promised Pašić that Russia would help.

The tsar planned to announce a "period preparatory to war" the next day, but Sazonov's pledge of support, which reached Belgrade shortly before the Austro-Hungarian ultimatum expired, did not detail what form Russian help would take. Lacking a specific pledge of military support from Russia, Pašić delivered a response to Giesl at the 6:00 p.m. deadline that was as conciliatory as Serbia could make it. He rejected point 6, but accepted point 5 with conditions, and accepted the rest of the ultimatum unconditionally. Pašić further proposed that, should his response be deemed unsatisfactory, the conflict be mediated either by the Permanent Court of Arbitration (established in 1899 at the Hague) or by the great powers of Europe collectively. While some historians have argued that Serbia would have accepted all of Austria-Hungary's demands if Russia had not offered its support, the evidence shows that the Serb leadership never intended to accept the ultimatum in its entirety and, in any event, the Russian offer of support on July 25 was too vague to influence Pašić's response to Vienna.

Following the instructions Berchtold had given him, Giesl informed Pašić on the spot that diplomatic relations between their countries were severed. Later that evening Francis Joseph authorized the implementation of Plan B, mobilizing seven army corps for an invasion of Serbia. Conrad designated the following Tuesday, July 28, as the first mobilization day, to facilitate the activation of the two corps whose harvest leave ended on the 25th (which included the VII Corps, based in southern Hungary, on the opposite side of the Danube from Serbia). In the hours before it responded to the ultimatum, Serbia had begun preparations to move the seat of government from Belgrade to the safety of Niš, 100 miles (160 km) to the southeast. That evening, as Austria-Hungary ordered its partial mobilization, Serbia ordered a full mobilization of its own army. Then, on the 26th, Russia began its "period preparatory to war," a premobilization based upon the decisions taken by the tsar and his ministers the day before. By the morning of Monday, July 27, when the statesmen of the other capitals of Europe first read Serbia's response to the ultimatum, including the appeal for mediation by the great powers, the time for mediation already had passed. Emboldened by the imminent Russian mobilization, Pašić certainly had no intention of being any more conciliatory than he had been in his initial response; indeed, now that he knew Serbia had a "blank check" of its own and could count on the support of Russia no matter what, he wished he had been less conciliatory two days earlier. Yet it soon became clear that, by accepting most of the points of the ultimatum, Pašić had scored a triumph in the court of international public opinion, even though Serbia had rejected the two points that really mattered and, if carried out, would have exposed the complicity of Serbian officers and officials in the assassination of the archduke. Austria-Hungary's formal declaration of war reached Belgrade just after noon on Tuesday, July 28. Thanks to the existing web of alliance commitments, eight days later eight countries, including five of the six great powers of Europe, would be at war with at least one of their neighbors.

The Dominoes Fall

Realizing that Europe could be on the brink of a general war, heads of state, ministers, and generals abruptly canceled their summer plans and returned to their capitals. On July 27 alone, Poincaré and Viviani broke off their Scandinavian tour and steamed for home, while William II cut short a Baltic cruise aboard his beloved yacht *Hohenzollern* to return to Berlin. Sir Edward Grey stepped up Britain's mediation effort, which on the 27th received the endorsement of France, but on the same day France assured Russia of its support in case of war, and Grey informed the German ambassador, Lichnowsky, that Britain would not remain neutral in a war pitting its Entente partners against Germany and Austria-Hungary. Grey overreached in making such a statement, which at that time most of his colleagues in the Liberal Asquith cabinet would not have supported, but at least one other minister was a step ahead of him: Winston Churchill, First Lord of the Admiralty, on that same fateful Monday ordered the British fleet not to disperse from a practice mobilization it had conducted over the weekend.

On the afternoon of July 28, shortly after the declaration of war, Austro-Hungarian artillery began shelling Belgrade across the Danube and Sava rivers; that evening, three river monitors from the navy's Danube Flotilla joined in the bombardment. The same day, without consulting his ministers or generals, William II appealed to Austria-Hungary to "halt in Belgrade" – to cross the Danube and occupy the Serbian capital, but then allow time for diplomacy to work – and also initiated a series of direct, personal exchanges with his cousin, Nicholas II, the so-called "Willy-Nicky" telegrams, all to no avail. Bethmann Hollweg likewise lost his nerve at midweek, earlier bravado notwithstanding; his wavering, and that of William II, understandably caused considerable anxiety in Vienna. Wednesday, July 29 proved eventful for all three Entente powers. Poincaré and Viviani landed at Dunkirk and hastened to Paris, where the president impressed upon the cabinet that in the present crisis France must have a united home front and the support of Britain, both of which could be achieved only by allowing Germany to be the aggressor. To ensure that French troops did nothing that could be considered provocative, Poincaré ordered those deployed along the border to pull back 6 miles (10 km) into France, a move they carried out the following day. Meanwhile, Grey presented his case for war to the rest of the cabinet in London, emphasizing his conviction that Germany would soon invade France via neutral Belgium (which, by that day, was alarmed enough to order a partial mobilization of its own), but his appeal failed to sway most of his colleagues. Finally, in St. Petersburg, Nicholas II ordered a general mobilization of the Russian Army, only to have second thoughts and countermand the order that evening. Besieged by protests from his generals and ministers, the following day the tsar relented, and the Russian mobilization was on again, effective July 31.

Russia's general mobilization gave Germany the war it wanted, and deprived Austria-Hungary of the war it thought it had achieved. Early on the afternoon of the 31st, an hour after the news reached Berlin, William II announced that war was imminent; Germany sent an ultimatum to Russia giving it until the following day to stop its preparations for war. A second ultimatum, to France, demanded not only a declaration of French neutrality should Germany and Russia go to war – reasonable enough if Germany's intention had been to limit the war to the Balkans and eastern Europe – but also German occupation of the French forts at Verdun and Toul, to last for the duration of the war, as a guarantee. Later the same day a third de facto ultimatum went to Austria-Hungary, as William II sent a telegram to Francis Joseph urging him to forget Serbia and focus instead on Russia, while Germany defeated France in the opening phase of the Schlieffen Plan. Francis Joseph had no alternative but to comply, for the sake of his own country's security as well as to support the Germans. Unfortunately for Austria-Hungary, the crushing news of Russia's mobilization and Germany's reaction to it came with its army in the midst of a deployment in the opposite direction. Conrad had reasoned that, if German pressure did not suffice to deter the Russians from intervening, a successful lightning strike against the Serbs certainly would. The initial mobilization order activated seven of the army's sixteen corps (*B-Staffel* plus *Minimalgruppe Balkan*) to carry out Plan B against Serbia, but on July 29, Conrad had raised the strength to eight corps (twenty-six divisions) by ordering III Corps, part of *A-Staffel*, to join *B-Staffel* and head south. Thus, he proceeded against Serbia with a strengthened Plan B involving half of the Austro-Hungarian Army, while taking no precautionary measures at all on the Russian frontier despite all the signs pointing toward Russian intervention. On July 31, after learning of Russia's general mobilization, the ministerial council in Vienna reaffirmed the decision to invade Serbia even though it would now also mean war with Russia and a general war for Europe. But the tables had turned completely since the Hoyos mission. Instead of fighting a war for its own limited goals in the Balkans, Austria-Hungary would be obligated to fight for broader German goals against the Triple Entente. After the ministers met, Francis Joseph issued a general mobilization order activating the army's remaining eight (*A-Staffel*) corps. Austria-Hungary did not want a war with Russia, especially one in which most of Germany's army, at least initially, would be occupied in the west, but at this stage its leaders could do little other than cling to Moltke's promise that even a general war would be short and decisive, and that Germany would "be finished with France in six weeks."

On August 1, after getting no response to its ultimatum to St. Petersburg, Germany proclaimed a general mobilization and declared war on Russia. France responded to its German ultimatum with a general mobilization of its own. That evening, Moltke took the first step in implementing his war plan by sending advance units of the German Fourth Army into neutral Luxembourg, which was occupied unopposed. The following day, alleging that the French Army stood on the verge of violating Belgian neutrality, the Germans delivered an ultimatum to Belgium demanding that their troops be allowed to pass through the country en route to France. In return, Germany promised to guarantee the territorial integrity of Belgium and its "possessions" (i.e. the Belgian Congo), and to pay for any supplies requisitioned or material damage done by its troops. On August 3, the Belgians rejected the ultimatum as "a flagrant violation of international law" and vowed to defend themselves against attack.[12] Undeterred, the Germans adhered to their timetable, declaring war on the French later that day and the Belgians the following morning. On the morning of August 4, Moltke ordered elements of the First, Second, and Third armies to cross the border into Belgium while, south of Luxembourg, the Fifth Army crossed into France and, farther to the south, the weaker Sixth and Seventh armies stood on the defensive in Lorraine and Alsace. Later on the 4th, the Reichstag voted 5 billion marks in war credits to cover the mobilization and the initial expenses of the war. The SPD's delegation voted unanimously in favor of the bill, confirming that the German government had, indeed, gotten the war it wanted. By being the first to initiate a general mobilization, Russia had cast itself in the role of aggressor in the eyes of the German public, including German socialists, and endowed the German cause with a sense of righteousness that blinded most Germans to the reality that their own leaders had escalated the war. When University of Leipzig history professor Karl Lamprecht spoke of "a single great feeling of moral elevation,"[13] he was far from alone. Indeed, in the first days of August 1914, very few Germans found fault with the Schlieffen Plan's logic that in order to defend itself against Russia, Germany had to attack France first and violate Belgium in the bargain.

For Sir Edward Grey, who had gotten too far ahead of most of his cabinet colleagues in his desire to bring Britain into the war, the German invasion of Belgium was a godsend, as nothing up to that point had worked to sway the non-interventionists in London: neither the occupation of Luxembourg, nor Germany's ultimatum to France, nor a threat by Grey to resign if Britain failed to support France, nor a threat by Asquith to resign if Grey went. In the House of Commons on the afternoon of August 3, the foreign secretary made his final appeal for war, linking British honor and interests not just to the fate of France, but to Belgium as well. After he spoke, Conservative leader Andrew Bonar Law and Irish Parliamentary Party leader John Redmond endorsed his remarks, but the key conversion came in his own Liberal Party. Germany's bullying of Belgium so outraged the leading non-interventionist, Chancellor of the Exchequer David Lloyd George, that it converted him overnight into a passionate supporter of British intervention. On the evening of the 3rd, after it became known in London that the Belgians had rejected the German ultimatum, Lloyd George supported a sharply worded British ultimatum to Berlin drafted by Asquith and Grey, demanding an end to all hostile action against Belgium. When this ultimatum expired at the end of the day on August 4, Britain declared war on Germany.

With this action France got the war it wanted, or at least war under the circumstances Poincaré had outlined upon his return from Russia. Britain supported France and, at least on the Western front, Germany was the clear aggressor. Looking back on the moment with great satisfaction, Poincaré observed that, internationally, "in contrast with Austro-German imperialism, France became … the living representative of right and of liberty," while domestically, "the *union sacrée*, to which I had appealed, sprang spontaneously … from every heart."[14] Indeed, having Germany cast in the role of aggressor was as important to French domestic unity as Russia's mobilization was to German domestic unity. The deep division between France's conservative Catholics and liberal secularists remained, but amid the declarations of war few doubted the need for Poincaré's "sacred union" to defend the endangered nation. In an important early sign of this unity, the Socialist Party rallied to the cause even though its leader Jean Jaurès, pacifist and critic of Poincaré, had been assassinated by a right-wing fanatic on July 31.

Britain's declaration of war all but completed the initial configuration of belligerents. On August 5, Montenegro demonstrated its solidarity with Serbia by declaring war on Austria-Hungary. The following day, the Dual Monarchy finally bowed to the inevitable and declared war on Russia. This started a new round of declarations, formalizing hostilities between Austria-Hungary and the countries already at war with Germany, and between Germany and the countries already at war with Austria-Hungary. The only European great power remaining on the sidelines, Italy, declared its neutrality on August 2, two days after condemning the Austro-Hungarian attack on Serbia as an act of aggression. The belligerents all mobilized unprecedented numbers of troops and deployed them at unprecedented speeds, and yet it took most of August for the first wave of combatants to be fully engaged. In the first three weeks of the month, Germany transported almost 4 million men and 600,000 horses on 11,000 trains of 54 cars each. At the peak of the mobilization, with seven of its eight armies headed west, Germany's Rhine bridges carried 560 trains per day. No other country had the infrastructure or the organization to move so many men so efficiently. The mobilization schedule of the Russian Army called for a total of just 360 trains per day, the Austro-Hungarian only 153.

Austria-Hungary faced the greatest challenges in mobilizing for war and experienced the greatest problems, owing to the need to abandon its original offensive against Serbia (Plan B) in order to fight Russia (Plan R). As of July 31, Conrad had five corps (the four corps of *B-Staffel* and one corps detached from *A-Staffel*) on southbound trains, to join the three corps of *Minimalgruppe Balkan* in smashing Serbia, leaving just the remaining eight corps of *A-Staffel* to face Russia. These five corps had to be turned around, but Conrad's own general staff railway bureau advised him that, aside from the lone *A-Staffel* corps, any attempt to reverse their course en route would cause complete chaos. His railway experts persuaded him that it would be better to allow the four corps of *B-Staffel* to detrain on the Serbian front, then re-embark on trains headed north; they assured him that the troops would still reach the Russian frontier no later than August 23, in the same number of days it would have taken them to get there under the original calculations of Plan R. This estimate proved to be wildly optimistic. When the fighting on the Russian front began in earnest, as scheduled, on the 23rd, the army had at its disposal only the nine corps originally assigned to *A-Staffel*. Half of *B-Staffel* (the equivalent of two corps) eventually trickled into place piecemeal between August 31 and September 8, eight to sixteen days later than promised. The remaining troops arrived either too late to participate in the initial battles or never arrived at all.

Conclusion: War by Accident or by Design?

In their volumes of work on the outbreak of World War I, too many scholars have lost sight of the fact that the shots fired on June 28, 1914, by Gavrilo Princip were the first shots of the war, and the archduke and his consort the first casualties. On that Sunday morning in Sarajevo, Serbia started World War I. The kingdom of Serbia was not a revolutionary state like the later Soviet Union or Islamic Republic of Iran, whose central authorities deliberately directed its interactions with the outside world on two levels: conventionally, via embassies and international organizations; and covertly, via revolutionary or terrorist activity. Nor was it an internally weak or failed state, such as Afghanistan at the end of the twentieth century, playing host to radical foreign non-state actors with whom its leaders shared a general sympathy. Rather, Serbia was a dysfunctional or semi-failed state that operated like a revolutionary state because a rogue element within its own army, supported or tolerated by elements within its political mainstream, operated an international terrorist organization. Serbia also differed significantly from true failed states in that it was unified internally behind a single national idea. It was the strength of this idea that made Serbia dangerous, because it caused so many Serbian leaders to condone the terrorists on the grounds that their ultimate goal, after all, was to fulfill the national idea.

Serbia's program of state-sponsored or state-condoned terrorism against Austria-Hungary provided the context in which the Dual Monarchy decided to resolve its Serbian problem by war in July 1914. It was willing to risk a broader conflict with Russia in pursuing this course, provided that it had the support of Germany. The leaders of the Dual Monarchy fully expected that the threat of German intervention on their behalf would suffice to compel Russia to back down and abandon Serbia to its fate, as it had in the Bosnian crisis of 1908–09. Thus, their ultimatum to Belgrade included demands that they knew the Serbs could not accept. Russia's general mobilization on Serbia's behalf handed German leaders the golden opportunity to launch the European war they had planned for, but in order to justify attacking France first, they sent an ultimatum to Paris that included demands that they knew the French could not accept. There was no equivalent to these ultimata on the side of the Entente; indeed, the Entente powers issued no such demands other than Britain's final ultimatum of August 4, threatening war if Germany did not cease military operations against Belgium immediately.

Thus, World War I hardly began by accident. Austria-Hungary risked a general war to get the local war it wanted, and Germany exploited its ally's local war to get the general war it wanted, in the process trapping the Dual Monarchy in a commitment to fight for German war aims, ultimately at Germany's direction. But the leaders in Vienna let the July Crisis slip from their control long before July 31, the day a general war became certain and Berlin began dictating their actions. Their decision to allow furloughed troops to return from harvest leave as scheduled had extended their timeline for action, giving the other powers too much leeway to steer events in other directions and too much time for the sympathetic international outrage over the archduke's assassination to die down. Aside from Russia's mobilization decisions, the Entente powers took no specific provocative steps during the crisis, but the linkage of Britain supporting France supporting Russia supporting Serbia tainted the Triple Entente with the responsibility of having backed the state whose goals and policies had led to the firing of the first shots. While Russia did not control Serbia's actions any more than Germany controlled Austria-Hungary, in both cases the assurances of support from a stronger ally emboldened the primary actor. In the tense days of early August 1914, few would have predicted that, of the countries most responsible for starting and escalating the war, only Serbia would emerge with its goals fulfilled.

SUGGESTIONS FOR FURTHER READING

Ferguson, Niall. *The Pity of War* (New York: Basic Books, 1999).

Keiger, John F. V. *Raymond Poincaré* (Cambridge: Cambridge University Press, 1997).

McMeekin, Sean. *July 1914: Countdown to War* (New York: Basic Books, 2013).

Mombauer, Annika. *Helmuth von Moltke and the Origins of the First World War* (Cambridge: Cambridge University Press, 2001).

Otte, T. G. *Statesman of Europe: A Life of Sir Edward Grey* (London: Allen Lane, 2020).

Smith, Leonard V., Stéphane Audoin-Rouzeau, and Annette Becker. *France and the Great War, 1914–1918* (Cambridge: Cambridge University Press, 2003).

Sondhaus, Lawrence. *Franz Conrad von Hötzendorf: Architect of the Apocalypse* (Boston, MA: Brill, 2000).

Strachan, Hew. *The Outbreak of the First World War* (Oxford: Oxford University Press, 2004).

Williamson, Samuel R., Jr. *Austria-Hungary and the Origins of the First World War* (London: Macmillan, 1991).

Wilson, Keith (ed.). *Decisions for War, 1914* (New York: St. Martin's Press, 1995).

NOTES

1. Franz Conrad von Hötzendorf, *Aus meiner Dienstzeit, 1906–1918, vol. 4* (Vienna: Rikola Verlag, 1921–25), 16–17.
2. Ljuba Jovanović, *The Murder of Sarajevo* (London: British Institute of International Affairs, 1925), 3.
3. Conrad, *Aus meiner Dienstzeit*, vol. 4, 34.
4. See Protocol of Common Ministerial Council, July 7, 1914, with Conrad's "secret" military remarks, in Conrad, *Aus meiner Dienstzeit*, vol. 4, 43–56.
5. "Vorbereitende Massnahmen," dated July 6, 1914, Österreichisches Staatsarchiv, Kriegsarchiv (hereafter KA), Generalstab, Operationsbüro, 695.
6. Conrad, *Aus meiner Dienstzeit*, vol. 4, 61.
7. Conrad, *Aus meiner Dienstzeit*, vol. 3, 667–73.
8. Quoted in Fischer, *War of Illusions*, 62.
9. Raymond Poincaré, *The Origins of the War* (London: Cassell, 1922), 187.
10. Austro-Hungarian ultimatum to Serbia, Vienna, July 22, 1914, text in wwi.lib .byu.edu/index.php/The_Austro-Hungarian_Ultimatum_to_Serbia_(English_ Translation).
11. Sazonov quoted in Jack Snyder, *The Ideology of the Offensive: Military Decision Making and the Disasters of 1914* (Ithaca, NY: Cornell University Press, 1984), 188.
12. German ultimatum to Belgium, August 2, 1914, and Belgian response, August 3, 1914, texts in www.firstworldwar.com/source/belgium_germanrequest.htm.
13. Lamprecht quoted in Roger Chickering, *Imperial Germany and the Great War, 1914–1918* (Cambridge: Cambridge University Press, 1998), 14.
14. Poincaré, *The Origins of the War*, 255.

La rue de Bruxelles   LOUVAIN (Belgium) Brussels street

Destruction of Louvain

On August 25, 1914, German troops razed much of Louvain, Belgium, and massacred 248 of its inhabitants, after the invaders came under fire in and near the town. Some 2,000 buildings were destroyed, including the university library, where more than a quarter of a million volumes were burned, along with priceless manuscripts, some dating from the twelfth century. While such instances of brutality and wanton destruction foreshadowed German behavior in occupied countries during World War II, in World War I they occurred mostly in Belgium in August 1914 (indeed, mostly in the days between August 20 and August 25) as Germans acted on fears of an organized Belgian guerrilla resistance that did not, in fact, exist. On the Balkan front, similar Austro-Hungarian brutalization of Serbian civilians likewise came mostly in the first weeks of the war.

3

The European War Unfolds

August–December 1914

August 5–16	Germans defeat Belgians in battle of Liège.
August 10	German warships *Goeben* and *Breslau* seek refuge at Constantinople.
August 14–23	Germans defeat French and BEF in battles of the Frontiers.
August 27–30	Germans defeat Russians in battle of Tannenberg.
September 5–9	Allied victory in the first battle of the Marne.
September 6–11	Russians defeat Austro-Hungarians in battle of Lemberg-Rawa Ruska.
September–October	"Race to the Sea" establishes continuous trench lines on Western front.
October–November	First battle of Ypres decimates BEF.
October–November	Onset of Russo-Turkish hostilities in Black Sea and Caucasus.
December 15	Serbs repel Austro-Hungarian invasion.
December	Russians initiate Carpathian "winter war."

The organized upheaval of the initial mobilization – the greatest such endeavor in human history up to that time – placed unprecedented millions of men into uniform, most of whom expected a decisive outcome by the following year at the latest. But the action soon stalemated on every front, and by the winter of 1914–15 degenerated into a test of wills. The greatest test came on the Western front, where the action included the three belligerents – Germany, France, and Britain – with the greatest capacity to sustain a modern war effort. The relative success or failure of the individual armies in the opening campaigns hinged on the efficiency of their mobilization, followed by command-and-control and logistics once the troops deployed to the various fronts. In physical and material terms, it became clear from the start that the sheer size of an army, if well supplied and efficiently led, carried more weight than its élan or spirit, and that artillery mattered more than anyone had imagined. The first five months of the war gave some indication of the horrors to come, from the carnage on stalemated fronts to atrocities against civilians in Belgium and the Balkans. Faced with a war far costlier, in human and material terms, than had been envisaged, the belligerents not only persisted in fighting, but articulated war aims that made a compromise peace impossible.

The German Invasion of Belgium

Thirty-seven days after the assassination of Francis Ferdinand, the first German troops crossed the frontier into Belgium and France. While Schlieffen had assumed Germany's northernmost troops, the First Army, would cross the Netherlands on their way west, Moltke anticipated that Britain might respond to the violation of Belgium by block-ading Germany, and recognized that a neutral Netherlands could serve as "the wind-pipe that enables us to breathe."[1] Indeed, Germany took 50 percent of Dutch exports mainly because of the transit trade, prompting one prewar British diplomat to call Rotterdam a "quasi-German" port.[2] Thus, under Moltke's 1911 revision of Schlieffen's war plans (see Perspectives 3.1), the 320,000 men of the First Army entered the fray via a bottleneck just 6 miles (10 km) wide, between the city of Liège and the Dutch border, in order not to violate Dutch neutrality. To their immediate left, the 260,000 men of the Second Army deployed through another bottleneck of the same width including the city of Liège and its southern suburbs. The German timetable allowed for the congestion but not the tenacious resistance of the 70,000 Belgian troops gar-risoning the city and its belt of formidable forts. After the Germans won the battle of Liège (August 5–16) the two armies used bridges in and near the city to complete their crossing of the Meuse on the 18th, just two days behind schedule. As the Germans swept through Belgium en route to the French border, the extent of their arc reached as far west as Brussels, with the First Army having the longest march, followed in turn (to its left or southeast) by the Second, Third, Fourth, and Fifth armies. The first three German armies subsequently entered France west of the point where the Meuse flows from France northward into Belgium, while the Fourth Army, which entered Belgium via Luxembourg, crossed the Meuse at Sedan. Only the Fifth Army, striking out of Lorraine, invaded France without passing through Belgium, retracing the elder Moltke's 1870 invasion route before bearing to the southwest to cross the Meuse north of Verdun. Moltke, joined by William II, directed the offensive from the headquarters of the High Command (the *Oberste Heeresleitung* or OHL), initially at Koblenz, then the city of Luxembourg.

Perspectives 3.1: The Schlieffen Plan

American political scientist Jack Snyder (born 1951) explained the manner in which the Schlieffen Plan turned Germany's darkest strategic fears into reality:

The Schlieffen Plan … made the fear of a two-front, general war in Europe a self-fulfilling prophecy. Because of the time pressures in the plan, any Russian mobilization would require an immediate German attack on France. Thus there could be no chance to localize a Balkan conflict – no chance for either side to posture militarily, negotiate, and demobilize. The Schlieffen Plan prepared for the worst case in a way that ensured that the worst case would occur.

Source: Jack Snyder, *The Ideology of the Offensive: Military Decision Making and the Disasters of 1914* (Ithaca, NY: Cornell University Press, 1984), 115.

• • • •

Terence Zuber (born 1948), a German-educated former US Army officer, brought the Schlieffen Plan controversy to a new level by alleging that the plan never existed in the first place, but was a postwar invention:

There never was a Schlieffen plan … The Schlieffen plan was invented by the General Staff to explain away their failure to win the 1914 Marne campaign. In fact, the German Army never had nearly enough troops to execute an operation as ambitious as the Schlieffen plan, and Schlieffen himself said so. This has not been recognized because the Schlieffen plan debate was in fact not really about military planning, but politics and "militarism". There is no mention of the Schlieffen plan before 1920.

Source: Terence Zuber, *Inventing the Schlieffen Plan: German War Planning, 1871–1914* (Oxford: Oxford University Press, 2002), 5. Reproduced with permission of Oxford University Press through PLSclear.

• • • •

British scholar Terence Holmes (born 1942) has rebutted Zuber's argument that the memorandum historians call the "Schlieffen Plan" could not have been a genuine war plan owing to the number of troops it required, which far exceeded the number Germany had at the time:

Despite the recent wave of attacks on his view that "there never was a 'Schlieffen plan'", Terence Zuber stands by his "central thesis", which is that the Schlieffen plan called for 96 divisions at a time when the German Army could deploy only 72. [Contrary to] Zuber's calculations … the Schlieffen plan called for 90 divisions, not 96. The official deployment plans of 1906 involved 78 divisions, including two of the ersatz corps that Zuber says were "non-existent". From the official discussion about those two ersatz corps we can prove that it would have been perfectly feasible to raise eight of them altogether, as required by the Schlieffen plan.

Source: Terence M. Holmes, "All Present and Correct: The Verifiable Army of the Schlieffen Plan," *War in History* 16 (2009): 98–115.

Even in the protracted action around Liège, the Belgian Army did not seriously impede the progress of the German offensive, yet the refusal to allow the invaders free passage to France irritated the Germans enough to have serious consequences for the Belgian people. From the start, civilians giving anything less than their complete cooperation to the German Army were liable to be shot. Mayors, policemen, and Catholic priests were most at risk of summary execution, ostensibly as potential catalysts for resistance, but most killings resulted from the panic that seized the German troops after they came under fire in or near a town. Their fear of guerrilla snipers or *francs-tireurs* harked back to the Franco-Prussian War of 1870–71, when their forefathers had faced armed irregulars operating behind the lines after Napoleon III's defeat at Sedan. There were no organized Belgian *francs-tireurs* in August 1914 and very few proven cases of German troops being fired upon by Belgians in civilian clothing, yet in the first weeks of the war some 6,500 Belgian civilians, including women and children, were shot out of hand in reprisals for alleged *franc-tireur* activity. Brussels, whose mayor discouraged resistance, fell to the First Army on August 20 with little loss of civilian life (see Box 3.1), but the same day a series of massacres began in smaller cities and towns. The worst atrocities were perpetrated by the Second Army on August 20 at Andenne (211 dead) and August 22 at Tamines (383 dead), by the Third Army on August 23 at Dinant (674 dead), and by the First Army on August 25 at Louvain (248 dead). In almost all cases massacres were accompanied by the deliberate destruction of property, in the case of Louvain the burning of some 2,000 buildings, including the university library. A Dutch eyewitness to the razing of Dinant commented that "a village on the side of a volcano could not have been more completely, more terribly annihilated."[3] Gruesome (and unsubstantiated) tales of Belgian civilians mutilating dead and wounded Germans, which circulated within the army and back to the home front like modern-day "urban legends," further fueled the paranoia, as did stories of Belgian women and even young girls bearing arms. Faith in the veracity of such accounts reached the highest levels. In his memoir of the campaign,

General Alexander von Kluck, commander of the First Army, noted that in the ruins of Louvain his men had found "corpses of women with rifles in their hands."[4] Such assertions figured prominently in subsequent German rebuttals to international criticism of their "rape of Belgium," though in embellishing and sensationalizing the accounts of German brutality, Allied propagandists themselves unwittingly discredited the accounts of the harshest Belgian suffering (see Online Essay 9). Nevertheless, the German Foreign Office remained nervous about the army's conduct in Belgium and frustrated by its inability to provide key specifics, in particular regarding "cruelties of Belgian irregulars against our wounded men, for which we have not found any evidence."[5]

Box 3.1 A British nurse in Belgium, August 1914

Esmee Sartorius served as a nurse throughout the war, first in Belgium, then in hospitals on the home front, and finally in Italy. In August 1914 she experienced the onset of the German occupation of Belgium before making her way home via neutral Holland:

Like so many others when war was declared, I applied at once to the St. John Ambulance, to which I belonged, to know if there was any possibility of their making use of me, my only recommendation being three months' training in the London Hospital… Three days later the British Red Cross got an appeal for forty nurses to be sent out to Belgium… and I was asked if I would go. I naturally accepted with alacrity, and August 14th found us in Brussels.

…Next day some of the nurses were sent to hospitals outside Brussels, and others, including M., my cousin (who was a fully trained nurse), and myself, were given posts in the Royal Palace, which posts, however, we never filled, as the next thing we heard was that the Germans were outside the gate of Brussels, and all the allied wounded were to be evacuated to Antwerp. We were then given the option of returning to England at once; some returned, but we, M. and I amongst others, elected to remain, as we were told we were wanted outside Brussels.

At 3 pm next day the Germans marched in; it was a soul-stirring sight, seeing these impassive and tired-looking troops marching in to what seemed like a deserted town, every door and window shuttered and barred, and not a civilian to be seen, or a sound to be heard, save the steady tramping of the German troops, regiment after regiment, guns, cavalry, Uhlans with their fluttering pennons on their lances. One felt that thousands of Belgians were waiting and watching behind their shuttered doors and windows, with bated breath and terrible anxiety lest anyone or anything should cause a disturbance, and so bring down the punishment of the enemy.

However, nothing happened, owing to the notices which had been posted up everywhere, and the wonderful influence of Burgomaster [Adolphe] Max, who had implored everyone to be careful and to give no cause or excuse for trouble. Brussels being an unfortified town, he had begged the people to help in a peaceful occupation. His words had the right effect and, after a time, doors and windows were opened, and cafes put their chairs and tables outside again, and the town gradually resumed its everyday life, but with a strong undercurrent of fear and consternation at the terrible feeling that the enemy was really in occupation, and Brussels under German rule.

Source: First published in *Everyman at War*, ed. C. B. Purdom (London: J. M. Dent, 1930), see www.firstworldwar.com/diaries/august1914.htm. All attempts to trace the copyright holder of the original work have been unsuccessful.

The German Invasion of France

The French Army completed its mobilization and forward deployment by August 18, days before the first German troops appeared on the border, yet it was unprepared to meet the invaders because its general staff had underestimated how many Germans were coming and miscalculated where they would cross the border. The German Western front deployment included nearly 1.5 million men in seventy-six infantry divisions (forty-five active and thirty-one reserve). French military intelligence accurately forecast the number of active divisions (anticipating between forty and forty-six), but seriously underestimated the number of reserve divisions and, thus, expected the overall size of the invading armies to be 13–18 percent smaller than they actually were. The error reflected the bias of conservative French Army leaders against reserves, forged in their peacetime opposition to the French Left's ideal of a "republican" short-service militia army. They kept their own reserves out of the front lines and assumed the Germans would do likewise. This miscalculation formed the basis for a second, equally serious error concerning the entry points of the invading forces. Because the French expected fewer Germans, their most pessimistic scenario had twenty-six enemy divisions transiting Belgium, all via the southeastern part of the country (south and east of the Meuse), entering France at a point east of where the Meuse bisects the Franco-Belgian border. But thanks to their use of so many reserves as front-line troops, the Germans sent thirty-four divisions through Belgium into France, with the arc of their advance reaching as far west as Brussels. Of these troops, just eight divisions crossed the Franco-Belgian border east of the Meuse, where the French expected as many as twenty-six, while twenty-six divisions crossed the border west of the Meuse, where the French had expected none (Map 3.1).

The requirements of Plan XVII, the French plan for an offensive into Alsace-Lorraine, further influenced French assumptions about what the German Army would do. The plan would work only if France deployed all of its armies on or east of the Meuse, and it would be irresponsible to concentrate so many French troops there if the Germans were expected to attack elsewhere. Thus, General Joseph Joffre, appointed commander-in-chief of the French Army in 1911, left the 110 miles (175 km) of potential front between the English Channel and the Meuse completely uncovered, in order to deploy just over 1 million men in five armies (twenty-one corps) from the Meuse eastward to Epinal, around 60 miles (100 km) from the Swiss border. At the onset of hostilities, the French First Army would advance from Epinal in the direction of Karlsruhe; the Second Army, from Nancy toward Saarbrücken; and the Third Army, from Verdun toward Kaiserslautern. The Fifth Army would stand guard along the Meuse east of Mézières and Sedan, in the sector where the French expected any Germans transiting Belgium to materialize. The Fourth Army, held in reserve, could assist the Fifth in stopping a German offensive or join the Third in its drive toward Kaiserslautern. Unlike

Map 3.1 Western front, 1914

the German war plan, which sought to envelop and destroy most of the French Army somewhere east of Paris, Plan XVII had no specific goal but assumed that a successful plunge into the German Rhineland would create the conditions under which Alsace-Lorraine could be recovered.

While the rival armies were still deploying to their borders the French actually initiated the action, sending elements of the First Army into Alsace on August 7, where they quickly took Mulhouse. Cheering crowds greeted their arrival, only to be disappointed when the Germans retook the town the next day. Meanwhile, in the countryside, most rural Alsatians greeted their liberators with indifference. French soldiers from departments far away wrote home with the shocking news that Alsatian peasants did not even speak French: "They all speak *Boche*. You never know if it's a compliment or an insult."[6] But if the French were wary of the Alsatians, the Germans did not fully trust them, either. Indeed, the German Army would send its Alsatian conscripts to the Eastern front, as long as there was an Eastern front to send them to.

The main encounters between the German armies advancing into France and the French armies advancing under Plan XVII, known collectively as the battles of the Frontiers, began over the next two weeks. They included four larger engagements: Lorraine (August 14–25); the Ardennes (August 21–23); Charleroi (August 21–23); and Mons (August 23–24). In the battle of Lorraine, also known as the battle of Morhange-Sarrebourg, the French First Army (General Auguste Dubail) joined the Second Army (General Noël de Castelnau) in facing the German Sixth Army (Crown Prince Rupprecht of Bavaria) and Seventh Army (General Josias von Heeringen). After the two French armies crossed the border, Castelnau quickly took Morhange and Dubail reached Sarrebourg, but a counterattack soon forced both of them to withdraw. Meanwhile, in the battle of the Ardennes, the French Third Army (General Pierre Ruffey) and Fourth Army (General Fernand de Langle de Cary) attacked the German Fifth Army (Crown Prince William) and Fourth Army (Duke Albrecht of Württemberg) as they emerged from the thick forests of Luxembourg and southern Belgium; the Germans promptly drove them back to Verdun and Sedan, respectively, inflicting heavy losses (see Box 3.2). To the northwest, in the battle of Charleroi, also known as the battle of the Sambre, the German Second Army (General Karl von Bülow) and Third Army (General Max von Hausen) nearly encircled the French Fifth Army (General Charles Lanrezac) after Joffre ordered it to advance into Belgium. The British Expeditionary Force (BEF) (General Sir John French), which landed at Boulogne and Le Havre starting on August 12, advanced on Lanrezac's left and met the German First Army (General Alexander von Kluck) in the battle of Mons. Upon realizing that he faced a German force more than twice as large as his own, General French fell back on Le Cateau, but not before the BEF had sustained 1,600 casualties. Meanwhile, in the battles of Lorraine, the Ardennes, and Charleroi, the French armies suffered 260,000 casualties, including 75,000 dead; of these, 27,000 were killed on a single day, August 22, in the simultaneous action of the three battles. The Germans also sustained significant losses in the battles of the Frontiers, though approximately 50,000 less than the French.

Box 3.2 A French historian in the ranks

Marc Bloch (1886–1944), historian and one of the founders (in 1929) of the Annales school, was shot by the Gestapo for his resistance activities during World War II. Earlier, he served in the French Army from 1905 to 1907 and again during World War I. In 1914, he experienced the army's mobilization, initial advance, and retreat as a sergeant in the 272nd Regiment:

Very early on the morning of August 4, I left for Amiens … At Amiens I found an extraordinarily animated city, its streets predictably teeming with soldiers … From August 11 to 21 the regiment remained in the region of the Meuse, first in the valley itself, where we guarded the bridges, and then on the right bank, close to the border. [On August 22] a very long and very hard march brought my company to Velosnes, a village right next to the Belgian border …

On the morning of the 25th we beat a retreat, and I realized that the hope [of the previous days] was misplaced … Owing to a delay in our order to move out, we were almost caught. Our rude awakening was followed by a forced march. On the way, we saw people abandoning their village in haste. Men, women, children, furniture, bundles of linen (and often the most disparate objects!) were piled on their wagons. These French peasants fleeing before an enemy against whom we could not protect them left a bitter impression, possibly the most maddening that the war has inflicted on us.

We were to see them often during the retreat, poor refugees crowding the roads and village squares with their wagons. Wrenched from their homes, disoriented, dazed, and bullied by the gendarmes, they were troublesome but pathetic figures … The next morning, while held in reserve on a plateau that dominated the left bank of the Meuse, we watched the smoke from burning villages rise into a shrapnel-speckled sky. The retreat lasted until September 5 …

Source: Marc Bloch, *Memoirs of War, 1914–15*. Translated, and with an Introduction by Carole Fink, reprint edn. (Cambridge: Cambridge University Press, 1991).

Following their defeat in the battles of the Frontiers, the Allies fell back on a line stretching from Paris eastward to Verdun, parallel to the River Marne. Notwithstanding the utter failure of Plan XVII, Joffre retained the confidence of his government, even as it decamped to Bordeaux, on his advice, during the night of September 2–3. In the greatest purge the army had seen since the French Revolution, Joffre fired two of his five army generals, Lanrezac and Ruffey, along with ten corps commanders, thirty-eight division commanders, and more than ninety brigadiers, in most cases citing their lack of aggressiveness, even though in the opening battles the cult of the offensive had inspired the French Army to squander more than a quarter of a million men. Joffre's treatment of his former protégé Lanrezac reflected his overall mentality. Condemned for being "hesitant" and "indecisive" at Charleroi, Lanrezac argued that standing and fighting there would have almost certainly resulted in "a new Sedan," the encirclement and destruction of the Fifth Army, but to no avail.[7] In a personal letter to the military governor of Paris, General Joseph Gallieni, Joffre praised Lanrezac as a great military thinker, but condemned his "pessimism" as a danger to the Fifth Army and to the success of the campaign as a whole.[8] Joffre never admitted that if Lanrezac had not saved the Fifth Army, the French would not have had the manpower they needed to stop the Germans days later at the Marne.

In an atmosphere approaching desperation, the French resorted to their reserves and fielded another two armies. The Sixth Army (General Michel Maunoury), culled from the Paris garrison, deployed just north of Paris, along the River Ourcq, while the Ninth Army (General Ferdinand Foch) deployed south of the Marne, between the Fourth and Fifth armies, supplemented by troops pulled from the Alsatian border, on the extreme right of the French Army, where Mulhouse had already been taken and lost twice. Meanwhile, Moltke had felt confident enough to weaken his own armies by detaching four divisions to reinforce East Prussia against a Russian invasion and another seven divisions to besiege the fortress of Maubeuge (where Joffre had left a garrison of 40,000) and to join German reserves in pursuing the Belgian Army in the direction of Antwerp. A week later, along the Marne, these eleven divisions would be sorely missed.

During the Allied retreat, the German First Army defeated the BEF a second time at Le Cateau (August 26), inflicting 8,000 casualties, and the Second Army repulsed a counterattack by the French Fifth Army at St. Quentin (August 29). After Le Cateau, Kluck assumed he had knocked the BEF out of the war, and with good reason. Deeply shaken by his initial losses, General French wanted to pull his troops out of the action and was stopped from doing so only by the personal intervention of the war secretary, Lord Kitchener, who came over from Britain to steady his nerves.

As the Germans neared Paris, Moltke ordered the First and Second armies to drive a wedge between the French capital and Joffre's armies to the east of it. Kluck protested that this move would expose the right (western) flank of his First Army as he passed Paris, but the OHL did not share his assessment of the risk (see Box 3.3). Complicating matters for the Germans, Lanrezac's Fifth Army retreated safely across the Marne to regroup south of Chateau-Thierry under its new commander, General Louis Franchet d'Esperey, while the BEF also made good its escape, clinging to the left (western) flank of the Fifth Army as it withdrew across the river. On September 3, Kluck's vanguard crossed the Marne halfway between Paris and Chateau-Thierry, and would soon meet the BEF south of the river. Bülow crossed the Marne too far east of Chateau-Thierry to encounter the Fifth Army, but soon ran into Foch's newly formed Ninth Army. Strains in German command-and-control became clear by the morning of the 4th, when Kluck spared no sarcasm in asking Moltke "to be informed of the situation of the other armies, whose reports of decisive victories have so far been frequently followed by appeals for support."[9] That evening Gallieni sensed an opportunity to engage the exposed flank of Kluck's army as it continued its march past Paris. Joffre agreed, and ordered Maunoury to attack with the fresh troops of the Sixth Army. Desperate for transport, Gallieni commandeered Paris taxicabs to drive the last reserves to the front.

Box 3.3 *"A difficult and risky undertaking"*

Alexander von Kluck (1846–1934), commander of the German First Army at the first battle of the Marne, gives his appraisal of the OHL's plan to seek a decisive battle east of Paris in the first week of September 1914:

I considered that to force the enemy away from Paris in a south-easterly direction (which would involve the passage of the Marne and the Seine) would be a difficult and risky undertaking. There would probably be initial successes, but it would be scarcely possible in the circumstances to continue the offensive until the enemy was decisively defeated or partially annihilated. Another group of four or five divisions was needed by the armies on the German right wing, in order to effectively guard the right flank against Paris and protect the long communications of the First and Second armies, if the advance was to be continued ... The Supreme Command, however, seemed to be firmly convinced that the garrison of Paris need not be taken into account for any operations outside the line of forts of the capital.

In fact, on the night of September 2–3 Moltke and the OHL had ordered Kluck to take responsibility for this threat with the forces already at his disposal, specifically "to follow in echelon behind the Second Army and to be responsible for the flank protection" of both armies against any French attack out of Paris. Kluck disobeyed the order on the grounds that it did not take into account the actual positions of the armies in the field. To comply would relinquish the initiative to the enemy and make it impossible to achieve the overall goal of decisive victory:

If the First Army, now a day's march ahead of the Second, was to get in echelon behind it, it would then become impossible to force the enemy in a south-easterly direction ... If it halted for two days so as to get in echelon behind the Second Army, the enemy's higher command would regain the complete freedom of action of which it had been deprived. Should the First Army hold back, the great success for which the Supreme Command was confidently striving ... could no longer be hoped for.

Source: Alexander von Kluck, *The March on Paris and the Battle of the Marne, 1914* (London: Edward Arnold, 1920), 94–97.

The following morning, just east of Paris, Maunoury fell upon Kluck's right flank, initiating a major battle that soon spread eastward up the Marne.

The Western Front: From the First Battle of the Marne to the First Battle of Ypres

The first battle of the Marne (September 5–9) began on the 36th day since general mobilization set the German war plan into motion, or M + 36. As long as Moltke's armies achieved a decisive victory over the French by M + 40, the Germans could honor their timetable for shipping most of the army east to face the Russians. But by September 5 most of the German armies were at least 80 miles (130 km) from their railheads, and their supply chain now depended upon horse-drawn wagons, overwhelmingly so, because more than half of the army's 4,000 trucks had broken down. On the eve of the battle Kluck informed Moltke that the First Army, whose position on the German right had required it to march the farthest and fight the most along the way, had "reached the limit of its endurance," and yet his troops, along with Bülow's Second Army, would face the hardest fighting along the Marne.[10] As the battle opened, Moltke ordered Kluck and Bülow to engage the BEF and French forces facing them south of the Seine, then turn their armies westward to attack Paris. But to deal with the flank attack by the new French Sixth Army, Kluck executed his turn sooner than Bülow, opening a gap of 30 miles (50 km) between the two German armies. Franchet d'Espérey's Fifth Army joined the BEF in exploiting this gap, and thus blocked the route that the OHL had ordered Bülow to take in his westward turn toward Paris.

The action quickly rippled eastward along the front, to the upper Marne and beyond, pulling in the German Third, Fourth, and Fifth armies against the French Third and Fourth armies, but the focal point remained the sector just east of Paris. There, with the deployment of Foch's new Ninth Army against the German Second Army, the Allies enjoyed a clear superiority in both men and artillery; furthermore, two of the three French armies engaged (the Sixth and Ninth) included fresh troops fighting their first battle. While Joffre took personal command of the Sixth Army and directed the battle from its field headquarters, Moltke established OHL headquarters at Charleville, near Sedan, and sent no instructions to either Kluck or Bülow, instead remaining true to the German doctrine of allowing the greatest possible initiative to commanders in the field. He waited until the 8th to dispatch a personal emissary to visit the five German armies engaged along the Marne, a mere lieutenant colonel who became the scapegoat (at least within the officer corps) for the ensuing order to retreat. Adding to the confusion, German field communications, excellent within each army, were nonexistent between armies, and Kluck and Bülow did not communicate directly by field telephone until the 9th. By then, each was blaming the other for the battle being lost, but the evidence appears worse for Bülow, who on the morning of the 9th initiated the general retreat by pulling his Second Army back across the Marne, without consulting either Moltke or Kluck, even though the Allies had not yet made a major break in his lines.[11] In four days of heavy fighting the French and Germans each suffered around 250,000 casualties, including 80,000 killed on the French side, while the BEF sustained 13,000, including 1,700 dead.

Coincidentally, the Germans lost the first battle of the Marne on M + 40, their self-imposed deadline for victory on the Western front. Moltke's critics cited his command-and-control problems as well as his decision, a week earlier, to send eleven of his divisions to fight elsewhere. The latter move paid dividends, however, in the capitulation of Maubeuge (September 8), which netted the Germans 40,000 French prisoners, and in the additional pressure on Antwerp, which the Belgians would abandon a month later. Within five days all five German armies engaged at the Marne had retreated to establish a new front running eastward from Noyon, anchored on its right by Kluck and Bülow on the high ground north of the River Aisne, and on its left by Crown Prince Rupprecht's Sixth Army, which stood opposite Verdun. By then the war minister, Erich von Falkenhayn (Figure 3.1), had been called to the OHL to replace Moltke, who suffered a nervous breakdown in the wake of the defeat. Falkenhayn took over on September 13, but the change was not formally announced until November 6. In the meantime, Moltke remained at headquarters to lend credence to the charade that all was still well, though

Figure 3.1 Erich von Falkenhayn

Erich von Falkenhayn (1861–1922) had a distinguished prewar career including seven years of service (1896–1903) in China, where he saw action during the Boxer Rebellion of 1900. Appointed war minister in 1913, he was the obvious choice to succeed Moltke as chief of the general staff following the German failure at the first battle of the Marne. Falkenhayn embodied the mannerisms and mentality of the Prussian officer corps, but (unlike his predecessors Schlieffen and Moltke, and his successors Hindenburg and Ludendorff) he did not believe in the doctrine of decisive victory. As early as November 1914 he recognized that, if the Triple Entente held firm, the Central Powers were doomed to defeat, and thereafter placed his hopes in knocking one of them out of the war (Russia in 1915, France in 1916). Sacked after the failure of his strategy of attrition at Verdun, Falkenhayn spent the rest of the war in a series of field commands, most notably in Romania (1916) and Palestine (1917).

the sacking of thirty-three generals indicated otherwise. As soon as they assumed their defensive positions, the German First and Second armies withstood an Allied onslaught in the first battle of the Aisne (September 13–28). The attack included the French Fifth and Sixth armies and the BEF, the latter taking another 12,000 casualties in the war's first action involving the assault and defense of trench lines. Falkenhayn responded by redeploying Heeringen's Seventh Army from Alsace to a position on the Aisne between the First and Second armies. As soon as it became clear that the heights above the Aisne could not be stormed, Joffre likewise turned to the eastern end of the front for manpower, redeploying Castelnau's Second Army from the border of Lorraine to the left of Maunoury's Sixth Army. As the fighting along the Aisne died down, Castelnau attempted to run the right flank of the German First Army west of Noyon. Kluck blocked the move, then attempted to turn Castelnau's left flank, also unsuccessfully. These failed flanking maneuvers signaled the start of the so-called "Race to the Sea," a series of encounter battles, most notably the first battle of Artois (September 27–October 10), in which the Allies and the Germans each repeatedly attempted to get around the exposed flank of their opponent, only to fail and dig in, in the process extending the continuous front closer to the English Channel (see Online Essay 1).

After bearing to the northwest from Noyon to Roye, the new trench lines headed due north toward Flanders in western Belgium, where King Albert, after ordering the evacuation of Antwerp (October 6–10), retreated behind the Yser with the five remaining divisions of the Belgian Army. Joffre reinforced Albert's troops with a makeshift force soon designated the French Eighth Army. Opposite Albert stood fresh German reserves plus the troops Moltke had detached earlier to besiege Antwerp, placed under the duke of Württemberg and the headquarters of the Fourth Army, which moved to Flanders after Falkenhayn redistributed their surviving original troops to reinforce German forces on the upper Aisne. To their south, across the French border, Falkenhayn filled the last gap on the German side of the line by redeploying Crown Prince Rupprecht's Sixth Army from Lorraine to Lille, opposite the new French Tenth Army (General Louis Maud'huy). After the first battle of the Aisne ended, the Allies agreed to redeploy the BEF alongside the Belgians in Flanders, where it could be more easily resupplied and reinforced through the Channel ports of Nieuwpoort, Dunkirk, and Calais. From just eight divisions (six infantry, two cavalry) in August, the BEF grew to include eight corps (six infantry, two cavalry) by December, when it was subdivided into the First Army (General Sir Douglas Haig) and Second Army (General Sir Horace Smith-Dorrien). Colonial troops helped man the continuous front created by the "Race to the Sea," including an Indian corps in the enlarged BEF and west African *Tirailleurs sénégalais* (Figure 3.2) in the French armies. Joffre appointed Foch as French northern sector commander and liaison to the Belgians and British. Foch, who had visited Britain three times as prewar War School commandant, thus further enhanced his résumé for his future role as supreme Allied commander.

Figure 3.2 Tirailleurs sénégalais

Troops of the "Senegalese rifles" at prewar maneuvers, Longchamp, 1913. They were recruited not just from Senegal (where the first such unit was raised, in 1857) but from all of French West Africa and French Equatorial Africa. Some 200,000 served in twenty regiments during World War I, including 135,000 on the Western front, the first of whom deployed in the autumn of 1914 to help hold the expanding trench lines during the "Race to the Sea." They were recruited as volunteers, but France's wartime manpower crisis prompted the army to use increasingly heavy-handed methods to fill their ranks. Protests against recruitment erupted in present-day Mali as early as 1915, and were suppressed with brute force. In the last year of the war, recruiting rebounded after the army introduced incentives such as better food, clothing, and the promise of postwar French citizenship. The *Tirailleurs sénégalais* saw action in most of the major battles on the Western front. They accounted for 30,000 of the 72,000 French colonial troops who lost their lives during the war.

The Belgians bore the brunt of the fighting in the battle of the Yser (October 16–30), and the BEF in the concurrent first battle of Ypres, in both cases with the support of French divisions; the German Fourth Army provided the opposition, reinforced at Ypres by part of the Sixth Army. Along the Yser, German artillery decimated the Belgians, whose most effective fire support came from British warships operating in the coastal waters on their left flank. Albert's troops suffered 15,000 casualties before the king authorized the flooding of the polders along the Yser, blocking what would have been the decisive final assault by German infantry. Meanwhile, to the immediate south of the Yser battlefield, the action around Ypres began on October 12 and did not die down completely until the end of November, with the heaviest fighting occurring between October 25 and November 13. Early in the battle the British took Passchendaele Ridge, the most significant high ground on a mostly flat landscape, then held it against repeated counterattacks in which the German troops included a small number of university and gymnasium student volunteers. German war propaganda exaggerated the role of these "children" and hailed their martyrdom as the *Kindermord bei Ypern*. The battle featured an unprecedented expenditure of artillery shells, which soon completely destroyed the city of Ypres behind the Allied lines. Based upon the rate at which it was using shells at Ypres and elsewhere, the German Army had only a six-day stock remaining when Falkenhayn broke off the attacks on the 13th. Throughout the autumn of 1914 a shell shortage caused considerable concern for all of the belligerents, but Ypres marked the first time it influenced an army's decision to end a battle.

From 1914 onward the three primary combatants on the Western front were able to offer their wounded better care than any previous armies, but as one recent analysis has pointed out, "these health care advances were counterbalanced by the greater gravity of the wounds inflicted," leaving the survival rate no better than for the wounded of the Napoleonic Wars.[12] The British Army sustained 85,000 casualties during the first five months of World War I, but its losses paled in comparison to those suffered by the other major combatants on the Western front in 1914: 850,000 for the French Army and 677,000 for the German, in the latter case a force also taking losses on the Eastern front. By the time the Ypres sector fell quiet in late November, the Germans had suffered nearly 135,000 casualties there, slightly more than the Allied total (58,000 British, at least 50,000 French, and 18,500 Belgian). The first battle of Ypres, the Western front's last action of the year, accounted for more than two-thirds of Britain's casualties for 1914 and destroyed most of what was left of the original BEF, Britain's prewar professional army.

The Balkan Front: The Austro-Hungarian Failure versus Serbia

Given the magnitude of the action unfolding on the Western front from the first days of August and the equally extensive clash on the Eastern front later in the month, the Balkans early on became the war's forgotten front. After the Russian mobilization of July 31 forced Austria-Hungary to alter its mobilization from Plan B (against Serbia) to Plan R (against Russia), the Dual Monarchy's deployment in the Balkans was supposed to be reduced to a holding action by the three corps assigned to *Minimalgruppe Balkan*, under the command of General Oskar Potiorek, military governor of Bosnia. Potiorek, despite a long-standing rivalry with Conrad, shared his desire to smash the Serbs. Under Plan B, he would have been the field commander of the invasion of Serbia and understandably felt robbed of the opportunity. Unfortunately for the overall Austro-Hungarian war effort, in August 1914 Potiorek determined to use the Balkan command to advance his own career at the expense of Conrad, whom he hoped to replace as chief of the general staff. Even after it became clear that the Russians were intervening and most of the army would have to deploy on the Eastern front, he kept as many troops as possible in his theater of the war, to win his own campaign against Serbia. Conrad finally agreed to let Potiorek keep the VIII (Prague) Corps, minus its cavalry division, because it contained thousands of Czechs whose loyalty he doubted should they be deployed against Russia. These troops, plus the three corps of *Minimalgruppe Balkan*, were paired to form the Fifth Army and Sixth Army, but when Potiorek finally invaded Serbia in force on August 12, his order of battle also included the Second Army (General Eduard von Böhm-Ermolli), consisting of the other three corps of *B-Staffel*, troops that should have been on their way to the Russian border by then, giving him 320,000 in all. To oppose him the Serbian Army mobilized more than 300,000 troops, counting all reserves and territorial forces, of which the 185,000 front-line troops (eleven divisions of infantry and one of cavalry) were organized into three corps-sized "armies." To their south, Montenegro added eighteen infantry brigades totaling 35,000–40,000 troops, but their poor training and antiquated armaments made them little better than militia. Crown Prince Alexander served as Serbian commander-in-chief, with his chief-of-staff, General Radomir Putnik, functioning as de facto commander. In addition to their superiority in numbers, the Austro-Hungarian forces also enjoyed a 2:1 advantage over Serbia in modern artillery pieces (744 guns to 381).

The Austro-Hungarian invasion began on August 12, touching off an ebb-and-flow of encounter battles over the next four months. Potiorek entered Serbia from the west, out of Bosnia, with 200,000 of his troops, while the rest of his forces held the line of the Sava and Danube on Serbia's northern border. Within days he suffered a defeat at the battle of Cer (August 16–19), where Putnik brought almost his entire army into the action. Afterward, Potiorek fell back into Bosnia and finally let go of the two *B-Staffel* corps he had not used in the campaign; the other two remained on the Balkan front for the rest of 1914. During September the opposing forces continued to spar across the border, before spending October replenishing their manpower and ammunition. Finally, in early November, Potiorek invaded Serbia from the north, across the Danube, as well as from the west, out of Bosnia. His troops advanced easily until the end of the month, when he ordered a pause to resupply before delivering what he assumed would be the knockout blow. He was confident enough to detach the Fifth Army to circle back to the north and take Belgrade, a symbolically important objective (long since evacuated by the Serbian government) that had been bypassed in the advance. Austro-Hungarian troops occupied Belgrade on December 2, but would not hold it for long. In late November France sent Serbia a desperately needed shipment of arms and ammunition, which reached Putnik's troops via Salonika (Thessaloniki) in neutral Greece, just as they braced themselves for Potiorek's final assault. On the day Belgrade fell Putnik ordered a counterattack that caught the Austro-Hungarian Army completely by surprise and dangerously dispersed; Potiorek's men were soon in headlong retreat, and by December 15 the invading forces had been driven from Serbian territory.

Both armies on the Balkan front of 1914 committed atrocities against civilians. Potiorek set the tone during the month between the archduke's assassination and the onset of war by rounding up a number of Bosnian Serb leaders on suspicion of disloyalty. The initial invasion of Serbia produced hard evidence to justify some of these detentions and many more, as the papers of a Serbian Army intelligence station at Loznica were captured intact, leading to the arrest on treason and espionage charges of more than 2,100 Bosnian Serbs, including 101 Orthodox priests. The greatest single massacre of Serbian civilians by Austro-Hungarian troops occurred on August 17 at Sabac, where at least eighty were shot. Many more were killed in smaller numbers in rural areas. While the actions of German troops in Belgium were rooted in their fear of phantom *francs-tireurs*, in Serbia there were numerous instances of armed Serbs not in uniform firing upon the invaders (although in some cases these were members of the army's last line of reserves, which lacked proper uniforms). As early as August 17 the commander of IX Corps, General Lothar von Hortstein, complained that he could no longer send out reconnaissance patrols because they were "all killed by the rural people." Austro-Hungarian troops reacted to such resistance by presuming an armed threat from all rural Serb civilians, shooting hundreds and burning countless farmhouses. In addition to the perceived danger, many appear to have acted on their visceral hatred and distrust of Serbs, whom they blamed for causing the war. As in Belgium, the invading troops were further incensed by gruesome tales of civilians mutilating their dead and wounded comrades, in the Austro-Hungarian case harking back to such incidents during the campaign to occupy Bosnia in 1878. Serbian troops behaved no better when they counterattacked into Austro-Hungarian territory in September, reserving the worst of their murder, rape, and plunder for the Bosnian Muslims. From the start of the war Muslims living in Serbia fled to Austrian lines and Bosnian Serbs to Serbian lines. On November 22, with Serbia apparently on the brink of defeat, Potiorek ordered the concentration in labor camps of all Serbian males aged between 16 and 60 residing in Austrian-occupied territory. Putnik's counteroffensive three weeks later canceled these plans before they could be implemented.[13]

Putnik's successful defense of Serbian territory earned his troops the respect of the Entente powers and provided a further (though unneeded) boost to national morale, but victory came at a high price: 118,000 casualties (including 22,000 dead), along with 45,000 men officially missing, including prisoners lost. Meanwhile, Austria-Hungary's 150,000 casualties (including 28,000 dead) and 74,000 prisoners lost paled in significance to the losses suffered by Conrad's armies on the Eastern front during the same months. Nevertheless, the initial Balkan campaign had been an embarrassing debacle, and afterward Potiorek did not wait to be sacked, instead submitting a request for retirement. Francis Joseph promptly accepted it, and at the end of the year gave the Balkan command to his cousin, Archduke Eugen. Thereafter, the Balkan front went dormant, as Austria-Hungary took advantage of the Serbian Army being in no shape to fight again anytime soon. Of the five corps Eugen inherited from Potiorek, three were sent to the Eastern front for the winter fighting in the Carpathians and the remaining two to the new Italian front in May 1915, leaving the Serbian border covered by little more than a defensive screen of second- and third-line reserves.

The Eastern Front: Tannenberg and Lemberg

On August 15, when Conrad met with Francis Joseph for the last time before departing Vienna for the Eastern front, the old emperor bid him farewell with as much optimism as he could muster: "God willing, all will go well, but even if it should go wrong, I will see it through."[14] He had no idea just how horribly wrong it would go, or that he would not live to see the end of it. Conrad and the titular head of the Austro-Hungarian *Armeeoberkommando* (AOK), Archduke Frederick, established their headquarters in the fortress city of Przemysl in Galicia. By the time they arrived, ten Austro-Hungarian cavalry divisions were conducting a reconnaissance in force into Russian Poland, at a depth of 90 miles (145 km), along 250 miles (400 km) of front east of the Vistula. Along the way, they encountered several Russian units en route to the front, fought pitched battles against dug-in infantry and dismounted cavalry, and sustained heavy losses. Nearly half of the army's total stock of horses was ridden to death or exhaustion in the week-long operation, which failed to gather much intelligence or disrupt the enemy deployment. The only genuine battle occurred east of Lemberg (L'viv) at Jaroslavice-Wolczkowce (August 21) between the Russian 10th Cavalry Division and the Austro-Hungarian 4th Cavalry Division. It was the largest cavalry engagement fought on any front during World War I, an indecisive clash in an indecisive opening act.

Conrad soon faced an unraveling strategic situation, as the thirteen divisions of Böhm-Ermolli's four *B-Staffel* corps, which were to constitute the Second Army, still had not arrived from the Serbian theater. In their absence, the Central Powers on the Eastern front deployed just forty-six infantry divisions against seventy-four Russian infantry divisions divided among six armies, with more behind them in two reserve armies. The Russian general staff resolved its dilemma as to which of the Central Powers to attack first by deciding to attack both simultaneously, a bold decision that ranked among the more rational calculations made in the summer of 1914, owing to the weakness of the forces Russia faced; it was also the most understandable, given the pleas the tsar received from Paris and Belgrade for a maximum effort to take pressure off the French and Serbian armies. On the border of East Prussia the Russians deployed their First and Second armies, reinforced to twenty-nine divisions to guarantee success against the nine divisions of the German Eighth Army. They allocated their remaining forty-five divisions to the Third, Fourth, Fifth, and Eighth armies against Austria-Hungary's thirty-seven divisions. Nicholas II appointed his cousin, Grand Duke Nicholas, commander-in-chief of this massive force, but the grand duke and his chief-of-staff, General Nikolai Yanushkevich, never produced a grand design for victory, instead approving or rejecting plans submitted by the individual army commanders. The degree of coordination would improve over time, but not until painful defeats drove home the need for change.

Despite the numerical inferiority of his German Eighth Army, General Maximilian von Prittwitz had difficulty obeying Moltke's orders to stand on the defensive. In the battle of Stallupönen (August 17) one German corps, 40,000 men, surprised General Pavel Rennenkampf's First Army, a force five times larger, inflicting 5,000 casualties and taking 3,000 prisoners while losing just 1,200 of its own men. The Germans were not so lucky when Prittwitz's entire army engaged Rennenkampf at the battle of Gumbinnen (August 20), where the Russians took advantage of their numerical superiority (192,000 troops, to 148,000 for the Germans) and made good use of their artillery to turn both German flanks, inflict 14,800 casualties against 16,500 of their own, and take 6,000 prisoners. In the wake of the defeat, Prittwitz panicked and ordered the Eighth Army to retreat all the way to the Vistula, conceding East Prussia to the Russians. Before he could execute the withdrawal, however, Moltke called General Paul von Hindenburg out of retirement to replace him, and assigned General Erich Ludendorff, fresh from a key role in the battle of Liège, to be his chief-of-staff.

The Russian invasion of East Prussia left the Germans in no position to take the pressure off Austro-Hungarian forces while they continued to await the arrival of the *B-Staffel* troops. Nevertheless, Conrad resolved to attack the Russians, a move the Germans encouraged, to draw the pressure off East Prussia while Hindenburg and Ludendorff arrived to take over there. The Austro-Hungarian First Army headed north, the Fourth Army northeast, and the Third Army east, arcing into Russian Poland, making their front broader and thinner with every passing day. In the battle of Krasnik (August 23–26) the First Army (General Viktor Dankl) outflanked the Russian Fourth Army (General Anton von Salza), forcing it to retreat; Russian officers taken prisoner at Krasnik gave Dankl's troops the supreme compliment, reporting that they had attacked with a ferocity greater "than that of the Japanese" in the Russo-Japanese War.[15] On the heels of this success, the Fourth Army (General

Moritz Auffenberg) nearly encircled the Russian Fifth Army (General Pavel Plehve) at the battle of Komarów (August 26–31), inflicting 40 percent casualties, taking 20,000 prisoners, and capturing 100 guns.

The last days of August were a bleak time for the Russians. On the heels of Dankl's victory at Krasnik and coinciding with Auffenberg's triumph at Komarów, Hindenburg and Ludendorff led a counterattack against the Russians that lasted from August 23 until September 2, climaxing in the battle of Tannenberg (August 27–30). The German Eighth Army, reinforced to 166,000 men, faced Rennenkampf's First Army, reinforced to 210,000, and Alexander Samsonov's Second Army, of 206,000 men. Despite being seriously outnumbered, the Germans enjoyed significant advantages. After Gumbinnen, Rennenkampf advanced toward Königsberg via a route north of the Masurian Lakes, while Samsonov advanced south of the lakes, leaving a gap between their armies. The two Russian generals had been bitter enemies ever since the Russo-Japanese War, barely communicated with one another, and did not coordinate their movements. When they did communicate, the Germans knew exactly what they were saying because, alone among the belligerents of 1914, the Russians used the new wireless radio technology for field communication without encrypting their messages. From the start of the battle Samsonov bore the brunt of the German attack, yet he did not ask Rennenkampf for help until the evening of the 28th, by which time he had fallen back toward the Russian border and was desperate for the First Army to prevent the Germans from encircling him. A belated relief attempt by Rennenkampf never got closer than 45 miles (72 km) from Samsonov, whom the Germans surrounded on the 29th. Distraught at the prospect of surrender, Samsonov shot himself that evening. The Second Army capitulated the next day. The Germans suffered less than 20,000 casualties at Tannenberg while inflicting 30,000; they also took 95,000 prisoners and captured more than 500 artillery pieces.

While the Germans were winning at Tannenberg, the tide started to turn against Conrad in eastern Galicia, where his Third Army (General Rudolf von Brudermann) suffered a defeat in the battle of Gnila Lipa (August 26–30) and had to fall back. Owing to Colonel Redl's prewar betrayal of Austria-Hungary's war plans, the Russians expected the main attack to come from Brudermann's sector and massed two armies – the Third (General Nikolai Ruzsky) and Eighth (General Aleksei Brusilov) – to meet him. On September 4, after Brudermann gave up Galicia's largest city, Lemberg, without a fight, Conrad sacked him in favor of General Svetozar Boroević, ironically a Serb (from the Krajina region of Croatia) who had distinguished himself as a corps commander in Auffenberg's army at Komarów. Conrad hoped the Germans would advance southward out of East Prussia after their victory at Tannenberg, to link up with Dankl's First Army and Auffenberg's Fourth Army advancing northward out of Galicia, but instead they followed the more logical course of turning on Rennenkampf's

First Army, which they defeated in the battle of the Masurian Lakes (September 9–14), ending the brief Russian incursion into East Prussia. Left to his own devices, Conrad ordered Boroević to retake Lemberg in a counterattack. During the ensuing battle of Lemberg-Rawa Ruska (September 6–11) the Third Army lacked sufficient artillery support for its advancing infantry and became bogged down at Gorodok, 35 miles (55 km) east of Przemysl. Meanwhile, strong Russian pressure on eastern Galicia and all along the front placed the First and Fourth armies in a vulnerable position; with Hindenburg not advancing southward out of East Prussia, they were left with no concrete objective and withdrew into Galicia. Half of Böhm-Ermolli's Second Army (from *B-Staffel*) finally redeployed from the Balkan front in time to join the other Austro-Hungarian armies in the desperate fighting around Lemberg, but Auffenberg failed to bring his Fourth Army into the battle quickly enough and became the scapegoat for the ensuing defeat (see Box 3.4). Conrad ordered a general retreat and on September 12 moved the AOK from Przemysl to Neu-Sandec (Nowy Sacz), 90 miles (145 km) to the west, where it remained for two months before moving another 100 miles (160 km) westward to Teschen (Tešin), which served as headquarters until early 1917. The loss of the battle of Lemberg-Rawa Ruska (in which the dead included one of his own sons) shook Conrad's confidence. An old friend remarked afterward that he "does not believe in his own historical calling to be the generalissimo of Austria against Russia."[16]

In their prewar discussions Moltke had told Conrad that Austria-Hungary would have to shoulder most of the burden on the Eastern front for six weeks while Germany defeated France. Conrad ordered the general retreat on Germany's M + 43, three days after the French won the first battle of the Marne. The German war plan had failed and with it the Austro-Hungarian war plan, and neither army had a backup plan. In the wake of the defeats at the Marne and Lemberg-Rawa Ruska, Conrad did not think the war was lost, but he no longer felt it could be won; the best the Central Powers could hope for was a negotiated peace, preferably after they had improved their military situation. Hindenburg sent Ludendorff to Neu-Sandec on September 18 to coordinate their next move against the Russians. They agreed to a counterattack at the end of September and, on Ludendorff's advice, Conrad left behind six divisions to garrison Przemysl. After one month of fighting, Conrad had conceded most of Galicia to the Russians, and lost 470,000 of the 800,000 men he had deployed on the Eastern front: 250,000 killed or wounded, 100,000 taken prisoner, and 120,000 left behind in Przemysl. The heavy casualties had included thousands of multilingual regular army officers and NCOs, whose early loss had long-term consequences for the cohesion of the multinational Habsburg army. In its battles against Austria-Hungary, Russia suffered barely half the casualties (210,000 killed or wounded and 40,000 taken prisoner) and lost only 100 guns while capturing 300.

Box 3.4 An Austrian violinist on the Eastern front

Fritz Kreisler (1875–1962), violinist and composer, served as a reserve officer in a Landsturm regiment of the Austro-Hungarian III Corps for the first month of the war, sustaining serious wounds in combat near Lemberg that brought his discharge from the service later in 1914:

We reached Vienna on August first. A startling change had come over the city since I had left it only a few weeks before. Feverish activity everywhere prevailed. Reservists streamed in by thousands from all parts of the country to report at headquarters. Autos filled with officers whizzed past. Dense crowds surged up and down the streets. Bulletins and extra editions of newspapers passed from hand to hand. Immediately it was evident what a great leveler war is. Differences in rank and social distinctions had practically ceased. All barriers seemed to have fallen; everybody addressed everybody else … The keynote of popular feeling was quiet dignity, joined to determination, with an undercurrent of solemn gravity and responsibility.
    … We proceeded to Graz … We traveled via Budapest to Galicia, and left the train at Strij, a very important railroad center south of Lemberg… We could not but surmise that we were going to be stationed there some time for the purpose of training and maneuvering. This belief was strengthened by the fact that our regiment belonged to the Landsturm, or second line of reserves, originally intended for home service … The next morning at four o'clock … suddenly orders for marching were given. After we had been under way for about three hours we heard far-away, repeated

rumbling … Not for a moment did we associate it with cannonading, being, as we supposed, hundreds of miles away from the nearest place where Russians could possibly be… We were thunderstruck at the sudden realization that the Russians had penetrated so deeply into Galicia … We started at once to dig our trenches.

A few days later, III Corps and the rest of the army faced a Russian onslaught:

We were … terribly outnumbered by the Russians, and … constantly had to retreat… On September 6th my battalion was ordered to take up a position commanding a defile which formed one of the possible approaches for the enemy. Here we awaited the Russians, and they were not long in coming … We heard a tramping of horses and saw dark figures swooping down upon us … My next sensation was a crushing pain in my shoulder, struck by the hoof of a horse, and a sharp knife pain in my right thigh. I fired with my revolver at the hazy figure above me, saw it topple over and then lost consciousness.

Kreisler survived his serious wounds, but ten weeks later he was declared 'invalid and physically unfit for army duty at the front or at home', and returned to civilian life.

Source: Excerpted from Fritz Kreisler, *Four Weeks in the Trenches: The War Story of a Violinist* (Boston, MA: Houghton Mifflin, 1915) available at www.gwpda.org/memoir/Kreisler/Kreisler.htm. Excerpts from *Frères de tranchées* (1914–18), by Marc Ferro, Malcolm Brown, Rémy Cazals, and Olaf Müller (© Perrin, 2005); see also www.gwpda.org/memoir/Kreisler/Kreisler.htm.

The Eastern Front: Warsaw and the Carpathians

In the first months of the war, the armies of the Eastern front, like their counterparts in the west, distinguished themselves most of all in their resiliency. Following the initial German victories in East Prussia and the Austro-Hungarian retreat from eastern Galicia, the opposing armies continued to spar all along the front, with the bloodiest action resulting from four counteroffensives by the Central Powers, two in the direction of Warsaw and two toward Przemysl. The two attacks on Warsaw (September 28–October 30 and November 11–25) matched the Austro-Hungarian First, Second, and Fourth armies and the new German Ninth Army (General August von Mackensen) against the Russian First, Second, Fifth, and Ninth armies of the "Northwest front" army group (General Nikolai Ruzsky, victor of Glina Lipa). In the first battle Mackensen advanced to within 12 miles (20 km) of Warsaw before being turned back. The concurrent first effort to relieve the siege of Przemysl, by Boroević's Austro-Hungarian Third Army, temporarily retook the fortress city (October 11–November 6) before losing it again. Finally, in the battle of Limanowa-Lapanów (December 3–9), fought southeast of Cracow, Conrad directed the Austro-Hungarian Fourth Army (now under Archduke Joseph Ferdinand), supplemented by Pilsudski's Polish Legion and a fresh German reserve division, in an attack on the Russian Third Army, now under General Radko Rusko Dimitriev, the former Bulgarian commander of the Balkan Wars, who had volunteered for Russian service at the outbreak of war. The Austro-Hungarian counteroffensive advanced 40 miles (64 km) eastward to the River Dunajec, relieving the pressure on Cracow (which would have been Russia's next objective) and turning back the westernmost Russian penetration of World War I. But Conrad lacked the reserves to press on to raise the siege of Przemysl, whose 120,000-man garrison became prisoners of the Russians in March 1915. Thus, the battles in Poland over the last three months of 1914 left both Warsaw and Przemysl in Russian hands, but at a considerable price. The two battles for Warsaw alone resulted in 160,000 Russian casualties against 77,000 for the Central Powers, continuing the Russian trend of suffering heavily in any battle involving German opponents, regardless of the outcome. Thanks at least initially to the persistence of Dimitriev, they lost another 115,000 in their repeated attacks on Przemysl, in which the colorful Bulgarian built upon his earlier record of squandering lives in fruitless frontal assaults.

William II responded to the initial failure to take Warsaw by appointing Hindenburg Supreme Commander in the East (*Oberbefehlshaber Ost* or "*OberOst*") with Ludendorff as his deputy, effective November 1. He granted them considerable autonomy from Falkenhayn and the OHL, but failed to persuade Francis Joseph to subordinate all Austro-Hungarian Eastern front forces to their command. Nevertheless, Conrad worked well enough with *OberOst* and in particular enjoyed good relations with Ludendorff, who praised the battle of Limanowa-Lapanów as "a splendid success of Austro-Hungarian arms."[17] Falkenhayn, in contrast, could barely conceal his contempt for Conrad. He typically dominated their meetings, only to have Conrad (the former war school professor and prolific author) send him a written rebuttal by courier the next day. These rejoinders served only to irritate Falkenhayn, who rarely showed interest in Conrad's opinions and dismissed Austria-Hungary as a "cadaver" long before it deserved the label.

In the first months of the war Conrad remained true to his conviction that an army had to continue to pursue the offensive relentlessly as long as the troops remained willing to attack. When the "Southwest front" army group (General Nikolai Ivanov), consisting of the Russian Seventh, Eighth, and Ninth armies, launched a winter offensive in the Carpathians in mid-December, Conrad started to pour troops into the snowy mountains, escalating an indecisive contest that all but destroyed the Austro-Hungarian regular army by the spring of 1915. Repeated frontal assaults against fixed enemy positions, usually without adequate artillery support, caused much of the carnage, but the snow and cold took their toll as well. On one particularly bitter night, 28 officers and 1,800 men of Boroević's Third Army froze to death at their posts. By the end of April, 600,000 of the 1.1 million Austro-Hungarian troops sent to the Carpathians had been killed, wounded, or taken prisoner. The Germans lost 32,000 of the 87,000 troops they contributed to the campaign as part of a new South Army (*Südarmee*) commanded by Falkenhayn's protégé, General Alexander von Linsingen. Falkenhayn did not send more because Hindenburg and Ludendorff had persuaded him to let them launch a winter offensive of their own out of East Prussia. Unlike the protracted agony in the Carpathians, *OberOst*'s northern offensive ended quickly in the indecisive second battle of the Masurian Lakes (February 7–22, 1915), where the German Eighth Army (General Otto von Below) and new Tenth Army (General Hermann von Eichhorn) met the new Russian Tenth Army (General Thadeus von Sievers) and Twelfth Army (General Pavel Plehve). The Germans nearly destroyed the Tenth Army, taking 100,000 prisoners, but their heavy losses (60,000 casualties, against 56,000 for the Russians) precluded a further advance. The indecisive outcome did nothing to diminish the reputations of Hindenburg and Ludendorff, but the same was not true for Conrad in the Carpathians, even though he, too, had inflicted heavy casualties on the troops of Ivanov's Southwest front. By the spring of 1915, his costly decision to pursue the winter campaign left him increasingly dependent on German support and further strained allied relations.

The Mediterranean: Turkey Joins the Central Powers

The Ottoman Empire occupied a crucial place in the international calculus of the summer of 1914. If it were on the side of the Entente or neutral, the war would be unlikely to spread to the Muslim colonial possessions of Britain and France or to Russia's large Central Asian Muslim holdings, the Triple Entente would control the Mediterranean and Black Sea, and the British and French could easily communicate with and supply the Russians. On the side of Germany and Austria-Hungary, the Ottoman Empire would block this potential lifeline at the Dardanelles and Bosporus, create an additional front for the Russian Army in the Caucasus, jeopardize Entente control over the Black Sea and at least the eastern part of the Mediterranean, and potentially revolutionize the Muslim world against all three Entente powers. Among the Ottoman Empire's Unionist leaders, Enver Pasha, holding the dual roles of war minister and chief of the general staff, emerged as the leading pro-German voice, but few of his colleagues shared his enthusiasm for an alliance with Berlin. Finally, on August 2, the day after Germany declared war on Russia, the Ottoman Empire's traditional arch-enemy, the Turks concluded a secret treaty with the Germans, while for the moment remaining officially neutral, in part to secure possession of their British-built dreadnoughts, two of which were scheduled to be turned over to Turkish crews at Newcastle the next day.

On August 3, with war apparently imminent between Britain and Germany, First Lord of the Admiralty Churchill seized the three dreadnoughts rather than let them fall into the hands of a potential future enemy. The British added the two completed dreadnoughts to their own navy later that month and broke up the third ship on its slip. The loss of the warships, which the Turks had already paid for, solidified anti-Entente sentiment in Constantinople and also made them more vulnerable at a time when it did not appear that the Germans could offer them any help at sea. Relief came when Germany's hostilities with France and Britain trapped two of its warships, the battle cruiser *Goeben* and light cruiser *Breslau*, in the Mediterranean with no hope of reaching the North Sea. Rather than join the Austro-Hungarian Navy in the Adriatic, they steamed for Constantinople, where they anchored on August 10. A week later they ran up the Turkish flag, the *Goeben* as *Yavuz Sultan Selim* and the *Breslau* as *Midilli*. In late September, after the British withdrew their naval mission, the German commander of the two warships, Rear Admiral Wilhelm Souchon, was made a vice admiral in the Ottoman navy and de facto commander of the Turkish fleet. A month later, Enver Pasha finally persuaded the rest of the cabinet to bring the Ottoman Empire into the war on the side of the Central Powers, but only after a trainload of gold worth 2 million Turkish pounds reached Constantinople from Berlin. On October 29, Souchon's warships shelled the ports of Odessa, Sevastopol, Novorossiysk, and Feodosia. Four days later, Russia declared war on the Ottoman Empire, followed, on November 5, by Britain and France. The Turks did not issue their reciprocal declarations of war until November 11, when Sultan Mehmed V, in his capacity as caliph, also proclaimed a jihad against the Triple Entente.

On November 2, the day the Russians declared war, a corps of their Caucasus Army crossed the border into Ottoman Armenia and advanced 15 miles (25 km) before encountering General Hafiz Hakki Pasha's Third Army, which forced them to withdraw. Enver Pasha then arrived to take personal command of the Third Army for the battle of Sarikamish (December 22, 1914–January 17, 1915), an ambitious attack all along the Caucasus front named after the town at the center of the line. Ottoman forces in the theater included 118,000 troops, facing a Russian Caucasus Army (General Alexander Myshlayevsky) of 65,000. Enver Pasha planned an ambitious campaign along a front of 775–930 miles (1,250–1,500 km), fought at an average elevation of 5,000–6,500 feet (1,500–2,000 m) in heavy snow. His entire army had barely 200 artillery pieces and fewer than seventy-five machine guns, and two of his divisions were deployed with no winter clothing. Resupply efforts suffered from a Turkish commitment, years earlier, not to build a railway line in the direction of the Caucasus without Russian approval. The Russians were better equipped and benefited from reinforcement by Armenian volunteers, whose enthusiasm won the praise of Nicholas II when the tsar visited the front late in the year. The climax of the battle came on December 29, when a Turkish bayonet assault failed to take the town of Sarikamish. Facing a Russian counterattack by a reinforced army of 100,000, the Turks fell back toward Erzerum, leaving the front line on Ottoman soil. Though it involved far fewer men for a much shorter period of time, the winter campaign in the Caucasus bore many similarities to the concurrent Carpathian campaign on the Eastern front. The Turkish Third Army suffered 47,000 dead, the Russian Caucasus Army 28,000; of these, 15,000 Turks and 12,000 Russians perished as a direct result of the weather. Remarkably few of the wounded survived (just 10,000 on the Turkish side). Enver Pasha had pursued the offensive against the advice of the head of the German military mission, Liman von Sanders. Afterward he returned to Constantinople, where he remained war minister and chief of the general staff until the last weeks of the war, never again attempting to command an army in the field. His decision to blame the fiasco on the disloyalty of the Armenians set the stage for the genocide that would soon be unleashed against them (see Chapter 12).

Conclusion

By the onset of winter the stalemated conflict had already been far bloodier and cost-lier than anyone had envisaged, yet the countries that went to war in August 1914 not only persisted in fighting but also raised the stakes for peace as the war dragged on. The Germans went farther than most in articulating war aims, the so-called "September program" of Bethmann Hollweg, formulated in the wake of the victory at Tannenberg and ironically dated September 9, the day of Germany's defeat at the first battle of the Marne. The program called for the creation of an economic *Mitteleuropa* under German domination, the annexation of Luxembourg, the relegation of Belgium and the Netherlands to German satellites, the liberation of Poland and Russia's non-Russian peoples (whose new states would form a buffer for Germany in eastern Europe), the annexation of some French territory, and the reduction of France to an economic dependent of Germany. The "September program" also revealed Berlin's revolutionary goals beyond Europe, as it included a radical redrawing of colonial borders in Africa, where the Belgian Congo would become the centerpiece of a German *Mittelafrika*. While no other government had such an ambitious program, all had war aims and none would accept a compromise settlement based upon the status quo ante. At least during the first three years of the war, public opinion in all countries generally favored a victorious peace, and such feelings only intensified as more men died, for without victory their sacrifice would be in vain.

While the success or failure of armies in the opening campaigns depended on the efficiency of their mobilization, then their command-and-control and logistics, the war of attrition placed a premium on the replacement of men, replenishment of *materiel*, and maintenance of strength especially in artillery. Germany had the most efficient mobilization, but the German advantage in command-and-control broke down once large-scale fighting began on the Western front and Moltke's armies were no longer advancing within narrowly prescribed parameters. After its failure at the Marne, the German Army's superiority in artillery and machine guns enabled it to establish and hold a continuous front deep in enemy territory. On the Eastern front, Germany enjoyed an even greater artillery advantage, but Russia, of course, had the superiority in numbers and had mobilized faster and more efficiently than expected. In their campaign against the Austro-Hungarian Army, the Russians enjoyed superiority in numbers of troops, artillery, and machine guns, and had the added advantage, thanks to the prewar treason of Colonel Redl, of knowing their enemy's war plans. Austria-Hungary's overall failure in the first months of the war was rivaled only by that of France, which likewise enjoyed no advantages over its primary opponent, Germany – either in its mobilization or initial implementation of war plans, or in manpower or firepower – and narrowly averted defeat just six weeks into the war. Joffre, like Conrad, pursued an aggressive offensive course completely inappropriate for his country's situation and resources. In the process, both generals destroyed enough of their own armies to make them dependent, for the rest of the war, on their allies. The fate of France, and that of the Allied cause against the Central Powers, hinged increasingly on the size and quality of the contribution that Britain would make on the Western front, and on the ability of the Entente to import war *materiel* from the neutral United States, a supplier unavailable to Germany owing to the British blockade in the North Sea. By the spring of 1915 this trade had assumed such a significance that Germany would resort to unrestricted submarine warfare in an effort to stem the flow of American munitions and other supplies to Britain and France. Paradoxically, amid the unprecedented bloodshed of an increasingly bitter war, ordinary soldiers early on adopted informal live-and-let-live arrangements with their adversaries wherever the lines stabilized. During lulls in the fighting, bored men at times engaged in shouting or singing matches with their enemies on the other side of no man's land, in some cases venturing out to fraternize or trade for alcohol or tobacco. On the Western front, a series of such incidents culminated in the "Christmas truce" of December 24–25,

1914, in Flanders, involving roughly two-thirds of the line held by the BEF, trenches on their northern flank held by the French Eighth Army, and the Germans of the Fourth and Sixth armies opposite them. The spectacle of widespread fraternization with the enemy disturbed the commanding officers on both sides so much that on subsequent Christmases artillery exchanges made a repetition of it impossible. Fraternization on such a scale would not be seen again until 1917 on the Eastern front, in the wake of the Russian Revolution.

SUGGESTIONS FOR FURTHER READING

Aksakal, Mustafa. *The Ottoman Road to War in 1914: The Ottoman Empire and the First World War* (Cambridge: Cambridge University Press, 2008).

Beckett, Ian F. W. *Ypres: The First Battle, 1914* (Harlow: Pearson Education, 2004).

Ferro, Marc, et al. *Meetings in No Man's Land: Christmas 1914 and Fraternization in the Great War* (London: Constable, 2007).

Herwig, Holger H. *The First World War: Germany and Austria* (London: Arnold, 1997).

—*The Marne, 1914: The Opening of World War I and the Battle that Changed the World* (New York: Random House, 2009).

Horne, John and Alan Kramer. *German Atrocities, 1914: A History of Denial* (New Haven, CT: Yale University Press, 2001).

Lyon, James. *Serbia and the Balkan Front, 1914: The Outbreak of the Great War* (London: Bloomsbury, 2015).

Porch, Douglas. *The March to the Marne: The French Army, 1871–1914* (Cambridge: Cambridge University Press, 1981).

Showalter, Dennis E. *Tannenberg: Clash of Empires* (Hamden, CT: Archon Books, 1991).

Van der Vat, Dan. *The Ship that Changed the World: The Escape of the Goeben to the Dardanelles in 1914* (Edinburgh: Birlinn, 2000).

NOTES

1. Quoted in Annika Mombauer, *Helmuth von Moltke and the Origins of the First World War* (Cambridge: Cambridge University Press, 2001), 94.
2. Herman de Jong, "The Dutch Economy during World War I," in Stephen Broadberry and Mark Harrison (eds.), *The Economics of World War I* (Cambridge: Cambridge University Press, 2005), 138–39.
3. Quoted in John Horne and Alan Kramer, *German Atrocities, 1914: A History of Denial* (New Haven, CT: Yale University Press, 2001), 39.

4. Alexander von Kluck, *The March on Paris and the Battle of the Marne, 1914* (London: Edward Arnold, 1920), 29.
5. Quoted in Horne and Kramer, *German Atrocities, 1914*, 238.
6. Quoted in Martyn Lyons, *The Writing Culture of Ordinary People in Europe, c. 1860–1920* (Cambridge: Cambridge University Press, 2013), 108.
7. Charles Louis Marie Lanrezac, *Le plan de campagne française et le premier mois de la guerre*, revised edn. (Paris: Payot, 1929), 173, 258.
8. Joffre to Gallieni, September 4, 1914, text in *Mémoires du Maréchal Joffre (1910–1917), Vol. 1* (Paris: Librairie Plon, 1932), 377.
9. Kluck to Moltke, September 4, 1914, quoted in Kluck, *The March on Paris*, 98–99.
10. Kluck to Moltke, September 4, 1914, quoted in Kluck, *The March on Paris*, 99.
11. Holger H. Herwig, *The Marne, 1914: The Opening of World War I and the Battle that Changed the World* (New York: Random House, 2009), 277.
12. Stéphane Audoin-Rouzeau and Annette Becker, *14–18: Understanding the Great War*, trans. Catherine Temerson (New York: Hill & Wang, 2002), 25.
13. Rudolf Jerabek, *Potiorek: General im Schatten von Sarajevo* (Graz: Verlag Styria, 1991), 162–65.
14. Franz Conrad von Hötzendorf, *Aus meiner Dienstzeit, 1906–1918, Vol. 4*, 399–400.
15. Josef Redlich, *Schicksalsjahre Österreichs, 1908–1919: Das politische Tagebuch Josef Redlichs,* Vol. 1, ed. Fritz Fellner, 2 vols. (Graz: Böhlau, 1953–54), August 26, 1914, 256.
16. Redlich, *Tagebuch*, Vol. 1, September 9, 1914, 270–71, and November 22, 1914, Vol. 1, 289.
17. Erich Ludendorff, *Meine Kriegserinnerungen 1914–1918*, 5th edn. (Berlin: E. S. Mittler & Sohn, 1920), 58.

Scharnhorst under full steam

Maximilian von Spee's flagship _Scharnhorst_ under full steam. The armored cruiser and its sister ship _Gneisenau_ (11,600 tons, six 8.2-inch [21-cm] guns, 7-inch [23-cm] armor, with a speed of 22 knots) were commissioned in 1907, but relegated to overseas duty after the emergence of the battle cruiser in 1908 rendered armored cruisers too weak for fleet service. During their 14,000-mile (25,000-km) odyssey from Tsingtao, China, to the Falkland Islands, the _Scharnhorst_, _Gneisenau_, and the light cruisers accompanying them were sustained by colliers and supply ships they met along the way, in operations made possible by the recent invention of the wireless telegraph.

4 The World War
East Asia, the Pacific, Africa

August 23, 1914	Japan declares war on Germany.
August	Allies seize German Samoa and Togo.
September–October	Japanese occupy German Micronesia (Marshalls, Carolines, Marianas).
September–November	Australians conquer Kaiser Wilhelmsland and Bismarck Archipelago.
October	Afrikaner "Maritz rebellion" against British in South Africa.
November 1	British naval defeat at battle of Coronel.
November 7	Germans surrender Tsingtao to Japanese.
November 8	German naval defeat at battle of the Falklands.
July 1915	South Africans complete conquest of German Southwest Africa.
February 1916	Allies complete conquest of German Cameroon.
November 1918	Surrender of last German forces in East Africa.

World War I, far more than World War II, centered on Europe, but within weeks of its outbreak the European war escalated into a world war, owing to the global nature of European colonial empires, commercial interests, and naval presence. While there would never be a non-European theater of the magnitude of the Pacific theater of World War II, the entry of Japan on the Allied side caused the fighting to spread to East Asia and the Pacific islands. The prewar naval arms race had brought a concentration of naval power in home waters, yet in the first months of the war European navies managed to carry the conflict to remote places that would not see hostilities in World War II, such as Tahiti, the coast of Chile, and the Falkland Islands. In contrast to World War II, there was also a protracted (though low-intensity) campaign in sub-Saharan Africa that lasted until the armistice. Aside from the Middle East, where events took longer to unfold and the fighting reached its climax much later, in the non-European theaters of World War I the Allies quickly, though not always easily, prevailed over German colonial forces, in each case leaving the outcome in little doubt by early 1915. During the war's first months, Allied (predominantly British) warships likewise swept the world's oceans of German cruisers, ending the naval war beyond European waters and the North Atlantic. This decisive success facilitated the unimpeded movement of men and supplies from around the world to bolster the Allied cause in Europe, and led Germany to make the fateful decision to embrace unrestricted submarine warfare.

The German East Asian Squadron: From Tsingtao to the Falklands

While the Japanese Navy never engaged the German East Asian squadron, Japan's entry into World War I provided the context for its flight from the Far East to the waters off South America, and for the subsequent failure of individual German cruisers to operate against Allied targets in the Pacific. For Japan, the war presented an opportunity to pursue long-term goals on the East Asian mainland, where it sought to replace European domination of China with its own, and in the western Pacific islands, valued as bases in the future competition with the United States for hegemony in the Pacific Ocean. A treaty of alliance with Britain, dating from 1902, provided Japan with a link to events unfolding in Europe. A mutual concern over Russian ambitions in the Far East led to the alliance, but British enthusiasm for it cooled after the decisive Japanese victory of 1905 led Russia to settle its differences with Britain in the Anglo-Russian Entente of 1907, freeing Japan to focus on its rivalry with the United States. Nevertheless, the alliance became active "if either signatory becomes involved in war with more than one Power,"[1] and thus obligated Japan to intervene as soon as Britain exchanged declarations of war with Austria-Hungary, after Germany. On August 15, two days after the onset of hostilities between Britain and Austria-Hungary, Japan demanded the disarmament or withdrawal of all German naval vessels in East Asian waters and the cession to Japan of Germany's Kiaochow (Jiaozhou) Bay territory with the base at Tsingtao (Qingdao). Eight days later, after the Germans refused to respond, the Japanese declared war. On August 24, their navy blockaded Kiaochow Bay with a formidable force including two dreadnoughts, one battle cruiser, pre-dreadnought battleships, and armored cruisers.

The commander of the German East Asian squadron, Vice Admiral Count Maximilian von Spee, had left Tsingtao on June 20, eight days before the assassination at Sarajevo, for a cruise through Germany's Micronesian island colonies (the Marianas, Carolines, and Marshalls) (Map 4.1) with his two best warships, the 11,600-ton armored cruisers *Scharnhorst* and *Gneisenau*. The light cruiser *Nürnberg* had left two weeks earlier, bound for the Pacific coast of Mexico, where it was to relieve the light cruiser *Leipzig*, deployed earlier to safeguard German interests threatened by the ongoing Mexican

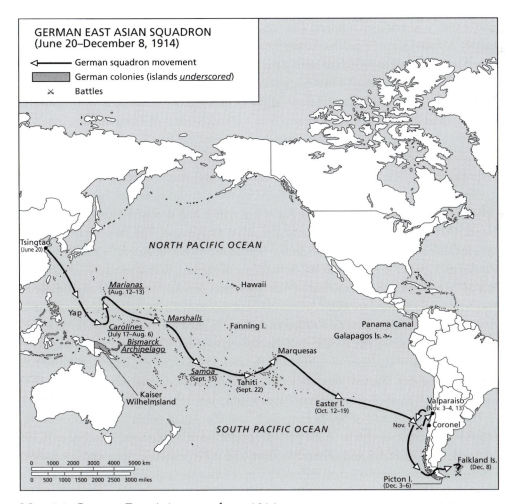

Map 4.1 German East Asian squadron, 1914

Revolution. Spee left behind at Tsingtao the light cruisers *Emden* and *Cormoran*, four gunboats, one destroyer, and the protected cruiser *Kaiserin Elisabeth*, the only Austro-Hungarian warship stationed outside European waters as of 1914. After the outbreak of war, but before Japan's entry, the Germans commissioned two auxiliary cruisers at Tsingtao: the Russian liner *Riasan*, captured by the *Emden*, which received the guns, crew, and name of the much smaller *Cormoran*; and the North German Lloyd liner *Prinz Eitel Friedrich*, which received the guns and crews of two of the gunboats. They escaped with the *Emden* before the Japanese blockaded Kiaochow Bay, accompanied by a flotilla of supply ships and colliers, seeking to catch up with Spee. The personnel from the remaining ships were ordered ashore, where they accounted for two-thirds of the 5,000 men deployed by the military governor, Captain Alfred Meyer-Waldeck, to defend Tsingtao against a Japanese siege commanded by General Mitsuomi Kaimo.

Kaimo's 60,000 men could have easily overwhelmed Meyer-Waldeck's tiny garrison, but he chose to tighten the noose around Tsingtao slowly, moving his troops forward under sufficient artillery support. They made their boldest advances at night and, ultimately, suffered just 415 deaths during the entire siege. Kaimo's deliberate pace allowed time for the British to send face-saving contributions – a pre-dreadnought battleship, a destroyer, and 1,500 troops – that made it an Allied operation rather than an exclusively Japanese one. On November 7, Meyer-Waldeck ordered the scuttling of the remaining warships and surrendered the garrison. The 4,600 defenders of Tsingtao were the largest body of prisoners taken by the Japanese during World War I and, in sharp contrast to their counterparts in World War II, were reasonably well treated, although the survivors ultimately were not repatriated to Germany and Austria until 1920.

The outbreak of hostilities found Spee in the Carolines, where he reunited the *Scharnhorst* and *Gneisenau* with the *Nürnberg*, which had reversed course at Honolulu rather than proceed as scheduled to the coast of Mexico. The three cruisers then sprinted full-steam back to Pagan in the Marianas, where on August 12 they met the *Emden* and *Prinz Eitel Friedrich*, escorting most of the supply ships and colliers coming out of Tsingtao; the rest, escorted by the *Cormoran* (ex-*Riasan*), joined the squadron two weeks later in the Marshalls. Provisioned and coaled for an extended voyage, Spee first detached the *Emden* to raid Allied commerce in the East Indies and Indian Ocean, then proceeded across the Pacific with the *Scharnhorst* and *Gneisenau*, accompanied at times by the *Nürnberg*, the *Cormoran*, and the *Prinz Eitel Friedrich*, attacking Allied targets along the way. The two armored cruisers did the most damage on September 22 at Tahiti, where they shelled the port of Papeete and sank a French gunboat (see Box 4.1).

The twists and turns of Spee's campaign, and the Allied effort to hunt him down, hinged upon advances made in the prewar revolution in wireless radio technology, led by Guglielmo Marconi and other inventors and entrepreneurs. Spee and his pursuers supplemented their wireless messages with exchanges delivered via undersea cable from various island outposts; island cable and wireless stations thus became targets for both sides.[2] The earliest casualties included the German wireless station on Yap in the

Box 4.1 **Trouble in paradise**

On October 7, 1914, the steamer *Moana* docked at San Francisco bringing passengers from Tahiti, among them a woman identified as "Miss Geni La France, a French actress," and New Zealand merchant E. P. Titchener. They gave the following eyewitness accounts of the shelling of Papeete, Tahiti, by the German cruisers *Scharnhorst* and *Gneisenau* on September 22, 1914:

La France: I was sitting on the veranda of the hotel, having a lovely holiday. Everyone was happy and contented. The sunshine was lovely and warm and the natives were busy at their work. I noticed two dark ships steaming up the little river, but was too lazy and "comfy" to take any interest in them. Suddenly, without any warning, shots began exploding around us. Two of the houses near the hotel fell with a crash and the natives began screaming and running in every direction. For a minute I didn't realize what was happening. But when another volley of shells burst dangerously near and some of the pieces just missed my head, I was flying, too.

… The shells from the German battleships [sic] kept breaking, and the explosions were terrible… The cries of the people were terrible. I was simply terror-stricken and could not cry for fear. I seemed to realize that I must keep my strength in order to reach the hills. We hid in the hills and the natives gave up their homes to the white people, and were especially kind to the women.

Titchener: From 8 o'clock until 10 the *Scharnhorst* and *Gneisenau* circled in the harbor, firing broadsides of eight-inch guns at the little gunboat *Zelle* [sic – *Zélée*] and the warehouses beyond. Only the American flag, which the American Consul hoisted, and an American sailing vessel also ran up, the two being in line before the main European residence section, saved that part of the town, for the German cruisers were careful not to fire in that direction.

It was plucky of the French to fire at all. At 7 o'clock we could see the two war vessels approaching, and soon made out they were cruisers … The Germans hoisted their flag and the *Zelle* fired two shots. The Germans swung around and fired their broadsides, and all the crew of the *Zelle* scuttled ashore. No one was hurt. The Germans continued to swing and fire. Their shells flew all over the town above the berth of the *Zelle* and the German prize ship *Walkure*, which the *Zelle* had captured … During the two hours of bombardment 1,000 shells from the big eight-inch guns of the cruisers fell and exploded in the town. The sound was terrific, and nobody blamed the natives for running away. With all the destruction, only three men were killed – one Chinaman and two natives.

The shelling sank the *Zélée* and *Walkure*, and caused an estimated $2 million of damage in Papeete, where two blocks of homes and businesses were destroyed. French officials set fire to a 40,000-ton coal depot to prevent it from falling into German hands.

Source: "Saw Papeete Razed by German Shells," *New York Times*, October 8, 1914.

western Carolines, destroyed by shellfire from the British armored cruiser *Minotaur* in early August, and the British cable station on Fanning Island (Tabuaeran), whose destruction by a landing party from the *Nürnberg* cut direct communication between Australia and Canada for two weeks in September. Wireless radio proved crucial to an impressive rendezvous that Spee orchestrated on October 12–14 at Easter Island, one of the most remote inhabited places on Earth. Steaming eastward across the Pacific, the *Scharnhorst*, *Gneisenau*, and *Nürnberg* made contact with the *Leipzig* and another light cruiser, the *Dresden* (both of which had operated independently as raiders since the declaration of war), at a distance of some 3,000 miles (4,800 km), when all were roughly 1,500 miles (2,400 km) away from the island. They coordinated not only their own rendezvous, but also that of seven colliers and supply ships stocked with fuel and provisions. From Easter Island, Spee's replenished warships steamed 2,000 miles (3,200 km) eastward to the coast of Chile, where they encountered a British force under Rear Admiral Sir Christopher Cradock off the port of Coronel. Cradock had left his base at Port Stanley in the Falkland Islands and rounded Cape Horn after an intercepted wireless message indicated that the *Leipzig* had called at Coronel. Unaware that Spee was sending all his transmissions via the *Leipzig*'s wireless in an attempt to mask the size and location of his force, Cradock expected to encounter only that lone light cruiser; indeed, he was convinced that the rest of Spee's squadron was far to his north, near the Galapagos Islands, en route to the recently opened Panama Canal, his fastest route home to Germany.

At the battle of Coronel (November 1, 1914) Spee's squadron faced two British armored cruisers, the 14,150-ton *Good Hope* and 9,800-ton *Monmouth*, both some-what older than the *Scharnhorst* and *Gneisenau*, along with the light cruiser *Glasgow* and the armed merchant cruiser *Otranto*. The pre-dreadnought battleship *Canopus* followed Cradock's cruisers at a distance, escorting his colliers. Despite his surprise at encountering five German cruisers instead of just one, Cradock engaged Spee without waiting for the *Canopus*. The two columns of warships closed shortly after 6:00 p.m., about 20 miles (32 km) offshore, in heavy seas and a southern springtime dusk that favored the Germans, who steamed on a southerly course east of the British line, which was soon silhouetted against the setting sun. The 8.2-inch (21-cm) guns of Spee's flag-ship recorded their first hits on Cradock's flagship *Good Hope* at 6:39 p.m., at a range of more than 11,000 yards (10,000 m); the *Gneisenau*, next in the German line, hit the *Monmouth* at 13,000 yards (11,900 m). Their punishing fire took its toll as the columns closed their distance by half, Spee estimating thirty-five hits against the *Good Hope* alone. The British flagship soon suffered a fatal explosion amidships, and went down with all hands. Spee reported no further resistance from the *Monmouth* after 7:20 p.m., but the crippled ship remained afloat until sunk by gunfire from the *Nürnberg* at 8:58 p.m., also with all hands. Cradock was among the 1,570 lost in the two sinkings. The *Otranto* and *Glasgow* escaped to return to the Falklands, en route warning the *Canopus* and the colliers to turn back. In contrast to the death toll on the British side, the only German casualties were two "slightly wounded" men aboard the *Gneisenau*. The *Gneisenau* sustained four hits, *Scharnhorst* two, the light cruisers none.[3]

Coronel was the first defeat suffered by a British squadron since the Napoleonic Wars, but Spee's victory had strategic as well as symbolic significance. Given the con-centration of British naval power in home waters – to face down the challenge of the

German fleet across the North Sea and secure the Channel for the BEF's operations in France – the loss of an overseas squadron, even one consisting of older warships, was devastating. Indeed, the debacle off Coronel put British forces on alert as far away as west Africa. But on a port call at Valparaiso after the battle, Spee gave a somber assessment of his own situation to an old friend living among Chile's large community of German expatriates:

I am quite homeless. I cannot reach Germany. We possess no other secure harbor anywhere in the world. I must fight my way through the seas of the world doing as much mischief as I can, until my ammunition is exhausted, or a foe far superior in power succeeds in catching me. But it will cost the wretches dearly before they take me down. [4]

After leaving Valparaiso, Spee took the squadron down the coast of Chile and around Cape Horn, to attack the British wireless station at Port Stanley in the Falkland Islands as a prelude to further operations in the South Atlantic. Despite the odds against him, he did not intend to give up anytime soon. The captain of the *Gneisenau*, Hans Pochhammer, recalled later that Spee, farther down the coast of Chile, had a shore party cut and stow several evergreens to ensure that the men of the squadron would have Christmas trees when the time came, because "who could say where we should be at Christmas?"[5] Most of them would be dead, thanks to the Admiralty's decision to respond to the defeat at Coronel by sending Vice Admiral Sir Doveton Sturdee to the South Atlantic with the battle cruisers *Inflexible* and *Invincible*. It was precisely the sort of overseas task for which these fast battleship-sized cruisers had been designed, and the only time during World War I that any vessel of the type undertook such a mission. As a precaution, the British had another two battle cruisers steam for the Panama Canal – the *Australia*, from Australian waters, and *Princess Royal*, from home waters – in case Spee chose that route into the Atlantic. Sturdee's battle cruisers reached the Falklands on December 7, by which time the *Canopus* and *Glasgow* had been reinforced by the armored cruisers *Carnarvon* and *Kent*, the light cruisers *Bristol* and *Cornwall*, and the armed merchant cruiser *Macedonia*.

To lay a trap for Spee at the Falklands, Sturdee kept his larger warships silent on the airwaves, as Spee had before the battle of Coronel. The Germans thus approached Port Stanley assuming the harbor would be either empty or nearly so; upon seeing that this was not the case, Spee called off the attack on the wireless station and decided to flee rather than fight. Sturdee gave chase with his entire squadron except the *Canopus*, which remained behind in Port Stanley. As the German ships steamed southeastward from the Falklands, they gradually lost their lead over the faster British battle cruisers. Facing the inevitability that his squadron would be destroyed, Spee broke off to the northeast with the *Scharnhorst* and *Gneisenau* in an attempt to lure the *Invincible* and *Inflexible* away from his three light cruisers, which could continue to function independently as raiders. Sturdee took the bait and pursued the *Scharnhorst* and *Gneisenau* with the two battle cruisers, whose 12-inch (30.5-cm) guns rained fire on their prey throughout the pursuit, the *Inflexible* firing 661 shells, *Invincible* 513.

Once the big guns found their range, and given his intention to go down fighting, Spee had no choice but to shorten the distance in order to give his own 8.2-inch (21 cm) guns a chance to hit the enemy ships. Thereafter the guns of the two armored cruisers scored twenty-two hits on the *Invincible* alone, but given the caliber of shells they were firing, they inflicted no serious damage, while the shorter range increased the punishment they had to absorb and hastened their own demise. After the *Scharnhorst* went down with all hands at 4:17 p.m., sunk by gunfire from a range of nearly 11,000 yards (10,000 m), Sturdee's battle cruisers closed on the *Gneisenau*, which they sank at 6:02 p.m. with fire from between 7,000 and 10,000 yards (6,400–9,100 m). Meanwhile, the light cruisers *Nürnberg, Leipzig,* and *Dresden* had scattered, chased, respectively, by the *Kent, Glasgow,* and *Cornwall*. Like Spee's armored cruisers, they refused to strike their flags even when hopelessly damaged. The *Kent* sank the *Nürnberg* at 7:27 p.m., and the *Glasgow* sank the *Leipzig* at 9:23 p.m. Only the *Dresden* could muster sufficient speed to escape; it was the newest of the German cruisers and the only one with turbine engines.

The British victory at the Falklands was even more decisive than the German victory at Coronel. Sturdee lost no ships and just ten men, while the Germans lost four of their five cruisers and 1,870 men. The dead included Spee, aboard the flagship *Scharnhorst*, and both of his sons, lieutenants aboard the *Gneisenau* and *Nürnberg*. Another 215 Germans, most of them from the *Gneisenau*, were rescued and taken prisoner. From their departure from Tsingtao in June 1914 until their destruction off the Falklands six months later, the ships of Spee's German East Asian squadron steamed almost exactly halfway around the world on their 15,000-mile (24,000-km) odyssey. Their voyage was unique in modern warfare, as no body of warships in the age of steam had traveled so far and for so long under such hostile conditions. Their defeat left the German Navy with no warship larger than a light cruiser still operating beyond European waters.

German High Seas Raiders

Following the battle of the Falklands, the Admiralty recalled the battle cruisers *Invincible* and *Inflexible*, along with the *Australia* and *Princess Royal*, to reinforce the British fleet in home waters. The ships remaining in South American waters focused on hunting down the *Dresden*, which returned to the Pacific after surviving the Falklands battle with the intention of making its way to the East Indies. The *Dresden* managed to sink just one Allied merchantman before engine trouble and lack of coal led its captain to request internment at Más a Tierra (Isla Robinson Crusoe) in the Juan Fernandez

Islands, 400 miles (640 km) west of the Chilean coast. On March 14, 1915, the *Kent* and *Glasgow* found it there and opened fire, ignoring the internment, prompting the *Dresden*'s captain to scuttle his ship.

While the operational history of Spee's squadron had been brief enough, the other German warships attempting to function beyond European waters fared even worse, as all were either sunk or blockaded by the time of the battle of the Falklands. The light cruiser *Emden* sank sixteen Allied ships (70,800 tons) in the East Indies and Indian Ocean, but its greatest success came against a target ashore: an oil depot at Madras, where it destroyed 346,000 tons of fuel in a 10-minute shelling on the night of September 22, 1914. The *Emden*'s victims included the Russian protected cruiser *Zhemchug*, sunk at Penang on October 28. Its career ended in the Cocos Islands on November 9, at the hands of the Australian cruiser *Sydney*, after it lingered too long to destroy a wireless station and cut an undersea cable. The light cruiser *Karlsruhe*, which had represented Germany at the opening ceremonies of the Panama Canal in August 1914, went on to sink sixteen merchantmen (72,800 tons) in the Caribbean before being lost to an accidental explosion on November 4, off the Lesser Antilles. The light cruiser *Königsberg*, on the German East African station when the war began, sank a number of merchantmen and the British protected cruiser *Pegasus* (off Zanzibar, on September 20, 1914) before being blockaded by British warships in the Rufiji River a month later. It remained a focal point of local Allied attention until it was finally sunk on July 11, 1915.

To supplement its cruising warships, Germany commissioned sixteen passenger liners and merchantmen to serve as auxiliary commerce raiders. The largest, the 24,900-ton North German Lloyd liner *Kronprinz Wilhelm*, sank fifteen ships (60,500 tons), but consumed too much coal to be a cost-effective raider and was given up for internment at Newport News, Virginia, in April 1915. The most successful was the 9,800-ton *Möwe*, which sank forty-one ships (186,100 tons) before being converted to a minelayer. The longest voyage belonged to the 16,000-ton *Prinz Eitel Friedrich*, commissioned at Tsingtao in August 1914, which followed Spee's squadron across the Pacific, rounded Cape Horn, and made it into the North Atlantic the following spring, logging around 25,000 miles (40,000 km), while sinking just eleven ships (33,400 tons) before giving itself up for internment at Newport News in April 1915. The most famous German raider – and the only sailing ship thus employed – was the three-masted windjammer *Seeadler*, commanded by Count Felix von Luckner, which sank sixteen vessels (30,100 tons) in an eight-month career before being wrecked on August 2, 1917 in the Society Islands. Of the sixteen German auxiliary cruisers, seven were eventually sunk or scuttled, four ended up interned in neutral ports, and two were lost to shipwreck. Few remained in service after the spring of 1915, when Germany began to use submarines as raiders against enemy commerce. While the *Unterseeboote* (U-boats) ultimately sank many times more Allied tonnage than German surface raiders, owing to their size and limited range few operated beyond European and Mediterranean waters, and those that did never left the North Atlantic, leaving the Allies free to use the rest of the world's oceans unmolested once the surface raiders were eliminated.

The Conquest of Germany's Pacific Colonies

Germany had few colonies to begin with, and the rapid conquest of most of them early in the war provided the context for the failure of the German high seas raiders, which consequently lacked a reliable network of bases for resupply and repairs. In the first three months of the war, Allied forces seized every German possession in the Pacific, starting on August 29, 1914, when an expeditionary force of 1,400 New Zealanders secured the surrender of German Samoa, complete with its coal depot and wireless station, without firing a shot. On September 11, 2,000 men from the Australian Naval and Military Expeditionary Force landed at Rabaul, capturing another coal depot and prompting the German defenders to destroy the wireless station at nearby Bita Paka. The Australians secured the surrender of the Bismarck Archipelago six days later, after minor skirmishing, and on September 24 went on to occupy Madang, the most significant settlement in Kaiser Wilhelmsland (northeastern New Guinea). Over the next two months they subdued the remaining German outposts on the mainland of New Guinea. With Spee's armored cruisers still at large at the time, these operations required a respectable escort, provided primarily by the Royal Australian Navy, led by the battle cruiser *Australia* until it joined Britain's Grand Fleet in the North Sea after the demise of Spee's squadron at the Falklands.

Meanwhile, Japanese naval forces deployed ostensibly to help hunt down Spee departed far too late to have any chance of catching him and instead focused their attention on securing the Marianas, the Carolines, and the Marshalls. Vice Admiral Yamaya Tamin's squadron, led by the battle cruiser *Kurama*, plodded along in Spee's wake as far as Eniwetok Atoll in the Marshalls, which it reached on September 29 (thirty-eight days after Spee had weighed anchor there). On October 3, Tamin occupied the German trading post on nearby Jaluit, then doubled back to the west – dropping the pretense of searching for Spee – and landed troops at key points in the Carolines, including Ponape (Pohnpei) on October 7 and Truk on October 12. A second squadron, commanded by Rear Admiral Tatsuo Matsumura in the battleship *Satsuma*, steamed due south behind Tamin, securing Yap and Palau in the western Carolines by October 7 and garrisoning Saipan in the Marianas on October 14. In contrast to the Australians and New Zealanders, the Japanese encountered no resistance on any of the islands they occupied and suffered no casualties. Indeed, for the war as a whole, Japan recorded less than 500 combat deaths, most of them in the siege of Tsingtao.

During these Micronesian operations, Japan and Britain made the pragmatic decision to consider the equator as a formal line of demarcation between the Japanese and
British (Australia–New Zealand) zones of occupation. While Grey characterized the
arrangement as a "temporary wartime measure," on December 1 the Japanese foreign
minister, Takaaki Kato, informed him that "the Japanese nation would naturally insist
on the permanent retention of all German islands north of the equator." He added his
expectation that Britain should support this position at the peace table once the war
ended.[6] Japan, indeed, would receive all of the Carolines, Marianas (minus US-owned
Guam), and Marshalls in 1919, by which time it was already treating them as permanent possessions. From west to east their newly acquired islands of Micronesia
stretched for some 2,600 miles (4,200 km), ensuring Japanese control over most of
the 4,000 miles (6,400 km) of ocean separating the US possessions of Hawaii and the
Philippines.

The Japanese occupation of German Micronesia thus represents a milestone on the
road to the Pacific theater of World War II, inasmuch as it ensured a future deterioration of the already tense relationship between Japan and the United States. Japan's
behavior in China following the fall of Tsingtao likewise pointed the way to World
War II, in that the Japanese began to act on their ambitions for the Chinese mainland.
During World War I the Republic of China, formally established on January 1, 1912,
following the overthrow of the Qing (Manchu) dynasty, existed in name more than in
fact, as foreign powers had annexed or leased most of the country's major seaports,
while regional warlords functioned as de facto rulers of the interior. Unable to assert
any authority, the founder and provisional president of the republic, Dr. Sun Yat-sen,
almost immediately relinquished the presidency to one of the warlords, General Yuan
Shih-kai, who became the primary target of the Japanese after the Germans surrendered their Kaiochow Bay enclave. Their pressure culminated on January 18, 1915, in
the infamous "Twenty-One Demands," which would have reduced China to a Japanese
protectorate. Yuan ultimately agreed to thirteen of the demands, incorporated into a
Sino-Japanese treaty signed on May 25. The Japanese thus solidified control over the
province of Shantung (Shandong), home to newly acquired Tsingtao and Kiaochow
Bay, as well as Port Arthur, Dairen, and the sphere of influence in Manchuria and Inner
Mongolia inherited from the Russians in 1905. Japan also received sweeping railway
concessions, mining concessions in Manchuria, and the opening of Manchuria and
Inner Mongolia to Japanese settlement. Japan claimed the right to veto non-Japanese
foreign investment in Manchuria, Inner Mongolia, and Shantung, as well as Fukien
(the mainland province opposite the Japanese territory of Taiwan), and insisted that
China should not make future agreements to lease or cede any of its coastal territory
to any country other than Japan.[7] The republic's legislature never ratified the treaty,
however, and after Yuan's death a subsequent Chinese government declared war on
the Central Powers (August 13, 1917) in order to gain access to the postwar peace

conference. There, Chinese leaders would count on the support of Britain and the United States to overturn the concessions Yuan had made to Japan, and would come away bitterly disappointed.

The War in Sub-Saharan Africa

The war in sub-Saharan Africa centered around Germany's four colonies: Togo, Cameroon, German Southwest Africa (modern-day Namibia), and German East Africa (modern-day Tanzania, minus Zanzibar, plus Rwanda and Burundi). Like the Pacific colonies, these territories were thinly defended and vulnerable to attack from nearby Allied lands. From the start it was clear that Germany could do nothing to save them, leaving their fate to be determined by the speed and force with which the Allies chose to attack them, and the resourcefulness (or lack thereof) of their local defenders (Map 4.2).

The west African colony of Togo was Germany's only self-sufficient overseas possession, thanks to the efficient cultivation of cocoa, cotton, and coffee. A narrow strip of land bordered by the British Gold Coast (modern-day Ghana) and French Dahomey (modern-day Benin), it was also the most vulnerable of the German African colonies. The Gold Coast regiment of the Royal West African Frontier Force (RWAFF), under Lieutenant Colonel F. C. Bryant, invaded Togo from the west on August 7, 1914, and was soon joined by a French force invading from Dahomey to the east. The 1,500 defenders (300 Germans and 1,200 Africans) capitulated after just nineteen days of fighting. Cameroon, 500 miles (800 km) to the east, was much larger and better defended, and required more resources to subdue. The initial British contribution included RWAFF units from Nigeria, Sierra Leone, Gambia, and the Gold Coast, under General Sir Charles Dobell, along with three Royal Navy cruisers and more than a dozen rivercraft from the Nigeria Marine, while the French contribution included one cruiser and a predominantly Senegalese infantry force. The cruisers provided artillery support for 2,400 British and 1,850 French troops who captured the colonial capital, Douala, on September 27. The Belgian Congo's *Force publique* soon joined other Allied forces attacking Cameroon from neighboring colonies, but the troops that had taken Douala stayed close to the coast to defend their conquests in case Spee's cruisers made an appearance. News of the German squadron's demise at the Falklands freed them to fight their way inland up the colony's main railway to Yaounde, Cameroon's other major city. An initial assault on Yaounde in the summer of 1915 failed, but a second offensive succeeded in taking the city on January 1, 1916. By then, the Allied force in Cameroon had grown to include 8,000 French, 6,400 British, and 500 Belgian troops, serving under British generals Sir Charles Dobell and F. H. G. Cunliffe and French general Joseph Aymerich. The last German outpost, at Mora in northern Cameroon, held out for another seven weeks after Yaounde, capitulating on February 18. After the fall of Yaounde most of the surviving German troops in the colony (about 600 Germans

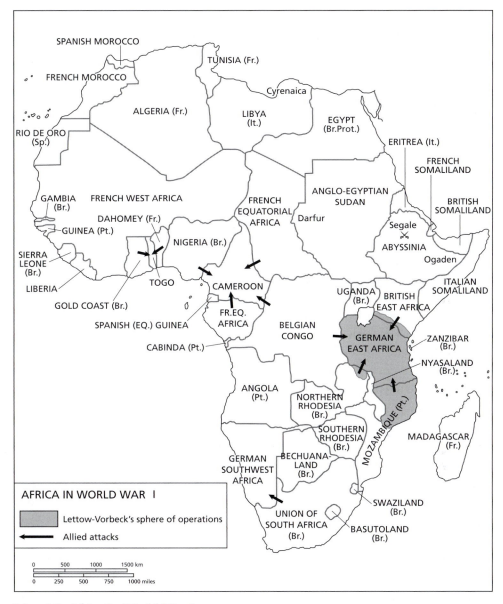

Map 4.2 Africa in World War I

and 6,000 Africans) crossed the border into Spanish (Equatorial) Guinea, where they were interned for the duration of the war.

Meanwhile, German Southwest Africa survived longer than it should have, owing to internal problems in South Africa, where the main fissure in the white population was not between speakers of English and Afrikaans but among the Afrikaners, pitting moderates, who had accepted British rule, against "old Boers," who had not. In August 1914 prime minister Louis Botha, a former Boer general who had emerged as the political leader of moderate Afrikaners, assured London that South Africa not only could defend itself, thus allowing the British garrison to depart for France, but would also undertake to invade Southwest Africa. With Spee's squadron still at large at the time, the British placed the highest priority on the destruction of the German wireless stations at Swakopmund and Lüderitz Bay; in September the Royal Navy destroyed the former with shellfire and landed a small South African detachment to seize the latter. Otherwise, the war got off to a slow start for Botha's Union Defense Force because the "old Boers" among South African officers saw Britain's predicament as a golden opportunity to reassert independence.

The Afrikaner rebellion against Botha's government took its name from Lieutenant Colonel S. G. "Manie" Maritz, commander of South African troops in the northern part of the Cape Colony, whose conspiracy with German officials across the border in Southwest Africa finally prompted Botha to sack him on October 8. Maritz went into open rebellion the following day, and on the 14th the prime minister declared martial law. With the help of his defense minister, General Jan Smuts, Botha led the loyal majority of the South African Army in a brief, decisive campaign that crushed the rebellion. When the main rebel force was defeated on October 24, Maritz fled to Southwest Africa. Isolated resistance in the Transvaal and Orange Free State collapsed by December, and the last rebel commandos, serving under Major Jan Kemp, surrendered on February 4, 1915, returning from Southwest Africa after having briefly joined Maritz and the Germans. By then, around 350 of the 12,000 men who joined the "Maritz rebellion" had lost their lives. In contrast to the Irish who rose against British rule at Easter 1916, "old Boer" rebels captured by the South African government were treated leniently. Most of the leaders received fines along with six- and seven-year prison sentences, only to be released early by Botha in 1916–17.

Within weeks of the surrender of the last rebels, Botha had mobilized a South African Army of 67,000 men for the invasion of Southwest Africa. Roughly two-thirds of this force saw action in the German colony, where they met stiff resistance from General Victor Franke's defense force (*Schutztruppe*) of 3,000 men, supplemented by a militia raised from among the colony's white settlers. In contrast to other German African colonial leaders, Franke was in no position to supplement his force with many African troops, the local population having been significantly reduced a decade earlier by the Herero genocide, Germany's response to the Herero rebellion of 1904. After Botha took the colonial capital, Windhoek, on May 12, 1915, Franke retreated to the north and made a last stand at Otavi on July 1, before surrendering his 2,000 remaining troops at Khorab eight days later.

Aside from small, isolated garrisons still holding out in Cameroon at the time, Colonel Paul Lettow-Vorbeck's East African Army was the only German military force still active in Africa on the first anniversary of the outbreak of the war. In August 1914, Lettow-Vorbeck had at his disposal just 3,000 soldiers and police, more than 90 percent of whom were local Africans, (Figure 4.1) to defend German East Africa. On August

15, one week after British warships shelled the colony's primary port, Dar-es-Salaam, Lettow-Vorbeck crossed into British East Africa (Kenya) and defeated an enemy force at Taveta. The same day, German artillery positions in Rwanda and Burundi began shelling villages along the eastern frontier of the Belgian Congo. Lettow-Vorbeck's first major victory came in the battle of Tanga (November 3–5, 1914), the colony's second largest port, where his 1,000 men beat back General Arthur Aitken's Indian Expeditionary Force of 8,000, inflicting heavy casualties. The War Office in London responded to the debacle by placing all British and Imperial forces in eastern Africa on the defensive until the defeat of the Germans in Southwest Africa, at which time South African troops would be sent to reinforce them. In the meantime, Lettow-Vorbeck's troops skirmished with enemy troops guarding the Kenyan border, while the British

Figure 4.1 A German *askari* leaving his family

This posed photograph illustrates the departure for war of a German East African *askari* (the word means "soldier" in Swahili, as well as in Arabic and other Middle Eastern languages). The Germans raised their first black African colonial troops in 1888 and eventually settled upon a highly selective recruiting process, after which inductees were subjected to rigorous training and draconian discipline. Thus, the German *askari* were considered elite troops by colonial African standards, and were also handsomely rewarded, being paid roughly double the wages of the British King's African Rifles (KAR), raised in neighboring British colonies. Their numbers also remained small. Germany employed no more than 11,000 of them during World War I, all close to home in the East African campaign. France, in contrast, raised twenty times as many black troops for the *Tirailleurs sénégalais*, of whom two-thirds served in Europe. Barely 1,000 German *askari* remained on active service in November 1918, when the last German East African forces surrendered.

focused on the German cruiser *Königsberg*, blockaded in the delta of the Rufiji River 100 miles south of Dar-es-Salaam. In the final attack on the *Königsberg* (July 11, 1915) two British Navy monitors sank the cruiser with the help of spotters from aircraft flying overhead. Before abandoning the wreck, the Germans dismounted its ten 4-inch (10-cm) guns for use ashore. Afterward, the surviving naval personnel joined Lettow-Vorbeck's army.

For the remainder of the war Lettow-Vorbeck benefited considerably from the tendency of his Allied opponents to look forward to the postwar redrawing of the map of sub-Saharan Africa. Britain and France were soon to formalize their partition of Togo and Cameroon (the French getting most of each), and Belgium, unrewarded for its participation in the Cameroon campaign, was keen to add the westernmost part of German East Africa (modern-day Rwanda and Burundi) to the Belgian Congo. Within the British camp, the India Office envisaged German East Africa as a future settler colony for Indians and a just reward for India's contribution to the war effort, and South African leaders – not content with the likely addition of Southwest Africa to the Union of South Africa – sought a role in the campaign there in order to stake a South African claim to East Africa as well. While Britain postponed a general election until after the war (and thus did not hold one from 1910 to 1918), all four dominions held elections during World War I, and in the case of South Africa the election of 1915 gave the party of Botha and Smuts an endorsement of their designs on German East Africa prior to the deployment of troops against Lettow-Vorbeck.

The first South Africans took the field in East Africa in January 1916, only to be routed by the Germans at Salaito Hill (Oldorobo), near Mount Kilimanjaro, on February 12. A week later Smuts received command of all British and Imperial troops in the region. Reinforced to 27,000 men, his army resumed the Allied offensive in the Kilimanjaro region, attempting for the first time to encircle Lettow-Vorbeck's main army at the battle of Reata (March 11, 1916). He failed to do so, but forced the Germans to abandon the area. The battle set the tone for the remainder of the campaign in East Africa, a war of maneuver in which the Allies (first under Smuts, eventually under General Jakobus "Jaap" van Deventer) repeatedly tried and failed to trap the elusive Germans, keeping Lettow-Vorbeck on the run without ever actually defeating him. Meanwhile, the Allies gradually took control of German East Africa. Belgian colonial troops attacked the colony from the northwest, taking Rwanda in May 1916 and Burundi in June. Another British colonial army advanced out of the southwest, from Northern Rhodesia (modern-day Zambia), and after Germany declared war on Portugal (March 9, 1916) a Portuguese colonial force from Mozambique attacked from the south. The last German supply ship slipped through the blockade on April 30; after German garrisons were forced to abandon Tanga (July 7) and Dar-es-Salaam (September 3), Lettow-Vorbeck lost all hope of resupply by sea. Facing 80,000 Allied troops by the end of 1916, his men were reduced to waging a guerrilla war in the southern portion of the colony, no longer attempting to defend territory. But supply problems and shortages of medicine

made it difficult for Smuts to bring his superior numbers to bear. Some of his white regiments suffered few combat losses yet were decimated by disease (for example, the 9th
South African Infantry, reduced from 1,135 men in February to just 116 in October).
Fortunately for the Germans, their smaller force did not require as much quinine to
keep its white troops free from malaria, and Lettow-Vorbeck did not hesitate to tailor
the size of his column to the amount of quinine at his disposal (see Box 4.2).

The South African army suffered 1,600 deaths in the East African campaign, four
times as many as it had in Southwest Africa, most of them during 1916. The campaign in general, and Smuts in particular, became increasingly unpopular with white
South Africans, especially as the absence of a decisive victory made it unlikely that
the dominion could successfully lay claim to German East Africa at the peace table.
Late in 1916, Smuts began to replace his South African, Rhodesian, and Indian troops
with black troops from the RWAFF, raised in Britain's west African colonies, and the
King's African Rifles (KAR), raised in Kenya, Uganda, and Nyasaland (modern-day
Malawi). By war's end the RWAFF had more than doubled in size, from seven to fifteen battalions, while the KAR grew even more dramatically, from three to twenty-two
battalions. Ultimately, five battalions of the RWAFF served in East Africa, along with
the entire KAR, the latter numbering more than 30,000 troops. For political reasons,
Smuts refused to employ black South Africans other than as porters and laborers. By
January 1917, when Smuts was called to London to join the Imperial War Cabinet,
black Africans accounted for more than half of the troops under British Imperial
command in East Africa. In the only major battle fought in the theater during 1917,
at Mahiwa (October 14–18) in the extreme southeast of the colony, Nigerians of the
RWAFF spearheaded the Allied attack. Lettow-Vorbeck called it his greatest victory
since Tanga, because the Allies lost half of their 5,000 men; he conceded, however, that
his own force of 1,500 could not afford the "very considerable" casualties of more than
500 suffered in the rearguard action, even though he had "completely defeated" the
enemy. [8] Mahiwa ended up being Lettow-Vorbeck's last stand in German East Africa
before he abandoned the colony and crossed into Mozambique (November 25, 1917).
That same week, a last-ditch effort to resupply him from home via Zeppelin failed
when the airship *L59*, carrying 15 tons of supplies, turned back over the Sudan and
eventually landed in Bulgaria.

For the next ten months the East African theater was limited to northeastern
Mozambique, where Lettow-Vorbeck's force spent much of the time chasing Portuguese
troops while, in turn, being chased by British colonial forces, primarily detachments
of the KAR. By August 1918 the dwindling German force was further weakened by the
influenza epidemic then making its way around the world. Lettow-Vorbeck decided to
abandon Mozambique and return to German East Africa (September 28), spending
just over a month in the southwest part of the colony before moving westward into
Northern Rhodesia (November 1). There, near Kasama on November 13, he learned
of the Armistice, and the provision that German colonial forces in East Africa must

Box 4.2 **Pragmatic warrior**

Figure 4.2 Paul von Lettow-Vorbeck

Despite being romanticized as the chivalrous "Lion of Africa," Colonel Paul von Lettow-Vorbeck (1870–1964), German commander in East Africa, enjoyed success as a field commander largely because of pragmatic decisions. These included a force reduction, described in his memoirs, which left behind more than 1,000 men to be captured by his pursuers just before he abandoned German East Africa for Portuguese Mozambique (November 25, 1917):

On November 17th I had to take a fateful decision at Nambindinga. The continual bush-fighting was threatening to consume all our ammunition. It would have been madness to go on with this fighting, which could not bring about a favorable decision. We had therefore to withdraw.

The supply question pointed the same way. Only by a drastic reduction of strength could we carry on with the stores in hand. Our supply area had been narrowed, fresh requisitioning had been interfered with by the enemy, and the produce of the land exhausted. The supply of quinine would last the Europeans a month longer. After the consumption of this the Europeans would certainly fall victim to malaria and its attendant evils; they would no longer be able to contend with the rigors of a tropical campaign. Only by reducing the number of Europeans to a minimum could enough quinine be ensured for each man to enable us to carry on the operations for months.

At the same time we had to reduce our total strength… [to] a smaller number of picked men with plenty of ammunition. It amounted to the reduction of our strength to about 2,000 rifles, including not more than 2,000 Europeans. All above this number had to be left behind. It could not be helped that among the several hundred Europeans and 600 Askari [African troops] that we were compelled to leave behind in the hospital at Nambindinga, there were men who would have liked to go on fighting and were physically fit to do so. Unfortunately, it must be admitted that among those who were left behind at Nambindinga, even among the Europeans, there were many who were not unwilling to lay down their arms. It is, however, worthy of mention that not only the majority of the Europeans, but also many Askari, were bitterly disappointed at having to remain.

Source: Paul von Lettow-Vorbeck, *My Reminiscences of East Africa*, 2nd edn. (London: Hurst and Blackett, 1920), 220–21.

capitulate to the Allies within one month. His troops surrendered at Abercorn, near the southern tip of Lake Tanganyika, on November 25.

By the time of the surrender, Lettow-Vorbeck's force had been reduced to 155 Germans and 1,156 African troops. He estimated that 14,000 men (3,000 Germans and 11,000

Africans) had served under him at one time or another, but the active force under his direct command was often barely one-tenth that size. Though not unique in this regard, he served as a symbol of the ability of the Central Powers to compel the Allies to spend significant resources in peripheral theaters, on land and at sea. While Lettow-Vorbeck's admirers (including many on the Allied side) romanticized him as a chivalrous warrior, the "Lion of Africa," this view stems mostly from his magnanimous treatment of enemy white soldiers and settlers. Indeed, the bigger picture was much grimmer. A veteran of the Boxer Rebellion and the Herero genocide, Lettow-Vorbeck pursued his campaign with little regard for the native peoples on either side. He conceded that his army had an attitude of "absolute callousness," especially after taking the war into Mozambique in 1917–18.[9] Once Lettow-Vorbeck gave up trying to hold or defend territory, the campaign degenerated into one of rival marauding columns living off the land, destroying communities along with their broader social and economic networks, leaving women and children especially vulnerable to being robbed, raped, kidnapped, bartered for supplies, or left to starve, if not murdered. A phenomenon common to all sides was what the Germans called their *Damenkolonie*, consisting of dependents of their African soldiers and porters, who clung to their column wherever it went.[10] It was an extreme version of the age-old camp follower phenomenon still common in European or American armies fifty or a hundred years earlier, but not seen in any other campaign of World War I.

Compared with the millions of men deployed on the fronts in Europe, and the tens of thousands killed in every major battle there, the size of the armies in sub-Saharan Africa and the losses they suffered appear minuscule. But their fluid campaigns, fought over vast rural areas that featured few roads and fewer railroads, in an environment inhospitable for horses and other beasts of burden, would have been impossible if not for the employment of large numbers of porters who served as the human supply chain for every army in the field. Historians have never come close to consensus on the number of black Africans mobilized in World War I or the overall number of casualties they suffered, as some sources count only the relatively small number of armed troops raised in a colony, while others also count the porters, who were often ten times as numerous (for example, the 250,000 porters mobilized by the Belgian Congo to support its *Force publique* of less than 20,000 soldiers) and whose deaths often went unrecorded. The total British Imperial death toll in the East African campaign (counting porters as well as soldiers) reached 100,000, of whom 45,000 were black Africans from Kenya, where they represented one-eighth of the adult male population. Of the 85,000 black South Africans enlisted in labor service during the war, 20,000 served as porters for the campaign against Lettow-Vorbeck, of whom nearly 1,200 died. Overall African civilian losses likewise are the roughest of estimates, owing to the nature of the fighting especially in East Africa, where the mobile tactics of Lettow-Vorbeck (especially in the war's last two years) generated hunger and disease that claimed untold numbers of lives. German East Africa had perhaps the war's greatest civilian death toll before the influenza epidemic of 1918, with an estimated 650,000 civilians and porters dying between 1914 and 1918. As early as January 1915, the burdens of war contributed to a rebellion against British rule in neighboring Nyasaland (Malawi) led by a most unlikely revolutionary, the Reverend John Chilembwe (see Box 4.3). Overall the conflict in sub-Saharan Africa was not inexpensive for the European powers in terms of lives or resources. By the time of the armistice in 1918 the theater had cost Britain an estimated £70 million, the equivalent of the entire British defense outlay in 1913, the last prewar peacetime year.

Box 4.3 "Our blood will surely mean something at last"

Reverend John Chilembwe (1871–1915), an American-educated Baptist minister, launched a brief, bloody revolt against British authority in Nyasaland (modern-day Malawi), sparked by local conditions exacerbated by the campaign against Lettow-Vorbeck in German East Africa. After attending Presbyterian and Baptist mission schools in Nyasaland, Chilembwe studied at the Virginia Theological College (today Virginia University of Lynchburg) from 1897 to 1900, key years in the development of this unlikely revolutionary:

[During his years of study in the United States, Chilembwe] imbibed the ideological ferment of African-American intellectual circles, and learned about John Brown and other abolitionists and emancipators. By 1900, Chilembwe was back in Nyasaland working for the American National Baptist Convention. Soon he had established a chain of independent African schools, constructed an impressive brick church, and planted crops of cotton, tea, and coffee. He sought to instill in fellow Africans a sense of self-respect.

In the years immediately preceding the 1915 rising, the area around Chilembwe's mission was hit hard by famine ... Moreover, William Jervis Livingstone, a local plantation manager, treated his laborers (many of them Chilembwe's parishioners) harshly and burned down Chilembwe's rural churches. Chilembwe complained loudly about racism. But his profound alienation followed the outbreak of

World War I in Europe, and the recruitment, which Chilembwe deplored, of Nyasa men for battles against the Germans in neighboring Tanzania. "We understand that we have been invited to shed our innocent blood in this world's war ... [But] will there be any good prospects for the natives after ... the war?" Chilembwe asked ... The remainder of his open letter, signed "in behalf of his countrymen," was a sharp protest against the neglect of Africans.

A month later, in January 1915, Chilembwe decided to "strike a blow and die, for our blood will surely mean something at last" ... He spoke to his 200 followers of the inspiration of John Brown, and warned them not to loot or to molest white women. On January 23, in different attacks, his men beheaded Livingstone, killed two other white men and several Africans while sparing a number of white women and children, looted an ammunition store in a large nearby town, and retreated to pray. When the rising failed to arouse local support, a forlorn Chilembwe fled toward Mozambique ... He was killed by African soldiers on February 3.

Chilembwe is revered as a hero in modern Malawi, which achieved independence in 1964. He was its first principled rebel, its first serious protester against colonial rule, and the first to shatter the widespread imperial belief that "the natives were happy" under foreign domination.

Source: Robert I. Rotberg, "Vita: John Chilembwe, Brief Life of an Anticolonial Rebel: 1871–1915," *Harvard Magazine* (March/April 2005).

Conclusion

In East Asia and the Pacific, World War I afforded Japan the opportunity to further enhance its great power status. After securing Taiwan, Korea, the Liaotung Peninsula, and a sphere of influence in Manchuria in its earlier victories against China and Russia, Japan added to its empire the former Chinese possessions of Germany plus three western Pacific archipelagos, the Carolines, Marianas, and Marshalls. In failing to engage Spee's squadron during its flight across the Pacific, the Japanese contributed nothing to the demise of the German Navy, yet at the end of the war the fall of Germany from the ranks of the world's naval powers would leave Japan with the third largest fleet behind Britain and the United States. None of the victorious Allies came away from World War I having gained such extensive strategic advantages at such little cost. During the war Japan also emerged as the primary tormentor of China, posing demands on the fragile republic that made the worst of the European "unequal treaties" imposed upon the late imperial regime seem mild by comparison. Thus, long before Japan's military occupation of Manchuria in 1931 and invasion of the remainder of China in 1937, World War I put in place the foundation for these future acts of aggression.

While the conquest of Germany's Pacific colonies, at least south of the equator, depended upon troops from Australia and New Zealand, both made greater contributions to the war effort elsewhere, and to the degree that World War I served an important formative role in their national identity, it hinged on more extensive sacrifices made farther from home. India played a role early in the war in East Africa but, likewise, helped the war effort of the British Empire to a far greater degree later and on other fronts. For South Africa, which the British had granted dominion status just four years before the war in a conciliatory gesture to the Afrikaners they had fought as recently as 1902, World War I had both short-term and long-term consequences. The "Maritz rebellion" of October 1914 caused great anxiety in Britain, yet its outcome affirmed that most Afrikaners had not just acquiesced in British rule, but were willing to defend the status quo with force against fellow Afrikaners. Compared with their Irish counterparts who rose against the British in April 1916, the rebels received lenient treatment, including Maritz himself, who served just three months in prison after finally returning home to face a treason trial in 1923. After World War I several leaders of the "Maritz rebellion" continued their struggle within the South African political system, using the National Party, founded in 1914, as their vehicle. Eventually, after World War II, they secured a majority of the dominion's whites-only electorate and formally established the apartheid system that endured for almost five decades thereafter.

Whether in East Asia, the Pacific islands, or sub-Saharan Africa, the victorious Allies established new regimes in the former German colonies, in most places as early as 1914–15, and afterward governed them as their own possessions, the postwar formality of League of Nations mandates notwithstanding. But much had changed in the century since the last time so much colonial territory had been redistributed among the great powers, at the end of the Napoleonic Wars. Europe's industrialization had left many more non-Western people integrated into the European-dominated world economy, not just as producers of raw materials but also as consumers. More significantly, exposure to Western ideals and European nationalism – ironically, almost always because of the educational efforts of Christian missionaries operating under the premises of the "White Man's Burden" – left a very small but also very significant number of colonial subjects unwilling to accept the continuation of life as it had been. By war's end the victorious Allies found this to be true even more so in their existing colonies than in the lands that had changed hands, as colonial leaders expected some general reward for the contributions their countrymen had made to the war effort. The postwar rhetoric of the peace conference, emphasizing democracy and national self-determination, raised expectations still higher, confirming the revolutionary impact that World War I had in so many of these lands, even though their anti-colonial movements moved on a slower trajectory than their counterparts in India and the Middle East.

SUGGESTIONS FOR FURTHER READING

Bennett, Geoffrey. *Coronel and the Falklands* (New York: Macmillan, 1962).

Gaudi, Paul. *African Kaiser: Paul von Lettow-Vorbeck and the Great War in Africa, 1914–1918* (New York: Caliber, 2017).

Paice, Edward. *Tip and Run: The Untold Tragedy of the Great War in Africa* (London: Weidenfeld & Nicolson, 2007). US edition *World War I: The African Front* (New York: Pegasus Books, 2008).

Peattie, Mark R. *Nan'yo: The Rise and Fall of the Japanese in Micronesia, 1885–1945* (Honolulu, HI: University of Hawaii Press, 1988).

Samson, Anne. *World War I in Africa: The Forgotten Conflict Among the European Powers* (London: I. B. Tauris, 2013).

Stephenson, Charles. *The Siege of Tsingtau: The German-Japanese War, 1914* (Barnsley: Pen & Sword Military, 2017).

Strachan, Hew. *The First World War in Africa* (Oxford: Oxford University Press, 2004).

NOTES

1. Article III of Anglo-Japanese alliance, January 30, 1902, text reproduced in www .firstworldwar.com/source/anglojapanesealliance1902.htm.
2. John Keegan, *Intelligence in War* (New York: Alfred A. Knopf, 2003), uses this campaign as a case study of the state of the art of wireless communication during World War I.

3. Spee's report of the battle, dated Coronel, November 2, 1914, is reproduced in wwi.lib.byu.edu/index.php/Graf_von_Spee%27s_Report. German accounts of the battle give all times as one hour earlier than British accounts.
4. Quoted in Hermann Kirchhof (ed.), *Maximilian, graf von Spee, der Sieger von Coronel: das Lebensbild und die Erinnerungen eines deutsches Seemanns* (Berlin: Marinedank-verlag, 1915), 73.
5. Hans Pochhammer, *Before Jutland* (London: Jarrolds, 1931), 186.
6. Quoted in Mark R. Peattie, *Nan'yo: The Rise and Fall of the Japanese in Micronesia, 1885–1945* (Honolulu: University of Hawaii Press, 1988), 45.
7. Japan's Twenty-One Demands (January 18, 1915; revised text April 26, 1915), Japanese Ultimatum to China (May 7, 1915), Chinese Reply to Japanese Ultimatum (May 8, 1915), texts reproduced in www.firstworldwar.com/source/21demands.htm.
8. Paul von Lettow-Vorbeck, *My Reminiscences of East Africa*, 2nd edn. (London: Hurst and Blackett, 1920), 213.
9. Lettow-Vorbeck, *Reminiscences*, 229.
10. See Michelle Moyd, "Gender and Violence," in Susan R. Grayzel and Tammy M. Proctor (eds.), *Gender and the Great War* (Oxford: Oxford University Press, 2017), 196–206.

Warschau unter Deutscher Besetzung
Einzug deutscher Kavalle

German troops enter Warsaw

In contrast to the trench warfare of the Western front, where the major offensives of 1915 barely moved the lines, on the Eastern front the Central Powers advanced until they conquered all of Russian Poland. After repulsing two attacks on Warsaw in autumn 1914, the Russians abandoned the city without a fight rather than risk having troops besieged there. Led by cavalry units, the German Ninth Army paraded into Warsaw on August 5, the day after the Russians departed. The victory failed to break the overall stalemate, however, as Tsar Nicholas II rejected a German overture for a separate peace.

5

The Deepening Stalemate

Europe, 1915

March 18	Anglo-French squadron fails to force Dardanelles.
April 25	Allied landings at Gallipoli.
April–May	Germans use chlorine gas at the second battle of Ypres.
May 2–10	Russian defeat at Tarnów-Gorlice.
May 23	Italy declares war on Austria-Hungary.
August	"Fokker scourge" marks onset of German air superiority.
August 5	Germans take Warsaw.
September 6	Bulgaria joins Central Powers.
September	Tsar Nicholas II assumes "personal command" of Russian Army.
September	First large-scale Allied gas attacks, by British in the battle of Loos.
October–December	Conquest of Serbia by Central Powers.
January 1916	Conquest of Montenegro by Austria-Hungary.
January 9	Last Allied troops evacuated from Gallipoli.

The first five months of the fighting left German troops in possession of most of Belgium and firmly entrenched in northeastern France, the Serbs holding their own in the Balkans, and the Russians occupying a vast swath of Austrian territory in the east and a smaller amount of Ottoman land on the Caucasus front. The generals debated their next moves with little interference from civilian leaders, none of whom yet advocated a negotiated settlement, despite the staggering human and material cost of the war thus far. In 1915 the belligerents focused primarily on recovering territories lost to enemy occupation, and this goal shaped the course of the war in its principal theaters. On the Western front, where the British Empire provided an ever-increasing share of the manpower, the French Army still shouldered most of the burden, and would absorb most of the losses, in Joffre's effort to expel the Germans from France. Meanwhile, on the Eastern front Falkenhayn directed the Central Powers in a major offensive designed to liberate Austria's occupied territories and also to conquer Russian Poland, in the hope that such a victory would enable German diplomacy to secure a separate peace with Russia. Britain and France anticipated the increased pressure on Russia and responded with an attempt to force the Dardanelles, an ill-fated campaign that left Britain and its Dominions focusing on the Gallipoli peninsula for much of the year. In general terms, the European war continued to escalate during 1915, with Bulgaria joining the Central Powers and reigniting the Balkan front, while Italy joined the Allies, opening up a new front in the Alps and on the Adriatic Sea.

The Western Front: First Battle of Champagne, Second Battle of Ypres, Second Battle of Artois

The Allies initiated almost all of the action on the Western front during 1915. Joffre's plan (Map 5.1) for the new year was set in motion in December 1914, shortly after the government returned to Paris from Bordeaux. It called for the French to drive northward into the Champagne region after breaking through between Rheims and the Argonne Forest, and for British and French armies to drive eastward after breaching the German lines in the Artois sector between the Franco-Belgian border and Arras. The attacks, if successful, would compromise the center of the enemy front and force a German withdrawal from France.

The first battle of Champagne began in earnest on December 20 and continued, with interruptions, until March 17. The German Third Army, now under the command of General Karl von Einem, bore the brunt of attacks spearheaded by Langle de Cary's French Fourth Army, making good use of its entrenched positions and superior machine-gun fire. In the three months of fighting each army suffered around 90,000 casualties, but nowhere did the French succeed in moving the front northward more than 2 miles (3 km). Because Falkenhayn had thinned their lines in order to provide

Map 5.1 Western front, 1915–17

more manpower for a spring offensive on the Eastern front, the Germans counterattacked only selectively. In one such case, at Soissons in mid-January, Colonel Hans von Seeckt orchestrated an infantry assault closely coordinated with a heavy preliminary artillery bombardment, initiating a practice employed by both sides in all of the rest of their battles during 1915. Thus began a cycle of trial and error warfare, in which the belligerents sought to combine tactics and technology to break the stalemate of trench warfare (see Online Essay 10).

The first Allied attempt at a preparatory shelling came at the battle of Neuve Chapelle (March 10–13) in the Artois sector, where Haig's First Army, including two British and two Indian divisions, attacked Crown Prince Rupprecht's Sixth Army after the war's most formidable bombardment prior to 1917. In the rapidly evolving air war (see Online Essay 3), the Royal Flying Corps provided aerial reconnaissance before the attack, photographing German positions, then assisted during the battle by bombing railways behind enemy lines. The British captured Neuve Chapelle within hours, but their offensive stalled before they reached the high ground of Aubers Ridge beyond it. After two days Rupprecht's troops counterattacked, pushing the British back to a line barely 1 mile (2 km) from their starting point, but failed to retake Neuve Chapelle, which Haig soon garrisoned with fresh Canadian troops. The battle confirmed that infantry could advance and hold ground against objectives properly identified through aerial reconnaissance and sufficiently pounded by a preliminary shelling. But after expending one-third of his stock of shells in the initial bombardment, Haig lacked the firepower to capitalize on what had been a promising start. While his casualties included 7,000 British and 4,200 Indian troops of the 40,000 engaged, the battle's greatest significance came in the recriminations afterward, as BEF commander Sir John French revealed the extent of the shell shortage to *The Times* war correspondent. *The Times* did not publish the story until May 14, but the ensuing storm of criticism, combined with the debacle then underway at Gallipoli, toppled Asquith's Liberal Government eleven days later. Asquith remained prime minister but in a coalition war cabinet, within which Lloyd George continued his wartime rise to power, holding the new portfolio of minister of munitions.

By then, the horror of trench warfare had been elevated to a new level with the use of poison gas by the Germans during the second battle of Ypres (April 22–May 25), the only Western front action initiated by Falkenhayn during 1915. By launching what appeared to be a major initiative in the west, Falkenhayn hoped to accentuate the element of surprise for the offensive the Central Powers would undertake against Russia in early May; he also intended to use the attack as a laboratory to test the battlefield effects of chlorine gas, developed for the German Army by Nobel prize-winning chemist Fritz Haber. It was not the first battle of World War I to feature the use of poison gas, but the first in which it was used with some effect. Three months earlier at Bolimów, west of Warsaw, cold weather and high winds had neutralized the impact of a bombardment of Russian positions with shells containing xylyl bromide tear gas. But the second battle of Ypres demonstrated the horrible usefulness of heavier-than-air gases such as chlorine, uniquely deadly for soldiers deployed in trenches. At second Ypres, the duke of Württemberg's Fourth Army deployed seven infantry divisions against Smith-Dorrien's Second Army, which included seven divisions of infantry (five British, one Indian, and one Canadian) plus three divisions of British cavalry. Allied forces in the sector also included two predominantly North African infantry divisions from the French Eighth Army and a Belgian division on Smith-Dorrien's far left. Initiating their attack late on the afternoon of April 22, the Germans released 168 tons of chlorine gas over 4 miles (6.4 km) of front. The gas cloud did the most damage in trenches manned by Moroccan and Algerian troops of the two French divisions. Those choosing to leave their trenches to avoid asphyxiation were riddled with machine-gun fire; within 10 minutes 6,000 of them were dead and most of the rest either blinded or otherwise incapacitated (see Box 5.1). Not anticipating such a decisive result, the Germans had not massed enough troops to exploit the sudden breach in the Allied lines, and those who advanced did so tentatively, owing to their own fear of asphyxiation. Smith-Dorrien quickly deployed British and Canadian troops to fill the gap, and the front held. On the morning of the 24th the Germans launched a second gas attack, this time against trenches held by the Canadian division, creating a temporary breach that enabled them to take the village of St. Julien. After Smith-Dorrien proposed a withdrawal to more secure lines just east of Ypres, Sir John French sacked him, but his replacement, General Herbert Plumer, soon executed the same withdrawal. German gas attacks on May 10 and May 24 were less decisive, but by the end of the five weeks of action the Germans had secured the higher ground east of Ypres, including Passchendaele Ridge, although the Allies still held the ruined city itself. In the process, the Germans inflicted twice as many casualties (59,000 British, 10,000 French) as they had sustained (35,000), mostly because of their use of chlorine gas. Thereafter, the Allies

Box 5.1 "The gas worked, and blind panic spread"

Excerpt from an anonymous British eyewitness account of the first successful battlefield use of poison gas, the release of 168 tons of chlorine gas by the German Army against the French 45th and 78th divisions (primarily Algerian and Moroccan troops), on the Western front at Ypres, April 22, 1915:

Utterly unprepared for what was to come, the [French] divisions gazed for a short while spellbound at the strange phenomenon they saw coming slowly toward them.

Like some liquid the heavy-coloured vapour poured relentlessly into the trenches, filled them, and passed on.

For a few seconds nothing happened; the sweet-smelling stuff merely tickled their nostrils; they failed to realize the danger. Then, with inconceivable rapidity, the gas worked, and blind panic spread.

Hundreds, after a dreadful fight for air, became unconscious and died where they lay – a death of hideous torture, with the frothing bubbles gurgling in their throats and the foul liquid welling up in their lungs. With blackened faces and twisted limbs one by one they drowned – only that which drowned them came from inside and not from out.

Others, staggering, falling, lurching on, and of their ignorance keeping pace with the gas, went back.

A hail of rifle fire and shrapnel mowed them down, and the line was broken. There was nothing on the British left – their flank was up in the air. The northeast corner of the salient around Ypres had been pierced. From in front of St. Julien away up north toward Boesinghe there was no one in front of the Germans.

Source: Charles F. Horne, ed., *Source Records of the Great War*, vol. 3 (Indianapolis: The American Legion, 1931), 146.

hastened to develop their own poison gases, ensuring that by the autumn of 1915 the new weapon would be used regularly by both sides. The French countered Haber's expertise by enlisting the help of their own Nobel prize-winning chemist, Victor Grignard, in the feverish race to introduce deadlier gases to the battlefield.

While most of the BEF was tied down in the second battle of Ypres, Haig's First Army joined the French Tenth Army (now under General Victor d'Urbal) in the second battle of Artois (May 9–15), attacking Crown Prince Rupprecht's Sixth Army. D'Urbal advanced on Vimy Ridge while, to his immediate north, Haig (reinforced to six divisions) advanced from Neuve Chapelle toward Aubers Ridge. The French attack came after an extensive artillery bombardment, conducted by nearly 1,100 guns over a five-day period (May 4–9); in contrast, the British attack followed a light 40-minute shelling on the morning of the 9th, as the concurrent action around Ypres left the BEF with little artillery to spare for Haig. As soon as the Allied infantry left its trenches it became clear that a number of German machine-gun nests had survived the shelling, especially along Aubers Ridge. On the first day of the offensive the British First Army suffered 11,000 casualties, prompting Haig to call off his attacks. Meanwhile, to the south, the French had better luck, in particular the troops of General Philippe Pétain's XXXIII Corps, but after six days d'Urbal's advance stalled, short of its objectives. French troops continued to skirmish with the Germans until June 25, without dislodging them from Vimy Ridge. The second battle of Artois cost the French 100,000 casualties and the Germans 75,000, in the war's most intense fighting since the first battle of the Marne. The French came away with a new appreciation of just how much the caliber of guns and weight of shells mattered in an artillery barrage, as most of their guns were 75-mm field cannon, excellent mobile artillery but too light to make a decisive difference in a preliminary shelling.

The Allied Failure at the Dardanelles

In the autumn of 1914, after the onset of trench warfare, Winston Churchill began to advocate the decisive use of British power around the periphery of Europe as an alternative to pouring more resources into the Western front. In his capacity as First Lord of the Admiralty, over the winter of 1914–15 he developed a plan calling for a column of Allied warships to force the Dardanelles, opening up the Turkish straits as a supply route from the Western Allies to Russia. The bold stroke might compel the Turks to sue for peace; at the least, Churchill calculated, it would force them to concentrate their power to defend Constantinople, relieving pressure not only on the Russians in the Caucasus but also on the British in Egypt. Best of all, he insisted, the operation could be accomplished with naval power alone.

Churchill's idea gained support when the stalemate on the Western front continued into 1915, but before acting on it, the British took decisive action to secure Egypt and the Suez Canal. Theoretically a part of the Ottoman Empire, Egypt had been independent since 1805 under the dynasty established by Muhammad Ali, whose descendants reigned under the title of khedive. Their lavish spending and borrowing from Western banks, along with the Anglo-French concession to dig the Suez Canal (opened in 1869), made Egypt a pawn of the European powers long before 1882, when Britain occupied the country to prop up the khedive's regime against an internal revolt. The khedive of Egypt at the onset of World War I, Abbas Hilmi II, cast his lot with the Central Powers and sought their aid to rid Egypt of its British occupiers, who responded, on December 18, 1914, by deposing him and formally declaring Egypt a British protectorate. Owing to his pro-Arab and pro-Islamist sentiments, the Young Turks soon exiled the ousted khedive to Vienna, but not before he supported the sultan's call to jihad against the Entente and the invasion of Egypt by the Ottoman VIII Corps, which on February 3, 1915, attacked British Imperial forces along the Suez Canal.

By the time of the attack General Sir John Maxwell's garrison included 70,000 men, its ranks swelled by troops from Australia, New Zealand, and India who had been arriving regularly via the Red Sea. They easily defeated the invading corps, which suffered 1,500 casualties against just 150 for the defenders. The debacle foreshadowed things to come for the Middle Eastern efforts of the Central Powers inasmuch as the Turkish commander, Jemal Pasha, faced inadequacies in firepower, supply, and transport, while the German general assigned to "assist" him, Baron Friedrich Kress von Kressenstein, could barely conceal his contempt for the Turks. To make matters worse, it became clear that the policies followed since 1908 by the Young Turk regime had so alienated the sultan's Arab subjects that the appeal to jihad did little to rally them against the British. No Arab religious or tribal leader publicly endorsed the invasion of Egypt, and many of the Syrian and Palestinian troops in VIII Corps deserted during the campaign.

The Ottoman defeat at the Suez Canal created an opening for the British to redeploy most of the Egyptian garrison for an attack on the Turkish straits, but Churchill initially persisted in his belief that the operation could be conducted with naval power alone, even though the presence of the German High Sea Fleet kept the British Navy's best capital ships in the North Sea and the presence of Austro-Hungarian dreadnoughts in the Adriatic likewise tied down the French Navy's dreadnoughts in the central Mediterranean. When the Allied bombardment of the outer forts of the Dardanelles began on February 19, Rear Admiral Sir John de Robeck's force included just two modern capital ships – the dreadnought *Queen Elizabeth* and battle cruiser *Inflexible* – backed by twelve British and four French pre-dreadnought battleships, and countless smaller warships. Following four weeks of preparatory shelling, de Robeck's ships attempted to force the Dardanelles at midday on March 18. Following closely behind a flotilla of minesweepers, the battleships steamed slowly into the straits three abreast, focusing their fire to silence the guns of the outer fortresses. The operation proceeded as planned until the Turks began to deploy batteries of horse artillery to fire on the screen of minesweepers. Because these batteries could be moved as soon as the guns of the battleships found their mark, the Allies could do little to counter their efforts. The minesweeping effort grew spotty, and at 2:00 p.m. one of the French pre-dreadnoughts struck a mine, sinking in less than 2 minutes with almost all hands. Mines soon sank two British pre-dreadnoughts, bringing the advance to a halt. The battle cruiser *Inflexible* also struck a mine but was towed safely out of the straits, as were two French pre-dreadnoughts badly damaged by shellfire from Turkish batteries during the withdrawal. Four other old battleships sustained lighter damage, leaving only the *Queen Elizabeth* and seven pre-dreadnoughts (six British and one French) to emerge from the Dardanelles unscathed.

The failure of the Allied navies led to the decision to form the Mediterranean Expeditionary Force (MEF) from the Egyptian garrison and deploy it to the Gallipoli peninsula, under the command of General Sir Ian Hamilton. On April 25, the spit of land forming the west bank of the Dardanelles was shelled by British and French warships, after which one French, two British, and two ANZAC (Australia-New Zealand Army Corps) divisions were carried to their beachheads not in purpose-built landing craft, like their World War II counterparts, but in columns of longboats towed by steam launches. A British infantry division landed at Cape Hellas, the tip of the Gallipoli peninsula, and the ANZAC divisions landed on the peninsula's Aegean coast. As diversions, the French division landed south of the mouth of the Dardanelles at Kum Kale prior to moving on to Cape Hellas, and a division of British marines (the Royal Naval Division) put ashore much farther up the Gallipoli peninsula at Bulair. The diversions had no effect, however, as six divisions of the Turkish Fifth Army, 84,000 men in all, held the heights to the north and south of the straits. Liman von Sanders, entrusted by Enver Pasha to organize the defenses, ordered General Mustafa Kemal (later known as Atatürk) (Figure 5.1) to deploy his division on the high ground just south of Suvla Bay, above what would soon be called Anzac Cove. In the initial landings of the 25th, 20,000 ANZACs secured a beachhead of three-quarters of a square mile (2 km²), which their best efforts over the next eight months did little to expand. Their failure owed much to Kemal, who recognized that the initial landing was not a feint and, by the evening of the battle's first day, engaged his entire division to contain it. The bloodiest fighting occurred in the first nine days after the landings, during which the ANZAC divisions (along with four battalions of the Royal Naval Division, sent down the coast from Bulair) suffered casualties that included 8,700 killed. The Turks lost nearly 20,000, by reinforcing Kemal's division and counterattacking repeatedly in an effort to force the ANZACs to withdraw. Thereafter both sides dug trench lines, the Turks on the high ground above the beaches and the Allies below, on the slope. Meanwhile, at Cape Hellas, the British 29th Division faced much lighter opposition but still lost 6,500 men in establishing its beachhead and advancing 3.5 miles (5.5 km) inland from the tip of

Figure 5.1 Mustafa Kemal

Mustafa Kemal (1881–1938) graduated from
the Ottoman military academy in 1902 and
joined the Young Turks shortly before their
successful coup in 1908. He served in Libya
during the Italo-Turkish War and in the
defense of Constantinople during the First
Balkan War. A lieutenant colonel in 1914, his
star rose quickly during World War I. Hailed
for his heroism while leading a division at
Gallipoli, he received a corps command
on the Caucasus front, where he became
head of the Second Army in 1917. He later
commanded the Seventh Army in Palestine.
In pursuit of his postwar goal of establishing a
secular republic, he formed a Turkish national
army that defeated Armenian and Greek
forces to secure the borders of the modern
Turkish state, proclaimed in 1923. He served
as president of Turkey until his death. In 1934
he was granted the surname Atatürk ("father
of the Turks") in recognition of his role in
founding the modern Turkish state.

the cape, where they, too, became bogged down in trench lines. Churchill's scheme
to break the stalemate of the Western front at the Dardanelles had only resulted in
another stalemate (see Online Essay 2).

British public and political reaction to the initial round of carnage at the Gallipoli
beachheads set the stage for the crisis that erupted when *The Times* published Sir
John French's revelation of the army's shell shortage. In agreeing to form a coalition
war cabinet under Asquith, Conservatives demanded as the price of their cooperation Churchill's resignation from the Admiralty, which followed on May 25. British
Navy leaders, who had never liked the idea of risking new capital ships at the Turkish
straits, promptly secured the return of the *Queen Elizabeth* and *Inflexible* to the North
Sea. Prudence dictated the move, as larger warships providing fire support for operations ashore were especially vulnerable to torpedo attack. During the month of May
1915 alone, another three British pre-dreadnoughts were lost off the Dardanelles, all
to torpedo attacks, two by *U21*, the first of dozens of German submarines sent to the
Mediterranean in the last three and a half years of the war. They were supplemented by
others shipped overland from Germany and assembled at Austro-Hungarian bases on
the Adriatic. The campaign was undertaken because the Austro-Hungarian Navy (with
just seven U-boats in the spring of 1915) lacked the submarine force to help the Turks

at the Dardanelles, and had greater concerns closer to home after May 1915, when Italy declared war on the Dual Monarchy. Because Italy did not declare war on Germany until August 1916, in the meantime all German U-boats in the Mediterranean were double-numbered as Austro-Hungarian. Almost three months after the spectacular debut of *U21*, another German submarine sank a British transport en route to the Dardanelles from Alexandria, drowning nearly 1,000 troops. The British also deployed undersea boats in the area, with much less dramatic results, although in December 1914 and again in August 1915 their submarines slipped through the Dardanelles to sink two Turkish pre-dreadnoughts.

Meanwhile, on the Gallipoli peninsula, over the eight months after their initial landings the Allies added another nine divisions to their original five, only to have the Turks reinforce their Fifth Army to sixteen divisions to contain them in their coastal enclaves. Two factors fueled the ensuing carnage: the Turks, like the French on the Western front, attacked repeatedly to expel the invaders from their soil, while the Allies attacked repeatedly in their quest to take the Turkish forts on the west bank of the Dardanelles, objectives that were maddeningly close to their own lines. Hamilton ultimately sought to break the stalemate by opening a third beachhead with a surprise landing of eight divisions at Suvla Bay. The ensuing battle of Sari Bair (August 6–21), named after the ridge dominating both Anzac Cove and Suvla Bay, featured the campaign's most intense fighting since early May. Individual actions included the infamous slaughter of two regiments of Australian Light Horse (fighting as infantry) at the Nek, in a tragically uncoordinated assault on the hill known as "Baby 700," and the bloody gains of the Australian 1st Division at Lone Pine, in what was supposed to have been a diversion. By the time the fighting died down the Allies had paid for their minor gains with more than 20,000 casualties. Kemal again emerged as Turkey's victorious hero, first anticipating Hamilton's choice of landing sites, then sweeping a force of New Zealanders from the crest of Chunuk Bair, which they had held for two days (August 8–10). Afterward the war of attrition continued along the trench lines, now at three coastal enclaves instead of two. Hamilton did not attempt another offensive before Lord Kitchener sacked him on October 15.

By then, Bulgaria's decision to join the Central Powers had forced the Allies to withdraw troops from Gallipoli for the defense of Serbia. To secure a route to their landlocked Balkan ally, the British and French concluded an agreement with the pro-Allied Greek prime minister, Eleftherios Venizelos, to allow them to land troops at Salonika, on the assumption that a Bulgarian invasion of Serbia would activate a Greco-Serbian defensive alliance dating from the Balkan wars, and bring Greece into the war on the side of the Allies. A British division from Suvla Bay and a French division from Cape Hellas were the first to arrive there, on October 5, followed by troops from Britain and France who could have been sent as reinforcements to the Gallipoli peninsula. The decision to evacuate the rest of the troops and abandon the Dardanelles campaign came on the recommendation of General Sir Charles Monro, Hamilton's replacement, shortly after his arrival at Gallipoli in late October, and was confirmed by Lord Kitchener after he visited the peninsula in mid-November. Naval forces successfully evacuated Anzac Cove and Suvla Bay on the night of December 19–20, and Cape Hellas on the night of January 8–9, 1916. The eight-month battle of Gallipoli (known to the Turks as the battle of Çanakkale, after the name of the local province) generated 251,000 Ottoman casualties, including 87,000 dead, and 141,000 Allied casualties, including 44,000 dead (among them 21,000 British, 10,000 French, 8,700 Australians, and 2,700 New Zealanders). At sea the British lost five of the twenty pre-dreadnoughts deployed in the Dardanelles campaign, the French, one of five, and the Turks, two of three. The Allied navies also torpedoed more than 56,000 tons of Turkish shipping in the vicinity of the straits, in the process losing eight submarines (four British and four French), most of them to mines.

The Western Front: Third Battle of Artois, Battle of Loos, Second Battle of Champagne

The temporary Anglo-French focus on the Dardanelles brought a lull in the action on the Western front that lasted the entire summer of 1915. Joffre took advantage of the respite to reorganize his forces into three army groups. Under the new arrangement Foch, in Flanders, and the First Army's Dubail, in Lorraine, both already functioning as de facto group commanders, continued in their roles for the northern and south-eastern sectors of the front. For the center of the line, Joffre elevated Castelnau to group commander and promoted Pétain to replace him as head of the Second Army. The Allies tried to implement Joffre's grand design again in the autumn, only this time better coordinated so that Allied troops attacked in the Artois sector and Champagne sector simultaneously in order to further strain the Germans. The third battle of Artois (September 25–November 4) featured a rematch of the same armies and commanders that had met at the second battle of Artois, only this time the French deployed 420 heavy guns to spearhead their four-day preparatory barrage. The volume of shelling still proved to be insufficient, however, and the advance of d'Urbal's Tenth Army stalled shortly after the offensive began, prompting Joffre to shift his reserves to the Champagne sector, where initial gains persuaded him that a breakthrough might be achieved.

The British component of the third Artois campaign, the battle of Loos (September 25–28), began not with a heavy bombardment but with the first large-scale Allied use of poison gas. Troops of Haig's First Army released 140 tons of chlorine gas on the morning of the 25th, prior to their initial assault on the German trenches west of Loos. Since the second battle of Ypres all armies had mass-produced their first primitive gas masks, which were too ineffective to inspire much confidence in the wearer; such was the case at Loos with the British, who experienced problems with their masks exacerbated by a wind shift that blew much of the gas back toward their own trenches. Nevertheless, British infantry breached the German lines and captured Loos. They failed to advance any farther, however, as their weak artillery failed to cut sufficient gaps in the German wire or to destroy many of the enemy's machine-gun nests. Within three days Haig's troops had to withdraw to their starting positions. By October the German Sixth Army, which had started the third Artois campaign with seventeen divisions, received additional reinforcements, giving Crown Prince Rupprecht more than enough troops to fend off further Allied attacks. The action at the third battle of Artois (including Loos) cost him just 20,000 casualties, against 50,000 for the British and 48,000 for the French.

Meanwhile, in the Champagne region, the French Second and Fourth armies led the assault. At the onset of the second battle of Champagne (September 25–November 6), German lines softened by a three-day preliminary shelling gave way, breached by troops funneled into forward trenches that French sappers had dug extraordinarily close to the German defenses. This new tactic, which came to be known as the "Joffre attack," quickly moved the front northward roughly 2 miles (3 km). The French took 25,000 prisoners and captured 150 guns before the advance stalled on October 6, dashing Joffre's hopes. Following more than three weeks of skirmishes, the Germans counterattacked on October 30 and by November 6 regained all the ground they had lost. His innovative tactics notwithstanding, Joffre remained wedded to the notion that, in the end, the spirit of his army mattered most, and somehow would compensate for all of its deficiencies. On the eve of the second battle of Champagne his general order to the troops underscored this belief: "Your élan is irresistible."[1] The battle cost the French another 145,000 casualties, the Germans 72,500, bringing France's losses for the year to roughly 1.1 million men killed, wounded, taken prisoner, or missing, against Germany's Western front casualties of 600,000. As bloody as the major battles had been, for each side more than half of the casualties came outside those clashes, in the day-to-day low-intensity war of attrition.

The indecisive bloodletting that set in during 1915 led to postwar criticism, especially in Britain, of the "criminal idiocy" of army leaders in squandering the lives of so many soldiers.[2] The juxtaposition, in postwar memory, of the bravery of the common soldiers and alleged incompetence of their generals became entrenched enough to survive the next world war, obscuring the reality that the generals of World War I did, indeed, learn from their failures, but could act on the lessons only rarely before new challenges led to new failures (see Perspectives 5.1). For example, during 1915 the Allies learned that their infantry could not hope to breach German trenches unless they used aerial reconnaissance to identify the weakest points in the enemy lines, cleared their way with an extensive bombardment by heavy artillery, and employed aircraft to bomb and strafe reserves that the Germans brought to the front to fill the breach. At that time, however, their numbers of heavy guns and the size of their stockpiles of shells remained insufficient to take advantage of what they now knew, and as they continued to improve their own production of guns and shells, the Germans did likewise, raising the stakes still higher. The German introduction of poison gas to the battlefield prompted the Allies to respond in kind, but it remained to be seen whether gas would serve any purpose other than to make the nightmare of trench warfare even worse for the average soldier. Meanwhile, in the budding air war, the frequency and intensity of aerial combat did not approach the levels of 1917–18, but during the autumn of 1915 the "Fokker scourge," as the British press called it, effectively swept British and French aircraft from the skies. German domination of the air left Allied commanders on the ground at third Artois, Loos, and second Champagne without aerial reconnaissance photographs, ironically only months after the value of such information had become universally accepted, and without the means to harass the enemy rear.

Perspectives 5.1: British generalship

British historian Adrian Gregory has suggested that the condemnation of the British High Command in World War I stems in part from the need for a "negative counterpoint" to a British effort in World War II that also featured significant, costly disasters:

The verdict of popular culture is more or less unanimous. The First World War was stupid, tragic, and futile … The criminal idiocy of the British High Command has become an article of faith … These incompetents butchered the flower of British manhood incessantly for four years without remorse or even, in many cases, awareness.

The disasters of British arms in the First World War are well known … By contrast, the litany of British catastrophes that makes up a large part of the Second World War is swept under the carpet… As an indictment of the stupidity of the "military mind", Britain's performance in the Second World War would be difficult to match … If "died in vain" means men being killed without contributing anything much to the final victory, then there should be more serious questions asked about 1939–1945. The British do not ask those questions because they have 1914–1918 instead. The extent to which the memory of the First World War has been reshaped as a negative counterpoint to a mythologized version of the Second World War cannot be overestimated.

Source: Adrian Gregory, *The Last Great War: British Society and the
First World War* (Cambridge: Cambridge University Press, 2008), 3–4.

• • • •

In his biography of Sir Douglas Haig, commander of First Army and, from 1916, the entire BEF, British historian J. P. Harris reflects the recent trend of judging British generalship less harshly:

Most historians seem now to accept that, whatever his other faults, Haig was very open to technological innovation, that the British army on the Western Front was highly experimental and innovative and that the British pushed the available military technology to its limits in the war's final year.

The revolution in Western Front scholarship that has taken place since the 1980s … has highlighted other issues, practically all of which were raised in some form during the war itself. Haig's capacity to adjust from open warfare to quasi-siege warfare conditions, his selection and employment of his staff, his relations with and employment of subordinate commanders, his handling of his artillery, his choice of battlefields for offensive operations, and his ability to 'read' battles and strategic situations are amongst these.

Source: J. P. Harris, Douglas Haig and the First World War
(Cambridge: Cambridge University Press, 2008), 2.

The Eastern Front: Tarnów-Gorlice and the German Peace Overture to Russia

Encouraged by the German intention to devote more resources to the Eastern front in 1915, Conrad visited Falkenhayn in Berlin three times during April to coordinate a spring offensive against the Russians, and came away pleased that the plan of attack would be based upon one of his own ideas. The two commanders agreed to integrate their forces so that Austro-Hungarian infantry would fight alongside German infantry and enjoy the support of superior German artillery. Such a combination had been attempted, successfully, at Limanowa-Lapanów in December 1914, where a German division had joined the Austro-Hungarian Fourth Army. For the May 1915 offensive of the Central Powers, the new German Eleventh Army received four Austro-Hungarian divisions to supplement its eight German divisions, and deployed on the front east of Cracow between the Austro-Hungarian Third and Fourth armies. Mackensen received overall command of the operation, with Hans von Seeckt, recently promoted to general after distinguishing himself at the first battle of Champagne, as his chief-of-staff. Falkenhayn relocated OHL headquarters to Pless in Silesia, about an hour's drive from the AOK in Teschen, to better coordinate the offensive.

Hope for better relations with the Germans balanced Conrad's disappointment over the bloody winter stalemate in the Carpathians, which ended in April with the Russians still at or near the crest of the mountain range, threatening Hungary. The "Carpathian winter" had cost his army 600,000 casualties, the Russians nearly as many, but Austria-Hungary (like France, in the west) could not afford to wage a war of attrition against a numerically superior foe. For Austria-Hungary, as for all other belligerents, most of the regular army of 1914 was gone by the spring of 1915, but owing to the unique character of the Dual Monarchy, its army had already begun to suffer problems with unit cohesion not seen elsewhere. Raw recruits and recalled reserves proved to be vulnerable to revolutionary nationalist and socialist agitation on the home front, while the reserve officers commanding them were less likely than career officers to be multilingual and thus had greater difficulty communicating with their troops. From the start of the war, Austria-Hungary had suffered the highest rates of prisoners lost of any of the belligerents; in particular, the number taken by the Serbs in the autumn of 1914 (74,000), from armies in which Croatians, Bosnians, and Czechs were the largest nationalities, concerned Conrad and the AOK. Finally, in April 1915, at the end of the Carpathian campaign, the 28th (Prague) Infantry Regiment surrendered en masse at the Dukla Pass, confirming Conrad's worst fears about the reliability of Slavic troops on the Russian front.

The Russians, meanwhile, were drifting into disarray. Their command-and-control had improved after Tannenberg but broke down again during the Carpathian campaign. When Grand Duke Nicholas ordered the reinforcement of Ivanov's army group for a further offensive on the Southwest front, where the Austro-Hungarian Army seemed on the verge of collapse, the army group commander on the Northwest front, the capable Ruzsky, refused to send troops to Ivanov and, in March 1915, resigned rather than see his front relegated to a secondary theater. The grand duke replaced him with General Mikhail Alekseev, Ivanov's chief-of-staff, assuming the two would continue to get along, but once in command of the Northwest front Alekseev proved to be little more cooperative than Ruzsky, sending his former superior just two divisions in time for the last Russian offensive of the "Carpathian winter." This lack of cooperation helped spare Conrad's army from destruction and caused the Russians to miss their best chance to invade Hungary. When the discord continued in the spring and summer of 1915, it nearly brought the Russian Army to its doom.

In the battle of Tarnów-Gorlice (May 2–10), Mackensen's troops spearheaded an offensive between the Vistula and the Carpathian foothills against the Russian Third Army, still under the Bulgarian General Dimitriev, but reinforced to 250,000 men (twenty-four divisions) since its defeat at Limanowa-Lapanów. The Central Powers made up for their inferior numbers with artillery firepower, as their infantry was backed by 700 guns (the most yet massed for a single battle on the Eastern front) against Dimitriev's 145. The fighting around the city of Tarnów and town of Gorlice began with a shelling on the evening of the 1st that decimated five Russian divisions by the time the infantry assault began the following morning. The Eleventh Army exploited the breach in the enemy lines and, with the Austro-Hungarian Fourth Army, quickly encircled most of Dimitriev's troops. By May 10, when Dimitriev finally ordered his remaining 40,000 troops to retreat eastward to Przemysl and the line of the San River, his army had suffered 70,000 casualties and lost 140,000 prisoners. For Russia the near-total destruction of the Third Army was a disaster greater than Tannenberg; in early June, after German troops captured Przemysl, Grand Duke Nicholas banished the colorful Bulgarian to a minor command in the Caucasus. While Tarnów-Gorlice was hailed at the time, and in most subsequent histories, as a "German" victory, Austria-Hungary provided 65 percent of the manpower directly involved in the breakthrough, but as the offensive continued to roll eastward Falkenhayn fueled its progress with fresh German divisions transferred from the Western front; by mid-June seven had arrived and an eighth was on the way. The advance soon compromised the entire Russian Southwest front, as the Russian Seventh, Eighth, and Ninth armies had to abandon their lines on the crest of the Carpathians or else risk being cut off as the Central Powers pushed eastward across their rear. Finally, on June 22, Böhm-Ermolli's Austro-Hungarian Second Army retook Lemberg, the provincial capital of Galicia. Though decisively beaten, the Russians made their pursuers pay for their gains. The forces involved in the offensive from Tarnów-Gorlice to Lemberg suffered 90,000 casualties, and even in victory Austria-Hungary lost most of another Czech regiment, the 36th, to desertion in the action near Przemysl.

As the Central Powers completed the liberation of Austrian Galicia, Falkenhayn pressured Bethmann Hollweg to make peace with Russia based on the status quo ante to enable Germany to focus on the Western front. Conrad, who had never wanted a war with Russia in the first place, supported him wholeheartedly, especially since Italy's declaration of war on Austria-Hungary in May 1915 gave him yet another opponent, in addition to Serbia, that he would rather be fighting. For an intermediary Bethmann Hollweg chose neutral Denmark's King Christian X, the tsar's first cousin. Complementary peace feelers included attempts at dialog with pro-German Russian aristocrats and family diplomacy via the minor German dynasties with connections to the Romanovs. But not everyone in the German political and military leadership wanted peace in the east, at least not until the expansionist goals of the "September program" had been achieved. This internal argument quickly became moot. On September 4, 1914, Britain, France, and Russia had agreed to pursue peace only in common; when Italy joined the Allies, they all renewed their pledge. Nicholas II received Danish envoy Hans Niels Andersen, but only to inform him that Russia would not conclude a separate peace.

The Eastern Front: The Conquest of Poland and the Tsar's "Personal Command"

Thus, Falkenhayn failed to achieve his intended goal in the east, even though the troops he and Conrad directed had won a dramatic victory. With the Western front quiet during the summer months of 1915, he resolved to eliminate the Polish salient altogether in a giant pincer movement, set in motion in mid-July (Map 5.2). The new German Twelfth Army (General Max von Gallwitz) moved southward from East Prussia toward Warsaw, supported by the German Ninth Army, now under Prince Leopold of Bavaria, which advanced on Warsaw from the west, via Lodz, engaging the Russian First,

Map 5.2 Eastern front, 1914–16

Second, and Fourth armies of Alekseev's Northwest front army group. Meanwhile, Mackensen's Eleventh Army, with the Austro-Hungarian First and Fourth armies on its flanks, advanced northward from Lemberg toward Lublin and Brest-Litovsk, across the rail lines linking Alekseev's armies to the Russian heartland.

Nicholas II's decision to continue fighting, honorable though it may have been, was hardly a rational choice, as his armies were so short of shells and ammunition that they could not fight much longer. Owing to a collapse in command-and-control within Ivanov's Southwest front army group, only Brusilov's Russian Eighth Army remained intact to oppose Mackensen's continued advance, leaving Alekseev's three Northwest front armies vulnerable to a double envelopment that would have left Russia in no condition to remain in the war. Alekseev appreciated the danger and ordered a retreat while his troops still had a way out. On July 30, the German Eleventh Army and Austro-Hungarian Fourth Army took Lublin, blocking a major rail line between Warsaw and the east and forcing Alekseev to ship retreating troops along the northern route through Bialystok and Vilna (Vilnius). On August 4, the Russians abandoned Warsaw (see Box 5.2) and, the following

Box 5.2 Warsaw falls to the Germans, August 4, 1915

Excerpts from American journalist Stanley Washburn's account of the fall of Warsaw, with reflections on its perceived significance at the time:

The game was up as far as Warsaw was concerned. Even if one had not been told verbally, the roads needed no interpretation. Mile after mile in unbroken column, plodding through the dust that rose above the road in clouds, was the endless column of caissons, transport carts, field kitchens, and the thousand and other odds and ends that belong to an army. But in this retreat, as in the many, many others that I have accompanied or rather preceded in Russia, there was nothing in the faces of the men to indicate whether they were retiring or advancing.

Wednesday, August 4th, Warsaw's last day ... was a perfectly still day, with hardly a cloud in the sky. Save for the dull booming of the guns over on the river there was absolute peace everywhere ... A few hours later the bridges were blown up and Warsaw was no longer Russian. The blowing up of the Vistula bridges marked the end of a distinct phase in the war, a phase which I believe history will ultimately judge as the zenith of the German strength in this war ...

From talks with innumerable prisoners there is no question in my mind that every German soldier believed from May 1st that the capture of Warsaw represented peace with Russia. Warsaw had come to represent the prize of the campaign, and from the German point of view its capture must represent to Russia the final failure of her armies. The rest of the war would be relatively simple: an independent peace with Russia, with trade agreements which would mean limitless resources to draw on for the war with France, against whom the entire strength in the east could be sent and Paris taken in a month. Then the long and slow preparation which every German hoped would mean the annihilation of England. From this point of view the outcome of the World War looked bright indeed to the troops who at last heard that the great prize was within their grasp. It seems, therefore, that while one cannot minimize the triumph of the Germans in actually taking Warsaw after so many months, one can but condemn the Germans for their failure to know beforehand that the capture of the city for which they made such endless sacrifices did not spell peace at all...

Having been with the Japanese in Manchuria [in 1904–05] and there becoming familiar with the extraordinary power of recuperation of the Russians, I felt reasonably confident that the men would not break and the critical period would be weathered and that the army would eventually get back onto a line where it could settle down for a sustained period of replenishment.

Source: Excerpted from Stanley Washburn, *Victory in Defeat: The Agony of Warsaw and the Russian Retreat* (London: Constable, 1916), 103–21.

day, the German Ninth Army occupied the city. Alekseev's armies completed their withdrawal from Poland just before the pincers closed on August 15, cutting the last rail line to Russia. Finally, on August 25, as the campaign began winding down, the German Eleventh and Austro-Hungarian Fourth armies moved on from Lublin to take Brest-Litovsk.

Hindenburg and Ludendorff's *OberOst* had no direct involvement in the Tarnów-Gorlice offensive or the subsequent attempted double envelopment of the Polish salient. During the same months, they kept busy directing an invasion of the Russian Baltic provinces by Below's Eighth Army, Eichhorn's Tenth Army, and General Otto von Lauenstein's new Niemen Army. At the culmination of their campaign, the Tenth Army secured Lithuania, taking Kovno (Kaunas) on August 18 and Vilna on September 19, but at a heavy price, suffering 50,000 casualties in the two weeks prior to the fall of Vilna. To the south, the Eighth Army encountered less opposition and took Grodno on September 3. To the north, along the Baltic coast, the Niemen Army's advance into Latvia stalled short of Riga after a detachment from the German Navy including two dreadnoughts, two pre-dreadnought battleships, and a battle cruiser lost the battle of the Gulf of Riga (August 8–19) to a much smaller Russian force. The city remained in Russian hands for another two years. While the Central Powers turned over the rest of their eastern conquests of 1915 to a civilian administration under a military governor, General Hans von Beseler, in the territories taken by the armies of *OberOst* a military administration directed by Ludendorff pursued a sociopolitical experiment aimed at bringing German order to the region and harnessing its resources to Germany's benefit. In many ways Ludendorff s program foreshadowed the grander schemes of the Third Reich in the Nazi-occupied territory of Poland and Russia, only without the genocide.

Ironically, given what would transpire in the same region a quarter of a century later, with few exceptions the Jews of Poland and western Russia greeted the Central Powers as liberators (Figure 5.2). The traditional persecution under the tsarist regime only accelerated during the spring of 1915, when Grand Duke Nicholas expelled tens of thousands of Jews from the vicinity of the front based on unfounded rumors that they were helping German troops infiltrate Russian lines. The most dramatic expulsion came on May 23 at Kovno, where a quarter of the population was Jewish. Meanwhile, in rural Lithuania, the retreating Russians brutalized the Baltic German minority in particular and Lutherans (Lithuanian as well as German) in general. Able-bodied men were forced to retreat with the Russian armies so that their labor could be denied to the German occupiers. These expellees joined a flood of refugees, mostly ethnic Russians, who fled to the east. By the time of the revolution, Russian Army defeats on the Eastern and Caucasus fronts would generate 6 million refugees, but the exodus out of Poland in 1915 accounted for most of them.

Figure 5.2 German patrol passes Jews on sidewalk

Two Orthodox Jews look on as a German patrol passes them in Neu Sandec, Austrian Galicia (present-day Nowy Sacz, Poland), in 1915, after the Central Powers had retaken the city from the Russians. In the wake of the next German occupation, in 1939, 90 percent of its Jewish community would perish in Nazi concentration camps, but the situation in World War I could not have been more different. Throughout Galicia, as well as in Russian Poland, Jewish populations typically welcomed German troops as liberators. If they suffered persecution during the war it came at the hands of the retreating Russians, who tended to view all Jews as German sympathizers. The area's Jews knew Neu Sandec as Sacz (its Yiddish name). Around one-third of the 25,000 residents were Jews, enough to support several synagogues and Jewish schools. Neu Sandec was also an important center of the Hasidic movement.

Weeks before the capture of Brest-Litovsk and Vilna brought an end to the German offensive in the east for 1915, Falkenhayn resolved to stop the advance as soon as the Polish salient had been eliminated and new front lines secured. The operation had failed to force Russia to the peace table but succeeded in contracting the Eastern front to around 800 miles (1,280 km) in length, along a line extending from just west of Riga on the Baltic due south to Czernowitz (Chernovtsy), the capital of the Austrian province of Bukovina, bordering neutral Romania. The dramatically shorter front would require far fewer troops to cover in the future, freeing more German manpower for the Western front. Indeed, the transfer of troops elsewhere became a pressing matter, because logistical problems had grown worse as the armies advanced eastward, far beyond their railheads, and the numbers at the front as of September could not be sustained, well-fed and healthy, for much longer. Since the outbreak of war thirteen months earlier, the German Army had experienced an illness rate on the Eastern front 50 percent higher than on the Western front, with thousands affected by typhus, malaria, and cholera; during the 1915 campaign Gallwitz's Twelfth Army, which stood just 60 miles (95 km) west of Minsk when Falkenhayn finally stopped it, had suffered the worst, reduced to half-strength by casualties and illness. The Russians did not help matters, for once it became clear that they would have to abandon Poland, they followed a scorched-earth policy during their retreat, laying waste to much of the eastern Polish territory that would be home to the new front and its immediate hinterland. The first German troops to leave the Eastern front, the ten divisions of Mackensen's Eleventh Army, went south rather than west, to the Balkan front, where Falkenhayn planned an autumn offensive with Bulgaria to knock Serbia out of the war.

In the wake of the loss of Poland, Nicholas II made the fateful decision to go to the front and take personal command of the armed forces for the duration of the war. In early September he left Petrograd (as the imperial city had been called for the past year, after the name St. Petersburg was deemed "too German") for a new headquarters established at Mogilev, 420 miles (680 km) south of the capital. His letter of September 5 to Grand Duke Nicholas, whom he reassigned to the Caucasus front, underscored the seriousness with which he would take his new role as commander-in-chief:

My duty to my country, which has been entrusted to me by God, impels me today, when the enemy has penetrated into the interior of the Empire, to take the supreme command of the active forces and to share with my army the fatigues of war, and to safeguard with it Russian soil from the attempts of the enemy.[3]

Because the tsar had no military training or experience, Alekseev, elevated from commander of the Northwest front army group to chief-of-staff in the tsar's headquarters, became de facto commander of the armed forces. General Aleksei Evert, who had replaced Salza as commander of the Fourth Army and safely extracted it from Poland, received command of a new Western army group holding the Russian center, while Ruzsky returned to head the Northern front (as the Northwest front was now called).

The Russian Army still outnumbered the armies of the Central Powers in the east, but in the first year of the war had suffered as many as 2.4 million casualties and lost 1 million prisoners; of these, 1.4 million of the casualties and almost all of the lost prisoners had come since May 1915. In comparison, since the start of the war Austria-Hungary had sustained 1.8 million casualties and lost 730,000 prisoners, while Germany's Eastern front casualties likely did not exceed 300,000, with only a few thousand prisoners lost. Despite improvements in domestic munitions production, Russia's own factories had not met the needs of the army and the trickle of imports from the Western Allies failed to make up the difference. To make matters worse, when the Russians retreated they abandoned precious stockpiles of munitions, most notably in

Warsaw and the nearby Vistula fortresses, that they could not replace. Thus, an army that had not been poorly equipped in August 1914 found itself in dire straits a year later. Despite its poor condition and the new burden of having the tsar at headquarters, the Russian Army would continue to show an inexplicable resilience, at least for another year.

The decisive defeat of the Russians failed to bring the Central Powers any closer together. Joint command-and-control remained a sensitive matter. Mackensen and Seeckt had directed the Tarnów-Gorlice offensive in the field, nominally under the command of Conrad, who issued orders to Mackensen only with Falkenhayn's consent. Even before the offensive Conrad had remarked to his mistress that "the role of the poor relation is unpleasant,"[4] but he would have to get used to it, for German achievements in the field only strengthened their hand within the alliance. In part to demonstrate Austria-Hungary's independence from Germany and the AOK's right to run its own operations, and in part out of his sincere conviction that Falkenhayn had stopped the campaign too soon, Conrad resolved to continue the offensive on his own. In the late summer of 1915 he used forty-seven under-strength divisions, 350,000 men in all, most of them from the First Army (now under General Paul Puhallo von Brlog), Böhm-Ermolli's Second Army, and Archduke Joseph Ferdinand's Fourth Army, to attack the Russians in the southern sector of the front, below the Pripet Marshes. Conrad hoped to envelop and destroy Brusilov's Eighth Army, then push through to take Kiev. He launched the offensive on August 26 and abandoned it on September 24, after a Russian counterattack pushed his armies back to their starting lines. During the four weeks of fighting Austria-Hungary lost another 230,000 men, including 100,000 taken prisoner. Many of the latter deserted en masse, among them large numbers of Czech and Ruthenian (Ukrainian) troops, along with some Bosnians. Conrad's own officers criticized the unrealistic offensive even while it was still underway, and afterward many wondered at the AOK's willingness to waste another quarter of a million men at a time when the Dual Monarchy was badly outnumbered along the new Italian front and had too few men to contribute to the upcoming conquest of Serbia on the revived Balkan front.

The Italian Front: The First Isonzo Battles

For the Allies, the intervention of Italy promised to compensate for the serious defeats Russia experienced on the Eastern front. Over the winter of 1914–15 Falkenhayn and other German leaders had hoped that Austria-Hungary would agree to purchase the neutrality of Italy with territorial concessions in the Alps and on the Adriatic, but the leaders of the multinational empire recognized that once they started ceding territory to satisfy the ethnic or nationalist claims of neighboring states there would be no end to it. Conrad warned Falkenhayn that the Italians might accept Austrian territory, then defect to the Entente at a later date, and irritated his allies with the sarcastic counter-proposal that Germany should buy France's neutrality by ceding Alsace-Lorraine. In the Treaty of London (April 26, 1915) Britain, France, and Russia promised Italy the southern Tyrol, Istria, and Dalmatia – Austrian lands that included not just ethnic Italians but hundreds of thousands of Germans, Slovenes, and Croatians as well – along with some Albanian and Turkish territory. While the terms of the treaty remained secret, from the start of the war Italy had done little to conceal its drift toward the Triple Entente. Its declaration of war on Austria-Hungary (May 23, 1915) came as no surprise to the Central Powers.

Falkenhayn rejected Conrad's pleas to release Austro-Hungarian troops from the Eastern front to man the Italian front; he had already moved several German divisions from the Western front to the east for the Tarnów-Gorlice offensive and could not afford to send more to make up for the transfer of Austro-Hungarian divisions elsewhere. Faced with no alternative, Conrad initially defended the Italian frontier almost entirely with reserve formations, including third-line Tyrol Home Guard (*Standschützen*). Archduke Eugen, in charge of the Balkan front since the retirement of Potiorek in December 1914, became Italian front commander, establishing a new headquarters in the Slovenian town of Marburg (Maribor). He brought with him the two remaining corps from the Serbian border, which formed the basis of a reconstituted Fifth Army. Conrad transferred two of his best army commanders from the Eastern front to serve as Eugen's field generals: Dankl, from the First Army, for the Alpine sector in the Tyrol; and Boroević, from the Third Army, for the front along the Isonzo River, which flowed from the Julian Alps southward into the northern Adriatic 12 miles (20 km) northwest of Trieste. Because the capture of the predominantly Italian city of Trieste, Austria-Hungary's primary seaport, remained the primary goal of the Italian Army throughout the war, most of the action on the Italian front would occur along the Isonzo, between Boroević's Fifth Army and the Italian Second and Third armies, while the Tyrol sector remained relatively quiet.

Officially, the Italian field army consisted of 900,000 men organized into thirty-five infantry divisions (ten of which were second-line reserves), twelve divisions of third-line militia, four cavalry divisions, a Guards (*Bersaglieri*) infantry division, and fifty-two battalions of Alpine troops. Within three weeks of the declaration of war Italy deployed 460,000 men along its 370-mile (600-km) border with Austria-Hungary, under the direction of General Luigi Cadorna, chief of the general staff since July 1914. Italy's relatively slow mobilization gave Austria-Hungary a month to prepare its defenses, and by late June it had 228,000 troops on the front. Though Cadorna's armies held a significant edge in numbers, their opponents had almost every other advantage. On the Italian front, more so than in any other theater of World War I, geography clearly favored the defender. In the rocky escarpment along the Isonzo, no less than in the

Alps, the terrain accentuated the advantages afforded by field fortifications, machine guns, and artillery. Making matters worse for Cadorna's troops, among the great powers Italy alone had weaker artillery and fewer machine guns than Austria-Hungary. Their 2,000 field artillery pieces included just 112 heavy guns, while the entire army had barely 600 machine guns, or two per regiment, one-third the Austro-Hungarian number. On the coastal flank of the Isonzo front, as in the Adriatic as a whole, the Austro-Hungarian Navy controlled the sea, the Italian Navy (reinforced by British and French units) contenting itself with blockading the mouth of the Adriatic from the boot-heel of Italy eastward to the coast of Albania. Italy suffered the consequences of conceding the Adriatic to the enemy on the first night of the war when the entire Austro-Hungarian fleet sortied from its main base at Pola (Pula) in Istria to steam along 300 miles (480 km) of undefended Italian coastline, shelling cities and towns and the coastal railway linking them, before returning to port completely unscathed.

Less tangible but perhaps most significant, the Austrians had enjoyed a psychological or moral advantage over the Italians ever since their wars of national unification, when Italy had not defeated Austria on land or at sea and achieved its goals only with the help of other powers. Unlike on the Eastern and Balkan fronts, where the events of 1914–15 had already given rise to doubts about the loyalty of the Slavic half of the Austro-Hungarian Army, against the Italians the same troops could be counted upon to be reliable, in particular the Slovenes and Croatians, whose homelands were most threatened by an Italian invasion. In general, Austria-Hungary found new energy in the campaign against a traditional, beatable foe. In the spring of 1915 a civilian population already strained by the manpower demands of the Eastern front produced more than 100 battalions of volunteers for the Italian front, most of them over- or under-aged males from the German Austrian populations of Carinthia, Carniola, and Styria, but some from as far away as Vienna, Salzburg, and Linz. Certainly, the circumstances under which Italy quit the Triple Alliance and joined the Entente further sharpened anti-Italian sentiments with a righteous indignation.

Along the Isonzo as well as in the Alps, Austro-Hungarian forces naturally chose the most favorable terrain for their defensive positions, in some cases very near the border, in others as much as 15 miles (24 km) behind it. In the first days of the campaign, Cadorna's armies advanced steadily from the prewar border, 2–10 miles (3–16 km) west of the Isonzo, up to the river itself, after which elements of the Second Army crossed the upper Isonzo near Caporetto (Kobarid), roughly 30 miles (50 km) from the sea, while to the south, the Third Army crossed the Isonzo at its mouth, capturing Monfalcone and its shipyard. At the center of the line, around the town of Gorizia, Boroević's troops held the line of the river and, in some places, its west bank. In the first battle of the Isonzo (June 23–July 7) Cadorna employed eighteen divisions in his first attempt to breach the lines Boroević had established with just six divisions of his own. He quickly recognized that he lacked the field artillery to prepare the way for a breakthrough even against an opponent so dramatically inferior in numbers. Bolstered by another two divisions that arrived during the battle, the Austro-Hungarian lines held. Afterward Cadorna established what would be his pattern for future battles by publicly admitting to only half the losses his army actually suffered, blaming his subordinates for his failures, then moving quickly to plot the next offensive. Italy received badly needed arms shipments from Britain and France, including hundreds of field guns, and by the onset of the second battle of the Isonzo (July 18–August 3) Cadorna had 840 guns, twice as many as Boroević, though most of the newly imported pieces were similar to the light field guns he already possessed. Despite spirited attacks, particularly on the slopes of Monte San Michele south of Gorizia, the front barely moved.

In the first ten weeks of the war, through the second battle of the Isonzo, Italy suffered 80,000 casualties. For Austria-Hungary such losses paled in comparison with those suffered on the Eastern front, but Italy lacked that frame of reference. Even Cadorna's artificially low figures made the first two battles of the Isonzo deadlier than all of Italy's wars of unification and colonial wars combined. Nevertheless, a month of Italian inaction prompted Joffre to visit Cadorna at his headquarters in Udine to urge him to resume his offensive and coordinate its timing with the autumn offensives on the Western front. He promised to send more artillery but no heavy guns, which the French themselves lacked. By the time of their next attack the Italians had increased their army and its firepower by more than half again, to include twenty-nine divisions and more than 1,300 guns. Meanwhile, the Austro-Hungarian Fifth Army, reinforced to twelve divisions, had brought its own artillery strength up to more than 600 guns, many of them heavier than anything the Italians possessed. Cadorna opened the third battle of the Isonzo (October 18–November 3) with a much more formidable preparatory shelling of Boroević's positions, followed by an attempted double envelopment of his stronghold at Gorizia. The Second Army attacked north of the city, the Third Army south of it, but both were stopped cold. Afterward Cadorna waited only a week before initiating the fourth battle of the Isonzo (November 10–December 2), during which his Second Army succeeded in taking some of the high ground north of Gorizia without breaking through to the city itself. In the two autumn battles the Italians sustained another 116,000 casualties against Austro-Hungarian losses of 74,000, prompting Cadorna to break off the offensive for the winter.

In the Isonzo battles of 1915 the Italians saw for themselves just how much the caliber of guns and weight of shells mattered in an artillery barrage. Like the Allies on the Western front in France, they repeatedly undertook frontal assaults after an insufficiently heavy preliminary bombardment had left too many of the enemy's field fortifications and machine-gun nests intact. For ordinary infantrymen, the consequences were devastating. During the first seven months of the campaign, troops on both sides also learned that the rocky terrain of their front would make their combat experience uniquely hellish, even by World War I standards. Limestone shrapnel multiplied the impact of the war's most lethal weapons, as every shell and every machine-gun round that struck a rock (as most did) sent deadly razor-sharp bits of it flying in every direction. Owing to the difficulty of digging into the rocky soil, trenches along the Isonzo tended to be shallower than on the Western front and offered the troops less protection. Just as serious to the survival rate of the troops, for the same reason more of the dead went unburied here than on any other front, or were consigned to shallower graves. As casualties mounted, with, ultimately, eleven battles of the Isonzo fought over the same ground, the stench and disease from unburied or inadequately buried corpses became a serious problem, while on both sides of the line the environment became increasingly demoralizing for the living.

The Italians, in particular, needed no further demoralization. While Austro-Hungarian morale on the Italian front remained higher than on the Eastern or Balkan fronts, as early as the end of the second battle of the Isonzo the Italian Army already experienced morale problems. From the time of Italy's entry into the war troops from the rural south suffered the lowest morale, owing to their deployment far from home, usually under northern Italian officers whose particular Italian dialect they could barely understand, officers who, in turn, too frequently treated them as racial inferiors, dismissing them as "Africans" owing to their dark complexion. Desertions, almost all to the home front rather than to the enemy, totaled 8,500 in 1915, 25,000 in 1916, and 50,000 in 1917. Instead of addressing issues of regional discrimination and homesickness, the army from the start blamed its morale problems on socialist or republican agitators and focused its vigilance against soldiers suspected of harboring those beliefs.

Notwithstanding Cadorna's best efforts to mislead the public about his army's defeats and casualties, the home front soon succumbed to an early case of war weariness. Italy's Liberal prime minister, Antonio Salandra, could offer his people little other than the hope that, if the Allies won the war, Italy would benefit from having contributed to their victory. By December 1915 the Italians were tying down eighteen Austro-Hungarian divisions, but they had to employ thirty-five divisions of their own to do so. The primary Italian war aim – the acquisition of the "unredeemed" lands of *Italia irredenta*, in the Alps and on the Adriatic – did little to fire the public imagination, especially as so few of the "unredeemed" Italians living under Austrian rule seemed enthusiastic about being liberated. Of the 800,000 Italians living in Austria-Hungary as of 1914, 110,000 served in its armed forces during the war, while only 2,700 fled to fight as volunteers on the Italian side. Like the French with the Alsatians during their brief incursion across the border in August 1914, Italy treated the Italians it liberated with a great deal of suspicion; after its initial modest advances in the Alps, the Italian Army interned 30,000 civilians from the South Tyrol in camps in Lombardy.

Analogous to Germany with the Alsatians, Austria-Hungary did not fully trust its own Italians despite their loyalty. From May 1915 onward Austro-Hungarian authorities systematically undermined that loyalty, removing 114,000 Italian civilians from the war zone in the South Tyrol to internment camps far from the front. Starting in 1916, when Tyrol's four *Kaiserjäger* (imperial rifle) regiments were redeployed from the Eastern front to the Alps, their substantial Italian minority (roughly 40 percent in each regiment) was gradually purged from the ranks, until by 1918 less than 5 percent remained. The army took this action despite losing just 500 Italian *Kaiserjäger* to deser- tion on the Eastern front in the first two years of the war. Eventually these and other Austro-Italians served in so-called "P.U. units," so designated because of the real or imagined "political unreliability" (*politische Unzuverlässigkeit*) of their nationality. Most "P.U. units" ended the war serving as military police in the occupied territories of Romania and western Russia. Such treatment, largely undeserved, would lead a major- ity of Austro-Italians to welcome "liberation" and incorporation into the kingdom of Italy when it came in November 1918.

The Balkan Front: Bulgaria and the Defeat of Serbia

With the summer offensive on the Eastern front winding down, Falkenhayn turned his attention to the Balkan front, where Bulgaria, on September 6, 1915, had joined the Central Powers and committed to open hostilities against Serbia within thirty days (Map 5.3). King Ferdinand I kept his country neutral for the first year of the war, but the setbacks of the Allies on the Eastern front and Gallipoli peninsula convinced him to act on his sympathies toward the Central Powers. For Bulgaria, the primary war aim remained unchanged from the Second Balkan War two years earlier: the acqui- sition of Macedonia, which Serbia had annexed at the end of the First Balkan War. While Conrad welcomed the resumption of war with Serbia – the war he had wanted in the first place – the circumstances made it a bitter pill to swallow. Bulgaria joined the alliance via bilateral negotiation with Germany, concluding a secret treaty dividing the spoils in the Balkans after Serbia's defeat. Even though Austria-Hungary had been included in the drafting of a military convention specifying Bulgaria's obligations in the field, it could not be denied that the final offensive in the Balkans, a traditional Austro-Hungarian sphere of influence, would be initiated by the Germans and the map redrawn afterward according to their wishes.

In any event, owing to his own recent decisions on the Eastern front and the demands of the new Italian front, Conrad's troops made only a modest contribution to the autumn campaign in the Balkans. Falkenhayn put Mackensen in overall command of the theater and gave Gallwitz (transferred from the Twelfth Army) operational command of the Eleventh Army, whose ten divisions redeployed from the Eastern front to the Danube, opposite northern Serbia. To join this force in attacking the Serbs from the north, Austria-Hungary sent the Third Army (now under General Hermann Kövess and, at four divisions, dramatically under-strength) to the Sava River in eastern

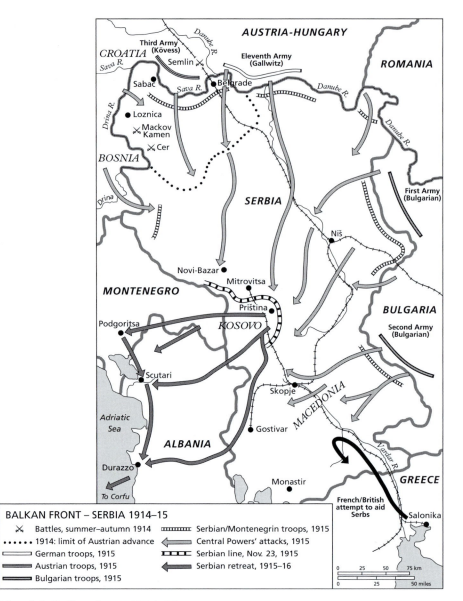

Map 5.3 Balkan front, 1914–15

Croatia. The Bulgarians fielded two small armies to attack the Serbs from the east, but at three divisions apiece each was even weaker than Kövess' force. As a concession to his ally, Falkenhayn agreed to send Mackensen's orders via Conrad and the AOK in Teschen, and to give Kövess two of Gallwitz's divisions to bolster the Third Army. On October 5 they began a preliminary shelling of Serbian positions along the Sava–Danube line, and over the following days Gallwitz and Kövess sent their armies across the rivers, while the Austro-Hungarian Navy's river monitors joined in the shelling of Belgrade. By the time the two Bulgarian armies finally crossed Serbia's eastern border on October 11, German and Austro-Hungarian troops were already in Belgrade. By the end of the month, Gallwitz and Kövess had advanced into northern Serbia to a line 40–70 miles (65–115 km) south of the Sava and Danube.

Serbia's definitive victory over the initial Austro-Hungarian invasion in December 1914 had made Putnik a national hero, but since then the old field marshal had been unable to do much to strengthen his forces. The first months of fighting had claimed many of his best troops, and a typhus outbreak in the winter of 1914–15 infected 500,000 Serbs and killed 200,000, including 70,000 soldiers. France and Britain provided little material assistance, faced with their own supply problems and, after May 1915, the challenge of helping Italy as well. Finally, after Bulgaria joined the Central Powers, they sent General Maurice Sarrail to Salonika to organize an Anglo-French "Army of the Orient," of which the first troops, a British division and French division from the Dardanelles, arrived on the day the Central Powers opened their campaign. Unfortunately for the Allies, Venizelos was not able to deliver on Greece's entry into the war. Bolstered by his pro-German general staff chief, Ioannis Metaxas, King Constantine refused to honor the Greco-Serbian defensive alliance and forced Venizelos to resign from office just before the first Allied troops landed. Because the Allies had violated Greek neutrality repeatedly since the start of the war – most notably, the French seizing Corfu as a base for their blockade of the mouth of the Adriatic, and the British occupying the Aegean island of Lemnos as a base for the Dardanelles campaign – the king's decision to keep Greece neutral did nothing to stop their reinforcement of Sarrail. In late October he received two divisions directly from France, which he planned to push up the Salonika-Belgrade railway through Skopje and Niš. In the end he could not move fast enough to save the Serbs, whose deployment against the German and Austrian invasion from the north left too few troops to fight the Bulgarians cutting across their rear from the east. By early November the Bulgarian Second Army (General Georgi Todorov) had advanced 50 miles (80 km) into Macedonia to take Skopje while, to its north, the Bulgarian First Army (General Kliment Boyazhdiev) took Niš. Ultimately, Todorov's army blocked Sarrail's divisions from linking up with the Serbs, and in early December they fell back on Salonika. By then, Putnik had made his last stand around Priština in the battle of Kosovo (November 10–December 4), against elements of the two Bulgarian armies and, on his northern flank, advance units of the German Eleventh Army. Putnik fought a rearguard action while his army, accompanied by a stream of refugees, retreated through neutral Albania to the Italian-occupied seaports of Durazzo and Valona. In the wake of the Salonika occupation, the Allies further compromised Greek neutrality by using Corfu as a safe haven for Serbia's government-in-exile and 133,000 troops evacuated over the winter of 1915–16 via the Albanian ports. In May 1916 the Allies shipped the Serbian troops on to Salonika, where they were rearmed and incorporated into Sarrail's army. Pašić and the Serbian government remained at Corfu, where the local municipal theater served as home to the Serbian parliament for the remainder of the war.

In December 1915, with the outcome of the campaign no longer in doubt, Falkenhayn withdrew most of Gallwitz's army and left it to Austria-Hungary and Bulgaria to complete the occupation of Serbia. In defeat the Serbs had suffered 94,000 casualties and lost 174,000 prisoners, against 67,000 casualties (37,000 Bulgarian, 18,000 Austro-Hungarian, and 12,000 German) for the Central Powers. From the AOK in Teschen, Conrad expressed satisfaction that the "Serbian pack of murderers" had paid the ultimate price for the crime of Sarajevo, but regretted that it had taken a general war to achieve the result, and that the Dual Monarchy would not benefit from the victory, having lost "the leading role in the Balkans" to Germany.[5]

Conclusion

In light of the overall condition of the Italian Army at the end of 1915, one wonders if an Austro-Hungarian breakthrough along the Isonzo – which would happen two years later, with German help, at Caporetto – could have come in 1915, if Conrad had not squandered so many troops in his own offensive against Russia after Falkenhayn halted the German effort in the east, or if Falkenhayn had opted to send German troops withdrawn from the east to the Italian front rather than to the Balkans. From the German perspective, the decision to crush the Serbs served the purpose of binding Bulgaria to the Central Powers and eliminating the Balkan front (except for the newly established Allied enclave at Salonika), but the Allies had expected little from the Serbs since the start of the war; indeed, their survival against the initial Austro-Hungarian invasion had been considered nothing short of miraculous. In contrast, the Allies had placed the highest hopes in Italy, whose declaration of war they believed would be the death knell of Austria-Hungary. If the Italians had been knocked out of the war within months of entering it, the blow would have been much harder for the Allies to bear than the loss of the Serbs, whom they assumed were living on borrowed time.

On the revived Balkan front, as on the Eastern front earlier in 1915, close cooperation between Germany and Austria-Hungary did not bring them closer together, even in victory. During the campaign, Falkenhayn infuriated Conrad by violating their command-and-control agreements, directing Mackensen as if he were any other German general leading an all-German operation. Nevertheless, Conrad proposed to Falkenhayn another major joint effort in 1916, against Italy. He was disappointed that Falkenhayn refused, opting instead to muster German strength for a war of attrition on the Western front, the strategy that would result in the indecisive bloodbaths at Verdun and the Somme. The rejection brought Conrad's relationship with Falkenhayn to a new low. In a defiant gesture of his independence from the Germans, he took back the Third Army from Mackensen and, after January 1, ordered Kövess to overrun Montenegro, which surrendered to Austria-Hungary on January 23, 1916. Kövess then pursued the retreating Serbs into northern Albania, took Durazzo, and established a front against the Italians, who retained Valona. The Germans considered the brief Montenegrin campaign hardly worth the effort, even though it did secure the hinterland of the Austro-Hungarian naval base at Cattaro, which German submarines operating in the Mediterranean had been using since May 1915.

Because of the continuing stalemate on the Western front and the rapid stagnation of the new fronts on the Isonzo and at Gallipoli, 1915 has been viewed as a year in which commanders, particularly on the Allied side, continued to ignore the realities they faced on the battlefields, squandering hundreds of thousands of lives in fruitless, unimaginative frontal assaults on enemy positions. The evidence shows otherwise. After the Germans, at Soissons in January 1915, provided an early example of how an infantry assault against trenches could succeed if closely coordinated with a heavy preliminary artillery bombardment, the Allies attempted the same tactic, and as early as Neuve Chapelle in March combined it with a primitive campaign of close air support, bombing and strafing the reinforcements the Germans attempted to bring to the front. Throughout 1915, however, the British, French, and Italians never had sufficient numbers of heavy guns to make the new tactical approach work; meanwhile, against the Russians on the Eastern front and in the destruction of Serbia on the Balkan front, the Central Powers demonstrated the crushing effectiveness of their artillery in breaching enemy lines and setting in motion offensives that made significant gains on the ground. By the end of 1914 it had already become clear that World War I would be an artillery war, challenging the industrial capacity of the home fronts to keep the guns supplied with shells. By demonstrating the need for a heavier bombardment to prepare the way for infantry assaults, the battlefield experiences of 1915 touched off a race to produce greater numbers of heavier caliber guns, along with a competition to develop and deploy entirely new weapons (such as poison gas in 1915, or the tank in 1916) that would serve as a tactical substitute for heavy artillery.

SUGGESTIONS FOR FURTHER READING

Dancocks, Daniel G. *Welcome to Flanders Fields: The First Canadian Battle of the Great War, Ypres 1915* (Toronto: McClelland & Stewart, 1988).

Gooch, John. *The Italian Army and the First World War* (Cambridge: Cambridge University Press, 2014).

Hall, Richard C. *Bulgaria's Road to the First World War* (Boulder, CO: East European Monographs, 1996).

Harris, J. P. *Douglas Haig and the First World War* (Cambridge: Cambridge University Press, 2008).

Hull, Isabel V. *Absolute Destruction: Military Culture and the Practices of War in Imperial Germany* (Ithaca, NY: Cornell University Press, 2005).

Liulevicius, Vejas G. *War Land on the Eastern Front: Culture, National Identity, and German Occupation in World War I* (Cambridge: Cambridge University Press, 2000).

Schindler, John R. *Isonzo: The Forgotten Sacrifice of the Great War* (Westport, CT: Praeger, 2001).

Thompson, Mark. *The White War: Life and Death on the Italian Front, 1915–1919* (New York: Basic Books, 2009).

NOTES

1. Joffre, General Order No. 43, September 23, 1915, text in *Mémoires du Maréchal Joffre*, 2: 88.
2. Adrian Gregory, *The Last Great War: British Society and the First World War* (Cambridge: Cambridge University Press, 2008), 3.
3. Charles F. Horne, ed., *Source Records of the Great War*, vol. 3 (Indianapolis: The American Legion, 1931), 321.
4. Conrad to Gina von Reininghaus, Teschen, April 17, 1915, KA, B/1450: 357.
5. Franz Conrad to Gina Conrad, Teschen, October 10, 1915, KA, B/1450: 357; Franz Conrad to Gina Conrad, Teschen, December 15, 1915, *ibid.*

Autumn reserves: Germany

The stalemating of all fronts by late summer 1914 dispelled the notion that decisive battles would decide the war within a matter of weeks. While Britain appealed for more volunteers, the home fronts of the continental countries (all of which had some form of compulsory service) endured call-ups of additional classes of reserves. Like the autumn 1914 reservists of other countries, the German soldiers pictured here were somewhat older than those mobilized in August and more likely to be family men. In this photograph, a wife (or perhaps fiancée or sister) helps a reservist carry his backpack to the railway station.

6 The Home Fronts, 1914–16

August 1914	Germany's "August Days."
August 1914	Collapse of Second Socialist International.
September 1914	Britain suspends implementation of Home Rule for Ireland.
January 1915	Germany initiates food rationing.
April 1915	Austria initiates food rationing.
May 1915	Italy's "Radiant May."
Summer 1915	Russian troops kill strikers at Kostroma and Ivanovo-Voznesensk.
July 1915	First food riots in Germany.
September 1915	Zimmerwald Conference of anti-war socialists.

In the summer of 1914 the outbreak of war featured what appeared to be an outpouring of pro-war sentiment in all countries, overwhelming the efforts of the Socialist International and other voices for peace. Those required to report for duty did so willingly or enthusiastically, and there was a rush to volunteer not only in Britain and the Dominions, where no service requirements existed, but to varying degrees also in the United States and other neutral countries. The home fronts were forced to respond when the anticipated short war dragged on into a second year. When heavy casualties created an ongoing need for fresh manpower, and the exhaustion of the initial stockpiles of munitions placed unprecedented demands on industry, women assumed an increasingly important role either as workers or as non-combatant volunteers, including under the Red Cross and other humanitarian organizations. In addition to revolutionizing labor relations and gender relations, in some quarters the war buoyed hopes for political revolution. Censorship and propaganda assumed a growing role in sustaining the effort of the home fronts amid these and other challenges, especially for the Central Powers once the Allied naval blockade began to affect food supplies.

The Myth of Popular Enthusiasm for War, Summer 1914

In popular memory and in historical accounts, World War I became the last war welcomed with widespread patriotic enthusiasm by civilian populations, and the days around August 1, 1914, were remembered for their last gasp of collective naiveté before the harsh reality of modern mass slaughter set in. For decades this myth went unchallenged before collapsing in the face of recent research and critical analysis. Almost all accounts of public sentiment on the outbreak of the war focused on the reaction of urban populations which, in all major belligerents except Britain and Germany, were in the minority. As more evidence emerges concerning the reaction of towns, villages, and rural areas, it has become clearer that a great number of civilians greeted the war with dismay. The traditional view of large crowds welcoming the declarations of war holds true only for Berlin and other major cities in Germany, and even for these urban areas recent scholarship has distinguished between "excitement," of which there was plenty, and actual "enthusiasm."[1] Indeed, Germany also witnessed the largest anti-war demonstrations. For Europe as a whole, a central problem appears to be the conflation (in memory and in subsequent histories) of enthusiasm for the coming of war and displays of patriotism when troops boarded trains for the front. While the former may not have been widespread, the latter certainly was, at large urban terminals, rural whistle-stops, and every sort of railway station in between. Regardless of how people felt about the war on a personal or political level, it became a matter of community pride to give the troops a proper send-off, and the enduring images from these occasions – the flags flying, bands playing, and crowds of loved ones cheering – dominated future memories of the summer of 1914.

Germany alone saw significant pro-war sentiment before the actual declarations of war. On the evening of July 25, within hours of Austria-Hungary's ultimatum to Serbia, a crowd of 10,000 assembled outside the palace in Berlin in the hope of catching a glimpse of William II, who had yet to cut short his annual Baltic cruise aboard the yacht *Hohenzollern*. The following day the crowds increased, and the phenomenon spread to other major cities. Because Germans had always been spectators in choreographed displays of patriotism, the government hardly knew how to react to the spontaneous expression of national feeling; in Berlin, the authorities even temporarily banned demonstrations in the center of the city. Anxiety went hand-in-hand with patriotic bravado, as the following week witnessed a run on the banks and grocery stores that did not subside for several days. On July 28, the day Austria-Hungary declared war on Serbia, 100,000 attended anti-war demonstrations sponsored by the Social Democrats in the working-class suburbs of Berlin; such protests throughout Germany that day and the next involved a total of 750,000 people. But on July 31, news of Russia's mobilization brought an end to anti-war protests, as the Social Democrats joined the other parties in rallying behind the government. The following day, when Germany declared its general mobilization, a crowd of 300,000 assembled outside the palace, where William II proclaimed that he saw "no more parties ... only Germans," concluding that "all that now matters is that we stand together like brothers."[2] The emperor invoked the image of the medieval *Burgfrieden*, the traditional peace within the castle or walled city to be maintained for the common good as long as the enemy stood at the gates.

After the declarations of war all countries involved in the July Crisis witnessed some degree of pro-war enthusiasm, including those for which the war would be disastrous. In Austria-Hungary, Conrad feared the general mobilization would spark widespread unrest, and yet men of all nationalities rallied to the colors without incident. An old friend of the AOK chief remarked that "the enthusiasm of the people for the war has been a great surprise to him."[3] Leon Trotsky, in the last days of his Vienna exile before departing for neutral Switzerland, remarked that "a most amazing crowd fill[ed] the fashionable Ring, a crowd in which hopes had been awakened."[4] At least initially, the Social Democratic Party's *Arbeiter-Zeitung* joined the rest of the Austrian press in publishing "excessively patriotic, even jingoistic" editorials.[5] Analyzing his own reaction to the outbreak of a war in which all three of his sons would serve, Sigmund Freud concluded that he had "suddenly mobilized libido for Austria-Hungary."[6] Writer Stefan Zweig later recalled that the subjects of Francis Joseph "felt what they should have felt in peacetime, that they belonged together."[7]

For good reason, the mood in France was far more sober. Future historian Marc Bloch, a sergeant in the French Army in 1914, remembered that "Paris during the first days of mobilization … was quiet and somewhat solemn." In contrast to the confident patriotism prevailing in Austria-Hungary (at least against Serbia) and in Germany, in France the public understood the likely cost of the struggle ahead. "The sadness that was buried in our hearts showed only in the red and swollen eyes of many women," Bloch recalled. "The men for the most part were not hearty; they were resolute, and that was better." Displays of patriotism took on a more defiant character, as "out of the specter of war, the nation's armies created a surge of democratic fervor."[8] The leaders of the Third Republic – a regime born in the midst of a French defeat at the hands of Germans in 1870 – from the start fully appreciated the gravity of their situation. From the first day of mobilization, no other government monitored public opinion more closely or, in the interest of maintaining morale, censored its own press more rigorously.

The British public, like its political leaders, took longer to respond to the crisis. On Sunday, August 2, as the cabinet deliberated its decision for war, British socialists staged a large anti-war demonstration in Trafalgar Square, London, and leading Anglican clerics across the country gave anti-war sermons; anti-war sentiments also prevailed among the nonconformist Protestant denominations, particularly Methodists and Baptists, especially in Wales, a hotbed of "pro-Boer" opposition to the South African war of 1899–1902. The following day, 10,000 people gathered outside Buckingham Palace for a patriotic demonstration, but the crowd would likely have been far smaller if it had not been a Monday bank holiday. Genuine enthusiasm for the war came only after it had been declared, and even then, the crowds were much smaller than in other countries. On the evening of August 4, as Britain's ultimatum to Germany lapsed without a response from Berlin, 12,000 assembled outside the palace and thousands more took to the streets elsewhere in London. But the outpouring was remembered as being much larger and preceding the actual declaration of war, in part thanks to the subsequent published accounts of those who wished it had been so. For example, David Lloyd George, keen to justify his own crucial change of heart on the question of war against Germany, later wrote of "warlike crowds that thronged Whitehall and poured into Downing Street, while the Cabinet was deliberating."[9]

Owing to the dearth of evidence for the countryside, almost all accounts of public sentiment on the outbreak of the war focus on Europe's cities. The relatively few contemporary accounts of rural reaction, invariably written by landowners, other local notables, their wives, or travelers passing through, recount an initial dismay or stoicism on the part of the common folk preceding any rallying to the national cause. For example, an American spouse of a landowner in Russian Poland recalled her peasant women crying upon hearing the news of war, so hysterically that she "was forced to threaten them with all sorts of punishment before they could be made to stop."[10] In rural Germany, where teachers and clergymen were asked afterward to submit accounts of local reactions to the outbreak of the war, the residents of a typical Bavarian village were "agitated and dismayed" by the mobilization, "and the wives of men liable for military service expressed their misery in no uncertain terms."[11] Finally, an Englishwoman transiting the Tyrol during the Austrian mobilization remarked at the "utter want of animation" on the part of the men she saw on the roads, coming down from their farms into the towns: "They plodded along the road or sat in groups … in an uncomplaining silence," showing neither despair nor enthusiasm for the cause to which they had been called. Like the vast majority of ordinary men mobilized in the summer of 1914, "they were parts of a vast machine set in motion for some reason unknown to them which they were unable either to accelerate or retard."[12]

Thus, a survey of the evidence reveals that in the summer of 1914 popular enthusiasm for the coming war manifested itself most dramatically in Germany, where the phenomenon was limited to the cities and towns, as the villages and farming communities appear to have reacted to the news with the same lack of enthusiasm as rural areas throughout Europe. Even among urban Germans, pro-war sentiments were far from universal; indeed, the Social Democratic Party mustered out the continent's largest anti-war demonstrations on July 28, the day Austria-Hungary declared war on Serbia. Nevertheless, many Germans later harked back fondly to the "August Days" of 1914 as a special time in which they had first experienced "a genuine sense of community." In a watershed moment in German political culture, the public had taken ownership of the nation; afterward the emperor remained the figurehead of nationalistic sentiment, but the people's sense of nationhood could no longer be directed from above in the traditional way. The moment, and the embellished memories of it, helped to lay the foundation for Hitler's National Socialism in that it created, for many Germans, an example of how a nationalist community could be united in a great cause and in a spirit that transcended the traditional divisive boundaries of social class.[13] Hitler himself certainly felt that way, after hearing the news of the declaration of war in Munich (see Box 6.1). This phenomenon of history remembered being at odds with the actual evidence of home-front attitudes from the summer of 1914 went beyond Germany. Eventually, in the victorious countries, memories of confident crowds cheering the onset of war and jubilant crowds celebrating the vindication of their efforts in November 1918 served as convenient bookends, though in many cases these memories, too, differed from the reality. For example, Londoners in the Armistice Day crowd of 100,000 gathered outside Buckingham Palace remembered a similar throng greeting the onset of war in 1914, when that earlier gathering had been barely one-tenth as large.

But an absence of genuine enthusiasm for war should not be interpreted as evidence of widespread anti-war sentiment. Especially in the cases of Austria-Hungary against Serbia, Germany against Russia in particular and "encirclement" by the Entente in general, France against Germany, and Britain (on behalf of Belgium) against Germany, the public for the most part accepted the argument that the war was defensive and the decision to fight it justifiable. And in a broader, often vaguer sense, ordinary people

Box 6.1 An Austrian in Munich welcomes the war

Adolf Hitler, born in Braunau, Austria, in 1889, moved to Munich in 1913 and served during the war as a foreign volunteer in a Bavarian regiment of the German Army (he finally became a German citizen in 1932, in order to be a candidate in the presidential election of that year). Hitler joined a jubilant crowd in Munich to welcome the declaration of war. He recalled the moment a decade later, in his political testament *Mein Kampf*:

The War of 1914 was certainly not forced on the masses; it was even desired by the whole people. There was a desire to bring the general feeling of uncertainty to an end once and for all. And it is only in the light of this fact that we can understand how more than two million German men and youths voluntarily joined the colors, ready to shed the last drop of their blood for the cause. For me these hours came as a deliverance from the distress that had weighed upon me during the days of my youth. I am not ashamed to acknowledge to-day that I was carried away by the enthusiasm of the moment and that I sank down upon my knees and thanked Heaven out of the fullness of my heart for the favor of having been permitted to live in such a time.

The fight for freedom had broken out on an unparalleled scale in the history of the world. From the moment that Fate took the helm in hand the conviction grew among the mass of the people that now it was not a question of deciding the destinies of Austria or Serbia but that the very existence of the German nation itself was at stake. At last, after many years of blindness, the people saw clearly into the future. Therefore, almost immediately after the gigantic struggle had begun, an excessive enthusiasm was replaced by a more earnest and more fitting undertone, because the exaltation of the popular spirit was not a mere passing frenzy. It was only too necessary that the gravity of the situation should be recognized. At that time there was, generally speaking, not the slightest presentiment or conception of how long the war might last. People dreamed of the soldiers being home by Christmas and that then they would resume their daily work in peace.

Whatever mankind desires, that it will hope for and believe in. The overwhelming majority of the people had long since grown weary of the perpetual insecurity in the general condition of public affairs. Hence it was only natural that no one believed that the Austro-Serbian conflict could be shelved. Therefore they looked forward to a radical settlement of accounts. I also belonged to the millions that desired this.

Source: Adolf Hitler, *Mein Kampf*, translated by James Murphy (London: Hurst and Blackett, 1939), eBook edition by Project Gutenberg of Australia, 2002.

joined their leaders in accepting World War I as something necessary or even beneficial for their country. While socialists saw the war as an opportunity for social leveling or perhaps more radical change, conservatives attached to it their hopes for a religious revival or a return to the values of bygone days. Across the spectrum of opinion, patriots in many countries viewed the war as a potential catalyst for "national renewal." Here, perhaps, lies the true tragedy of the civilian reaction on the home front at the outbreak of the war. To a variety of degrees and for a variety of reasons, too many people in 1914 considered war acceptable.

Nationalism Trumps Socialism: From the July Crisis to Zimmerwald

The Second Socialist International, established in 1889, enjoyed significant advantages over the First International (the International Workingmen's Association) of 1864–76, whose leaders had included Karl Marx and Friedrich Engels. Whereas the First International operated on the basis of individual membership, including anarchists as well as socialists, and had been dominated by figures (like Marx and Engels) too radical to live in their own countries, the Second International functioned as an international alliance of Marxist socialist political parties. Among the parties in Europe's six leading countries, the French Socialist Party, which from 1905 called itself the French Section of the Socialist International (*Section Française de l'Internationale Ouvrière* or SFIO), identified itself most closely with the Second International. Its counterparts were the Italian Socialist Party, the German and Austrian Social Democratic parties, the British Labour Party, and the Russian Social Democratic Labor Party.

While, in theory, all Marxist socialists subscribed to Marx's vision of the inevitable worldwide proletarian revolution, pragmatic and moderate forces dominated the Second International. The influence of each of the parties within it hinged on their performance at the polls, and this, in turn, depended upon whether the electoral laws of the individual countries discriminated against working-class voters, and the success of the parties in overcoming such obstacles. Thus, the German SPD (which in the 1912 legislative elections polled 35 percent of the popular vote and won 27 percent of the seats) was in a better position to dominate the Second International than the French SFIO (1914: 17 percent of the vote and seats), the Austrian Social Democrats (1911: 16 percent of the seats), the Italian Socialist Party (1913: 7.5 percent of the vote, 9 percent of the seats), and the British Labour Party (1910: 6 percent of the vote and seats). The Russian Marxist socialists, divided after 1903 into the radical Bolsheviks and more moderate Mensheviks, represented the revolutionary fringe of the Second International. Even after the reforms Nicholas II granted in the wake of the Revolution of 1905, a restricted franchise limited the two parties to a combined 15 of 448 seats in the 1912 Duma elections (3 percent). The Bolsheviks understood they had nothing to lose by being unabashedly revolutionary.

Reflecting their faith in social class as the primary human identity and their goal of international working-class solidarity, the parties of the Second International steadfastly condemned nationalism for the "national prejudices" its adherents had "systematically cultivated … in the interest of the ruling classes for the purpose of distracting the proletarian masses." The Second International likewise took a firm stand against militarism. Its 1907 congress reminded members of "the duty of the working class and particularly of its representatives in the parliaments to combat the naval and military armaments with all their might … and to refuse the means for these armaments," as well as "to exert every effort … to prevent the outbreak of war." The only possible good that could come from a war would be the opportunity "to utilize the economic and political crisis created by the war to rouse the masses and thereby to hasten the downfall of capitalist class rule."[14]

The 1912 extraordinary congress of the Second International, convened in Basel during the First Balkan War, issued a manifesto observing perceptively that "the overcoming of the antagonism between Germany on the one hand, and France and England on the other, would eliminate the greatest danger to the peace of the world, shake the power of tsarism which exploits this antagonism, render an attack of Austria-Hungary upon Serbia impossible, and secure peace to the world."[15] Thereafter the SPD, SFIO, and Labour Party redoubled their efforts to improve relations between their countries, but to no avail. At the climax of the July Crisis of 1914, the International Socialist Bureau (the permanent executive of the Second International, headquartered in Brussels since 1900) met in emergency session on July 29, to issue a last-ditch appeal to "the workers of all nations concerned ... to further intensify their demonstrations against the war, for peace, and for the settlement of the Austro-Serbian conflict by international arbitration." In particular, the bureau called upon the SPD and SFIO to "exert the most energetic pressure upon the governments of their respective countries."[16] The leaders of the Second International envisaged an international general strike as the last chance for stopping a general war, but their plans came to nothing. Paradoxically, while the summer of 1914 found the international socialist movement arguably as strong and united as it had ever been, or ever would be, one of the first and most enduring revolutionary legacies of World War I was the destruction of that solidarity and the permanent splintering of the socialist Left. The last hopes of a socialist action to stop the escalation of the war died on August 4, when the SPD's Reichstag delegation voted unanimously in support of war credits to fund the German mobilization.

The general unity of the SPD behind the German war effort, forged in the belief that the Second Reich had no choice but to mobilize in the face of Imperial Russia's general mobilization, remained firm as long as Nicholas II remained on the throne and Germany's socialist leaders could justify the war as a struggle against tsarist autocracy. Nevertheless, the first cracks in the *Burgfrieden* appeared in December 1914, when the SPD's Karl Liebknecht became the first Reichstag member to vote against supplementary war credits, then joined with other anti-war SPD members to form the Spartacus League (*Spartakusbund*), precursor of the postwar Communist Party of Germany (KPD). By the following summer, Liebknecht's anti-war colleagues within the SPD's Reichstag delegation included Adolf Hoffmann and Georg Ledebour, who represented Germany at the Zimmerwald Conference (September 5–8, 1915), convened near Bern, Switzerland, by anti-war critics of the Second International. Of the thirty-eight delegates from ten countries (including all of the major belligerents except Britain), nineteen signed the "Zimmerwald Manifesto" (see Box 6.2), calling for "a peace without annexations or war indemnities," guaranteeing "the right of self-determination of nations."[17] Future leaders of the Bolshevik Revolution played key roles at Zimmerwald. Trotsky drafted the manifesto and Lenin signed it, although Lenin and seven other delegates (the so-called "Zimmerwald Left") also condemned it as insufficiently revolutionary. The Zimmerwald Left's founders and subsequent followers included radical leftists from most of Europe's Marxist socialist parties, many of whom would later heed Lenin's call to establish Communist parties and send representatives to the Communist International (Comintern), founded in Moscow in 1919. Within the context of World War I, however, the deliberations at Zimmerwald were more significant for introducing into the discourse the concepts of national self-determination and peace without annexations or indemnities, concepts that would gain popularity during the last two years of the war.

Box 6.2 **The Zimmerwald Manifesto**

On September 21, 1915, the socialist peace conference at Zimmerwald issued the following statement on the war, drafted by Leon Trotsky:

Workers of Europe!

The war has lasted for more than a year. Millions of corpses lie upon the battlefields … Whatever may be the truth about the immediate responsibility for the outbreak of the war, one thing is certain: the war that has occasioned this chaos is the outcome of Imperialism, of the endeavors on the part of the Capitalist classes of every nation to satisfy their greed for profit by the exploitation of human labor and of the treasures of Nature …

But we Socialist parties and working-class organizations … have invited the workers *to suspend their working-class struggle* … They have voted the ruling classes the credits for carrying on the war. They have put themselves at the disposal of their Governments for the most varied services … and *thus have taken upon themselves the responsibility for this war, its aims, its methods.* And just as Socialist parties failed separately, so did the most responsible representative of the Socialists of all countries fail: the *International Socialist Bureau* …

In this intolerable situation … we representatives of Socialist parties, of Trade Unions, or of minorities of them … summon the working class to reorganize and begin the struggle for peace. This struggle is also the struggle for liberty, for Brotherhood of nations, for Socialism. The task is to take up this fight for peace, for a peace without annexations or war indemnities … *The right of nations to select their own government must be the immovable fundamental principle of international relations.*

Organized Workers! Since the outbreak of the war you have put your energies, your courage, your steadfastness at the service of the ruling classes. Now the task is to enter the lists for your own cause, for the sacred aims of Socialism, for the salvation of the oppressed nations and the enslaved classes, by means of the irreconcilable working-class struggle. It is the task and the duty of the Socialists of the belligerent countries to take up this struggle with full force; it is the task and the duty of the Socialists of the neutral countries to support their brothers by all effective means in this fight against bloody barbarity. Never in the history of the world has there been a more urgent, a more noble, a more sublime task, the fulfillment of which must be our common work. No sacrifice is too great, no burden too heavy, to attain this end: the establishment of peace between the nations …

Workers of all countries, unite!

Source: Marc Ferro, *The Great War, 1914–1918*, trans. Nicole Stone (original emphasis) (London: Routledge & Kegan Paul, 1969), 165–69.

Understanding the Rush to Volunteer: Britain, the Empire, and Elsewhere

On August 6, 1914, just two days after Britain declared war on Germany, the iconic recruiting poster of Lord Kitchener made its first appearance, featuring the caption "Your King and Country Need *You!*" King George V and Britain, indeed, needed volunteers, as the regular army of 1914 included just six divisions of infantry and one of cavalry, and the reserve Territorial Force (another fourteen infantry divisions and fourteen cavalry brigades) consisted of men who had enlisted for "home service" only. As a traditional maritime power with a small standing army, Britain was the only European great power that did not have conscription, and thus depended upon volunteers to expand its army for service on the continent. After first "inviting" the Territorials to volunteer for overseas service (most did), the government issued an appeal for an additional 500,000 volunteers. By August 31, enlistments were averaging 20,000 per day, and on September 3 the Army recorded 33,304, the war's highest total for any single day. The week of August 30–September 5, with 174,901 enlistments, was the biggest week. By the end of September total enlistments topped 760,000.

While Britain's regular army eventually doubled in size and the Territorials quadrupled, Kitchener initially focused on populating his so-called "New Army" divisions. These were amalgamated from "Pals battalions," groups of classmates, football teammates, coworkers, and neighborhood friends enticed to volunteer by the guarantee that they would serve together with their "pals" in the same units. By the end of September 1914, fifty cities and towns across Britain had raised at least one Pals battalion; Manchester led the way, eventually raising fifteen. The obvious drawback of the Pals battalions – that so many of the young men of an individual city neighborhood or provincial town could be killed in a single battle or even on a single day – did not become apparent until the battle of the Somme, by which time the introduction of conscription had ended their deliberate recruitment. Perhaps the most jarring example of this unintended consequence came on the morning of the first day at the Somme, when the 11th Battalion of the East Lancashire Regiment, a Pals battalion of 700 men from Accrington, suffered 585 casualties (235 killed, 350 wounded) within a span of 20 minutes, a horrific burden for a small town to bear. Even a year before the Somme, heavy casualties had begun to depress voluntary enlistments to levels that could not sustain Britain's war effort. By the summer of 1915, following the disastrous start of the Gallipoli campaign, the army was averaging 70,000 enlistments per month, fewer than it had per *week* in August and September 1914. Such numbers prompted Britain to resort to conscription early the following year.

Voluntary enlistments in the countries with conscription typically involved men no longer on active duty seeking to return to service rather than waiting to be called up. In other cases, men drafted earlier, in peacetime, and rejected as physically unfit volunteered and were accepted under the lower wartime standards. Germany pro-cessed 250,000 volunteers not otherwise called up, France 350,000. Across Europe, thousands of teenaged boys not yet liable for the draft enlisted with the permission of their parents or, in some cases, without it, leaving home and lying about their age to the recruiters. France, with a minimum age of just 17, led the way in enlisting teenagers. Beyond Europe, thousands of emigrants and expatriates went to great lengths to make their way to their home countries in order to serve. In perhaps the most tragic case, in November 1914 Spee's squadron processed hundreds of volunteers in Chile after the battle of Coronel, from among the local German expatriates as well as the crews of German merchantmen trapped by the war in Valparaiso harbor; dozens were accepted for enlistment, almost all of whom perished a month later when Spee's cruisers were sunk off the Falklands.

There are no reliable figures for the number of men from neutral countries who vol-unteered to fight on one side or the other in World War I, but certainly the United States, from 1914 to 1917, accounted for the greatest share. The 35,600 Americans serving in the Canadian Army dwarfed the smaller American contingents serving in the British or French armies. The most celebrated volunteers were the 267 Americans in the French Army air service's Lafayette Flying Corps (the most famous component of which was the pursuit squadron known as the Lafayette Escadrille), but many more Americans – an estimated 1,700 – served in Britain's Royal Flying Corps. Among other neutrals far from the action, the countries of Latin America, eight of which eventually followed the United States into the war, combined to send 10,000 volunteers to the British Army.

As with the issue of overall enthusiasm for the war, the desire to volunteer for ser-vice was far from universal. Even where strong initially – such as in Britain and the Dominions, where the armed forces relied upon it – the rush to volunteer proved to be ephemeral, and by the end of the war Australia stood alone as the only significant belligerent not to have resorted to conscription. For every under-age or over-age vol-unteer, there were others of prime military age who exploited every available loophole or exemption to stay out of the army. And for every emigrant or expatriate who risked life and limb to return to his home country to serve, there were many more emigrants – especially from Austria-Hungary, Russia, and Italy – who thanked their good fortune at having left Europe before the war started and had no desire to return home, at least as long as the fighting continued.

Home-Front Politics: The Central Powers

Within days of the onset of war, various versions of martial law or a state of siege went into effect throughout the warring countries of Europe, as legislators dutifully passed or acquiesced in extensive restrictions on civil liberties. On August 4, the

day the German Reichstag approved the initial round of war credits, it also delegated most of its powers to the Bundesrat (the legislative upper house, appointed by
the governments of the German states) for the duration of the war. It retained only
the power of the purse, to be exercised when necessary, usually every four or five
months, to approve further funding for the war. In a bad case of bureaucracy run
amok, wartime Germany had a military administrative structure for civilian life,
charged with implementing martial law, imposed on top of a civilian structure of
government that continued to exist, both supplemented by a host of new agencies
created by the Bundesrat (and often housed in the war ministry) charged with various aspects of managing the economy for the good of the war effort. Thus, at least
in the duplication of agencies and the resulting confusion over lines of authority,
the last years of the Second Reich foreshadowed the administrative chaos of the
Third Reich.

Despite these structural inefficiencies the home front remained governable as long
as the leading political parties remained faithful to the *Burgfrieden*. At least initially
the war effort enjoyed the unqualified support of almost all of the country's leading
intellectuals, ninety-three of whom signed a manifesto in October 1914 (see Box 6.3)
reflecting their naive, patriotic acceptance of their government's account of the origins
of the war and the German Army's conduct in Belgium. Virtually every internationally
acclaimed German scientist signed the document except Albert Einstein, who supported a countermanifesto appealing "to Europeans" to transcend nationalism for the
sake of their common civilization (see Box 6.4). He was one of just four professors at
the University of Berlin to sign it, but the number of doubters grew as the war dragged
on. Bethmann Hollweg found it ever more difficult to satisfy the more conservative
parties, on the one hand, which demanded a victorious peace with territorial annexations (along the lines of what the chancellor himself had proposed in his program of
September 1914), and the SPD, on the other hand, which found itself supporting a war
that no longer looked much like a defensive struggle against tsarist autocracy. After
Liebknecht, in December 1914, became the first SPD Reichstag deputy to reject further funding for the war, his party formally censured him, but the following year more
of his colleagues joined him in his public dissent from the *Burgfrieden*. In December
1915, twenty SPD deputies opposed war credits and another twenty-two abstained
from voting.

In Austria-Hungary, the onset of the war brought no change in parliamentary political life in the Austrian half of the empire, because the prime minister, Stürgkh, had
suspended the chaotic twenty-two-party Reichsrat in March 1914 in response to the
obstructionist behavior of the Czech parties and the Social Democrats, and once again
resorted to government by decree using Francis Joseph's emergency powers. With
the onset of war and martial law, Stürgkh deferred to military officials who, at least

until 1916, exercised greater authority over civilian life in Austria than in Germany. Meanwhile, the Hungarian prime minister, Count István Tisza, kept the parliament in Budapest in session as a means of providing greater legitimacy for his own wartime actions; politically, he could afford to do so, as the narrow Hungarian franchise (offering voting rights to just 10 percent of the population) gave him a far more predictable and cooperative legislature than the universal male suffrage of the Austrian half of the empire gave Stürgkh's Reichsrat.

Box 6.3 Manifesto of the ninety-three German intellectuals

On October 4, 1914, ninety-three leading German intellectuals issued a spirited defense of their country's role in the origins of the war and its conduct once the fighting began. Signatories included Max Planck and no fewer than twelve other past or future Nobel Prize winners:

As representatives of German Science and Art, we hereby protest to the civilized world against the lies and calumnies with which our enemies are endeavoring to stain the honor of Germany in her hard struggle for existence … As heralds of truth we raise our voices against these.

It is not true that Germany is guilty of having caused this war. Neither the people, the Government, nor the "Kaiser" wanted war …

It is not true that we trespassed in neutral Belgium. It has been proved that France and England had resolved on such a trespass, and it has likewise been proved that Belgium had agreed to their doing so. It would have been suicide on our part not to have been beforehand.

It is not true that the life and property of a single Belgian citizen was injured by our soldiers without the bitterest defense having made it necessary …

It is not true that our troops treated Louvain brutally. Furious inhabitants having treacherously fallen upon them in their quarters, our troops with aching hearts were obliged to fire a part of the town, as punishment. The greatest part of Louvain has been preserved…

It is not true that our warfare pays no respects to international laws. It knows no undisciplined cruelty. But in the east, the earth is saturated with the blood of women and children unmercifully butchered by the wild Russian troops, and in the west, dumdum bullets mutilate the breasts of our soldiers …

It is not true that the combat against our so-called militarism is not a combat against our civilization, as our enemies hypocritically pretend it is. Were it not for German militarism, German civilization would long since have been extirpated …

We cannot wrest the poisonous weapon – the lie – out of the hands of our enemies. All we can do is proclaim to all the world, that our enemies are giving false witness against us … Have faith in us! Believe, that we shall carry on this war to the end as a civilized nation, to whom the legacy of a Goethe, a Beethoven, and a Kant, is just as sacred as its own hearths and homes.

Source: Excerpted from Professors of Germany, "To the Civilized World," *The North American Review* 210, no. 765 (August 1919): 284-85. *The World War I Document Archive* (online), Brigham Young University Library, available at wwi.lib.byu.edu/index.php/Manifesto_of_the_Ninety -Three_German_Intellectuals.

Box 6.4 A "Manifesto to Europeans"

In response to the "Manifesto of the ninety-three," later in October 1914 the University of Berlin physiologist Georg Nicolai circulated the following "Manifesto to Europeans," written with the help of Albert Einstein. Aside from Nicolai and Einstein, just two of their colleagues signed it:

Never before has any war so completely disrupted cultural cooperation ... Anyone who cares in the least for a common world culture is now doubly committed to fight for the maintenance of the principles on which it must stand. Yet, those from whom such sentiments might have been expected – primarily scientists and artists – have so far responded, almost to a man, as though they had relinquished any further desire for the continuance of international relations. They have spoken in a hostile spirit, and they have failed to speak out for peace. Nationalist passions cannot excuse this attitude, which is unworthy of what the world has heretofore called culture ...

Technology has shrunk the world. Indeed, today the nations of the great European peninsula seem to jostle one another much as once did the city-states that were crowded into those smaller peninsulas jutting out into the Mediterranean. Travel is so widespread, international supply and demand are so interwoven, that Europe – one could almost say the whole world – is even now a single unit. Surely, it is the duty of Europeans of education and goodwill at least to try to prevent Europe from succumbing, because of lack of international organization, to the fate that once engulfed ancient Greece! Or will Europe also suffer slow exhaustion and death by fratricidal war?

The struggle raging today can scarcely yield a "victor"; all nations that participate in it will, in all likelihood, pay an exceedingly high price. Hence it appears not only wise but imperative for men of education in all countries to exert their influence for the kind of peace treaty that will not carry the seeds of future wars, whatever the outcome of the present conflict may be ...

The first step in this direction would be for all those who truly cherish the culture of Europe to join forces – all those whom Goethe prophetically once called "good Europeans."... If, as we devoutly hope, enough Europeans are to be found in Europe ... we shall endeavor to organize a League of Europeans. This league may then raise its voice and take action.

We ourselves seek to make the first move, to issue the challenge. If you are of one mind with us, if you too are determined to create a widespread movement for European unity, we bid you pledge yourself by signing your name.

Source: Ronald W. Clark, *Einstein: The Life and Times* (New York: HarperCollins, 1984), 229–30. (Reprinted by permission of SLL/Sterling Lord Literistic, Inc. © by Ronald Clark.)

Home Front Politics: The Allies

The governments of the leading Allies enacted restrictions on civil liberties no less extensive than those of the Central Powers. Even in Britain, traditionally the most liberal of Europe's great powers, the Defence of the Realm Act (August 8, 1914) made citizens liable to arrest without warrant, imprisonment without charges being filed, and trial before courts-martial for violation of an ever-growing list of restrictions on what they could say and do, all in the name of national security and wartime exigency. Asquith's attempt to continue with the same peacetime Liberal government lasted until May 1915, when the scandal over the army's shell shortage coincided with the disastrous start of the Gallipoli campaign to force him to form a wartime coalition. In addition to Churchill's resignation from the Admiralty, other significant changes included Lloyd George exchanging the Exchequer for the new post of minister of munitions. Throughout the war Britain experienced more strikes than France or Germany, involving greater numbers of workers, including major actions during 1915 by metalworkers on the Clyde in Scotland and coal miners in South Wales. Asquith considered using the Defence of the Realm Act to outlaw strikes, but feared that it would undermine the cohesion of the home front.

Ireland, meanwhile, drifted toward rebellion as frustration over the postponement of Home Rule (suspended on September 18, 1914, for the duration of the war) gradually eroded the power base of John Redmond and the Irish Parliamentary Party. Most of the predominantly Catholic, pro-Home Rule Irish Volunteers heeded Redmond's call to support the war effort, including his own brother, who was later killed on the Western front, and his son, decorated for his bravery there. But Kitchener and the war ministry refused their request to form units under their own (Catholic) officers or to use their traditional flags and insignia. At the same time, Kitchener, revealing prejudices shared by most British senior officers, gave these same privileges to the Protestant, anti-Home Rule Ulster Volunteers. The unequal treatment hurt recruiting in Ireland's Catholic south, and heavy Irish casualties on the Gallipoli peninsula caused further discouragement. By the end of 1915 Sinn Féin and the Irish Republican Brotherhood campaigned openly against British Army recruiting efforts, while the Irish Volunteers drilled and marched in the towns and villages of the south. Redmond's decision to reject Asquith's invitation to join the coalition government further tipped the balance toward eventual confrontation, as the Conservatives brought into the cabinet included some of the staunchest opponents of Home Rule.

For Russia, the onset of war brought the suspension of parliamentary government, but not before the Duma dutifully approved the funding for the army's mobilization. Thereafter, the task of governing fell to Nicholas II and his cabinet, headed by prime minister Ivan Goremykin, a 74-year-old conservative nonentity recently called out of retirement, whose only virtue was his loyalty to the tsar. By August 1914, the Duma's Bolshevik delegation had dwindled to five members; they voted against the war credits and, afterward, continued to publicly oppose the war. In November, the government had them arrested and, after trials and convictions, exiled to Siberia. Amid the crackdown on dissent, the material demands of the war effort quickly drove Russia's small, overburdened working class to breaking point, and when strikes broke out in the spring and summer of 1915, they were met with brute force. Troops shot and killed striking workers in June at Kostroma and in August at Ivanovo-Voznesensk; the thirty deaths in the latter case sparked three days of protest strikes in Petrograd. Faced with growing discontent, and with the Russian Army in full retreat out of Poland, Nicholas agreed to reconvene the Duma, but his refusal to replace Goremykin and his cabinet with a "ministry of national confidence" drove almost all of the parties into opposition, even those that still staunchly supported the war effort. The Constitutional Democrats (Kadets), Octobrists, and Nationalists created a center-right "Progressive bloc" committed to the transformation of Russia into a genuine constitutional monarchy whose ministers would be responsible to the legislature. In early September, when Nicholas departed for the front, leaving the Romanov court in the hands of Empress Alexandra and a circle of advisors including the eccentric holy man, Grigori Rasputin, Goremykin's own cabinet refused his request that they endorse the tsar's decision. In February 1916 Nicholas replaced Goremykin with Baron Boris Stürmer, a favorite of Rasputin, then further discredited himself by allowing Stürmer to serve concurrently as interior minister and, from July 1916, as foreign minister, too, replacing Sazonov. With the war going badly and the home front collapsing, the German-surnamed Stürmer and German-born Alexandra became lightning rods for conspiracy theories that gained widespread credence within Russia. It did not help that, in making their decisions, Nicholas, Alexandra, and Stürmer all ignored the Duma, fueling a crisis in which an ever broader spectrum of political figures joined a growing number of generals in opposing the continuation of the status quo.

Imperial Russia, despite its weaknesses, played a central role in the war effort of France, and not just on the battlefield. The existence of an extensive Eastern front helped to shore up a shaky home front, in that it gave the French public a reasonable hope for victory that it would not have the next time it faced a German invasion, in 1940. Among the major belligerents France in 1914–15 suffered more casualties, per capita, than any other country, and in the first weeks of the war lost 6 percent of its territory to foreign occupation, more than any other country in the entire war. Yet Poincaré's *union sacrée* held and morale did not collapse, in part because France enjoyed the unique advantage of having been invaded by an enemy it had done nothing to provoke; indeed, a deep conviction in the righteousness of the country's cause left the French public less susceptible to the effects of bad news from the front.[18] The German invasion generated a million refugees – one out of every forty French citizens – who flocked to Paris or points farther south and west. The burden of resettling and providing for these migrants caused serious strains, and yet in 1914–15 France experienced relatively little labor unrest. In and around Paris, the Department of the Seine experienced just nineteen strikes in the first nineteen months of the war, involving a total of less than 400 workers. Under the *union sacrée* the cabinet of René Viviani (and that of his successor, Aristide Briand, after October 1915) encompassed a broader spectrum of political opinion than the wartime government of any other country. Its members ranged from Catholic conservatives on the right to the SFIO's Jules Guesde, considered a radical voice within the Second International, on the left, and included every leading politician except the Radical Party's Georges Clemenceau, who refused to join it despite his strong support for the war. Instead, Clemenceau used the newspaper he edited as a vehicle with which to criticize the leadership of Viviani and Briand, as well as Joffre and the generals, often running foul of the censors. The SFIO, like the German SPD, voted unanimously for war credits in August 1914, but began to see its own radical left drift into opposition to the war during 1915. In an early sign of things to come, on May Day the secretary of the union of metalworkers, Alphonse Merrheim, defied the censors by publishing a denunciation of the war. Later that month, in an effort to head off labor disputes that could hurt war production, Viviani appointed the SFIO's Albert Thomas to the post of Undersecretary for Munitions in the War Ministry. Thomas proved to be so effective that Briand, in December 1916, rewarded him with full ministerial status.

In Italy, a divided home front spent the first nine months of the war debating the alternatives of intervention or continued neutrality. Pope Benedict XV's preference for Italy to remain neutral influenced many conservative Catholic Italians, while the Italian Socialist Party succeeded where the other larger parties of the Second International had failed, in maintaining its anti-war posture. In June 1914, the Socialists had shown their power in the "Red Week" general strike, involving a million workers in the north-central provinces of the Marches and Romagna, and threatened to turn out similar numbers to keep Italy neutral. Nevertheless, during the winter of 1914–15 most of the leading Italian newspapers supported the Liberal prime minister, Antonio Salandra, in his pro-Entente interventionist position, and their views helped shape public opinion. The journalists supporting the war included Benito Mussolini, editor of the Socialist Party newspaper *Avanti!*, who very publicly abandoned his party's anti-war stance in a piece published in October 1914. Afterward he quit the Socialists and, with French money, established his own interventionist paper, *Il Popolo d'Italia*, which in postwar Italy would become the mouthpiece of his Fascist movement. The last weeks before the Italian declaration of war, later enshrined in patriotic memory as "Radiant May," actually featured several demonstrations against the war as well as for it, many by crowds exceeding 100,000, and frequent, bloody clashes between pro- and anti-war activists in all major cities. After Italy entered the war, the Socialists remained opposed to it, but lost the support of those who, like Mussolini, preferred to combine their socialism with nationalism. Interventionists ranged from traditional Liberals like Salandra, acting out of sheer opportunism, to passionate racial nationalists like Gabriele d'Annunzio, who hoped the modern Italian nation would finally prove itself on the battlefield and wash away the shame of its less than glorious past. But alone among the great powers, Italy could not claim to have entered the war for defensive reasons, and the passions unleashed for and against Italy's opportunistic war only further divided the country.

Hardship and Social Change

Throughout urban Europe, the onset of war brought immediate and noticeable changes to daily life. Measures to save fuel and energy affected the regularity of night-time public transportation as well as electric and gas lighting. Nightlife was curtailed as restaurants and cafés closed earlier than usual, and the recently established cinemas shut down entirely. Public places featuring music labored under new expectations of propriety, with bands and orchestras limited to patriotic or serious songs, and Germany even banned dancing until late in the war. By 1915, however, shows and concerts to benefit war charities had begun to revive public entertainment, while cinemas screened carefully censored war-related films to packed houses. Meanwhile, inflation struck all countries and only worsened as the war continued. It tended to be a social leveler, as simple economics dictated that it benefited debtors over creditors, whose fixed accounts receivable were no longer worth as much in real terms. Wartime inflation thus proved to be a boon to farmers with mortgaged property, while the rise in food prices caused a relative increase in the income and status of all farmers. With the obvious exception of areas directly affected by the position of the front lines, these factors generally enriched rural Europe at the expense of the cities. In urban areas, the lower middle class suffered the worst; petty tradesmen, clerks, and low-ranking civil servants soon saw their cost of living far outstrip their buying power.

Mobilization affected the economy more profoundly in France than anywhere else. Of the male working population of 12.6 million, 2.9 million were called up in August 1914, and another 2.7 million by June 1915; ultimately, 75 percent of French males aged 20–55 would be in uniform at some time during the war. But, ironically, the country suffering the greatest shortage of military manpower was also the first to grant leave to large numbers of workers to return home to the factories. With war *materiel*, especially shells, running dangerously low, the French government recognized that its efforts to bring more female and migrant labor into war industries could not work fast enough to head off a crisis. Thus, in November 1914, the army began to release men whose skills made them more valuable in the factories than at the front. Furloughs expanded after the SFIO's Thomas took charge of munitions production, reaching 500,000 by the end of 1915, enough for the army to finally stop the practice out of concern for its own manpower. While the vast majority of furloughs were legitimate, managers in some industries abused the policy to rescue male relatives from the trenches even if they had never worked in factories; such cases, when exposed, naturally undermined the morale of families with husbands or sons still at the front. The wartime French workforce had to compensate for the productivity of the country's occupied territories, which included 55 percent of its coal mines and produced 80 percent of its steel. Fortunately, the ten lost departments (of the total eighty-seven) produced a far smaller share of the French food supply. Nevertheless, by the end of 1915 meat was in short supply and the government grew concerned about unrest over the general rise in food prices. In November, a Paris police report indicated that people were "much more concerned about the high cost of living than … with the progress of military operations."[19]

Germany was the first of the great powers to ration food, owing to the combined effects of the Allied blockade, the loss of trade with Russia (its main prewar source of grain), and the wartime reduction of agricultural imports from Austria-Hungary. In January 1915, the German government implemented bread rationing. By May, the price of food in Germany had increased by 65 percent over the last prewar month, compared with a 35 percent rise in Britain during the same period. The onset of shortages and rationing had a disproportionate effect on poorer Germans. Throughout the war there would be a greater class-based inequality of civilian sacrifice in Germany than in Britain or France, even though its home front was more heavily regulated. In the autumn of 1914, the war ministry appointed Walther Rathenau, head of AEG (Germany's General Electric), to lead its new War Raw Materials Division, charged with limiting production of consumer goods and increasing output of munitions. But Germany would run out of food long before it ran out of munitions. The government erred in capping food prices at artificially low levels (as did Russia and Austria-Hungary), giving the relatively inefficient German agricultural sector no incentive to increase production. Indeed, if not for trade with its neutral neighbors, Germany's situation would have become desperate even earlier. In the years 1914–16 the Netherlands exported virtually all of its agricultural surplus to Germany, and Denmark remained an important source of dairy products. In the latter case, the Danes could not keep up with German demand; by the autumn of 1915 Germany suffered a milk shortage, and butter was in such short supply that stores selling it were stormed and looted during riots in July in Chemnitz and in December in Berlin.

For Austria-Hungary, the Russian occupation of Galicia in 1914–15 affected the food supply much more than the Allied blockade at the mouth of the Adriatic. Because Galicia accounted for one-third of the arable land in the Austrian half of the Dual Monarchy, its loss caused an immediate grain shortage. Food shortages began to hit the larger cities in October 1914, with the situation in Vienna exacerbated by the influx of 200,000 Galician refugees, mostly impoverished, many of them Jews. The first market queues for milk and potatoes appeared in Vienna early in 1915; in April, Austria introduced rationing of flour and bread, expanded during 1916 to include milk, coffee, and sugar. Austria introduced two meatless days per week in 1915, extended to three in 1916. Because the constitutional compromise of 1867 had left Austria and Hungary as separate economic entities, each had its own wartime rationing policies. The Hungarian half of the empire, more overwhelmingly rural and agrarian than the Austrian, offered more generous civilian rations, leaving Austrians to allege that Hungarians were taking care of themselves to the detriment of the common cause. Such feelings were not unjustified, as Hungary temporarily banned food exports to Austria at the beginning of 1915. For the year Austria received just 36 percent of the grain it would normally import from Hungary.

The Red Cross and Humanitarian Volunteers

In the first month of the war, the Red Cross emerged as the most important organization for civilian volunteerism. The International Committee of the Red Cross, founded in 1863 by Swiss humanitarian Henri Dunant, first provided aid to wounded soldiers the following year, in Bismarck's War of 1864 against Denmark. By 1914 it had grown into a coordinating organization for forty-five national Red Cross societies. While idealists traditionally point to the growth of the Red Cross during World War I as evidence of a common European humanitarianism, more recent scholarship suggests that most volunteers were drawn to Red Cross service as a way to support their own country's war effort. Indeed, the single greatest wartime initiative of the Red Cross, for the benefit of prisoners of war, appears to have been rooted in a pragmatic transnational reciprocity rather than pure humanitarianism.[20]

When the war dragged on into a second year with no end in sight, all belligerents faced challenges in accounting for prisoners lost, processing those taken, and providing for the long-term care of POWs. Among the millions ultimately captured, Germany alone took 220,000 French prisoners in the first five months of the war and 360,000 Russian prisoners by March 1915, before the conquest of Russian Poland. The International Red Cross created a registry of those missing or assumed captured that grew to include the names of 7 million persons, 2 million of whom were eventually located in prison camps. Ultimately the Red Cross delivered 2 million parcels to POWs, as well as 20 million letters to and from them. Because the prewar Geneva conventions had been signed under the auspices of the Red Cross, the international organization took responsibility for monitoring wartime compliance, eventually sending inspectors to more than 500 POW camps across Europe. The national Red Cross organizations of neutral countries played a leading role in this effort, starting in 1915 when Austria-Hungary and Russia agreed to allow the Danish Red Cross to inspect POW camps in both countries.

As the richest and most populous neutral country, the United States had an especially active humanitarian volunteer effort. In the Commission for Relief in Belgium, led by future president Herbert Hoover, Americans coordinated the feeding of occupied Belgium (and, ultimately, of German-occupied France) with help from Spain, which cosponsored the organization, and the Netherlands, which transshipped the aid via Rotterdam. In addition to Belgian relief, the American Red Cross chartered 341 ships to send US$1.5 million worth of aid to Europe before the US entered the war; its medical initiatives included a partnership with the Rockefeller Foundation to fight the 1915 typhus epidemic in Serbia. Under the Red Cross and other charities, Americans funded and staffed field hospitals and ambulance services. The latter became a popular way to get to France for college-aged men with the means to pay their own expenses; six Ivy League schools alone accounted for almost 1,000 ambulance drivers, including Harvard's E. E. Cummings. Subsequent volunteer drivers included teenagers Ernest Hemingway, employed on the Italian front, and Walt Disney, en route to France when the Armistice was signed.

The International Committee of the Red Cross and its national societies all were chaired by men, often members of royal families (such as Prince Charles of Sweden) or retired political leaders (such as former president William H. Taft in the United States). In every country, women in Red Cross leadership roles tended to be spouses of prominent men. These included Lady Helen Munro-Ferguson, wife of the governor-general of Australia, who founded the Australian Red Cross in August 1914, and Lady Julia Drummond, widow of a Canadian senator, who moved to London during the war to head the Canadian Red Cross Information Bureau. Despite their lack of representation at the highest level of the organization, women accounted for most volunteers in most countries, as the humanitarian mission made Red Cross work a socially acceptable outlet for them.

For a woman seeking direct involvement in the war, the traditionally female role of nurse offered the greatest opportunity. In Britain, the Imperial Military Nursing Service and Territorial Force Nursing Service, combined, had barely 2,300 trained professional nurses at the onset of war. Their numbers were soon supplemented by tens of thousands of amateur nurses serving in "Voluntary Aid Detachments," cosponsored by the Red Cross and the Order of St. John of Jerusalem. Members of these detachments, colloquially referred to as "VADs," were typically unmarried middle-class women who shared the same social background and circumstances as most volunteer nurses in other countries. Their official minimum age for service in Britain was 21, for service abroad 23, but it was not uncommon for the minimum age to be waived. A much smaller number of women served in Britain's First Aid Nursing Yeomanry (FANY), a uniformed service with no direct equivalent in other countries. Adventures of FANYs included driving ambulances in France and riding horseback to and from duties at field hospitals in the Balkans. Unlike VADs, whose expenses could be covered by Red Cross philanthropy if their families lacked the resources to subsidize them, most FANYs were daughters of the upper class whose families paid all of their expenses. By the end of the war, 80,000 VADs and FANYs had served, but twice that number had applied and been turned away.

When France faced invasion in August 1914, so many women sought to help in nursing and other auxiliary services that the government asked them to stop volunteering and just stay home. Soon enough, the need to care for massive numbers of wounded provided plenty of opportunity for volunteer nurses, even in field hospitals near the front, which the army's Military Health Service (*Service de Santé Militaire*) initially had placed off-limits for women. Ultimately wartime France deployed 100,000 nurses; of these, roughly 10,000 were nuns from Catholic religious orders, 30,000 paid professionals recruited from 1916 onward, and the rest volunteers serving under the auspices of three Red Cross women's organizations. Despite their relatively small numbers, the nuns served as conservative role models for the rest. In France, as well as in Britain, volunteer nurses were hailed as heroines, romanticized long before the success of some of their postwar memoirs cemented their place in popular memory of the war years.

The purely humanitarian motive to serve was strongest among doctors, nurses, and supporting personnel from neutral countries. In addition to the American Red Cross, the Danish Red Cross was active on all fronts (driven in part by a national rivalry of its own, with the Swedish Red Cross). After British nurse Edith Cavell, a prewar expatriate working in occupied Belgium, was shot by the Germans in October 1915 for helping stranded and straggling Allied soldiers escape via the neutral Netherlands, it became rare for nurses from belligerent countries to serve behind enemy lines. A notable exception came on the Eastern front, where Russia from the start had difficulty recruiting nurses, as the country's nobility and relatively small middle class only had so many daughters to contribute. The Russian Red Cross mobilized just 4,000 nurses in 1914 and 25,000 by 1916; thus Russia welcomed nurses from Allied and neutral countries to help care for its wounded soldiers, and from the Central Powers to assist with the large number of POWs it held, nearly all of whom were Austro-Hungarian.

While nursing was the highest-profile form of female volunteerism, nurses accounted for a tiny fraction of the vast legion of women in wartime Red Cross work, whose number in Britain alone reached 3 million. For married women, wartime voluntary activity under the Red Cross more frequently mirrored prewar charitable and social work. Sewing and knitting circles that, in peacetime, would have done work for the poor formed the basis for much larger efforts to produce supplementary articles for the armed forces, with socks being in high demand especially for soldiers in the trenches on the Western front. Likewise, women with peacetime experience as organizers and fundraisers for charities lent their energy to sending letters and parcels to troops at the front and POWs, and to raising money for the Red Cross. Such activities, part-time in nature, were compatible with traditional obligations to home and family. Compared with women serving later in uniformed auxiliaries such as Britain's Women's Royal Naval Service and Women's Army Auxiliary Corps (see Chapter 11), or those who went to work in munitions factories, women engaged in Red Cross work – from nursing to sewing to correspondence and fundraising – did so within established prewar parameters of gender and class, and thus encountered little controversy in their work.

Other preexisting organizations with expanded wartime roles included the Young Men's Christian Association and the Salvation Army, which were particularly significant to the English-speaking countries. Both built upon their already extensive social missions to provide support services on the home front and also moved quickly to develop a presence in the war zone. Starting in October 1914 in Le Havre, the YMCA established hundreds of centers behind the lines in France, with the goal of providing wholesome venues for rest and relaxation for soldiers on leave. The YMCA eventually sponsored musical entertainment, cinemas, and participatory athletics, as well as libraries, guest speakers, and Bible study. The Salvation Army likewise established a presence behind the front lines, providing religious services, food and fellowship, and was the first private charity to deploy volunteer ambulances.

Box 6.5 A farewell to "provincial young-ladyhood"

Vera Brittain (1893–1970), daughter of a prosperous Midlands mill owner, left her studies at Somerville College, University of Oxford, shortly before her twenty-second birthday to become a volunteer nurse. She served from 1915–18 in hospitals in France and Malta, during which time her brother, her fiancé, and two close friends all were killed in combat or died of wounds. Through her memoir of the war years, *Testament of Youth* (1933), she became one of the iconic voices of Britain's "Lost Generation":

'And what is your age, nurse?' the Matron inquired, after hearing the necessary details of my Devonshire Hospital experience. 'Twenty-three,' I replied, promptly but mendaciously, giving the minimum age at which I could be accepted in an Army hospital [in France] ... Since I looked, in the provincial excessiveness of my best coat and skirt, an unsophisticated seventeen, she probably did not believe me, but ... she accepted the bold statement at its face value, and promised to apply for me in October ...

After following the progress of the new Allied expedition to Salonika, and ... journalistic outbursts over the shooting of Nurse Cavell, [we] read, rather sadly, in *The Times* of October 15th, the customary account of the opening of the Michaelmas Term at Oxford ... On the following day, as if to justify my decision to remain away from college, my orders came ... telling me to report at the 1st London General Hospital, Camberwell, on Monday, October 18th ...

The leaves were falling fast, and a misty twilight quenched the autumn tints into greyness. Now that the moment of departure had come, I felt melancholy and a little afraid. The next morning, soberly equipped in my new VAD uniform, I took ... the early train to London, and turned my back forever upon my provincial young-ladyhood.

Source: Vera Brittain, *Testament of Youth* (1933; reprint ed. New York: Seaview Books, 1980), 179–80, 203–04.

Women and Gender Relations

From the start of the war the changing role of women was most evident in Britain. While historians continue to debate whether the aid British women gave to the war effort led directly to their voting rights in 1918, the leading suffrage organizations did their part by encouraging women to rally to the cause. The mainstream National Union of Women's Suffrage Societies (NUWSS) funded the Scottish Women's Hospitals, front-line medical units organized by Edinburgh-trained surgeon Elsie Inglis, Scotland's leading suffragist, and staffed entirely by women. Meanwhile, Emmeline Pankhurst's Women's Social and Political Union (WPSU), the most radical of the suffrage organizations, adapted its confrontational tactics to new ends in supporting the "white feather girls," a loose movement that publicly shamed men who had not volunteered for military service. In March 1915, the Board of Trade created the Register of Women for War Service, broadly defined as "paid employment of any kind" that freed a man for military service. The registry soon included 124,000 women, who took jobs in government offices, military bases, and hospitals, as well as in the private sector. Women typically were paid significantly less than men doing the same jobs, especially in the munitions factories, where they began to appear in greater numbers after the expansion of the munitions industry under the direction of Lloyd George. The first round of unrestricted submarine warfare in 1915 (see Chapter 8) did not disrupt imports to Britain enough to spark a food shortage; nevertheless, fears of the consequences of a rural labor shortage led to the creation, in 1915, of the Women's Land Army (Figure 6.1), to recruit female volunteers (mostly from towns and villages) to replace farm labor lost to military service. British farmers thus were in a better position to respond to the offer of higher prices for greater production, and with the help of female labor cultivated land not farmed for decades.

France had less success in recruiting women war workers, in part because of the government's generous "separation allowances" to the spouses and children of men called up by the army. Indeed, compared with Britain, where families of modest means complained that their "terrible" allowances amounted to little more than "starvation money,"[21] in France the formula gave many working-class or peasant women a greater household income than their husbands had earned in peacetime, and thus no incentive to leave the home for work in munitions factories. As of October 1915, French war industries registered just 75,000 female workers, most of whom had already been at work, but in jobs where wages were far lower than those offered by the munitions factories, such as domestic service or the textile industry. The latter continued to produce for the domestic market, including the Paris fashion industry, which still set international trends. In 1915, skirts known as "war crinolines" became popular despite a scandal over their revealing calf-length. The fashion caught on, with the 1916 iteration accompanied by the irreverent slogan "the war is long, but the skirts are short."[22] That year the trend spread to London and, despite the war, to Berlin. Of course, high fashion

Figure 6.1 Women's Land Army

Fears of a rural labor shortage in Britain led to the creation of the Women's Land Army, originally known as the Women's Land Service Corps. Low wages discouraged enrollment by women from poorer families, who needed better-paying work to help their families meet basic needs. Thus, most volunteers were from families financially secure enough to accommodate their absence, and most otherwise would not have been doing paid work. Not surprisingly, such women often had no previous experience with manual labor of any kind, much less farm work, even though most came from towns and villages. By some estimates 60 percent of those who volunteered were dismissed as unfit. The Women's Land Army grew to include 260,000 volunteers by the spring of 1918. They provided a valuable supplement to Britain's agricultural labor and eased fears of food shortages at a time when increasing numbers of people from the countryside were migrating to the cities for work in munitions factories.

remained irrelevant to the vast majority of French women, for whom the only clear trend was the growing prevalence of black clothing, traditional for those mourning a lost loved one. Years later one Frenchman who had experienced the war as a child recalled that, by the end of 1915, his own widowed mother "no longer stood out in the crowd" because of the sheer number of women wearing black as a consequence of the French Army's staggering losses at the front.[23]

With millions of men removed from civilian life as of August 1914, and millions more called up afterward, women accounted for an ever-growing majority of the home-front population. When historians first turned their attention to the World War

I home front, their focus primarily on Britain and the United States, secondarily on Germany and France, and almost exclusively on the urban experience led them to conclude that a social revolution had occurred in the years 1914–19, forever changing gender relations. Women entered the workforce in unprecedented numbers, and for the first time large numbers of young, single women earned independent incomes. This led to the assertion of social independence, reflected in the skimpier clothing, shorter hairstyles, and looser morals (including public drinking and smoking, along with premarital and extramarital sex) that broke with lingering Victorian norms and foreshadowed the Roaring Twenties, while women's contribution to the war effort led to an increase in legal rights, most notably the right to vote, granted immediately after the war in Britain, the United States, Germany, and Austria. In recent years social and cultural historians have done valuable work in exposing these myths, albeit without making much progress toward a new synthesis on what actually happened or might have happened. Some have argued that the war reinforced traditional gender relations as much as it overturned them, citing the role of wartime propaganda underscoring the notion that marriage and motherhood were a woman's natural roles, and looking forward to the victorious peace in which these norms could be restored. In any event, it now appears that the changes ascribed to a wartime revolution in gender relations occurred more gradually and were more limited or, in some cases, more temporary than earlier accounts would have us believe. The war did little, if anything, to increase opportunities for women in the workplace on a permanent basis. In the United States, fewer women were employed outside the home in 1920 than in 1910, while in Germany, despite the deaths of 1.8 million able-bodied men in the years 1914–18, the proportion of the female population working outside the home stood at 35.6 percent in 1925, only a modest rise from 31.2 percent in 1907. Even in France, which suffered 1.3 million war dead and another 1.1 million men "severely wounded with permanent work incapacity," the workforce in 1919 included just 200,000 more women than it had in 1913, leading one analyst to conclude that "continuity … dominates the facts, even if mentalities may have changed more."[24] Finally, and perhaps most important of all, assertions concerning revolutionary changes in sexual norms and behavior ignore the basic realities of the time. Long after World War I few women had access to birth control and abortion remained illegal (except in Russia, where the new Bolshevik regime would grant women abortion on demand in November 1920).

Conclusion

August 1914 witnessed widespread enthusiasm for the war once it was declared, if not sooner. Because nationalism proved to be stronger than socialism, World War I became a watershed in the history of the socialist movement, which would never again be as united as it was in July 1914. The rush to volunteer, impressive at first, especially in Britain and the Dominions, dissipated by 1915, leading to consideration of conscription in every country that still had a volunteer army. Finally, by the end of 1915 Russia and Austria-Hungary had already learned what Italy was soon to find out: that they lacked the ability to sustain a modern war effort without substantial help from their friends. Meanwhile, the three belligerents with the greatest such capacity – Britain, France, and Germany – each managed the home front in its own way, and effectively enough. Britain introduced unprecedented restrictions on its hallowed civil liberties, while postponing both conscription and rationing for as long as possible. In France, the most politically inclusive wartime government paradoxically applied the most vigorous censorship to what had been, arguably, Europe's most vigorously free press, and exploited to the fullest the unifying circumstances under which the country had been forced to fight. For Germany, the unity of the home front lasted as long as it did anywhere else, but for different reasons. The layers of bureaucracy, old and new, may have been inefficient, but they reinforced what many observers, at the time and afterward, explained as a cultural predisposition to submit to authority. Unfortunately, they also failed to impose sacrifices equally on the whole of society, and thus the Germans experienced less wartime social leveling than the British or French. Even though many Germans would later hark back to the sense of community that prevailed in August 1914, the barriers dividing the social classes were only temporarily and superficially bridged. By the end of 1915 this fatal internal flaw had not yet become apparent, either on the home front or within the German military, but in another three years the strains of warfare would expose it in both places.

SUGGESTIONS FOR FURTHER READING

Becker, Jean-Jacques. *The Great War and the French People*, trans. Arnold Pomerans (New York: St. Martin's Press, 1986).

Chickering, Roger. *The Great War and Urban Life in Germany: Freiburg, 1914–1918* (Cambridge: Cambridge University Press, 2007).

Darrow, Margaret. *French Women and the First World War: War Stories of the Home Front* (Oxford: Berg Publishers, 2000).

Fell, Alison S., and Christine E. Hallett (eds.) *First World War Nursing: New Perspectives* (London: Routledge, 2013).

Gatrell, Peter. *Russia's First World War: A Social and Economic History* (Harlow: Pearson Education, 2005).

Grayzel, Susan. *Women's Identities at War: Gender, Motherhood, and Politics in Britain and France during the First World War* (Chapel Hill, NC: University of North Carolina Press, 1999).

Grayzel, Susan R., and Tammy M. Proctor (eds.) *Gender and the Great War* (Oxford: Oxford University Press, 2017).

Gregory, Adrian. *The Last Great War: British Society and the First World War* (Cambridge: Cambridge University Press, 2008).

Healy, Maureen. *Vienna and the Fall of the Habsburg Empire: Total War and Everyday Life in World War I* (Cambridge: Cambridge University Press, 2004).

Newman, Vivien. *We Also Served: The Forgotten Women of World War I* (Barnsley: Pen and Sword History, 2014).

Verhey, Jeffrey. *The Spirit of 1914: Militarism, Myth, and Mobilization in Germany* (Cambridge: Cambridge University Press, 2000).

NOTES

1. Jeffrey Verhey, *The Spirit of 1914: Militarism, Myth, and Mobilization in Germany* (Cambridge University Press, 2000), 71.
2. Quoted in Verhey, *The Spirit of 1914*, 65–66.
3. Josef Redlich, *Schicksalsjahre Österreichs, 1908–1919: Das politische Tagebuch Josef Redlichs, Vol. 1*, ed. Fritz Fellner (Graz: Böhlau, 1953–54), August 26, 1914, 252.
4. Leon Trotsky, *My Life* (New York: Charles Scribner, 1931), 233–34.
5. John W. Boyer, *Culture and Political Crisis in Vienna: Christian Socialism in Power, 1897–1918* (Chicago: University of Chicago Press, 1995), 370.
6. Sigmund Freud to Sándor Ferenczi, August 23, 1914, in *The Correspondence of Sigmund Freud and Sándor Ferenczi, Vol. 2* (Cambridge, MA: Belknap Press of Harvard University Press, 1993–2000), 12–14.
7. Stefan Zweig, *The World of Yesterday: An Autobiography* (New York: Viking Press, 1943), 223.
8. Marc Bloch, *Memoirs of War, 1914–1915*, trans. Carole Fink (Ithaca, NY: Cornell University Press, 1980; reprint edn. Cambridge University Press, 1991), 78.
9. Quoted in Adrian Gregory, *The Last Great War: British Society and the First World War* (Cambridge: Cambridge University Press, 2008), 10.
10. Laura de Gozdawa Turczynowicz, *When the Prussians Came to Poland: The Experiences of an American Woman During the German Invasion* (New York: G. P. Putnam, 1916), 5, 11.
11. Reception of the news of mobilization in Walburgskirchen, Bavaria, August 1, 1914, quoted in Benjamin Ziemann, *War Experiences in Rural Germany, 1914–1923*, trans. Alex Skinner (Oxford: Berg, 2007), 19.
12. Mary Houghton, *In the Enemy's Country: Being the Diary of a Little Tour in Germany and Elsewhere during the Early Days of the War* (London: Chatto & Windus, 1915), 24–25.
13. Peter Fritzsche, *Germans into Nazis* (Cambridge, MA: Harvard University Press, 1998), passim; quoted from 29; see also Verhey, *The Spirit of 1914*, 23–27.

14. Resolution adopted at the Seventh Congress of the Second Socialist International, Stuttgart, August 18–24, 1907, available at www.marxists.org/history/international/social-democracy/1907/militarism.htm.

15. Manifesto adopted at the Extraordinary Congress of the Second Socialist International, Basel, November 24–25, 1912, available at www.marxists.org/history/international/social-democracy/1912/basel-manifesto.htm.

16. Resolution of the International Socialist Bureau, Brussels, July 29, 1914, available at www.workers.org/marcy/cd/sambol/bolwar/bolwar06.htm.

17. Manifesto of the International Socialist Conference, Zimmerwald, Switzerland, September 1915, available at www.marxists.org/history/international/social-democracy/zimmerwald/manifesto-1915.htm.

18. Jean-Jacques Becker, *The Great War and the French People*, trans. Arnold Pomerans (New York: St. Martin's Press, 1986), 139–40.

19. Quoted in Becker, *The Great War and the French People*, 137.

20. Heather Jones, "International or Transnational? Humanitarian Action during the First World War," *European Review of History* 16 (2009): 697–713.

21. Quoted in Gregory, *The Last Great War*, 286.

22. Quoted in Irene Guenther, *Nazi Chic? Fashioning Women in the Third Reich* (Oxford: Berg, 2004), 28.

23. Quoted in Stéphane Audoin-Rouzeau and Annette Becker, *14–18: Understanding the Great War*, trans. Catherine Temerson (New York: Hill & Wang, 2002), 179.

24. Pierre-Cyrille Hautcouer, "The Economics of World War I in France," in Stephen Broadberry and Mark Harrison (eds.), *The Economics of World War I* (Cambridge: Cambridge University Press, 2005), 199–200.

The face of war, Germany 1916

Youth and fatigue show on the face of a soldier of a storm troop unit. Such soldiers represented the cream of the crop in the mid-war German Army, handpicked for their physical fitness, trained in special tactics, and armed with automatic weapons, hand grenades, and flamethrowers. But aside from the steel helmet (newly issued in 1916, replacing the traditional spiked helmet), this soldier's kit appears improvised and his uniform shabby; judged by appearance alone, he has far more in common with the surrendering German of November 1918 than the confident German of August 1914.

7 Raising the Stakes

Europe, 1916

The onset of trench warfare on the Western front made a deep impression on Falkenhayn, who recognized earlier than most other German generals that the Central Powers simply lacked the manpower and resources to win a war of attrition against the Allies. Indeed, on November 18, 1914, he informed Bethmann Hollweg that "as long as Russia, France, and England hold together, it will be impossible for us to beat our enemies such that we will get an acceptable peace. We would instead run the danger of slowly exhausting ourselves."[1] Thus, he broke with a German way of war that called for the "annihilation" of the enemy, instead seeking what Moltke the Elder, and Napoleon and Clausewitz before him, had advocated before the cult of the offensive took their legacy to grotesque extremes: the destruction of enemy field armies as a prerequisite to the achievement of war aims through diplomacy.[2] Yet this approach, which had worked for the elder Moltke and Bismarck in the Wars of German Unification, had failed in 1915, invalidating the assumption that such victories in the field would lead to a diplomatic solution. Having fully invested their people in a modern war effort, Russia had rejected overtures for a separate peace despite its serious losses in Poland, and Serbia had refused to capitulate even after the Central Powers occupied all of its territory. But Falkenhayn did not expect the same sort of tenacity from Germany's own allies. In an audience with William II on January 24, he remarked that he did not believe that Austria-Hungary and the Ottoman Empire could be counted upon to continue the struggle "beyond autumn of this year."[3]

While Conrad did not share Falkenhayn's pessimism, earlier in January 1916 he asked the political leaders of the Dual Monarchy to define what they would consider an acceptable end to the war. Led by foreign minister Count István Burián, who had replaced Berchtold a year earlier, the ministers all agreed that a peace safeguarding the "prestige" and "interests" of Austria-Hungary would be possible only after a decisive victory against Italy. Conrad then renewed his request for German participation in an offensive on the Italian front, but Falkenhayn rejected it again, arguing that the OHL had determined its course for 1916 already, and given the scope of his plans for the Western front, he could spare no German troops to join in an offensive against Italy or to replace Austro-Hungarian troops transferred from the Eastern front for that purpose. Conrad then made the fateful decision to proceed with an offensive on the Italian front using Austro-Hungarian resources alone. The determination of the AOK and the OHL to pursue their own strategies and objectives in 1916 proved to be disastrous for both. In contrast to the Central Powers, the Allies resolved to cooperate more closely than before. On December 6–8, 1915, at French headquarters in Chantilly, northeast of Paris, Joffre and Sir John French met with General Yakov Zhilinsky, prewar chief of the Russian general staff, and representatives from the Italian and Serbian armies to work out a general plan for a series of coordinated offensives on all fronts. They assumed that Germany would be "slowing down the process of attrition, to be in a condition to continue the struggle indefinitely," and would build upon its successes of 1915 on the

Eastern front by focusing once again on the defeat of Russia.[4] The planned Allied offensives had obvious territorial goals (the liberation of occupied lands on the Western and Eastern fronts, and the capture of Trieste on the Italian front) but, in general, aimed at engaging the Central Powers in a war of attrition they were bound to lose in the long run, the sort of war the Allies assumed they wanted to avoid. Their grand design had yet to be implemented when Falkenhayn confounded the Allies on both points, not only launching his own campaign of attrition, but doing so on the Western front, at Verdun.

Verdun

Why did the Germans adopt a strategy that played to the strength of the Allies? In the first seventeen months of the war, the French had suffered more than 1.9 million casualties, including 590,000 men killed. The OHL's Intelligence Section estimated that France would face a manpower crisis by September 1916 if its losses in the upcoming year continued at the rate of 1914–15. Falkenhayn reasoned that an acceleration of the rate of loss would break the French Army completely, and he planned to accomplish this by mounting an attack of unprecedented strength at a specific point on the front, which the French could withstand only by sustaining so many casualties that they would destroy themselves. Thus, even though Falkenhayn believed Germany could not win a long-term war of attrition against the Allied coalition as a whole, he pinned his hopes on a short-term war of attrition focusing on France alone. It was, as one historian has noted, a "cold, self-wasting calculation," for its fulfillment would require the deliberate sacrifice of hundreds of thousands of German troops.[5]

Falkenhayn chose to attack at Verdun, a stronghold of twenty forts in rolling hills along the upper Meuse commanding a salient between the central and southeastern sectors of the Western front. Verdun also had great symbolic significance, having been a fortress town since Roman times, acquired by France from the Holy Roman Empire in 1648, and the last French fortress to capitulate in the Franco-Prussian War of 1870–71. The French could be counted upon to attempt to hold Verdun regardless of the cost, making it the ideal point for the Germans to attack. Crown Prince William's Fifth Army, reinforced to a staggering forty-one divisions (with fifteen more in reserve), spearheaded the assault. The German battle plan called for an unprecedented artillery bombardment, budgeting 3 million shells for the first eighteen days of the battle, a rate of fire to be sustained by more than thirty trainloads of munitions arriving in the sector every day. On the morning of February 21 the attack began, with more than 800 heavy guns, almost 400 light guns, and 200 mortars pounding a sector of the front just 10 miles (16 km) wide, prior to the initial advance by ten divisions of infantry. Their artillery included 12-inch (305 mm) Skoda howitzers, on loan from Austria-Hungary, the

15-inch (381 mm) "Long Max" railway gun, and the 16.5-inch (420 mm) "Big Bertha." The advancing troops were led by eight companies armed with a new weapon, the flamethrower, and all wore the distinctive new steel helmets that would become standard for the German Army for the remainder of World War I and all of World War II. Joffre had anticipated at least a diversionary attack at Verdun and gave Pétain's Second Army three divisions to reinforce the five already stationed in the salient, along with another three in reserve, backed by nearly 400 light and 250 heavy guns. Seriously outnumbered in manpower and artillery, the French could not stop the Germans from storming the heights east of the Meuse to take Fort Douaumont, the highest fortified place in the sector, on February 25, but at that point German lines came within range of French artillery on high ground west of the Meuse, and their advance halted. In the first five days of the battle the French lost 24,000 men, almost 15,000 of them prisoners, but within the first ten days the Germans lost 26,000. The Fifth Army launched a second major assault in early March and a third in early April, which Pétain repulsed amid mounting casualties on both sides.

Given the ferocity of the action, Pétain recognized early on that fresh, well-supplied troops would be the key to holding Verdun. Rather than have the Second Army decimated and its morale broken while other French armies stood idle in quieter sectors, Joffre agreed to rotate most of his troops through the battle. The French Army opened the year with ninety-three divisions on the Western front, and by July 1 sixty-six of them had seen action at Verdun, though no more than twenty-five (including sector reserves) were ever there at any given time. In contrast, on the German side, just forty-eight divisions rotated through the battle, fewer than the fifty-six (including reserve divisions) that had been allotted to the sector in February. Pétain's supply chain depended upon convoys of trucks plying the winding *voie sacrée*, the "sacred road" from Bar-le-Duc to Verdun. In one crucial eight-day period (February 27–March 6), the Second Army received 190,000 reinforcements and 23,000 tons of munitions via this route. Thanks to the introduction of the Nieuport 11 biplane, the French Army Air Corps recovered from the "Fokker scourge" of the previous autumn and dominated the skies over Verdun (see Online Essay 3). As a result, no German aircraft ever bombed or strafed the *voie sacrée*. Air superiority also benefited French artillery spotting (either by aircraft or by tethered balloons defended by aircraft) and enabled the French to disrupt German artillery spotting.

At the end of the first phase of the battle Pétain's immediate superior, Langle de Cary, who had succeeded Castelnau as central army group commander during the winter, infuriated Joffre by ordering French troops to retreat from the Woevre plain, on the front east of Verdun. Joffre responded by sacking Langle and elevating Pétain to replace him. General Robert Nivelle, in turn, succeeded Pétain as commander of the Second Army. After Fort Vaux, the last of the major outer-belt forts on the east bank of the Meuse, fell on June 7, the Germans renewed their attacks using phosgene gas.

They also introduced storm troop tactics, using handpicked squads of troops armed with automatic weapons, hand grenades, trench mortars, and flamethrowers against French machine-gun nests and other strong points that artillery barrages could not reliably neutralize. During the second half of June, the Germans very nearly achieved a breakthrough, causing a political crisis in Paris. Thus far the *Union sacrée* had precluded criticism of Joffre or the conduct of the war, but on June 22 the storm finally broke. The Chamber of Deputies (albeit in secret session) pilloried the commander, with the most damning criticism coming from future war minister André Maginot, then convalescing from wounds he had received as a sergeant leading a platoon at Verdun. The following day Nivelle practically willed the Germans to stop, concluding his most famous order of the day with the line that became his promise to Joffre, and to the French nation: "they shall not pass (*Ils ne passeront pas*)." Fortunately for the French defenders, the combined effects of Aleksei Brusilov's offensive on the Eastern front (from June 4) and the British offensive along the Somme (from July 1) made it impossible for Falkenhayn to sustain his offensive at Verdun after July 12, when the Germans were stopped at Fort Souville, 2.5 miles (4 km) from the citadel.

On August 29 the cumulative setbacks of 1916 caused William II to sack Falkenhayn. By then, the Germans had inflicted 315,000 French casualties at Verdun at a cost of 281,000 of their own, or a ratio of 1.1:1, a far cry from the goal of 3:1 or 5:2 that Falkenhayn had set to justify his strategy. The Germans transitioned to the defensive and pulled most of their troops from the sector, inviting a counteroffensive that began six weeks later. Nivelle initiated the French attack and quickly eclipsed Pétain as the hero of Verdun. He enjoyed the support of Joffre, who visited frequently during the autumn weeks, and the able assistance of the new commander of the Verdun forts, General Charles Mangin, most recently commander of the Third Army. The French began to employ the creeping barrage tactic adopted by the British at the Somme in mid-July, in which the shells rained down just in front of the advancing infantry, creating the opportunity for them to take enemy trenches before the defenders could come out from under cover to resume their normal defensive positions. They made the tactic more effective by having their infantry advance much closer (just 90–100 yards or 80–90 m) behind the curtain of falling steel. The counteroffensive also featured new 400 mm howitzers mounted as railway guns, equivalent (if not superior) to Krupp's "Big Bertha." Firing from tracks 8 miles (13 km) southwest of Verdun, their shelling set both Fort Douaumont and Fort Vaux ablaze on October 23; a Moroccan regiment stormed the former on the 24th, and French forces finally secured the latter on November 2. The counteroffensive continued until December 18, by which time the front line at the center of the Verdun salient in Caumieres Wood stood just half a mile (0.8 km) south of its original location. The ten months of fighting generated 377,000 French casualties against 337,000 German. Officially, the French acknowledged 162,000 dead, the Germans 82,000, though the latter likely topped 140,000.

The battle of Verdun certainly ranked as the most geographically concentrated prolonged bloodletting of the war, as virtually all of its dead fell within an area of 10 square miles (26 km²), within which 10 million shells were fired, equaling 1.35 million tons of steel. Six villages in the sector were completely destroyed and never rebuilt, including Fleury, on the Meuse heights between Fort Douaumont and Fort Souville, which changed hands sixteen times during the battle.

The Somme

Of all the other campaigns of 1916, the battle of the Somme (July 1–November 18), initiated by the Allies in the northern sector of the Western front, 120 miles (195 km) west-northwest of Verdun, had the most immediate effect on the ability of the Germans to persist in following Falkenhayn's strategy. Planning for the offensive had begun the previous December, led by Sir Douglas Haig, who succeeded Sir John French as commander of the BEF shortly after the Chantilly conference. The force at his disposal bore little resemblance to the British Army of 1914. War secretary Lord Kitchener, who died a month before the action began on the Somme (on a mission to Russia, when his ship struck a mine), had raised 2.5 million volunteers since the war began; when the initial flood of enlistees declined to a trickle, Parliament passed the Military Service Act (January 27, 1916) establishing conscription. The expanded force included a regular army of twelve divisions, backed by thirty of Kitchener's "New Army" divisions and, eventually, sixty divisions of reserves from the Territorial Force. After the original BEF was subdivided into the First and Second armies in December 1914, the Third Army (General Sir Edmund Allenby) was created in October 1915 and Fourth Army (General Sir Henry Rawlinson) in February 1916. British industry provided the growing force with a quality and quantity of weaponry, munitions, and supplies that were the envy of the other Allies, though not without glitches (most notably the significant number of "dud" shells that failed to explode when fired at the Somme). The rapid expansion of the army also exacerbated the shortage of competent leadership at all levels, diluting a pool of qualified officers already thin because Britain's prewar regular army had been so small, and so many officers were lost in the first months of the war.

Haig's plan focused on the point where the Somme, flowing from east to west, toward the Seine, crossed the north-south lines of the opposing armies, near the juncture of the British and French sectors of the front. The main thrust of the British-led advance would come north of the river, on either side of an old Roman road built on a straight line from Albert 12 miles (19 km) northeastward to Bapaume. Owing to Falkenhayn's emphasis on Verdun, the Allies enjoyed a tremendous initial superiority over the German forces opposing them: the ten divisions of the Second Army (now under General Fritz von Below), backed by just 844 guns, which enjoyed the sole advantage of being dug-in along a low, wooded ridge dotted with abandoned villages they had fortified. The attacking force consisted of the fifteen divisions of Rawlinson's Fourth Army, supported on their left (northern) flank by two divisions from Allenby's Third Army and, on their right (south), by the eleven divisions of the French Sixth Army (General Marie Émile Fayolle). Allied artillery included around 3,000 guns, half British, half French, including 400 heavy guns, giving them an advantage in that category for the first time in a major battle. As at Verdun, air superiority gave the Allies an advantage in artillery spotting, and enabled them to disrupt German artillery spotting, at least for the first two months of the battle. The main weakness of the attackers stemmed from their competing visions of how to exploit these advantages. Haig, a former cavalryman, envisaged artillery and infantry creating a deep breach in the enemy front that would be exploited by cavalry, restoring movement to the campaign and culminating in a decisive encounter battle somewhere in the German rear. Rawlinson, in contrast, believed British artillery and infantry could not overcome more than one enemy trench line at a time, leaving no opening for the cavalry, and recognized that his troops lacked the skill and training to win an encounter battle with the Germans. He advocated a "bite and hold" approach, consolidating hard-won gains piecemeal in a methodical campaign to push the enemy back. These competing visions led to a fateful compromise: while Rawlinson, indeed, intended to "bite and hold" the first German trench line, the preparatory shelling would be dispersed over all three German trench lines, to prepare for the breach in depth that Haig wanted.

The preliminary bombardment began on June 24 and continued until the infantry assault on the morning of July 1, by which time 12,000 tons of shells, some 1.7 million rounds, had been fired. Supplementing the efforts of the artillery, the British attempted the greatest mining effort of the war thus far, digging seventeen tunnels under the first line of German trenches and packing some of them with as much as 20 tons of explosives, all of which were detonated at the start of the battle. The Germans had never experienced an assault of such ferocity (see Box 7.1) but they recovered quickly, as the dispersed bombardment failed to destroy their deeper dugouts and fortified machine-gun emplacements, and left much of their wire intact. Meanwhile, the gaps in the front created by the mining operations were often impassible. British troops were supposed to advance under a creeping barrage, but the gap between the barrage line and the first line of infantry was too great for the tactic to work as designed. All of these factors combined to make July 1, 1916, the bloodiest day in the history of the British Army. Of their seventeen divisions, sixteen saw action, suffering a staggering 57,470 casualties including 19,240 men killed, most of them by machine-gun fire. The six German divisions opposing them lost 8,000 men, including 2,200 prisoners. Meanwhile, to their south, along the banks of the Somme, the eleven divisions of the French Sixth Army fared much better against the four German divisions they faced, mostly because Fayolle, a former artillery instructor at the École de guerre, had insisted upon a preliminary

Box 7.1 *"Gigantic forces of destruction"*

Lieutenant Alfred Dambitsch comments on the new methods and technologies employed by the British and French armies against the Germans at the Battle of the Somme:

In respect to new methods and machines, the present French and British offensive is the last word. The aim of any offensive in modern warfare is the destruction of the enemy. This is the object of the present offensive, the idea being to enclose us in a tactical ring by simultaneous bombardment with long-range guns from the front and the rear. Accordingly the greedy beast began eating at the back lines of the German front. First of all our third and second trenches were incessantly bombarded, mostly by heavy artillery, of which the enemy had concentrated unprecedented masses in the sector of attack. It was dugouts which had to be battered down, so that at the moment of assault all the defenders, except a few survivors, and all the machine guns might be buried. Our second and third trenches were bombarded in order to prevent our bringing up reserves.

... The battering down of our advanced trenches was almost exclusively left to the heavy artillery and trench mortars, especially the latter. The French have made great improvements in this weapon lately. For the destruction of our trenches they exclusively employed those of the heaviest caliber, and they now throw their mines with greater accuracy and over longer ranges than formerly. Opposite my company no fewer than six mortars were placed. They were worked uninterruptedly, throwing hundreds of aerial torpedoes on our position from the first to the third trenches. They tore up our wire obstacles from the ground, poles and all, and threw them all over the place, crushing the dugouts if they fell on them, and damaging the trenches. In a very short time great portions of our trenches had been flattened out, partly burying their occupants. This fire lasted for seven days, and finally there came a gas attack, also of an improved kind.

The deepest impression left on me was not a feeling of horror and terror in face of these gigantic forces of destruction, but an unceasing admiration for my own men. Young recruits who had just come into the field from home, fresh twenty-year-old boys, behaved in this catastrophic plowing and thundering as if they had spent all their life in such surroundings, and it is partly thanks to them that the older married men also stood the test so well.

Source: firstworldwar.com/diaries/somme_dambitsch.htm.

shelling focused on the enemy's forward trenches. *"Magnifique préparation,"* he noted in his diary, resulting in the near-total destruction of the first line of German defenses in his sector.[6] His methodical advance continued for several days, pushing forward as far as 6 miles (10 km) in some places, taking 12,000 prisoners and 70 guns before slowing because of the British failure to the north.

Falkenhayn soon reinforced Below with seven divisions from the German reserve, while Haig committed the British Reserve Army (General Sir Hubert Gough), soon renamed the Fifth Army, to which he transferred the northern half of the Fourth Army, seven of Rawlinson's fifteen divisions. The Reserve Army had been formed to exploit the gap Haig had hoped would open in the enemy lines. Instead, these troops now took over the sector of the battlefield on Rawlinson's left. By July 13 the British had lost another 25,000 men, while securing the first line of German trenches along their 18-mile (29-km) sector of the battlefield. Below's Second Army, meanwhile, lost men at less than half the British rate, but by July 10 had still registered 40,200 killed, wounded, missing, or taken prisoner, far more than the Germans had lost in the first ten days at Verdun. As Falkenhayn continued to reinforce the sector, stripping troops from the German Sixth Army to the north and artillery from Verdun, he reassigned Below to command a reconstituted First Army north of the Somme, including some of his former troops bolstered by reserves, while General Max von Gallwitz (only recently brought to Verdun from Macedonia) took command of what remained of the Second Army, on Below's left, straddling the Somme. In late August Crown Prince Rupprecht of Bavaria assumed the role of group commander for both armies.

Meanwhile, Haig resolved to keep the Germans occupied in as many places as possible, to prevent Falkenhayn from redeploying troops to the Somme. The largest of his complementary attacks, the battle of Fromelles (July 19–20) on the Artois sector, 50 miles (80 km) north of the Somme, included the first use of Australian troops on the Western front and had the distinction of being Australia's costliest 24 hours of the war, with over 5,500 casualties, many more than fell on any single day at Gallipoli. Australians serving in Gough's Reserve Army joined the action at the Somme four days after the engagement at Fromelles, seizing Pozieres on the Albert–Bapaume road. By then, the rest of the empire had already begun to make its contribution. One of Haig's two divisions of Indian cavalry saw action as early as July 14, the same day that a South African brigade made its debut. The Canadians (see Box 7.2) and New Zealanders saw their first major action on September 15. Ultimately the 53 infantry divisions Haig commanded at the Somme included four from Australia, four from Canada, and one from New Zealand. The South African infantry brigade served in a British division, as did a regiment from Newfoundland (not a Canadian province until 1949) which was among the units decimated on the first day of the battle. The only Indians to see action at the Somme were cavalrymen, as the BEF's two Indian infantry divisions had been redeployed to the Middle East late in 1915.

After the Germans called off their offensive at Verdun, Joffre expanded the battle at the Somme by having the French Tenth Army (General Joseph Micheler) join the action south of the river, on the right of Fayolle's Sixth Army. Shortly thereafter, on September 15, the British Fourth Army launched the most robust Allied attack since July 1. Following a three-day shelling that expended more than 800,000 rounds, Rawlinson used tanks to spearhead the offensive by fifteen divisions on the front opposite Flers and Courcelette. The 28-ton Mark I tanks, "land battleships" based on a concept promoted by Winston Churchill earlier in the war, lumbered forward at 3mph (5km/h) and helped push the Germans back over half a mile (1 km) along a sector 6 miles (10 km) wide, modest gains but still the greatest since the first day of the battle. British troops captured Flers, the Canadians took Courcelette, and German casualties included 4,000

Box 7.2 A Canadian infantryman at the Somme

Excerpt from a letter by Private William H. Gilday, 82nd Battalion, Canadian infantry, to his sister, describing his experiences at the battle of the Somme:

We went into the front line one night. Fritz shelled us as we were going in and of course got a few of our men. We remained in the trench until morning without being bothered much, and then the snipers got busy. I believe if you had put a nickel up just above the parapet so they could see it, they would sure knock it down.

About noon that day we got the order to go over the top. So over we went. I know you think that they run, holler, yell and such like, but that is not the case. At least, it was not so on that occasion, for we walked very grim and quiet. I can speak only for myself, for until I struck the barbed wire, my mind simply stood still. I did not think of anything at all. Something hit me on the leg and tore my pants. Then my mind worked overtime. The noise was maddening, bullets whizzed by me singing their death song, shrapnels were screaming overhead and shells were bursting in every direction. The air was filled with iron and lead and practically all my comrades fell.

I cannot for the life of me imagine how I happened to escape. I don't know how anyone could have survived it. However, several others as well as myself reached the German trenches, but there were only two Huns in that part. We had no officers and only a wounded sergeant and eight men; so not knowing what to do, held that end, for the men on our left never reached the trench. I stayed in there for hours, shivering with fear and expecting every minute to be the next. That afternoon I got into another trench with some more men and a few officers. Near midnight we were again ordered to go over the top. Once again I succeeded in getting safely across, but as before, there were only a few Huns to greet us. They ran leaving everything, even their rifles …

We were in three days and three nights and I had some pretty narrow shaves. God sure made a good job of taking care of me, for I felt rather sick. I wish I could tell you everything that happened, but you would never realize how things are. I got a bullet right through my left breast pocket, and it passed through my paybook and some photos. I am enclosing one of the photos that was pierced, so you can keep it as a souvenir. The pellet never touched me.

The pierced photograph was of Gilday's brother, Clem, of the Canadian Engineers, who was killed in action in France later that month.

Source: First published in the *Calgary Daily Herald*, November 6, 1916, available at www .canadiangreatwarproject.com/transcripts /transcriptDisplay.asp?Type=L&transNo=27.

---

prisoners. Of the forty-nine tanks sent from Britain to France for the offensive only thirty-two made it to the front; of these, just nine advanced ahead of the infantry as planned, while another nine crossed no man's land to engage the enemy but could not keep up with the infantry. Mechanical problems accounted for most of the attrition, yet Haig recognized the value of the new invention, continued to use tanks sporadically during the last weeks of the battle, and asked the War Office for a thousand more.

At the time, the deployment of the first tanks paled into insignificance compared to the concurrent restoration of German air superiority thanks to the Albatros D2, the aircraft that the "Red Baron," Manfred von Richtofen, flew over the Somme battlefield, where he recorded the first of his eighty kills. In late September Crown Prince Rupprecht remarked that "the fact that our flyers are getting the upper hand is of prime advantage to our artillery."[7] From then until the end of the battle seven weeks later, the Allies were no longer able to disrupt German aerial artillery spotting or protect their own spotters from the enemy. This disadvantage contributed to the ineffectiveness of Haig's armies in their attempts, at Joffre's urging, to mount further attacks on the Somme after the French began their counteroffensive at Verdun in mid-October.

The action at the Somme finally ended on November 18, a month before Verdun. While it had been primarily a British battle, their fifty-three divisions had been joined by forty-four French divisions, many of which also rotated through Verdun. Against them, the Germans ultimately committed fifty divisions of their own, two more than saw action at Verdun. The human toll at the Somme exceeded the losses in the much longer battle at Verdun: 622,000 Allied casualties (420,000 British and Imperial, 202,000 French), including 146,000 killed or missing, against German losses of 429,000, including 164,000 killed or missing.

The Italian Front: Conrad's Tyrol Gamble

By the end of 1915 the Austro-Hungarian Army had lost 3.2 million men killed, wounded, or taken prisoner. Nevertheless, in January 1916, while Kövess and the Third Army were conquering Montenegro, the makeshift Seventh Army (General Karl Pflanzer-Baltin) withstood a Russian attack on the southern sector of an Eastern front that had been relatively quiet since September 1915; thereafter, it appeared unlikely Russia would attempt another major offensive anytime soon. By March, fresh conscripts and convalesced wounded men had restored the army's strength to 2.3 million, including 900,000 combat-effective troops. Together, these factors restored Conrad's confidence that he could win a victory without German help, by redeploying some of his best troops from the Eastern front for action against Italy. Conrad's plan called for fourteen divisions to attack out of the Tyrol salient, hooking to the south and east toward Venice and the Adriatic. Such a stroke would isolate the main body of Cadorna's army, deployed in northeast Italy, and leave the rest of the Italian peninsula virtually defenseless. If it succeeded, it would likely knock Italy out of the war. The build-up itself posed the main obstacle, as no army in history had attempted an offensive in the Alps involving so many troops. Because almost all of Dankl's existing Alpine forces were second- and third-line units suitable only to stand on the defensive, six of the divisions had to be brought in from the Eastern front and seven from either Boroević's Fifth Army on the Isonzo or the Balkans. Owing to the physical limitations of the Austrian rail network in the Alps (which could bring just forty-five trains per day into the Tyrol), the 1,450 trains needed to carry the troops and their supplies would take longer than normal to get them into place, making secrecy problematic.

An unusually mild winter through February led Conrad to believe he could launch the offensive in early April, but heavy snows after March 1 disrupted his plans, cutting the daily number of trains in half and hampering both the deployment of troops and the placement of artillery for the preliminary bombardment. In early April, when Conrad had hoped to attack, 8 feet (2.4 m) of snow blanketed the staging areas, and soldiers already at the front were issued snow shovels to clear the way. Thousands of troops exhausted themselves on such duty, and avalanches alone killed 600 men. Meanwhile, the Austro-Hungarian concentration in the Alps became common knowledge. On April 13 Italian and French newspapers reported relatively accurate figures of the build-up; by then, Cadorna had started to shift troops to the Italian First Army (General Roberto Brusati) on the Tyrol frontier, away from the Second and Third armies in the Isonzo sector, which had been quiet all winter except for the brief, inconclusive fifth battle of the Isonzo (March 9–17). Conrad had hoped for a decisive 2:1 advantage in the Tyrol sector, but by the start of the offensive Brusati had been reinforced to 114,000 troops backed by 850 guns, against the 157,000 men and 1,200 guns Conrad mustered for the Austro-Hungarian side. Thus, the concentration of fourteen divisions in the Tyrol did not give him the local numerical superiority he had hoped for, but at the same time had seriously weakened the Central Powers on the Eastern front as well as the Austro-Hungarian lines on the Isonzo, where transfers to the Alps reduced Boroević's Fifth Army to just 195,000 men, against 403,000 in the Italian Second and Third armies.

Even without German involvement, a command-and-control controversy plagued the operation from the start. Conrad divided his troops between Dankl's new Eleventh Army (nine divisions) and a new iteration of the Third Army (five divisions) under its old commander, Kövess, transferred from Montenegro. Dankl and Kövess were trusted protégés of Conrad, but because he remained at AOK headquarters in Teschen throughout the operation, they took orders from General Alfred Krauss, chief-of-staff at Archduke Eugen's Italian front headquarters in Marburg. Krauss numbered among Conrad's leading critics and did not get along with either Dankl or Kövess. Dankl resented having the heir to the throne, Archduke Charles, as one of his corps commanders, all the more so because Krauss skewed the battle plan to ensure local victory for Charles' XX Corps, leaving the rest of Dankl's army short of artillery. Falkenhayn, belatedly informed of the upcoming offensive, suggested that the fourteen divisions involved would better serve the cause of the Central Powers at Verdun. This proposal only made Conrad all the more determined to proceed alone against the Italians, reasoning that regardless of the outcome, at least the bloodletting would come in pursuit of Austro-Hungarian, not German, objectives. The revised starting date of May 15 resulted from a projection of the daily rate of snow melt down to 8 inches (20 cm), according to conventional wisdom, the maximum depth in which infantry could fight.

Dankl's Eleventh Army occupied the western sector of the Tyrol front and had the most ambitious objectives. His main thrust was to go southeastward from Rovereto through the Vallarsa to Schio and, ultimately, to Vicenza. On the left (eastern) flank of his army, Archduke Charles' XX Corps received the task of taking Arsiero. Farther to the northeast, one wing of Kövess' smaller Third Army was to advance through the Val d'Assa from Verle toward Asiago, while the other penetrated as deep as possible into the Val Sugana, along the Brenta River toward Bassano.

The bitter divisions among the Austro-Hungarian generals spilled over from the planning stage into the operation itself. While Dankl fumed, Archduke Charles' XX Corps plodded slowly toward its objectives even though it faced lighter opposition and enjoyed better artillery support than any other formation. On May 29, XX Corps took Arsiero and the III Corps of Kövess' Third Army took Asiago. By the end of the month the offensive had captured 40,000 Italians and 380 of their guns, but success in the center stood in sharp contrast to the failure on both flanks. By early June the main body of Dankl's army remained stuck in the Vallarsa to the west, while on the northeastern end of the sector, the main body of Kövess' Third Army had stalled in the Val Sugana. In terms of territory occupied, the offensive reached its high-water mark on June 15, long after the overall plan had clearly failed. On June 24–26, the Third and Eleventh armies pulled back to more defendable positions, abandoning both Arsiero and Asiago. At its deepest point the offensive had pushed the Italians back only 15 miles (24 km), and after the retreat, the greatest secured gain anywhere along the front was just 12 miles (19 km). Austro-Hungarian losses (killed, wounded, sick, missing, and prisoners lost) amounted to 43,000 men, compared with 76,000 for the Italians. On the Western front similar gains at such a cost would have been acceptable, but Conrad and the AOK had expected victory, and the failure to break through had a devastating effect on the morale of the commanding generals as well as the troops involved. Archduke Eugen sacked Dankl, who joined Conrad in blaming the failure of the offensive on Krauss, but Krauss and Archduke Charles held Conrad accountable on the grounds that the general idea of pushing fourteen divisions through the Alps into Italy failed to account for basic realities of geography.

The Eastern Front: Brusilov's Steamroller

As the fighting stalemated on the Italian front, the focus shifted back to the east. Just as the French, earlier in the year, had pressured the Russians to act against the Germans to relieve the pressure on Verdun, the Italians begged them to distract Austria-Hungary from the Tyrol offensive. An earlier attempt to respond to the French pleas had led to Russia's worst defeat of the war thus far, after Nicholas II authorized a late winter attack by elements of the Northwest army group (General Aleksei Kuropatkin) and Western army group (General Aleksei Evert) northwest of Minsk, against the German Tenth Army (General Hermann von Eichhorn). The battle of Lake Naroch (March 18–April 14) ended in disaster for the Russians, who attacked with a numerical advantage of nearly 5:1 (350,000 to 75,000), yet suffered five times as many casualties as the Germans (100,000 to 20,000) despite preparing the battlefield with their heaviest artillery bombardment of the war thus far. Afterward Evert and Kuropatkin advocated a defensive stand for the rest of 1916, citing Russia's shortages in artillery and shells. These losses would be difficult to replace, as by 1916 Russian munitions factories supplied just one-third of the army's shells and one-third of its bullets, and the Western Allies, already strapped by the demands of their own armies, struggled to make up the difference.

In the wake of the debacle at Lake Naroch, the tsar gave command of the Southwest army group to General Aleksei Brusilov, whose Eighth Army had distinguished itself as the best of the Russian armies in the war thus far. Brusilov immediately called for a major spring offensive all along the front. Over the weeks that followed, he persuaded the tsar to allow him to open the offensive with an attack on the Austro-Hungarian sector of the front opposite his own army group, after which the armies under Evert and Kuropatkin would join him in a general advance. Brusilov's group – the Seventh, Eighth, Ninth, and Eleventh armies – included forty divisions of infantry and fifteen of cavalry, roughly 650,000 men in all. By the start of the offensive they were reasonably well armed, albeit with an eclectic mix of weaponry and munitions. Thousands of Brusilov's men carried Japanese rifles imported via the Trans-Siberian Railway, and two corps went into battle with Austro-Hungarian rifles captured in 1915. His artillery included 1,938 guns, almost 100 more than the enemy armies opposing them, though all but 168 were light field guns. His modest stockpile of munitions included gas shells imported from the Western Allies.

On June 4 the "Brusilov offensive" began, targeting a sector of the enemy lines in which Falkenhayn's protégé Linsingen commanded an army group consisting of the Austro-Hungarian First, Second, Fourth, and Seventh armies, along with the mixed Austro-German *Südarmee*. Since the end of the previous summer's action, Falkenhayn had removed eighteen divisions from the sector and Conrad six. While these redeployments had bolstered their offensives on other fronts, the five armies were left with fewer men overall (470,000 Austro-Hungarian troops in thirty-seven divisions of infantry and eleven of cavalry, along with 30,000 Germans in two infantry divisions) than Brusilov's four. The AOK, focused on the action in the Alps, continued to dismiss the possibility of a Russian offensive right up to the day it was launched, discounting reports of enemy sappers digging new forward trenches closer to Austro-Hungarian lines. Brusilov ordered the digging to prepare for a "Joffre attack," imitating the tactic used by the French at the second battle of Champagne the previous autumn. He sent his armies forward after an intense barrage kept brief by the limitations of his own artillery. Far from suffering the consequences, the Russians benefited from having not signaled where the attacks could be expected or churned up the ground the attacking infantry would have to cross. The combination of surprise and speed ensured a decisive breakthrough.

The Russians made their greatest initial gains at the two ends of Brusilov's sector. In the south, the Ninth Army pushed Pflanzer-Baltin's Seventh Army back to the foothills of the Carpathians, inflicting casualties of 57 percent (most of them killed or wounded) in the first two weeks of the fighting. On June 18, the Russians took Czernowitz (see Box 7.3), the only large city to change hands as a result of the offensive. In the north, the Eighth Army routed Archduke Joseph Ferdinand's Fourth Army, which suffered losses of 54 percent (most of them taken prisoner or deserted) and ceased to be an effective fighting force. Some of the front-line units the Russians overran suffered catastrophic losses. On a single day, June 5, 77 percent of the men of the 1st (Vienna) Reserve Regiment were killed in action. As in the Eastern front battles of 1915, Austria-Hungary's Czech troops proved to be particularly unreliable, with the 8th (Moravian) Infantry Regiment deserting en masse. The collapse of the Fourth Army opened a gap in the front 13 miles (20 km) wide, through which Brusilov's troops quickly advanced 47 miles (75 km) to the west. Although the center of the breach, at Lutsk in the western Ukraine, was over 300 miles (480 km) east of Teschen, the Russian breakthrough caused a panic at the AOK. Conrad advised his wife to leave for Vienna because "the situation is too dangerous."[8]

On June 8, Conrad went to Berlin to determine how to limit the damage. Even though Falkenhayn had removed three times as many divisions as Conrad from the threatened sector, the front that had collapsed was Austro-Hungarian and the troops taken from it most recently had been the six divisions Conrad sent to the Tyrol. Thus, the disaster strengthened Falkenhayn's already strong hand, overshadowing his own risky decision to weaken the German presence not just south of the Pripet Marshes, but all along the Eastern front. Indeed, at the time of Brusilov's attack, the army groups of Evert and Kuropatkin outnumbered the German armies standing opposite them by a staggering 750,000 men, but Falkenhayn had gambled that, given the outcome of the battle of Lake Naroch in March, the same Russian generals would not attack again regardless of their numerical superiority. He was right. Even though the Russian plan called for the ninety divisions of Evert and Kuropatkin to join Brusilov in a general offensive, by mid-June the tsar's chief-of-staff, Alekseev, had heard nothing but excuses from them. He finally gave part of Evert's group (the Third Army) to Brusilov along with a new Guards Army and all available reinforcements and supplies. Thus, the behavior of the tsar's generals served only to focus even more of Russia's resources against Austria-Hungary rather than Germany, increasing Conrad's woes and further weakening him vis-à-vis Falkenhayn. To get the Germans to send troops to the southern sector of the Eastern front, he had to call off his offensive against Italy and transfer troops of his own back to the east, ultimately eight divisions, along with Kövess and the headquarters of the Third Army. Conrad also accepted greater German control over the Austro-Hungarian forces deployed against Russia, as German staff officers were attached to

Box 7.3 "For the third time our poor villages were burning"

Excerpt from an anonymous Polish landowner's account of the Brusilov offensive (June), as experienced from the Austro-Hungarian side of the front near Czernowitz:

During the night of June 12th–13th terrific artillery fire was heard in the town [Czernowitz]. Somewhere near a battle was raging. For the third or fourth time since the beginning of the war we were passing through that experience. I went to the army command to ask advice. A staff-captain had just arrived with news from the front. The Austrian troops were resisting. Still, after the front between the Dniester and Pruth had once been broken there was no other natural line for resistance … "How long can we hold out?" was my question. The old general looked at me and answered: "Only our rearguards are now engaged; our forces are gathering a few miles from here. If our flank near Horodenka holds out overnight we shall not evacuate the town."

I returned to Sniatyn. Small groups of inhabitants were standing about the streets, commenting on the news. Artillery and ammunition were at full speed passing through the town for the front. A few regiments of infantry marched through at night. The horizon was red with the glow of fires. For the third time our poor villages were burning. Whatever had survived previous battles was now given up to the flames. Homeless refugees, evacuated from the threatened villages, were passing with their poor, worn-out horses and their cows – all their remaining wealth. In perfect silence; no one complained;

it had to be. Mysterious cavalry patrols and dispatch-riders were riding through the streets. No one slept that night. In the morning the first military transports passed through the town. The retreat had begun. Questions were asked. The Magyar soldiers quietly smoked their pipes; there was no way for us of understanding one another. Only one of them, who knew a few German words, explained, "Russen, stark, stark, Masse" (Russians, strong, strong, a great mass).

… Suddenly the gun-fire stopped and the expert ear could catch the rattling of machine guns. The decisive attack had begun. All a-strain, we were awaiting news. Some soldiers appeared round the corner of the road, slightly wounded. Then a panic began. Some one had come from a neighboring village reporting that he had seen Cossacks. Soon refugees from the villages outside were streaming through the town. General confusion. Children were crying, women sobbing. A mass flight began. Again cavalry and dispatch-riders. Then a drum was heard in the square. It was officially given out that the situation was extremely grave and that whoever wished to leave the town had better do so immediately. We had to go. As I was mounting the carriage I perceived in the distance, near the wood on the hill, a few horsemen with long lances – Cossacks from Kuban. They were slowly emerging from the forest and approaching the town. "Drive ahead!" I shouted to the coachman.

Source: Charles F. Horne, ed., *Source Records of the Great War*, vol. 4 (Indianapolis: The American Legion, 1931), 201–02.

each of the Austro-Hungarian armies in Linsingen's army group. Mackensen's former chief-of-staff, Seeckt, became chief-of-staff of Pflanzer-Baltin's Seventh Army before assuming the same role, in July, with a new mixed Austro-German Twelfth Army under Archduke Charles, promoted from his corps command in the Alps after the end of the Tyrol offensive.

By June 14, the first four divisions of German reinforcements reached the endangered sector of the front, where they led Linsingen's efforts to rally the remnants of the Austro-Hungarian Fourth Army (now under General Karl von Terztyanszky) and seal the worst of the breaches in the line. Falkenhayn intended for the additional German troops to counterattack and return the front to the line of June 4, but the reinforcements could not offset the large number of Austro-Hungarian casualties, deserters, and prisoners lost, and with the onset of the Anglo-French offensive at the Somme on July 1, no more would be coming. By the end of the first week of July, the Central Powers had just 421,000 troops to counter Brusilov's reinforced strength of 711,000, odds that made merely stopping his steamroller a significant victory. For the next two and a half months, the opposing armies launched indecisive attacks and counterattacks. On Brusilov's southern flank, Russian troops made it to the crest of the Carpathians in early August before being pushed back, while on the northern flank, his repeated attempts to break through to the eastern Polish railway junction at Kovel generated casualties far out of proportion to the strategic significance of the objective. As the campaign continued, Brusilov reverted to fighting the way he had in 1914 and 1915, better than most other Russian generals but without the tactical ingenuity that had made the initial phase of his offensive so successful. Unimaginative frontal assaults without sufficient artillery support generated enormous Russian casualties, which by mid-summer surpassed those of the Central Powers.

To stop the Brusilov offensive, Falkenhayn ultimately redeployed eighteen German divisions (eight from the Western front, eight from elsewhere on the Eastern front, and two from Macedonia) and also arranged for two Turkish divisions to be sent to the front via Bulgaria, occupied Serbia, and Hungary. By the time the tsar, on September 21, ordered an end to offensive operations, the Russian armies along the front south of the Pripet Marshes stood at least 20 miles (32 km) and in some places 50 miles (80 km) west of their lines of June 4. Aside from the Russian conquest (subsequently lost) of almost all of Austrian Galicia in September and October of 1914, Brusilov's offensive gained and secured more ground than any Allied offensive of the war thus far. Overall, during the three and a half months of fighting, some 370,000 Austro-Hungarian troops had been killed or wounded, with another 380,000 taken prisoner. In achieving the victory, Brusilov lost a million men (including 58,000 to desertion) and pushed his army to the brink of mutiny. Thus, Brusilov's offensive was a watershed for both sides, leaving Austria-Hungary unable to continue functioning as an autonomous military power and Russia with an army ripe for revolution.[9]

The debacle on the Eastern front contributed to William II's decision to sack Falkenhayn on August 29, but Conrad, as the weaker ally (and the one whose sector of the front had collapsed), bore the brunt of the criticism. Francis Joseph and nominal AOK head Archduke Frederick had both questioned the wisdom of weakening the defenses against Russia for the sake of the offensive against Italy, and as recently as June

1, Conrad had assured the emperor that the Eastern front would hold. As Brusilov's troops continued to push westward, the civilian leaders of Austria-Hungary lost confidence in Conrad to such an extent that they began to trust the Germans more than they trusted him. Burián and the foreign ministry staff called for all future Austro-Hungarian offensives to be undertaken only after consultation with the Germans. Building upon the command concessions Conrad had made in the first week of Brusilov's offensive, on July 18 Hindenburg and *OberOst* received command of all Austro-Hungarian forces north of Lemberg. At the same time Archduke Charles received titular command of the front south of Lemberg but with Seeckt remaining as his chief-of-staff, an arrangement that made Seeckt the de facto commander of the sector. With his own government abandoning him, Conrad could not resist the humiliating German takeover. Afterward his old friend, jurist and politician Josef Redlich, remarked that "Conrad remains *pro forma* in Teschen, but he has nothing more to say."[10]

The Balkan Front: Romania Enters the War

In the summer of 1914 Romanian nationalists had clamored for war against Austria-Hungary and the annexation of the Habsburg province of Transylvania, home to 3 million ethnic Romanians. The government of King Carol I, a Hohenzollern cousin of William II, kept Romania neutral, but the country's slow drift toward the Allies began in October 1914, when Carol died, leaving the throne to his more opportunistic nephew, Ferdinand I. As the war stalemated, Ferdinand's pragmatic prime minister, Ion Bratianu, exploited Romania's neutrality to the fullest, negotiating with both sides for the best terms. The Romanians still feared Russia more than they wanted Transylvania, but in offering them the opportunity to take the Habsburg province the Allies did much better than the Central Powers, who could promise only the predominantly Romanian Russian province of Bessarabia (Moldova). Finally, over the summer of 1916, the early success of the Brusilov offensive and the concurrent bullying of Greece by the Allies (see section below) made Bratianu anxious about Romania's fate if it did not join them. Yet Bratianu drove a hard bargain, insisting that Sarrail's "Army of the Orient" launch an offensive against Bulgaria from the Salonika pocket as a precondition to a Romanian offensive into Transylvania. Hard pressed on the Western front, the French and British could not spare the troops to reinforce their Salonika army until mid-August, and thus the Romanians refused to formalize their commitment to the Allies until that time. In the Treaty of Bucharest (August 17, 1916) the Allies promised Romania extensive territorial gains at the expense of Austria-Hungary – Transylvania, Banat, and Bukovina – in exchange for the Romanian invasion of Transylvania. In addition to the Anglo-French promise to attack Bulgaria from the Salonika pocket, the Russians pledged to continue Brusilov's offensive and to deploy three divisions along the Black Sea, south of the mouth of the Danube, to prevent Bulgaria from retaking southern Dobruja, which it had ceded to Romania at the end of the Second Balkan War. On August 27, Romania declared war on Austria-Hungary (Map 7.1).

Romania's entry into the war reopened a third Allied front against the Dual Monarchy, one much longer (at roughly 400 miles or 645 km) than the Italian front. The Allies placed high hopes in Romania, as they had in Italy fifteen months earlier, assuming the added burden would break Austria-Hungary. The need for still more troops to cover yet another front further exposed the folly of Falkenhayn's strategy of attrition on the Western front. For the second time in less than three months, Germany would have to save Austria-Hungary from disaster, only this time Conrad could spare no troops of

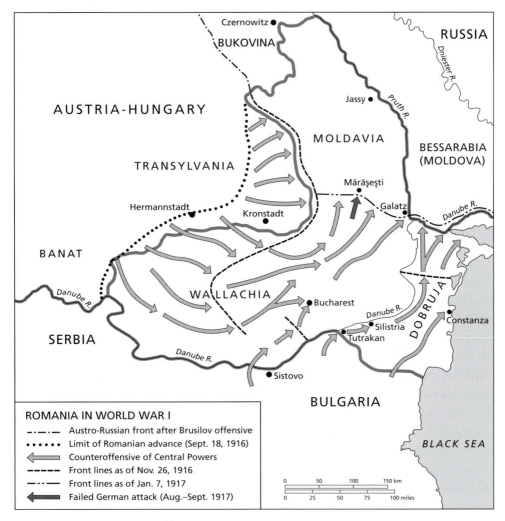

Map 7.1 Romania in World War I

his own to help meet the new threat. He had already withdrawn more than half of the manpower from the Tyrol to reinforce the Eastern front; meanwhile, along the Isonzo, Boroević's Fifth Army was down to nine divisions (against Cadorna's twenty-two) and had just lost Gorizia in the sixth battle of the Isonzo (August 6–17), absorbing another 40,000 casualties. Conrad assigned General Arthur Arz von Straussenberg to defend Transylvania with a reconstituted First Army initially consisting of just one and a half regular divisions supplemented by local third-line reserves (*Landsturm*) and customs police, 34,000 men in all, against a Romanian invading force more than ten times larger.

Under the circumstances, Romania could be defeated only through the joint effort of all four Central Powers, with the sort of close cooperation that would be possible only under a unified command. Falkenhayn, who had long advocated a unified Central Powers command, would have no role in it. Romania's decision to join the Allies did not surprise him but discredited him nonetheless, because he had assured William II that it would not happen for at least another month, after the predominantly agrarian country had completed its harvest. For the emperor, this crucial miscalculation was the last straw. On August 29, he replaced Falkenhayn with Hindenburg (Figure 7.1(a)), who brought Ludendorff (Figure 7.1(b)) with him from *OberOst* to serve as his chief-of-staff at the OHL. Prince Leopold of Bavaria replaced Hindenburg on the Eastern front, but his chief-of-staff, General Max Hoffmann (formerly *OberOst*'s third-in-command, after Hindenburg and Ludendorff), served as de facto commander. During September the Central Powers ratified agreements making the German emperor their supreme allied commander, a concession that gave Hindenburg and Ludendorff control over the Austro-Hungarian, Bulgarian, and Ottoman armed forces. A secret annex to the agreement, included at Conrad's insistence, obligated the Germans to consult Francis Joseph on matters related to the "territorial integrity" of the Dual Monarchy.

Romania, a country of 8 million with a regular army of 160,000 men, mobilized 440,000 for combat units including twenty-three infantry divisions grouped into four armies. The Allied war plan called for three of the armies to invade Transylvania: the First Army and Second Army from the south, out of Wallachia, and the Fourth Army from the east, out of Moldavia. The Third Army (General Alexandru Averescu) stood on the defensive along the Danube in the Dobruja basin, Romania's outlet to the Black Sea, backed by the Russian "Dobruja Detachment" (General Andrei M. Zaionchkovsky) consisting of three Russian divisions and a division of ethnic Serb deserters from Bosnian and Croatian regiments of the Austro-Hungarian Army. Further deterring a Bulgarian invasion of Romania, Sarrail's force in the Salonika pocket, reinforced to include 320,000 men in twenty divisions (six French, six British, six Serbian, one Italian, and one Russian) (Figure 7.2), would attack the Bulgarians in Macedonia. The Central Powers countered with a plan calling for Arz's First Army to push the Romanian Fourth Army back into Moldavia, while a reconstituted German Ninth Army counterattacked against the First and Second armies and advanced on Bucharest.

Figure 7.1 (a) Hindenburg and (b) Ludendorff

Field Marshal Paul von Hindenburg (1847–1934) and General Erich Ludendorff (1865–1939) shared responsibility for the same victories and defeats, though public attention focused on Hindenburg, while those who knew better credited Ludendorff with being the brains behind the old field marshal. Called out of retirement in August 1914 to lead the Eighth Army in East Prussia, Hindenburg from the start benefited from the expertise of Ludendorff, who in the war's first days had masterminded the reduction of the Belgian fortresses at Liège. Their victory at Tannenberg catapulted them to national fame, and within months they became commander and chief-of-staff for the German Eastern front. In August 1916, the sacking of Falkenhayn led to the elevation of Hindenburg to head of the OHL, with Ludendorff once again following as his chief-of-staff. Thereafter, they functioned as de facto rulers of Germany, having their way in every significant policy decision and charting the course that led to their country's defeat.

Hindenburg and Ludendorff assigned the Ninth Army to Falkenhayn, thus giving him the opportunity to redeem his reputation in the field. Meanwhile, Mackensen received command of a "Danube Army" in northern Bulgaria, including the Bulgarian Third Army (four divisions) supplemented by two Turkish divisions and smaller German and Austro-Hungarian components, with the initial goal of invading Dobruja and cutting off Romania's access to the sea. The Central Powers contained Sarrail's force with the same three armies that had been watching the Salonika pocket since the previous December: the German Eleventh, the Bulgarian First, and the Bulgarian Second.

The experience of Romania in the wars of 1912–13 had an unfortunate effect on its approach to the campaign of 1916. In contrast to the bloody trials of Bulgaria and Serbia, Romania had remained neutral in the First Balkan War against the Ottoman

Figure 7.2 Vietnamese troops in Salonika

The Allied effort in the Salonika pocket grew to include twenty divisions by 1916, enough to make possible the offensive that established the Macedonian front. But even as the Allied governments devoted more resources to the theater, it never rose above secondary significance in their overall strategy. In addition to the polyglot nature of the force there (including British, French, Italian, Serbian, and Russian divisions, joined eventually by Greeks), the front often became a dumping-ground for commanders, officers, and units not wanted elsewhere, such as these *Tirailleurs annamites* from southern Vietnam. The French colonial *Tirailleurs indochinois* were far less numerous and less highly regarded than their African counterparts. They eventually grew to include eight regiments: four of *Tirailleurs tonkinois* (from northern Vietnam and Laos), two and a half of *Tirailleurs annamites*, and one and a half of *Tirailleurs cambodgiens* (from Cambodia). Many officers and soldiers involved in southeast Asia's post-1945 conflicts received their first training and combat experience in their ranks.

Empire, then determined the outcome of the Second Balkan War merely by intervening against Bulgaria and marching on Sofia, a campaign in which it fought very little and suffered few casualties. Thus, the Romanians went to war in 1916 with an exaggerated sense of their military capabilities, and their misplaced confidence exasperated the Russians in particular. Alekseev considered them to be more trouble than they were worth, and Zaionchkovsky characterized his assignment to Dobruja as "a punishment for some crime I did not even know I had committed."[11] In the opening days, the invasion unfolded at a leisurely pace, as the Romanians did nothing to exploit their dramatic initial superiority over the Austro-Hungarian defenders. They quickly took Hermannstadt (Sibiu) and Kronstadt (Brasov), but failed to advance deeper into Transylvania, instead settling into shallow trench lines all along the front.

The tide soon turned against them, as the end of Brusilov's offensive on September 21 allowed the Central Powers to transfer divisions from the Eastern front to Transylvania. Arz's First Army and Falkenhayn's Ninth were reinforced to six divisions apiece (in each case, a mixture of German and Austro-Hungarian units). Their subsequent victories in the battles of Hermannstadt (September 26–29) and Kronstadt (October 7–9) highlighted a systematic effort to push the Romanians back to the crest of the Carpathians. It helped their cause that, at the start of the campaign, Mackensen had taken less than a week to reconquer southern Dobruja for the Bulgarians, quickly driving Zaionchkovsky's forces back toward the mouth of the Danube. His Danube Army captured the key fortresses of Tutrakan (September 6) and Silistria (September 8), taking 40,000 prisoners, before moving into northern Dobruja with the goal of seizing Constanza, Romania's primary seaport. As Mackensen's methodical advance on Constanza continued, the Romanians shifted troops from Transylvania to the defense of northern Dobruja, so many that by late October, their First, Second, and Fourth armies – which had enjoyed a 10:1 advantage over the defenders of Transylvania two months earlier – were reduced to a combined strength of just ten divisions, numerically inferior to the twelve that Falkenhayn and Arz deployed against them. By the beginning of November the Central Powers had pushed all Romanian troops out of Transylvania; Arz gave up two of his divisions to Falkenhayn, then used the remainder of the First Army to hold the line of the Carpathians along Transylvania's prewar eastern border, while the Ninth Army pushed southward over the mountains to carry the campaign into Wallachia. Mackensen, meanwhile, shifted part of the Danube Army 130 miles (210 km) upriver to Sistovo, where it crossed the Danube on November 23–25 and linked up with the Ninth Army on the 26th. The Germans entered Bucharest on December 6, and by the end of the year occupied all of Wallachia and Dobruja.

In just over three months of fighting, Romania suffered casualties of 163,000 killed, wounded, or missing and lost 147,000 prisoners. Three of its four field armies were routed and dispersed. Ferdinand I and his prime minister, Bratianu, moved the capital to Jassy (Iasi) in Moldavia, where the Romanian Second Army, now under Averescu, served as a catalyst for continued resistance as long as Russia remained in the war. The decisive nature of the Romanian campaign of 1916 vindicated the decision of the Central Powers to create a unified command, and also foreshadowed its future functioning. Against Romania, Austria-Hungary provided the greatest share of the manpower for the Central Powers (46 percent, compared with 22 percent for Germany and a combined 32 percent for Bulgaria and the Ottoman Empire), but because the Germans provided the planning and leadership, they received most of the credit for the success. Dreams of the future exploitation of Romanian wheat and oil buoyed the spirits of the home front in Austria-Hungary as much as Germany, but the victory did nothing to revive the prestige of Conrad or the AOK. By the time the unified command was established, Germany was already subsidizing the war effort of Austria-Hungary at a rate of 100 million marks per month. By the end of the year, Austro-Hungarian troops would be issued the new German steel helmets, and all new uniforms were tailored not in their own pike grey but in German field grey, from cloth imported from Germany. To sustain this effort, the OHL introduced the Hindenburg Program later in 1916, under which it militarized the German home front and pressured Austria-Hungary to do the same (see Chapter 11). Thus, the OHL believed Germany could continue to supply itself and its allies, and get them to better supply themselves.

The outcome of the Romanian campaign brought Alekseev's worst fears to fruition: in the autumn of 1916 the Russians had to extend their lines another 200 miles (320 km) southward, to the Black Sea, to prevent the Central Powers from invading Ukraine out of occupied Romania. The new sector of the front, which followed the Carpathian border between eastern Transylvania and Romania before turning eastward through Galatz to reach the sea, could be covered only by thinning the rest of the Eastern front and committing all of Russia's reserves. The lack of depth of the front, along with the fatigue of the troops, made further offensive operations problematic, but the Russians were able to hold their lines because the Central Powers were just as exhausted and likewise had to cover a greater length of front than before Romania had entered the war. The Russian Army's first serious mutiny occurred on the night of October 1–2 in a Siberian unit, starting a trend that accelerated as the year drew to an end. In December 1916 alone, more than a dozen Russian units refused to obey various orders.

Romania's rapid collapse in the autumn of 1916 rendered Sarrail's offensive out of the Salonika pocket irrelevant, despite its modest gains. From their first attacks on September 12, the Allies made good use of their superior numbers in a successful drive westward along the rail line from Salonika to Monastir (Bitola) in the southwest corner of Macedonia, which they secured on November 19. By the time the offensive ended on December 11, Sarrail's troops had linked up with Italian forces occupying the southern half of Albania, and thus expanded the Salonika pocket into a continuous Macedonian front. Along with Monastir, they liberated a narrow strip of Serbian territory adjacent to the Greek border totaling 400 square miles (1,040 km²), but at a considerable cost: 50,000 casualties (among them 27,000 Serbs), against 53,000 for the Bulgarians and 8,000 for the Germans. Confirming the modest nature of the gains (and a lack of faith that they were permanent), Pašić and the Serbian government remained at Corfu rather than move to Monastir.

Between Two Alliances: The Ordeal of Greece

On August 30, 1916, three days after Romania entered the war, the protracted struggle between King Constantine, brother-in-law of William II, and his former prime minister, Eleftherios Venizelos, over the continuation of Greek neutrality finally came to a head when Colonel Epaminondas Zymbrakakis led a coup of pro-Allied Greek army officers in Salonika. With their support, Venizelos soon established a provisional government there, rewarding Zymbrakakis with a promotion to general and command of a new "National Army." Venizelos' authority was accepted in the parts of Greece already under Allied occupation and in most of the Aegean islands; the Allies did not formally recognize the provisional government, but its creation emboldened them to bully the royal government in Athens even more than before. After seizing the Greek Navy in October, the Allies demanded that the Greek Army surrender to them a list of equipment and munitions including ten batteries of mountain artillery sorely needed by Sarrail for his drive on Monastir.

When the royal government refused the demand, the Allies deployed the French dreadnought *Provence* and four pre-dreadnought battleships to shell Athens. On December 1, 2,000 British and French marines landed in the Greek capital, but royalist troops under General Metaxas forced them back to their ships, inflicting more than 200 casualties before a settlement was arranged giving the Allies six of the mountain batteries (alas, too late to help Sarrail's offensive). In the wake of the Allied landing, royalist troops and civilians attacked supporters of Venizelos in Athens. The provisional government at Salonika then declared Constantine deposed, while Constantine issued a warrant for the arrest of Venizelos. Amid the standoff, the Allies finally recognized the provisional government, and Allied warships blockaded the ports of the mainland areas still loyal to the king. At the same time, the establishment of a continuous front from Salonika on the Aegean to the Albanian coast at the mouth of the Adriatic effectively left Greece behind Allied lines. These developments combined to doom Constantine's quest to keep his country united and neutral.

Conclusion

At the end of 1916 the situation along Europe's battle lines was not unfavorable for the Central Powers. Falkenhayn had failed to bleed the French Army into submission at Verdun, but the Germans had withstood the attack at the Somme and enabled their allies to fend off Brusilov's offensive in the east. Austria-Hungary failed to achieve a breakthrough in the Tyrol but continued to hold Trieste, repulsing three more Italian offensives in the seventh, eighth, and ninth battles of the Isonzo (September–November 1916). The concurrent Romanian campaign demonstrated the benefits of the unified command established by the Central Powers in the late summer. In addition to occupying almost all of Romania, they remained in possession of most of Belgium and Serbia, all of Montenegro, northeastern France, Russian Poland, and Lithuania, while the Allies held only a small amount of Austro-Hungarian territory (Gorizia, Bukovina, and eastern Galicia). Yet despite the generally positive balance sheet, the alliance of the Central Powers was in worse shape than ever. Conrad never forgave Falkenhayn for refusing to follow up the 1915 conquest of Serbia with a knockout blow against Italy, against whom a small fraction of the German manpower wasted at Verdun would have made a tremendous difference. Conrad enjoyed far better relations with Hindenburg and Ludendorff than with Falkenhayn; Ludendorff, in particular, considered him a tragic figure, a commander of "rare vision" whose army "was not strong enough to carry out his bold designs."[12] But when it came to amassing power for Germany at the expense of Austria-Hungary, Conrad's new partners were worse than Falkenhayn. Conrad observed that the German drive to dominate the alliance had accelerated "not only in the military realm … but also in the political realm." After guarding his country's prerogatives jealously for two years, by August 1916 he accepted the "necessity" of a closer "alignment" between Austria-Hungary and Germany, but did so with a distinct lack of enthusiasm. Later in the autumn of 1916 he confided in his wife his exasperation with the "high-handedness and impertinence, which has made the north Germans so hated throughout the world."[13]

In sharp contrast, the trials and disappointments of 1916 only made the Allies stronger. In particular, the Somme reassured the French that the British were irrevocably committed to the war, and thus solidified their alliance at a time when France still had the larger army on the Western front (2.8 million men at year's end, to Britain's 1.6 million) but, owing to the casualties it had endured thus far, could no longer bear the brunt of the fighting there. The burden had already begun to shift during the last six months of 1916. Even though the war would go on for another two years, the French had suffered most of their casualties by the end of the fighting at Verdun; the British, in contrast, suffered 80 percent of their casualties between the first day of the Somme and the Armistice. For the Germans as well as the Allies, the overlapping ordeals of Verdun and the Somme generated unprecedented numbers of casualties labeled as shellshock, a catchall for a wide variety of maladies ranging from physical brain damage to psychological trauma (see Online Essay 5). On the other fronts, both Britain and France remained concerned about Russia, disappointed in Italy, and shocked that Romania had fought so poorly. Their shameless bullying of Greece, which Germany with some justification claimed was no different than its own treatment of Belgium, would soon gain them another ally of dubious value.

Tactical innovations in 1916 included the nascent storm troop tactics employed by the Germans at Verdun, in which specially armed and trained squads attacked enemy strong points in advance of the general assault; the emulation of the "Joffre attack" at the start of the Brusilov offensive, when the Russians narrowed the open ground to be crossed by sapping forward trenches closer to the enemy; the British mining operations that opened the action at the Somme by quite literally blowing holes in the enemy's front lines; and the British reinvention of the creeping barrage, later used to better effect by the French at Verdun. All had the same goal, to limit the casualties to infantry crossing no man's land, yet 1916 was bloodier than 1915 had been, because all armies continued to have difficulty applying new tactics consistently and competently, or replicating tactics (their own and those of other armies) that had worked elsewhere. The fate of British infantry on the first day of the Somme – where too many men faced too much open ground to cross, following a creeping barrage that was too far ahead of them – served as the most sobering single example of how things could go terribly wrong even when those planning the battle knew better. As for new technologies, gas attacks continued throughout 1916 but the development of more effective gas masks limited their effectiveness, and it remained to be seen whether the tank would evolve quickly enough to become a decisive weapon. The arms race in the air continued to affect the balance of power in the skies over the Western front, with the Allies recovering a measure of superiority early in the year, only to have the Germans take it back again in the autumn. Aircraft continued to have their greatest practical use in reconnaissance, especially artillery spotting, as artillery remained the decisive weapon for all armies on all fronts. Throughout 1916 the Allies remained inferior to the Central Powers in artillery, but clearly narrowed the gap, especially in numbers and quality of heavy artillery pieces.

Throughout Europe, the recriminations stemming from the unprecedented carnage of 1916 brought down military and political leaders. Aside from Germany, where Falkenhayn gave way to Hindenburg and Ludendorff in the midst of the great battles at Verdun and the Somme, and Italy, where the prime minister who brought the country into the war, Antonio Salandra, fell from power in the wake of Austria-Hungary's Tyrol offensive, the changes all came in the last weeks of the year. In Britain, Haig survived and even received a promotion to field marshal on New Year's Day, but the prime minister was not so lucky. Asquith, whose eldest son died at the Somme, resigned on December 5. Two days later Lloyd George succeeded him, after having spent the previous six months as Kitchener's successor at the War Office. In France, the human toll of the war finally caught up with Joffre during the last week of the fighting at Verdun. On December 13, Nivelle, a colonel at the beginning of the war, leapfrogged Pétain to become commander of the French armed forces. Poincaré cushioned Joffre's fall by promoting him to marshal of France on the day after Christmas, then sent him to visit the United States after it declared war. In Austria-Hungary, Emperor Francis Joseph died on November 21, at the age of 86. His 29-year-old great-nephew, Archduke Charles, succeeded him, and at least initially appeared to stand by Conrad, whom he promoted to field marshal four days into his reign. But on December 2, Charles assumed personal command of the Austro-Hungarian armed forces, and after clashing repeatedly with Conrad over the winter, replaced him with Arz on February 27, 1917. Finally, in Russia, the disastrous casualties of 1916 further discredited the Imperial Russian government, prompting a group of political and military leaders to deputize Alekseev as their spokesman to demand that Nicholas II grant reforms. Alekseev could not bring himself to do so, and instead cited ill health to justify taking several weeks' leave. In the meantime, his circle remained convinced that the German-born Empress Alexandra was deliberately sabotaging the war effort but could do nothing about it; they did finally act against her eccentric advisor, Grigori Rasputin, assassinating him on December 29. The Romanovs remained on the throne for just eleven weeks after his death.

SUGGESTIONS FOR FURTHER READING

Buckingham, William F. *Verdun 1916: The Deadliest Battle of the First World War* (Gloucestershire: Amberley Publishing, 2016).

Dowling, Timothy C. *The Brusilov Offensive* (Bloomington, IN: Indiana University Press, 2008).

Duffy, Christopher. *Through German Eyes: The British and the Somme, 1916* (London: Weidenfeld & Nicolson, 2006).

Foley, Robert T. *German Strategy and the Path to Verdun: Erich von Falkenhayn and the Development of Attrition, 1870–1916* (Cambridge: Cambridge University Press, 2005).

Gilbert, Martin. *The Somme: Heroism and Horror in the First World War* (New York: Henry Holt, 2006).

Hart, Peter. *The Somme: The Darkest Hour on the Western Front* (New York: Pegasus Books, 2008).

Jankowski, Paul. *Verdun: The Longest Battle of the Great War* (Oxford: Oxford University Press, 2014).

Philpott, William. *Bloody Victory: The Sacrifice of the Somme and the Making of the Twentieth Century* (Boston, MA: Little, Brown, 2009).

Prete, Roy A. "Joffre and the Origins of the Somme: A Study in Allied Military Planning," *Journal of Military History* 73 (2009): 417–48.

Smith, Leonard V. *The Embattled Self: French Soldiers' Testimony of the Great War* (Ithaca, NY: Cornell University Press, 2007).

Torrey, Glenn E. *The Romanian Battlefront in World War I* (Lawrence, KS: University Press of Kansas, 2011).

NOTES

1. Quoted in Isabel V. Hull, *Absolute Destruction: Military Culture and the Practices of War in Imperial Germany* (Ithaca, NY: Cornell University Press, 2005), 215.
2. See Robert T. Foley, *German Strategy and the Path to Verdun: Erich von Falkenhayn and the Development of Attrition, 1870–1916* (Cambridge: Cambridge University Press, 2005), 124–25, and Hull, *Absolute Destruction*, 215–17.
3. Quoted in Foley, *German Strategy*, 182.
4. Memorandum, Second Allied Military Conference, Chantilly, December 6, 1915, available at www.firstworldwar.com/source/chantillymemo.htm.
5. Hull, *Absolute Destruction*, 220.
6. Diary entry for July 1, 1916, in Émile Fayolle, *Cahiers secrets de la grande guerre*, ed. Henry Contamine (Paris: Plon, 1964), 164–65.
7. "Battle of the Somme, by Crown Prince Rupprecht," September 28, 1916, available at www.firstworldwar.com/source/somme_rupprecht.htm.
8. Franz Conrad to Gina Conrad, Teschen, June 6, 1916, KA, B/1450: 357.
9. For an elaboration on this thesis see Timothy C. Dowling, *The Brusilov Offensive* (Bloomington, IN: Indiana University Press, 2008).
10. Josef Redlich, quoted from *Schicksalsjahre Österreichs, 1908–1919: Das politische Tagebuch Josef Redlichs, Vol. 2*, ed. Fritz Fellner (Graz: Böhlau, 1953–54), July 9, 1916, 127.
11. Quoted in Dowling, *The Brusilov Offensive*, 154.
12. Erich Ludendorff, *Meine Kriegserinnerungen 1914–1918*, 5th edn. (Berlin: E. S. Mittler & Sohn, 1920), 85.
13. Franz Conrad, "Denkschrift über das Verhältniss der ö.u. Monarchie zu Deutschland," n.d. ("in Teschen 1916 begonnen," after September 1916), KA, B/1450: 143; Conrad to Gina, Teschen, November 16, 1916, KA, B/1450: 357.

British Grand Fleet at sea, spring 1916

In a war that witnessed the emergence of the submarine as an offensive weapon and the commissioning of the first aircraft carriers, battle fleets and their capital ships (dreadnoughts and battle cruisers) still mattered. Though World War I featured just one fleet-scale naval engagement, at Jutland (May 31–June 1, 1916), the superiority of Britain's surface fleet remained the key to its ability to keep Germany blockaded throughout the war. The devastating consequences of the blockade vindicated the prewar sacrifices Britain made to out-build Germany in capital ships. At the time this photograph was taken, Britain had forty-two ships to Germany's twenty-two.

8 The War at Sea, 1915–18

January 24, 1915	British victory at battle of Dogger Bank.
March–September 1915	First round of German unrestricted submarine warfare.
May 7, 1915	German U-boat sinks Cunard liner *Lusitania*.
May 31–June 1, 1916	German tactical victory at battle of Jutland.
February 1917	Germans resume unrestricted submarine warfare.
March 1917	Mutiny in Russian Baltic fleet.
May 1917	Allies adopt anti-submarine convoy system in Atlantic.
May 15, 1917	Austro-Hungarian victory at battle of the Otranto Straits.
July 1917	Unrest in Austro-Hungarian fleet at Pola.
July–August 1917	Unrest in German High Sea fleet at Wilhelmshaven.
February 1918	Austro-Hungarian naval mutiny at Cattaro.
July 19, 1918	First raid by aircraft from carrier (HMS *Furious*).
October 1918	Mutinies at Pola and Wilhelmshaven.

After the destruction of Spee's squadron at the battle of the Falklands in December 1914, the focus of the war's naval dimension shifted, for the duration, to European waters. For most surface vessels this meant the North Sea and the Adriatic, as the Allied navies adopted a strategy of "distant blockade" against Germany (on a line between Scotland and Norway) and against Austria-Hungary (across the Otranto Straits, between the boot-heel of Italy and Albania). While the Admiralty had planned for a more comprehensive economic warfare, leveraging Britain's dominant position in international finance along with its sea power,[1] the naval blockade alone proved to be devastating enough. For Germany, a prewar net importer of food, at war with Russia, its main prewar source of grain, the inability to trade by sea arguably was the single most important factor in its ultimate defeat. Indeed, at war's end, Herbert Asquith, still mourning the son he had lost at the Somme, conceded as much. "With all deference to our soldiers," the former prime minister concluded, "this war has been won with sea power."[2]

In their quest to keep the Central Powers blockaded, the surface fleets of the Allies enjoyed a considerable advantage, thanks to their decisive edge in capital ships (dreadnoughts and battle cruisers). Following the losses and gains of the Ottoman Navy in August 1914, and the Admiralty's acquisition of a Chilean dreadnought then nearing completion in a British shipyard, the Allies had eighty capital ships built or building (Britain, forty-five; France, twelve; Japan, twelve; and Russia, eleven) against thirty-one for the Central Powers (Germany, twenty-six; Austria-Hungary, four; and Turkey, one). The neutral states of 1914 accounted for another twenty-seven (the United States, fourteen; Italy, six; Spain, three; Brazil, two; and Argentina, two), of which the American, Italian, and Brazilian totals would eventually swell the Allied advantage still more. But the logic of distant blockade dictated that the Allies would risk their own capital ships only on the rare occasions when the Central Powers sent out theirs in attempts to challenge the status quo. Thus, naval strategists planning for capital ship engagements instead got a war in which light cruisers and destroyers saw far more action than dreadnoughts and battle cruisers. Because the Allies enjoyed an insurmountable supremacy in those smaller warship types, too, the Central Powers attempted to revolutionize naval warfare by giving a central, offensive role to the submarine, a vessel originally conceived for a peripheral, defensive role (primarily as a harbor defender, against enemy blockade). In refocusing their efforts on undersea warfare, they left their capital ships to rust at anchor for much of the war, with dire consequences for the morale of most of their seamen. In 1917–18 Germany and Austria-Hungary (along with Russia, whose Baltic and Black Sea fleets had been similarly idled) experienced serious naval mutinies, and revolutionary movements in all three countries attracted significant numbers of sailors.

Dogger Bank

The first five months of the war featured no naval battles in which each of the opposing forces included dreadnoughts or battle cruisers. In the only action in European waters – the first battle of Helgoland Bight (August 28, 1914) – a British force led by five battle cruisers under Vice Admiral David Beatty destroyed half of Rear Admiral Leberecht Maass' squadron of light cruisers, inflicting serious casualties (712 dead, including Maass). Like Sturdee at the Falklands four months later, Beatty demonstrated just how decisive the firepower of capital ships would be in any surface action against older or smaller warships.

With an eye toward reducing Britain's overall 3:2 ratio of superiority in capital ships, the German strategy called for Rear Admiral Franz Hipper's battle cruiser squadron to raid the British North Sea coast in order to lure part of the Grand Fleet out of its main base at Scapa Flow and into battle with the main body of dreadnoughts of the High Sea Fleet, under Admiral Friedrich von Ingenohl, in the hope of achieving a decisive victory that would even the odds. Hipper's shelling of Hartlepool and Scarborough on December 16 nearly resulted in a big battle, as the two fleets narrowly missed contact. Admiral Tirpitz, administrative head of the navy, later lamented that "Ingenohl had the fate of Germany in the palm of his hand" that day, yet could not get the desired engagement.[3] At the time, the British still had six battle cruisers either in the Mediterranean or not yet returned from the pursuit of Spee, leaving the Grand Fleet with a capital-ship advantage of just 27:21 and the chances of a German victory better than they would ever be again.

Capital ships of the two fleets finally met at the battle of Dogger Bank (January 24, 1915), in the fishing grounds of the central North Sea, after Ingenohl ordered Hipper to disrupt the work of "intelligence trawlers" the Admiralty had deployed among the fishing boats there. Shortly after daybreak, Hipper's three battle cruisers and the armored cruiser *Blücher*, approaching from Wilhelmshaven, made contact with five battle cruisers under Beatty, approaching from the British battle cruiser base at Rosyth. Hipper promptly turned for home, and a furious pursuit ensued. By 9:05 a.m. the British had closed enough to begin firing. The 15,800-ton *Blücher*, the smallest ship in the battle, brought up the rear of Hipper's column and bore the brunt of enemy fire that it could not return, as its 8.3-inch (21-cm) guns were outranged by the 12-inch (30.5-cm) guns of the British battle cruisers. Ultimately, a shell from the *Princess Royal*, fired at more than 19,000 yards (17,400 m), penetrated the deck of the *Blücher* and ignited ammunition below. The armored cruiser capsized and sank at 1:13 p.m., with almost all hands (792 dead). Two of the three German battle cruisers sustained damage, as did two of the five British battle cruisers. Beatty's flagship *Lion* took seventeen hits and had to be towed back to Rosyth.

The battle of Dogger Bank had consequences far out of proportion to its modest size and scope. The loss of the *Blücher* – ironically, neither a dreadnought nor a battle cruiser – demonstrated to William II what could happen to one of his dreadnoughts or battle cruisers in an ill-conceived or unlucky future battle. After the defeat he sacked

Ingenohl for failing to keep the main body of the High Sea Fleet close enough to come to Hipper's aid and trap Beatty's battle cruisers. Ingenohl's successor, Admiral Hugo von Pohl, found himself hamstrung by the emperor's fear of losing his capital ships in action, a fear that doomed the German surface fleet to inactivity for most of the rest of the war.

Unrestricted Submarine Warfare: Round One, 1915

The submarine, developed before the war as a short-range defensive weapon, demonstrated its offensive potential less than two months into the war, on September 22, 1914, when the German *U9* torpedoed and sank the old British cruisers *Aboukir, Hogue*, and *Cressy* (1,459 dead) off the Dutch coast, all within less than an hour. When it came to attacking merchant vessels, initially the Germans respected norms designed for surface warships – allowing crews to abandon ship, then providing for their safety – but their respect for international law waned as it became clear that Britain, in closing Germany's ports, had no intention of honoring the provisions of the Declaration of London (1909) asserting the right of food shipments and nonmilitary cargo to pass through a blockade. After *U17* torpedoed and sank a British merchantman off the Norwegian coast on October 20, German submarine commanders gradually became more aggressive in their targeting of unarmed vessels and less circumspect about the fate of those aboard the ships they sank. At the same time, they continued their attacks on British warships, by February 1915 adding a pre-dreadnought battleship and two light cruisers to the three armored cruisers claimed in the initial action (see Online Essay 4).

In the wake of the defeat at Dogger Bank, William II favored a more aggressive submarine campaign as a means to cause serious harm to the Allied war effort without risking his dreadnoughts and battle cruisers. By then, too, the last of the German surface raiders was being hunted down, and naval leaders felt the need to do something to contest Allied control of the world's shipping lanes. Tirpitz agitated tirelessly for a more aggressive approach, and as early as November 1914 advocated unrestricted submarine warfare. Finally, on February 4, 1915, Germany proclaimed a "blockade" of its own against Britain, warning that all merchant vessels in the waters around the British Isles were liable to destruction. Thus began the first phase of unrestricted submarine warfare, culminating on May 7 in the sinking of the 30,400-ton Cunard liner *Lusitania* by *U20* off the coast of Ireland, with the loss of 1,198 lives, including 128 American citizens, a key event in turning the United States against Germany (see Box 8.1). In response to a formal US government protest, Foreign Secretary Gottlieb von Jagow alleged that the *Lusitania* had "Canadian troops and munitions on board,"[4] inaccurate regarding the former but not the latter, as the *Lusitania*'s own ship's manifest listed 5,671 cases of cartridges and ammunition, along with 189 containers of unspecified "military goods." Nevertheless, American public and political opinion for the most part rejected the German argument that the ocean liner was a legitimate target of war.

Box 8.1 **A survivor's story**

Excerpt from a letter by Isaac Lehmann of New York, a first-cabin passenger aboard the *Lusitania* and one of the 761 survivors of the sinking, to his brother, Henry Lehmann:

I was sitting on deck after luncheon talking with Mr Pearson, the traction magnate, and Mr Medbury ... Suddenly there came an explosion, and I remarked to Mr Medbury, "I'll bet we have been torpedoed." I ran down below to my cabin to get the lifebelt from the rack, but it was gone. Then I gathered up my papers, and met Steward Barnes, who got another lifebelt, which I buckled on and went to the top deck, where the boats were. One was swung out from the davit, but it recoiled and killed about forty people.

At this moment the ship lurched wildly to starboard. At the same time there was an explosion inboard, apparently from the boilers, which took me up with it into the air and then I fell into the water, going down several feet, it seemed. When I came to the surface I managed to grasp an oar, and kept afloat with my lifebelt.

While I was in the water I saw a sight that I shall never forget. There were two men clinging to an upturned water cooler, and being upright, it managed to float. One of the poor chaps tried to get on top and managed to do so, but he upset the cooler and they were both drowned.

There was no panic on board, but if the *Lusitania* had only kept afloat a little longer many more lives would have been saved.

Source: "Lifeboat's Recoil Killed 40: Oar and Belt Kept Isaac Lehmann Afloat, He Writes," *New York Times*, May 25, 1915.

The sinking of the *Lusitania* also further hardened the resolve of the British home front; indeed, one recent analysis confirms that it was "the greatest single atrocity of the war in British eyes" and the issue of whether the ship "was carrying munitions ... was absolutely beside the point."[5] Conspiracy theorists, at the time and for years afterward, fantasized that Churchill had orchestrated the sinking in order to bring the United States into the war, although the Admiralty was responsible at least for the cynical calculation that Britain could not lose by using passenger liners to import war *materiel* from the United States: most cargoes would make it through, and every ship torpedoed would bring the Americans closer to declaring war on Germany.

Unrestricted submarine warfare forever linked the undersea boat with the German Navy, ironically so, because the Germans had trailed each of the three navies of the Triple Entente in prewar submarine development. Before 1914, Germany had completed just thirty-six submarines, and when the campaign began at the end of February 1915 the navy still had just thirty-seven U-boats in service. During the next seven months the Germans rarely maintained more than six of them on patrol around the British Isles, yet they demonstrated their destructive potential by sinking 787,120 tons of merchant shipping (89,500 in March 1915, 38,600 in April, 126,900 in May, 115,290 in June, 98,005 in July, 182,770 in August, and 136,050 in September) against a total loss of fifteen submarines. The campaign was extended into the Mediterranean when

Austria-Hungary added its own small U-boat force to the campaign, after opening its Adriatic bases to German submarines to facilitate their operation off the Dardanelles. Despite the apparent success, the first round of unrestricted submarine warfare ended in September 1915, when an old rival of Tirpitz, Admiral Henning von Holtzendorff, became operational chief-of-staff (chief of the *Admiralstab*) of the German Navy. Holtzendorff joined the chancellor, Bethmann Hollweg, and the head of the OHL, Falkenhayn, in persuading William II that the level of antagonism the campaign generated in the United States and other neutral countries far outweighed the material losses that the small U-boat force had caused.

The Germans faced sobering facts regarding the number of submarines and crews needed for a truly decisive effort: hundreds of U-boats, not dozens, built in sufficient numbers to account for their very short service lives, and manpower likewise trained in sufficient numbers to make good the high losses at sea. By early 1916, Falkenhayn recognized that this grim calculus followed the same logic of the campaign of attrition he planned to unleash at Verdun; along with Holtzendorff, he reconsidered his position of the previous autumn and joined Tirpitz in advocating a more aggressive course. On February 29, Holtzendorff authorized an "intensified" submarine campaign, but Bethmann Hollweg opposed subsequent efforts to get the emperor to resume unrestricted submarine warfare. While William II wavered, U-boat commanders grew increasingly aggressive, torpedoing Allied merchantmen without warning. The matter came to a head after *U29* sank the passenger ferry *Sussex* in the English Channel on March 24, prompting Woodrow Wilson to threaten to break diplomatic relations if Germany did not end the campaign (see Perspectives 8.1). At this stage Bethmann Hollweg's reasoning prevailed, and the "intensified" campaign stopped. The decision infuriated Tirpitz enough to prompt his retirement from the Imperial Navy Office.

Jutland, 1916

After succeeding Pohl as commander of the High Sea Fleet in January 1916, Vice Admiral Reinhard Scheer persuaded William II to allow the German capital ships to resume regular sorties. Scheer intended to repeat the same strategy that had resulted in defeat a year earlier, using Hipper's battle cruisers to lure part of the British Grand Fleet into battle with the main body of the High Sea Fleet, in the hope of achieving a decisive victory that would reduce or eliminate Britain's surface fleet superiority. Unlike Ingenohl on the day of Dogger Bank, however, Scheer planned to keep the German dreadnoughts close enough to come to Hipper's aid and destroy the British forces that came out to chase him. Sorties in March and April of 1916 brought no contact with British capital ships, but Scheer's third sortie, on May 31, resulted in the battle of Jutland (Map 8.1), the largest naval engagement of the war. In the predawn hours of the 31st, five battle cruisers under Hipper's command steamed northward

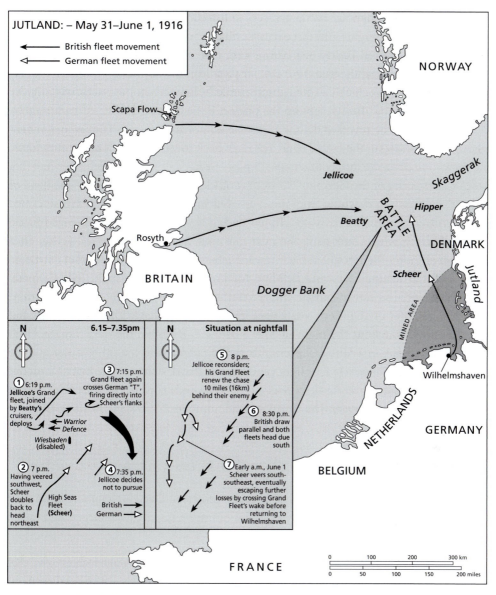

Map 8.1 Jutland, 1916

from Wilhelmshaven, parallel with the coast of Danish Jutland, in the direction of the Skaggerak, with Scheer's sixteen dreadnoughts, six pre-dreadnoughts, and a host of smaller warships following some 50 miles (80 km) behind. As in the battle of Dogger Bank, Beatty's battle cruisers came out of Rosyth to intercept Hipper, followed by the rest of the Grand Fleet, under Admiral Sir John Jellicoe, out of Scapa Flow, coincidentally also roughly 50 miles behind. Owing to a recent exchange of ships between Beatty and Jellicoe, Beatty had six battle cruisers and four dreadnoughts, and Jellicoe had twenty-four dreadnoughts and three battle cruisers.

Hipper encountered Beatty just before 4:00 p.m. that afternoon, and immediately turned south, drawing the pursuing British squadron toward Scheer's superior force. During the hour-long chase German gunfire sank the British battle cruisers *Indefatigable* and *Queen Mary*, but Beatty kept up the pursuit until sighting Scheer's dreadnoughts. Around 5:00 p.m. he reversed course and steamed northward, with Hipper and Scheer giving chase, drawing the entire High Sea Fleet back toward Jellicoe's advancing force. As the two fleets came into contact at 6:15 p.m., Beatty's ships joined Jellicoe's line in a west-east crossing of the German "T," pounding Hipper's battle cruisers at the head of Scheer's column, approaching from the south. During this phase the British lost a third battle cruiser, the *Invincible*, while Hipper had to abandon the badly damaged battle cruiser *Lützow*, which sank early the next morning. Scheer broke off the action after less than an hour, then doubled back toward Jellicoe's line for another brief exchange before finally turning away and heading for home around 5:30 p.m. Jellicoe made the fateful decision not to pursue the retreating Germans, only to change his mind at 8:00 p.m., after giving them a safe lead in the ensuing chase. The battle continued sporadically throughout the night of May 31/June 1. By dawn the next day the High Sea Fleet was back in Wilhelmshaven, minus the *Lützow* and ten other warships: the pre-dreadnought *Pommern;* four light cruisers; and five destroyers. The British suffered much heavier losses: three battle cruisers, three armored cruisers, one destroyer flotilla leader, and seven destroyers. The German dead numbered 2,551, the British 6,097.

Perspectives 8.1: Unrestricted submarine warfare

On April 18, 1916, Woodrow Wilson formally protested German submarine warfare as a violation of "long established" principles of international law, concerning cruiser warfare:

The law of nations in these matters, upon which the Government of the United States based that protest, is not of recent origin or founded upon merely arbitrary principles set up by convention. It is based, on the contrary, upon manifest principles of humanity and has long been established with the approval and by the express assent of all civilized nations … If it is still the purpose of the Imperial Government to prosecute relentless and indiscriminate warfare against vessels of commerce by the use of submarines, without regard to what the Government of the United States must consider the sacred and indisputable rules of international law and the universally recognized dictates of humanity, the Government of the United States is at last forced to the conclusion that there is but one course it can pursue.

Source: Charles F. Horne, ed., *Source Records of the Great War*, vol. 4
(Indianapolis: The American Legion, 1931), 93, 95.

• • • •

American legal scholar Earl Willis Crecraft (1886–1950) initially applauded the entry of the United States into the war on the grounds that it upheld the long-standing American principle of freedom of the seas, only to regret after the peace settlement that the United States had abandoned its "honorable neutrality." In his book *Freedom of the Seas* (1935) Crecraft gave an even-handed analysis typical of mainstream American academia as war clouds began to gather over Europe once again:

Because Americans became so hostile to Germany over the submarine, they have paid little attention … to the German argument that Great Britain was waging a war of starvation against civilian populations, and that the submarine was the effective weapon as an instrument of retaliation. In the eyes of America, Germany had become the chief aggressor against neutral maritime rights. The spread of this conviction led to our entering the war.

… It may happen that Great Britain's maritime practices, when viewed by those who have paid dearly for them in the past, may in the long run appear equally as aggressive as the German practices of 1915 and 1916 … If opposing belligerents continue to arm their merchantmen and to institute "food blockades," the temptation to give a free hand to submarines will exist as long as the latter are built… Acts of aggression are to be condemned of course; but so are acts that provoke aggression.

Source: Earl Willis Crecraft, *Freedom of the Seas*
(New York: Appleton Century, 1935), 122–23.

A London journalist best summed up the post-Jutland strategic situation: the prisoner had assaulted its jailer but was now safely back in its cell.[6] Nevertheless, the Germans, having outperformed expectations, claimed Skaggerak (their designation for the battle) as a great victory, while the British, expecting a triumph on the order of Trafalgar, emerged bitterly disappointed. Jellicoe and Beatty (or, more accurately, their supporters within the officer corps) each blamed the other for opportunities missed. Meanwhile, in Germany, an officer corps historically fragmented by infighting rallied around Scheer, excusing his tactical errors at Jutland, as did William II, who rewarded him with a promotion to full admiral and the Iron Cross *Pour le Merite*, the country's highest military decoration. At the end of 1916 Beatty became commander of the Grand Fleet, when Jellicoe was appointed First Sea Lord. Scheer would finally turn over command of the High Sea Fleet to Hipper in August 1918, then spend the last months of the war in the new post of Chief of the Supreme Navy Command.

Aside from Scheer's good luck and Jellicoe's moments of caution, Jutland turned out the way that it did largely because of the sturdier construction of the German capital ships, the unsafe handling of unstable powder supplies aboard the larger British warships, and poor fire control especially on the British side. The durability of the German capital ships was impressive enough. Four of the five battle cruisers absorbed heavy punishment, but only one was lost. Germany's newest dreadnoughts each sustained 5–10 hits, but none was seriously damaged. Regarding powder supplies, critics have noted the low quality of British cordite, the lack of flash-tight doors below heavy gun turrets on the British battle cruisers, and the remarkably careless way in which propellants were moved from magazines to turrets. Catastrophic magazine explosions claimed the battle cruisers *Invincible, Indefatigable*, and *Queen Mary*, and the armored cruiser *Defence*, bringing instant death to most of their crews. Indeed, the three battle cruisers accounted for more than half of the British dead at Jutland (3,339), and with just twenty-eight men surviving them. As for fire control, the battle demonstrated the superiority of German range-finding devices and the inadequacy of British gunnery training, especially in the battle cruisers, which performed very poorly. None fared worse than the *New Zealand*, which fired 420 shots during the battle, more than any other capital ship, and scored just four hits.

Unrestricted Submarine Warfare: Round Two, 1917–18

For the German Navy, the celebration of the "victory" at Jutland soon gave way to gloom, upon the realization that the battle had done nothing to alter the strategic situation in the North Sea. In a report to William II dated July 4, 1916, Scheer advocated a renewal of unrestricted submarine warfare and, in the meantime, active surface operations integrating U-boats with battle fleet sorties. When Scheer took the High Sea Fleet out again on sorties in August and October 1916, and a portion of it out on a third sortie in November, submarines accompanied his capital ships and attempted to lay traps for British capital ships lured out of their bases. On each of these occasions, Scheer encountered the Grand Fleet's screening vessels rather than its dreadnoughts or battle cruisers, and his U-boats managed to sink just two light cruisers, both during the August sortie. Meanwhile, the British, employing the same tactic against the Germans, had much greater success, as submarines operating with the Grand Fleet's screen of light cruisers and destroyers torpedoed (but did not sink) three of Scheer's dreadnoughts over the course of the three sorties.

While not decisive, these developments sufficed to make both navies far more cautious in their deployment of capital ships. In a letter to Jellicoe on September 6, Beatty cited the adage "when you are winning, risk nothing."[7] A week later the two admirals agreed that British dreadnoughts and battle cruisers should not be risked south of 55° 30'N, a line crossing the North Sea from Newcastle to the German-Danish border. Scheer likewise agreed with William II that further fleet-scale operations were not worth the risk. The High Sea Fleet attempted just one more sortie into the North Sea, in April 1918, with the same result as the post-Jutland sorties of 1916: no British capital ships encountered, and one German dreadnought torpedoed (but not sunk) by a British submarine. Otherwise, for the last two years of the war (November 1916–November 1918) few of the capital ships of the High Sea Fleet left port other than to stand watch in the Helgoland Bight while German minesweepers cleared channels for the U-boats to sortie. An exception came in October 1917, when Scheer sent ten dreadnoughts and a battle cruiser – nearly half of the battle fleet – through the Kiel Canal and into the Baltic to secure the Gulf of Riga (see Chapter 9).

Meanwhile, in the autumn of 1916 Germany began a restricted submarine campaign that sank more tonnage in five months than the unrestricted campaign of 1915 had in seven months, owing to the larger number of U-boats now deployed. Adhering (at times only loosely) to internationally accepted prize rules, the Germans sank 231,570 tons in September 1916, 341,360 in October 1916, 326,690 in November 1916, 307,850 in December 1916, and 328,390 in January 1917. Surfaced U-boats did most of the damage, as 80 percent of the victims were warned before being sunk, and 75 percent were sunk by the deck gun rather than by torpedoes. Remarkably, during these five months the Germans lost just eleven submarines.

Hoping for even more decisive results, on January 9, 1917, William II met with Hindenburg, Ludendorff, Bethmann Hollweg, and the chief of the *Admiralstab*, Holtzendorff, to discuss the resumption of unrestricted submarine warfare. The previous month Holtzendorff had authored a memorandum estimating that the Allies had just 3 million tons of surplus shipping capacity remaining; thus, if Germany sank 600,000 tons per month for five months, Britain would have to sue for peace. Allowing an extra, sixth month for the U-boats to do their work, he calculated that an unrestricted campaign begun by February 1 could win the war by August 1. The emperor accepted his arguments, as did Bethmann Hollweg, who, earlier in the month, had seen a peace overture to the Allies come to nothing (see Chapter 9). The chancellor announced the campaign in the Reichstag on January 31 (see Box 8.2). While the specifics of Holtzendorff's formula remained secret, the public promise of victory by August 1 buoyed the spirits of a hungry home front then in the midst of the "turnip winter" (see Chapter 11). For their part, Hindenburg and Ludendorff could hardly believe their luck that the navy had positioned itself to shoulder the blame if the war did not end well. They soon authorized trench leaflets informing the troops that "our *Admiralstab* assumes full responsibility, that by the end of July or beginning of August, England will ask us for peace."[8]

Embracing the challenge, navy leaders agreed to abandon two dreadnoughts and five battle cruisers then under construction, to free up shipyard personnel and resources to build more U-boats. While, with hindsight, this decision came too late, logically it could not have come earlier, because Germany had invested too much in capital ship construction over too many years for it to be abandoned prior to Jutland and the definitive failure of the surface fleet to deliver on Tirpitz's prewar promises. When the campaign resumed, the German Navy had 105 U-boats, one-third of which were at sea. German submarines claimed 520,410 tons of Allied shipping in February 1917, 564,500 tons in March, and a staggering 860,330 tons in April, a monthly total never surpassed even by Hitler's U-boats in World War II. Another 616,320 tons were sunk in May and 696,725 tons in June.

Box 8.2 "The best and sharpest weapon"

In a speech to the Reichstag on January 31, 1917, Theobald von Bethmann Hollweg (Chancellor 1909–17) explained why Germany and Austria-Hungary were resuming unrestricted submarine warfare at that particular time:

In the first place, the most important fact of all is that the number of our submarines has very considerably increased as compared with last spring, and thereby a firm basis has been created for success. The second co-decisive reason is the bad wheat harvest of the world. This fact now already confronts England, France and Italy with serious difficulties. We firmly hope to bring these difficulties by means of an unrestricted U-boat war to the point of unbearableness. The coal question, too, is a vital question in war. Already it is critical, as you know, in Italy and France. Our submarines will render it still more critical. To this must be added, especially as regards England, the supply of ore for the production of munitions in the widest sense, and of timber for coal mines. Our enemy's difficulties are rendered still further acute by the increased lack of enemy cargo space. In this respect time and the U-boat and cruiser warfare have prepared the ground for a decisive blow.

... A few days ago Marshal von Hindenburg described to me the situation as follows: "Our front stands firm on all sides. We have everywhere the requisite reserves. The spirit of the troops is good and confident. The military situation, as a whole, permits us to accept all consequences which an unrestricted U-boat war may bring about, and as this

U-boat war in all circumstances is the means to injure our enemies most grievously, it must be begun." The Admiralty Staff and the High Seas Fleet entertain the firm conviction – a conviction which has its practical support in the experience gained in the U-boat cruiser warfare – that Great Britain will be brought to peace by arms. Our allies agree with our views. Austria-Hungary adheres to our procedure also in practice. Just as we lay a blockaded area around Great Britain and the west coast of France, within which we will try to prevent all shipping traffic to enemy countries, Austria-Hungary declares a blockaded area around Italy. To all neutral countries a free path for mutual intercourse is left outside the blockaded area. To America we offer, as we did in 1915, safe passenger traffic under definite conditions, even with Great Britain.

No one among us will close his eyes to the seriousness of the step which we are taking. That our existence is at stake everyone has known since August 1914 ... In now deciding to employ the best and sharpest weapon, we are guided solely by a sober consideration of all the circumstances that come into question, and by a firm determination to help our people out of the distress and disgrace which our enemies contemplate for them. Success lies in a higher Hand, but, as regards all that human strength can do to enforce success for the Fatherland, you may be assured, gentlemen, that nothing has been neglected.

Source: Charles F. Horne, ed., *Source Records of the Great War*, vol. 5 (Indianapolis: The American Legion, 1931), 9–11.

German leaders calculated that the benefits of resuming unrestricted submarine warfare would justify the risk of the United States intervening in the war. The American declaration of war against Germany on April 6 had no effect on the land war in 1917, as it would take more than a year for the United States to deploy significant forces on the Western front. In contrast, the US Navy, the world's third largest, behind the British and German, became a factor immediately, although its principal asset – a battle fleet of fourteen dreadnoughts – had little relevance given the changing circumstances of the naval war. Rear Admiral William S. Sims, newly appointed commander of US forces in European waters, focused immediately on the U-boat threat and was shocked that Jellicoe had no answer for it. While Holtzendorff had underestimated by half the amount of surplus tonnage available to the Allies, in just three months the Germans had sunk nearly a third of the 6 million tons actually needed to trigger a crisis, which the First Sea Lord estimated would come by November 1 at the latest. Sims advocated a comprehensive convoy system to counter the U-boat threat. The British Navy had escorted some troopships since 1914 but, because a convoy had to move at the speed of its slowest member, merchant captains resisted the extension of the practice to include all unarmed ships, preferring to take their chances at outrunning any submarines they encountered. Many junior officers in the British Navy favored a convoy system, as did Lloyd George, and a skeptical Jellicoe finally authorized it on April 30, at which time the prime minister credited Sims with the breakthrough.

The following week, American destroyers joined British destroyers in anti-submarine patrols out of Queenstown, Ireland, becoming the first US Navy ships actively engaged in the war. They soon provided most of the ships there and at Brest, France, while British escort craft operated out of Buncrana on the north coast of Ireland and Devonport on the Channel. The first convoys crossed the Atlantic in June 1917; thereafter, the volume of Allied shipping increased while losses to U-boats fell dramatically, to 555,510 tons in July, 472,370 tons in August, 353,600 tons in September, and 302,600 tons in November. Amid the declining losses, the campaign still far surpassed Holtzendorff's target of sinking 3 million tons by August 1, but failed (by less than a million) to reach Jellicoe's crisis point of 6 million tons by November 1. Nevertheless, the tonnage sunk in October (466,540) and December (411,770) underscored the continued seriousness of the U-boat threat, and on the first anniversary of the resumption of unrestricted submarine warfare, the overall shipping tonnage at the disposal of the Allies was still decreasing. The threat to Allied shipping from Austro-Hungarian submarines and German submarines operating from Austro-Hungarian bases in the Adriatic necessitated a convoy system in the Mediterranean as well, including an American force based at Gibraltar and a significant Japanese squadron (one cruiser and fourteen destroyers) at Malta. In the Mediterranean as well as the Atlantic, convoys plus improved tactics in anti-submarine warfare led not only to lower losses in shipping tonnage, but to higher German losses in U-boats sunk – forty-three in the months of August through December 1917, compared with just nine in February, March, and April.

In addition to implementing convoys, the Allies also invested heavily in anti-submarine mining operations. Starting in 1915 the British attempted to close the eastern approach to the English Channel by deploying a floating anti-submarine barrage between Dover and Calais. The barrage consisted of nets dragged by armed trawlers and auxiliary steamers known as "drifters," eventually supplemented by mines. The Dover Barrage sank just two U-boats in the years 1915–17 before claiming perhaps a dozen in 1918. The vulnerable drifters endured regular raids from German destroyers based at the Belgian ports of Ostend and Zeebrugge, at least until British raids on those ports in April and May 1918 disrupted the effort. In the end the Dover Barrage succeeded only as a deterrent, as most German submariners avoided the risk and took the longer northern route, around Scotland, to get to and from the Atlantic. Starting in March 1918, the British and American navies attempted to close this route, too, by deploying the so-called Northern Barrage. By October the Allies accomplished the monumental task of assembling nets and sowing 70,000 mines between the Orkney Islands and Norway, but the results (six or seven U-boats sunk) hardly justified the massive effort.

The war's last engagement between British and German capital ships, the second battle of Helgoland Bight (November 17, 1917), resulted when Beatty sent Vice Admiral T. W. D. Napier with a force led by three battle cruisers to disrupt German minesweepers clearing routes for U-boats, leading to an encounter with two dreadnoughts guarding them. The operation marked the only time that British capital ships ventured south of the 55° 30'N "risk nothing" limit set in September 1916 by Jellicoe and Beatty, and the results were negligible, with neither side losing a ship. Napier's failure contributed to Lloyd George's decision to replace Jellicoe as First Sea Lord with Admiral Sir Rosslyn Wemyss. With the approval of Wemyss, in April 1918 Beatty sought to increase the likelihood of another fleet-scale surface action by moving the entire Grand Fleet from Scapa Flow to the battle cruiser base at Rosyth, 250 miles (400 km) closer to Wilhelmshaven, but the overwhelming superiority of the British surface fleet – further reinforced in December 1917 by five American dreadnoughts – made it even less likely that the High Sea Fleet would come out again.

Throughout 1918 U-boats continued to shoulder the burden of the German war effort at sea and took a heavy toll right up to the autumn, sinking 295,630 tons in January, 335,200 in February, 368,750 in March, 300,070 in April, 296,560 in May, 268,505 in June, 280,820 in July, and 310,180 in August. Thereafter, the collapse of the German war effort brought a dramatic decline in the activity of U-boats, which sank just 171,970 tons in September, 116,240 in October, and 10,230 in the first eleven days of November. The totals for the final year of the war included 166,910 tons sunk by six long-range U-boats deployed along the Atlantic seaboard of the United States. One of them laid a mine off Long Island which, on July 19, sank the armored cruiser *San Diego*, the only larger US warship lost in World War I. But the U-boats failed miserably where it mattered most, defying the assumptions of the OHL that they would prevent significant numbers of American soldiers from being shipped to Europe. By the time of the Armistice, 2,079,880 US troops had made the crossing safely. German submarines did not sink a single inbound troop transport on the high seas; of those sunk after arriving in European waters but before reaching port, the greatest loss of life came in February 1918 in *UB77*'s sinking of the *Tuscania*, a British troopship carrying over 2,000 American soldiers, of whom 166 died. Despite their failure to turn the war in favor of the Central Powers, the leading U-boat commanders ranked among the most celebrated war heroes on a home front whose civilians suffered increasing hardship as the war progressed and the Allied blockade continued. Chief among them were the German Navy's Lothar Arnauld de la Perière, whose submarines sank 189 Allied merchantmen (446,700 tons), along with two Allied gunboats, and for the Austro-Hungarian Navy's much smaller undersea effort, Georg von Trapp, whose submarines sank twelve Allied merchantmen (45,670 tons), along with a French armored cruiser and an Italian submarine.

The War in the Adriatic

The war in the Adriatic began in earnest when Italy entered the war on the side of the Entente. Under an Anglo-French-Italian naval convention concluded at Paris on May 10, 1915, Admiral Luigi of Savoy, duke of the Abruzzi, received command of the First Allied Fleet, predominantly Italian and based at Brindisi. The existing Allied force under Admiral Augustin Boue de Lapeyrère, predominantly French since the outbreak of war, was redesignated the Second Allied Fleet and given a base at Taranto, much closer to the mouth of the Adriatic than its initial anchorage at Corfu. On May 23, within hours of Italy's declaration of war, Austro-Hungarian naval commander Admiral Anton Haus sortied with his entire fleet and conducted a punitive bombardment of the Italian coastline, supplemented by air raids on Venice and Ancona. By the time Abruzzi's warships left Brindisi, the Austro-Hungarian fleet had returned safely to Pola.

In the nine months of fighting before Italy entered the war, Austria-Hungary had lost just one light cruiser and one torpedo boat, while the vastly superior Allied force sent no capital ships into the Adriatic after December 1914, when a U-boat torpedoed and nearly sank the French dreadnought *Jean Bart*. Lapeyrère grew even more cautious after April 1915, when Trapp's *U5* sank the armored cruiser *Léon Gambetta* (684 dead) off the Italian boot-heel. Italy likewise rarely operated larger warships in the Adriatic after July 1915, when it lost two armored cruisers to submarine attacks within a span of eleven days. That September, the Italian Navy was further shaken when Austrian saboteurs blew up the pre-dreadnought *Benedetto Brin* at Brindisi. The Allies took solace in their successful evacuation of Serbian soldiers and civilians from ports in Albania to Corfu, after the Central Powers crushed Serbia and occupied all of its territory. Over the course of nearly 250 individual passages in the winter of 1915–16, they lost just four transports, all to mines.

At sea as well as on land, Italy's entry into the war did not have the desired impact for the Allies. Throughout the war Abruzzi feuded with Lapeyrère and his successor as French (and overall Allied) commander, Vice Admiral Louis Dartige du Fournet, over alleged lack of support, prompting the French and British to send more help to the mouth of the Adriatic, thus enabling the Austro-Hungarian "fleet in being" at Pola and Cattaro to tie down an ever-greater number of Allied warships that could have been put to better use elsewhere. Italian insecurities grew as they continued to lose battleships without losing (or even fighting) a battle. In August 1916, Austrian saboteurs struck again, this time at Taranto, where they blew up the dreadnought *Leonardo da Vinci*, and four months later an enemy mine claimed the pre-dreadnought *Regina Margherita* off Valona, Albania. The Italian Navy prioritized its own efforts at sabotage and unconventional weaponry, without immediate results. Finally, in December 1917, a high-speed Italian motor torpedo boat, *MAS9*, penetrated the harbor defenses at Trieste and sank the Austro-Hungarian pre-dreadnought *Wien*.

While the Allies conceded it virtually free run of the Adriatic, the Austro-Hungarian Navy experienced the same essential reality at Pola and Cattaro as the German Navy at Wilhelmshaven. A hungry home front demanded that the blockade be broken, and yet it was just as powerless to force open the mouth of the Adriatic as its German counterpart was to break the blockade in the North Sea. Austria-Hungary had a much smaller submarine force than Germany (twenty-seven U-boats, of which no more than twenty were in service at any one time), but likewise embraced the submarine as its best bet to counter the blockade, and participated actively in the unrestricted submarine warfare campaigns of 1915 and 1917–18. The Allies responded to the threat by deploying the Otranto Barrage, on the model of the Dover Barrage, at the mouth of the Adriatic in 1915–16. In the battle of the Otranto Straits (May 15, 1917), the most successful anti-barrage raid of the war, Captain Miklós Horthy and an Austro-Hungarian force led by three light cruisers sank fourteen of the forty-seven Otranto drifters, along with two destroyers and one freighter, while losing no ships of his own. The Allies subsequently reinforced the Otranto Barrage but, like its counterpart at Dover, it did not justify the expenditure of resources required for its maintenance. Indeed, in over three years it registered just two confirmed successes, netting one Austro-Hungarian and one German submarine. Meanwhile, Horthy's successful raid on the Otranto Barrage established him as the rising star of the Austro-Hungarian Navy. In March 1918 he was promoted to rear admiral and – over the heads of twenty-eight admirals senior to him – placed in command of the fleet.

Horthy's extraordinary advancement, coming in the wake of a serious mutiny at Cattaro, temporarily brought new life to the Austro-Hungarian Navy, but it saw no further action after June 10, 1918, when the dreadnought *Szent István* was torpedoed and sunk by the Italian *MAS15* off Premuda Island as it made its way from Pola down the Dalmatian coast with its three sister-ships for an attack on Allied forces at the Otranto Straits. Horthy had hoped to replicate, with the dreadnought squadron, the previous spring's successful raid by light cruisers and destroyers against the Otranto Barrage, but the loss of the *Szent István* forced him to cancel the operation. Afterward Austro-Hungarian morale plummeted, dashing Horthy's hopes of revitalizing the fleet. In the last weeks of the war, the reversals suffered by the Central Powers on land forced the Austro-Hungarian Navy to abandon its most exposed stations. The river monitors and patrol boats of its Danube Flotilla, which had advanced all the way into the Black Sea and up Ukrainian rivers following the collapse of Russia in 1917, withdrew back up the Danube when Bulgaria left the war, and as Italian troops advanced northward through Albania, the navy abandoned Durazzo on October 2. The Austro-Hungarian Navy fought its last battle that day, an engagement typical of its war effort in the Adriatic in that it achieved a tactical success against overwhelming odds: a force of two destroyers, two submarines, and one torpedo boat evacuated the Durazzo garrison and returned safely to Cattaro after withstanding attacks by a combined Anglo-French-Italian-American force including eight cruisers and sixteen destroyers supported by torpedo boats, *MAS* boats, submarines, and bombers from the British and Italian air services. The Austro-Hungarian *U31* inflicted the only casualty of the battle, damaging a British cruiser with a torpedo hit.

Naval Mutinies

For the navies of the Central Powers, the emphasis on submarine warfare affected more than just *materiel* and construction policies. The most highly regarded junior officers were given command of U-boats, and others went to the light cruisers and destroyers, leaving less capable men to take their places aboard the battleships and larger cruisers. In sharp contrast to the typical World War I submarine, where two or three junior officers lived at close quarters with their crew of two or three dozen men, sharing in all of their hardships, every larger warship was a microcosm of the society of the country it represented, and for the Central Powers – as for Russia – the differences were extreme. During the last two years of the war, the inexperience or mediocrity of shipboard "middle management" exacerbated the problem of the social gulf between officers and seamen, at a time when the relative inactivity of the big ships would have caused increased tensions in any event. Life in port also meant closer contact with the home front, making the sailors of the German, Austro-Hungarian, and Russian fleets more likely to see their own hardships in the broader context of conditions within their countries as a whole (see Chapters 9 and 11).

In July 1917, discontent over food shortages sparked the first demonstrations in the Austro-Hungarian fleet at Pola. Order was restored fairly easily, and Haus' successor as navy commander, Admiral Maksimilian Njegovan, was lenient toward the seamen involved. Three months later, the Austro-Hungarian Navy suffered its first and only desertion of a vessel at sea when a Czech machinist and a Slovene boatswain's mate seized their torpedo boat and defected to Italy. Njegovan and Austro-Hungarian leaders considered it an isolated incident, but coming in the wake of the demonstrations at Pola it raised fears, especially in Germany, that the Austro-Hungarian fleet would be infected by the political problems the Austrian home front had begun to experience after Emperor Charles reconvened the Reichsrat in May 1917 and eased censorship.

The German Navy, too, suffered unrest in the summer of 1917, likewise reflecting the war weariness of the home front. At Wilhelmshaven in early June, the crew of the dreadnought *Prinzregent Luitpold* received better food after a hunger strike. Anticipating further demonstrations, Tirpitz's successor, Admiral Eduard von Capelle, authorized the creation of "food committees" aboard all ships of the fleet, but few captains set these up until their crews forced them to. The situation deteriorated still more after the passage of the Reichstag's Peace Resolution in mid-July. The fleet became increasingly politicized, and an estimated 5,000 sailors joined the anti-war Independent Social Democratic Party (USPD). The first half of August was particularly tense, with some sailors refusing all orders. The *Prinzregent Luitpold* was again at the center of the strikes, but four other dreadnoughts and a light cruiser were also affected. Scheer reacted decisively in breaking the strikes. Courts martial meted out a total of 360 years in prison terms to the mutineers, and two of their leaders were executed.

The problems of social divisions, short rations, and general inactivity were even greater for the Russian Navy than for the German or Austro-Hungarian navies, and left the crews of the tsar's fleet increasingly susceptible to revolutionary agitation. Since their commissioning late in 1914, the Russian Baltic Fleet's four dreadnoughts had spent most of the war anchored at Helsinki. In March 1917, shortly after the abdication of Nicholas II, unrest in the fleet culminated in the murder of its commander, Vice Admiral Adrian Nepenin, and several other officers. Revolutionary committees took over many of the ships, and by the summer most were sympathetic toward Lenin and the Bolsheviks. It was against this much-weakened foe that the German Navy launched its largest Baltic operation of the war, securing the Gulf of Riga in October 1917. After the demise of Russia's Provisional Government three weeks later, the sailors devoted their energies to the new Bolshevik regime, becoming its most loyal followers.

Meanwhile, in the Black Sea Fleet, the fall of Nicholas II did not usher in the same sort of disorder. Under the command of Vice Admiral Alexander Kolchak, the fleet had maintained a more active regimen, dominating the Black Sea and winning its own war against the Turkish Navy despite the best efforts of the Ottoman commander, Admiral Wilhelm Souchon, whose German-crewed battle cruiser *Yavuz Sultan Selim* (ex-*Goeben*) served as flagship. After the tsar's abdication Kolchak's crews formed revolutionary committees, but morale remained higher than in the Baltic Fleet and relations between officers and their crews deteriorated more gradually. By June 1917, the situation was grim enough for Kolchak to resign in frustration, but the fleet remained capable of action right up to the eve of the Bolshevik Revolution. On November 1, Kolchak's successor, Rear Admiral Alexander Nemits, left Sevastopol with two dreadnoughts, three pre-dreadnoughts, and five smaller escorts on a last sortie against Turkish forces at the mouth of the Bosporus. Before the operation was complete, however, the crew of the flagship mutinied, giving Nemits no choice but to return to port. One week later, the new Soviet Russian government suspended all offensive naval operations.

The ensuing winter witnessed strikes of an unprecedented scale on the home fronts of the Central Powers, including more than a million workers during January 1918. The German Navy did not mutiny at that point, but the Austro-Hungarian Navy suffered serious unrest at Cattaro (February 1–3). The Cattaro mutiny started aboard the armored cruiser *Sankt Georg*, where the captain was shot in the head but, miraculously, not killed. Along with better food and working conditions, the mutineers demanded an end to Austria-Hungary's dependence upon Germany, endorsed Lenin's appeal for a peace without annexations or indemnities, and called for a good-faith response to the Fourteen Points that Woodrow Wilson had proposed less than four weeks earlier (see Chapter 9). The mutiny began to collapse after army artillery fired on the red-flagged harbor watch *Kronprinz Rudolf*, killing one sailor and wounding several others. The arrival of three pre-dreadnoughts from Pola on the morning of February 3 caused the remaining mutineers to surrender. The uprising had included sailors of all nationalities of the empire, confirming that war weariness and socialist politics – not the centrifugal forces of nationalism – were its strongest influences. Afterward, the navy executed four mutineers and imprisoned almost 400 more.

The navies of the Central Powers experienced no further serious unrest until the last days of the war. In his capacity as Chief of the Supreme Navy Command, Admiral Scheer was not willing to have the High Sea Fleet finish the war without a fight. On October 24, in connivance with Hipper (since August 1918 chief of the High Sea Fleet) and without consulting the emperor or the chancellor, he adopted the infamous Operations Plan 19, which would have sent Germany's remaining eighteen dreadnoughts and five battle cruisers on a suicidal raid in the direction of the Thames estuary. The sortie was scheduled for October 29, but sailors learned of the scheme two days earlier, and between the 27th and the 29th the crews of seven dreadnoughts and four battle cruisers mutinied (see Box 8.3). When the rebellion spread to two more dreadnoughts on October 30, Scheer and Hipper gave up their plan. Hipper then made the fateful decision to disperse his mutinous capital ships, sending some up the Elbe River and others

Box 8.3 "Every injustice shall find its revenge"

Excerpt from the diary of Richard Stumpf, seaman from Bavaria and eyewitness to the naval mutiny at Wilhelmshaven, where he served aboard the battleship Helgoland, October 29, 1918:

Soon thereafter we heard that the stokers on three battleships had deliberately allowed the fires to die down and had even extinguished them. At this time about a hundred men from *Von der Tann* were running loose about town; *Seydlitz* and *Derffinger* were missing men. Thus the fleet could not have sailed even if there had been no fog. It is sad, tragic, that it could go so far as this. But somehow even with the best of intentions I cannot suppress a certain sense of *Schadenfreude.** What has happened to the almighty power of the proud captains and staff engineers? Now at last, after many years, the suppressed stokers and sailors realize that nothing, no, nothing can be accomplished without them. Can this be possible? After having lived for such a long, long time under this iron discipline, this corpse-like obedience, it appears hardly possible.

As late as a few months ago I would have laughed at anyone who suggested that our people would simply throw up their hands at the approach of our enemy. Long years of accumulated injustice have been transformed into a dangerously explosive force which now erupts with great power all around. My God – why did we have to have such criminal, conscienceless officers? It was they who deprived us of all our love for the Fatherland, our joy in our German existence, and our pride for our incomparable institutions. Even now my blood boils when I think of the many injustices I have suffered in the navy. "Every injustice shall find its revenge." Never has this old motto been truer than now.

On the *Thüringen*, the former model ship of the fleet, the mutiny was at its worst. The crew simply locked up the petty officers and refused to weigh anchor. The men told the captain that they would only fight against the English if their fleet appeared in German waters. They no longer wanted to risk their lives uselessly.

… Now the revolution has arrived! This morning I heard the first flutter of its wings. It came like lightning. Unexpectedly it descended with one fell swoop and now holds all of us in its grip. Even though I was in the midst of things, I did not realize how quickly word spread this morning to "prepare to demonstrate on shore." The Division Officer, the First Officer and the Adjutant came down to our quarters and asked us in a crestfallen manner what it was that we wanted … We replied, "we shall parade in the streets to obtain our rights."

* transl.: pleasure derived from the misfortunes of others.

Source: Richard Stumpf, *War, Mutiny, and Revolution in the German Navy: The World War 1 Diary of Seaman Richard Stumpf*, trans. and ed. Daniel Horn (New Brunswick, NJ: Rutgers University Press, 1967), 418–20.

through the Kiel Canal into the Baltic, unwittingly enabling the sailors to serve as the catalyst for the revolution that swept through most northern German ports in the days before the Armistice. On November 5 sailors aboard the dreadnought *König* killed two officers who tried to stop them from replacing the imperial naval standard with a red flag; otherwise, mutineers gained control of the fleet with little resistance and no further deaths.

During the same days, the Austro-Hungarian Navy likewise succumbed to a general mutiny. As in the High Sea Fleet, the first open unrest came on October 27. Three days earlier, the army's front against Italy had collapsed in the face of a major offensive, leaving Trieste and Pola vulnerable to conquest by land. At the same time, in the south, the Italian conquerors of Albania had advanced to within 60 miles (90 km) of Cattaro. By October 29, most of the warships were in the hands of their crews. The Germans abandoned their Austro-Hungarian submarine bases, heading for home aboard twelve U-boats after scuttling another ten. Acknowledging the impending dismemberment of his empire, on October 30 Emperor Charles decided to turn the fleet over to the Yugoslav National Council. The following day, Horthy relinquished command of the ships at Pola to Slovene and Croatian officers loyal to the council, and on November 1 a similar transition occurred at Cattaro. In both cases, all seamen not belonging to the south Slav nationalities received immediate furloughs. Meanwhile, Charles assigned the navy's Danube Flotilla to Hungary. As a postscript to the collapse of the Austro-Hungarian Navy, the twelve German U-boats that fled the Adriatic at the end of October all made it home safely, although not until after the collapse of their own country and its navy. On November 9, the day of William II's abdication, *UB50* torpedoed and sank the pre-dreadnought *Britannia* off Cape Trafalgar. It was the last warship casualty of World War I.

The Birth of Naval Aviation

The aircraft carrier, like the submarine, first emerged as an important warship type during World War I, but only toward the end of the conflict, because naval aviation had a later prewar start and developed at a slower pace. After the outbreak of the war, the British Navy supplemented its lone prewar seaplane tender, the 7,080-ton *Ark Royal*, with other, smaller tenders, three of which participated in the British Navy's first air raid against a German target, the Cuxhaven Zeppelin base, on December 25, 1914. The raid caused little damage, and of nine seaplanes launched, just three survived to be picked up by the tenders. Throughout the rest of the war the British remained the leader in naval aviation, deploying seaplane tenders and primitive carriers in most operations on or near the coast, starting with the *Ark Royal* off Gallipoli. By the end of the war the British Navy had deployed thirteen such vessels; otherwise, only the French Navy (with five) and the Russian Black Sea Fleet (with eight) commissioned seaplane tenders.

In November 1915, the British achieved the first successful wartime deck launch of a wheeled airplane, and in September 1916 demonstrated that an airplane could land on a deck after hooking an arrestor cable. These breakthroughs led to the decision to build the carrier *Argus* (Figure 8.1) on the hull of an unfinished ocean liner and convert the new battle cruiser *Furious* into an aircraft carrier. On July 19, 1918, the *Furious* became the first carrier to launch and recover wheeled aircraft in a successful air raid, conducted by seven Sopwith Camels on the Tondern Zeppelin sheds in Schleswig-Holstein. The *Argus* was commissioned too late to see action. At the Armistice, Britain had a third aircraft carrier under construction and was building a fourth on the hull of a dreadnought originally laid down in Britain for the Chilean Navy. In 1919, work began to convert the battle cruisers *Glorious* and *Courageous* to aircraft carriers, giving Britain six built-and-building before any other navy had one.

Figure 8.1 HMS *Argus*

After experiments in September 1916 demonstrated that aircraft could land successfully after hooking an arrestor cable, the British Navy began to convert the unfinished passenger liner *Conte Rosso* into the 14,450-ton flush-deck carrier *Argus*. At the same time, the new battle cruiser *Furious* was fitted with separate launching and landing flight decks fore and aft of its centerline funnel and superstructure. The *Furious* entered service first, in March 1918, but the design was not a success, as a large net on its afterdeck failed to prevent aircraft from crashing into the funnel. This was not a problem aboard the *Argus*, which had no superstructure at all. It entered service in September 1918 and conducted its first successful deck landings on October 1, 1918, thus becoming the world's first truly operational aircraft carrier. The navy painted the *Argus* in "dazzle" camouflage and planned to use it in a torpedo-bombing raid on Kiel, but the war ended before the operation could take place.

At that stage few admirals were moved to re-envisage war at sea based upon the meager results of naval aviation in World War I, but Sir Charles Madden, commander-in-chief of the Atlantic Fleet and future First Sea Lord, was bold enough to call for the future British Navy to be built around a core of twelve carriers. Britain's leading military aviator, Air Marshal Hugh Trenchard, became famous for repeatedly stating "I do not claim to be able to sink a battleship,"[9] but across the Atlantic, his counterpart Colonel William "Billy" Mitchell took an openly antagonistic stance toward the US Navy. Under Mitchell's direction, in July 1921 aircraft from the US Army Air Corps bombed and sank the former German dreadnought *Ostfriesland* near the mouth of Chesapeake Bay. This demonstration silenced Mitchell's critics in the US Navy, who had insisted that even a defenseless stationary battleship could not be sunk by aircraft alone. The battleship had withstood every previous technological breakthrough, including the submarine, but in the long run it would not survive the challenge from the air.

Conclusion: A Revolution in Naval Warfare?

At sea, as on land, in a losing effort the Central Powers inflicted more damage and casualties than they sustained. This was especially true in the largest classes of warships. Germany lost one battle cruiser and Austria-Hungary one dreadnought, while Britain lost two dreadnoughts and three battle cruisers, Italy one dreadnought, and Russia (before leaving the war in December 1917) one dreadnought. In pre-dreadnought battleships, Germany and Austria-Hungary each lost one, while Britain lost eleven, France four, Italy two, and Russia one. Among the major non-European combatants, Japan lost a dreadnought to a magazine explosion and the Ottoman Navy lost a pre-dreadnought, while US losses were limited to smaller warships. Thus, the British Navy lost as many of the most modern capital ships (dreadnoughts and battle cruisers) as all other belligerents combined and, for pre-dreadnought battleships, one more than the total lost by all other navies. Fortunately for Britain and for the Allies in general, the British victory in the prewar naval arms race provided such a wide margin of material superiority that such losses could be sustained without seriously jeopardizing the war effort.

As the war progressed, the greatest threat to British (and overall Allied) command of the sea came from German submarines, but Allied (especially Anglo-American) cooperation ultimately sufficed to neutralize the danger, and at sea as well as on land, offensive strategies brought significantly higher casualties for the attacker than for the defender. Germany lost 178 of 335 U-boats (53 percent) and its junior partner in unrestricted submarine warfare, Austria-Hungary, lost 8 of 27 (30 percent). Allied rates of submarine losses were much lower: 43 of 269 submarines (16 percent) for Britain, 13 of 72 (18 percent) for France, 8 of 75 (11 percent) for Italy, and 9 of 61 (15 percent) for

Russia, through December 1917. In the end, the German undersea campaign made life miserable for the British and their allies, but it did not win the war for the Central Powers or, in a general sense, revolutionize naval warfare. In the end, the survival of Britain's superior surface fleet ensured its national security and naval preeminence, and facilitated a naval blockade that succeeded where Germany's U-boats failed, in determining the outcome of the war.

SUGGESTIONS FOR FURTHER READING

Gordon, Andrew. *The Rules of the Game: Jutland and British Naval Command* (Annapolis, MD: Naval Institute Press, 1996).

Halpern, Paul G. *The Battle of the Otranto Straits: Controlling the Gateway to the Adriatic in World War I* (Bloomington, IN: Indiana University Press, 2004).

Hathaway, Jane (ed.) *Rebellion, Repression, Reinvention: Mutiny in Comparative Perspective* (Westport, CT: Praeger, 2001).

Herwig, Holger H. *"Luxury" Fleet: The Imperial German Navy, 1888–1918*, revised edn. (Atlantic Highlands, NJ: Humanities Press, 1987).

Philbin, Tobias R. *The Battle of Dogger Bank* (Bloomington, IN: Indiana University Press, 2014).

Sondhaus, Lawrence. *The Great War at Sea: A Naval History of the First World War* (Cambridge: Cambridge University Press, 2014).

Sondhaus, Lawrence. *German Submarine Warfare in World War I: The Onset of Total War at Sea* (Lanham, MD: Rowman & Littlefield, 2017).

Tarrant, V. E. *Jutland: The German Perspective* (Annapolis, MD: Naval Institute Press, 1995).

Yates, Keith. *Flawed Victory: Jutland 1916* (New York: Naval Institute Press, 2000).

NOTES

1. See Nicholas A. Lambert, *Planning Armageddon: British Economic Warfare and the First World War* (Cambridge, MA: Harvard University Press, 2012).
2. Quoted in Lance E. Davis and Stanley L. Engerman, *Naval Blockades in Peace and War: An Economic History since 1750* (Cambridge University Press, 2006), 211.
3. Quoted in Alfred von Tirpitz, *My Memoirs*, 2 vols. (New York: Dodd, Mead & Co., 1919), 2: 285.
4. "The Sinking of the Lusitania – Official German Statement," Foreign Minister Gottlieb von Jagow, Berlin, May 28, 1915, in Charles F. Horne, ed., *Source Records of the Great War*, vol. 3 (Indianapolis: The American Legion, 1931), 198.

5. Adrian Gregory, *The Last Great War: British Society and the First World War* (Cambridge: Cambridge University Press, 2008), 61.
6. Paul G. Halpern, *A Naval History of World War I* (Annapolis, MD: Naval Institute Press, 1994), 328.
7. Quoted in Halpern, *A Naval History of World War I*, 331.
8. Quoted in Matthias Erzberger, *Erlebnisse in Weltkrieg* (Stuttgart: Deutsche Verlags-Anstalt, 1920), 251.
9. Quoted in Geoffrey Till, *Airpower and the Royal Navy, 1914–1945: A Historical Survey* (London: Jane's Publishing, 1979), 158.

Wilson and Lenin

Woodrow Wilson (1856–1924) is the only career academician to become president of the United States. His reputation as a reformer while president at Princeton (1902–10) led to his election as governor of New Jersey (1910) then US president (1912). He entered the White House with an agenda for domestic reform, remarking that "it would be an irony of fate if my administration had to deal chiefly with foreign affairs."

Vladimir Ilyich Ulyanov (1870–1924) became a sworn opponent of the tsarist regime after his elder brother was executed for plotting to assassinate Alexander III. First imprisoned in 1895, he was sent to Siberia (1897) to a camp near the Lena River, source of his later alias "Lenin." He spent most of 1900–17 in exile abroad, becoming a central figure in the Russian Social Democratic Labor Party and head of its Bolshevik faction (1903).

9 Wilson, Lenin, and Visions for Peace

December 12, 1916	Bethmann Hollweg's peace overture
January 22, 1917	Wilson's "peace without victory" speech; Lenin's last speech in Zurich; Bloody Sunday anniversary strikes in Russia.
February 3	United States breaks diplomatic relations with Germany.
March 1	"Zimmermann telegram" released to American press.
March 15	Abdication of Nicholas II.
April 6	United States declares war on Germany.
April 9–16	Lenin returns to Russia.
June	First American troops arrive in France.
July–August	Russian defeat in "Kerensky offensive."
November 2–3	First US combat deaths on Western front.
November 7–8	Bolshevik Revolution in Russia.
December 15	Soviet Russia signs armistice with Central Powers.
January 8, 1918	Wilson's "Fourteen Points" speech to Congress.

On December 12, 1916, as the French counterattack at Verdun finally fizzled out, German chancellor Bethmann Hollweg made a peace overture to the Allies via the United States. President Wilson eagerly embraced the chance to serve as mediator. He had sought the role previously, but peace missions to Europe by his chief advisor, Colonel Edward House, in February 1915 and again in January 1916, had come to nothing, as the cotton baron-turned-financier (whose colonelcy had been granted by a Texas governor) returned home both times convinced that Britain and France wanted the United States to commit to an "entangling alliance" of the sort George Washington had warned against, while Germany wanted nothing less than total victory.

On December 18, Wilson asked both sides to share their terms. While the German chancellor responded with a vague statement, refusing to share specifics before negotiations began, the Allies on January 10, 1917, issued a list of demands ultimately incorporated into the postwar treaties, including the cession of Alsace-Lorraine to France and the dismemberment of Austria-Hungary in order to grant freedom to its Italian, Romanian, and Slavic nationalities. Bethmann Hollweg, anticipating an unacceptable outcome to his overture, agreed the day before the Allied statement that Germany should resume unrestricted submarine warfare. Wilson, meanwhile, held out hope for a negotiated settlement and, in a speech to Congress on January 22, implored the belligerents to accept a "peace without victory." Nine days later, he received notice from the German government of the resumption of the unrestricted U-boat campaign, couched as a response to his speech. Outraged, Wilson broke diplomatic relations with Germany on February 3.

In light of the submarine offensive that followed, the Allies at the time (and most scholars since, especially in Anglo-American circles) have assumed the German peace overture was insincere, though recent scholarship – focusing on the Allied response – has suggested instead that the Allies emerged from the year of Verdun, the Somme, and Jutland more determined than the Germans to achieve a victorious peace.[1] At the time, German generals and admirals, though frustrated that Bethmann Hollweg had delayed William II from unleashing the U-boats, came to view the overture as beneficial in making the resumption of unrestricted submarine warfare appear as a response to Allied intransigence. But, outside of Germany, few believed that events had unfolded in a sequence that gave Germany the moral high ground. Wilson, in characterizing the Allied demands of January 10 as the foundation for a reasonable peace, showed the extent to which he was already prejudiced in favor of their perspective. In the absence of peace talks the war continued into a fourth year, during which the Allies would add the United States to their ranks but lose Russia. These revolutionary developments – the United States showing its potential to act as a leading great power, and the replacement of the tsar's government, ultimately, with the first communist regime – would change the world forever.

Wilson's Drift Toward War, 1914–17

The resumption of unrestricted submarine warfare in February 1917 prompted the United States to go to war with Germany two months later, but American involvement in World War I did not start in April 1917. In its sentiments, policies, and actions, the United States had abandoned genuine neutrality long before it entered the war. Over the first thirty-two months of the conflict, the Americans provided the Allies with tens of thousands of volunteers, billions of dollars' worth of munitions, and, most important of all, billions of dollars in loans, initiating a process that, by 1918, transformed the country from a debtor to the world's leading creditor. Meanwhile, Woodrow Wilson moved gradually from a posture of strict neutrality to one of leading the United States into an unprecedented full-scale involvement in a war in Europe.

Few would have predicted that the war erupting in Europe in August 1914 would escalate to involve the United States, which, alone among the world powers, had no alliance commitments binding it to any of the other powers. For a number of reasons, American intervention on the side of the Allies appeared particularly unlikely. Of the 92 million Americans recorded in the 1910 census, 10 percent listed German as their first language. In addition to the millions of immigrants from Germany and Austria-Hungary, those from Ireland (overwhelmingly Catholic and anti-British) and Russia (almost all Jews escaping tsarist persecution) were more likely to favor the Central Powers over the Entente, as were many Americans of German or Irish heritage. Of the other seven world powers, Japan alone had a strained relationship with the United States, which worsened after the Japanese invoked their British alliance to join the Allies and seize Germany's western Pacific island colonies, astride the route from Hawaii to the Philippines, then bullied China with their Twenty-One Demands. Finally, the United States throughout its history had championed the cause of freedom of the seas and, as early as the Napoleonic Wars, had asserted its right as a wartime neutral to trade with whomever it wanted. Thus, of all the issues that might draw the United States into the conflict, the Allied blockade of the North Sea and Adriatic, closing the ports of the Central Powers to American shipping, appeared to be the one most offensive to American sensibilities.

Wilson's secretary of state, William Jennings Bryan – the unsuccessful Democratic nominee in three of the four presidential elections preceding Wilson's victory in 1912 – was an even more unlikely warrior than the president. Bryan rejected the prewar movement for American "preparedness," championed by former president Theodore Roosevelt, as a sort of criminal enterprise, believing that the mere possession of the means to wage a modern war would, inevitably, lead the United States to commit acts of aggression abroad: "this nation does not need burglar's tools unless it intends to make burglary its business."[2] In the wake of the sinking of the *Lusitania*, Roosevelt lambasted Wilson for his timid response to the deaths of 128 American citizens, in particular the assertion that the United States was "too proud to fight," but Bryan considered the president's response too harshly anti-German, and in June 1915 resigned from the cabinet. In the presidential election of 1916, both Wilson and his Republican opponent, Charles Evans Hughes, advocated neutrality but with "preparedness." On the strength of the campaign slogan "He Kept Us Out of War," Wilson won re-election but by the narrowest margin (until 2004) for any sitting American president.

By the time of Wilson's re-election, the United States had developed a considerable financial and economic stake in an Allied victory, despite the president's initial conviction that funding or supplying either side would compromise American neutrality. In November 1914 France began borrowing from New York banks, and in August 1915 foreign countries received permission to sell bonds on the American financial market. By April 1917 the Allies had raised US$2.6 billion in this way, mostly through the firm of J. P. Morgan, and another US$2 billion by liquidating some of their prewar investments in American securities. In contrast, German bonds sold through the firm of Kuhn Loeb failed to attract much interest. Meanwhile, American munitions exports increased from US$40 million in 1914 to almost US$1.3 billion in 1916, and the overall value of exported manufactured goods from US$2.4 billion (6 percent of the gross national product or GNP) in 1914 to US$5.5 billion (12 percent of GNP) in 1916, with orders from the Allied countries accounting for almost all the growth. The war-generated economic boom gave the United States an average annual trade surplus of US$2.5 billion for the years 1914–17, up dramatically from the prewar average of US$500,000. During the period of American neutrality, the sales of munitions and supplies brokered by J. P. Morgan alone accounted for more than one-quarter of all US exports.

While the relative popularity of Allied bonds over German bonds reflected the preference of American investors, the Allied blockade made it virtually impossible for American firms to export anything to the Central Powers, even if they wanted to. Wilson protested the blockade as soon as it was implemented but took no action against it; once the Allies became dependent upon American capital, munitions, and supplies he never considered withholding these in order to force an end to the blockade, even though its comprehensive scope (including food and medicine) clearly violated international law. Before resigning as secretary of state, Bryan urged Wilson to condemn the Allied blockade – most notably in the president's statement following the sinking of the *Lusitania*, in order to balance his condemnation of German unrestricted submarine warfare – but he refused to do so. Indeed, most American leaders, and the public in general, remained unsympathetic to German attempts to equate the U-boat "blockade" of the British Isles with the Allied blockade of Germany.

Box 9.1 The Zimmermann telegram

On January 19, 1917, German foreign secretary Arthur Zimmermann (1854–1940) informed the German ambassador in Mexico City that unrestricted submarine warfare would be resumed effective February 1, and gave him instructions on how to proceed should the United States declare war on Germany:

On the first of February we intend to begin submarine warfare unrestricted. In spite of this, it is our intention to endeavor to keep neutral the United States of America. If this attempt is not successful, we propose an alliance on the following basis with Mexico: That we shall make war together and together make peace. We shall give general financial support, and it is understood that Mexico is to reconquer the lost territory in New Mexico, Texas, and Arizona. The details are left to you for settlement …

You are instructed to inform the President of Mexico of the above in the greatest confidence as soon as it is certain that there will be an outbreak of war with the United States and suggest that the President of Mexico, on his own initiative, should communicate with Japan suggesting adherence at once to this plan; at the same time, offer to mediate between Germany and Japan. Please call to the attention of the President of Mexico that the employment of ruthless submarine warfare now promises to compel England to make peace in a few months.

After the British intercepted and decoded the telegram, President Wilson authorized its publication on March 1,

further inflaming an American public already incensed by the resumption of unrestricted submarine warfare. In a speech to the Reichstag on March 29, Zimmermann inexplicably confirmed the authenticity of the telegram, which skeptical Americans had denounced as a British forgery, and defended the "patriotic" motives behind it:

I instructed the Minister to Mexico, in the event of war with the United States, to propose a German alliance to Mexico, and simultaneously to suggest that Japan join the alliance. I declared expressly that, despite the submarine war, we hoped that America would maintain neutrality. My instructions were to be carried out only after the United States declared war and a state of war supervened. I believe the instructions were absolutely loyal as regards the United States. General Carranza [Venustiano Carranza Garza, president of Mexico] would have heard nothing of it up to the present if the United States had not published the instructions which came into its hands in a way which was not unobjectionable … When I thought of this alliance with Mexico and Japan I allowed myself to be guided by the consideration that our brave troops already have to fight against a superior force of enemies, and my duty is, as far as possible, to keep further enemies away from them … Thus, I considered it a patriotic duty to release those instructions, and I hold to the standpoint that I acted rightly.

Source: Charles F. Horne, ed., *Source Records of the Great War*, vol. 5 (Indianapolis: the American Legion, 1931), 43–46.

After US protests led to the suspension of unrestricted submarine warfare in September 1915, Germany resorted to acts of sabotage within the United States to stem the flow of supplies to the Allies (reasoning, somehow, that such a course would be less inflammatory than the U-boat campaign). The operation was funded through the

German embassy in Washington and initially included the military attaché, Franz von Papen, future German chancellor and key figure in bringing Hitler to power in 1933. The most significant plot to come to fruition resulted, in the predawn hours of July 30, 1916, in a spectacular explosion on Black Tom Island in New York harbor, the primary shipping point for munitions exports to Britain and France. The ignition of 1,000 tons of munitions shook the earth at a level exceeding 5.0 on the Richter scale, caused an estimated US$20 million of damage (including serious damage to the nearby Statue of Liberty) and injured several hundred people, but owing to the late hour and the rapid evacuation of the island, only seven died. The following day's *New York Times* cautioned readers against jumping to the conclusion that the blast had been perpetrated by "alien plotters against the neutrality of the United States," but conceded that "the destruction of so large a quantity of Allied war material must prove cheering news to Berlin and Vienna."[3]

In February 1917, after the resumption of unrestricted submarine warfare prompted Wilson to break diplomatic relations with Germany, the British revealed to the Americans that they had intercepted and decoded a telegram sent by Arthur Zimmermann, Jagow's successor as German foreign secretary, to the German embassy in Mexico City. The "Zimmermann telegram" (see Box 9.1), drafted in anticipation of an American declaration of war against Germany, promised Mexico the return of three southwestern US states in exchange for its entry into the war, and sought Mexican help in getting Japan to quit the Allies and join the Central Powers. After securing proof that it was not a British forgery, on March 1 Wilson released the text of the telegram to the American press. Long considered to have been crucial to turning American public opinion decisively in favor of US intervention on the side of the Allies, the telegram now appears to have affected Wilson more than anyone else, causing him to lose hope in the possibility of peace. His cabinet, Congress, and the public already had made up their minds, with majorities already favoring war.

Revolution in Russia: Nicholas II Overthrown

Early in the new year, the Russian home front finally broke under the weight of the human toll of the war, the food shortages resulting from the mobilization of so many millions of peasant farmers, and the working conditions in the country's overburdened factories. On January 22, the day of Wilson's "peace without victory" speech, the tsar's government faced the most serious demonstrations since the Revolution of 1905, held to commemorate the twelfth anniversary of the Bloody Sunday massacre that had marked the onset of the upheaval of that year. In Petrograd alone, 150,000 workers went out on strike. Large numbers of protesters also took to the streets in

Moscow and in cities as far away as Kharkov and Baku. The unrest grew over the next six weeks and became increasingly radicalized, culminating on March 8 in a demonstration by 200,000 Petrograd workers calling for an end to the tsarist regime and the war. Nicholas II's critics among Russia's political and military leaders had already concluded the previous autumn that only decisive change could save the country. Speaking in the Duma in November 1916, Pavel Miliukov, leader of the Kadets, ended a litany of criticism of prime minister Stürmer and the government's conduct of the war with the question, "What is this? Stupidity or treason?"[4]

As Russia entered its fourth year of war, the army's human shortcomings ranked as its greatest problem. Thanks to the efforts of the Allies to get munitions into Russia via Archangel in the north and Vladivostok in the east, Russian troops were better supplied in 1917 than at any time since 1914. But the leadership, from the tsar at Mogilev down to the generals in the field, left much to be desired, while the manpower, historically Russia's greatest strength, was melting away. By the beginning of 1917 the Russian Army had lost 2.7 million men killed or wounded and more than 4 million prisoners. Another 2.3 million served in the interior in garrisons, which included a volatile mixture of fresh conscripts, veteran soldiers convalescing from wounds, and troublemakers too unreliable for the front. Events would soon show that the garrisons were also unreliable against demonstrators.

In the face of the crisis, the loose circle of politicians, generals, and noblemen best positioned to take action could not reach a consensus on what to do, and aside from murdering Rasputin, none of them acted until the tsar unwittingly forced their hand by responding to the street demonstrations with orders to dissolve the Duma and use force against the protesters. On March 10, troops deployed to disperse the demonstrations joined them instead, sparking a full-scale mutiny of the Petrograd garrison. Two days later the Duma defiantly proclaimed the formation of the Provisional Government. On the 13th, Nicholas attempted to return to the capital from Mogilev but only made it as far as Pskov, where representatives of the Duma met him and urged him to abdicate. On the 15th, Alekseev, recently returned to duty from his extended sick leave, confirmed that most Russian generals felt the tsar should give up the throne. He reported their verdict to the tsar, and that evening Nicholas abdicated, bypassing his sickly son, Aleksei, in favor of his brother, Grand Duke Michael. The following day Michael refused the throne, instead calling on the Russian people to obey the Provisional Government until a Constituent Assembly could be elected to determine the future constitution of the country (see Box 9.2). The relatively bloodless revolution claimed 169 lives, most of them in Petrograd, including a handful of officers shot by their men. Vice Admiral Nepenin, commander of the Baltic fleet, was the highest-ranking officer to be murdered. Revolutionary sailors soon controlled most Russian warships.

Box 9.2 **The Romanovs renounce the Russian throne**

On March 15, 1917, Nicholas II abdicated in favor of his brother, Grand Duke Michael:

In the midst of the great struggle against a foreign foe, who has been striving for three years to enslave our country, it has pleased God to lay on Russia a new and painful trial. Newly arisen popular disturbances in the interior imperil the successful continuation of the stubborn fight. The fate of Russia, the honor of our heroic army, the welfare of our people, the entire future of our dear land call for the prosecution of the conflict, regardless of the sacrifices, to a triumphant end. The cruel foe is making his last efforts and the hour is near when our brave army, together with our glorious allies, will crush him.

In these decisive days in the life of Russia, we deem it our duty to do what we can to help our people to draw together and unite all their forces for the speedier attainment of victory. For this reason we, in agreement with the State Duma, think it best to abdicate the throne of the Russian State and to lay down the Supreme Power. Not wishing to be separated from our beloved son, we hand down our inheritance to our brother, the Grand Duke Michael Alexandrovich, and give Him Our blessing on mounting the throne of the Russian Empire … We call on all faithful sons of the fatherland to fulfill their sacred obligations to their country by obeying the Tsar at this hour of national distress, and to help him and the representatives of the people to take Russia out of the position in which she finds herself, and to lead her into the path of victory, well-being, and glory. May the Lord God help Russia!

The following day, March 16, Michael in effect renounced the throne by declaring that he would accept it only if it were offered to him by a popularly elected assembly:

A heavy burden has been laid on me by my brother who has passed over to me the imperial throne of Russia at a time of unprecedented war and popular disturbances. Animated by the thought which is in the minds of all, that the good of the State is above other considerations, I have decided to accept the supreme power only if that be the desire of our great people, expressed at a general election for their representatives to a Constituent Assembly, which should determine the form of government and lay down the fundamental laws of the Russian Empire. With a prayer to God for his blessings, I beseech all citizens of the Empire to subject themselves to the Provisional Government, which is created by and invested with full power by the State Duma, until the summoning, at the earliest possible moment, of a Constituent Assembly, selected by universal, direct, equal, and secret ballot, which shall establish a government in accordance with the will of the people.

Source: *Documents of Russian History, 1914–1917*, ed. Frank Alfred Golder (New York: The Century Co., 1927), 297–99.

For the Allies, the abdication of Nicholas II raised hopes as well as fears. In Britain, France, and Italy, liberals and socialists led a chorus of optimists who assumed the Provisional Government could fare no worse than the tsarist regime and would probably govern better. But others doubted Russia's new leaders could master the increasingly volatile situation within the country. For all his weaknesses, the tsar had been a known quantity, and under his direction Russia had been a reliable ally, shouldering more than its share of the war's burdens. The greatest fear, common in all Allied capitals, was that the Provisional Government would pull Russia out of the war. Such a development would send shock waves from Flanders to the Persian Gulf, enabling Germany to focus on the Western front in France and Austria-Hungary to mass its forces against Italy, while the Ottoman Empire could concentrate its war effort against British and Imperial troops in Mesopotamia and the British-sponsored Arab revolt in the Hejaz (see Chapter 12). Thus, from the outset the Provisional Government came under great pressure from London, Paris, and Rome (soon joined by Washington) to stay in the war.

This pressure fell on a government that never really controlled Russia. While, in theory, it inherited the full powers of the tsarist regime, the Provisional Government from the start had to accept a "dual power" arrangement with the network of soviets (councils), led by the Petrograd Soviet, which had been formed across the country by revolutionary workers and peasants. On March 14, the Petrograd Soviet issued its famous Order Number One, sanctioning the creation of soviets within the armed forces and, in effect, ending traditional military discipline in Russia. The order affirmed that the soviets within each military unit would control its weapons and were bound to obey the orders of the Provisional Government only if they did not conflict with the orders of the Petrograd Soviet. Because the Provisional Government made the fateful decision to keep Russia in the war, Alekseev and the generals faced the prospect of fighting the Central Powers in 1917 hamstrung by the requirement that every officer must justify every order to his troops, down to the lowest level.

The United States Declares War

The initial revolution in Russia and the abdication of Nicholas II removed the embarrassment Wilson would have felt in bringing the United States into a war against German autocracy in league with the greatest autocrat of all. On March 20 the cabinet unanimously endorsed war; thereafter, the president came round to the notion that, having failed in his quest to shape a lasting peace as a neutral mediator, he could do so by making the United States the key contributor to an Allied victory. He finally asked Congress for a declaration of war on April 2, in a lengthy address to Congress (see Box 9.3) that touched off four days of debate. On April 4, the Senate authorized hostilities by a vote of 82:6, followed on April 6 by the House of Representatives, 373:50. The "no" votes in the Senate included George W. Norris of Nebraska, who alleged that "we are going into war upon the command of gold … I feel that we are about to put the dollar sign on the American flag."[5] Dissenters in the House included Representative Jeanette Rankin of Montana, one of a dozen states to allow full voting rights to women at that time; Rankin also cast the lone dissenting vote against World War II.

Figure 9.1 Wilson asks Congress to declare war

On April 2, 1917, two months after the resumption of unrestricted submarine warfare, President Woodrow Wilson asked Congress to declare war on Germany. His detailed speech sparked two days of debate in the Senate and four in the House of Representatives, both of which granted his wish but not without dissent (six "no" votes in the former and fifty in the latter). The deliberations contrasted sharply with the next such occasion, December 8, 1941, after Japan's attack on Pearl Harbor, when Congress took just forty minutes to give President Franklin Roosevelt a near-unanimous declaration of war (one representative voting "no") after his brief seven-minute speech requesting it.

Unlike Italy in 1915, Romania in 1916, and Greece later in 1917, the United States joined the Allies as an "associated power" rather than by concluding a treaty tying itself to the prewar Triple Entente. In refusing to join the Entente, Wilson sought to preserve his own free hand to shape a peace settlement not necessarily bound by the territorial promises the Allies had made to each other since 1914. Joining the Entente would also have committed the United States to fight all the Central Powers, and Wilson wanted war with Germany alone. The United States finally declared war on Austria-Hungary in December 1917, but never opened hostilities with Bulgaria or the Ottoman Empire, although it did break diplomatic relations with them. A host of countries that had suffered economic hardship because of unrestricted submarine warfare followed the lead of the United States in joining the Allies as "associated powers," including Liberia and

Box 9.3 **Wilson asks Congress to declare war**

Excerpts from President Woodrow Wilson's speech to the US Congress, April 2, 1917, asking for a declaration of war against Germany:

The present German submarine warfare against commerce is a warfare against mankind. It is a war against all nations. American ships have been sunk, American lives taken, in ways which it has stirred us very deeply to learn of, but the ships and people of other neutral and friendly nations have been sunk and overwhelmed in the waters in the same way. There has been no discrimination. The challenge is to all mankind. Each nation must decide for itself how it will meet it. The choice we make for ourselves must be made with a moderation of counsel and a temperateness for judgment befitting our character and our motives as a nation. We must put excited feeling away. Our motive will not be revenge or the victorious assertion of the physical might of the nation, but only the vindication of right, of human right, of which we are only a single champion.

… I advise that the Congress declare the recent course of the Imperial German Government to be in fact nothing less than war against the government and people of the United States; that it formally accept the status of belligerent which has thus been thrust upon it; and that it take immediate steps not only to put the country in a more thorough state of defense but also to exert all its power and employ all its resources to bring the Government of the German Empire to terms and end the war … I have said nothing of the Governments allied with the Imperial Government of Germany because they have not made war upon us or challenged us to defend our right and our honor … I take the liberty, for the present at least, of postponing a discussion of our relations with the authorities at Vienna.

It is a distressing and oppressive duty, Gentlemen of the Congress, which I have performed in thus addressing you. There are, it may be, many months of fiery trial and sacrifice ahead of us. It is a fearful thing to lead this great peaceful people into war, into the most terrible and disastrous of all wars, civilization itself seeming to be in the balance. But the right is more precious than peace, and we shall fight for the things which we have always carried nearest our hearts – for democracy, for the right of those who submit to authority to have a voice in their own Governments, for the rights and liberties of small nations, for a universal dominion of right by such a concert of free peoples as shall bring peace and safety to all nations and make the world itself at last free.

On April 6, the Senate and House of Representatives voted for war. The United States waited another eight months before declaring war on Austria-Hungary, on December 7.

Source: Charles F. Horne, ed., *Source Records of the Great War*, vol. 5 (Indianapolis: The American Legion, 1931), 109–11, 115–17.

---

eight Latin American states (Brazil, Costa Rica, Cuba, Guatemala, Haiti, Honduras, Nicaragua, and Panama), while another four South American countries (Bolivia, Ecuador, Peru, and Uruguay) severed diplomatic relations with Germany but did not declare war. Aside from Brazil, which deployed a naval division for Atlantic convoy duty, none of them contributed armed forces to the war effort, but all played their part in seizing German assets, including merchant ships that had been granted internment in their neutral ports. Wilson welcomed their involvement as confirmation of the righteousness of the Allied cause, the crusade of democracy against German imperialism. The American entry into the war also affected the countries that chose to remain neutral, who lost the most powerful champion of their international rights especially in maritime matters. The Dutch in particular suffered the consequences, as the United States joined Britain in requisitioning Dutch merchant ships for its own wartime use.

Lenin From Exile to the "Sealed Train"

From his wartime exile in Switzerland, Lenin did not foresee the abrupt collapse of the tsarist regime. Speaking before a socialist youth group in Zurich on January 22 – the same day that Wilson's "peace without victory" speech coincided with the first large street demonstrations in Petrograd – he mused that "we old folks may not live to see the decisive battles of the coming revolution."[6] On March 15, the day he first heard news of the revolution and the imminent abdication of the tsar, he began plotting his return home, with the route across Germany appearing the most promising. Lenin's Bolshevik Party had remained small and its leaders were all in exile or in prison, but they were well known to the Central Powers. Austria-Hungary had provided sanctuary for Lenin and every other significant Bolshevik at one time or another before August 1914 and, after the war forced most of them to seek refuge in Switzerland, a German agent had contacted Lenin there as early as May 1915. As soon as it became clear the Provisional Government that replaced the tsarist regime would not sue for peace, Germany became keenly interested in fomenting a second revolution that would destabilize Russia enough to knock it out of the war. After Lenin contacted Berlin via the German ambassador to Switzerland, Zimmermann and the Foreign Office began to discuss the terms under which Germany would provide passage to the Bolshevik leader and a select group of his followers. While Zimmermann struck the bargain that sent Lenin home to Russia, the OHL endorsed it wholeheartedly. Two years later, Ludendorff remarked that "from a military point of view his journey was justified, for Russia had to be laid low."[7]

Zimmermann finalized the plan with one eye on the United States, amid a greater sense of urgency after Wilson, on April 2, asked Congress for a declaration of war. While some German leaders doubted the United States could draft, train, and transport a large army to Europe, all recognized that Germany's fate now likely hinged on ending the war in the east in time for its efforts to be focused on the Western front in order to achieve victory there before American reinforcements could arrive. They approved Zimmermann's arrangements on the 5th, one day before the US declaration of war, and on the following Monday, April 9, Lenin, his wife Nadezhda Krupskaya, and thirty others crossed the Swiss-German border. The two railway cars placed at their disposal (a coach and a baggage car) were "sealed" by mutual agreement. Lenin, anticipating accusations of being a German agent, wanted as little interaction as possible with the

Germans as he crossed their territory, while the Germans, for obvious reasons, were very careful about which of their own people would have contact with such dangerous revolutionaries.

On April 11, Lenin's entourage left their train at Sassnitz on the Baltic, took a ferry to Malmö in southern Sweden, then proceeded again by rail via Stockholm to Haparanda at the border of Sweden and the Russian grand duchy of Finland. There, the traveling party disembarked for a brief sleigh ride to the Finnish town of Tornio, where they boarded a Russian train for the final leg of the journey to Petrograd. Krupskaya later recalled that, when a young lieutenant came into their coach and engaged Lenin in a debate about the war and Russia's future, "soldiers began squeezing into the car until there was no room to move" and "stood on the benches so as to better see and hear."[8] During the afternoon of April 16, as they crossed southern Finland and neared their destination, Lenin fretted that the train would be too late for them to get a cab from the station to his sister's home in Petrograd. He also speculated that it would not matter, for they would all be arrested upon their arrival.

When they pulled into Petrograd's Finland Station at 11:10 p.m. on the evening of the 16th, they were overwhelmed by their reception. Searchlights swept across the tens of thousands of people crowded into the square and the surrounding streets, some of them carrying torches, all eager to see or hear the returning hero. Lenin and Krupskaya finally made their way from the station to their destination several blocks away in an armored car, from which Lenin had to alight at least a dozen times to deliver brief, impromptu speeches to the crowd in exchange for their leave to travel another block or two. In his initial address, an eyewitness remembered, Lenin expressed his belief that "any day may see the general collapse of European capitalism. The Russian revolution you have accomplished has dealt it the first blow, and has opened a new epoch."[9] Three days later, in his "April Theses," Lenin railed against the Provisional Government's attempt to channel the people's revolutionary fervor to revive the war effort; instead, he denounced "Russia's part in a predatory imperialist war" and called for "a truly democratic peace" in which "all annexations [would] be renounced." He called on his followers to provide "no support for the Provisional Government" and advocated its replacement "not [by] a parliamentary republic ... but a Republic of Soviets."[10]

It seemed farfetched at the time, but seven months later, Lenin got his wish, a Soviet Russia that certainly could not have been created without him – or without the cooperation of Imperial Germany in providing him with the "sealed train." Throughout those months the Germans would continue to aid his cause, and their own, by further undermining the discipline of the Russian Army. With the encouragement of their superiors, German troops fraternized with their counterparts all along the Eastern front; as winter gave way to spring, the commanders of the Russian Fifth, Tenth, and Twelfth armies reported such overtures, which culminated in a widespread fraternization on May 1, the international workers' holiday. Meanwhile, along the Austro-Hungarian sector of the front, widespread fraternization occurred on Eastern Orthodox Easter Sunday, April 15. Long before the Germans understood the reciprocal danger, Lenin recognized that fraternization could be used to spread the virus of revolution from Russia to the Central Powers. He made the Bolshevik position clear in a *Pravda* editorial of April 28: "Long live fraternizations. Long live the worldwide people's socialist revolution."[11]

To Europe With the AEF: "Lafayette, We Are Here"

Woodrow Wilson's self-righteous idealism, firmly rooted in his Protestant Christian faith, combined with the imperialism and nationalism of Theodore Roosevelt and the Republican opposition to endow the American war effort with a crusading zeal. Wilson had asked Congress to declare war before making a definitive decision about whether to send troops to Europe; indeed, some members of Congress assumed America's naval and industrial contribution would suffice. But in welcoming a French mission under Joffre to the White House on May 2, Wilson assured the marshal that the US would ship an expeditionary force to France "just as soon as we could send it."[12] He abandoned his long-standing opposition to conscription in part because Roosevelt asked for permission to form and lead a unit of volunteers, along the lines of his "Rough Riders" of the Spanish-American War, and Wilson had no intention of allowing his political nemesis to command troops in France. Congress authorized the draft later that month (see Chapter 11). In the meantime, the US Army laid the foundation of the American Expeditionary Force (AEF) by enlisting hundreds of thousands of volunteers in the existing regiments of the regular army and National Guard.

In choosing the commander of the AEF, Wilson passed over General Leonard Wood, a Roosevelt protégé, fellow "Rough Rider," and former army chief-of-staff, in favor of General John J. "Black Jack" Pershing, commander of the recent American intervention in Mexico against Pancho Villa. Wilson then gave Pershing greater leeway in determining American military strategy and policy than any other wartime president ever had, or ever would in the future. Pershing faced a daunting task. The United States had a peacetime army significantly smaller than the prewar forces of either Belgium or Serbia, including barely 100,000 regulars backed by 125,000 poorly trained National Guardsmen. During the Mexican intervention, the National Defense Act of June 1916 had authorized the expansion of the wartime strength of the regular army to 286,000 men and put the National Guard under the control of the War Department rather than state governors, but conscription ultimately facilitated the creation of a force fourteen times that size. To accommodate that growth, after the declaration of war the US Army built an infrastructure of camps and bases as the men were reporting for duty, granted rapid promotions to most of its veteran officers, and filled the enormous demand for junior officers by promoting NCOs and granting commissions after a three-month course.

Shortly after these processes had begun, Pershing and his staff arrived in France in June 1917 amid great fanfare, along with 14,000 troops of the American 1st Division, too few to make a difference on the Western front but enough to raise spirits when parading through Paris. Pershing endeared himself to the French public by paying homage to Napoleon at his tomb in the Invalides, where he kissed the emperor's sword, but another, more private gesture had greater significance for the Americans. On July 4, Pershing's staff made a pilgrimage to the 12th Arrondissement on the east side of Paris, to visit the grave of the Marquis de Lafayette in Picpus cemetery. There, the general's aide, Lieutenant Colonel Charles E. Stanton, uttered the famous words "Lafayette, we are here" (often, incorrectly, attributed to Pershing, upon his arrival in France a month earlier). Just as the French hero of the American Revolution had played a central role in securing the independence of the United States, Pershing's AEF had arrived to help liberate France from the Germans.

Amid the daunting task of raising, training, and transporting the AEF to Europe, Pershing had to deal with the impatience of the French and British, who wanted American troops amalgamated into their divisions as soon as they arrived in France. Assistant chief-of-staff General Tasker Bliss warned Secretary of War Newton Baker that the AEF could "simply be parts of battalions and regiments of the Entente Allies. We might have a million men there and yet no American army and no American commander."[13] Pershing received no specific instructions from Wilson on how to deal with the amalgamation question, but the president expected to have a central role at a postwar peace conference, which could be secured only if the troops of the AEF were organized and trained as an American army and given responsibility for their own sector of the Western front, where the contribution of the United States in defeating Germany would be clearly demonstrated. Owing to a strategic decision to use the available shipping tonnage to transport men rather than equipment, the AEF used French machine guns and artillery, British and French tanks, and was supported by American pilots flying British and French planes. Thus, additional months of training were necessary before deployment to the front, to ensure a basic competence and familiarity with the weaponry. The 1st Division finally went to the trenches in October 1917, in a quiet sector near Nancy in Lorraine. The US Army's first combat deaths followed on the night of November 2–3.

Kerensky and the Delusion of Revolutionary War

Following the abdication of the tsar, Alexander Kerensky, a leader of the Socialist Revolutionary (SR) Party, was the only member of both the Provisional Government and the Petrograd Soviet, and thus provided a crucial link between the two. After the new prime minister, Prince Georgi Lvov, appointed Kerensky war minister, he brought Brusilov to headquarters at Mogilev to replace Alekseev as overall commander of the army. General Vasili Gourko, recently appointed commander of the Western army group (replacing Evert, the only senior general to oppose the tsar's abdication), recalled later that no one yet "understood the danger which threatened the ... fighting capabilities" of the army as a result of the revolution; instead, "all were hypnotized, and compared the Russian Revolution with the great French Revolution," giving "special attention ... to the successes of French arms after the revolution."[14] Kerensky reflected this optimistic revolutionary idealism. He believed "democratization" would revive the spirit of the army, enabling it to spread the democratic revolution to other countries. The Provisional Government's egalitarian vision of the "nation in arms" even included female soldiers, serving in fifteen women's battalions, one of which would see combat in the summer of 1917.

On his tours of the front, Kerensky won the support of the troops (whom he insisted should address him as "comrade") as well as their officers, reaffirming Order Number One while also attempting to restore some semblance of command authority. He also received a vote of confidence from the First All-Russian Congress of Soviets after it convened in Petrograd on June 16. Overruling the Petrograd Soviet, which on May 15 had called for a "peace without annexations or indemnities," a majority consisting of the SR Party and the Menshevik faction of Russian Marxists readily embraced the wishful thinking of the French revolutionary model offered by Kerensky and authorized him to launch an offensive at his discretion. Lenin's Bolsheviks, a minority at the congress, voiced their opposition in the strongest terms and thus established themselves as the party of choice for anti-war revolutionaries. Given the volatile nature of Russian politics, Kerensky moved quickly alter securing the endorsement of the congress. He gave Brusilov permission to proceed with an offensive he hoped would result in a morale-boosting victory, affirming the fighting ability of Russia's "democratic" army and increasing the credibility of the Provisional Government both at home and abroad.

During preparations for the Kerensky offensive, fraternization stopped and desertions declined dramatically. In his address to the troops on the eve of the battle, Brusilov urged "the Russian Revolutionary army" to embrace the tasks of "defending our freedom and exalting our great revolution."[15] The offensive began on July 1, spearheaded, as in 1916, by the Southwest army group, consisting of Brusilov's old Eighth Army (now under General Lavr Kornilov), along with the Seventh and Eleventh armies, which together included forty infantry and eight cavalry divisions, backed by 1,328 guns. Their opponents included replenished versions of some of the same formations routed by Brusilov the previous summer: the Austro-Hungarian Second and Third armies and the Austro-German *Südarmee*, twenty-six divisions in all, backed by 988 guns. Within days the Russians had advanced 20 miles (32 km), roughly half-way to Lemberg, and nearly captured the Drohobycz oil fields (see Online Essay 8). Hindenburg and Ludendorff had to redeploy eleven German divisions from France and three Austro-Hungarian

Figure 9.2 Alexander Kerensky

Kerensky (1881–1970) had much in common with Lenin. They were born in Simbirsk on the Volga, to acquainted families, the sons of schoolteacher fathers who became school superintendents (indeed, Kerensky's father served under Lenin's father and, in turn, was among Lenin's teachers). Both earned law degrees at St. Petersburg University, then embraced the cause of revolution. In contrast to Lenin, Kerensky was jailed only briefly and never exiled. After the Revolution of 1905 he became a prominent defense attorney in political trials of revolutionaries. He joined a faction of the non-Marxist Socialist Revolutionary (SR) party and served in the Duma from 1912–17. During 1917 he had the unique role of being in both the Provisional Government and the Petrograd Soviet. As war minister (and, later, prime minister), he wore a uniform despite having no military experience. The disastrous offensive that bore his name sealed his government's fate. Toppled in the Bolshevik Revolution, he refused to support either side in the subsequent civil war. He spent the rest of his life in exile, first in France, then in the United States.

divisions from the Isonzo to hold the front. By the time most of them arrived the offensive had already lost momentum, as Brusilov learned quickly that Order Number One made it impossible to sustain attacks in the face of heavy losses.

German divisions then led a counterattack (July 19–August 3) that left the Russian Army completely broken. By the time the fighting stopped, the Central Powers had advanced 150 miles (240 km) to the east and retaken all the Austro-Hungarian territory in eastern Galicia and Bukovina that had been left in Russian hands the previous year, including the city of Czernowitz. In the five weeks of fighting each side lost around 60,000 men killed or wounded, but for the Russians massive desertions (for the first time, more to the rear than to the enemy) swelled total losses to 400,000, leaving the Provisional Government with no effective forces south of the Pripet Marshes. Brusilov blamed the collapse on "the criminal propaganda of the Bolsheviks" (see Box 9.4), but Austro-Hungarian propaganda leaflets also played a role in the latest round of a leaflet war that Russia and Austria-Hungary had engaged in since August 1914. In any event, after the defeat officers and NCOs labeled as "Bolshevik" anyone who shirked his duty. But blaming the Bolsheviks only enhanced their reputation in the eyes of war-weary soldiers. Within the remnants of the armies of the Southwest group, the number of Bolshevik cells would grow from 74 in July to 173 in September and 280 in November.

Box 9.4 "The criminal propaganda of the Bolsheviks"

General Aleksei Brusilov, commander of the Russian Army's 1916 "Brusilov offensive," also served as commander of the 1917 "Kerensky offensive," named for Alexander Kerensky, the war minister and, later, head of the Provisional Government. Two weeks after a promising start, by July 21–22 the operation failed amid Bolshevik-inspired desertions, as recounted in Brusilov's official dispatches from those days:

July 21st: After strong artillery preparation, the enemy persistently attacked our detachments on the Pieniaki-Harbuzow front [on both sides of the headwaters of the Sereth and 20 miles south of Brody]. At first all these attacks were repelled.

At 10 o'clock, July 19th, the 607th Mlynoff Regiment, situated between Batkow and Manajow (in the same region), left their trenches voluntarily and retired, with the result that the neighboring units had to retire also. This gave the enemy the opportunity for developing his success.

Our failure is explained to a considerable degree by the fact that under the influence of the extremists (Bolsheviks) several detachments, having received the command to support the attacked detachments, held meetings and discussed the advisability of obeying the order, whereupon some of the regiments refused to obey the military command. The efforts of the commanders and committees to arouse the men to the fulfillment of the commands were fruitless.

July 22nd: Our troops, having manifested absolute disobedience to the commanders, continued to retreat to the River Sereth, part giving themselves up as prisoners.

Only the 155th infantry division in the district of Dolzanka-Domamoricz, and the armored cars which fired on the German cavalry on the Tarnopol road, put up any opposition to the enemy.

With immense superiority in forces and technic [sic] on our side in the sections attacked, the retreat continued almost without a break. This was due to the absolute instability of our troops and discussions as to whether to obey or not to obey orders of commanders, and to the criminal propaganda of the Bolsheviks.

Source: Charles F. Horne, ed., *Source Records of the Great War*, vol. 5 (Indianapolis: The American Legion, 1931), 253–54.

The Bolshevik Revolution: Russia Leaves the War

On July 16–17, in the last days of the Kerensky offensive, the Bolshevik Red Guards (armed factory workers and army deserters) launched a premature attempt to seize power in Petrograd in the name of the soviets. The episode of the "July Days" resulted in some 400 deaths – more than twice as many as the revolution in March – and forced Lenin into temporary exile in Finland, but otherwise did little to harm his cause. As the only revolutionary party advocating peace, the Bolsheviks continued to gain support among soldiers in the wake of the Kerensky offensive. When Prince Lvov resigned on July 21, just after the Central Powers began their counterattack, Kerensky became prime minister of the Provisional Government and thus the prime target for Lenin's withering criticism. Thanks to a generous subsidy from the Germans, by July the Bolsheviks were publishing forty-one daily newspapers with a circulation of 320,000. Their rise in popularity within the army complemented an increase in support from among workers, especially in the capital, which put them closer to their goal of taking over the Petrograd Soviet.

Kerensky played into their hands by sacking Brusilov on July 31 and placing the army in the hands of the charismatic, ambitious Kornilov. Kerensky, in turn, ordered Kornilov to resign on September 9 for plotting to make himself dictator of Russia. Kornilov rejected the order, and defended his actions by alleging that "the Provisional Government, under the pressure of the Bolshevik majority in the soviets, is acting in complete harmony with the German General Staff."[16] With troops loyal to Kornilov threatening to march on Petrograd, Kerensky allowed the Red Guards, whom he had disarmed after the July Days, to recover their weapons and organize the defense of the capital. Sailors from the Kronstadt base of the Baltic fleet and Bolshevik sympathizers in the Petrograd garrison joined them. They arrested 7,000 suspected supporters of Kornilov, including hundreds of officers, and alerted railway workers not to let his trains get through. Bolshevik agents then fanned out from the capital and turned the detachments of idled troops against their officers. Kerensky called Alekseev out of retirement to replace Kornilov. He returned, reluctantly, and on September 14 obeyed the prime minister's order to arrest Kornilov, whom he imprisoned at Bykhov, near Mogilev. His actions saved the Provisional Government, at least for the moment. After just twelve days back in office, Alekseev gave way to Nikolai Dukhonin, at 41 one of the youngest generals in the Russian Army (though technically Kerensky assumed the role of army commander-in-chief himself, with Dukhonin as his chief-of-staff). The Kornilov affair thus left the army hierarchy in complete confusion and Kerensky hopelessly weakened. In the capital he was absolutely dependent on the Petrograd Soviet, and beyond it he exercised authority only with the approval of the growing network of local soviets.

Figure 9.3 Democratic peace

A detachment of Bolshevik Red Guards poses in Petrograd, October 1917, with a banner declaring their support for the "democratic peace" promised in Lenin's April Theses. The Red Guards consisted of armed factory workers and army deserters, supplemented in Petrograd by sailors from the Russian Baltic Fleet. Those pictured here are mostly workers from the "Triangle" factory. There were never more than 7,000 Red Guards at any time during 1917, but their numbers sufficed to secure control of Petrograd after Lenin seized power in the name of the Soviets (November 7–8).

Heartened by the clear signs that their investment in Lenin would pay off, the Germans patiently awaited the Bolshevik takeover and the separate German-Russian peace that would follow it. In the meantime, they limited their military operations to Riga, which the German Eighth Army (now under General Oskar von Hutier) took in a brief action on September 1–3, opened with the first large-scale use of the storm troop tactics previewed in 1916 at Verdun and employed later in 1917 at Caporetto and Cambrai. The German Navy, which had failed in its previous bid to secure the Gulf of Riga in August 1915, followed up with a second attempt (October 12–20) involving half of the High Sea Fleet, which landed troops on Ösel and Dagö islands while dreadnoughts drove off a badly outnumbered Russian flotilla. The loss of Riga and its gulf left the Germans in control of the entire Baltic except the Gulf of Finland. In his report to the Provisional Government following the debacle, Dukhonin observed that in terms of sea power "we are in effect back to the age of Tsar Aleksei," father of Peter the Great, founder of the Russian Navy.[17] Hindenburg's remarks on the aftermath of the Riga operation reflected the German view that the campaign in the east was over. "The structure of the Russian front became ever looser. It became clearer with every day that passed that Russia was too shaken by internal agitation to be capable of any military demonstration within a measurable time."[18]

Meanwhile, the Bolsheviks secured majorities in the soviets in Petrograd (September 22) and Moscow (October 2), and Lenin returned from Finland to plan his seizure of power. On October 23, the Bolshevik central committee approved his appeal for an "armed insurrection," over the protests of Grigori Zinoviev, Lev Kamenev, and other party leaders. According to Karl Marx, the proletariat would rise spontaneously once its economic circumstances had become intolerable, and nothing could be done to hasten or delay the event; indeed, Marx specifically rejected "putschism," the seizure of power by coup d'état. But Lenin persisted in the face of such misgivings, laying plans for his coup to coincide with the meeting of the Second All-Russian Congress of Soviets, which convened in Petrograd on the evening of November 7. By then, Kerensky could claim the loyalty of just 3,000 of the 200,000 troops in and around the capital – mostly officers, cadets, and members of the Petrograd Women's Battalion. In the middle of the night of November 7–8, when the Red Guards stormed Kerensky's offices in the Winter Palace, they met with little opposition (see Box 9.5). The Congress, controlled by the Bolsheviks and their Left SR allies, welcomed the news of the coup and set about appointing the new Soviet government, headed by

Box 9.5 **The Bolsheviks storm the Winter Palace**

American journalist and communist activist John Reed (1887–1920) rode the wave of Bolshevik supporters into the Winter Palace in Petrograd on the night of November 7–8, 1917. This excerpt from Reed's *Ten Days that Shook the World* (1919) captures the chaos of that night:

In the light that streamed out of all the Winter Palace windows, I could see that the first two or three hundred men were Red Guards, with only a few scattered soldiers. Over the barricade of firewood we clambered, and leaping down inside gave a triumphant shout as we stumbled on a heap of rifles thrown down by the *yunkers* [teenaged army cadets serving in the palace guard] who had stood there. On both sides of the main gateway the doors stood wide open, light streamed out, and from the huge pile came not the slightest sound.

Carried along by the eager wave of men we were swept into the right hand entrance ... A number of huge packing cases stood about, and upon these the Red Guards and soldiers fell furiously, battering them open with the butts of their rifles, and pulling out carpets, curtains, linen, porcelain plates, glassware ... The looting was just beginning when somebody cried, "Comrades! Don't touch anything! Don't take anything! This is the property of the People!"... Many hands dragged the spoilers down. Damask and tapestry were snatched from the arms of those who had them ... Roughly and hastily the things were crammed back in their cases, and self-appointed sentinels stood guard. It was all utterly spontaneous.

... "Clear the Palace!" bawled a Red Guard, sticking his head through an inner door. "Come, comrades, let's show that we're not thieves and bandits. Everybody out of the Palace except the Commissars, until we get

---

Box 9.5 **The Bolsheviks storm the Winter Palace (continued)**

sentries posted." Two Red Guards, a soldier and an officer, stood with revolvers in their hands. Another soldier sat at a table behind them, with pen and paper. Shouts of "All out! All out!" were heard far and near within, and the Army began to pour through the door, jostling, expostulating, arguing. As each man appeared he was seized by the self-appointed committee, who went through his pockets and looked under his coat. Everything that was plainly not his property was taken away, the man at the table noted it on his paper, and it was carried into a little room. The most amazing assortment of objects were thus confiscated; statuettes, bottles of ink, bed-spreads worked with the Imperial monogram, candles, a small oil-painting, desk blotters, gold-handled swords, cakes of soap, clothes of every description, blankets. One Red Guard carried three rifles, two of which he had taken away from *yunkers*; another had four portfolios bulging with written documents. The culprits either sullenly surrendered or pleaded like children. All talking at once the committee explained that stealing was not worthy of the people's champions …

Source: First published in *Ten Days that Shook the World* (1919), available at www.marxists.org/archive/reed/1919/10days/10days/ch4.htm.

Lenin as chairman of the Council of People's Commissars (Sovnarkom). Their take-over preempted elections to the Constituent Assembly, promised since March and finally held on November 25–27. The SRs, strong among Russia's peasant majority, polled twice as many votes as the Bolsheviks, leading Lenin to order Soviet troops to disperse the assembly when it attempted to convene on January 18, 1918. But getting into power proved to be easier than staying in power, as the Russian Civil War (1918–21) would demonstrate.

Conclusion: Competing Visions or Compatible Visions?

On the day after the Bolshevik coup, Lenin called for an immediate end to the war, building upon the Petrograd Soviet's earlier appeal for a "peace without annexations or indemnities," which, in turn, echoed the Zimmerwald Manifesto of September 1915. To facilitate negotiations, he proposed a three-month armistice on all fronts (see Box 9.6). While awaiting a response from the other belligerents, he asserted the Sovnarkom's authority over the Russian Army, abolished traditional ranks, titles, and medals, and established the principle of elected leadership for all military units. Dukhonin, formally named commander-in-chief in one of Kerensky's last official acts, initially remained head of the army. After receiving no response to his peace appeal from foreign governments, on November 21 Lenin directed Dukhonin to open armistice talks with the Germans. Given the general's recent actions – he had spent the week after the Bolshevik Revolution attempting to rally support for Kerensky, then allowed

Kornilov and other anti-Bolshevik generals to escape from prison – Dukhonin not surprisingly refused to obey Lenin's orders. Dismissed the following day, he remained defiant and was still at headquarters in Mogilev when his Bolshevik successor, Nikolai Krylenko, arrived on December 3. By then, Dukhonin's last loyal troops had abandoned him, leaving no one to stop Krylenko's Red Guard escort from murdering him on the spot. Twelve days later, the Soviet Government concluded an armistice with the Central Powers, ending the war on the Eastern front.

Box 9.6 Lenin's Decree on Peace

On November 8, 1917, the day after seizing power, Lenin presented to the Second All-Russian Congress of Soviets his appeal to all belligerents to conclude an immediate peace:

The Workers' and Peasants' Government … drawing its strength from the Soviets of Workers', Soldiers', and Peasants' Deputies, proposes to all warring peoples and their governments to begin at once negotiations leading to a just democratic peace … without annexations (i.e., without the seizure of foreign territory and the forcible annexation of foreign nationalities) and without indemnities.

The Russian Government proposes to all warring peoples that this kind of peace be concluded at once; it also expresses its readiness to take immediately, without the least delay, all decisive steps pending the final confirmation of all the terms of such a peace by the plenipotentiary assemblies of all countries and all nations. […]

The government considers that to continue this war simply to decide how to divide the weak nationalities among the powerful and rich nations which had seized them would be the greatest crime against humanity, and it solemnly announces its readiness to sign at once the terms of peace which will end this war on the indicated conditions, equally just for all nationalities without exception. […]

The government abolishes secret diplomacy, expressing, for its part, the firm determination to carry on all negotiations absolutely openly and in view of all the people. It will proceed at once to publish all secret treaties ratified or concluded by the government of landlords and capitalists [i.e. the Provisional Government] from March to November 7, 1917. […] We have to fight against the hypocrisy of the governments, which, while talking about peace and justice, actually carry on wars of conquest and plunder. Not one single government will tell you what it really means. But we are opposed to secret diplomacy and can afford to act openly before all people. We do not now close nor have we ever closed our eyes to the difficulties. […]

Wars cannot be ended … by one side alone. We are proposing an armistice for three months – though we are not rejecting a shorter period – so that this will give the suffering army at least a breathing spell and will make possible the calling of popular meetings in all civilized countries to discuss the conditions [of peace]. […]

While addressing to the governments and peoples of all countries the proposal to begin at once open peace negotiations, the government, for its part, expresses its readiness to carry on these negotiations by written communications, by telegraph, by parleys of the representatives of different countries, or at a conference of such representatives.

Source: https://www.firstworldwar.com/source/decreeonpeace.htm. Originally published in *Izvestiia*, November 9, 1917.

During the months of Lenin's rise to power in Russia, Wilson had made several speeches articulating his own revolutionary vision of a world reshaped by American ideals. The fall of the tsarist regime enabled him to characterize the "war to end all wars" as a struggle of representative governments against autocracy, to "make the world safe for democracy." Amid the lofty abstractions he gradually distilled a more specific program for peace, the Fourteen Points, presented to a joint session of Congress on January 8, 1918 (see Box 9.7). His sixth point included an appeal to fair play for Russia: "The treatment accorded Russia by her sister nations in the months to come will be the acid test of their good will, of their comprehension of her needs as distinguished from their own interests, and of their intelligent and unselfish sympathy." But Wilson's outline of American peace terms, drafted without consulting the Allies, came at a time when none of them yet recognized the legitimacy of the Soviet Government and all still hoped Russia would somehow remain in the war, even though, by then, two months had passed since the Bolshevik Revolution and three weeks since the German-Soviet armistice.

Box 9.7 **Wilson's Fourteen Points**

Excerpts from President Woodrow Wilson's speech to the US Congress, January 8, 1918, outlining his war aims and peace agenda:

The program of the world's peace, therefore, is our program; and that program, the only possible program, as we see it, is this:

I.   Open covenants of peace, openly arrived at, after which there shall be no private international understandings of any kind but diplomacy shall proceed always frankly and in the public view.

II. Absolute freedom of navigation upon the seas, outside territorial waters, alike in peace and in war ...

III. The removal, so far as possible, of all economic barriers and the establishment of an equality of trade conditions among all the nations consenting to the peace and associating themselves for its maintenance.

IV. Adequate guarantees given and taken that national armaments will be reduced to the lowest point consistent with domestic safety.

V.   A free, open-minded, and absolutely impartial adjustment of all colonial claims ...

VI. The evacuation of all Russian territory and such a settlement of all questions affecting Russia as will secure the ... opportunity for the independent determination of her own political development and national policy and assure her of a sincere welcome into the society of free nations under institutions of her own choosing; and, more than a welcome, assistance also of every kind that she may need and may herself desire. The treatment accorded Russia by her sister nations in the months to come will be the acid test of their good will, of their comprehension of her needs as distinguished from their own interests, and of their intelligent and unselfish sympathy.

VII. Belgium ... must be evacuated and restored ...

Box 9.7 Wilson's Fourteen Points (continued)

VIII. All French territory should be freed and the invaded portions restored, and the wrong done to France by Prussia in 1871 in the matter of Alsace-Lorraine … should be righted, in order that peace may once more be made secure in the interest of all.

IX. A readjustment of the frontiers of Italy should be effected along clearly recognizable lines of nationality.

X. The peoples of Austria-Hungary, whose place among the nations we wish to see safeguarded and assured, should be accorded the freest opportunity of autonomous development.

XI. Rumania, Serbia, and Montenegro should be evacuated; occupied territories restored; [and] Serbia accorded free and secure access to the sea …

XII. The Turkish portions of the present Ottoman Empire should be assured a secure sovereignty, but the other nationalities which are now under Turkish rule should be assured … an absolutely unmolested opportunity of an autonomous development, and the Dardanelles should be permanently opened … under international guarantees.

XIII. An independent Polish state should be erected which should include the territories inhabited by indisputably Polish populations, which should be assured a free and secure access to the sea …

XIV. A general association of nations must be formed under specific covenants for the purpose of affording mutual guarantees of political independence and territorial integrity to great and small states alike.

Source: Margaret MacMillan, *Paris 1919: Six Months that Changed the World* (New York: Random House, 2001), 495.

Lenin, repudiating the commitments of a government he considered illegitimate, and Wilson, joining the war as an "associated power" of the Allies to avoid being bound by commitments his cobelligerents had made earlier, both appeared uniquely poised to help bring about a just peace. As the war's last winter set in, their appeals resonated with war-weary soldiers, sailors, and workers on both sides, many of whom saw no incompatibility in the visions they had articulated; indeed, Lenin and Wilson would be quoted, at times interchangeably, in the manifestos of mutineers and strikers during the widespread unrest of the months to come. But the army of Lenin's Russia was melting away, while Wilson's America was feverishly building an army to tip the balance in the war of attrition in Europe. Lenin had seized power by force in a country in chaos, which, at the end of 1917, ranked below even Italy as the weakest of the great powers, while Wilson, emboldened by re-election the previous year, confidently led to war a country poised to become the strongest of the great powers. Thus, in the circle of governments, the simple facts of power politics caused Lenin's voice to be disregarded while Wilson's ideals, if not heeded, were at least accommodated. Allied leaders were in no position to resist the American president's characterization of their war as one being fought for universal rights and freedoms, even if they had been so inclined. The entry of the United States into the war would give the Allies men – millions of men – to go with the capital, munitions, and supplies they were already receiving from American sources. To the French and British, little else mattered at that stage.

SUGGESTIONS FOR FURTHER READING

Abraham, Richard. *Alexander Kerensky: First Love of the Revolution* (New York: Columbia University Press, 1987).

Katkov, George. *Russia 1917, the Kornilov Affair: Kerensky and the Breakup of the Russian Army* (London: Longman, 1980).

Grotelueschen, Mark Ethan. *The AEF Way of War: The American Army and Combat in World War I* (Cambridge: Cambridge University Press, 2007).

Rabinowitch, Alexander. *The Bolsheviks Come to Power: The Revolution of 1917 in Petrograd* (New York: W. W. Norton, 1976).

Smythe, Donald. *Pershing: General of the Armies* (Bloomington, IN: Indiana University Press, 1986).

Trask, David F. *The AEF and Coalition Warmaking, 1917–1918* (Lawrence, KS: University of Kansas Press, 1993).

Traxel, David. *Crusader Nation: The United States in Peace and the Great War, 1898–1920* (New York: Alfred A. Knopf, 2006).

Tucker, Robert W. *Woodrow Wilson and the Great War: Reconsidering America's Neutrality, 1914–1917* (Charlottesville, VA: University of Virginia Press, 2007).

Volkogonov, Dmitri. *Lenin: A New Biography*, trans. and ed. Harold Shukman (New York: The Free Press, 1994).

Woodward, David R. *The American Army and the First World War* (Cambridge: Cambridge University Press, 2014).

NOTES

1. See Horst Afflerbach, *Auf Messers Schneide: Wie das Deutsche Reich den Ersten Weltkrieg verlor* (Munich: Verlag C. H. Beck, 2018), 243–47.
2. Quoted in D. Clayton James and Anne Sharp Wells, *America and the Great War, 1914–1920* (Wheeling, IL: Harlan Davidson, Inc., 1998), 22.
3. *New York Times*, July 31, 1916, 1.
4. Quoted in Thomas Riha, *A Russian European: Paul Miliukov in Russian Politics* (South Bend, IN: University of Notre Dame Press, 1969), 310.
5. Quoted in David M. Kennedy, *Over Here: The First World War and American Society* (Oxford: Oxford University Press, 1980; reprinted edn., 2004), 21.

6. Quoted in Dmitri Volkogonov, *Lenin: A New Biography*, trans. and ed. Harold Shukman (New York: The Free Press, 1994), 104.
7. Erich Ludendorff, *Ludendorff's Own Story: August 1914–November 1918, Vol. 2* (New York: Harper & Brothers Publishers, 1919), 126.
8. Nadezhda Krupskaya, *Memories of Lenin* (London: Lawrence & Wishart, 1970), 294.
9. Quoted in Edmund Wilson, *To the Finland Station* (New York: Farrar, Straus & Giroux, 1972), 549.
10. V. I. Lenin, "The Tasks of the Proletariat in the Present Revolution ('April Theses')," in *The Lenin Anthology*, ed. Robert C. Tucker (New York: W. W. Norton, 1975), 295–300.
11. Quoted in Marc Ferro, "Russia: Fraternization and Revolution," in *Ferro et al., Meetings in No Man's Land: Christmas 1914 and Fraternization in the Great War* (London: Constable, 2007), 220.
12. Quoted in David R. Woodward, *The American Army and the First World War* (Cambridge University Press, 2014), 92.
13. Quoted in Frederick Palmer, *Bliss, Peacemaker: The Life and Letters of General Tasker Howard Bliss* (New York: Dodd, Mead & Co., 1934), 153–54.
14. Basil Gourko, *War and Revolution in Russia, 1914–1917* (New York: Macmillan, 1919), 335.
15. "Aleksei Brusilov, 'Address to the Revolutionary Army,' July 1, 1917," in Charles F. Horne, ed., *Source Records of the Great War*, vol. 5 (Indianapolis: The American Legion, 1931), 250–51.
16. Kornilov's Proclamation, September 11, 1917, text in John Shelton Curtiss, *The Russian Revolutions of 1917* (Princeton, NJ: Van Nostrand Anvil Books, 1957), 143–44.
17. Quoted in Alexander Rabinowitch, *The Bolsheviks Come to Power: The Revolution of 1917 in Petrograd* (New York: W. W. Norton, 1976), 225.
18. Paul von Hindenburg, *Out of My Life*, vol. 2, trans. Frederic Appleby Holt (New York: Harper, 1921), 80.

Italian retreat from Caporetto

Troops of the Italian Second Army retreat along the Udine–Codroipo road in northeast Italy after being routed by Austro-Hungarian and German forces at Caporetto in the upper Isonzo valley. In the twelfth battle of the Isonzo (October 24–November 19, 1917), better known as the battle of Caporetto, Italy lost nearly half of its army and the Allies almost lost Italy, during the same days that the Bolshevik Revolution ended Russia's involvement in the war. Caporetto became better known to the English-speaking world after being dramatized in Ernest Hemingway's novel, *A Farewell to Arms* (1929), and in two films (1932, 1957) based on the novel.

10 Upheaval and Uncertainty

Europe, 1917

March	Germans withdraw to Hindenburg Line.
April–May	French defeat in "Nivelle offensive."
April–September	Mutinies in French Army.
June 29	Greece joins the Allies.
Summer	Allies recover air superiority over Western front.
July–November	Third battle of Ypres (Passchendaele).
October–November	Twelfth battle of the Isonzo (Caporetto).
November 20	First use of tanks en masse, by British at Cambrai.
December 9	Romania signs armistice with Central Powers.

Germany's decisions to resume unrestricted submarine warfare and to facilitate Lenin's return to Russia led to the two most significant developments of 1917, but at no time during the year was it clear how the combination of the United States entering the war and Russia leaving it would affect the outcome. While the trade-off appeared to doom the Central Powers in the long run, within the ongoing war of attrition the departure of the Russians would deprive the Allies of their largest army at a time when the Americans were not yet in a position to make good the loss. And for all those in the Allied camp who took heart in Wilson's articulation of the new ideological clarity of their cause, on both sides there were many more who reacted to the events in Russia with the apprehension (or the hope, depending upon one's perspective) that the example might be replicated elsewhere. Thus, throughout the year, instances of retreat or surrender (along with strikes on the various home fronts) were seen as harbingers that the war might be destined to end not in victory or defeat but in a revolution toppling many, if not all, of the existing governments.

Unable to afford a repeat of the bloody battles of 1916, the Central Powers resolved to remain on the defensive during 1917 while the U-boats (and the Bolsheviks) did their work. On the Western front, the Germans fundamentally changed the war on the operational and tactical levels by unveiling the Hindenburg Line. This newly fortified front, constructed from Lille to Verdun, in some places 30 miles (50 km) behind the former front, bore witness to their intention to stand on the defensive, in particular, the Siegfried section (*Siegfriedstellung*) built south of Arras, across the bulging salient German troops had fought so hard to defend in the battle of the Somme. By March 20, the Germans completed their retreat to the new front; afterward, Ludendorff had local commanders implement a new "defense in depth," brainchild of Colonel (later General) Fritz von Lossberg, making full use of the Hindenburg Line's machine guns in concrete pillboxes and more formidable wire, trenches, dugouts, and bunkers. During 1917 these changes further underscored the difference between the war in the west and the war on the other fronts, where weary armies faced each other across far more malleable lines.

The Western Front: Arras and Vimy Ridge, the Nivelle Offensive

After resolving to replace Joffre as commander of the French armed forces, both Poincaré and Briand favored promoting the more aggressive Nivelle, architect of the counteroffensive at Verdun, over the head of the more cautious Pétain, architect of the earlier defense against the German onslaught. Nivelle's subsequent revision of plans for the Allied spring offensive of 1917 reflected his characteristic boldness. Whereas Joffre had assumed that British and Imperial forces would take the lead in the new year with French forces supporting them, Nivelle reversed their roles: the attack would be led by his own French armies at the center of the front along the River Aisne, a sector quiet since the autumn of 1914. In contrast to the methodical, relatively unambitious "bite-and-hold" tactics that Rawlinson's forces had used to achieve modest gains at the Somme, Nivelle argued that the entire depth of the enemy front could be breached in just two days. His plan called for a massive preliminary shelling along 50 miles (80 km) of the front between Soissons and Rheims, to be followed by a creeping barrage that would provide immediate support for an attack by waves of infantry spearheaded by tanks. The artillery support, he argued, would enable a frontal assault to break through multiple lines of German trenches and succeed in reaching the enemy artillery line – usually 6 miles (10 km) behind the front – in a single attack. Nivelle was so confident of success that he refused a late winter request by Franchet d'Esperey to have his northern army group attack while the Germans in his sector were retreating to their new positions on the Hindenburg Line, because it would draw resources away from the big push. But by shortening their front, the Germans put themselves in a better position to respond to an Allied offensive no matter where it struck; this, plus the broader factors of the initial Russian revolution and the impending American declaration of war, cast doubts over the wisdom of the plan as its start date drew nearer. Pétain, deeply hurt at having been passed over, intrigued against Nivelle and led the opposition to the plan within the army. Among the political leaders, Poincaré continued to support Nivelle, but on March 20 Briand fell from power in a cabinet reshuffle; the new premier, Alexander Ribot, appointed a war minister, Paul Painlevé, who made no secret of his opposition to Nivelle and the offensive. Poincaré finally convened a war council at Compiègne on April 6 – coincidentally, the day the United States entered the war – in a last-ditch attempt to clear the air. In the end Nivelle received a vote of confidence, but only after he threatened to resign.

Nivelle impressed the British more than his own countrymen. Thanks to his English mother he spoke English fluently, and did not hesitate to use it to his advantage in talks with France's allies. Early in 1917 he nearly persuaded Lloyd George to sack Haig in favor of Gough; the prime minister did not make the move (fearing a political backlash), but agreed to subordinate British forces to Nivelle's overall command for the upcoming offensive. Haig supported Nivelle because he let him launch his own offensive in the vicinity of Arras, as a diversion to the French thrust at the German center, and also promised French support for a British offensive in Flanders later in the year. North of Arras, Haig deployed the British First Army (now under General Sir Henry Horne) and Allenby's Third Army against the German Sixth Army (now under General Ludwig von Falkenhausen). First Army's Canadian Corps was assigned the task of taking Vimy Ridge, where enemy forces had been dug in ever since the "race to the sea" in the autumn of 1914, defying all attempts to dislodge them. Meanwhile, to the southeast of the town, Gough's Fifth Army was to assault the German line near

Bullecourt. Over the winter, all three British armies had been reinforced with conscripts, the first of whom arrived in France late in 1916, after the battle of the Somme. Their artillery spotting would improve during 1917 thanks to the introduction of the Sopwith triplane, superior to the German Albatros D3, but the new planes were not deployed in sufficient numbers to affect the action at Arras, where Richtofen's squadron ensured that Germany continued to enjoy the air superiority it had wrested from the Allies the previous autumn (see Online Essay 3).

In preparation for the battle of Arras (April 9–May 17), the British bombarded Vimy Ridge for three weeks and the rest of the 24-mile (39-km) sector for five days. In expending a record 2.7 million shells, they sought to make up in quantity what they lacked in targeting quality, as the Royal Flying Corps lost seventy-five planes in the days immediately preceding the battle, seriously compromising the direction of the shelling. Nevertheless, with the help of an effective creeping barrage, Haig's armies pushed the Germans back almost 4 miles (6 km) during the battle's first six days, in part because the terrain on the eastern slope of Vimy Ridge made it difficult for Falkenhausen to fully implement Lossberg's "defense in depth." Highlighting the success, the Canadian Corps took most of its objectives on the battle's first day and secured Vimy Ridge by April 12. But as a diversion for Nivelle's main offensive, the attack failed. Falkenhausen held his front without calling in reserves from elsewhere, and after their initial successes, Haig's armies made no further gains during four more weeks of intense fighting. The British lost almost 160,000 men, against 120,000–130,000 casualties for the Germans. The Somme, a much longer battle, had generated many more killed and wounded, but if measured in terms of casualties per day, Arras (with an average daily loss exceeding 4,000) was Britain's bloodiest battle of the war. Afterward, the sector remained quiet until the autumn, when it came alive again with artillery exchanges and gas attacks during the third battle of Ypres (Passchendaele), though the front remained unchanged (see Box 10.1).

The main spring offensive, which evolved into the second battle of the Aisne (April 16–May 9), began the day after the action at Arras stalemated. To lead the attack, Nivelle assembled a new "reserve army group," consisting of the Fifth, Sixth, and Tenth armies, commanded by the latter army's former head, Micheler. His forces were flanked on the right by Pétain's central army group, which would contribute its westernmost army, the Fourth, to the offensive. Micheler's Fifth and Sixth armies (nineteen divisions, with 128 tanks) opened the battle by attacking the German Seventh Army (General Max von Boehn), while the Fourth Army joined the action on the second day, advancing from its position east of Rheims to attack Fritz von Below's First Army. They made less progress than anticipated, for a variety of reasons. Aerial reconnaissance gave the Germans plenty of advance warning that they were coming, and a shortage of howitzers made the preliminary bombardment lighter than Nivelle wanted. The shelling proved to be ineffective against most features of the new German "defense in depth,"

Figure 10.1 Canadians in machine-gun pits at Vimy Ridge

Troops of the British First Army's Canadian Corps in machine-gun pits during the assault on Vimy Ridge. In the first four days of the battle of Arras (April 9–12, 1917), four Canadian divisions drove three divisions of the German Sixth Army from the ridge north of the town, taking 4,000 prisoners. Canadian casualties included 3,600 dead and 7,000 wounded. The battle was not the war's first action involving Canadian troops nor the most strategically important, yet it was celebrated, at the time and over the decades that followed, as the first occasion on which the Canadian divisions, raised from all parts of the country, fought together, and successfully, as a corps. In Canadian history, Vimy Ridge occupies a place in "birth of the nation" narratives analogous to Gallipoli for Australians (though the debate over the myth and reality of its significance is not quite as fraught). In 1922 France granted Canada 250 acres (100 hectares) on Vimy Ridge for a memorial park, and in 1936 a monument was dedicated on the site.

and, as for the British at Arras, German air superiority made it difficult for the French to spot their own artillery. The creeping barrages were uncoordinated and some troops advanced without proper artillery support. Nivelle's 13-ton Schneider CA1 tanks were of little help to the infantry; they were roughly half the size of the British Mark I tanks used at the Somme and far less effective, with seventy-six lost on the first day of the battle. Finally, the terrain in the sector Nivelle chose for the attack posed formidable natural obstacles, including the rugged south face of the Chemin des Dames ridge

Box 10.1 *"A spot of gas"* at Vimy Ridge, 1917

Excerpt from a memoir written by Harold Saunders, British infantry private, describing the action at Vimy Ridge in October 1917, featuring gas attacks by both sides:

The most awesome and in some ways most dreadful thing I ever saw was a kind of ceremonial gas attack in the autumn of 1917. We withdrew from the front line to the support trench, so that the engineers could operate on the ground between. It was a still moonlit night, one of those nights when the guns on both sides were quiet and there was nothing to show there was a war on. The attack began with a firework display of golden rain. The fireworks petered out and a line of hissing cylinders sent a dense grey mist rolling over No Man's Land. What breeze there was must have been exactly right for the purpose. But the unusual silence, the serene moonlit sky, and that creeping cloud of death and torment made a nightmare scene I shall never forget. It seemed ages before Jerry realized what was afoot. At last, however, the first gas alarm went and I think most of us were glad to think he would not be taken unawares. Presently the gongs and empty shell-cases and bars of steel were beating all along his front, almost as though he was welcoming in the New Year. But I was haunted for hours afterwards by the thought of what was happening over there.

Sympathy was blown sky-high the next night, however. We were going out to rest and shortly before the relieving troops were due Jerry started one of the fiercest barrages I ever experienced. The relief could not come up. The trenches were crowded with men all packed up and unable to go, and it rained – heavens, how it rained! Hour after hour we stood there in the rising flood, helpless as sheep in the pen, while the guns did their worst. It was six in the morning before we got back to the rest billets, more dead than alive. Even then there was no rest for me. I was detailed to parade for battalion guard in four hours. Battalion guard was a spit and polish business, and a full day would not have sufficed to remove nine days' mud from my uniform and clean my saturated equipment. A scarecrow guard of deadly tired men eventually paraded. We had done our best to get clean, but neither the sergeant-major nor the adjutant, both looking fresh and beautiful, applauded our efforts. Very much the contrary, in fact. But we were all past caring what they thought or said about our appearance.

The next time I went into the line a spot of gas sent me out of it for good. I did not know American troops were in France till I found myself in one of their hospitals at Etretat. The nurses and doctors were gentle beyond anything I ever experienced … A week later I was in Blighty, the soldier's Promised Land. Six months afterwards I appeared in the streets again as a civilian with a profound hatred for war and everything it implies.

Source: First published in *Everyman at War*, ed. C. B. Purdom (J. M. Dent, 1930), available at www .firstworldwar.com/diaries/trenchesatvimyridge.htm. (All attempts at tracing the copyright holder of the original work were unsuccessful.)

behind the German trench lines and, most significantly, the Aisne itself, a wide river that cut across the battlefield from east to west, in one place between the opposing armies. Nivelle's plan called for his troops to cross these obstacles plus a second river, the Ailette, and a second ridge, all in just two days.

Within the first four days of the offensive the French took 20,000 prisoners and captured 147 guns, but at a horrific cost of 118,000 casualties, including 40,000 on the first day, and without securing the Chemin des Dames ridge. The daily use of creeping barrages, on top of the protracted preliminary bombardment, soon led to a shell shortage, while the shocking casualties of April 16–20 caused a breakdown in the French Army's medical service. Given the doubts that had preceded it, the offensive's initial failure left Nivelle facing a scrutiny the likes of which Joffre had never experienced in any of his disasters. On April 23 Poincaré himself telephoned the commander to voice his concerns. Nivelle persisted amid growing pessimism from both Pétain and Micheler, and by May 4–5 French troops had captured most of the Chemin des Dames ridge. But by the time the fighting ended on May 9, they had advanced no farther than 2 miles (3 km) in any part of the sector. The French recorded a total of 187,000 casualties against 103,000 for the Germans (including their 20,000 prisoners lost). Afterward there was no shortage of critics to condemn both the general and his offensive. Perhaps most damning was the assessment of Nivelle later given by General Sir William Robertson, chief of the Imperial General Staff: "I always thought his plan was ridiculous and certainly had no confidence in him as commander-in-chief."[1]

As the battle was winding down, Lloyd George came to Paris with Robertson to discuss future Allied strategy. They brought with them Jellicoe, to underscore the existential threat posed by the U-boat war (at a time when the Anglo-American convoy system had been agreed to, but not yet implemented). While the British acknowledged that Nivelle had to be replaced, they were concerned that the defensive mindset of his likely successor, Pétain, would result in the French doing very little fighting at all. Meetings of the leading British and French generals – Robertson, Haig, Nivelle, and Pétain – resulted in a commitment to keep up the pressure on the Germans, but "with limited objectives" rather than grand designs, making "the fullest use of our artillery" to inflict losses on the enemy "with the minimum loss possible" to Allied infantry.[2] Just as Lloyd George had agreed to place Haig's armies under Nivelle's overall command for the spring offensives, the French premier, Ribot, agreed to place the French First Army under Haig's overall command for a fall offensive in Flanders.

Lloyd George and Robertson returned to London unaware that Nivelle's failure at the second battle of the Aisne would be followed by the French Army's most serious breakdown of discipline and morale of the entire war. The wave of disobedience soon spread throughout the army, affecting units not even involved in the offensive. War minister Painlevé sacked Nivelle on May 15 in favor of Pétain, and on the same day made Foch army chief-of-staff. Pétain restored order through a combination of patriotic appeals and firm discipline, and by not calling upon the army to do anything beyond the terms of the recent Anglo-French agreement. Nevertheless, the mutiny did not subside until mid-September, by which time it had affected 54 of the army's 114 infantry divisions. These months also witnessed unprecedented fraternization between French and German troops across no man's land; aside from the typical exchange of French food for German tobacco, each side sought newspapers from the other, a sign that neither fully trusted their own government to tell them the truth about the war or the revolution in Russia. The French mutinies, coinciding with the collapse of Russian resistance on the Eastern front, demoralized the French home front (see Chapter 11) but did not precipitate the same magnitude of crisis that forced Russia out of the war. During the mutiny 20,000 French troops deserted to the Germans, an unprecedented number for the Western front, but minuscule by the standards of desertion in the Russian or Austro-Hungarian armies. Unlike the Russian Army that same summer, the French Army remained intact and held its positions, and even units in mutiny could be counted upon to defend their positions against enemy attack.

Figure 10.2 Robert Nivelle

Robert Nivelle (1856–1924) joined the French army in 1878 upon graduation from the Ecole Polytechnique. After reaching only the rank of colonel by 1913, he advanced rapidly during the war owing to his expertise in artillery. He succeeded Pétain as commander of the French Second Army at Verdun, and in June 1916 issued his famous order of the day, "*Ils ne passeront pas!* (They shall not pass!)" His effective use of creeping barrage was key to the French counterattack that autumn, leading to his extraordinary appointment to succeed Joffre as French commander-in-chief. Born to a French father and English mother, Nivelle used his fluency in English to his advantage in interactions with British political and military leaders during his brief time in command. After his failed offensive, he was named head of French forces in North Africa. He was the most prominent French general not invited to the postwar festivities in Paris in the summer of 1919.

Recent scholarship has cast doubt over the degree to which the Nivelle offensive actually caused, rather than merely triggered, the French Army mutinies of 1917. The case for Nivelle's responsibility rests primarily on his raising of false hopes for victory prior to the offensive; even here, other factors must be taken into account, including the success of the Canadians at Vimy Ridge just one week earlier and press reports characterizing the German withdrawal to the Hindenburg Line as a retreat, both of which led the average French soldier to expect that the enemy could and would be pushed back. The broader developments of the spring of 1917 also played a part. For war-weary front soldiers, the decision of the United States to declare war (when it did not yet have an army to contribute) appeared more likely to extend the war than to end it, and thus hurt morale more than it helped. The tsar's abdication and the radical democratization of the Russian Army likewise affected the French army, directly so in that two Russian brigades, deployed on the Western front as a token of Franco-Russian solidarity, received orders from Petrograd (coincidentally on April 16, the first day of the Nivelle offensive) to elect soviets and conform to Order Number One. The brigades actually fought well on the first day of the offensive before being sent to the rear, where they later mutinied and joined a May Day demonstration. Widespread strikes on the home front on and after May 1 also coincided with the spread of mutiny to divisions not engaged in the Nivelle offensive. Indeed, the overall chronology of the mutinies, most of which occurred in the weeks after Nivelle was sacked, calls into question the credit long given to Pétain for ushering in calm and order with his May 15 appointment. A parallel debate over what actually constituted "mutiny" has caused considerable disparity in estimates of the overall number of mutineers, from a low of 25,000 to a high of 88,000, while the number of divisions affected has been revised upward from the official figure of 54 to as many as 78. In any event, Pétain clearly faced a very serious crisis and ultimately dealt with it effectively, restoring discipline more by "carrot-and-stick" than by harsh measures. Of more than a hundred death sentences, only two dozen were carried out.[3]

The Eastern Front: The Czechoslovak and Polish Legions

In July 1917, at the onset of the Kerensky offensive, the Russians temporarily broke the front of the Austro-Hungarian Second Army when their own Eleventh Army deployed Czechoslovak legionnaires, recruited from earlier deserters, opposite the Dual Monarchy's predominantly Czech 35th and 75th Infantry regiments. Even though the two regiments had good prior service records, thousands of troops abandoned their positions to join their countrymen in the Russian ranks. Aside from the division of ethnic Serb deserters (from Bosnian and Croatian regiments of the Austro-Hungarian Army) in Zaionchkovsky's "Dobruja Detachment" during the Romanian campaign the previous autumn, the Czechoslovak legion serving in the Kerensky offensive represented Russia's most significant use of Austro-Hungarian deserters in the war thus far. Russian efforts to recruit troops from among Czech prisoners dated from August 1914, but until 1917 few had seen action. The initiative gained momentum when the Czech nationalist leader and future Czechoslovak president Tomáš Masaryk visited Russia from his London exile shortly after the tsar's abdication, accompanied by his former student, Slovak nationalist leader Milan Štefánik. Both considered the legion critical to strengthening the case for the establishment of a Czech-Slovak state after the war. To facilitate their recruiting efforts in Russia, the French Army gave Štefánik, a French citizen and military pilot, the rank of general prior to their trip. While the vast majority of the 210,000 Czechs and Slovaks in Russian captivity showed no interest in the legion, enlistments improved dramatically during and after the visit. This overall success obscured the fact that, despite Štefánik's prominent role alongside Masaryk, less than 10 percent of the legionnaires were Slovaks. Thus, the initiative foreshadowed the Czech domination of the postwar project to cobble together a nation-state for the two related nationalities. By 1918 the Czechoslovak legion included 61,000 men. Ironically, they would be known to history mostly for their role in fighting the Bolsheviks during an epic retreat across Siberia to Vladivostok after the outbreak of the Russian Civil War.

The Czech contribution to the Allied cause, though modest, dwarfed that of the Poles on the side of the Central Powers. Pilsudski's Polish legion had served in the Austro-Hungarian Army on the Eastern front since 1914, but remained small and insignificant. The Central Powers hoped to enlarge it after November 1916, when they recognized an "independent" kingdom of Poland and sparked a wave of Polish desertions from the Russian Army by announcing the news via a propaganda leaflet drop. But few of the deserters chose to volunteer for the legion; indeed, Ludendorff, the leading proponent of German exploitation of the resources of occupied Poland, always considered plans to mobilize Polish soldiers unrealistic. Nevertheless, in April 1917 the Germans created a Polish Army on the foundation of Pilsudski's legion; it grew to include 21,000 men by July, when the Germans precipitated a crisis by demanding that Polish troops swear an oath to William II. Pilsudski and most of his men refused. The 3,000 legionnaires from Austrian Galicia were then drafted into the Austro-Hungarian Army and sent to the Italian front, while another 15,000 who refused the oath, including Pilsudski, were interned in Germany. The remaining 3,000 men took the oath and served alongside the Germans, ultimately under the auspices of the Polish Regency Council, formed in September 1917. By the end of the war their force grew to include 9,000 troops, who went on to become the nucleus of the postwar Polish Army. The Germans kept Pilsudski in prison for the duration of the war. Three days after the armistice, he became the first head of state of the Republic of Poland.

Greece Enters the War, Romania Departs

Greece began the year divided between the provisional government of Venizelos at Salonika, recognized by the Allies, and the royal government of King Constantine, still on the throne following the ill-conceived Allied attack on Athens in December 1916. To avoid further armed conflict with the Allies (as well as a civil war between his own troops and those loyal to Venizelos), in January 1917 Constantine withdrew his entire army to the south of Greece where, in a further concession, he furloughed all but 10,000 troops. The political standoff continued for another five months, by which time the provisional government's General Zymbrakakis had built his National Army to a strength of over 60,000, enough to march on Athens and dethrone Constantine. By merely threatening to do so, Venizelos forced the hand of the Allies, who agreed to do it for him. On June 11, they landed 9,500 troops on the isthmus of Corinth, cutting off the main body of the royal army from Athens, after which French politician Charles Jonnart, as Allied High Commissioner for Greece, quickly arranged Constantine's departure on behalf of the country's new "protecting powers." The removal of the king – characterized by Jonnart as a liberation of the country and restoration of its constitution (see Box 10.2) – culminated three years of Allied violations of Greece's national sovereignty and territorial integrity. Constantine went into exile in Switzerland, along with his eldest son, Crown Prince George, after issuing a statement that carefully avoided the word "abdication." He eventually returned to the throne and, upon his death, George would succeed him. In the meantime, Venizelos returned to the capital in triumph, to govern a superficially reunited country, while Constantine's second son, Alexander, occupied the throne. Greece formally declared war on the Central Powers on June 29.

Greece's entry into the war came with far less risk than the analogous move by Romania in 1916, as the Allies had already established the Macedonian front along its northern border and were in full control of Greek waters. Greece was thus secured from suffering the same fate as Romania, which had been crushed by the Central Powers within months of joining the Allies. Romanian perseverance in Moldavia served as the only bright spot for the Allies on the Eastern front during 1917, though it was tested severely after the failure of the Kerensky offensive, when the counterattack by the Central Powers broke the Russian front to the north. At that point Mackensen attempted to deliver a final blow to Averescu's Romanian Second Army, the reconstituted Romanian First Army (General Eremia Grigorescu), and the Russian Fourth Army (General Alexander Ragoza), which were holding the Moldavian front south of Brusilov's retreating armies. In the battle of Mărășești (August 6–September 8) the Romanians, with Russian help, registered their only success of the war, beating back Mackensen's attack. The engagement generated more than 60,000 casualties for the Central Powers against 27,000 for the Romanians and 25,000 for the Russians. The

Box 10.2 The Allied takeover of Greece

Charles Jonnart (1857–1927), former French senator, foreign minister, and governor-general of Algeria, served briefly as Allied High Commissioner for Greece during 1917. In this capacity he arranged for King Constantine, on June 14, to turn over the throne to his son Alexander. His proclamation on that occasion hailed the Triple Entente as Greece's liberators and protectors:

France, Great Britain, and Russia desire to see Greece independent, great, and prosperous, and they mean to defend the noble country, which they have liberated, against the united efforts of the Turks, Bulgarians, and Germans. [...]

Berlin until now has commanded Athens and has been gradually bringing the people under the yoke of the Bulgarians and Germans. We have resolved to reestablish the constitutional rights and unity of Greece. The protecting powers have in consequence demanded the abdication of King Constantine. But they do not intend to touch the constitutional monarchy. They have no other ambitions than to assure the regular operation of the Constitution ... which King Constantine has ceased to respect.

Greeks! The hour of reconciliation has come. Your destinies are closely associated with those of the protecting powers. Your ideal is the same. Your hopes are the same. We appeal to your wisdom and patriotism. The blockade is now raised. Every reprisal against the Greeks, no matter by whom, will be pitilessly suppressed. No attempt against the public order will be tolerated. The property and liberty of all will be safeguarded. A new era of peace and work is opening before you. [...]

Long live Greece, united, great, and free!

Source: Charles F. Horne, ed., *Source Records of the Great War*, vol. 5 (Indianapolis: The American Legion, 1931), 239–40.

dead included Lieutenant Ecaterina Teodoroiu, one of the war's few female combat officers, hailed in Romania as a modern-day Joan of Arc. The victory at Mărășești did little to improve the Romanian strategic situation, which became hopeless following the Bolshevik Revolution. On December 9, six days before the Soviet Russian armistice with Germany and Austria-Hungary, Romania concluded an armistice of its own with the Central Powers, and went on to sign a treaty of peace with them in May 1918.

The Western Front: Messines, Passchendaele, Cambrai

Faced with the relative inactivity of the French after the Nivelle offensive, British and Imperial forces assumed responsibility for carrying the war to the Germans on the Western front for the rest of 1917. Haig shifted the action to the north, where Plumer's Second Army initiated the battle of Messines (June 7–14), attacking a small bulge in the lines of the German Fourth Army (now under General Sixt von Arnim), 3 miles (5 km) south of Ypres. Plumer's troops had not been involved in a major battle in more than two years, but had been busy since 1916 digging thousands of meters of tunnels across no man's land and under the German positions along Messines Ridge. In the predawn hours of June 7, after a seventeen-day preliminary bombardment, the British opened the battle by detonating mines in nineteen of the tunnels. History's largest man-made explosion to date, audible in London, blew the crest off of the ridge and killed 10,000 Germans on the spot. Plumer then sent nine divisions (including one each from Australia and New Zealand) forward under a creeping barrage supported by tanks and supplemented by gas attacks, and within hours secured all of his objectives. Over the next week the Second Army held its gains against a series of German counterattacks. Plumer's troops inflicted 25,000 casualties, slightly more than they suffered, and took 7,000 prisoners.

The meticulous planning and successful execution of the attack at Messines raised British expectations going into the ensuing battle of Passchendaele, or the third battle of Ypres (July 31–November 10). Haig spearheaded the attack with Gough's Fifth Army, relocated from the Somme sector to the ruins of Ypres, where it was flanked on the south by Plumer's Second Army and on the north by the French First Army (General François Anthoine), the only French formation remaining in the Flanders sector. Their opponents included Arnim's Fourth Army and, on its right (northern) flank, the German Fifth Army, reconstituted since its decimation at Verdun and now under Max von Gallwitz. Taking the attack at Messines as a sign that a bigger offensive would follow in the Ypres sector, the Germans spent the intervening weeks further improving defenses already strengthened over the prior months to reflect Lossberg's "defense in depth." The Allies, meanwhile, became more assertive in the air war, following the introduction of Britain's Sopwith Camel and France's SPAD S13 during the spring and summer. The fighting began on July 31, after a fifteen-day preliminary shelling, when Gough's Fifth Army, supported on its left by the French, attacked Pilckem Ridge. The Allies suffered 32,000 casualties in a single day in order to advance 3,000 yards (2,770 m) and secure a total of 18 square miles (47 km²) of territory. During August heavy rains reduced the battlefield to a quagmire, rendered British tanks useless (Figure 10.3), and escalated the cost of every Allied gain. In September, as the rains abated, Haig shifted the weight of the offensive to Plumer's Second Army on Gough's right, but British and Imperial forces continued to pay dearly for very modest successes, for example, taking another 36,000 casualties to advance 2,750 yards (2,540 m) and gain another 9 square miles (23 km²) of territory in the battles at Menin Road (September 20–25) and Polygon Wood (September 26–October 3). A week later, amid a resumption of heavy rain, Gough's army returned to the fray in a thrust toward Poelcappelle, supported on its flanks by Plumer and Anthoine, but achieved only modest results.

Haig nevertheless remained confident that the Germans had lost much of their strength and ordered his armies to proceed with an assault on their main objective, Passchendaele Ridge. The II ANZAC Corps bore the brunt of the first day of the attack, October 12; another 13,000 Allied casualties included 2,700 from the New Zealand division, making it the bloodiest single day in that country's history. The following week, Plumer's Second Army received four Canadian divisions to relieve the battered ANZACs, and these troops spearheaded the final push to secure the ridge (October 26–November 10), highlighted by their capture of the town of Passchendaele on November 6. The Canadians suffered more than 16,000 casualties at the third battle of Ypres, three-quarters of them in the last sixteen days of the battle. Among Dominion forces their losses were surpassed only by the Australians, whose five divisions sustained 38,000 casualties during the offensive, including 26,000 in October, the bloodiest month in Australia's history. In three and a half months of fighting the Allies had advanced no more than 5 miles (8 km) at any point along the front, at a cost of 245,000 British and Imperial and 8,500 French casualties, against 200,000 for the Germans. In overall casualties, Passchendaele ranked as the British Empire's costliest battle of the war other than the Somme.

The staggering cost of the modest victory at Passchendaele left the Allies with no reserves to exploit their subsequent breakthrough at the battle of Cambrai (November 20–December 7), where the British Third Army, now under General Sir Julian Byng, attacked the sector of the German front held by the Second Army (General Georg von der Marwitz). After a preparatory shelling by 1,000 guns, Byng used 476 tanks massed across a front of 6 miles (10 km) to lead an attack by six infantry divisions, followed by two cavalry divisions tasked with exploiting the anticipated breach in the German lines. Demonstrating that Lossberg's "defense in depth" was not impregnable, the British advanced farther in six hours than they had in three and a half months at Passchendaele. Byng's cavalry could not follow up on the initial breakthrough, but the infantry secured a salient just over 5 miles (8 km) deep. Marwitz, reinforced to twenty divisions, launched his counterattack on November 30. In the most extensive use yet of storm troop tactics on the Western front, the Germans deployed squads armed with automatic weapons, hand grenades, trench mortars, and flamethrowers to infiltrate and break the enemy front before their general infantry assault. The week-long counterattack left the British with no net territorial gain, and by the end of the battle each army had suffered roughly 45,000 casualties. Nevertheless, both the British and the Germans were heartened by the result. Almost two-thirds of Byng's tanks (297 of 476) made it through the battle without being destroyed, ditched, or stalled, clearly demonstrating their worth when used in sufficient numbers on reasonably flat, dry terrain. In 1918 the use of tanks would play an increasingly significant role in Allied operations, as would storm troop tactics on the German side.

Figure 10.3 Stuck in the mud at Passchendaele

A year after the British Army introduced tanks at the Somme, it pinned great hopes on them at Passchendaele, only to have too many ditch in muddy conditions. Two weeks of preliminary shelling, extensive use of creeping barrages in the initial infantry advance, and heavy rains combined to create a quagmire in which just 19 of the 136 tanks involved in the initial attack made it past the first German trench line. On August 2 most tanks were withdrawn; the battle went on for another ninety days, but tanks saw action on just ten days and in modest numbers, with no more than three dozen being deployed at any given time.

Though the United States declared war on Germany on April 6, none of the Western front battles of 1917 involved American troops. After arriving in France piecemeal in June and July, the 1st Division of the American Expeditionary Force (AEF) underwent training in Lorraine before replacing French troops on the front near Nancy in October. Few American troops would arrive in France until 1918, after the first men conscripted in the spring and summer of 1917 had completed their basic training in the United States. Two days before the American declaration of war on Germany, the first troops of a new Allied country deployed on the Western front – from Portugal. Germany had declared war on Portugal in March 1916, after the Portuguese government honored a British request to seize German ships interned in its ports. Unrestricted submarine warfare had caused considerable hardship in Portugal, whose biggest trading partner was Britain; furthermore, its largest colonies, Angola and Mozambique, both bordered German colonies and had been threatened by the war in sub-Saharan Africa. In addition to participating in the colonial war, Portugal in August 1916 committed to send troops to the Western front, the first of which arrived in April 1917. Two divisions ultimately served with the British First Army on the northernmost sector of the front in France, just south of the Franco-Belgian border.

The Italian Front: The Road to Caporetto

After dismissing Conrad as chief of the general staff in February 1917, Emperor Charles had refused his request to retire and instead assigned him to command an army group in the Tyrol, consisting of the Austro-Hungarian Tenth and Eleventh armies (the former under Krobatin, recently ousted from the war ministry). Conrad expected another chance to launch an offensive out of the Alps, but instead saw one-third of his troops sent to the Isonzo to reinforce Boroević's Fifth Army. In the battle of Monte Ortigara (June 9–29) Conrad's shrinking forces withstood an attack by the Italian Sixth Army, inflicting 23,000 casualties, but otherwise saw no action, while Boroević fended off ever larger offensives. In the tenth battle of the Isonzo (May 12–June 8) Cadorna deployed thirty-eight divisions against Boroević's fourteen, and in the eleventh battle of Isonzo (August 19-September 12), fifty-one against twenty. These two battles together caused 315,000 Italian and 235,000 Austro-Hungarian casualties, and brought the front to within 9 miles (15 km) of Trieste. Cadorna remained oblivious to the impact of such losses on the morale of his own army, and was confident that one more push in the autumn would secure that prize (Map 10.1).

Following the collapse of the Kerensky offensive, Charles asked William II for permission to transfer more of his troops from the Eastern front to the Isonzo, to enable Austria-Hungary to launch its own offensive against Italy, with German support limited to heavy artillery. Given the state of his armed forces and their performance in the war thus far, Charles' faith in the Austro-Hungarian Army appeared barely more realistic than Kerensky's recent faith in the Russian Army, but his generals had always been confident they could beat the Italians, an enemy that virtually all of Austria-Hungary's nationalities could be counted upon to fight against. The OHL feared the consequences of such an operation regardless of its outcome, as a face-saving victory against the Italians would leave Charles with little incentive to keep his country in the war, while a defeat might force Austria-Hungary to sue for peace. Both for the sake of maintaining their ally and maintaining control over their ally, Hindenburg and Ludendorff sent General Otto von Below with six divisions from the Eastern front to spearhead Charles' offensive. Upon their arrival on the upper Isonzo they joined nine Austro-Hungarian divisions to form the new Fourteenth Army, positioned between Krobatin's Tenth Army in the eastern Tyrol and Boroević's Fifth Army on the lower Isonzo. The German arrivals, plus the Austro- Hungarian troops redeployed from Conrad's army group, gave the Central Powers thirty-five divisions on the Isonzo to forty-one for Italy,

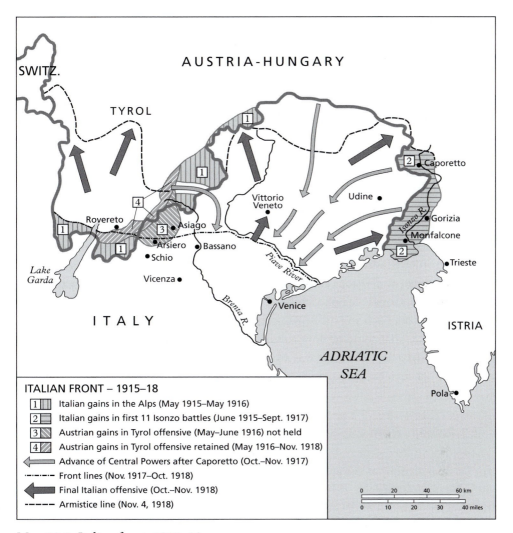

Map 10.1 Italian front, 1915–18

but in the Fourteenth Army's 15-mile (24-km) sector opposite Caporetto (Kobarid), Below's fifteen divisions – backed by 1,845 guns – enjoyed a decisive local superiority over two corps of the Italian Second Army (General Luigi Capello). Austro-Hungarian deserters gave the Italians ample warning of what was to come, but Cadorna believed the attack would be a diversion, with the real enemy offensive coming from Conrad's sector in the Tyrol, not across the Isonzo. After all, there had been eleven battles of the Isonzo to date, Italy had initiated all of them, and none had its focal point so far upstream.

The twelfth battle of the Isonzo, also known as Caporetto, began in a heavy rain in the predawn hours of October 24. The attack followed a plan Conrad had first devised in 1908 and proposed to the OHL as recently as January 1917, to punch a hole in the Italian lines on this relatively quiet sector of the front. It was made more effective by a crushing preparatory barrage, followed by gas shelling and infiltration of the Italian front lines by storm troopers (whose leaders included Lieutenant Erwin Rommel). The Austro-Hungarian Army, confident that its propaganda offensive had helped to bring about the recent collapse of the Russians in the east, also blanketed Italian lines with demoralizing leaflets. Below's opening blow created a gap in the Italian lines 20 miles (32 km) wide, enabling his troops to advance 14 miles (22 km) and take 20,000 prisoners on the first day alone. The breach compromised the entire Second Army, sending it into headlong retreat, and also forced the withdrawal of the armies on its flanks. The Italian Third Army, practically within sight of Trieste, fell back in the face of an attack by Boroević's Fifth Army, while the Italian Fourth Army, in the Alps on the eastern Tyrol border, headed south with Krobatin's Tenth Army in pursuit. While these forces withdrew in an orderly fashion, the retreat of Capello's Second Army became a disorganized rout in which entire divisions surrendered after being outflanked or cut off by the rapid enemy advance. Gorizia fell on October 28 and Udine two days later (see Box 10.3).

On October 30, Foch and his British counterpart, Robertson, arrived to consult with Cadorna about what could be done to turn the tide. Cadorna refused to take responsibility for the debacle. "The army was swarming with worms," he ranted, and "the internal enemy" of socialist propaganda, defeatism, and cowardice had caused its demise.[4]

Box 10.3 **Retreat from Caporetto**

Excerpt from an account of the evacuation of Udine, October 27–28, 1917, by British author and journalist Perceval Gibbon (1879–1926), who witnessed the Italian retreat as a war correspondent:

During October 27th the civilians of the threatened districts of Udine and its adjoining villages began their flight westward ... Udine poured itself along the great level highway which runs westward toward the cities of the plain, and by Sunday morning [the 28th] the poor little town with its shuttered shops and vacant streets ... had taken on the air of a cemetery [...]

Toward noon it was evidently time to leave. I think I was the last civilian to go. I took a last look around from the summit of Castle Hill. Rain squalls inhabited the wide landscape like a population. Roads seemed to crawl and writhe with their dense westward traffic, and from Cividale, where the army had set fire to military depots, there arose great spires of flame and smoke [...]

My own way rearward was by the great road which runs through Codroipo, Pordenone, and Treviso. It was a river running bank-high with the population of the retreat – vehicles four abreast crawling at the pace of the slowest, guns and caissons, private motor cars and donkey carts, soldiers on foot, and all that infinitely pitiable debris of war, the weary women and crying children whom Germany has made homeless. It is these last who give to every retreat its air of tragedy and disaster.

Source: Charles F. Horne, ed., *Source Records of the Great War*, vol. 5 (Indianapolis: The American Legion, 1931), 324–25.

On the advice of Foch and Robertson, France and Britain soon refused to send aid unless Cadorna was replaced. The rout finally subsided on November 3, and four days later the front stabilized at the Piave River. On November 9, King Victor Emmanuel III sacked Cadorna in favor of General Armando Diaz, and by the 21st, two days after the fighting ended, six French and five British divisions had arrived from the Western front to help hold the line. The four weeks of fighting cost the Central Powers 30,000 casualties, but had been nothing short of catastrophic for Italy, which suffered 40,000 casualties and lost at least 265,000 prisoners (half of the Italian total for the entire war), 3,000 machine guns, and 3,150 artillery pieces, along with 5,400 square miles (14,000 km^2) of territory inhabited by a civilian population of 1 million. The disaster reduced the size of the Italian Army by half, from sixty-five divisions to thirty-three. While German leadership and artillery support had been decisive, the Central Powers had achieved a great victory with a force in which more than 80 percent of the troops were Austro-Hungarian. Men of all nationalities had fought well, including a number of Slavic units whose earlier performance on the Eastern front had been questionable. As early as November 30, the OHL started to withdraw Below's German troops for redeployment to France. Boroević received the Austro-Hungarian divisions from Below's army and, in January, became group commander over his former Fifth (Isonzo) Army and a reconstituted Sixth Army, which held the Piave line for the next eleven months with little German help.

Conclusion

As the year of upheaval and uncertainty drew to a close, the grand strategy of Hindenburg and Ludendorff appeared to have been vindicated. On the Western front the Germans conserved their strength, while the Allies paid dearly for minor gains. The failure of the Nivelle offensive had left the French Army wracked by mutinies, apparently incapable of further offensive action. On the Italian front, the Austro-Hungarian army, too, seemed incapable of offensive action, but the German contribution of a mere six divisions and a few dozen batteries of artillery made it strong enough to almost knock Italy out of the war. Yet for the Allies, the debacle at Caporetto and the reduction, by half, in the size of the Italian Army paled in significance to the total collapse of the Russian Army amid two revolutions that led, finally, to the signing of an armistice by the Bolshevik government. The demise of Russia created a hopeless situation for Romania, which likewise left the war. As 1917 ended, the Central Powers and Soviet Russia opened peace talks at Brest-Litovsk, which the OHL anticipated would soon result in a definitive end of hostilities in the east and allow the transfer of German troops to the west for the final push against Paris in 1918.

But amid this generally positive picture for the Central Powers, some significant clouds had appeared on the horizon. The resumption of unrestricted submarine warfare had brought the United States into the war, and the German and Austro-Hungarian navies both experienced mutinies. On the home front, the food shortages and hardships of the winter of 1916–17 fueled doubts that the war could be brought to a victorious end, leading to a peace resolution in the German Reichstag and anti-war criticism in the reconvened Austrian Reichsrat (see Chapter 11). Meanwhile, on the Allied side, with the notable exception of Russia the other major belligerents had less reason to doubt that their home fronts would hold. Thanks to the leadership of Lloyd George and the growing sacrifices of the Dominions, the British Empire succeeded in keeping the Allied cause viable while the United States mobilized its armed forces and economy for war. Finally, in November 1917, the appointment of Georges Clemenceau as French premier and Vittorio Orlando as Italian prime minister put in place political leaders capable of rallying their exhausted countries to meet the challenges of one more year of war. That month, at Lloyd George's suggestion, the Allies created a Supreme War Council, headquartered at Versailles, but did not yet follow the example of the Central Powers in creating a unified command.

On a tactical level, 1917 brought further innovations to the war in the field. The Germans refined the storm troop tactics previewed at Verdun, employing them extensively and successfully at Riga, Caporetto, and Cambrai. British mining operations on the model of those used at the Somme were employed more extensively at Messines, but the preparation time required made them unfeasible for widespread use, and in any event during 1917 both sides became more adept at detecting when the enemy was tunneling under their lines. In the artillery war, the Allies refined the creeping barrage to a point where at Passchendaele, British and Imperial troops advanced just 40 yards behind the curtain of falling shells. Finally, at Cambrai, the British demonstrated how decisive tanks could be if used in appropriate numbers on the right terrain. During 1917 mustard gas joined chlorine and phosgene in the chemical arsenal, and the widespread use of gas shells or gas canisters that could be fired from special launchers minimized the risks for the attacker, but gas remained a supplementary tool rather than a decisive weapon. In the air war, the ebb and flow of the past two years continued, with the introduction of new fighter designs putting the skies back into play for the Allies from the summer of 1917 until the summer of 1918, improving their artillery spotting at a time when they were finally closing the gap in heavy artillery. The biggest problem for the Allies in 1917 remained human error at the highest levels of command, in particular the poor decisions made by Nivelle in choosing to launch his offensive across the Aisne, and by Haig in selecting the ground east of Ypres for his big push in the summer and autumn. Cambrai demonstrated that tanks could be decisive against Lossberg's "defense in depth," but at both the second battle of the Aisne and the battle of Passchendaele the terrain made tanks irrelevant. In both battles, as in so many of the actions in 1915 and 1916, when innovation failed the commanders defaulted to a reliance on brute force, with horrific consequences for their soldiers. At the end of 1917 few would have predicted that Britain's military leaders, within a year, would take the lead in the Allied effort to figure out how to win a modern war.

SUGGESTIONS FOR FURTHER READING

Cook, Tim. *Vimy: The Battle and the Legend* (London: Allen Lane, 2017).

Cornwall, Mark. *The Undermining of Austria-Hungary: The Battle for Hearts and Minds* (Basingstoke: Macmillan, 2000).

Lloyd, Nick. *Passchendaele: A New History* (New York: Basic Books, 2017).

Morselli, Mario. *Caporetto 1917: Victory or Defeat?* (London: Routledge, 2001).

Murphy, David. *Breaking Point of the French Army: The Nivelle Offensive of 1917* (Barnsley: Pen & Sword Military, 2015).

Smith, Leonard V. *Between Mutiny and Obedience: The Case of the French Fifth Infantry Division during World War I* (Princeton, NJ: Princeton University Press, 1994).

Williams, Charles. *Pétain* (London: Little, Brown, 2005).

NOTES

1. Quoted in Elizabeth Greenhalgh, *The French Army and the First World War* (Cambridge: Cambridge University Press, 2014), 199.
2. See Greenhalgh, *The French Army and the First World War*, 201–10.
3. Quoted in Elizabeth Greenhalgh, *Victory through Coalition: Britain and France during the First World War* (Cambridge University Press, 2005), 150.
4. Quoted in John R. Schindler, *Isonzo: The Forgotten Sacrifice of the Great War* (Westport, CT: Praeger, 2001), 258.

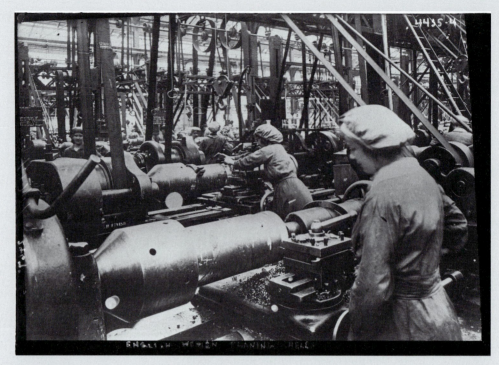

British women in a shell factory

Britain employed more women in war industries than any other country in World War I. By August 1916, 340,000 held positions controlled by the War Office, including women such as these, working in munitions factories, while another 766,000 were employed in the civilian sector. Many jobs were opened to them only because of the suspension of legislation dating as far back as the Factory Act of 1833, which barred women from dangerous occupations. Indeed, most of their opportunities lasted only as long as the war. Nevertheless, their involvement in the economy was responsible for Britain experiencing a greater degree of wartime social change than other countries.

11 The Home Fronts, 1916–18

January 1916	Military Service Act authorizes conscription in Britain.
April 1916	Ireland's Easter Rising.
Autumn 1916	Hindenburg Program militarizes German war industries.
November 1916	Emperor Francis Joseph dies.
December 1916	Lloyd George becomes British prime minister.
January 1917	London press makes first reference to "flappers."
April 1917	Stockholm Conference of anti-war socialists (to January 1918).
May 1917	Selective Service Act authorizes conscription in the United States.
July 1917	German Reichstag passes Peace Resolution.
October 1917	Orlando becomes Italian prime minister, introduces rationing.
November 1917	Clemenceau becomes French premier, introduces rationing.
January 1918	War's worst strikes cripple Germany and Austria-Hungary.
January 1918	Britain initiates food rationing.
March 1918	Representation of the People Act enfranchises British women.
March 1918	Influenza pandemic begins.

During the last half of the war, the European powers with the greatest capacity to wage modern war each experienced serious crises on their home fronts. Britain resorted to conscription and suppressed a rebellion in Ireland. France endured a crisis of home-front morale mirroring that of the army and a collapse of the *union sacrée*, with the war still far from being won. Germany likewise experienced the collapse of the *Burgfrieden*, coinciding with the unprecedented militarization of its home front under the Hindenburg Program and the struggle to feed the civilian population during the "turnip winter." Among the weaker great powers, Austria-Hungary appeared doomed to follow Russia down the path of disintegration, as revolutionary thinking spread among its nationalities following the death of Francis Joseph, while in Italy, as in France, the collapse of the army's morale threatened the home front as well. In the last half of the war strong civilian leaders emerged to rally the civilian population in each of the three leading European Allies – David Lloyd George in Britain, Georges Clemenceau in France, and Vittorio Orlando in Italy – while in the United States, the ideals of Woodrow Wilson lent a veneer of unity to a degree of domestic upheaval not seen since the country's civil war a half-century earlier. Finally, amid growing sentiment for peace on the European home fronts, the international socialist movement again tried, and failed, to facilitate a compromise peace, while in America, few other than socialists opposed the war once it was declared. These developments confirmed the degree to which nationalism had triumphed over socialism, and, at least in Europe, foreshadowed the division of the Left between socialism and communism in the wake of the Bolshevik Revolution.

Conscription Comes to Britain, the Dominions, and the United States

Owing to the decline in the number of volunteers for the British Army during the last months of 1915, the public was not surprised when the Asquith Government, on January 5, 1916, introduced a conscription bill to Parliament. The Labour Party alone opposed conscription but did so only in theory, as its MPs did not take a stand against it in the House of Commons. The Military Service Act, passed on January 27, authorized the conscription of all physically fit unmarried men aged 18–41, exempting widowers with children and men employed in a list of "reserved professions," including clergymen, teachers, and many industrial workers. A second bill in May extended the service liability to married men aged 18–41, with the provision that single men would be taken first. Amid the British Army's manpower crisis during the German spring offensive of 1918, Parliament extended the age ceiling to 51 and reduced exemptions for men employed in industry; at that stage Lloyd George benefited from the support of the Labour Party in getting the unions to accept the conscription of previously exempt workers. British conscription legislation allowed for conscientious objection, but only for Quakers or others with clear pacifist convictions who could prove that they had held such beliefs before the war. Even those whose claims were considered legitimate ended up at the front in khaki nevertheless, in a Non-Combatant Corps tasked with digging trenches, removing land mines, and erecting or repairing the wire in no man's land, as well as recovering the wounded and carrying them to hospitals in the rear. Starting in January 1917, less strenuous noncombatant roles, in particular clerical staff positions, were held by women serving in the Women's Army Auxiliary Corps (WAAC), which enrolled 57,000 volunteers by war's end (see Box 11.1).

Box 11.1 A girl's contribution

Excerpt from a memoir written after the war by a woman identified only as "Mrs A. B. Baker," who entered the WAAC in 1917 at the age of 18:

This is a girl's contribution. It has few thrills. First, as to why I went: At home, my father was too old to go. Also, he had the farm. My sister and I have no brother. Many relatives lived near us. All had men-folk who could go to fight – and did. Uncles, cousins, and cousins' sweethearts were all in the trenches or in training for the trenches. Three or four times a week an aunt or a cousin would bring in her letter from the Front, and read it proudly. They were anxious of course. One cousin was killed. One uncle was wounded. But they were proud, above all. They said that Father and Mother were lucky, to have no one about whom they need be anxious.

… I do not know what Mother felt. I quickly discovered that Father did not count himself lucky. Their pity hurt his pride. With him, it was not only pride. The farm had been the family's for two hundred years. The country meant more to Father than flags waved and glib patriotic cant uttered. The old sorrow that he had no sons had become, I guessed, a new bitterness. To be brief, there you have

the reason why I joined the WAACs. I joined first and told my home-folks afterwards. (I had to call myself twenty-one. They would allow no girl under twenty-one to go to France. I meant to go to France. But I was not nineteen.) Mother was upset. Father said little. Yet I knew that he was glad.

… I had got to France, but I had not got to the War. I was never very near the line. The devilish guns rumbled day and night. By day, the click-clacking of my typewriter keys drowned the rumbling of the guns. In that, I see now, lay a parable. I saw only unheroic monotony, then. By night, the rumbling grew louder and seemed nearer. Wakeful, I would make impossible plans to get hold of a Tommy's uniform, in it to break camp and to make my way to the line. There I was to be a second Lady of the Lamp, or something equally ridiculous. It was all very schoolgirlish and absurd, I have no doubt. But, then, I was absurd, and I had been a schoolgirl not so very long before.

Source: First published in *Everyman at War*, ed. C. B. Purdom (J. M. Dent, 1930), available at www .firstworldwar.com/diaries/storyofawaac.htm. (All attempts at tracing the copyright holder of the original work were unsuccessful.)

Among the Dominions, Canada and South Africa had provisions for conscription if enough volunteers could not be raised, while Australia and New Zealand did not. South Africa had conscripts in its prewar peacetime army and perhaps as many as half of the 146,000 white South Africans who served in World War I were drafted. In contrast, Canada did not use conscripts until the last year of the war, under terms that became law in August 1917; ultimately, they accounted for 100,000 of the 620,000 men serving in the wartime Canadian Army, though fewer than half of them deployed to Europe before the Armistice. In both cases, the reluctance of a non-English-speaking population to volunteer (the Afrikaners in South Africa and the Québécois in Canada) drove the decision to use conscription. The Québécois accounted for 28 percent of Canada's population but, in the years 1914–17, just 5 percent of the army's volunteers; indeed, the 35,600 Americans who served in the Canadian Army in those years out-numbered the Québécois. But Americans accounted for only a small portion of the 49 percent of the foreign-born troops in Canadian service, most of whom were immi-grants to Canada from the British Isles. Of all the dominions, Australia fielded the most homogeneous army; more than 99 percent of the 332,000 men serving overseas in the AIF were of British (including Irish) descent, and 35 percent had been born in the British Isles. The Australian public opposed conscription and twice (in October 1916 and December 1917) rejected it in referenda. The issue was not so controversial in New Zealand, which enlisted 14,000 volunteers in the first week of the war alone – a remarkable figure for a country of just 1.1 million people – but ultimately could not meet its army's needs through voluntary enlistments. In June 1916, the parliament in Wellington passed a conscription law over the opposition of just four MPs, and ulti-mately just over one-quarter of the 103,000 New Zealanders to serve overseas were conscripts. By war's end 42 percent of the country's males of military age had been inducted, and of these, 16 percent were killed and another 40 percent wounded. Of all participants in World War I, only Serbia suffered higher per capita casualties than New Zealand.

The United States had no tradition of universal military service, and conscription had only been attempted there during the last years of its civil war (unsuccessfully, by both the Union and Confederate armies). Nevertheless, the Selective Service Act of May 1917 (Figure 11.1) met with little resistance, and of the millions drafted just 20,000 applied for conscientious objector status. The act required all males aged 21–30 to register for conscription, extended in January 1918 to those aged 18–45. Most con-scripts went into new "National Army" units analogous to the "New Army" divisions created by Kitchener in Britain. By the time the United States discontinued the draft in 1919, conscripts accounted for 2.8 million of the 4 million men inducted into the army (the 600,000 men in the navy and 80,000 in the marines were almost all volunteers). Reflecting the diversity of the country, half a million of the conscripts were foreign-born and 13 percent were African American. Three-quarters of the immigrants were not proficient in English; many were not even citizens, as the conscription law applied to US residents regardless of their citizenship status. Along with rural whites and African Americans, urban immigrants contributed to the alarmingly high overall percentage of inductees (31 percent) who were illiterate in the English language. Owing to the recent influx of immigrants from southern and eastern Europe, Catholics accounted for 42 percent of all inductees and Jews 6 percent, prompting the Knights of Columbus and Jewish Welfare Board to volunteer to help serve the needs of their co-religionists at the various camps and bases. The unexpectedly large number of Jews entering service resulted in the US Army commissioning rabbis to serve as its first Jewish chaplains.

Figure 11.1 Conscription, American style

Under the Selective Service Act of 1917, the United States used a lottery to determine the order (by birthday) in which conscripts would be inducted, a method still employed as late as the Vietnam War. The United States went on to abolish the draft in 1920, reintroduce it in 1940, then abolish it again in 1973. In this photograph, Secretary of War Newton D. Baker, blindfolded, draws the draft order from a glass fishbowl. Baker was an unusual choice to preside over the greatest military build-up the United States had yet attempted. An avowed pacifist whose only elected office had been mayor of Cleveland, Ohio, he came to the War Department in 1916 as a compromise choice whose main qualification was his personal loyalty to President Wilson.

Ireland's Easter Rising

In September 1914 the Asquith Government suspended Home Rule for twelve months or the duration of the war. The delay raised doubts that the bill would ever be implemented in the form passed by Parliament and, despite the best efforts of Redmond and the Irish Parliamentary Party, undermined the Catholic population's support for the British war effort. Starting in 1915, Sinn Féin and the Irish Republican Brotherhood actively discouraged enlistment; by April 1916, Ireland's Catholic majority, 74 percent in the 1911 census, had provided just 56 percent of the 97,000 Irish volunteers for the British Army. Asquith's conscription bill of January 1916 excluded Ireland not because its manpower was not needed, but because the prime minister feared sparking a general revolt there at a time when the demands of the Western front had left Britain with almost no troops in Irish garrisons.

Planning for an Irish uprising against Britain intensified shortly after World War I began. Sir Roger Casement, one of the founders (in 1913) of the Irish Volunteers, went into exile in Germany and spent the next year and a half attempting, unsuccessfully, to recruit an "Irish brigade" from among British prisoners of war of Irish origin. Casement, a Protestant, was not fully trusted by other Irish Republican leaders and not a member of the Irish Republican Brotherhood, which sent one of its own leaders, Joseph Plunkett, to Berlin in 1915 to secure weapons for a rebellion. Plunkett succeeded in getting the Germans to commit to providing a shipload of 20,000 rifles, 10 machine guns, and ammunition for an uprising scheduled for Easter Sunday, 1916. Patrick Pearse, chosen by the brotherhood to lead the uprising, called for the Irish Volunteers to assemble across the country, only to have the plot unravel on Easter weekend, when Casement was arrested shortly after German submarine *U19* landed him on the coast of Kerry, and a supply ship with the munitions (disguised as a Norwegian freighter) missed the rendezvous point offshore and returned to Germany. On Easter Monday, April 24, after a bitter dispute over whether the operation should continue as planned without the German arms, Pearse, Plunkett, and five other members of a self-appointed Irish Provisional Government proclaimed the creation of the Irish Republic (see Box 11.2). Most of the Irish Volunteers failed to heed their call to rise, and just over 1,000 rebels assembled to seize key points in Dublin. The war had left barely 1,300 British troops in the Dublin garrison, but these were quickly reinforced and by the following Saturday, April 30, the last of the rebels surrendered. Beyond Dublin the Easter Rising featured only minor skirmishing, in the counties of Galway, Louth, Meath, and Wexford. The dead included 116 British troops, 16 policemen, 64 rebels, and 254 civilians, most of the latter caught in the crossfire of the six days of street fighting in Dublin. Around 400 soldiers and police and more than 2,000 Irish (mostly civilians) were wounded. In early May, the British tried and executed Pearse, Plunkett, and thirteen others identified as rebel leaders. Casement suffered the same fate three months later, following a treason trial in London.

Box 11.2 **Proclamation of the Irish Republic**

On April 24, 1916, Easter Monday, seven members of a self-appointed Irish Provisional Government – Thomas J. Clarke, Sean MacDermott, Thomas MacDonagh, P. H. Pearse, Eamonn Ceannt, James Connolly, and Joseph Plunkett – issued the following proclamation of Ireland's independence from Britain, signaling the start of the "Easter Rising":

Irishmen and Irishwomen: In the name of God and of the dead generations from which she receives her old tradition of nationhood, Ireland, through us, summons her children to her flag and strikes for her freedom.

Having organized and trained her manhood through her secret revolutionary organization, the Irish Republican Brotherhood, and through her open military organizations, the Irish Volunteers and the Irish Citizen Army, having patiently perfected her discipline, having resolutely waited for the right moment to reveal itself, she now seizes that moment, and, supported by her exiled children in America and by gallant allies in Europe, but relying in the first on her own strength, she strikes in full confidence of victory.

We declare the right of the people of Ireland to the ownership of Ireland, and to the unfettered control of Irish destinies, to be sovereign and indefeasible. The long usurpation of that right by a foreign people and government has not extinguished the

right, nor can it ever be extinguished except by the destruction of the Irish people. In every generation the Irish people have asserted their right to national freedom and sovereignty; six times during the past three hundred years they have asserted it in arms. Standing on that fundamental right and again asserting it in arms in the face of the world, we hereby proclaim the Irish Republic as a Sovereign Independent State. And we pledge our lives and the lives of our comrades-in-arms to the cause of its freedom, of its welfare, and of its exaltation among the nations.

… Until our arms have brought the opportune moment for the establishment of a permanent National Government, representative of the whole people of Ireland and elected by the suffrages of all her men and women, the Provisional Government, hereby constituted, will administer the civil and military affairs of the Republic in trust for the people.

We place the cause of the Irish Republic under the protection of the Most High God, Whose blessing we invoke upon our arms, and we pray that no one who serves that cause will dishonour it by cowardice, inhumanity, or rapine. In this supreme hour the Irish nation must, by its valour and discipline and by the readiness of its children to sacrifice themselves for the common good, prove itself worthy of the august destiny to which it is called.

Source: http://www.firstworldwar.com/source/ irishproclamation1916.htm.

While cracking down on the rebels, Asquith moved quickly to try to defuse the Irish question, appointing Lloyd George to mediate between Redmond and Protestant Unionist leader Sir Edward Carson. Negotiations collapsed when Redmond refused to accept Ulster remaining in the United Kingdom in exchange for immediate Home Rule for the rest of Ireland. The following summer, after becoming prime minister, Lloyd George summoned all Irish parties to an Irish Convention in Dublin, but Sinn Féin, committed to a wholly independent Irish Republic, refused to participate. The convention came close to advocating Home Rule for a united Ireland over Ulster's objections (prompting Carson to resign from Lloyd George's cabinet), before collapsing in March 1918 after the twin blows of Redmond's death and the British Army's manpower crisis in the face of the German offensive launched that month. At Lloyd George's urging, Parliament approved Home Rule but linked it to the extension of conscription to Ireland, over the opposition of the Irish Parliamentary Party. The conscription issue unified southern Ireland against Britain as never before. Moderates, Sinn Féin radicals, and Catholic bishops alike rallied behind the Irish Anti-Conscription League, which staged a general strike in April. The crisis abated over the summer, as the failure of the German offensive and the deployment of significant numbers of American troops in France eased British manpower concerns. In June, Lloyd George rescinded the latest Home Rule offer and let the conscription issue die. Ultimately, Ireland raised just 43,000 recruits for the British Army in the thirty-one months after the Easter Rising, a sharp decline from the 97,000 raised in the first twenty-one months of the war. Nevertheless, the conscription episode had fateful consequences. In December 1918, in the first postwar elections to the House of Commons, Sinn Féin won 70 percent of the Irish seats and the Irish Parliamentary Party just 6 percent. The unification of the majority of Irish Catholics behind the cause of complete separation from Britain set the stage for the postwar armed struggle for Irish independence.

The Central Powers: "Turnip Winter" and Total War

On August 31, 1916, two days after succeeding Falkenhayn as head of the OHL, Hindenburg proposed a doubling or tripling of most areas of war production, setting new quotas that could not be achieved without imposing a greater degree of military control over civilian labor. Though known as the Hindenburg Program, the production quotas and the measures needed to achieve them were drafted and monitored by Ludendorff, the field marshal's quartermaster general and second-in-command, and his subordinate, Colonel Max Bauer, building upon the foundation established earlier by the industrialist Rathenau and the War Raw Materials Division. On December 2, 1916, the Reichstag approved the linchpin of the program, the Patriotic Auxiliary Service Law, providing for the compulsory employment of all males aged 17–60 not in the armed forces. Because the measure could not succeed without the support of the unions and the parties most sympathetic to them, Bethmann Hollweg included in the bill language recognizing the right of workers to organize and to submit labor disputes to arbitration. He also wisely dropped some of the more extreme ideas of Ludendorff and Bauer, such as lowering the minimum working age to 15, applying the law to women as well as men, denying rationed food to those not engaged in "productive" employment, and closing the universities for the duration of the war, except for war-related scientific research. The bill passed by a wide margin, 235:19, on the strength of a heretofore unusual coalition of progressive liberals, the Catholic Center Party, and the SPD, but with 143 abstentions, mostly from the two conservative parties and the center-right National Liberals (normally taken for granted by German chancellors), who feared the long-term consequences of Bethmann Hollweg's sweeping concessions to workers. Members of the anti-war faction of the SPD accounted for the rest of the abstentions and cast all of the "no" votes.

Under the unified command structure of the Central Powers, the Hindenburg Program applied to Austria-Hungary as well as to Germany, at least when it came to the production quotas. The OHL allowed the AOK and the Austrian and Hungarian governments to determine how they would achieve the goals. The new expectations came at the worst possible time for the Dual Monarchy. In October 1916, the Austrian home front was rocked by the sensational assassination of the prime minister, Count Stürgkh, gunned down in the restaurant of a Vienna hotel by anti-war activist Friedrich Adler, son of Viktor Adler, founder and head of the Austrian Social Democratic Party. Then, a month later, the death of Francis Joseph removed the empire's most important symbol of multinational unity. Austro-Hungarian industry could not meet the unrealistic quotas of the program (for example, doubling the production of bullets and shells), and the attempt to do so only strained the empire's weak transportation system and encouraged the centrifugal tendencies within its multinational workforce.

In February 1917, Rathenau advised Ludendorff that the Hindenburg Program would fail without the "ruthless closure" of non-essential businesses, a halt to the construction of expensive and unnecessary new factories, decisive action to prevent the "complete collapse" of the German railways, and above all, a "radical reform" of the program's administration, which had become a "legislative monster" employing 150,000 people.[1] The OHL heeded Rathenau's advice only in suspending the building of new factories. The railways, militarized under General Wilhelm Groener, head of the recently created War Office, continued to suffer from a coal shortage and a deteriorating infrastructure not properly maintained since 1914. Against Ludendorff's wishes, the OHL concluded that the civilian economy could not be shut down without turning the public against the war. Finally, the Germans seemed incapable of organizing or reorganizing anything without a net increase in the number of bureaucrats involved. The Reichstag did not help matters by passing a series of amendments to the service law of December 1916, exempting students, farmers, and some white-collar workers, in the process ensuring that the German working class would continue to bear the brunt of supporting the war effort. By May 1917, the 120,000 new workers mustered into the factories since the passage of the law included just 36,000 compelled to work because of it; most of the rest (75,000) were women. The Hindenburg Program would not have had the workers it needed if Germany had not granted leave to skilled workers in the army, as France had done earlier, but on a far greater scale. As of September 1916, the war ministry had already exempted 1.2 million workers from military service, and by

July 1917 the Hindenburg Program added another 700,000. Such extensive labor leaves would not have been possible if the Central Powers had not resolved to stand on the defensive for 1917. Ultimately, just over 2 million of the estimated 3 million additional workers needed for the program came from foreign sources: 100,000 Belgians deported to Germany; 600,000 Poles who voluntarily or involuntarily came to Germany to work, mostly in agriculture; and the rest Russian prisoners of war who, like the Poles, worked mostly in agriculture, freeing rural Germans to work in war industries. From the German point of view these efforts to exploit the manpower of defeated or occupied lands left much to be desired. They would be repeated in the Third Reich, with a brutality sufficient to yield greater results.

The outcome of the Hindenburg Program is difficult to assess because, as one historian has noted, so much of it reflected the "smoke and mirrors" of domestic propaganda.[2] In any event, by the winter of 1917–18 the Central Powers had a surplus in most weapons, and when they lost the war, it was not because of a shortage of *materiel*. In the final analysis, the OHL used the Hindenburg Program to expand its own power on all levels: within the army, over the war ministry; within Germany, over the civilian population; and within the alliance, over the war effort of Austria-Hungary. While German industrialists reaped huge profits, workers also saw their wages rise thanks to Bethmann Hollweg's concessions to them. The government's official recognition of the role of unions also sparked their dramatic revival: German union membership had collapsed to 1.2 million in 1916, the lowest total in over a decade, then nearly doubled to 2.2 million by 1918. But the labor force of newly empowered unionized workers, rural transplants, women, and foreign deportees produced at a far lower rate per person employed than Germany's prewar industrial laborers; indeed, one recent analysis gives the "rather devastating" estimate that productivity declined during the war by at least 20 percent.[3]

Germany and Austria-Hungary implemented the Hindenburg Program at a time of increasing shortages on the home front. Though most of the other belligerents, to varying degrees, followed their example, the Germans led the way in introducing what would be called "recycling" a half-century later: the massive, systematic salvaging, reduction, and reuse of objects and materials of all kinds. The food supply became especially problematic after Britain concluded an agreement with the Netherlands in 1916, under which half of Dutch agricultural exports (almost all of which had gone to Germany in 1914–16) would now go to British markets. Food imports to Germany from (or through) Denmark and Switzerland also declined owing to the concerns those countries had about maintaining their own food supplies. By early 1916, German food rationing included everything except green vegetables, fruits, poultry, and game (Figure 11.2). The War Food Office was created in May 1916, ostensibly to rationalize the supply system, but it could do nothing in the face of poor German grain harvests (21.8 million tons in 1916 and 14.9 million in 1917, down from 30.3 million in 1913). Within the Dual Monarchy, Hungary continued to starve Austria, reducing its grain

Figure 11.2 German women queuing for food

Wartime food shortages in Germany led to scenes such as this one, in which civilians (almost always women) spent several hours per week standing in food queues. In January 1915, Germany became the first of the belligerents to introduce wartime food rationing, owing to the combined effects of the British blockade, the loss of trade with Russia (its main prewar source of grain), and the wartime reduction of agricultural imports from Austria-Hungary. The situation worsened as, by 1916, food imports to Germany from (or through) the neighboring neutral countries also declined. Poor grain harvests in Germany (the 1917 yield being less than half that of 1913) only exacerbated the crisis. Substitute (*ersatz*) food and drink were used more extensively on the home fronts of Germany and Austria-Hungary than anywhere else, as a means of replacing items in short supply.

shipments to 3.3 percent of prewar levels in 1916 and 1.9 percent in 1917. The grain shortage combined with the army's requisitioning of fodder to make it difficult for farmers to maintain their livestock. By 1917 German meat consumption stood at 25 percent of prewar levels, and the sale and slaughter of dairy cattle for meat naturally led to a shortage of dairy products even in rural areas. With the average civilian diet reduced to less than 1,000 calories per day, many mothers sacrificed their own diets for the sake of their children; thus, only in the war's last year did German and Austrian family physicians begin to observe widespread cases of malnutrition among children. In July 1916, the city of Berlin opened its first publicly run kitchen and by the end of September there were eleven of them, plus seventy-seven centers to distribute food to the public. Use of the kitchens peaked in February 1917, in the midst of the "turnip winter," named after the vegetable most available on the home fronts of the Central

Box 11.3 "A new front emerged – it was held by women"

Ernst Gläser (1902–63) experienced the winters of 1916–17 and 1917–18 as a teenager on the German home front, and included his experiences in the novel *Jahrgang 1902* (*Born in 1902*), first published in 1928:

"This is going to be a hard winter," sighed my mother on one of those days … The meal consisted of a couple of slices of fat-free sausage, daintily cut-up turnips, which were held together by a thin sauce, and three potatoes per person. The bread … was like clay. We sat waiting, almost praying, in front of this meal. Perhaps, we thought, it would change miraculously to match our desires. While I was opening my napkin apathetically and lethargically – for we had been eating the same thing almost daily for months – my mother put her hand on the back of my neck, ran her hand almost fearfully through my hair and said softly and indistinctly: "I can't do anything about it … tomorrow perhaps I can get a couple of eggs and some meat … don't be so sad … perhaps I can also get some white flour …" She wept. "But mother," I lied, "this tastes very good, although of course the other things would be even better." I picked up my spoon and dug enthusiastically into the pale turnips.

… The winter remained hard until the end. The war began to leap from the fronts and press onto civilians. Hunger destroyed unity; within families, children stole rations from one another. August's mother … prayed and lost weight. The food that she was allotted she distributed to August and his siblings, and she kept only a minimum for herself. Soon the women who stood in the gray lines in front of the stores were talking more about their children's hunger than about their husband's deaths. The war switched the sensations that it offered.

A new front emerged. It was held by women. Against the "Entente" of military police and male civilian inspectors who could not be spared for military service. Every pound of butter that was surreptitiously obtained, every sack of potatoes that was successfully concealed at night was celebrated in families with the same enthusiasm as the victories of the armies had been celebrated two years earlier. Soon many fathers, who were stationed in regions where food was grown and who had the power to requisition from the enemy population, were sending packages of food to their families via comrades who were on furlough.

… Actually we enjoyed this change, for it awakened our sense of adventure. It was wonderful and dangerous to steal away from farmhouses with forbidden eggs, to throw oneself into the grass when a policeman turned up, and to count the minutes by one's heartbeat. It was wonderful and grand to dupe these policemen and to be celebrated as a hero by one's mother after a lucky triumph.

Source: Ernst Gläser, *Jahrgang 1902* [*Born in 1902*] (Berlin, 1931), 290–93, translated by Jeffrey Verhey and Roger Chickering for *German History in Documents and Images*, available at germanhistorydocs.ghi-dc.org/sub_document. cfm?document_id=960&language=english.

Powers. While the government assumed a greater social welfare role in Germany, Austria-Hungary relied heavily upon existing private and community charities for food distribution and other war relief work. Because these charities had been organized by and for the individual nationalities, the principle of "each nation only cares for its own" guaranteed a considerable variation in the distribution of hardship and only exacerbated ethnic tensions.[4]

Overall, the class-based inequality of sacrifice continued to be more of a problem in Germany and Austria-Hungary than in Britain or France. During the last half of the war, the meager meals and austere lives of ordinary people contrasted sharply with the quality and quantity of food available to wealthy families on country estates or to "paying customers" at urban hotels and night spots. Germany's dancing ban of 1914 eventually gave way, and in the cities gambling and illicit sex flourished, along with a black market that made virtually everything available but at a price out of the reach of most people. Meanwhile, in rural areas, farmers (or, more typically, their wives and children) battled policemen and food inspectors tasked with preventing hoarding, but by 1918 hoarding as well as theft of food had become common (see Box 11.3). Austria witnessed the most extreme manifestations of the food shortage. In July 1917, troops quelling food riots in Moravia killed twenty-one civilians, and by the following January as many as 25,000 people could be found in a single food queue in Vienna. Germany, along with Austria-Hungary, also rationed new clothing, since the Allied blockade deprived both countries of their only sources of cotton, and wool and leather were also in very short supply.

Among working-class Germans, shortages and the decline in buying power provided the underpinning for social unrest, especially in the wake of the "turnip winter." While just 129,000 workers struck in 1916, the number skyrocketed to 668,000 in 1917 before receding to 392,000 in 1918. In the war's last year the worst strikes came in January, threatening preparations for the German spring offensive. During 1918, Austria-Hungary experienced far greater labor unrest than Germany, with 600,000 workers striking on a single day, January 16. The Austro-Hungarian Army pulled seven divisions from the front to help break the strikes and round up the growing number of deserters on the home front; they netted 44,000 in the first three months of 1918 alone.

The Central Powers: War-Weariness and the Promise of Reform

The "turnip winter" featured Bethmann Hollweg's unsuccessful peace overture, the resumption of unrestricted submarine warfare, and the ensuing breakdown in relations with the United States, but for Germany these developments paled in significance to the unexpected revolution in Russia, which shook the solidarity of the home front as nothing had before. In 1914, most Germans had rallied behind the war effort out of a general patriotism, but the Left supported the war (and the SPD voted for war credits) because Russia had mobilized first. Thereafter, most of the SPD had embraced the war as a defensive struggle against tsarist autocracy and the wrongheaded Western powers that supported it, and remained true to the *Burgfrieden* even though the victories of the Central Powers had long since minimized the Russian threat. The abdication of Nicholas II and the establishment of the Provisional Government reminded them that the reason they had supported the war in the first place no longer existed. The demise of the tsar's government, by default, made the Allies a group of constitutional democracies and the Central Powers the most autocratic states in Europe, giving credence to Wilson's subsequent characterization of the war as a struggle of freedom against autocracy. Recognizing that this new reality put German liberals and socialists in an awkward position, Bethmann Hollweg persuaded William II to issue a promise of postwar constitutional reform. The emperor's speech, on April 7, the day after the United States entered the war, included few specifics other than a promise to end the archaic three-class voting system (which allocated legislative seats by tax bracket) used for state elections in Prussia, which encompassed two-thirds of the territory of the German Empire. In any event, William II's remarks came too late to preserve the unity of the home front under the *Burgfrieden*. One day earlier, the anti-war faction of the SPD finally broke away to establish the Independent Social Democratic Party (USPD), offering an overtly pacifist, revolutionary alternative to war-weary workers and military personnel. With Karl Liebknecht serving a prison sentence following a treason conviction for his anti-war activity, Hugo Haase assumed leadership of the new party. The collapse of tsarist autocracy likewise spurred the Austro-Hungarian leadership to embrace a future of political reform, while at the same time unwittingly encouraging revolutionary elements within the Dual Monarchy. In May 1917, Emperor Charles reconvened the Austrian Reichsrat, which had last met in March 1914, and accepted the resignation of the venerable Hungarian prime minister, Tisza, after he refused to broaden the traditionally exclusive Hungarian franchise.

The actions of William II and Charles in the spring of 1917, meant to rally public support and calm the home front in the wake of the "turnip winter," only served to raise the expectations of parties and peoples traditionally excluded from power. In the Dual Monarchy virtually all nationalities and political parties began to focus on the postwar future and their likely places in it, while in Germany a gulf opened between those who wanted Hindenburg and Ludendorff to lead the country to a victorious peace (including territorial annexations, indemnities, and economic exploitation of defeated countries) and those who advocated a compromise peace. The latter tended to doubt the wisdom of unrestricted submarine warfare and feared the long-term consequences of the United States joining the Allies. In June, Reichstag deputy Eduard David led an SPD delegation to a socialist peace conference at Stockholm (see section below) with the permission of Bethmann Hollweg, who saw propaganda value in the exercise, especially since the Allied powers were not allowing their socialists to attend. But the next time the Reichstag was summoned to approve additional war credits, David and his SPD colleagues Friedrich Ebert and Philipp Scheidemann joined Matthias Erzberger of the Catholic Center Party in surprising the chancellor with a peace resolution (see Box 11.4). Especially for Erzberger, indications that the OHL did not believe its own rhetoric about the U-boat campaign forcing Britain to the peace table by August 1

Box 11.4 **The Reichstag calls for a negotiated peace**

On July 19, 1917, the German Reichstag approved by a vote of 212:126 the following resolution, rejecting any peace including annexations, indemnities, or economic exploitation, the sort of peace then being advocated by the high command of Hindenburg and Ludendorff:

As on August 1, 1914, so also now on the verge of a fourth year of war, the words of the speech from the throne still hold: "We are not impelled by the lust of conquest."

Germany took up arms in defense of her freedom, her independence, and the integrity of her soil. The Reichstag strives for a peace of understanding and a lasting reconciliation of peoples. Any violations of territory, and political, economic, and financial persecutions are incompatible with such a peace.

The Reichstag rejects any plan which proposes the imposition of economic barriers or the solidification of national hatreds after the war. The freedom of the seas must be maintained. Economic peace alone will lead to the friendly association of peoples. The Reichstag will promote actively the creation of international organizations of justice.

However, as long as the enemy governments refuse to agree to such a peace, as long as they threaten Germany and her allies with conquest and domination, so long will the German people stand united and unshaken, and they will fight until their right and that of their allies are made secure.

Thus united, the German people remain unconquerable. The Reichstag feels that in this sentiment it is united with the men who have fought with courage to protect the Fatherland. The undying gratitude of our people goes out to them.

Source: https://www.firstworldwar.com/source/
reichstagpeaceresolution.htm.

triggered the move. The resolution passed on July 19 by a margin of 212:126, with 59 abstentions, supported by the same coalition of parties (progressive liberals, Center, and SPD) Bethmann Hollweg had used to pass the Patriotic Auxiliary Service Law the previous December. Once again the "no" votes and abstentions came from the conservative parties, National Liberals, and anti-war socialists (now constituted as the USPD), only with far fewer of them abstaining.

In a genuine parliamentary democracy the vote of July 19 would have toppled the government and compelled the country to negotiate peace, but under the German constitution it had the status of a nonbinding resolution. William II, Hindenburg, and Ludendorff officially ignored the peace resolution, but before it even passed the Reichstag they blamed Bethmann Hollweg for failing to keep it from reaching the floor. At the insistence of the generals, the emperor sacked the chancellor on July 14 and replaced him with a man of their choice, the jurist Georg Michaelis. The first commoner to hold the office of German chancellor, Michaelis had been an administrator in the food rationing bureaucracy since 1914, most recently as Prussian state commissioner of nutrition, but he lacked the political experience needed to manage the Reichstag. He remained in office only until the next crisis, in October, sparked by a Reichstag speech in which Admiral Eduard von Capelle, Tirpitz's successor at the Imperial Navy Office, accused the

USPD of fomenting revolutionary activity in the fleet and among dockyard workers but without providing specific evidence. After the SPD rallied to support the USPD, William II replaced Michaelis with Count Georg von Hertling, a member of the conservative wing of the Catholic Center Party and, for the past five years, prime minister of Bavaria.

As the war entered its last months, the home-front developments of the past two years set the stage for the ultimate crises that Imperial Germany and Austria-Hungary would face. The definitive end of the *Burgfrieden* left Germany deeply divided. The political Right, reorganized after September 1917 under the banner of the new Fatherland Party, kept faith with Hindenburg and Ludendorff in their quest for victory, and attempted to rally the public first behind the notion that the U-boat campaign would still work, then that a final offensive in the West would lead to victory. Meanwhile, the peace resolution of July 1917 put the Center Party and the moderate Left on record supporting a compromise to end the war, and the emergence of the USPD presaged the revolution in store for Germany in the winter of 1918–19. The Fatherland Party would not survive the war, but its rhetoric foreshadowed the postwar recriminations concerning the German home front, accusing the parties of the peace resolution and the USPD of defeatism and treason. Meanwhile, in Austria-Hungary, the leaders of a number of the nationalities had already gone into exile in Paris, London, and Rome long before Charles reconvened the Reichsrat in May 1917; the Allied response to Bethmann Hollweg's peace overture of December 1916 confirmed their success in lobbying for independent states in the event of an Allied victory. In Germany as well as Austria-Hungary, the shortages of food and other essentials made it difficult for ordinary people to believe that the Central Powers would emerge victorious, even though the front lines remained on enemy soil. The conquest of most of Romania by the end of 1916 allowed Germany and Austria-Hungary to take a share of its harvest the following year, but the occupation of Ukraine in the spring of 1918 (see Chapter 13) came too late to be of any benefit. Even then, the victors argued over the spoils; a minor crisis erupted in April 1918 when barges loaded with Romanian grain for Germany were seized on the Danube at Vienna by local authorities desperate to feed their city. In both countries, the war exposed the inherent inequalities of the social class structure, inequalities that the governing authorities lacked the will or insight to remedy. The inability of the Central Powers to enforce a more equitable sharing of the burdens of the war demoralized their home fronts and left fewer of their citizens confident that the war could be won or would lead to a better future.

France in Crisis: Clemenceau and the End of the *Union Sacrée*

For the French home front, the weight of the sacrifice at Verdun and the war-weariness of soldiers home on leave began to affect the mood of the civilian population long before Nivelle's debacle along the Aisne in the spring of 1917. Confidence in Russia, a key element to French home-front morale ever since 1914, collapsed following the abdication of the tsar. The American declaration of war the following month did little to help, although the well-publicized arrival of the first AEF troops in June 1917 rekindled some hope for the future. While the Americans, like the British before them, marveled that certain quarters of Paris featured a social life incongruous with the bloody stalemate of the nearby front, by 1917 the night clubs and cabarets had lost much of their luster. Even the fashion industry fell into line with the new pessimism, producing more somber women's dress designs to replace the scandalously short calf-length "war crinolines" of 1915–16. But amid the new sobriety of style the color black was seen less than before, owing to a "breakdown in funeral and mourning etiquette" especially evident in urban areas.[5] By war's end France had 600,000 widows (to 500,000 for Germany and 200,000 apiece for Britain and Italy), making the experience of losing a husband unexceptional.

The failure of the Nivelle offensive brought the first significant public rejection of the *union sacrée* by members of the French Left. Prominent advocates of peace included Joseph Caillaux and Louis-Jean Malvy of the Radical Party. Caillaux, a prewar premier, purportedly met with German agents on wartime trips abroad, while Malvy, interior minister in Ribot's cabinet, secretly funneled money to newspapers advocating peace without victory. In June 1917, during a debate in the Chamber of Deputies over whether France should send a delegation to the socialist peace conference at Stockholm (see section below), future Nazi collaborator Pierre Laval, then an SFIO deputy representing Aubervilliers, spoke in favor of the measure: "Whether you like it or not, a wind of peace is blowing through the country … The means of giving hope to the troops and confidence to the workers … is Stockholm!"[6] But by a 5:1 margin the chamber defeated a motion to send a delegation. The verdict came much to the dismay of munitions minister Albert Thomas, the last prominent SFIO member in the cabinet, who had visited Stockholm in April, at the start of the conference, en route home from a special mission to the Provisional Government in Petrograd. He finally resigned from the cabinet in September, causing the fall of Ribot as premier. By then Malvy had been forced to resign after Clemenceau, his leading critic, produced evidence that the defeatist newspapers he supported had also received funds from German agents. While President Poincaré weighed the options of forming a government under Caillaux, which would seek peace with the Germans, or Clemenceau, which would fight to the finish, war minister Painlevé formed a short-lived center-right cabinet without the support of the SFIO. In November, Poincaré opted for Clemenceau.

Like Painlevé, Clemenceau formed a center-right cabinet that excluded the SFIO, but he retained just three of his predecessor's eighteen ministers. He promptly sent a strong message to the defeatists by ordering the arrest of Caillaux and Malvy on treason charges. Clemenceau also asserted a degree of civilian control over the military notably absent early in the war, when the politicians gave Joffre a free hand to indulge in his bloody fiascos, but in the process he also defended the army from its detractors. Speaking to the Senate in December 1917, the premier rebutted criticism of Pétain with the assertion that "I alone am responsible here … General Pétain is under my orders; I cover him fully."[7] While his frequent visits to the front line helped to rally the troops, the fiery 76-year-old lived up to his nickname "the Tiger" by rallying the home front his own way. In the course of this "second mobilization," Clemenceau preferred to bully his opponents rather than reach out to them, leaving the *union sacrée* dead in the public sphere as well as the governing coalition.

Clemenceau assumed power just as France was finally experiencing a food crisis of sorts, rooted in the government's wartime policy of allowing leaves from military service for factory workers but not for farming labor. French agriculture gradually broke down under its own manpower crisis; in 1916, 35 percent of farmland went uncultivated, compared with 15 percent the previous year. In general, food remained more plentiful throughout the war in France than in any other major belligerent country, but in the spring of 1917 the cost of it rose dramatically, with some items doubling or even tripling in price during the Nivelle offensive. Clemenceau finally introduced partial bread rationing in November 1917, applied in cities and towns with populations of 20,000 or more. In general, France distributed the burden of the food situation more equitably than Germany or Austria-Hungary, but less so than Britain. By the last year of the war there were long queues and high prices for most essentials. Soldiers home on leave were allowed to jump the queues, a questionable benefit that too often resulted in their families and civilian friends burdening them with the shopping.

In and around Paris, the Department of the Seine experienced just 100 strikes in 1916, involving fewer than 12,000 workers, but in 1917 labor unrest escalated to more than 300 strikes idling almost 250,000. The largest single strike – by 100,000 Paris munitions workers, most of them women – coincided with the worst of the mutinies that followed the Nivelle offensive. By June 1917, soldiers released to the factories accounted for 36 percent of the workforce in France's war industries, but things were about to change. Under the Mourier Law of August 1917, the army received the right to recall to the front any reservists aged 24–35 who had been granted leave in 1914–15 (or never inducted in the first place) because they were factory workers. The measure caused a collapse in morale among the men affected and their families, fueling strikes and workplace vandalism. Shortly after becoming premier, Clemenceau responded decisively to acts of sabotage by workers in munitions factories and power plants, threatening to deploy troops against them. The number of strikes in the Seine department fell to 150 in 1918, involving just over 200,000, as the French munitions industry used foreign labor to replace workers recalled under the Mourier Law. Because foreign workers risked summary deportation if they struck, the greater share of foreigners in the workforce minimized the impact of strikes in the last year of the war. For the war as a whole, France imported 330,000 workers from elsewhere in Europe, the majority of them from Spain, and 300,000 from beyond Europe, including 223,000 from French colonies, most of the rest from China. The combination of the Mourier Law and the influx of foreign workers fueled anti-foreign sentiment in French factory towns; one working-class wife in Le Creusot argued that the foreigners "should rightly be sent to the front and our husbands allowed to stay in the workshops."[8] While violence against foreign workers, especially colonials and Chinese, peaked amid the labor unrest of 1917, incidents persisted into 1918. Many individual beatings and killings of non-white workers came as vigilante punishment for their social or sexual relationships with French women. In May 1918 a series of strikes intended to last until the war ended collapsed after just ten days, not only because of the lack of support from foreign workers but also the unwillingness of the French public to support such actions in the midst of the final German offensive.

The last German drive on the French capital placed added burdens on the civilian population, as Gotha bombers and long-range railway guns caused just enough death and destruction to rattle the public. The first air raid, on the night of January 30–31, involved fifty planes dropping ninety-three bombs; during March, as the German ground offensive began, further raids killed 120 Parisians. Meanwhile, the Germans used their "Paris guns" on forty-four days between March 23 and August 9, when the front was close enough for the city to be within their 80-mile (130-km) range. At that distance targeting was even less precise than in aerial bombing, and the 181 shells fired killed just 256 people. More than the bombing or shelling, the threat of a German breakthrough induced an exodus from the capital, the likes of which had not been seen since August 1914. Until late June, when the German advance slowed to a halt, Paris continued to experience "the slow hemorrhaging of her population," with thousands per day leaving.[9] By early August the stations of Paris were busy with people returning home, who would soon join the troops in hailing Clemenceau as "the father of victory."

There was, of course, another French home front, in the part of France behind German lines, where the clocks were set to German time (one or two hours ahead of French time, depending upon the season) and the local population endured the arbitrary and often brutal policies of the occupation regime. Even under the Hindenburg Program significant numbers of French workers were not deported to Germany, yet some were sent to Belgian factories and many more employed as forced labor away from their homes within occupied France. The logic behind some German policies remains a mystery, unless the goal was merely to confuse, humiliate, or further demoralize the French population. One such example came at Easter 1916, when 20,000 French women and girls from Lille were required to undergo gynecological examinations, for no apparent reason, before being deported to other locales in the occupied zone. Compared with other countries facing similar situations, wartime France followed very lenient policies toward French women seeking abortions or arrested for infanticide as a consequence of being impregnated by a German soldier, policies clearly influenced by the context of France having been the first country whose population had practiced birth control on a widespread basis, a country where abortion remained a crime but was rarely punished. In the well-publicized infanticide case of Joséphine Barthélemy, left carrying a German soldier's child when the enemy evacuated her home village of Meurthe-et-Moselle, the accused offered only the defense that "I did not want a child born of a *boche* father." In her acquittal in January 1917, the court accepted the reasoning of her attorney that her murder of her own infant son was "an act of war," for which she should be considered a "war heroine."[10] But especially as the war dragged on, policies of compassion toward those most affected by the German occupation or forced from their homes by the invasion broke down in the face of practical realities. Local officials in the provinces often had difficulty distinguishing between genuine refugees displaced from their homes by the war (and thus entitled to welfare subsidies) and those who had voluntarily left their homes near the front lines or even in Paris because they no longer felt safe living there. In the resulting confusion, some refugees did not receive the help their government intended for them.

Orlando and the Revitalization of the Italian Home Front

Italy's counterpart to Clemenceau, Vittorio Orlando, came to power less than three weeks before him in the autumn of 1917. A legal scholar from Palermo, Orlando was Sicily's most prominent Liberal politician. He had held four cabinet posts since 1903, serving most recently as interior minister in the government of Paolo Boselli, successor to Salandra. He became prime minister five days after the front broke at Caporetto, and soon demonstrated a unique combination of personal qualities that proved to be what Italy needed at that moment. When it came to home-front morale and depth of support for the war, Italy's experience contrasted sharply to that of France. While widespread appreciation of the gravity of France's situation led to the *union sacrée* at the start of the war, with the misgivings and disunity coming later, Italy entered the war deeply divided and suffered an endemic crisis in morale, fueled by doubters on both the Left and the Right. In July 1917, Socialist Party deputy Claudio Treves coined the famous slogan "not another winter in the trenches," and the following month Catholics were shaken by Pope Benedict XV's "peace note" which posed the question, "is the civilized world to become nothing more than a heap of corpses?"[11] Caporetto, however, provided the sort of clarity for Italy that August 1914 had produced in France. Thus, the temporary breakdown of the Italian front in the autumn of 1917 had the opposite effect in Italy to that of the failure of the Nivelle offensive in France, and the Italians, though much closer to military collapse, never seriously contemplated a compromise peace. Invoking the same sort of spirit that had recently died in France, Orlando called his cabinet of all parties the *Unione Sacra*, Italy's *union sacrée*.

Aside from the prime ministers, General Alfredo Dallolio, coordinator of munitions production, ranked as the most significant figure on the Italian home front. Under his direction, industrial workers granted leave from the army remained subject to military discipline and, along with their nonmilitary counterparts, often worked 16-hour days. A system of binding arbitration sufficed to eliminate most strikes but favored factory owners over workers; wages, adjusted for inflation, were 27 percent lower in 1917 than in 1913. The government established almost 2,000 factories during the war, 84 percent of them in the already industrialized north and north-central regions of the country, but struggled to provide housing and social services for the greater number of workers, many of whom were migrants from the impoverished south. Like the French Army, the Italian Army did not grant wartime work leaves to peasants and thus strained the agricultural base of a country that could normally feed itself. Thanks largely to the efforts of peasant women, food production never dipped below 90 percent of prewar levels, but the dramatic reduction of remittances from Italian emigrants abroad made life even harder for poorer Italians, many of whom depended on the assistance of relatives in the Americas. The loss of this income during the war also affected the economy as a whole, since the sum total of emigrant remittances had covered 40 percent of Italy's trade deficit in prewar years. Rationing and price controls, first attempted in 1916, became unavoidable by the summer of 1917, which saw food shortages from Calabria in the south to Piedmont in the north, including the war's worst food riots, at Turin in August. A system of ration cards, introduced in October 1917, met with rejection in the countryside but worked well enough in the cities. Overall, the discipline imposed upon Italy's wartime workers did not apply to their corrupt bosses (whose scandals forced Dallolio's resignation in May 1918) or to the middle and upper classes in general.

The British Home Front under Lloyd George

In Britain, food rationing came later than elsewhere but the program, once implemented, was more comprehensive and spread the burden more equitably than the rationing regimes of other countries. Even though Britain's food supply depended upon imports from overseas, the resumption of unrestricted submarine warfare in February 1917 led not to compulsory rationing but to a vigorous campaign to conserve food and eliminate waste. Lloyd George's government waited until January 1918 before imposing food rationing, starting in Greater London. The program, extended to the rest of the country by April, included every food and drink except tea, cheese, and bread. Britain waited so long to introduce rationing in part because, in contrast to Germany, it hesitated to add the cost of the supervisory bureaucracy to an already-enormous war outlay. Even before the onset of rationing Parliament had approved a budget for the 1917–18 fiscal year (£2.7 billion) thirteen times larger than the last peacetime budget, for 1913–14. During those same four years the standard rate of income tax had risen from 6 percent to 30 percent, and ultimately Britain funded just over 18 percent of its war expenses with taxation rather than borrowing, far more than any other country.

Despite being spared from hunger, Britain in the last half of the war continued to suffer more strikes involving more workers and more lost workdays than any other belligerent power. In 1916, 581 strikes idled 284,000 workers; in 1917, the figure rose to 688 strikes involving 860,000 workers. Asquith and, after December 1916, Lloyd George did not think it was feasible for factory workers to be conscripted and assigned to workplaces on a military model. Instead, in response to the Hindenburg Program, Britain established the voluntary National Industrial Service under the direction of Neville Chamberlain, who received a cabinet-level appointment (his first) and the goal of attracting 500,000 workers to war industries. Chamberlain resigned eight months later, by which time the failed program had placed just 20,000 workers in factory jobs. Strikes continued to be a problem throughout 1918, disconnected from the increasingly positive news from the battlefields. On August 21, two weeks after British and Imperial troops began the final Allied offensive against the Germans, 150,000 miners struck in Yorkshire. Even London's "bobbies" were not immune to labor unrest; on August 30, 14,000 policemen struck for a pay raise.

Britain ultimately employed more women in war industries than any other country in World War I, and their involvement in the wartime economy was responsible, directly or indirectly, for Britain experiencing a greater degree of social change and social leveling. By August 1916, 340,000 were working in munitions factories and other jobs controlled by the War Office, along with 766,000 in the civilian sector. So many working-class women left domestic service for the higher wages offered by the war industries that by 1918 only the wealthiest households still had maids. By April 1918, the Women's Land Army had reached 260,000 volunteers, whose work on Britain's farms helped ease concerns about food shortages even as more people from the countryside continued to migrate to work in munitions factories, making London and other cities increasingly crowded and lively. Early closing times were imposed on pubs (and would remain in place, in revised form, until 1988) but not on night clubs, which flourished especially in London, where the theaters also experienced a wartime boom. Among young women with the means to indulge in such entertainment, precursors of the postwar "flappers" (a term that first appeared in the London press in January 1917) began to appear in public sporting hairstyles and clothing that were a revolutionary departure from prewar norms. Although historians continue to debate the degree to which the contribution of women to the British war effort resulted directly in the granting of suffrage, by March 1918, when Parliament passed the Representation of the People Act by a wide margin, so many women were engaged in such visible roles in society and the economy that it would have been unconscionable to deny them the vote any longer. The new law gave the vote to all women aged 30 and older, making them 43 percent of the electorate in the next general election, held in December 1918. Ten years later they received the vote at 21, under the same terms as men.

Britain experienced only sporadic air raids during World War I, yet the resulting deaths and destruction helped to harden the resolve of the home front. German Zeppelins began bombing coastal cities in January 1915, then extended their range to London that May, before venturing farther north to bomb the cities of the Midlands and even Edinburgh. Gotha bombers made their first appearance over London in May 1917, followed in January 1918 by much larger Staaken R6 bombers The R6 raids continued until May, by which time they had dropped 30 tons of bombs. The raids by aircraft, like the earlier Zeppelin raids, caused more outrage than panic. *The Times* account of a raid in June 1917 confirmed that such actions accomplished little for the enemy other than "to increase the utter and almost universal detestation in which he is held by the people of this country."[12]

From the onset of his coalition ministry in December 1916, Lloyd George presided over the most stable and unified of the Allied governments. The cabinet included former Conservative prime minister Arthur Balfour as foreign secretary, along with Winston Churchill, back from his brief tenure as an army officer in the trenches in France, who from July 1917 held Lloyd George's former portfolio as munitions minister. The prime minister was the only Liberal in the five-man Imperial War Cabinet, which included three Conservatives, one Labour Party member, and (from June 1917) South Africa's Jan Smuts. Especially for South Africa and Canada, but also for Australia and New Zealand, contributions to the war effort came with the expectation of greater autonomy from Britain in the postwar world. At the opening session of the Imperial Conference of 1911, Asquith had assured his colleagues from the Dominions that "each of us are … masters in our own house" in domestic affairs, but reaffirmed the traditional British view that foreign policy could be controlled only from London.[13] This position softened considerably during the war, and from the creation of the Imperial War Cabinet to the ratification of the Statute of Westminster in 1931, the Dominions achieved an ever-greater voice in their external affairs, and ultimately the status of independent states bound to Britain by choice, as equals.

War Comes to America

The American role in the war was revolutionary, but no less than the role of the war in the development of the United States, where it justified an increase in the power of the federal government at the expense of the individual states and, within the federal government, the power of the executive branch at the expense of the legislature. A series of laws including the Espionage Act (June 1917) and Sedition Act (May 1918) imposed restrictions on civil liberties along the lines of similar laws enacted in Europe in 1914.

Socially, the war helped to transform the United States in three important ways: by serving as an impetus for the extension of voting rights to women; as a catalyst for the "Great Migration" of African Americans from the rural South to the industrial centers of the North; and as an "Americanizing" influence for a country in which one-third of the people were either immigrants or children of immigrants.

The women's suffrage movement in the United States, like the movement in Britain, featured a large mainstream organization, the National American Woman Suffrage Association (NAWSA), analogous to the British NUWSS, and the smaller, more radical National Woman's Party (NWP), founded in 1916 by Alice Paul on the model of Pankhurst's WPSU, which she had joined while residing in Britain before the war. Owing to the delayed entry of the United States into the war, its suffrage movement overlapped in part with the peace movement. The Women's Peace Party (WPP), established in 1915, counted social activist Jane Addams among its leaders, and shared members with both the NAWSA and the NWP, at least until April 1917, when the NAWSA rallied behind the war effort. The NWP did not, and instead intensified its protests, criticizing Wilson's global crusade for democracy as a fraud as long as women in his own country were denied the vote. Thus, confrontational scenes nearly identical to those played out before the war in Britain – with women being arrested, going on hunger strikes, and being force-fed while in captivity – were repeated in the United States in 1917–18. Wilson opposed women's suffrage in his 1912 campaign and took no position on it in 1916 (even though, by then, several states had already granted it). In January 1918, after he publicly endorsed the cause, a women's suffrage bill passed the House of Representatives but failed in the Senate. That September, Wilson went to Capitol Hill in an attempt to persuade the senators that the suffrage bill was "vital to the winning of the war."[14] The war was over by the time Congress finally approved a constitutional amendment barring gender-based suffrage discrimination; it was ratified by the requisite three-quarters of the states in August 1920, in time to give women aged 21 and over the vote in the presidential election that November. In his speech urging the Senate to pass the suffrage bill, Wilson observed that "this war could not have been fought … if it had not been for the services of the women." But most of these services were unpaid, through the Red Cross and other charities; indeed, American war-related industries registered just 1 million women workers and, as in the French case, most of them had already been employed at other lower-paying jobs outside the home. In the United States, as in Europe, such wartime gains in access to employment were even more temporary in World War I than they would be in World War II. Reflecting the ephemeral nature of wartime job opportunities, the US census of 1920 showed just under one-quarter of the female population over age 16 as part of the paid workforce, a slight decline from 1910.

World War I brought more dramatic change for African Americans than for American women. When the United States entered the war more than 90 percent of

American blacks still resided in the former slaveholding states, but the wartime "Great Migration" saw 500,000 of them move from southern farms to northern cities to work in defense and other industries; the trend continued during the 1920s, bringing another 800,000 African Americans to the North. The census of 1920 registered a net decrease in black population in most southern states, while New York, Pennsylvania, Ohio, and Illinois had the greatest gains. The influx of African Americans sparked wartime race riots in several northern cities. The first, and worst, came in July 1917 in East St. Louis, Illinois, leaving at least 100 people dead, most of them black. The following summer further race riots erupted in New York, Washington, Philadelphia, and Chicago. Racial violence also rippled across the southern states, home to most of the sixty African Americans lynched during 1918, up from thirty-six in 1917. Wartime training of black troops at southern bases led to clashes rooted in local Jim Crow laws, most notably in August 1917 in Houston, where a fight left fifteen local whites and four black soldiers dead, and resulted in the execution of another fourteen black soldiers after courts martial. The wave of racial violence peaked in 1919 before subsiding in the early 1920s. Most African American leaders supported the war effort, either because they considered it an opportunity for the cause of civil rights or feared a backlash if they did not. Harvard-educated sociologist W. E. B. DuBois encouraged blacks to "forget our special grievances and close our ranks ... with our own white fellow citizens."[15] The most notable dissenter, newspaper editor A. Philip Randolph, spent the war in prison after advocating an African American boycott. Among the racial minorities in the AEF, the 368,000 African Americans were by far the largest group. The army commissioned black officers only to command black troops; Wilson, a segregationist despite his overall progressive views, intervened personally to ensure that the highest-ranking black officer in the prewar army, a lieutenant colonel, did not see active duty during the war. Pershing did not share the prejudices against African American troops typical of officers in the segregated army of his time. He always spoke highly of the four prewar black regiments, in particular the 10th Cavalry, which he had commanded in Cuba during the Spanish-American War. These views were the source of his nickname "Black Jack," sanitized by the press from his service nickname, "N – Jack." Of course, such sentiments only went so far, as the status and treatment of African American soldiers did not rank high on Pershing's list of wartime concerns. Upon arrival in France, most were sent to labor units, and the AEF's two black combat divisions, the 92nd and 93rd, fought under French command on the French sector of the front.

Mexican Americans followed the same wartime migration pattern as African Americans, only on a far smaller scale. Their prewar population of roughly 250,000 lived almost exclusively in the states of Texas, New Mexico, Arizona, and California, but during the war they began to establish a presence in the upper Midwest. In addition to the northern migration of Mexican Americans, during and immediately after the war at least 70,000 Mexicans immigrated legally and perhaps another 100,000 illegally, mostly to take agricultural jobs. Among the alien population, draft-age men were inducted only if they declared their intention to become US citizens. "Non-declarant" alien conscripts were automatically exempted from service, but they also forfeited their right to seek citizenship at a later date. Few Mexican aliens (less than 6,000) chose induction for the sake of achieving future citizenship, and a large number of Mexican American citizens apparently fled to Mexico to avoid military service; as a result, the census of 1920 recorded twice as many Mexican American females as males. The US Army did not segregate its Hispanic inductees and, statistically, their service pattern remains difficult to trace. The same was true of conscripts from among 180,000 Asian Americans, a population deliberately kept small by the US bans on Chinese (1882) and male Japanese (1907) immigrants, at a time when European immigrants enjoyed an open door. In contrast to their Mexican immigrant counterparts, the Asians registered far fewer "non-declarants" among their conscripts, because so many Chinese and Japanese males embraced military service as a means to become citizens after the war. World War I also helped to change the status of the Native American population of the United States. The defeat of the last free tribe in 1890 had left all surviving "Indians" confined to federal reservations, and until an act of Congress in 1924 they, too, were considered resident aliens because of their status as citizens of the various indigenous nations. Like Asian Americans, Native Americans tended to view military service as an opportunity rather than a burden; nearly one in five adult male Native Americans, 17,000 in all, served in the army during World War I. In sharp contrast to the other racial minorities, they were highly regarded as soldiers and (albeit often for stereotypically racist reasons) more likely than white soldiers to be used as scouts, messengers, or snipers. The World War II practice of using Native Americans, speaking their indigenous languages, as radiomen began in the AEF in the last two months of the war. In general, the US Army sought to use military service as an instrument of "Americanization" for immigrant draftees, but in the end pragmatism prevailed over patriotic idealism. Accommodations included exceptions to English-only training policies, but without abandoning the overall goal of Americanizing immigrant troops.

Wartime Anti-Germanism in the United States and Britain

Germany held the distinction of being the ancestral homeland of more US citizens than any other place outside the British Isles. The rest of the American population tended to admire German Americans and value their contributions to the development of the country, and held the German language and culture in high regard. Yet with the American declaration of war on Germany, public pressure, combined with the desire of most German Americans to demonstrate that they were Americans first, brought an abrupt end to most German-language newspapers, most German-specific social and cultural activities, and the use of the German language in Lutheran and Reformed church services. Some symphonies even banned Bach and Beethoven. German-language courses (taken by a quarter of all US high school students) all but disappeared from the schools. The American Protective League and local patriotic committees harassed German Americans who did not appear sufficiently enthusiastic about the war, and shops run by German Americans endured boycotts. Many families "Americanized" or anglicized their names (for example, from Schmidt to Smith) or at least the names of their businesses. In Cincinnati, where 60 percent of the population had German heritage, all German-language books were removed from the public library. Book burnings were staged across the country, while streets, neighborhoods, suburbs, and towns lost their German names, along with some foods (such as sauerkraut becoming "liberty cabbage") and breeds of dogs (dachshunds becoming "liberty hounds"). The war was also a boon to the Women's Christian Temperance Union and other groups favoring the prohibition of alcohol. With German American brewers such as Anheuser-Busch of St. Louis, Pabst of Milwaukee, and Stroh of Detroit in no position to lobby against it, a Congress in which more than two-thirds of the representatives in each party favored prohibition easily passed it into law in December 1917; the resulting Eighteenth Amendment to the US Constitution was approved by the requisite number of states thirteen months later. Amid the wave of discrimination, nearly half a million German citizens residing in the United States were photographed and fingerprinted, and 2,300 were interned as dangerous enemy aliens, but few were subjected to physical violence. The lone German American lynched during the war, coal miner Robert Prager of Maryville, Illinois, met his fate in nearby Collinsville hours after making "disloyal" remarks at a local Socialist Party meeting. Though most contemporary newspaper headlines echoed the *St. Louis Post-Dispatch* in characterizing the action as a "German Enemy of U.S. Hanged by Mob,"[16] Prager no doubt met his fate because he was a socialist as well as a German (see section below).

During the last year of the war, Lloyd George ordered the intensification of anti-German propaganda efforts in Britain, for the domestic audience as well as to undermine the Central Powers abroad (see Online Essay 9). Newspaper magnate Lord Beaverbrook helped fan the flames of popular anti-Germanism within Britain, which by war's end manifested itself in ways similar to the American anti-Germanism of 1917–18, only with far fewer Anglo-Germans than German Americans to target. There were no "liberty hounds" in Britain, but the English Kennel Club officially declared German Shepherds to be "Alsatians," a decision that stuck for sixty years. Of course, the most prominent Anglo-Germans were the royal family itself and other fixtures of the British aristocracy who shared some of their German roots. In June 1917, King George V distanced the dynasty from its German origins by changing its name from the House of Saxe-Coburg-Gotha to the House of Windsor, and ordering all members of the royal family to relinquish their German titles. A number of British aristocratic families, most of them related to the royal family, followed suit, for example, Battenberg becoming Mountbatten.

The Failure of Anti-War Socialism, from Stockholm to St. Louis

In April 1917 the International Socialist Bureau (the permanent executive of the Second International, headquartered in Brussels before the war) reconvened at Stockholm in neutral Sweden. The more radical International Socialist Committee, formed in September 1915 at the Zimmerwald Conference, quickly followed suit. Led by their representatives from the neutral Scandinavian countries and the Netherlands, they issued a joint appeal for a peace conference to be held in Stockholm. The Central Powers accepted the offer. Eduard David led the German SPD delegation that arrived in June, and Viktor Adler led the Austrian Social Democratic contingent. Hungary's small socialist party sent a separate delegation. On the Allied side, France was not alone in its refusal to support the conference. Italy, the United States, and the Provisional Government of Russia likewise declined to send delegates. Lloyd George initially agreed to let future Labour prime minister Ramsay MacDonald attend, then changed his mind.

The conference soon degenerated into a series of meetings involving the Scandinavian and Dutch hosts and any foreign socialist leaders who could make their way to Stockholm. In addition to the delegates from the Central Powers, these included a variety of Russian revolutionaries attending in defiance of the Provisional Government. Lenin initially supported the conference but did not attend and eventually condemned it for being tainted by Germany's "selfish and predatory imperial interests,"[17] strong words indeed, coming from Russia's leading beneficiary of German largesse. Notwithstanding his role in drafting the Reichstag's peace resolution the following month, the SPD's David delivered the standard German defense of his country's actions. In a June 6 speech in Stockholm, he categorically rejected German war guilt, blaming the war instead on the prewar encirclement of Germany by the Entente "syndicate."[18] Austria-Hungary approached the conference in a far more conciliatory and hopeful frame of mind. In correspondence with the soon-to-be-ousted Count Tisza, foreign minister Count Czernin defended his decision to allow Adler's delegation to go to Sweden: "If they secure peace, it will be a socialistic one," but "after the war, we shall be forced to have a socialist policy whether it is welcome or not." Czernin "consider[ed] it extremely important to prepare the Social Democrats" for what he saw as their leading role in postwar Austria, in foreign as well as domestic policy.[19] But the leaders of the Stockholm initiative lost all hope of ever convening a conference after the Bolshevik coup in Russia, when Lenin issued his own appeal for an international peace conference, reiterating the 1915 Zimmerwald principle of a "peace without annexa-tions or indemnities." Their series of meetings ended in January 1918, nine months after they began.

The onset of the Stockholm Conference coincided with the US entry into the war, which in turn sparked a vigorous response from American socialists. On April 7, 1917, one day after Congress declared war on Germany, the Socialist Party of America attracted 200 delegates to an "emergency national convention" in St. Louis, which pro-duced an anti-war resolution characterizing the actions of Wilson and Congress as "a crime against the people of the United States and against the nations of the world." Such inflammatory language obscured the sound reasoning of much of the rest of the document, including the assertion that "democracy can never be imposed upon any country by a foreign power by force of arms."[20] Given the mood of the American home front, the strong anti-war posture of the Socialist Party soon made its members prime targets of US federal authorities operating under the Espionage and Sedition acts, patriotic officials at the state and local levels, and citizen groups such as the American Protective League. It did not help that so many American socialists were German Americans (including at least 20 percent of the delegates at the St. Louis convention). Socialist leaders jailed for anti-war activities included Eugene Debs, a union organizer of Alsatian descent, who in the presidential election of 1912 had won 6 percent of the vote (still the largest share ever for a socialist candidate). Debs remained incarcerated through the election of 1920, when he ran a write-in campaign for president from his jail cell and won 3.4 percent of the vote. Nevertheless, World War I and the Bolshevik Revolution weakened and divided American socialists, just as it weakened and divided the Left in European countries.

The Influenza Pandemic

The transport of the AEF to Europe had a devastating unintended consequence, trigger-ing the global spread of a strain of influenza deadlier than any the world had yet seen. While historians continue to debate exactly where and when the virus first appeared, the illness afflicting soldiers and civilians alike in Europe by summer 1918 traces back to an outbreak in early March at Fort Riley, Kansas, where 100 men reported sick with the same symptoms on the same morning. Initially called the "three-day fever," it dif-fered from most influenza outbreaks in that so many of its victims were between the ages of 20 and 40. The virus soon spread throughout the United States, then became a pandemic thanks to the transport of American troops and their infection of the crews of the troopships that carried them abroad, as well as the Allied soldiers they served with in France. These included men from all over the British and French empires who, in turn, spread the virus to Africa, Asia, and the Pacific when they returned home. By

May 1918 the virus had spread to the Allied armies in France, and soon thereafter to German troops advancing and taking prisoners during their spring offensive. In June it made its first appearance in India, at Bombay. Out of concern for morale, the belligerent governments censored reporting about the extent and severity of the influenza outbreak. Some of the earliest and most accurate reporting came out of neutral Spain, leading the press and public health officials to label the pandemic "Spanish influenza," a designation used in the United States as early as July 1918.

After a brief summer respite, the virus reappeared on August 27 among sailors in Boston, Massachusetts, only in a far deadlier form. Within a week, dozens of American soldiers awaiting transport to Europe were dying every day, either from influenza or the bacterial pneumonia that followed it, often just four or five days after being in perfect health. This more lethal strain of the virus appeared almost simultaneously at Brest, France, and at Freetown, Sierra Leone, like Boston major ports of embarkation or debarkation for troops. That autumn it ravaged the German Army, then spread to the hungry home fronts of Germany and Austria-Hungary. The weekly influenza death rate in Britain peaked at more than 4,000 in the last week of October. Meanwhile, in France, the flu claimed 1,200 lives per week in Paris alone, but owing to vigorous wartime censorship the pandemic was not mentioned in the French press until mid-month, when Clemenceau's son-in-law died from the virus. By the end of 1918 Germany had recorded 400,000 deaths from influenza, Britain 170,000, but the United States remained the hardest hit, with 450,000. In October alone 195,000 Americans died from the illness, including 4,597 in Philadelphia in a single week, and 851 in the city of New York on a single day, October 23. In many cities concern about infection kept crowds down when news of the Armistice arrived. In San Francisco, 30,000 people took to the streets wearing face-masks to celebrate the end of the war, but despite the precaution the city experienced another flare-up of flu cases in December.

By the time it subsided in 1919, an estimated 28 percent of all Americans had been infected by the virus and 675,000 had died from it. Germany likely suffered more than half a million deaths, France 400,000, Italy 350,000, Britain 228,000. Japan lost at least as many as Britain and perhaps close to 400,000. Deaths in Russia certainly surpassed all of these, adding to the millions lost in the civil war there. Among the Dominions, Canada recorded 50,000 deaths, Australia 12,000, New Zealand 8,500. The latter included 2,200 Maori, whose death rate of 42.3 per thousand far eclipsed the white New Zealander rate of 5.8 per thousand, foreshadowing the devastating toll that influenza would levy during 1919 among Pacific islanders. The former German Samoa suffered the most, the dead there including 30 percent of the adult male population, but where the governing authorities moved quickly to establish effective quarantines, entire native populations were spared, for example, in American Samoa and French New Caledonia, neither of which recorded a single fatality. Figures for China or the

African colonies remain near guesswork, but the available data for certain cities (for example, Addis Ababa, Abyssinia, where 10,000 died) points to a heavy death toll. No country suffered as much as India, where as many as 20 million died in the twelve months after the virus first appeared in June 1918. For the pandemic as a whole, the overall mortality rate reached 2.5 percent, twenty-five times the norm for influenza, and 5 percent in India.

The worldwide death toll from the virus for decades was estimated to have been around 20 million, mostly in Europe and North America, but by the end of the twentieth century, as researchers came to appreciate the scope of the pandemic in India and the Asia/Pacific region, the figure was revised upward to 50 million, with some scholars speculating that as many as 100 million may have perished. It is now believed that at least 20 percent of the human population was infected at some time during 1918–19. It is difficult to imagine that the pandemic would have achieved such proportions if not for World War I. The camps, troopships, trenches, and hospitals of the warring countries served as incubators for the virus, and the transport to Europe and home again of millions of men accelerated its spread worldwide. Without the victims of the influenza pandemic, the death toll of World War I stands at a fraction of the human cost of World War II, but with them included, the gap narrows considerably.

Conclusion

As the war entered its final year, the Allied countries, minus Russia, had withstood their worst military and domestic crises and, with the entry of the United States, looked forward to a better future, while for the Central Powers the worst was yet to come. The warring countries had one thing in common when it came to their home fronts: they were reaping the whirlwind of public belligerency they had sown earlier, and became victims of their own propaganda to drive their peoples on. Notwithstanding the best efforts of the pacifists, by 1918 there were, arguably, more proponents of peace in uniform than in civilian dress. Indeed, military personnel on visits home frequently remarked that hatred of the enemy ran much deeper there than in the trenches. For example, a German officer on leave was dismayed at the thoughts of "hatred and revenge" that consumed the home front, while a British officer observed that home "looked strange to us soldiers. We could not understand the war-madness that ran wild everywhere … The civilians talked a foreign language, and it was newspaper language. I found serious conversation with my parents all but impossible."[21] Even in Austria-Hungary, the remaining belligerent most desperate for peace, the last-ditch peace initiatives of Emperor Charles, when revealed by the Allies, would be denounced on the home front as treason. As the generals continued their struggle to master the strategic, tactical, and logistical factors that would produce the ultimate victory, the politicians faced the increasingly thorny problem of coming up with an outcome to the war that would be acceptable to the public.

Especially in the last half of the war, strikes served as the most dramatic manifestation of home-front tensions. In numbers of strikers alone, Britain appeared to suffer the most serious wartime labor unrest, yet in judging the magnitude of those strikes as a threat to the country's stability, it must be recognized that Britain, historically, had Europe's least politically radical labor movement. In the years 1914–18, as before, most British workers struck because of the circumstances of their own labor, not a desire to topple the prime minister, change their overall system of government, or change their government's external policies. They struck in circumstances that gave them the greatest likelihood of achieving their goals, and the war merely presented them with a greater number of those opportunities. In contrast, for all of the continental powers, the prospect of labor unrest affecting the strength of the army at the front, causing a breakdown leading to invasion and defeat, made large-scale strikes far more dangerous than in Britain, which in this regard had much more in common with the United States or the Dominions. Indeed, for France and Italy, a front line standing on the national soil cast all wartime labor unrest in a different light, and any workers striking as they would in peacetime certainly risked enjoying far less public support. In Germany and Austria-Hungary, as well as Imperial Russia before March 1917, the absence of fully functional parliamentary systems and the past history of how each of these governments dealt with socialism and organized labor provided a very different context, making every strike a political statement and, on some level, a protest against the regime and its policies.

SUGGESTIONS FOR FURTHER READING

Allen, Keith. "Food and the German Home Front: Evidence from Berlin," in Gail Braybon (ed.), *Evidence, History and the Great War: Historians and the Impact of 1914–18* (New York: Berghahn Books, 2003), 172–97.

Barry, John M. *The Great Influenza* (New York: Viking, 2004).

Capozzola, Christopher. *Uncle Sam Wants You: World War I and the Making of the Modern American Citizen* (Oxford: Oxford University Press, 2008).

Gregory, Adrian, and Senia Paseta (eds.) *Ireland and the Great War: "A War to Unite Us All"?* (Manchester: Manchester University Press, 2002).

Jeffery, Keith. *Ireland and the Great War* (Cambridge: Cambridge University Press, 2000).

Kennedy, David M. *Over Here: The First World War and American Society* (Oxford: Oxford University Press, 1980; reprinted edn., 2004).

Pollard, John F. *The Unknown Pope: Benedict XV (1914–1922) and the Pursuit of Peace* (London: Geoffrey Chapman, 1999).

Roberts, Mary Louise. *Civilization without Sexes: Reconstructing Gender in Postwar France, 1917–1927* (Chicago, IL: University of Chicago Press, 1994).

Townshend, Charles. *Easter 1916: The Irish Rebellion* (Chicago, IL: Ivan R. Dee, 2005).

Wills, Clair. *Dublin 1916: The Siege of the GPO* (Cambridge, MA: Harvard University Press, 2009).

Winter, Jay and Jean-Louis Robert. *Capital Cities at War: Paris, London, Berlin, 1914–1919* (Cambridge: Cambridge University Press, 2007).

See also titles under *Suggestions for further reading* for Chapter 6, "The Home Fronts, 1914–16."

NOTES

1. Quoted in Walther Rathenau, *Walther Rathenau, Industrialist, Banker, Intellectual, and Politician: Notes and Diaries 1907–1922*, ed. Hartmut Pogge von Strandmann (Oxford: Oxford University Press, 1985), 216–18.
2. Holger H. Herwig, *The First World War: Germany and Austria* (London: Arnold, 1997), 263.
3. See Albrecht Ritschl, "Germany's Economy at War, 1914–1918 and Beyond," in Stephen Broadberry and Mark Harrison (eds.), *The Economics of World War I* (Cambridge: Cambridge University Press, 2005), 47.
4. See, for example, Tara Zahra, "Each Nation Only Cares for its Own: Empire, Nation, and Child Welfare Activism in the Bohemian Lands, 1900–1918," *American Historical Review* 111 (2006): 1378–402.
5. Quoted in Stéphane Audoin-Rouzeau and Annette Becker, *14–18: Understanding the Great War*, trans. Catherine Temerson (New York: Hill & Wang, 2002), 179.
6. Quoted in John Williams, *The Home Fronts: Britain, France and Germany, 1914–1918* (London: Constable, 1972), 214.
7. Quoted in Leonard V. Smith, Stéphane Audoin-Rouzeau, and Annette Becker, *France and the Great War, 1914–1918* (Cambridge University Press, 2003), 143.
8. Quoted in Jean-Jacques Becker, *The Great War and the French People*, trans. Arnold Pomerans (New York: St. Martin's Press, 1986), 142.
9. Becker, *The Great War and the French People*, 315.
10. Stéphane Audoin-Rouzeau, *L'enfant de l'ennemi (1914–1918): Viol, avortement, infanticide pendant la Grande Guerre* (Paris: Aubier, 1995), 13–31.
11. Benedict XV, Peace Note of August 1, 1917, quoted in Patrick J. Houlihan, *Catholicism and the Great War: Religion and Everyday Life in Germany and Austria-Hungary, 1914-1922* (Cambridge: Cambridge University Press, 2015), 199.
12. *The Times* (London), June 13, 1917, quoted in Barry D. Power, *Strategy Without Slide-rule: British Air Strategy, 1914–1939* (London: Croom Helm, 1976), 55.

13. Quoted in W. K. Hancock and R. T. E. Latham, *Survey of British Commonwealth Affairs, Vol. 1* (London: Oxford University Press, 1964), 3.

14. Wilson, Speech to the US Senate, September 30, 1918, text in *Ripples of Hope: Great American Civil Rights Speeches*, eds. Josh Gottheimer, Bill Clinton, and Mary Frances Berry (New York: Basic Civitas Books, 2003), 148–49.

15. Quoted in Christopher Capozzola, *Uncle Sam Wants You: World War I and the Making of the Modern American Citizen* (Oxford: Oxford University Press, 2008), 34.

16. *St. Louis Post-Dispatch*, April 5, 1918, 1.

17. Lenin, "The Stockholm Conference," September 8, 1917, text in Lenin, *Collected Works*, vol. 25 (Moscow: Progress Publishers, 1977), 269–77.

18. Eduard David, *Wer trägt die Schuld am Kriege? Rede, gehalten in Stockholm, am 6.juni 1917* (Berlin: Vorwärts, 1917).

19. Quoted in George V. Strong, *Seedtime for Fascism: The Disintegration of Austrian Political Culture, 1867–1918* (London: M.E. Sharpe, 1998), 165–66.

20. "The Socialist Party and The War," adopted at the St. Louis National Emergency Convention, April 14, 1917, text in Alexander Trachtenberg (ed.), *The American Labor Year Book, 1917–18* (New York: Rand School of Social Science, 1918), 50–53.

21. Quoted in Williams, *The Home Fronts*, 102, 125.

Indian lancers entering Haifa, 1918

Indian cavalry of the Jodhpore and Mysore Lancers, 16th (Imperial) Cavalry Brigade, entering Haifa, September 21, 1918. Cavalry accounted for a small fraction of the 580,000 Indian combat troops serving overseas, but they played a key role in securing Allied control over cities and towns throughout Mesopotamia and Palestine, and in routing Turkish formations in retreat. During 1918, Indian cavalry often operated with air support, which reduced obstacles too formidable for them to handle themselves. In the last weeks of the war they were the first Allied troops into Damascus, Beirut, Aleppo, and Mosul.

12 The World War
The Middle East and India

November 1914	Anglo-Indian invasion of Mesopotamia.
April 1915	Armenian genocide begins.
March 1916	British Imperial forces repel Sanusi invasion of Egypt.
June 1916	Sharif Hussein of Mecca declares Arab independence.
October 1916	T. E. Lawrence arrives at Mecca, becomes liaison to Arab revolt.
November 1916	Anglo-Egyptian force defeats, kills sultan of Darfur.
December 1916	Lucknow Pact unites Indian leaders in quest for Home Rule.
March 1917	Anglo-Indian forces take Baghdad.
November 1917	Fall of Gaza, onset of British invasion of Palestine.
December 1917	Jerusalem falls to British Imperial forces.
September 1918	Battle of Megiddo completes British conquest of Palestine.
October 1	Lawrence and Arabs enter Damascus.
October 30	Ottoman Empire signs armistice.

Failure at Gallipoli in 1915 did nothing to change the underlying Allied convictions regarding the significance of the Ottoman Empire for the war as a whole. While another direct strike at the Dardanelles and Constantinople was out of the question, from the eastern Sahara across the Middle East to the Arabian desert, Allied forces and their surrogates continued to engage the Turks and those loyal to them. With the Western front consuming an ever-greater share of the manpower of Britain and the Dominions, the resources of India became indispensable to the war effort in the Middle East. Returning to India to assume an increasingly prominent role in the Indian National Congress, Mohandas K. (Mahatma) Gandhi saw an opportunity in this turn of events and supported the war, reasoning that a strong showing would strengthen India's hand in its relationship with Britain. German attempts to subvert British rule in India failed miserably, but, thanks largely to T. E. Lawrence, Britain fared better in its attempt to foment an Arab revolution against the Ottoman Empire. In the long run Britain would be burned by the flames of nationalism and anti-colonialism it had fanned for the sake of rallying most Indians and Arabs behind the Allied cause, but within the context of World War I the ends appeared to justify the means, especially since the British had no intention of giving India the degree of self-government that it wanted, and they and the French had no intention of rewarding the Arab contribution with postwar independence. Just as the wartime movements in India and the Arab world foreshadowed future developments, Turkey's Armenian genocide presaged subsequent state-sponsored attempts to exterminate specific civilian populations. On the fringes of the war in the Middle East, local conflicts from Darfur to Ethiopia and Somalia likewise pointed the way to a grim future.

The Mesopotamian Campaign: India's Great War

From their initial efforts to defend Egypt through the evacuation of the Gallipoli beachheads in the winter of 1915–16, the Allies kept their efforts against the Ottoman Empire focused on the lands bordering the eastern Mediterranean (Map 12.1). Thereafter, the spotlight shifted to the Persian Gulf and Mesopotamia (modern-day Iraq), where the British had opened a theater of action on November 6, 1914, the day after they declared war on the Turks, sustained largely by troops from India. While Indian troops fought in Europe and played a significant role in sub-Saharan Africa, only in Mesopotamia would they account for a majority of Allied manpower throughout the war. Indeed, in recognition of the primary role of India in sustaining the campaign, for much of the war it would be directed by the India Office rather than the War Office.

Map 12.1 Middle East in World War I

The Mesopotamian campaign began when an Anglo-Indian landing force of 600 men stormed the Turkish fort at Fao, guarding the Persian Gulf approach to the Shatt-al Arab waterway in the Tigris-Euphrates delta. By the end of November 1914, 7,000 Allied troops had garrisoned nearby Abadan Island, since 1908 home to the refineries of the Anglo-Persian Oil Company, and proceeded upriver to occupy Basra. The Abadan refineries stood at the terminus of a pipeline 140 miles (225 km) long, leading inland to the company's oil fields in southwestern Persia, the source of much of the Royal Navy's petroleum (see Online Essay 8). Britain placed the highest strategic priority on securing these resources, and once they were secured it was not a foregone conclusion that a full-scale occupation of all of Mesopotamia would be attempted. But the very ease with which these first moves succeeded spawned ambitions that began to take on a life of their own when the Turkish governor and military commander in Mesopotamia, Halil Pasha (uncle of Enver Pasha), decided to keep his troops on the defensive in the vicinity of Baghdad. Even there, the Turks had difficulty keeping their troops supplied and reinforced, as the Ottoman sector of the famed Berlin-to-Baghdad railway (under construction since 1888) remained unfinished. As of 1914, the 1,255-mile (2,020-km) journey from Constantinople to Baghdad still took at least twenty-one days, employing trains over five segments of track and horse-drawn wagons or coaches over four segments of dirt road.

By the time the Turks finally attempted to retake Basra, the Anglo-Indian forces there had grown to include two divisions. In the battle of Shaiba (April 11–14, 1915), fought on the outskirts of Basra, Lieutenant General John Nixon deployed just 7,000 of his men to defeat Suleiman al-Askary's army of 12,000 Turks backed by 10,000–15,000 Arab tribesmen, in the process inflicting 6,000 casualties while sustaining only 1,200. In the wake of the disaster al-Askary committed suicide and local Turkish resistance collapsed. With the support of the viceroy of India, Lord Charles Hardinge, Nixon sought permission to take Baghdad as soon as possible, as a first step in the conquest of Mesopotamia. Over the months that followed, as the prospects at Gallipoli grew increasingly grim, Nixon's vision of an easy march on Baghdad gained considerable political appeal. Though slowed by spring floods and intense summer heat (reaching 45°C, or 113°F, as early as June), the troops he sent forward reached Nasiriya (July 24), then Kut (September 26), just 100 miles (160 km) from Baghdad. In late October, Asquith's cabinet sanctioned an assault on Baghdad by the unit that had taken Kut, Major General Charles Townshend's 6th Indian Division. Townshend was promised another two divisions "as soon as possible" but in the meantime was to proceed with the troops at hand.[1]

In the battle of Ctesiphon (November 22–24, 1915), fought among ancient ruins along the Tigris 25 miles (40 km) from Baghdad, Townshend's 12,000-man division met 18,000 Turks under General Albay Yûsuf Nûreddin Bey, advised by Field Marshal Colmar von der Goltz. Called out of retirement in 1914 to the post of German military governor of Belgium, Goltz, at age 72, was deemed to be of greater use in the Ottoman Empire, where he had served as a military advisor from 1883 to 1895. His presence made little difference at Ctesiphon, where despite their numerical disadvantage Townshend's men forced the Turks out of their forward trench lines and fought them to a bloody draw, inflicting 9,500 casualties while suffering 4,300 of their own. Afterward both armies abandoned the field, the Turks to Baghdad and Townshend to Kut, where he soon found that his exhausted division could not be supplied adequately at such a distance from Basra.

Goltz, drawing on the resources of Baghdad, soon followed Townshend to Kut, laying siege to the city on December 7 and strengthening his forces thereafter. Ultimately,

Goltz commanded nearly 80,000 Turks encircling the city, and some of the British Army's Middle East experts began to argue that Kut could be saved only by an acceleration of efforts to turn the Arab population against their Ottoman rulers. But Nixon rejected the meddling of "experts from Oxford" who came to Basra to advise him on how to win over the local Arabs, among them Captain T. E. Lawrence of the Cairo Intelligence Office, who had done field work in Mesopotamia as an archaeologist before the war.[2] Nixon returned to India in January 1916, after the failure of an initial relief expedition; his successor, Lieutenant General Percival Lake, presided over another two relief attempts that fared no better. By the time Townshend surrendered Kut (April 29, 1916), another 1,746 of his men had died. In addition to the loss of the 6th Indian Division, British Imperial forces suffered 23,000 casualties in the three failed relief attempts against just 10,000 for the Turks. Townshend spent the rest of the war confined in relative comfort in Constantinople, while 4,000 of the 10,000 troops he surrendered were worked to death in Turkish prison camps; revelations of their fate led to his disgrace after the war. Meanwhile, Nixon, Lake, and several other British officers associated with the debacle saw their military careers end as a result.

The crisis at Kut prompted Kitchener to send British troops to Mesopotamia, including the 13th Division, recently evacuated from Gallipoli, which arrived in time to participate in the last futile relief attempt. Following the surrender of Kut, the commander of the 13th, Lieutenant General Frederick Stanley Maude, succeeded Lake as commander of the Anglo-Indian Army and integrated the theater into the overall British war effort, taking orders directly from the War Office in London rather than from the India Office via the colonial government in Delhi. The reinforcement of Maude's command to 50,000 men marked the turning of the tide in the Mesopotamian campaign, coinciding, on the Turkish side, with the death of Goltz, who succumbed to typhus in Baghdad during the last days of the siege of Kut, leaving the incompetent Halil Pasha to resume command. The completion of key tunnels in the Taurus mountains in January 1917 left just one significant gap in Baghdad's rail link with Constantinople (which, alas, would not be completed until 1940), but their opening came too late to shore up the Ottoman position in Mesopotamia; indeed, the tunnels only facilitated the more rapid redeployment of thousands of Halil Pasha's troops from Mesopotamia via Damascus to the Hejaz to fight against the growing Arab revolt. Against a weakened adversary, Maude's army easily retook Kut (February 23, 1917), overwhelming a Turkish force half its size. He then advanced quickly on Baghdad, where Halil Pasha made a weak attempt at a last stand. Maude's army routed the Turks, taking 15,000 prisoners, and entered the city on March 11. By then the Arab revolt in the Hejaz was well underway, and the population of Baghdad gave the Anglo-Indian Army a rousing welcome. Eight days later, in his "Proclamation of Baghdad," Maude declared that "our armies do not come into your cities and lands as conquerors or enemies, but as liberators." Acknowledging Sharif Hussein of Mecca's declaration of Arab independence made nine months earlier, he closed his address by assuring his audience of Britain's col-laboration "in realizing the aspirations of your race."[3] After pausing to consolidate his gains, Maude resumed the offensive in the autumn of 1917, battling the Turks at Tikrit and Ramadi, but he did not live to see the end of the campaign. In mid-November he died of cholera, oddly enough in the same house in Baghdad where Goltz had died of typhus nineteen months earlier.

After Major General William Marshall succeeded Maude, the focus shifted to occupying the country. Troops from India now poured into Mesopotamia, swelling Marshall's ranks to 350,000 men by year's end, an army one historian has character-ized as "astonishingly inactive."[4] Aside from quelling a major uprising, centered on Najaf, in May 1918, Marshall's troops saw little action until the last days of the war, when Lloyd George, looking ahead to the postwar partition of the Ottoman Empire, ordered him to secure the oil fields around Mosul. For this purpose Marshall deployed an Anglo-Indian force under Major General Alexander Cobbe, which defeated Ismail Hakki Bey's Turkish Sixth Army in the battle of Sharqat (October 29–30, 1918), fought 140 miles (225 km) north of Baghdad. Two weeks later, after the Ottoman Empire concluded an armistice with the Allies, a division of Indian cavalry from Cobbe's force occupied Mosul unopposed.

Historians and military analysts have drawn comparisons between the Anglo-Indian campaign in Mesopotamia and the US-led invasion of Iraq in 2003. In both cases, the invaders underestimated the challenges posed by advancing on Baghdad while relying on an ever longer and more vulnerable supply chain stretching back to the Persian Gulf. Both invading forces faced outbreaks of looting and lawlessness in localities abandoned by the former authorities; the British, responding faster than the Americans ninety years later, restored order by deploying a police force recruited from Muslim Indians. Much like the Americans decades later, the British reached out to the oppressed Shiite majority of the country in overtures backed by generous cash bribes to tribal leaders, yet still had difficulty earning their trust. Both faced their greatest challenges from the Sunni minority. During World War I, most of Mesopotamia's Sunni tribes honored the sultan's call to jihad and joined the Turks in resisting the invaders, while throughout the country, German agents matched or topped British bribes to tribal leaders, in some cases fomenting unrest in cities and towns already taken by Anglo-Indian forces. They achieved their greatest success with the large, predominantly Shiite Muntafiq confed-eration, which remained loyal to the Turks long after the onset of the Arab revolt in June 1916, even as support for the Ottoman cause among other Arab tribes began to erode. The civilian population did not fully acquiesce in the Anglo-Indian occupation until September 1917, when Maude's victory at Ramadi finally prompted the Muntafiq to change sides. Ninety years later the US experienced similar problems with tradi-tional tribalism after overthrowing Saddam Hussein's dictatorship, and once again, the acquiescence of the Muntafiq proved critical to the foreign occupation.[5]

Owing to the central role of Indian troops in Mesopotamia, the ebb and flow of the campaign influenced wartime events in south Asia. In February 1916, during the siege of Kut, Gandhi made a speech at the dedication of Banaras Hindu University challenging Indians to seize control of their own political fate. Referring to the Afrikaners of South Africa, where he had lived and worked from 1893 to 1914, Gandhi concluded that the British had no respect for a people unwilling to assert their own right to freedom, and would grant self-government to India only if the Indian people, like the Afrikaners in the Anglo-Boer War, first stood up to them (see Box 12.1). In a departure from his

Box 12.1 "If we are to receive self-government, we shall have to take it"

Excerpts from a speech by Mohandas K. (Mahatma) Gandhi, February 4, 1916, on the occasion of the ceremonial laying of the cornerstone of Banaras Hindu University. The address was cut short following his provocative remark concerning South Africa, which the British had granted dominion status in 1910, just eight years after the end of the Boer War:

The Congress has passed a resolution about self-government, and I have no doubt that the All-India Congress Committee and the Muslim League will do their duty and come forward with some tangible suggestions. But I, for one, must frankly confess that I am not so much interested in what they will be able to produce as I am interested in anything that the student world is going to produce or the masses are going to produce. No paper contribution will ever give us self-government. No amount of speeches will ever make us fit for self-government.

… I honor the anarchist for his love of the country. I honor him for his bravery in being willing to die for his country; but I ask him – is killing honourable? Is the dagger of an assassin a fit precursor of an honourable death? I deny it. There is no warrant for such methods in any scriptures. If I found it necessary for the salvation of India that the English should retire, that they should be driven out, I would not hesitate to declare that they would have

to go, and I hope I would be prepared to die in defense of that belief. That would, in my opinion, be an honourable death.

… We should have an empire which is to be based upon mutual love and mutual trust. Is it not better that we talk under the shadow of this college than that we should be talking irresponsibly in our homes? I consider that it is much better that we talk about these things openly. I have done so with excellent results before now. I know that there is nothing that the students do not know. I am, therefore, turning the searchlight towards ourselves. I hold the name of my country so dear to me that I exchange these thoughts with you, and submit to you that there is no room for anarchism in India. Let us frankly and openly say whatever we want to say to our rulers, and face the consequences if what we have to say does not please them.

… If we are to receive self-government, we shall have to take it. We shall never be granted self-government. Look at the history of the British Empire and the British nation; freedom-loving as it is, it will not be a party to give freedom to a people who will not take it themselves. Learn your lesson if you wish to from the Boer War. Those who were enemies of that empire only a few years ago have now become friends …

Source: First published in *The Selected Works of Mahatma Gandhi, vol. 6: The Voice of Truth, Part I, Some Famous Speeches*, 3–13, available at www.mkgandhi.org/speeches/bhu.htm.

belief in nonviolence, he encouraged Indians to enlist in the army, reasoning that "if the Empire wins mainly with the help of our army, it is obvious that we would secure the rights we want."[6] While such appeals did not yield great results, it was of some consolation to the British that they remained more popular than the Germans in the eyes of most Indians. A German-sponsored Indian Independence Committee, established in August 1914, included anti-British activists residing in Germany, Switzerland, and the United States, for the most part university students (both Hindu and Muslim) supplemented by dissident Bengali Muslims and Punjabi Sikhs. The Germans quickly learned what the British already knew, and had benefited from for decades: that British rule alone held together a south Asian subcontinent divided not just between Hindus, Muslims, and Sikhs, but by dozens of different regional languages and cultural identities, making it practically impossible to get Indians to form a common front against British rule. But amid the wartime strains vague pan-Indian ideas coalesced into an Indian vision of a self-governing Dominion. In the Lucknow Pact of December 1916, Muhammad Ali Jinnah committed the Muslim League to support the predominantly Hindu Indian National Congress in a common campaign for Home Rule within the British Empire. Jinnah, at the time a member of both organizations, was the main architect of the pact, which included a plan for Hindu-Muslim power sharing in a future Indian government.

From the Sahara to the Horn of Africa

The war in the Sahara, as well as in Abyssinia and Somaliland (the future Ethiopia and Somalia), was much more closely connected to the war in the Middle East than to the war in sub-Saharan Africa. From November 1914 onward, the British and their Entente partners feared that Mehmed V's proclamation of jihad would inflame the region, yet ultimately the greatest threats to their interests arose not from Muslim desires to heed the sultan's religious appeal, but because of local circumstances: in Libya, where the Sanusi had continued to resist an Italian takeover begun in the Italo-Turkish War of 1911–12; in northern Somalia, where the Sahili continued their earlier resistance to British colonial control; in western Sudan, where Anglo-Egyptian forces battled the sultan of Darfur; and in Abyssinia, where the ancient Christian monarchy passed into the hands of an unstable young emperor sympathetic toward Islam. The first three conflicts featured small, traditional desert forces mounted on horses or camels, armed with rifles and sabers, but at times supported by armored cars, aircraft, and machine-gun units. The fourth ultimately involved a clash of the largest armies deployed during World War I outside Europe.

The Sanusi of Cyrenaica (northeastern Libya), an order of Sufi Muslims, resisted the Italian annexation of Libya during and after the Italo-Turkish War, retreating southward into the desert once Italy established control over the country's Mediterranean coast. Thus, the Sanusi became a factor in World War I when Italy joined the Entente in

May 1915. Their leader, Grand Sanusi Sayyid Ahmad, had close ties to Constantinople, in part because Ottoman war minister Enver Pasha and the leading Turkish general, Mustafa Kemal (Atatürk), had both served with the Sanusi during the Italian war. Sayyid Ahmad had always enjoyed good relations with the British and hesitated to attack them in neighboring Egypt, but in early 1916 he finally did so, urged on by Turkish advisors including Enver Pasha's own brother, Nuri Bey. A force of 5,000 Sanusi crossed some 200 miles (320 km) of western Egyptian desert and emerged at the oasis of Siwa, just 360 miles (580 km) west of the Nile, alarming the British and raising fears for the security of Egypt and the Suez Canal. The 1st South African Brigade, recently arrived in Britain from the former German Southwest Africa and destined for the Western front, instead re-embarked for Egypt to deploy against the Sanusi. General Henry Lukin commanded the 5,800-man brigade after its arrival in Alexandria; supplemented by British aircraft and armored cars, the South Africans gradually secured Egypt's western border. By March 1917 the Sanusi had been chased back into Libya, where they continued to skirmish with the Italians for several months until Sayyid Ahmad abdicated as Grand Sanusi in favor of Sayyid Idris, his pro-British kinsman. Sayyid Idris promptly made peace with the British and Italians, both of whom recognized him as "emir of Cyrenaica."

A similar, but more stubborn, threat plagued British Somaliland (northern Somalia), where the Dervishes of the Muslim Sahili order enjoyed local prominence. Theologically they shared much in common with the puritanical Sanusi (although not their Sufi mysticism) and the Wahhabi of Arabia, whose beliefs would provide the foundation for the postwar Saudi Arabian kingdom. Sahili leader Sayyid Muhammad Abdille Hassan, nicknamed "the Mad Mullah" by his adversaries, did not need the sultan's call for jihad to inspire him to take up arms; indeed, he had been at war with the British on and off since 1899, and as recently as March 1914 his Dervishes had shocked the British with a raid on the colonial capital, Berbera. Once the war began, the Somaliland Field Force (SFF), consisting of Indian troops and local Somalis mounted on camels, intensified their campaign against the Sahili. In contrast to the Sanusi, the Sahili were poorly armed and no match for the SFF which, though smaller in number (with just 1,250 troops in 1914–15), had Maxim guns mounted on camels and were supported by artillery. By February 1915, the SFF had pushed Mullah Hassan and his 6,000 supporters into the eastern part of the colony near the tip of the Horn of Africa, where they were contained for the remainder of the war. In 1919, as part of a postwar experiment to give the RAF a prominent role in colonial "policing," the British began to use aerial bombing and strafing to reduce the number of Dervishes. Sahili resistance finally collapsed in 1920, after Mullah Hassan died of smallpox.

Of the four threats the Allies faced on the African fringe of the Middle East, only the one in Darfur was largely of their own making. The Anglo-Egyptian government of Sudan, established at Khartoum in 1898, had been unable to subdue the western Sudanese region of Darfur, a hornet's nest of thirty distinct black African and Arab tribes speaking fourteen different languages, whose only commonalities were their Muslim faith and their fierce independence. As an expedient, they recognized Ali Dinar (leader of the Fur, a black African tribe) as "sultan of Darfur."[7] In a series of events that bore some similarity to the onset of the genocidal bloodletting in the same region early in the twenty-first century, Arab tribes supported by the government in Khartoum became increasingly aggressive in their age-old rivalry with the various black African tribes that constituted a majority of the population of Darfur. After 1914 they received a sympathetic hearing (and modern firearms) from British colonial administrators, who saw the conquest of Darfur as a catalyst for rallying Sudanese Arab support for their own regime. For his part, Ali Dinar responded favorably to overtures from Nuri Bey's Ottoman mission in Libya. He did not heed the Turkish sultan's appeal for jihad, but in May 1915 declared his own jihad against the British and began to mobilize his forces. While the Entente powers feared how dangerous Ali Dinar would become if he managed to get German weaponry via Turkish agents in Libya, his troops remained too few in number and too ill-equipped to be of much threat to their interests. The following spring, just as Sayyid Ahmad's Sanusi were being expelled from Egypt, the sultan of Darfur faced an Anglo-Egyptian invasion by the Darfur Field Force (DFF): 2,000 Egyptian and Sudanese troops under the command of British Lieutenant Colonel P. V. Kelly, supplemented by Arab irregulars. On May 22, 1916, the DFF inflicted a decisive defeat on Ali Dinar's 3,600-man army at the village of Beringia (Birinjia), a few miles east of the sultan's capital, El Fasher. In the brief engagement, Ali Dinar's troops suffered 357 casualties before abandoning the field in disarray; the DFF, meanwhile, lost just twenty-six killed and wounded, and occupied El Fasher two days later. Over the next six months, the DFF gained more local allies as Ali Dinar's supporters gradually deserted him. Finally, on November 6 at Juba (Giubu), the sultan was killed in a predawn raid on his camp. By then, the actions of the British and their Egyptian and Sudanese surrogates had fueled a cycle of retaliatory atrocities between the Arab and black African tribes in and around Darfur, facilitating a deepening of hatreds that endured after order was restored. In January 1917, Darfur's de facto independence came to an end, as the region was formally annexed to Anglo-Egyptian Sudan.

Perhaps the most puzzling challenge the Allies faced in the region came in Abyssinia, the ancient homeland of black African Christianity, where Emperor Iyasu V had succeeded his grandfather, Menelik II, in December 1913. When the war began the following year both sides actively courted Abyssinia, which was Africa's second most populous state (after British Nigeria) and the only one in modern times to defeat a European power attempting to conquer it (Italy, in 1896). The impulsive Iyasu spent an inordinate amount of time in the country's eastern Muslim region, the Ogaden; unlike most previous Abyssinian emperors he enjoyed good relations with his Muslim subjects, leading the Germans and Turks to believe he was leaning toward the Central Powers. In August 1915, the British accused him of sending supplies across the border to support the Sahili insurgency of Mullah Hassan in British Somaliland, and one month later Italian agents reported that Iyasu had converted to Islam. Historians remain divided over whether the conversion actually took place, but for the next year the British lived in fear that Iyasu would proclaim a jihad and use Abyssinia's large army to overrun their own much smaller forces in neighboring Egypt, Sudan, Somaliland, and Kenya. They need not have worried, because during the same year Iyasu's relations with the leaders of his country's powerful Christian nobility, which had yet to agree to formally crown him as emperor, deteriorated markedly, until his excommunication by the Orthodox Christian Church made his coronation out of the question. In September 1916, he was deposed in a coup that installed his aunt Zewditu (Zauditu) as empress, with his cousin, Ras Tafari Makonnen (the future Emperor Haile Selassie), as regent and heir apparent, exercising power behind the throne. Iyasu did not go quietly. His father, Ras Mikael, the late Menelik's son-in-law, commander of the Abyssinian Army on its northern border with Italian Eritrea, marched on the capital of Addis Ababa with 80,000 troops to support his claim to the throne. General Habte Giyorgis, loyal to the regency, deployed 120,000 troops to block his way. At the battle of Segale (October 27, 1916), fought 40 miles (65 km) north of the capital, they met in what was, by far, the largest military engagement on the African continent during World War I. The two sides suffered 10,000 casualties in the five-hour battle, which ended in Ras Mikael's defeat and capture. Iyasu remained at large within Abyssinia until taken prisoner after the war. Although it was never clear that Iyasu would have brought Abyssinia into the war on the side of the Central Powers, his ouster, and the rise to prominence of the future Haile Selassie, was considered a victory for the Entente. Abyssinia remained neutral, and its large army remained on the sidelines.

From the Sahara to the Horn of Africa, the darkest hours for the Allies in general, and for Britain in particular, came in the spring of 1916. Against the backdrop of the Turkish victories at Gallipoli and Kut, hostilities opened against Ali Dinar in Darfur, just as Sayyid Ahmad's Sanusi were being driven out of Egypt, at a time when Mullah Hassan's Sahili had been contained (but not definitively beaten) in Somaliland, and Iyasu V was still the emperor (albeit uncrowned) of Abyssinia. Fortunately for the Allies, these four threats, while coinciding, remained uncoordinated. If Sayyid Ahmad, Ali Dinar, Mullah Hassan, and Emperor Iyasu had anything in common, it was that they received little more than moral support from the Turks and even less from Germans.

Arabia, Palestine, Syria

Although it was not apparent at the time, the turning point of World War I in the Middle East came on June 27, 1916, when Sharif Hussein bin Ali, the 62-year-old emir of Mecca, declared the independence of the Arab people from the Ottoman Empire as well as their religious freedom from the caliph, Sultan Mehmed V (see Box 12.2;

Box 12.2 **The emir of Mecca declares Arab independence**

Figure 12.1 Sharif Ali of Mecca

Excerpts from the declaration of Arab independence from the Ottoman Empire, issued by Sharif Hussein bin Ali (1854–1931), then emir of Mecca, on June 27, 1916:

In the Name of God, the Merciful, the Compassionate, this is our general circular to all our Brother Moslems ... It is well known that of all the Moslem Rulers and Emirs, the Emirs of Mecca, the Favored City, were the first to recognize the Turkish Government. This they did in order to unite Moslem opinion and firmly establish their community, knowing that the great Ottoman Sultans (may the dust of their tombs be blessed and may Paradise be their abode) were acting in accordance with the Book of God and the Sunna of his Prophet (prayers be unto him) and were zealous to enforce the ordinances of both these authorities.

... The Emirs continued to support the Ottoman State until the Society of Union and Progress [the "Young Turks"] appeared in the State and proceeded to take over the administration thereof and all its affairs. The result of this new administration was that the State suffered a loss of territory which quite destroyed its prestige, as the whole world knows, was plunged into the horrors of war and brought to its present perilous position, as is patent to all.

... All this evidently did not fulfil the designs of the Society of Union and Progress ... It has put forth other innovations touching the fundamental laws of Islam (of which the penalties for infringement are well known) after destroying the Sultan's power, robbing him even of the right to choose the chief of his Imperial Cabinet or the private minister of his august person, and breaking the constitution of the Caliphate of which Muslims demand the observance.

... We are determined not to leave our religious and national rights as a plaything in the hands of the Union and Progress Party. God (blessed and exalted be He) has vouchsafed the land an opportunity to rise in revolt, has enabled her by His power and might to seize her independence and crown her efforts with prosperity and victory ... Her principles are to defend the faith of Islam, to elevate the Muslim people, to found their conduct on Holy Law, to build up the code of justice on the same foundation in harmony with the principles of religion, to practice its ceremonies in accordance with modern progress, and make a genuine revolution by sparing no pains in spreading education among all classes according to their station and their needs.

... We raise our hands humbly to the Lord of Lords for the sake of the Prophet of the All-Bountiful King that we may be granted success and guidance in whatsoever is for the good of Islam and the Moslems. We rely upon Almighty God, who is our Sufficiency and the best Defender.

Source: First published in *Source Records of the Great War, vol. 4,* ed. Charles F. Horne, National Alumni, 1923, available at www.firstworldwar.com/source/arabindependence_hussein.htm.

Figure 12.1). In the prewar years Hussein's role as guardian of Islam's holy places and de facto ruler of the Hejaz (al-Higaz) made him a figure of political and religious significance within the Arab world, and opponents of the Ottoman sultan considered him a potential caliph. Hussein's own goals – formal autonomy for the Hejaz and recognition of his Hashemite family as hereditary sharifs of Mecca – were far more modest, yet incompatible with the Young Turk vision of making the Ottoman Empire a unitary Turkish national state. In October 1914, just before the outbreak of hostilities between Britain and the Ottoman Empire, the British offered to recognize Hussein as caliph and establish a protectorate over the "Arab nation."[8] Like other Arab leaders living under Ottoman rule, Hussein was slow to break with the Turks but also unenthusiastic about supporting them, for example, in their failed initial attack on Egypt in February 1915. Meanwhile, Hussein's sons Abdullah and Faisal negotiated with various agents of both sides and with Arab nationalist leaders. Faisal spent much of the first half of the war in Damascus, considered the most likely center of an Arab revolt, but by the winter of 1915–16 Turkish authorities had suppressed the Arab nationalists there, convincing Hussein and his sons that any uprising would have to be based in the Hejaz. Faisal returned home to Mecca ostensibly to help his father raise volunteers from among the Arab tribes of the desert to support a second Turkish attack on Egypt. These troops instead turned against the Turks in skirmishing that began near Medina on June 5, 1916, some three weeks in advance of Hussein's formal declaration of Arab independence.

The Turks initially reassured the Germans that Hussein's actions would have no broader significance beyond the Hejaz, and both agreed to proceed with their planned second invasion of Egypt from Palestine. Kress, still serving as de facto Ottoman commander there, was eager to avenge the defeat he had suffered in the first Turkish drive to the Suez Canal in February 1915 (see Chapter 5). This time his army of 18,000 Turks advanced from Gaza along the Mediterranean coast of the Sinai until they were stopped at Romani, 25 miles (40 km) short of the canal, by General Sir Archibald Murray's newly formed Egyptian Expeditionary Force (EEF). In the battle of Romani (August 3–5, 1916) the 10,000-man EEF sustained 1,000 casualties, while killing, wounding, or capturing just over half of Kress' force. The EEF included elements of two British infantry divisions, but mounted infantry units – Australia and New Zealand Light Horse – were largely responsible for Murray's victory.

Afterward the Turks abandoned their designs on Egypt and, with German encouragement, focused instead on containing the Arab revolt and holding Mesopotamia. The connection between these two objectives blurred in the months that followed; as early as August 1916, German consular officials in the part of Mesopotamia still under Ottoman control noted local Arab sympathies for the sharif's call to rise against the Turks. By the end of 1916, the forces of Hussein and his sons had not made dramatic conquests, but their holdings included the city of Mecca and the nearby Red Sea ports of Jidda and Rabigh, securing their line of supply and communication to the outside world. They threatened Medina and the Hejaz railway to the north, and had isolated the Turkish garrison of Yemen to the south. The French soon joined the British in recognizing Hussein as "king of the Hejaz," sending military advisors to Mecca, and funneling surplus weaponry (mostly older small arms) to the Arabs through Jidda. However, France's quest for influence in the Middle East on a par with that of Britain, in anticipation of a postwar partition of the Ottoman Empire, foundered on a lack of cash, as Paris could not match the £50,000 per month that London provided as a subsidy to Hussein.

Among the Allied military advisors sent to Mecca, none had a greater impact than Lawrence (Figure 12.2), whose arrival from Cairo in October 1916 coincided with the arrival in Medina of a Turkish corps dispatched from Damascus via the Hejaz railway. Of the 50,000 Arab rebels some 45,000 were ill-trained irregulars, described by Lawrence as "rather casual, distrustful fellows, but very active and cheerful."[9] In the face of the subsequent Turkish advance from Medina most of them melted away, leaving Lawrence to fear for the survival of the revolt should the Turks retake the holy city. Winning the trust of Abdullah and Faisal, Lawrence persuaded them that Mecca could best be saved by raiding the Hejaz railway and threatening the Ottoman supply chain, something their remaining irregulars could do very effectively. In January 1917, a small Royal Navy landing party assisted them in capturing of the port of Wejh (al-Wajh), 315 miles (510 km) up the Red Sea coast from Rabigh and better suited as a supply depot for the new campaign. The raids sufficed to force the Turkish corps to abandon its move against Mecca and fall back on Medina, where it remained entrenched until the Armistice, though in a weakened state after dispersing half of its strength along the Hejaz railway to guard its lifeline to Damascus. During the course of the raids the Arab forces shifted their center of gravity northward, in July 1917 taking the port of Aqaba, 280 miles (455 km) north of Wejh, with the help of the Bedouin sheik Auda ibn Tayi, whose tribes controlled the northern Arabian desert east of the Jordan River.

Thanks largely to the work of American journalist Lowell Thomas, who accompanied him in the desert during 1918, Lawrence unwittingly went down in history as "the uncrowned king of Arabia" and "commander-in-chief of many thousands of Bedouins," with a record embellished and distorted perhaps more than that of any other person involved in World War I.[10] A complex man who alternately loved and shunned the limelight, Lawrence tried to set things straight in his own memoir of the campaign, calling it "an Arab war, waged and led by Arabs, for an Arab aim, in Arabia." He reiterated that he "never held any office among the Arabs" and "was never in charge of the British mission with them."[11] After his initial key role in persuading Hussein's sons that Mecca could best be defended by attacking the Hejaz railway, his primary tasks were to make sure they continued to see the coincidence of their interests with

Figure 12.2 Lawrence of Arabia

T. E. Lawrence (1888–1935) first traveled to the Middle East in 1909, to research his Oxford BA thesis on Crusader castles. He returned to the Ottoman Empire to work as an archaeologist from 1911 to 1914. During World War I, Lawrence put his fluent Arabic and knowledge of the Arab lands to good use, initially as an army intelligence officer in Cairo, then, from October 1916, as liaison to the Arab revolt. American journalist Lowell Thomas, who accompanied Lawrence for part of 1918, helped to make him an international celebrity. Lawrence's massive memoir, *The Seven Pillars of Wisdom* (1922), and its abridged version, *Revolt in the Desert* (1927), further enhanced his image. In between these projects Lawrence escaped the public eye by returning to the military, first the Royal Air Force, then the Royal Tank Corps, each time serving under an assumed name. Ultimately, he returned to the academic life, producing a translation of Homer's *Odyssey* prior to his death in 1935 in a motorcycle accident.

those of Britain, to facilitate their efforts in getting more Arab tribes to join them (usually with cash subsidies), and to keep the lot moving up the Hejaz railway in the general direction of Damascus.

Beyond Lawrence and the Hejaz, the British made similar efforts elsewhere in Arabia to unite the Arab tribes behind Hussein's revolt. Captain William Shakespear, distant cousin (several generations removed) of the Elizabethan playwright, won over Abdul Aziz ibn Saud of Riyadh, emir of the Nejd and imam of the puritanical Wahhabi sect of Islam. Shakespear even died in Saudi service at the battle of Jarrab (January 24, 1915), at the hands of the pro-Ottoman Rashidi. At a reception held in Kuwait in November 1916, ibn Saud joined the Arab princes of the Persian Gulf in a declaration of support for the sharif of Mecca and the Arab revolt (see Box 12.3), but he was dissatisfied with his meager British subsidy of £5,000 per month – one-tenth of the amount the sharif of Mecca was receiving – and did little to earn it other than to fight his own archenemies, the Rashidi, whom he would have been fighting anyway.

While the British initiatives elsewhere in Arabia had no direct bearing on the course of the war, the fall of Aqaba, at the mouth of the Jordan River, roughly 150 miles (240 km) due south of Jerusalem and the same distance east of Suez, made Lawrence, Faisal, and Abdullah players in the British quest to invade Palestine with forces based in Egypt. After checking the Turkish advance against the Suez Canal in August 1916 at Romani, Murray had sent his subordinate, General Sir Charles Dobell, across the northern Sinai with an advance guard of the EEF. In January 1917 Dobell took Rafah, just 19 miles (31 km) from Gaza, which the Turks had fortified under the direction of Kress, but in the first (March 26) and second (April 19) battles of Gaza, the EEF failed to capture the Ottoman stronghold, in the process suffering 9,800 casualties against 4,800 for the Turks. In June, shortly before Lawrence and the Arabs took Aqaba, General Sir Edmund Allenby arrived in Egypt to replace Murray. He faced a muddled strategic situation in which the British (and overall Allied) goals remained ill-defined. That autumn the foreign secretary, Arthur Balfour, issued his famous declaration promising Britain's postwar help in "the establishment in Palestine of a national home for the Jewish people,"[12] but as late as September 1917 Sir Mark Sykes, co-author, with France's François Georges Picot, of a 1916 agreement for the postwar Allied partition of the Ottoman Empire, noted that "the war cabinet still had not agreed on how far Allenby should go in Palestine."[13] Only the prime minister seemed sure. Lloyd George, who, like Churchill in World War II, sought to exploit weaknesses around the periphery of enemy-held territory, favored a robust campaign in Palestine. In his last interview with Allenby before the general's departure for Cairo, he made it clear that he wanted "Jerusalem before Christmas."[14]

Shortly after his arrival Allenby left the comfort of Cairo for Rafah, assuming command of the EEF at the front. He built up the EEF into ten divisions of infantry (of

Box 12.3 **Gertrude Bell on the emergence of ibn Saud**

The British archaeologist Gertrude Bell (1868–1926), initially denied a wartime posting to the Middle East, served in France as a nurse before being assigned, in 1915, to the Arab Bureau at Cairo, where she renewed her prewar acquaintance with T. E. Lawrence. Assigned to the Persian Gulf in 1916, she gave the following account of the wartime visits to Kuwait and Basra of Abdul Aziz ibn Saud, future founder of the kingdom of Saudi Arabia:

Ibn Saud's connection with us has received public confirmation in a durbar of Arab sheikhs held at Kuwait on November 20 … In a speech as spontaneous as it was unexpected, Ibn Saud pointed out that, whereas the Ottoman Government had sought to dismember and weaken the Arab nation, British policy aimed at uniting and strengthening their leaders …

Ibn Saud is now barely forty, though he looks some years older. He is a man of splendid physique, standing well over six feet, and carrying himself with the air of one accustomed to command … As a leader of irregular forces he is of proved daring, and he combines with his qualities as a soldier that grasp of statecraft which is yet more highly prized by the tribesmen … Abdul Aziz has drawn the loose mesh of tribal organization into a centralized administration and imposed on wandering confederacies an authority which, though fluctuating, is recognized as a political factor …

If the salient feature of the Kuwait durbar was the recognition by the assembled Arab chiefs of the good will of Great Britain towards their race, it was the presence of an unchanging type of desert sovereignty, among conditions so modern that they had scarcely grown familiar to those who created them, which gave Ibn Saud's visit to Basra its distinctive colour. In the course of a few hours the latest machinery of offence was paraded before him. He watched the firing of high explosives at an improvised trench and the bursting of anti-aircraft shells in the clear heaven above. He travelled by a railway not six months old and sped across the desert in a motor-car to the battlefield of Shaaibah, where he inspected British infantry and Indian cavalry, and witnessed a battery of artillery come into action. In one of the base hospitals … he was shown the bones of his own hand under the Roentgen ray. He walked along the great wharves on the Shatt el-Arab, through the heaped stores from which an army is clothed and fed, and saw an aeroplane climb up the empty sky. He looked at all these things with wonder, but the interest which he displayed in the mechanism of warfare was that of a man who seeks to learn, not of one who stands confused, and unconsciously he justified to the officers who were his hosts the reputation he has gained in Arabia for sound sense and distinguished bearing.

Source: Excerpted from Gertrude Bell, *The Arab War*, (London: The Golden Cockerel Press, 1940), ch. 4: "Ibn Saud."

which three were mounted infantry), a force three-quarters British with the balance being made up of ANZAC and Indian troops. At Lawrence's behest he also increased the British subsidy of the Arab revolt to £200,000 per month. Meanwhile, the Germans sent Falkenhayn to assume overall direction of the defense of Palestine. Kress, now de facto commander of the Turkish Eighth Army, was reinforced to ten divisions and extended his trench lines from Gaza 30 miles (50 km) eastward to Beersheba, almost halfway to the Jordan River. Allenby opened the third battle of Gaza (October 31–November 7, 1917) by having his mounted divisions turn the Turkish left flank at Beersheba. In the climax of the action on October 31, the 4th Australian Light Horse Brigade thundered across 4 miles (6.5 km) of open ground under artillery and machine-gun fire to breach Beersheba's defenses, forcing the evacuation of the town. Two days later, Allenby began the infantry assault on Gaza itself, supported by an artillery barrage and six tanks. On November 7, British forces took the city, and the entire Gaza-Beersheba line crumbled. The battle cost the attackers 18,000 casualties and the defenders 13,000, but Allenby's troops also took 12,000 prisoners.

After Allenby breached the Gaza–Beersheba line, Falkenhayn deployed the Turkish Seventh Army (General Fevsi Pasha) on the inland (left) flank of Kress' Eighth Army in order to block a British drive up the road from Beersheba through Hebron and Bethlehem to Jerusalem. In the battle of El Mughar Ridge (November 13) a daring charge by 800 British mounted infantry, reminiscent of the action of the Australian Light Horse at Beersheba two weeks earlier, enabled Allenby to drive a wedge between Kress' Eighth Army, which retreated up the coast to Jaffa, and Fevsi Pasha's Seventh Army, which fell back on Jerusalem. After detaching a corps to pursue Kress and secure Jaffa, Allenby deployed the rest of the EEF against Fevsi Pasha's army in the battle of Jerusalem (December 8–26). On the first day of the action British forces attacked the city simultaneously from the west, through Deir Yassin, and the south, through Bethlehem, breaching the Turkish defenses in both places. Jerusalem fell on December 9 and Allenby entered the city two days later, thus meeting Lloyd George's deadline with two weeks to spare. Skirmishing continued in the hills around Jerusalem while Falkenhayn reinforced the Seventh Army for a major counterattack on December 25–26, which Allenby's troops withstood. Meanwhile, on the coast, a British victory over Kress' Eighth Army on December 21–22 secured the port of Jaffa as a base for supplying Jerusalem. The Jerusalem campaign as a whole cost the Turks 25,000 casualties against 18,000 for the British and Imperial troops. After the defeat, the Germans reassigned Falkenhayn to the Eastern front, leaving Liman von Sanders in charge of the defense of Palestine.

Lacking clear instructions on what to do after taking Jerusalem, in February 1918 Allenby sent an EEF column to take Jericho, 15 miles (24 km) to the east, then sent his Light Horse divisions across the Jordan on two unsuccessful raids (March 21–April 2 and April 29–May 5) against the Hejaz railway at Amman. By then his army bore little resemblance to the force he had taken over the previous summer, as the onset of the German offensive on the Western front brought the withdrawal to France of most of his British troops and their replacement with raw recruits from India. Once three-quarters British, the EEF emerged from the changes half-Indian. Muslim troops accounted for 29 percent of the new arrivals, and some of them promptly deserted to the Turks. The three Light Horse divisions (one British, one Australian, and one mixed ANZAC) were among those remaining intact and thus were the units Allenby subsequently relied upon the most. After the failure of the raids on Amman, the EEF dug in along a front anchored on the Mediterranean north of Jaffa and the Jordan River north of Jericho, securing the hilltops with redoubts and blocking the valleys and ravines with barbed wire. During the summer Liman von Sanders made only one serious attempt to break the front, on July 14, when he used two battalions of German storm troopers to clear the way for a Turkish division to attack at Abu Tellul in the Jordan valley, only to have the effort repulsed by the vigorous work of the Australian 1st Light Horse Brigade. Allenby's army lost another two divisions of British troops over the summer, but by September finally began to regain the manpower needed for offensive operations thanks to the arrival of another four Indian divisions (including two of cavalry), two battalions from the West Indies, an Armenian Legion raised in France, and a Jewish Legion of Zionist volunteers, including future Israeli prime minister David Ben Gurion, bringing the total strength of his polyglot force to nearly 70,000. Allenby lost his small tank detachment in the spring of 1918 and never got it back, but by September he had seven squadrons of aircraft (six British RAF, one Australian), an armored car detachment, and an artillery park of 540 guns. Opposite him in northern Palestine and across the Jordan around Amman, the three armies under Liman von Sanders had dwindled to just 35,000 men, backed by 400 guns.

For the ultimate Allied offensive Allenby was finally able to coordinate operations with Lawrence and the Arabs. Faisal's army emerged from the desert on September 17 to join the armored car detachment and air squadrons in raiding Deraa (Dar'a), around 50 miles (80 km) north of Amman, where a spur from Haifa joined the Hejaz railway. The action cut the only rail and telegraph lines linking Liman von Sanders' armies with Damascus. Two days later, after Allenby feinted a build-up on his eastern flank along the Jordan, shelling by the Royal Navy against Turkish lines north of Jaffa signaled his true intention, as he attacked from his western flank with nearly two-thirds of his army. Following the breakthrough his main force hooked to the north and east, scattering the Turkish Eighth Army before it, while the rest of his troops attacked all along the front. After the initial breakthrough, the battle hinged on the coordination of rapidly advancing mounted troops and supporting aircraft. An Indian cavalry brigade raced 50 miles (80 km) to Nazareth, chasing Liman von Sanders from his headquarters on September 20, and another Indian brigade rode to Haifa to secure it the following day. Mustafa Kemal, brought in by Liman von Sanders to command the Turkish Seventh Army, evacuated his headquarters at Nablus on the night of September 20–21, to avoid being surrounded, but the following day found him pinned against the Jordan River to the east, where the RAF added to his misery by bombing and strafing his troops.

The action of September 19–21, somewhat arbitrarily called the battle of Megiddo (Armageddon) after the ancient battle site at the center of the action, left the British in complete control of Palestine. Allenby's EEF sustained just 5,300 casualties in completely routing the Turkish Seventh and Eighth armies, which lost 20,000 of their 24,000 men. The outcome made the position of the 11,000-man Turkish Fourth Army in and around Amman untenable, and it withdrew northward to Damascus, destroying Arab villages as it retreated. Faisal's army, accompanied by Lawrence, pursued the retreating Turks and twice fell upon them (September 27–28), killing 5,000 stragglers. Meanwhile, on the 26th, the ANZAC Mounted Division secured Amman and subsequently took the surrender of other Turks retreating up the Hejaz railway from the south, who feared their fate at the hands of the Arabs. By the end of the month 75,000 Turks had surrendered to British and Imperial forces, including much of the garrison of Damascus, after the Australian Mounted Division and a division of Indian cavalry, advancing via the Golan Heights following the battle of Megiddo, circled the city on September 29–30 and blocked its garrison's escape routes to the north.

After Faisal entered Damascus on October 1, Lawrence's efforts to establish him there as "King of the Arabs" ran afoul of Allenby, who soon arrived with a French liaison officer in tow, as the Sykes-Picot agreement called for Syria, along with Lebanon, to become a French protectorate. As recently as June 1918 the Arabs had received further assurance that they would enjoy "complete and sovereign independence" in any lands they liberated themselves,[15] but now they learned the British would honor that promise only in the strictest sense, as, indeed, they had received some sort of help in liberating everything other than trackless desert. Whether or not Lawrence was deliberately misled by his own superiors, he clearly underestimated their intention to enforce prior arrangements the Allied governments had made concerning the Arab lands. Having overplayed his hand, he departed for leave in Britain, disappointed and exhausted, to resurface again as Faisal's primary advocate at the Paris Peace Conference. The ensuing month featured little further action. Indian cavalry secured Beirut on October 8 and, along with Arab troops, Aleppo on October 26. Four days later the Armistice of Mudros ended hostilities between the Ottoman Empire and the Allies.

Throughout 1917 and 1918 the Arabs rarely had more than 10,000 fighters along the Hejaz railway, but tied down Ottoman forces many times the size of their own. Lawrence estimated that by war's end, they had killed or wounded 35,000 Turks, captured another 35,000, and secured Hussein's tutelage over 100,000 square miles (260,000 km²) of territory, all while suffering very light casualties. More significantly, the Arab revolt tied down enough Ottoman troops to enable the more conventional British and Imperial campaigns in Mesopotamia and Palestine to achieve victory. Indeed, if the Arabs had heeded Mehmed V's call to jihad and actively supported the Turkish war effort, any Allied efforts in these areas would have been no more successful than the landings at Gallipoli.

The Armenian Genocide

The vision of the Young Turks, to revitalize the Ottoman Empire as a secular, constitutional Turkish national state, threatened the Armenians at least as much as it did the Arabs. While the Young Turk program included legal equality for all nationalities and freedom of religion, it also established Turkish as the official language of government and education, with the clear goal of assimilating ethnic and religious minorities. The Armenians had lived in eastern Asia Minor and the Caucasus region since ancient times, and in the Middle Ages also colonized Cilicia, on the Mediterranean coast northwest of Syria, where their last independent kingdom fell in 1375. Armenians had lived peacefully for centuries as one of many Orthodox Christian minorities under Turkish rule, but their situation deteriorated during the 1800s as the Ottoman Empire began to disintegrate. While their Christian brethren in the Balkans established their own nation-states, Armenians endured increasing persecution and occasional violence, including massacres in 1895 and 1909. Imperial Russian conquests in the Caucasus region brought part of the Armenian population under tsarist rule, prompting some to view the Russians as their likely deliverers from further persecution. After the outbreak of war, the enthusiasm with which some Caucasus Armenians welcomed the initial Russian invasion in the winter of 1914–15 gave the Ottoman government a pretext for vigilance against all Armenians, culminating in Enver Pasha's February 1915 order disarming Armenian soldiers in the Ottoman army. Up to that point Turkish policy was only slightly harsher than that of its allies in dealing with suspect loyalties of ethnic minorities, for example the Germans not using their Alsatian troops on the Western front or the Austrians not using their Italian troops on the Italian front. But Germany did not react to the people of Mulhouse welcoming French troops in 1914 by attempting to murder all of them after the town was retaken, nor did Austria-Hungary react to the Serbs of Bosnia and Croatia welcoming Serbian troops in 1914 by attempting to murder all of them after those provinces were secured. Only in the Ottoman Empire did suspicion of loyalty of an ethnic minority lead to genocide, as measures ostensibly rooted in state security escalated into mass murder.

On April 24, 1915, the eve of the Allied landings at Gallipoli, interior minister Talaat Pasha sent ciphered telegrams to army commanders and provincial governors declaring that the Armenian minority was in a general state of rebellion. He ordered the arrest of Armenian leaders throughout the empire and the deportation of Armenians from the Caucasus front and other strategically sensitive places. The sweeping condemnation rested on scant evidence; days earlier, the Armenian minority in the eastern city of Van had taken up arms to defend itself against a local crackdown Talaat Pasha himself had ordered, and held out against Ottoman forces until General Nikolai Yudenich brought the Russian Caucasus Army to their rescue the following month. By then, most of the Armenian leaders rounded up on the night of April 24–25 had been murdered, and eager enforcement of the deportation order had degenerated into a genocide. To ensure the requisite ruthlessness, Talaat Pasha isolated or removed the few Ottoman officials who opposed his policies. Armenians died all over the empire, but the desert death camps at Ras-ul-Ain and Der-ez-Zor became especially notorious. Many also died in eastern Asia Minor, after a Turkish counterattack in July forced the Russians to abandon Van, sparking the mass murder of Armenians who did not retreat with them. At the end of August, just four months after authorizing the deportations of Armenians, Talaat Pasha informed the German embassy in Constantinople that the measures had been stopped and "the Armenian question no longer exists."[16] He issued further "stop" orders throughout 1916 and after his appointment, in February 1917, to serve as the sultan's grand vizier (prime minister), indicating that the killing had continued; meanwhile, no one was ever prosecuted for continuing to kill Armenians. Their only salvation came in the continued fluidity of the Caucasus front throughout the genocide. Yudenich went back on the offensive in 1916, securing Erzerum in January and Trebizond (Trabzon) in April. These Russian successes saved some Armenians, but most survivors remained at the mercy of Ottoman forces.

While the Ottoman state was not modern enough or efficient enough to engage in the sort of industrial mass murder that Nazi Germany perpetrated in World War II, the initial phase of the process bore some resemblance to the ghetto policy initiated in 1939 by the Germans for the Jews under their control. Armenians were concentrated in certain neighborhoods of cities, their remaining wealth extorted in exchange for food, while disease and starvation reduced their numbers. The final phase likewise resembled Nazi Germany's forced marches of Jews in 1945, as columns of Armenians were driven on meandering routes with many dying or being killed along the way. In their case, the most common final destination was the desert of northern Syria and northern Iraq, where almost all of the survivors of the marches perished. In another similarity to the Holocaust, ordinary Ottoman Muslims, Kurds as well as Turks, apparently needed little encouragement to participate in the genocide; throughout the country, regular and irregular military formations and the gendarmerie willingly participated in the robbery, rape, and brutal murder of large numbers of Armenians. Indeed, ethnic and religious hatred and local enthusiasm appears to have been the key to translating Talaat Pasha's orders into a campaign of mass murder. Nevertheless, the Ottoman state bore responsibility for the extermination of Armenians, most directly for those drafted into the army, as disarmed Armenian soldiers serving in labor battalions typically were shot as soon as they finished a project or had otherwise outlived their usefulness. The sheer viciousness of the campaign was reflected in the collateral killing of other non-Muslims, especially those known variously as Assyrian, Syrian, or Chaldean Christians, hundreds of thousands of whom were caught up in the Armenian genocide.

In December 1915, the *New York Times* reported that a million Armenians had already perished, and German sources later in the war spoke of just 100,000 survivors

Box 12.4 A German eyewitness condemns the Armenian genocide

Excerpts from a report by Dr. Martin Niepage, a teacher at the German Technical School in Aleppo, urging action by the German government to stop the Armenian genocide:

When I returned to Aleppo in September, 1915, from a three months' holiday at Beirut, I heard with horror that a new phase of Armenian massacres had begun ... which aimed at exterminating, root and branch, the intelligent, industrious, and progressive Armenian nation, and at transferring its property to Turkish hands.

...In order, I was told, to cover the extermination of the Armenian nation with a political cloak, military reasons were being put forward, which were said to make it necessary to drive the Armenians out of their native seats, which had been theirs for 2,500 years, and to deport them to the Arabian deserts ... After I had informed myself about the facts and had made inquiries on all sides, I came to the conclusion that all these accusations against the Armenians were, in fact, based on trifling provocations, which were taken as an excuse for slaughtering 10,000 innocents for one guilty person, for the most savage outrages against women and children, and for a campaign of starvation against the exiles which was intended to exterminate the whole nation ... In the neighborhood of the German Technical School, at which I am employed as a higher grade teacher, there were ... seven or eight hundred exiles dying of starvation. We teachers and our pupils had to pass by them every day.

still living under Turkish rule. Such figures touched off a controversy that continues to this day, with Turkish, Armenian, and other scholars publishing widely differing statistics on the number of Armenians in the Ottoman Empire as of 1914, as well as the number of victims and survivors. By the most conservative estimates, somewhere between 600,000 and 1 million Armenians died in the genocide.[17] Another ongoing controversy concerns the alleged German role in the Armenian genocide, accentuated by historians too eager to link it to the Nazi German extermination of Jews, who typically cite Hitler's remark, "who still talks nowadays about the extermination of the Armenians?" in brushing off the concerns of his generals about the consequences of killing civilians on the Eastern front of World War II.[18] While on the German home front the SPD's Karl Liebknecht and the Center Party's Matthias Erzberger were the only leading political figures ever to speak out about the persecution of Turkey's Armenian minority, less publicly German and Austro-Hungarian diplomats serving in the Ottoman Empire protested the killings from the start. A number of Germans living, working, or stationed in the Ottoman Empire were alarmed by the genocide and made efforts to bring it to the attention of their government, which they assumed – incorrectly – must not have known about it. Some of their accounts expressed fears that Germany would be held accountable for the atrocities (see Box 12.4). The evidence shows that the leading German officials in the Ottoman Empire, at the worst, acquiesced in the genocide, doing nothing to stop it.[19]

Box 12.4 A German eyewitness condemns the Armenian genocide (continued)

..."*Ta'alim el aleman*" ("the teaching of the Germans") is the simple Turk's explanation to everyone who asks him about the originators of these measures ... They cannot believe that their Government has ordered these atrocities, and they hold the Germans responsible for all such outrages, Germany being considered during the war as Turkey's schoolmaster in everything. Even the mullahs in the mosques say that it was not the Sublime Porte but the German officers who ordered the ill-treatment and destruction of the Armenians. The things which have been passing here for months under everybody's eyes will certainly remain as a stain on Germany's shield in the memory of Orientals.

...I know for a fact that the Embassy at Constantinople has been informed by the German Consulates of all that has been happening. As, however, there has not been so far the least change in the system of deportation, I feel myself compelled by conscience to make my present report ... Even apart from our common duty as Christians, we Germans are under a special obligation to stop the complete extermination of the half-million Armenian Christians who still survive. We are Turkey's allies and, after the elimination of the French, English and Russians, we are the only foreigners who have any say in Turkish affairs ... It is utterly erroneous to think that the Turkish Government will refrain of its own accord even from the destruction of the women and children, unless the strongest pressure is exercised by the German Government.

Source: First published in *Source Records of the Great War*, vol. 3, ed. Charles F. Horne, National Alumni, 1923, available at www.firstworldwar.com/diaries/armenianmassacres.htm.

The collapse of Russia during 1917 left the survivors of the Armenian genocide in an even more precarious situation. In the Treaty of Brest-Litovsk (see Chapter 13) the Soviet government formally pulled Russia out of the war and, as part of the capitulation, abandoned non-Russian territory including much of the Caucasus. Two months later, in May 1918, independent republics were proclaimed in Georgia, Azerbaijan, and Armenia, the latter with its capital at Yerevan. That summer a Turkish army under Nuri Bey skirted the Armenian republic's territory in advancing eastward to support Azerbaijan against Russians still in occupation of Baku, where thousands of Armenians had also sought refuge. The British intervened belatedly, with a small force under General Lionel Dunsterville which advanced from Mesopotamia across northwestern Persia to reinforce Baku temporarily before, in September, evacuating the Armenians there. Dunsterville's quixotic campaign was hardly a rescue mission, as Britain's primary interest was in denying Baku's oil to the Central Powers (see Online Essay 8) and seizing the Russian Caspian Flotilla. Armenia would make its case for independence the following year at the Paris Peace Conference. It was little consolation to the Armenians that the last Ottoman sultan, Mehmed VI, issued a postwar proclamation promising an investigation into the genocide and "justice" for its victims (see Box 12.5).

Box 12.5 Turkey's last sultan promises justice for the Armenians

Mehmed VI (1861–1926) became sultan on July 3, 1918, upon the death of his brother. His government concluded an armistice with the Allies on October 30. The following brief proclamation, issued on December 6, acknowledges wartime "mistreatment" of the Armenian people and promises an investigation, which never took place. He abdicated in 1922:

My sorrow is profound at the mistreatment of my Armenian subjects by certain political committees acting under my government.

Such misdeeds and the mutual slaughter of sons of the same fatherland have broken my heart. I ordered an inquiry as soon as I came to the throne so that the fomenters might be severely punished, but various factors prevented my orders from being promptly carried out.

The matter is now being thoroughly investigated. Justice will soon be done and we will never have a repetition of these ugly events.

Source: First published in *Source Records of the Great War*, vol. 3, ed. Charles F. Horne, National Alumni, 1923, available at www.firstworldwar.com/source/mohammedvi_proclamation.htm.

Conclusion

As ineffective as the Germans and Turks were in using the call to jihad or other persuasions to incite Muslim resistance to the British on the western and southern fringe of the Middle East, from Libya to Darfur to Somalia, they were even more ineffective along the northern and eastern fringe, where schemes to penetrate Persia and Afghanistan never amounted to anything. Yet, as in so many aspects of the naval war, from the Sahara to India the Central Powers managed to tie down considerable Allied resources at little cost to themselves. Indeed, even after the sharif of Mecca declared Arab independence from the Turks, the British feared the Arabs would defect to a pro-German Muslim front that would endanger their interests throughout the region. While the Germans sent just 20,000 troops to the Ottoman Empire during World War I, almost 500,000 British and Imperial troops (most of them Indian) were garrisoned across the Middle East by 1918, and the British concluded a series of expedient agreements with their French allies, with various Arab leaders, and even with the leaders of the Zionist movement, in an effort to cover all contingencies. Historians may speculate about the impact that an additional 500,000 troops would have had if deployed on the Western front; far more certain were the devastating consequences, still reverberating a century later, of the contradictory agreements and broken promises.

In terms of manpower, India's role in World War I in the Middle East far exceeded that of the Arabs themselves. Without Indian troops, the British would have had great difficulty finishing the campaign in Palestine to their satisfaction and could never have occupied Mesopotamia. In the latter case, the end of the war brought renewed challenges to a British regime backed, after the Paris Peace Conference, by the authority of a League of Nations mandate. The inability of Britain to impose its will on the country resulted in Iraq becoming independent within fifteen years, the first of the mandates to achieve such status, ironically at a time when India was still not independent or even self-governing. India's long quest for freedom finally ended in success after World War II, but the years 1914–18 were crucial to the struggle. For Indians, as for so many other Asians and Africans, the experience of World War I exposed the myth of European superiority. Afterward, when the implied promise of Dominion status went unfulfilled, the sense of betrayal created the conditions under which Gandhi assumed direction of an increasingly aggressive mass movement against British rule.

SUGGESTIONS FOR FURTHER READING

Bloxham, Donald. *The Great Game of Genocide: Imperialism, Nationalism, and the Destruction of the Ottoman Armenians* (Oxford: Oxford University Press, 2005).

Göçek, Fatma Müge, Norman Naimark, and Ronald Grigor Suny (eds.) *A Question of Genocide: Armenians and Turks at the End of the Ottoman Empire* (Oxford: Oxford University Press, 2010).

Grainger, John D. *The Battle for Palestine, 1917* (Woodbridge: Boydell Press, 2006).

Hughes, Matthew. *Allenby and British Strategy in the Middle East, 1917–1919* (London: Taylor & Francis, 1999).

Kieser, Hans-Lukas. *Talaat Pasha: Father of Modern Turkey, Architect of Genocide* (Princeton, NJ: Princeton University Press, 2018).

Mack, John E. *A Prince of Our Disorder: The Life of T.E. Lawrence* (London: Weidenfeld & Nicolson, 1976).

Martin, Bradford G. *Muslim Brotherhoods in 19th-century Africa* (Cambridge: Cambridge University Press, 1976).

McKale, Donald M. *War by Revolution: Germany and Great Britain in the Middle East in the Era of World War I* (Kent, OH: Kent State University Press, 1998).

Suny, Ronald Grigor. *"They Can Live in the Desert but Nowhere Else": A History of the Armenian Genocide* (Princeton, NJ: Princeton University Press, 2015).

Theobald, Alan Buchan. *Ali Dinar: Last Sultan of Darfur, 1898–1916* (London: Longman, 1965).

Wolpert, Stanley. *Gandhi's Passion: The Life and Legacy of Mahatma Gandhi* (Oxford: Oxford University Press, 2002).

NOTES

1. Ronald William Millar, *The Death of an Army: The Siege of Kut, 1915–1916* (Boston, MA: Houghton Mifflin, 1970), 12.
2. Millar, *The Death of an Army*, 132–33.
3. Lieutenant General Sir Stanley Maude, "Proclamation of Baghdad," March 19, 1917, available at wwi.lib.byu.edu/index.php/The_Proclamation_of_Baghdad.
4. Cyril Falls, *The First World War* (1960; reprint edn Barnsley: Pen & Sword Military, 2014), 310.
5. See Donald M. McKale, *War by Revolution: Germany and Great Britain in the Middle East in the Era of World War I* (Kent, OH: Kent State University Press, 1998), 211–12; Youssef Aboul-Enein, "The First World War Mesopotamian Campaigns: Military Lessons on Iraqi Ground Warfare," *Strategic Insights* 4(6) (June 2005), available at www.hsdl.org/?search=&searchfield=&all=The+First+World+War+Mesopotamian+Campaigns%3A+Military+Lessons+on+Iraqi+Ground+Warfare&collection=public&submitted=Search.
6. Quoted in Stanley Wolpert, *Gandhi's Passion: The Life and Legacy of Mahatma Gandhi* (Oxford: Oxford University Press, 2002), 97.
7. See Alan Buchan Theobald, *Ali Dinar: Last Sultan of Darfur, 1898–1916* (London: Longmans, 1965).
8. McKale, *War by Revolution*, 75.
9. T. E. Lawrence, "Evolution of a Revolt," *Army Quarterly* 1(1) (October 1920), available at archive.org/stream/LawrenceTheEvolutionOfARevolt/Lawrence%20The%20Evolution%20of%20a%20Revolt_djvu.txt.
10. Lowell Thomas, *With Lawrence in Arabia* (New York: Grosset & Dunlap Publishers, 1924), 3, 5, and passim.
11. T. E. Lawrence, *The Complete Seven Pillars of Wisdom: The "Oxford" Text* (Fordingbridge: J. and N. Wilson, 2004), 5.
12. Balfour Declaration, November 2, 1917, available at www.firstworldwar.com/source/balfour.htm.
13. Quoted in Matthew Hughes, "Command, Strategy and the Battle for Palestine, 1917," in Ian F. W. Beckett (ed.), 1917: *Beyond the Western Front* (Leiden: Brill, 2009), 118.
14. David Lloyd George, *War Memoirs, vol. 2* (London: Odhams, 1938), 1090.
15. Quoted in David Stevenson, *The First World War and International Politics* (Oxford: Oxford University Press, 1988), 296.
16. Quoted in Wolfgang Gust (ed.), *The Armenian Genocide: Evidence from the German Foreign Office Archives, 1915–1916* (New York: Berghahn Books, 2014), 71.
17. Ronald Grigor Suny, *"They Can Live in the Desert but Nowhere Else": A History of the Armenian Genocide* (Princeton, NJ: Princeton University Press, 2015), 347.
18. Quoted in Suny, *"They Can Live in the Desert but Nowhere Else"*, 347. See also Stefan Ihrig, *Justifying Genocide: Germany and the Armenians from Bismarck to Hitler* (Cambridge, MA: Harvard University Press, 2016).
19. For the best recent account of the German role see Donald Bloxham, *The Great Game of Genocide: Imperialism, Nationalism, and the Destruction of the Ottoman Armenians* (Oxford: Oxford University Press, 2005), 115–33.

Allied commanders Pétain, Haig, Foch, and Pershing

General Philippe Pétain (1856–1951), Field Marshal Sir Douglas Haig (1861–1928), Marshal Ferdinand Foch (1851–1929), and General John J. Pershing (1860–1948). The Allies finally created a unified command in March 1918, agreeing to elevate Foch to Supreme Allied Commander. He had a strained relationship with Pétain and Haig, who resented the growing control he exercised over their armies, and Pershing aggravated all three with his reluctance to allow American divisions to be assigned to British and French armies. Nevertheless, they got along well enough to guide the Allied armies to victory against their weary German foe.

13 Endgame
Europe, 1918

March 3	Treaty of Brest-Litovsk ends war on Eastern front.
March–July	German offensive on Western front.
April	"Sixtus Affair" reveals Austro-Hungarian quest for separate peace.
July–August	Allied victory in second battle of the Marne.
Summer	Fokker D7 restores German air superiority.
August 8–11	Combined-arms attack gives Allies decisive breakthrough at Amiens.
August–November	"Hundred Days offensive" liberates France, half of Belgium.
September	Allied offensive knocks Bulgaria out of war.
October–November	Franco-Serbian offensive liberates Serbia.
October–November	Italian victory in battle of Vittorio Veneto.
November 3	Austria-Hungary signs armistice.
November 9	William II abdicates.
November 11	Germany signs Armistice.

As the war entered another new year, the military and political landscape of Europe still looked very different than it would just ten and a half months later. Germany prepared to unleash its first major offensive on the Western front since Verdun two years earlier, this time with the goal of winning the war, not just inflicting casualties. For the Germans victory would come none too soon, as they had long doubted that their alliance partners, Austria-Hungary and the Ottoman Empire, could continue fighting much longer. On the Allied side it remained to be seen whether Britain could fight any better than it had at Passchendaele the previous year, or whether France and Italy could still fight at all. Confident in their own *materiel* and tactical preparations, Hindenburg and Ludendorff likewise had reason to believe that the great uncertainties on the strategic level would play out in their favor. The German-Soviet armistice of December 1917 had ended the fighting on the Eastern front, German U-boats were still sinking Allied tonnage faster than it could be replaced, and as of January 1918 just 175,000 troops had reached France from the United States, none of whom had yet seen significant action. The home fronts were another matter. Now that Russia was out of the war and both France and Italy had survived the temporary breakdowns of 1917, the Central Powers would face the greatest challenges in keeping their civilian populations behind the war effort.

The Western Front: From "Michael" to the Marne

Germany's spring offensive of 1918 was its greatest effort on the Western front since August 1914, but differed from the earlier operation in many ways. Instead of a single, sustained push along a broad front, Ludendorff planned a series of blows from Flanders to the Champagne, hoping one of the attacks would achieve a "Tannenberg," encircling and destroying an individual enemy army, thus leaving a gap in the Allied lines that would compromise the entire front. Success would hinge on the concentration of overwhelmingly superior forces at the point of attack, since the Germans began the year marginally inferior to the Allies in artillery (14,000 guns to 18,500) and aircraft (3,700 to 4,500), and dramatically inferior in tanks, with only ten against some 800 Allied tanks of all designs. For supply they had barely one-quarter as many trucks as the Allies, leaving their march to the Marne dependent, as in 1914, primarily on horse-drawn wagons. The German food shortage also reduced the army's daily ration to 2,500 calories per man, significantly less than the Allied norm. For example, in the Italian Army – the least well-fed of the Allied armies of 1918 – the ideal was 4,000 calories per man, the reality just over 3,000. The deficiencies in *materiel* and supplies left the Germans even more dependent on the performance of their infantry, which Ludendorff reorganized to put the most physically fit troops in "attack" divisions and the young and the middle-aged in numerically weaker "trench" divisions, assigned to hold the quieter sectors of the front. By the onset of spring the treaty of Brest-Litovsk (see "Endgame in the East," below) had formally ended the war against Russia and allowed the OHL to redeploy thirty-three divisions to France, raising the German total there to 192, but their headcount of manpower at the front (1.4 million men) revealed that the average division was at half-strength.

Fortunately for the Germans, by 1918 the French and British armies had reduced their own infantry divisions to just 9,000 men (from 12,000), to free manpower for the artillery, air and tank corps, and after the downsizing fielded just 157 divisions (99 French, 58 British) on the Western front. American divisions were three times as large (at 28,000) but only six of them had made it to France. Thus, despite their superiority in *materiel* and supplies, the Allies had little choice but to plan to stand on the defensive in 1918. On December 19, 1917, the chief of the Imperial General Staff, Robertson, informed the Imperial War Cabinet that the British Army had "no offensive plans in mind at present" and "must act on the defence for some time to come."[1] General Fayolle, recently named commander of the French reserve army group, speculated that significant American manpower would only be brought to bear "in eighteen months," certainly not before June 1919.[2] Before the emergency created by the German spring offensive, Pershing, too, assumed US troops would not see much combat until 1919. Haig predicted 1920, and feared that in the meantime, Britain would so weaken itself by bearing the brunt of the fighting that "America would get a great pull over us" in the postwar world. It was enough to make him advocate a compromise peace.[3] Lloyd George and the war cabinet did not share his pessimism and considered 1918 an opportunity to weaken Germany's allies by shoring up the Italian front against Austria-Hungary and the Macedonian front against Bulgaria, while keeping the pressure on the Ottoman Empire in Palestine and Mesopotamia. The French agreed, and committed to continue their efforts on the Italian and Macedonian fronts. Critics of this strategy included Robertson, whose conclusion that it diverted too many troops from the Western front contributed to his decision to resign in February 1918.

The first phase of the German plan (Map 13.1), codenamed "Michael," led to the second battle of the Somme (March 21–April 5), for which Ludendorff massed the Second Army (General Georg von der Marwitz), Seventeenth Army (General Otto von Below), and Eighteenth Army (General Oskar von Hutier), totaling seventy-six divisions (700,000 troops), backed by 6,600 guns and nearly 1,100 aircraft, against a 70-mile (113-km) sector between Arras and the River Oise. The British lines opposite them were held by just twenty-six divisions of infantry and three of cavalry, supported by 2,700 guns, divided between the Third Army (General Sir Julian Byng) and Fifth Army (General Sir Hubert Gough), the latter insufficiently dug in, having taken over most of its 42 miles (68 km) of front from the French during the winter. To preserve the element of surprise, the Germans decided to forgo days of preliminary shelling in favor of a brief, crushing bombardment in the predawn hours of March 21, after which they moved forward in a dense fog and overwhelmed the British front trenches. Following modest first-day gains, the Germans exploited unusually dry weather conditions to advance as far as 30 miles (50 km) by the sixth day. Haig later rewrote his diary entries for those tense days, to allege that Pétain, Lloyd George, and even King George V each had "lost his nerve" or were "in a funk" in the midst of the defeat.[4] It was a vain attempt to mask his own paralyzing loss of nerve. Indeed, on March 25 Haig told Robertson's successor, General Sir Henry Wilson, that victory or defeat – not just in this battle, but for the entire war – depended upon how much help the French could send him.

With the fate of the common Anglo-French war effort hanging in the balance, on March 26 Poincaré, Clemenceau, Pétain, and Foch met with Haig, Wilson, and Lord Alfred Milner, the latter representing Lloyd George and the Imperial War Cabinet, at Doullens, not far behind the collapsing British front. Clemenceau proposed making Foch supreme commander, with authority to "coordinate" Allied operations. Wilson, an old friend of Foch from his prewar visits to Britain, helped make the choice unanimous.

Figure 13.1 British and French troops in rifle pits

After the German spring offensive breached the trench lines of the British Third and Fifth armies, the Western Allies faced an advancing enemy on open ground for the first time since 1914. The prospect of the Germans driving a wedge between the British and French sectors of the front prompted the French to rush troops to fill the breach. This rare photograph shows British and French troops together in shallow rifle pits, late March 1918, awaiting the next German onslaught.

Map 13.1 Western front, 1918: German offensive

Foch's defiance vindicated their judgment: "the moment is … as in 1914 on the Marne; we must dig in and die where we stand if need be."[5] Aside from Pétain, who was deeply shaken by Haig's pessimism, the French kept their wits better than the British and took grim satisfaction in their role in stabilizing the front. While the Germans reinforced their offensive with another fourteen divisions, on the Allied side Foch committed the

French Sixth Army (General Denis Auguste Duchêne) along the Oise, then bolstered Gough's shattered army with ten infantry and five cavalry divisions from Fayolle's reserve army group. By the time the Germans broke off their attacks on April 5, they had advanced another 10–15 miles (16–24 km) at the center of the bulge to take Noyon and Montdidier, just 70 miles (110 km) from Paris. In sixteen days the Germans suffered 239,000 casualties but inflicted 248,000 (178,000 British and Imperial, 70,000 French), while capturing 90,000 prisoners (almost all British and Imperial) and 1,300 guns. The BEF had not lost so many men in such a short time in the entire war. Overall, the debacle discredited Gough more than anyone else. Afterward, Haig sacked him and pulled what was left of the Fifth Army out of the line.

The Germans opened the second phase of the offensive, codenamed "Georgette," just four days after "Michael" ended, initiating the fourth battle of Ypres (April 9–29), also known as the battle of the Lys. Their attack focused on the twenty-nine divisions of the British First Army (General Sir Henry Horne) and Second Army (General Herbert Plumer) in the Flanders sector, using sixty-one divisions of the German Fourth Army (General Sixt von Arnim) and Sixth Army (General Ferdinand von Quast), including eleven divisions that had participated in "Michael." The Germans made their greatest gains against the First Army along the River Lys, smashing Horne's two Portuguese divisions and advancing 12 miles (19 km) in five days, taking Armentières and Merville. The front stalled there, but to the north, where Belgian troops were drawn into the battle, the Germans retook Passchendaele Ridge and advanced to the ruins of Ypres. Despite their gains the Germans again failed to achieve a breakthrough and, in the process, suffered 123,000 casualties, roughly the same as they inflicted. The battle was the bloodiest in the history of Portugal, which sustained 7,400 casualties, mostly from the 2nd Division, commanded by future Portuguese president Manuel Gomes da Costa.

The third phase of the German offensive, codenamed "Blücher-Yorck," led to the third battle of the Aisne (May 27–June 6). Ludendorff concentrated twenty-eight divisions of the German Seventh Army (General Max von Boehn) against the Chemin des Dames sector, where the eleven French and three British divisions of Duchêne's Sixth Army held the hard-won gains of the previous spring's Nivelle offensive. Pétain had ordered Duchêne to maintain a "defense in depth," in emulation of the German strategy of the previous year, but instead Duchêne concentrated his forces along the heights north of the River Aisne. Following the heaviest German artillery barrage of the war, in which more than 3,700 guns fired 2 million shells in just four and a half hours, Boehn's infantry easily broke Duchêne's front. On the first day alone they advanced 12 miles (19 km) along a front 25 miles (40 km) wide, the greatest single-day gain by either side since the onset of trench warfare on the Western front. Exploiting the breach, Ludendorff committed the First Army (General Fritz von Below) and Third Army (General Karl von Einem) to the battle. On May 29 the Germans took Soissons, and the following day their advance cavalry units reached the Marne. By the eighth day they had advanced 30 miles (50 km) and consolidated a foothold on the Marne at Chateau-Thierry, 56 miles (90 km) from Paris. By the time the Allies stabilized the front on June 6, they had suffered 127,000 casualties (98,000 French, 29,000 British), the Germans roughly 130,000. In the wake of the debacle Pétain sacked Duchêne in favor of General Jean Degoutte but saw much of his control over French forces pass to Foch, whose initial vague powers of "coordination" of Allied operations had been redefined to "strategic direction."[6]

The United States accepted Foch as supreme Allied commander one week after the Doullens conference (March 26), and in early May, Pershing agreed to assign AEF divisions to the other Allied armies as an emergency measure. The first of these saw action in the battle of Cantigny (May 28), fought just northwest of Montdidier, where the American 1st Division retook a village in German hands since the end of "Michael" seven weeks earlier, then held it against several counterattacks. Within days Americans also saw action just west of Chateau-Thierry, where the battle of Belleau Wood (June 1–26) grew out of the third battle of the Aisne, but continued for another three weeks after the rest of the sector fell quiet. Two AEF divisions, supported by a British corps and elements of Degoutte's Sixth Army, engaged five German divisions, retaking the forest in a battle that destroyed virtually every tree in it and generated 10,000 casualties on each side. A brigade of US Marines led the attack at Belleau Wood, earning the nickname "devil dogs" ("*Teufelhunden*") from their opponents for their fearless human-wave tactics.

With the action at Belleau Wood still underway, the Germans began the fourth phase of their offensive, codenamed "Gneisenau." On June 9, Hutier's Eighteenth Army attacked southward along the Montdidier–Noyon sector, while Boehn's Seventh Army pushed westward from Soissons, hoping to join forces near Compiègne and encircle the French forces opposite them. Each advanced 6 miles (10 km) on the first day before the French finally demonstrated their own mastery of "defense in depth." Over Pétain's objections, Foch gave General Charles Mangin the French Tenth Army with orders to lead an immediate counterattack, and on June 11–12 his three French and two American divisions turned the tide. Once again the Germans practically traded losses with the Allies, suffering 30,000 casualties to 35,000 for the French and Americans.

Second Battle of the Marne: Turning Point in the West

By the time the Germans launched the fifth and final phase of their offensive, which led to the second battle of the Marne (July 15–August 6), they had 207 divisions to 203 for the Allied armies, but the latter included an ever-growing number of American divisions, each as large as a German corps, and thus had achieved numerical superiority in troops. Influenza had weakened both sides, yet the Germans, on short rations and exhausted from their efforts thus far, no doubt suffered worse. Ludendorff's plan for the final attack called for Boehn's Seventh Army, supported by the Ninth Army (General Bruno von Mudra), to push across the Marne from the bulge created by "Blücher-Yorck," while Einem's Third Army joined the First Army (now under General Johannes von Eben) in attacking southward on the quiet Champagne sector east of the French stronghold of Rheims. The German attacks, involving fifty-two divisions in all, were backed by more than 600 heavy guns. Another successful French "defense in depth" stopped Einem and Eben on the first day, but along the Marne, Boehn pushed Degoutte's French Sixth Army across the river and established a foothold on the south bank 9 miles (14 km) wide and 4 miles (6 km) deep. The Germans were closer to Paris than at any time since September 1914.

By July 18 the Allies had stabilized their lines, and Foch coordinated a counterstroke against the "Blücher-Yorck" bulge by four French armies – the Sixth (Degoutte), Tenth (Mangin), Fifth (General Henri Berthelout), and Ninth (General Antoine de Mitry) – bolstered by eight large AEF divisions, four British divisions, and two Italian divisions. The Sixth and Tenth armies, whose combined nineteen French and four American divisions were backed by 2,100 guns, 350 tanks, and 1,000 aircraft, spearheaded the operation. On the first day the American 3rd and 26th divisions joined a French division in surprising the Germans at Chateau-Thierry, advancing without a preliminary artillery shelling but under an effective creeping barrage. The German lines broke, forcing Boehn to withdraw all his troops north of the Marne (see Box 13.1). By the time the battle ended on August 6, the Allies had retaken nearly all of the "Blücher-Yorck" bulge and advanced to the Soissons-Rheims line, along the River Vesle. Thus, the second battle of the Marne was as decisive as the first had been in September 1914. The Allies suffered 134,000 casualties (95,000 French, 17,000 British, 12,000 American, 10,000 Italian) but inflicted 139,000, in addition to capturing more than 29,000 German soldiers and nearly 800 guns.

Between the onset of "Michael" on March 21 and the high-water mark at the second battle of the Marne on July 18, the action on the Western front generated more casualties than any single front had seen in any four-month period since August–December 1914. The French topped the Allies in casualties with 433,000, followed by British and Imperial forces with 418,000, while Germany's casualties, 641,000 killed or wounded, equaled almost half of its front-line strength of March, and the best troops, those in the "attack" divisions, had suffered the most. The prisoners lost at the second battle of the Marne – the most ever within such a short period of time – caused some in Berlin to fear that the army's morale had started to break. In any event, the tide had clearly turned. Chancellor Hertling recalled later how hope had turned to despair in the first days of the battle: "On the 18th even the most optimistic among us knew that all was lost. The history of the world was played out in three days."[7]

Box 13.1 "The Americans kill everything!"

Excerpt from a memoir by Kurt Hesse, junior officer in the 5th Grenadier Regiment, 36th Infantry Division, describing the high-water mark of the spring offensive of 1918, and the American role in forcing the Germans back across the Marne:

My troop, the Grenadier Regiment No. 5, was to cross at the right flank of the 36th Infantry Division near Jaulgonne at two places ... There was thorough confidence in the leaders; but there was an indefinite feeling that the affair would not succeed ...

The enemy had taken several prisoners from us [and] from here and there we heard of deserters. In defiance of all war experiences little had been done to keep our purpose secret.

... The enemy fire increased each day. When on July 13th we moved to the places of preparation, thick clouds of gas lay on the wood of Jaulgonne ... Scarcely ever have I experienced such a dark night as the one from July 14th to 15th. In the woods one could not see one's own hand in front of one's eyes, and ran against trees. The ground was smooth and slippery, the air filled with gas; now and then there was a roaring, for the enemy sent across some heavy grenades. This lasted hour after hour ... The crossing is comparatively quick ... The railroad tracks are crossed, the railroad station Varennes taken after a short fight, we go on past the road Moulins-Varennes – already 1,000 m south of the Marne! – and

up the southern slopes of the valley. Suddenly from the right there are sounds of sharp firing and screams. In the morning mist, in the high grain field, one can see storm columns advance, dressed in brown – Americans!

... On the afternoon of July 15th it was possible to improve the line somewhat ... but this did not change anything in the final result of the day. It was the severest defeat of the war! ... Never have I seen so many dead, nor such frightful sights in battle. The Americans on the other shore had completely shot to pieces in a close combat two of our companies. They had lain in the grain, in semicircular formation, had let us approach, and then from 30 to 50 feet had shot almost all of us down. This foe had nerves, one must allow him this boast; but he also showed a bestial brutality. "The Americans kill everything!" That was the cry of horror of July 15th, which long took hold of our men.

... Like salvation we welcomed the command: "Front to be withdrawn behind the Marne!" In the night between the 18th and 19th of July we withdrew ... Low spirits took hold of most of the men. So infinitely many dear comrades we had left over there. Many of them we had not been able to lay in the earth. It had all been like a warning: your turn too is coming! Thus thought the man at the front.

Source: Charles F. Horne, ed., *Source Records of the Great War*, vol. 6 (Indianapolis: The American Legion, 1931), 249–50, 252, 255–57.

Why had the offensive failed? Right up to July 18 the spirit of the German Army was generally good, but breaches of discipline had been frequent. Too often, hungry troops stopped to indulge in the food and wine found in the trenches they captured, slowing their progress. At the same time, a deterioration in military decorum prompted frequent reminders to junior officers and soldiers of their obligation to salute their superiors and to maintain proper bearing. Like the Allies in their offensives of 1915–17, the Germans in 1918 typically owed their initial breakthroughs to innovative tactics and good use of technology, but reverted to brute force as soon as their attacks stalled, escalating their own casualties. They failed to achieve a "Tannenberg" any-where along the Western front, and after nearly trapping the British Fifth Army in the first days of "Michael," they never came close again. German generals criticized the fragmented, probing nature of the offensive, and as early as "Georgette," the high cost of modest gains caused officers and soldiers alike to lose their faith in ultimate victory. If Ludendorff had a grand strategic design, it was to drive a wedge between the British and French sectors of the front. After he failed to do so, the advances made in subse-quent attacks, up to and including "Blücher-Yorck," muddled his thinking by putting Paris tantalizingly close to the German grasp.

The Balkan Front: The Collapse of Bulgaria and Liberation of Serbia

In December 1917, General Adolphe Guillaumat succeeded Sarrail as Allied com-mander on the Macedonian front. He inherited what Ludendorff had derisively dis-missed as "the greatest Allied internment camp," a large multinational army pinned down by a smaller enemy force, suffering from morale problems born of boredom along with disproportionately high losses from disease. Guillaumat raised morale and readiness by improving sanitation and supply, while his integrated staff standardized tactics in key areas such as the use of artillery and poison gas. By the time General Franchet d'Esperey arrived in June 1918 to replace Guillaumat, his army had lost two of its six British divisions, withdrawn for service in the Middle East, and had finally disarmed its Russian division, whose soldiers were put to work as laborers. These losses were more than made good by the addition of nine divisions of Greek troops, of whom the three National Army divisions of General Zymbrakakis were the most reliable. In the Greek Army's first significant engagement of the war, the battle of Skra-di-Legen (May 29–31, 1918), Zymbrakakis led these three divisions, supported by a French bri-gade, in the storming and capture of a fortified Bulgarian position near Mount Paikon, north of Salonika, suffering 2,800 casualties and taking 1,800 Bulgarian prisoners (Map 13.2).

By the end of the summer of 1918, there were 300,000 Allied troops on the Macedonian front, spearheaded by thirty-one infantry divisions (eleven French, nine Greek, seven Serbian, and four British). In mid-September they launched a general offensive against the Bulgarians. Franchet d'Esperey attacked along the central and western sectors of the front with the French and Serbs, while General George Milne and the British attacked along the eastern sector; the Greek Army contributed two divisions to each, and held the rest of its troops in reserve. On September 15, follow-ing a day-long preparatory barrage, Franchet d'Esperey ordered his troops forward. In the battle of Dobro Pole (September 15–21) at the center of the front, one Serb

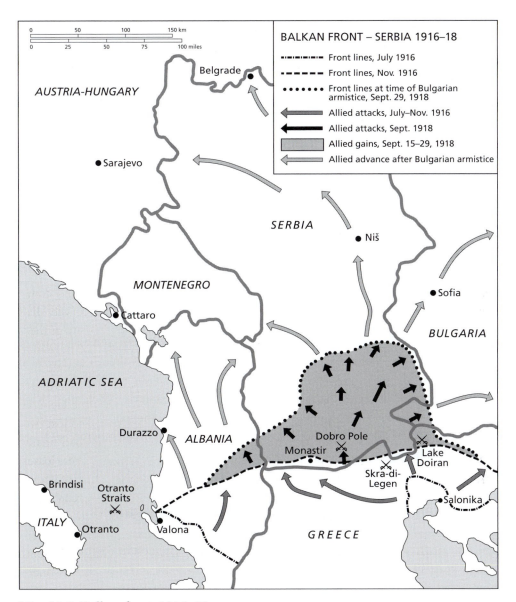

Map 13.2 Balkan front, 1916–18

and two French divisions achieved a breakthrough, compromising the flanks of the Bulgarians holding the line to the west and east. Meanwhile, on the eastern end of the front, Milne's troops attacked entrenched Bulgarian forces at Lake Doiran (September 18–19) and were repulsed with heavy losses (3,900 British and 3,900 Greek casualties, against 2,700 Bulgarian). It was the single costliest battle of the war for the Greeks, though more embarrassing for the British. But the defeat at Dobro Pole forced the

Bulgarians to abandon their position at Lake Doiran, and within days their entire army was in headlong retreat, with some units succumbing to mutiny. On September 29, representatives of King Ferdinand I signed an armistice, pulling Bulgaria out of the war. Four days later Ferdinand abdicated in favor of his son, who assumed the throne as King Boris III.

Following the collapse of Bulgarian resistance, Lloyd George ordered Milne to march eastward, against Constantinople, rather than northward into Serbia or Bulgaria. He began his advance on October 1, reinforced by a French division. The Greeks chose to follow in Milne's wake and seize Western Thrace, since 1913 Bulgaria's outlet to the Aegean. Meanwhile, on the opposite end of the front, the Italians advanced to occupy northern Albania as it was evacuated by Austro-Hungarian forces. Thus, it fell to French and Serbian troops to liberate occupied Serbia, an easy enough task, because the Dual Monarchy's garrison there had dwindled to just 21,000 troops, barely half as many as were assigned to hold neighboring Montenegro. To prepare for their return home, Pašić and the government in exile had negotiated the Corfu Declaration (July 20, 1917) with exiled Croatian and Slovenian leaders, laying the groundwork for postwar Serbia to expand into the kingdom of Yugoslavia. Meanwhile, the army at Salonika purged surviving Black Hand members, a process highlighted by the trial and execution of the infamous "Apis," Colonel Dragutin Dimitrijević, in June 1917. French and Serbian troops entered Belgrade on November 5, 1918; within days Pašić reached the capital, where he soon had the aging Serbian monarch, Peter Karageorgević, proclaimed "King of the Serbs, Croats, and Slovenes." At the peace conference the following year, Pašić performed masterfully in ensuring that the victorious powers remembered Serbia as the first victim, rather than the perpetrator, of World War I.

The Italian Front: The Collapse of Austria-Hungary

The last Austro-Hungarian offensive of the war had the strangest of origins: the revelation, in April 1918, that Emperor Charles had conducted a secret peace initiative a year earlier using his brother-in-law, Prince Sixtus of Bourbon-Parma, a Belgian Army officer, as his special agent to negotiate with the French. When Clemenceau broke the "Sixtus Affair" by publishing a letter Charles had addressed to the French government in March 1917, the alliance of the Central Powers experienced its greatest strain thus far. Charles promptly issued a denial and William II accepted his word; in public, they could do little else. The following month, when the two emperors met at German headquarters in Spa, Belgium, the Germans tested Charles' loyalty by demanding another Austro-Hungarian offensive against the Italians, this time without German assistance. On May 12, Charles agreed, reluctantly, to undertake the offensive, even though it meant calling up young men born in 1900 to ensure sufficient numbers at the front.

From his post as army group commander in the Tyrol, Conrad called for a repetition of his failed offensive of 1916, a thrust out of the Alpine salient hooking toward the Adriatic, arguing that this time it would succeed because of the timing (summer, rather than spring) and his own personal command of the Austro-Hungarian Tenth and Eleventh armies, which would spearhead the operation. Boroević disagreed, advising the emperor to use his army group, consisting of the Austro-Hungarian Fifth and Sixth armies, to attack across the Piave River against the main body of the Italian Army. Charles and his staff made the fateful decision to allow both of them to attack simultaneously, dividing the available resources (fifty-seven divisions and 6,800 guns) to give Conrad most of the artillery and Boroević most of the infantry. Opposing them stood sixty-nine Allied divisions (fifty-eight Italian, six French, and five British) coordinated by Diaz, Cadorna's successor as chief of the Italian general staff. The battle of the Piave River (June 15–23), so designated because the Alpine component involved significantly fewer troops on both sides, opened with an Austro-Hungarian thrust across the Piave that established a foothold on the south bank 15 miles (24 km) wide and 5 miles (8 km) deep; meanwhile, in the Tyrol, Conrad's army group also gained ground, taking 10,000 Italian prisoners. In contrast to its performance at Caporetto eight months earlier, this time the Italian Army recovered quickly, and Diaz orchestrated robust counterattacks in both sectors. Conrad's troops were soon forced back to their starting lines; Boroević held his ground longer, and with much heavier losses, before retreating back across the Piave. Thus, Austria-Hungary's last great gamble of the war ended in defeat, at a cost of 150,000 casualties and 25,000 prisoners lost against 80,000 casualties for the Allies. The failure of the attacks discouraged the army enough to render it incapable of further offensive action. Afterward, on the eve of the second battle of the Marne, both sides lost troops to the Western front, as Diaz sent eight divisions (four French, two British, and two Italian) to France, while Austria-Hungary sent four. Charles made Conrad the scapegoat for the failure of the offensive, sacking him on July 15 under the guise of granting his request to retire, which he had made seventeen months earlier upon being dismissed from the AOK.

Diaz waited until the collapse of Austria-Hungary was imminent before heeding Orlando's call for a final victory that would put Italy in a better position for the postwar peace conference. Symbolically, he chose the anniversary of the battle of Caporetto to open the battle of Vittorio Veneto (October 24–November 2), unleashing an Allied force equivalent to fifty-seven divisions (fifty-one Italian, three British, and two French, with smaller US and Czechoslovak formations), backed by 7,700 guns, against fifty-two Austro-Hungarian divisions, backed by 6,000 guns. The Allies blanketed the enemy front with propaganda leaflets – the culmination of a year-long campaign in which the Italians (with the aid of Lord Northcliffe and the British) avenged the Austro-Hungarian demoralization of the Italian Army before Caporetto

– and as soon as the offensive opened, it became clear that the Dual Monarchy's forces were disintegrating. On October 30 the Italian Eighth Army (General Enrico Caviglia) took Vittorio Veneto, breaking the front between Boroević's Fifth and Sixth armies and the two Austro-Hungarian armies in the Tyrol. Roads and railway lines to the north were soon clogged with retreating units, bands of deserters heading for home, and some civilian refugees. Austria-Hungary handed over its navy to the Yugoslav National Council at Pola (October 31) and Cattaro (November 1) before agreeing to a truce with Italy on November 2. The following day an armistice was signed at Padua that came into effect on the 4th, just as Italian troops finally entered Trieste. The Allies suffered 38,000 casualties in the final offensive (of which all but 500 were Italian) against 135,000 for the Austro-Hungarian Army, which also lost 360,000 prisoners by the time the armistice formally ended hostilities. The lopsided casualty ratio resulted when the Italians continued to attack an enemy that had stopped fighting. The prisoners, most of whom were held well into 1919, included all former Austro-Hungarian soldiers not fortunate enough to have deserted the front before November 4.

By the time the fighting on the Italian front officially ended, the internal collapse of the Dual Monarchy was well underway. On October 16 Emperor Charles declared that "Austria is to become a federal state in which each race [sic] will create its own constitutional status in the territory in which it dwells."[8] The promise of federalization sent the leaders of the various nationalities scrambling to create their own governments, while soldiers garrisoning the home front followed the Russian example in joining with urban workers to establish revolutionary councils. On October 21, the German Austrian representatives in the Austrian Reichsrat declared themselves to be the provisional national assembly of a "German-Austrian state." On the 25th, Count Mihály Károlyi, leader of the Hungarian opposition Independence Party, established a Hungarian National Council; on the 28th, the Czechoslovak National Council in Prague proclaimed the establishment of Czechoslovakia, after which the Allies recognized Tomás Masaryk as its provisional president; and on the 30th, the "German-Austrian state" formed a government with Social Democrat Karl Renner as chancellor. On October 31, in a last-ditch attempt to save Hungary for the Habsburgs, Charles recognized Károlyi as Hungarian prime minister, but the same day, soldiers supporting Károlyi assassinated the retired prime minister, Count Tisza, symbol of Hungarian loyalty to the Habsburgs. On November 1, Károlyi's government called home all Hungarian troops still serving on the Italian front, accelerating the collapse there. The nascent German Austrian government waited until November 12, the day after Charles left Vienna, to proclaim the "Republic of German Austria" and, at the same time, the *Anschluss* or union of Austria with Germany.[9] Over the months that followed they would learn that Wilson's principle of national self-determination did not apply to the German population of Austria.

Endgame in the East: From the Baltic to the Black Sea

The German-Soviet armistice of December 15, 1917, left Lenin's inner circle divided over what to do next. The Soviet premier favored an immediate peace on whatever terms the Germans offered, to enable the new regime to set about the tasks of rebuilding and communizing Russia, but Nikolai Bukharin spoke for the revolutionary idealist majority in advocating the immediate pursuit of world revolution. Leon Trotsky advocated the middle ground of "no war, no peace," under which Soviet Russia would drag out the peace negotiations at Brest-Litovsk for as long as possible in the hope that the Central Powers would succumb to revolution. Heartened by news of massive strikes in Germany and Austria-Hungary, in January 1918 the Soviet leadership approved Trotsky's formula. Russia also released the 2 million prisoners of war it held, most of whom were Austro-Hungarian, in the hope that they would take the revolution home with them; some of them did, and eventually became significant political figures (most notably the future Austrian socialist leader Otto Bauer, Hungarian communist leader Béla Kun, and Yugoslav communist leader Josip Broz Tito). Trotsky, as commissar for foreign affairs, took charge at Brest-Litovsk, where he soon found that the OHL's General Hoffmann had no patience for his revolutionary tactics. On February 9, the Central Powers increased the pressure for a definitive settlement by concluding a separate peace with Ukraine. The following day, Trotsky formally declared "no war, no peace," announcing that Soviet Russia considered hostilities to have ended but would not sign a peace treaty. On February 18, the Central Powers called the Bolshevik bluff and resumed the war, sending their troops eastward, unopposed, all along the front. German troops occupied Minsk later that day, prompting local nationalists to proclaim an independent Belarus. After a bitter debate in which Bukharin and the idealists again advocated an immediate world revolution, Trotsky agreed with Lenin that Soviet Russia had no alternative but to accept Germany's terms (Map 13.3).

Now it was Germany's turn to stall. When informed of the Soviet capitulation, Ludendorff persuaded Hindenburg to allow the troops to continue marching eastward, to occupy more territory for Ukraine, Belarus, and the other eastern vassal states the Germans planned to create. Thus, at this crucial moment, Ludendorff's long-range vision from his days at *OberOst* – of an eastern Europe of German satellites, formed at Russia's expense, that would serve the future economic needs of the Reich – took precedence over the immediate need to end the war in the east and redeploy German troops to the Western front, the very reason the OHL had wanted to send Lenin back to Russia in the first place. After two weeks the Central Powers broke off the march, and in the Treaty of Brest-Litovsk (March 3) the Soviet government recognized the independence of Finland, Estonia, Latvia, Lithuania, and Belarus, as well as Ukraine. At the insistence of the Ottoman grand vizier, Talaat Pasha, the Russians relinquished their claims to all of the Caucasus territory they had seized from the Turks since 1878.

Map 13.3 Eastern front, 1917–18

Soviet Russia also agreed to pay reparations to Germany, eventually fixed at 6 billion marks, and signed the treaty without securing the release of the enormous number of Russian prisoners, more than 95 percent of whom had survived the war (1.4 million in Germany, 1.2 million in Austria-Hungary). The territory lost by Russia included 34 percent of its population, 32 percent of its arable land, 54 percent of its industry, and 89 percent of its coal mines. Lenin justified the treaty on the grounds that "we have no army" and "must make use of every possible breathing-space to retard imperialistic attacks on the Soviet Socialist Republic."[10] His only consolation came in his faith that Germany would be defeated sooner or later, making the concessions temporary. He could not have imagined that it would happen just eight months later.

The OHL withdrew troops from the east as soon as the treaty was signed, to reinforce the German offensive on the Western front that began later that month. But initially, forty-three of the seventy-six divisions in the east as of March 3 remained there, to guard the territories Russia had surrendered. Because Russian opponents of Lenin considered the Treaty of Brest-Litovsk proof that he had been a German agent all along, the settlement triggered a civil war that had been brewing ever since the Bolshevik Revolution. On March 11, Lenin abandoned Petrograd for the security of the Kremlin in Moscow, while Trotsky, in his new role as commissar for war, set about the task of building the "Worker-Peasant Red Army." With the notable exception of Brusilov, virtually all prominent generals of the tsarist army joined the so-called White armies, as did Kolchak, the most respected admiral in the navy. Fortunately for Lenin, rejection of the Bolsheviks was the only thing the Whites had in common, as their ranks included every other Russian political party and persuasion, from revolutionary SRs and Mensheviks to advocates of absolute monarchy. Because the imperial family, in internal exile since March 1917, was the only catalyst that might unite a significant number of Whites, Lenin ordered the murder of Nicholas II, along with his wife and children, after they fell into the hands of the Bolsheviks in July 1918 at Ekaterinburg.

The first months of the Russian Civil War (1918–21) were intertwined with the endgame of World War I in the east. Shortly after the Bolsheviks quit the war, Allied troops landed at Murmansk and Archangel on the White Sea, as well as at Vladivostok, ostensibly to secure stores of military supplies their countries had sent to Russia while it was still fighting the Central Powers. In all three cases, Allied forces fell into informal alliances with local Whites. Meanwhile, because most of the White armies based their operations in Russia's recently ceded territories – from Finland in the north to the Caucasus in the south – these areas, too, became embroiled in the civil war. The Germans sent troops to Finland in April and to Georgia in June, in both cases welcomed by the local regimes as protectors against the Red Army. German designs on the oil resources of the Caspian Sea caused them to hedge their bets between the Bolsheviks and the Turks until the latter took Baku in September, alas, too late to make any difference in the war. The Central Powers were more concerned with exploiting their command of the Black Sea to use it, along with the Ukrainian rivers and the Danube, to ship the much-anticipated Ukrainian grain harvest to their hungry home fronts. The Austro-Hungarian Navy even detached monitors and patrol boats from its Danube Flotilla for convoy duty on the Dnieper, Dniester, and Bug rivers, but when harvest time came, the Central Powers squabbled over the spoils until their exploitation became a moot point, in September, when the collapse of Bulgaria forced the Austro-Hungarian

Flotilla to withdraw back up the Danube, effectively closing the route. Meanwhile, the Allies feared the Germans would form their own Black Sea fleet from the battle cruiser *Yavuz Sultan Selim* (ex-*Goeben*) and captured units of the Russian Black Sea Fleet, and thus maintained considerable naval forces of their own in the eastern Mediterranean. It was aboard one of these ships, the British pre-dreadnought *Agamemnon*, anchored off Mudros, that the Turks signed their armistice with the Allies on October 30.

Endgame in the West: From Amiens to the Armistice

Would it have made a difference if more German divisions had been sent west early enough to join in the spring offensive? Hindenburg and Ludendorff did not have the luxury of analyzing their failure before the next crisis broke (Map 13.4). On August 8, just two days after the fighting ended at the second battle of the Marne, the Allies achieved a stunning success east of Amiens, breaking the front and inflicting the German Army's worst single-day losses of the war thus far. The battle of Amiens (August 8–11) targeted the bulge in the front created by the "Michael" offensive of March and April, with the reconstituted British Fourth Army (General Sir Henry Rawlinson) spearheading the attack against Marwitz's German Second Army. The Fourth Army included fifteen divisions of infantry (five Australian, five British, four Canadian, and one American) plus three British cavalry divisions, supported by nearly 1,400 guns, 1,100 French and 800 British aircraft, along with 414 tanks, in terrain well suited for their use. Like the Americans and French at Chateau-Thierry, Rawlinson's troops attacked without the prior warning of a preliminary bombardment, jumping off in a thick predawn fog. With the Australians and Canadians setting the pace, they made good progress under a well-timed creeping barrage. For the combined-arms assault, Foch gave Haig operational command over the twelve divisions of the French First Army (General Marie-Eugène Debeny), which joined the battle on Rawlinson's right on August 9. By the 11th, the two Allied armies had overwhelmed six of Marwitz's fourteen divisions and created a gap in the front 15 miles (24 km) wide. The tanks were key to forcing the Germans to retreat 12 miles (19 km), but just thirty-eight were still operational on the 11th and six on the 12th, giving the Germans a chance to recover. The OHL followed the usual protocol of committing more troops and attempting an immediate counter-attack, in this case with Hutier's Eighteenth Army (fifteen divisions), but this time the standard response failed utterly, as the troops seemed to lack the strength and will to retake any ground at all. By the end of the battle, the Allies had suffered 42,000 casualties (22,000 British and Imperial, 20,000 French), the Germans 41,000, plus 33,000 prisoners lost. Most of the German retreat came on August 8, which Ludendorff called "the black day of the German army," but not because of the lost ground: 16,000 troops had surrendered in one day, confirming the OHL's fears from the second battle of the Marne that the spirit of the army was breaking (see Box 13.2).

Map 13.4 Western front, 1918: final Allied offensive

The battle of Amiens marked the onset of the "Hundred Days offensive" of the Allies, including a first phase of roughly seven weeks pushing the Germans back to the Hindenburg Line, followed by a second phase of six weeks during which the line was breached, forcing Germany to sue for peace. The first phase included the reduction of the "Michael" bulge through the persistent effort of three British armies (Rawlinson's Fourth, Byng's Third, and Horne's First), plus Debeny's French First Army. The battles of Bapaume (August 21–29), Mont St. Quentin (August 31–September 4), Havrincourt (September 12), and Epehy (September 18–19) featured heavy fighting often spear-headed by the Canadian Corps (General Sir Arthur Currie) or Australian Corps (General Sir John Monash). At Havrincourt, the New Zealand Division and two British divisions drove out a larger enemy force, revealing that the Germans could no longer be counted upon to hold even where they enjoyed local superiority. The Australians carried the day at Epehy and took another 12,000 prisoners, but the bloody fighting resulted in the mutiny of one of Monash's battalions, a sign that, even with victory in sight, there were limits to how far Allied commanders could push their troops. During 1918 the Australians took more than their share of enemy-held territory, capturing a

Box 13.2 Hindenburg describes the British breakthrough of August 8, 1918

The field marshal attributes the breakthrough to the effective use of tanks and aircraft, and notes that afterward, panic and enemy propaganda left his army in no shape to hold the front:

On the morning of August 8th our comparative peace was abruptly interrupted. In the southwest the noise of battle could clearly be heard. The first reports ... were serious. The enemy, employing large squadrons of tanks, had broken into our lines on both sides of the Amiens-St. Quentin road. Further details could not be given. The veil of uncertainty was lifted during the next few hours ... The great tank attack of the enemy had penetrated to a surprising depth. The tanks, which were faster than hitherto, had surprised Divisional Staffs in their headquarters and torn up the telephone lines which communicated with the battle front.

... The wildest rumors began to spread in our lines. It was said that masses of English cavalry were already far in the rear of the foremost German infantry lines. Some of the men lost their nerve, left positions from which they had only just beaten off strong enemy attacks and tried to get in touch with the rear again ... Other influences made themselves felt. Ill humor and disappointment that the war seemed to have no end, in spite of all our victories, had ruined the character of many of our brave men... In the shower of pamphlets which was scattered by enemy airmen our adversaries said and wrote that they did not think so badly of us; that we must only be reasonable and perhaps here and there renounce something we had conquered.

Then everything would soon be right and we could live together in peace, in perpetual international peace ... There was, therefore, no point in continuing the struggle. Such was the purport of what our men read and said. The soldier thought it could not be all enemy lies, allowed it to poison his mind and proceeded to poison the minds of others.

On August 8th our order to counter-attack could no longer be carried out. We had not the men, and more particularly the guns, to prepare such an attack, for most of the batteries had been lost on the part of the front which was broken through. Fresh infantry and new artillery units must first be brought up, by rail and motor transport. The enemy realized the outstanding importance which our railways had in this situation. His heaviest guns fired far into our back areas. Various railway junctions, such as Peronne, received a perfect hail of bombs from enemy aircraft, which swarmed over the town and station in numbers never seen before.

... I had no illusions about the political effects of our defeat on August 8th. Our battles from July 15th to August 4th could be regarded, both abroad and at home, as the consequence of an unsuccessful but bold stroke, such as may happen in any war. On the other hand, the failure of August 8th was revealed to all eyes as the consequences of an open weakness. To fail in an attack was a very different matter from being vanquished on the defense.

Source: Charles F. Horne, ed., *Source Records of the Great War*, vol. 6 (Indianapolis: The American Legion, 1931), 282–86.

disproportionate number of German troops and guns, but their units had a desertion rate four times the BEF norm (most likely because Australia did not allow its deserters to be shot) and a disturbing number of cases of soldiers killing their own officers. Exhausted by the hard-driving Monash, the Australian Corps finally had to be pulled from the line on October 5, and saw no further action in the war. The rest of the troops in Haig's group fought on, maintaining their edge over the Germans owing to "superior supplies and a lower level of exhaustion."[11]

During these same weeks, on the front east of Verdun, Pershing finally had enough troops to form the American First Army, officially on August 30. In the battle of St. Mihiel (September 12–16) he deployed fourteen AEF divisions backed by a French colonial corps, 2,900 guns, 1,500 aircraft, and more than 400 tanks to attack a salient occupied by the German Fifth Army (under the command of Marwitz, fresh from the debacle at Amiens), not knowing that the Germans had already started to evacuate the area the previous day. Upon his arrival Marwitz had found the Fifth Army completely demoralized; the troops of two Austro-Hungarian divisions sent from Italy to reinforce it were even derided as "war prolongers" ("*Kriegsverlängerer*") and "strikebreakers" by their German comrades.[12] The commander of one of these divisions, General Josef Metzger, remarked with smug satisfaction that the Germans were no longer "so loud-mouthed" ("*großschnäuzig*"). He noted the irony of their "tank fright" ("*Tankfurcht*"), which caused their lines to waver at the mere sight of attacking tanks,[13] a weapon their own army had not seen fit to mass-produce (Figure 13.2). Nevertheless, the Americans paid dearly for their victory at St. Mihiel. When heavy rain and mud rendered the tanks ineffective, Pershing resorted to the same sort of frontal assaults that had earned the AEF high praise, and heavy losses, at Cantigny, Belleau Wood, and Chateau-Thierry. The Allies suffered 13,700 casualties while inflicting 7,500, but captured 16,000 prisoners and 400 guns.

During the Hundred Days offensive, Foch's lifelong faith in the cult of the offensive served the Allies well. With ever-growing numbers at his disposal and an ever-weaker enemy before him, his own casualties mattered little to him. He recognized that the Allied armies could be stopped only if they attacked piecemeal, allowing the Germans to check them by shifting their divisions from one sector to another. To prevent this from happening, for the second phase of the offensive he devised a three-pronged attack against the Hindenburg Line. North of the Somme, the same armies Haig had just used to reduce the "Michael" bulge – the British First, Third, Fourth, and French First – would drive eastward along a line from Cambrai across the Sambre and into southern Belgium. To their north, the Belgian Army (twelve divisions), Plumer's British Second Army (ten divisions), and Degoutte's French Sixth Army (six divisions), redeployed from the Marne, formed a group nominally commanded by King Albert but de facto by Degoutte, which would push from Ypres across northern Belgium toward Antwerp. Finally, on the eastern sector of the front, Pershing's American First Army

Figure 13.2 German eighteen-man tank

The German army was slow to embrace the tank. The most popular model, pictured here, was
the 30-ton Daimler-Benz A7 V, armed with one 2.25-inch (57-mm) gun and six machine guns,
requiring a crew of eighteen. It was slow and unstable, and its minimal ground clearance limited its
off-road maneuverability. Just twenty were produced and only ten deployed, all in 1918 in France, in
support of the German spring offensive.

would redeploy west of Verdun to attack the Hindenburg Line in the Argonne Forest,
then advance up the left bank of the Meuse toward Sedan, joined on its left by the
French Fourth Army (General Henri Gourand). The attacks began in late September.

The efforts of the British First, Third, and Fourth armies were once again led by
the Australian and Canadian corps. At the Canal du Nord (September 27–October 1)
the Canadians attacked across the waterway to rout the German Seventeenth Army.
At the St. Quentin Canal (September 29–October 10) the Australians, in their last
battle, breached the Hindenburg Line with the help of two AEF divisions attached
to Rawlinson's Fourth Army. In the second battle of Cambrai (October 8–10) the
Canadians took the thinly defended city with very few casualties, then continued to lead
the way a week later in the battle of the Selle (October 17–25), where the New Zealand
Division also figured prominently along with King Albert's Belgians, advancing on the
British left. Finally, at the second battle of the Sambre (November 4), advance elements
of the three British armies joined the French First Army in securing 50 miles (80 km)

of the Sambre for the main body of their armies to cross. The German failure to hold the line of the Sambre compromised their control over all of southern Belgium, which the Allies stood poised to liberate a week later. Most of these battles, like the earlier action after Amiens, included conventional assaults involving the customary tools of World War I – artillery bombardments, gas, machine-gun fire – rather than innovative tank tactics or close air support by planes. The Allied armies continued to suffer heavy losses in pushing back a beaten enemy (see Box 13.3). The BEF as a whole sustained 314,000 casualties during the Hundred Days offensive, among them just over 49,000 Canadians, mostly because of the heavy reliance on infantry attacks. After Amiens, large numbers of tanks were used only at the St. Quentin Canal and in the walkover at the second battle of Cambrai.

Box 13.3 "If a shell has got your name on it, it will get you"

Excerpt from a memoir written by A. B. "Ken" Kenway, British artilleryman, describing the action at Messines Ridge (October 3, 1918):

We were half-way back to the trench when suddenly there were four or five explosions, following quickly one on another. We flung ourselves flat on our faces … We lay there a few minutes waiting; then there was another salvo of shells and, peeping up, I saw a cloud of black smoke and a fountain of earth rise in the air over the trench where Bob and the others were. We waited a little while, but, as nothing else came over, we made a dash towards the trench.

God! What a sight met our eyes! A shell had landed right among the boys. It was a slaughterhouse – just a mass of mangled flesh and blood. Bob's head was hanging off… Jimmy Fooks was squatting on his haunches, not a mark on him, quite dead, killed by the concussion. You couldn't tell which was Harris and which was Kempton – what was left of them was in pieces. I was numbed. I felt as if a great weight was pressing on my head. I was choking.

In a dream I heard the sergeant's voice, "For God's sake get away. Get to hell out of it before they start again." He had been asleep in the gun-pit and was untouched. Somehow I got back to the lorry which was waiting to take us back. Then I broke down and between my sobs I cursed the Germans.

… We knew the enemy was beaten; we knew it couldn't last much longer, and at this time, after three years in France and the end so near, Bob must be killed! Harris, who had left a young bride in England – killed! Jimmy Fooks, whose time was nearly up – killed! And Kempton, who was due for leave – killed also! Why hadn't they come across to the cookhouse with Thomas and me? Why hadn't the relief come up in time?

If either of these things had happened Bob would still be alive. And then I remembered his fatalism – "It's no use worrying, Ken. If a shell has got your name on it, it will get you; it will turn round corners to get you," and it had done that to Bob and the others; it had found its way into that trench and got them.

They left them where they fell and covered them over. The trench which they dug to give them shelter in life proved to be their grave, and sheltered their bodies in death.

Source: First published in *Everyman at War*, ed. C. B. Purdom (J. M. Dent, 1930), available at www.firstworldwar.com/diaries/messinesoctober1918.htm. (All attempts at traring the copyright holder of the original work were unsuccessful.)

Meanwhile, to the north, the campaign of King Albert's army group, known to history as the fifth battle of Ypres (September 28–November 11), actually started at the ruined city in western Flanders but continued, methodically, to the northeast, gradually beating back the German Fourth and Sixth armies, and liberating the coastal districts of Belgium in moving toward its goal of Antwerp. The Germans temporarily held up Plumer's British Second Army at Courtai (October 14–19), while the Belgians took Ostend (October 17) and Bruges (October 19), then reached the Belgian-Dutch border on October 20. By the time of the Armistice, King Albert's group had pushed its front 45 miles (72 km) east of their starting points, but Brussels and Antwerp remained in German hands.

Of the twenty-nine AEF divisions to see action before the Armistice, Pershing used twenty-two in the Meuse–Argonne offensive (September 26–November 11), which turned into the biggest single battle of the Hundred Days. Owing to the unusually large size of the American divisions (28,000 men apiece) Pershing deployed more than 600,000 troops in all, eventually divided between a separate First Army (General Hunter Liggett) and Second Army (General Robert Bullard). In contrast, their opponents, including the forty-four German divisions of Army Group Gallwitz, totaled no more than 450,000. The Germans fortified the rugged terrain of the Argonne Forest, negating the Allied advantages of nearly 4,000 guns and 200 tanks, and more than 800 aircraft. The Americans broke the Hindenburg Line in early October, but in the first five weeks of fighting advanced just 10 miles (16 km) beyond it. Thereafter, the German front wavered, allowing the Americans to advance another 10 miles in just two days (November 1–3) and 10 more in the last week of the war, to reach the outskirts of Sedan alongside Gourand's French Fourth Army, which had been advancing on their left. The battle continued until the Armistice, by which time it had cost the Americans 117,000 casualties, the French 70,000, and the Germans as many as 120,000. The American losses included 26,000 killed, still the largest number of combat deaths in any single battle in US history. The Meuse-Argonne also produced three of the most remarkable American stories of World War I: the survival of the "lost battalion" of the 77th Division; Sergeant Alvin York of the 82nd Division capturing 132 Germans single-handedly; and the decorations won by the unwanted warriors of the African American 93rd Division, which served in Gourand's army, wearing French uniforms. During the autumn offensive of the AEF, influenza killed 10,000 of Pershing's soldiers and sent another 100,000 to hospital. Including men who succumbed while still in training in the United States, the American military flu casualties for those weeks rise to 25,000 dead and nearly 350,000 hospitalized.

Amid their retreat the only bright spot for the Germans came in the air war, where the introduction of the Fokker D7 biplane had tipped the balance back in their favor (see Online Essay 3). But the recovery of air superiority came too late to affect the overall effort of a seriously weakened army. By the time the Allies launched their autumn offensive the combined effects of the flu and summertime battle losses had reduced most German divisions to shells of a few thousand men, and just forty-seven were considered to be combat-ready. On September 29, the three Allied thrusts against the Hindenburg Line prompted Ludendorff to inform William II and German political leaders that "the condition of the army demands an immediate armistice in order to avoid a catastrophe."[14] The army and the monarchy had lost the war but, in Ludendorff's cynical calculation, they could still emerge from the fiasco with their reputations intact. Just as the OHL earlier had embraced unrestricted submarine warfare as a way to make the navy appear responsible for Germany's fate, Ludendorff now urged the emperor to turn over the government to the Reichstag parties that had supported the peace resolution of July 1917, to ensure that they would be blamed for what was certain to be an unfavorable outcome. His strategy for the endgame spawned the "stab in the back legend" ("*Dolchstosslegende*"), promoted by Hindenburg and Ludendorff, and embraced after November 1918 by Germany's disillusioned war veterans and disoriented nationalists struggling to make sense out of the defeat. According to their twisted logic, the home front's socialists and liberals had undermined the army, then betrayed their country by concluding a dishonorable peace. Anti-Semites added Germany's Jews to their list of "November criminals," ignoring the 30,000 Iron Crosses awarded to Jewish soldiers and their 12,000 combat deaths.

Before the Reichstag was told the truth about the war, William II, on September 30, declared that, henceforth, Germany would be a constitutional monarchy with a chancellor responsible to a Reichstag majority. Hertling was replaced by the liberal Prince Max of Baden, whose cabinet included leaders of the SPD, Catholic Center Party, and progressive liberals. On October 2, Ludendorff's deputy, Major Baron Erich von der Bussche, shocked the Reichstag with the news that "we cannot win the war," and that the new government would have to seek "the breaking-off of hostilities, so as to spare the German people and their allies further sacrifice."[15] Thus, on October 5, it fell to Prince Max to inform Wilson of Germany's willingness to negotiate peace based on the Fourteen Points. In a subsequent note on the 21st, he made a formal appeal for an armistice, accompanied by a pledge to evacuate the territories Germany still occupied. He also had the navy end unrestricted submarine warfare and call home its remaining U-boats. He had less luck in moderating the destructive behavior of the army, which followed a scorched-earth policy as it withdrew from France, including flooding mines and dynamiting railway bridges. On October 23, to appease the Left at home, Prince Max ordered the release of political prisoners, including Karl Liebknecht, whose first act as a free man was to visit the Soviet Russian embassy in Berlin. On the 26th, under pressure from Prince Max, William II appointed General Groener to replace Ludendorff, who then fled to Sweden rather than trust his safety to the increasingly volatile German home front.

Thus, the army's inability to stop the advancing Allies had dire consequences for Imperial Germany, prompting political reforms and peace overtures that raised expectations of an imminent end to the war. But with revolution in the air on the home front, the army experienced only isolated mutinies. Why did defeat and retreat not cause it to collapse? The German Army had a foundation of strong discipline, and even under the extreme strains of the last months of the war it carried out few death sentences (less than fifty for the entire war, compared with 600 for France and nearly 350 for Britain and its empire). In contrast to the Imperial Russian and Austro-Hungarian armies, whose internal fissures divided officers from soldiers, for most German soldiers "officer hate" ("*Offizierhass*") focused on senior officers alone. By 1918, most soldiers recognized junior officers as fellow-sufferers in the ordeal of the trenches and trusted them not to squander their lives in a lost cause. The large-scale surrenders that started at the second battle of the Marne reflected this solidarity, as most were led by captains or lieutenants who considered their soldiers too exhausted to keep fighting.[16] The army continued to retreat in an orderly fashion, to fight but not attack, and to lose ever-greater numbers of prisoners – 385,500 during the Hundred Days battles alone – without losing its overall cohesion or leaving gaps in the lines that would cause the front to break.

The German Navy lacked a similar cohesion, and thus had much more in common with its Imperial Russian and Austro-Hungarian counterparts (see Chapter 8). While the army, though battered, remained intact, on October 27 the fleet at Wilhelmshaven mutinied rather than obey orders to embark upon one last, fatal sortie against the British. At the end of the month Admiral Hipper dispersed the mutinous warships to the northern German ports, where the sailors soon became catalysts for local revolutionary activity. On November 1, three days after William II departed Berlin to meet with Hindenburg and the generals at Spa, Liebknecht issued a stirring appeal for a German revolution (see Box 13.4), sparking fears among Prince Max and his Reichstag supporters, as well as Allied leaders, that the Imperial government would give way to a Bolshevik-style regime. On the 4th, a Monday, sailors joined workers in seizing control of Kiel, and the following day the revolution spread to Hamburg and Bremen. As the week progressed workers throughout the country took to the streets. On the 6th, SPD leader Ebert pleaded with Groener to persuade William II to abdicate in favor of one of his sons, in order to preserve the constitutional monarchy. The following day, Hanover and Frankfurt joined the coastal cities in establishing revolutionary soviets or councils (*Räte*), while in Munich, USPD leader Kurt Eisner, jailed earlier for anti-war activism, proclaimed a Bavarian "soviet republic" ("*Räterepublik*").

Amid the deterioration of the German Army, Navy, and home front, Wilson responded to Prince Max's overture of October 5 as quickly as circumstances would allow him. The main problem with the chancellor's proposal for a peace based on the Fourteen Points was that the program had been proclaimed unilaterally by Wilson and never endorsed by the Allied governments. To secure their support for the Fourteen Points, he dispatched his advisor, Colonel House, on the next convoy to France, where he arrived on October 25. Wilson also empowered House to represent him in the drafting of specific armistice terms. House found that British, French, and Italian leaders generally agreed with the American position that the world should be reordered, starting in Europe. Most notably, Point IV, arms reduction, would be applied vigorously to Germany but not at all to the victorious powers, and the "autonomous development" references in Point X and Point XII, concerning the Habsburg and Ottoman nationalities, were now taken to mean outright independence, requiring the dismemberment of both empires. Thus, the Fourteen Points now justified a revolutionary agenda of the victors, including the wholesale redrawing of borders, the permanent weakening of Germany, and the destruction of its allies, all couched in Wilsonian idealism. By November 4, the Allied Supreme War Council agreed to all of the Fourteen Points except for Point II, concerning freedom of the seas, which the British found too restrictive (because, for example, it would have made illegal their absolute blockade of Germany, so critical to the Allied victory). The Allies also reserved the right to demand reparations from Germany, an issue not addressed in the Fourteen Points but certainly in the air ever since the Zimmerwald Manifesto's appeal for a "peace without annexations or indemnities." The following day, Wilson informed the Germans that the Supreme War Council had accepted the Fourteen Points, with the two noted reservations, and had empowered Foch to present the armistice terms.

Box 13.4 "End the war yourselves, and use your weapons against the rulers"

Excerpt from Karl Liebknecht's appeal for an immediate German revolution (November 1, 1918):

Comrades! Soldiers! Sailors! And you workers! Arise by regiments and arise by factories. Disarm your officers, whose sympathies and ideas are those of the ruling classes. Conquer your foremen, who are on the side of the present order. Announce the fall of your masters and demonstrate your solidarity.

Do not heed the advice of the Kaiser Social Democrats [of the majority SPD]. Do not let yourselves be led any longer by unworthy politicians, who play you false and deliver you into the hands of the enemy.

Stand fast like many of the genuine Social Democrats [of the USPD] in your companies and regiments. Seize the quarters of your officers; disarm them immediately. Make sure that your officers sympathize with you. In case they do so, let them lead you. Shoot them immediately in case they betray you after they have declared themselves supporters of your cause.

Soldiers and marines! Fraternize! Take possession of your ships. Overpower first your officers. Place yourselves in communication with your comrades on land and seize all harbors and open fire, if necessary, on loyal groups.

Workers in munitions factories: You are the masters of the situation. Stop work immediately. From this moment on you are only making bullets which will be used against you and yours. The bullets which you now make will never reach the front.

Stop making bayonets which will be thrust into your entrails by the knights of the Government. Arise, organize, seize weapons and use them against those who plan to make slaves of you after they have made their own peace. End the war yourselves, and use your weapons against the rulers.

Source: First published in *Everyman at War*, ed. C. B. Purdom (J. M. Dent, 1930), available at firstworldwar.com/source/germancollapse_liebknecht.htm. (All attempts at tracing the copyright bolder of the original work were unsuccessful.)

On the morning of Friday, November 8, a German delegation headed by Center Party leader Matthias Erzberger, principal author of the July 1917 peace resolution, met the Allied delegation, headed by Foch, in a railway coach in the forest of Compiègne, not far from Foch's headquarters. The armistice terms were harsher than the Germans expected, including the immediate demobilization of the army, internment of all but the oldest ships of the navy, and the surrender of the most lethal weapons including all submarines, late-model artillery and machine guns, Fokker D7 aircraft and bombers. All German military personnel were to withdraw to the country's 1914 borders, minus the west bank of the Rhine, where Alsace-Lorraine was to be returned to France and the rest (including the bridgehead cities of Cologne, Coblenz, and Mainz) occupied by Allied troops. The Germans had to return all Allied prisoners (535,000 French, 360,000 British, 133,000 Italians), but German POWs would remain in Allied hands (429,000 in France, 329,000 in Britain) until the signing of a definitive peace. The blockade would also remain in force until that time. Given 72 hours to sign the document, Erzberger sought further instructions, but by then Berlin was in chaos, as was OHL headquarters at Spa. On Saturday morning, November 9, Groener met with thirty-nine generals at Spa to gauge whether they thought their troops would march home, at the behest of William II, to "reconquer" the home front from "Bolshevism." After only one general gave him an unequivocal "yes," Groener informed the emperor that "the army will march home in peace and order" but "it no longer stands behind Your Majesty."[17] Hindenburg, a silent witness to the painful conversation, offered no support for Groener or consolation for his emperor before Prince Max phoned from Berlin to report the desertion of the capital's garrison, and to recommend William II's immediate abdication as the only way to save the monarchy. The emperor went to lunch mulling abdication and returned to the shocking news that Prince Max had already announced it in Berlin, then resigned in favor of Ebert, who was to appoint an imperial regent. Within an hour came word that the new chancellor's SPD colleague Scheidemann had proclaimed a republic, apparently to preempt Liebknecht's anticipated proclamation of a soviet republic. Later that afternoon William II boarded his imperial train and left Spa for the Netherlands, where he would live in exile until his death in 1941. Amid the confusion, Erzberger did not receive authority to sign the Armistice until Ebert finally sent it late Sunday evening. Shortly after midnight on Monday, November 11, Erzberger and the German delegation returned to the railway coach in the forest of Compiègne. In three hours of further discussions Foch made only minor alterations to the terms of the armistice, which Erzberger and his colleagues signed at 5:00 a.m. Foch and Admiral Sir Rosslyn Wemyss, Britain's First Sea Lord, signed for the Allies. The time for the cease fire was set at 11:00 a.m. that morning, the eleventh day of the eleventh month. World War I had ended, but the global revolution it had sparked continued.

Conclusion

After the war, German soldiers subscribing to the "stab in the back legend" would recount that they were shocked on the morning of November 11 when the guns suddenly fell silent, and outraged to learn that they would be demobilizing and going home, unlike the Allies, who would follow them into Germany as far as the Rhine. They blamed Germany's defeat on home-front treachery, on the grounds that they had not been defeated in the field. But embracing the bigger lie required them to lie, too. Since August 8 the German Army had not launched a successful counterattack anywhere on the Western front, and had not been able to hold its ground anywhere that the Allies attacked. While the front never broke, it had been pushed back day by day, week by week, for more than three months, until the Allies had retaken all of France and almost half of Belgium. Imperial Germany collapsed politically because it had been defeated militarily. Regardless of how they recalled the moment later, most German soldiers no doubt greeted the Armistice with relief rather than shock or dismay, for it spared their country from an invasion that their beaten army could no longer prevent, and spared their own lives.

The pivotal battle of 1918, at Amiens, reflected the culmination of the evolution of warfare over the past four years (see Online Essay 10). The British had provided a glimpse into the future of what the combination of well-coordinated infantry, artillery, tanks, and aircraft could accomplish. They restored mobility to the Western front by dealing the Germans a blow from which they could not recover. But ironically, after achieving the key breakthrough by showing signs of appreciating modern combined-arms warfare, British and Imperial troops did not replicate the feat in another major battle for the rest of the war, instead driving the retreating Germans ahead of them with brute force, just as the other Allied armies did.[18] While the British achievement cannot be denied, to Foch (and, indeed, to all who remained true to the cult of the offensive) such operational and tactical refinements played less of a role in the achievement of victory than the relentless application of superior manpower, once that manpower became available. Embracing this approach in 1918, Britain and France both lost troops they could not replace, at a time when the United States was deploying more men every day. Thus, World War I ended as it had begun, as a war of attrition, but one which accentuated the American role in the endgame in Europe.

Indeed, when he informed the Reichstag that the war was lost, Major von der Bussche explained that "the enemy, owing to the help he has received from America, is in a position to make good his losses" and could draw upon "an almost inexhaustible supply of reserves."[19] In January 1917, Germany risked the resumption of unrestricted submarine warfare assuming that, if the United States declared war, the U-boats would prevent American troop transports from reaching Europe. But in the eighteen months of transatlantic convoy (May 1917–November 1918) no transports were sunk on the high seas and very few in coastal waters after the crossing, where losses were minimal. A total of 2,079,880 American soldiers made it safely to Europe. In terms of expectations versus reality, the utter failure of the German Navy to disrupt the flow of American troops to the Western front ranks among the most remarkable developments in the history of warfare. Thanks to their safe passage, in November 1918 the US Army alone had as many men on the Western front (1.4 million) as the German Army when it launched its spring offensive in March, and had another 700,000 in France but not yet deployed to the front. Behind them stood 2 million more at camps and bases in the United States, awaiting transport to Europe as soon as they completed basic training. While some scholars, especially in Britain and the former Dominions, argue that the American effort was ineffective or even inconsequential (see Perspectives 13.1), given the nature of combat during World War I the AEF did not have to fight particularly well to make a difference. In sheer numbers of casualties 1918 was bloodier than 1917, but thanks to the United States, the Allies could now replace men faster than the Germans could kill them. That sobering calculus determined the outcome of the war, and not just in the German decision to seek an armistice. In November 1918 the French still had the largest Allied army, but the number of Americans deployed on the Western front had surpassed the number of troops from Britain and the Dominions as well as from France. By then, Clemenceau and Foch shared Haig's fear, articulated earlier in the year, that "America would get a great pull over us" the longer the war continued.[20] Thus France and Britain were receptive to the German overture in part because they recognized that, should the war last into 1919, the American role in the war would only grow larger and, with it, the American role in shaping the peace.

Perspectives 13.1: The American military contribution

Australian historian Elizabeth Greenhalgh (1944–2018) emphasized the AEF's dependence upon the French Army for most of its equipment and its reluctance to accept French training for combat on the Western front:

As for the USA, France had supplied most of the AEF's weapons and had tried to make its C-in-C [Pershing] follow the French lead. The French Army had supplied instructors and interpreters, but General Pershing preferred his own methods. Relations with Pershing and the American armies were complicated: respect for the New World's youth and enthusiasm was mixed with exasperation that the C-in-C of those young and enthusiastic doughboys would not accept the lessons of experience gained the hard way.

Source: Elizabeth Greenhalgh, *The French Army and the First World War* (Cambridge: Cambridge University Press, 2014), 404.

• • • •

British historian Peter Hart (born 1955) ranks among the critics of the AEF's performance, but concedes it played an important supporting role in the final victory:

Although the Americans continued to advance [in 1918] they were still losing far too many men. It was due to a combination of reasons: their simplistic tactics, poor communications, sometimes inadequate leadership, the thoroughly hostile terrain, and, of course, the German army ... And yet when all was said and done, the Americans did fight hard in the closing months of the war. Their huge armies were now not only theoretically depressing German morale as a future threat, but they had joined the British and French in battering away at the overstretched and doomed German defences.

Source: Peter Hart, *1918: A Very British Victory*
(London: Weidenfeld & Nicolson, 2008), 438–39.
(Reprinted with permission of The Orion Publishing Group, London.)

• · • •

American historian David Woodward (born 1939) places the AEF at the center of the Allied achievement of victory over Germany, despite its relatively brief engagement:

The prospect of future American help in 1917 encouraged the French and British to fight on and caused Ludendorff to take desperate steps in 1918 to achieve a victor's peace before US forces dramatically tipped the military balance in the Entente's favor ... The American offensive at Meuse-Argonne played a significant, arguably decisive, role in abruptly and unexpectedly ending the war in November 1918 ... Although involved in intense combat for only some 110 days, the AEF played an essential role in preventing the Second Reich from establishing hegemonic control of Europe.

Source: David R. Woodward, *The American Army and the First World War*
(Cambridge University Press, 2014), 3, 378–79.

SUGGESTIONS FOR FURTHER READING

Boff, Jonathan. *Winning and Losing on the Western Front: The British Third Army and the Defeat of Germany in 1918* (Cambridge: Cambridge University Press, 2012).

Chernev, Borislav. *Twilight of Empire: The Brest-Litovsk Conference and the Remaking of East-Central Europe, 1917–1918* (Toronto: University of Toronto Press, 2017).

Cornwall, Mark. *The Undermining of Austria-Hungary: The Battle for Hearts and Minds* (London: Macmillan, 2000).

Ferrell, Robert H. *America's Deadliest Battle: Meuse-Argonne, 1918* (Lawrence, KS: University Press of Kansas, 2007).

Greenhalgh, Elizabeth. *Foch in Command: The Forging of a First World War General.* (Cambridge: Cambridge University Press, 2011).

—*Victory through Coalition: Britain and France during the First World War* (Cambridge: Cambridge University Press, 2005).

Gumz, Jonathan. *The Resurrection and Collapse of Empire in Habsburg Serbia, 1914–1918* (Cambridge: Cambridge University Press, 2009).

Lloyd, Nick. *Hundred Days: The Campaign That Ended World War I* (New York: Basic Books, 2014).

Neiberg, Michael S. *Foch: Supreme Allied Commander in the Great War* (Washington, DC: Brassey's, 2003).

— *The Second Battle of the Marne* (Bloomington, IN: Indiana University Press, 2008).

Rabinowitch, Alexander. *The Bolsheviks in Power: The First Year of Soviet Rule in Petrograd* (Bloomington, IN: Indiana University Press, 2007).

Travers, Tim. *How the War was Won: Command and Technology in the British Army on the Western Front, 1917–1918* (London: Routledge, 1992).

Watson, Alexander. *Enduring the Great War: Combat, Morale and Collapse in the German and British Armies, 1914–1918* (Cambridge: Cambridge University Press, 2008).

Woodward, David R. *Trial by Friendship: Anglo-American Relations, 1917–1918* (Lexington, KY: University Press of Kentucky, 2003).

NOTES

1. Quoted in David R. Woodward, *Trial by Friendship: Anglo-American Relations, 1917–1918* (Lexington, KY: University Press of Kentucky, 2003), 116.
2. Diary entry for March 19, 1918, in Émile Fayolle, *Cahiers secrets de la grande guerre*, ed. Henry Contamine (Paris: Plon, 1964), 259.
3. Quoted in J. P. Harris, *Douglas Haig and the First World War* (Cambridge: Cambridge University Press, 2008), 425.
4. Harris, *Douglas Haig and the First World War*, 457.
5. Quoted in Michael Neiberg, *Foch: Supreme Allied Commander in the Great War* (Washington, DC: Brassey's, 2003), 63.
6. Neiberg, *Foch*, 64–65, 69.
7. Quoted in Robert H. Zieger, *America's Great War: World War I and the American Experience* (Lanham, MD: Rowman & Littlefield, 2000), 98.
8. Imperial Manifesto Federalizing the Austrian Lands, October 16, 1918, text in Malbone W. Graham, Jr., *New Governments of Central Europe* (New York: Henry Holt, 1926), 501.

9. Article II, Austrian Constitution of November 12, 1918, text in Graham, *New Governments of Central Europe*, 508.

10. Quoted in John W. Wheeler-Bennett, *Brest Litovsk: The Forgotten Peace, March 1918* (London: Macmillan, 1938; reprinted edn. New York: W. W. Norton, 1971), 280.

11. Alexander Watson, *Enduring the Great War: Combat, Morale and Collapse in the German and British Armies, 1914–1918* (Cambridge University Press, 2008), 183.

12. Manfried Rauchensteiner, *Der Tod des Doppeladlers: Österreich-Ungarn und der Erste Weltkrieg* (Vienna: Verlag Styria, 1993), 589.

13. Metzger to Conrad, near Verdun, September 6, 1918, KA, B/1450: 208.

14. Quoted in Hajo Holborn, *A History of Modern Germany, 1840–1945* (Princeton, NJ: Princeton University Press, 1982), 502.

15. Major Freiherr von der Bussche's Address to the Reichstag of the Recommendations of the German High Command, October 2, 1918, available at www.firstworldwar.com/source/germancollapse_bussche.htm.

16. Watson, *Enduring the Great War*, 231, 234, and passim.

17. John W. Wheeler-Bennett, *Wooden Titan: Hindenburg in Twenty Years of German History, 1914–1934* (New York: William Morrow, 1936), 197, 199.

18. See Tim Travers, *How the War was Won: Command and Technology in the British Army on the Western Front, 1917–1918* (London: Routledge, 1992), 175–76 and passim.

19. Bussche's Address to the Reichstag, October 2, 1918, available at www.firstworldwar.com/source/germancollapse_bussche.htm.

20. Harris, *Douglas Haig and the First World War*, 425; Elizabeth Greenhalgh, *Foch in Command: The Forging of a First World War General* (Cambridge: Cambridge University Press, 2011), 490.

Clemenceau, Wilson, Lloyd George

French premier Georges Clemenceau (1841–1929), US president Woodrow Wilson (1856–1924), and British prime minister David Lloyd George (1863–1945), photographed leaving a session of the Paris Peace Conference, Palace of Versailles, June 1, 1919. Their deliberations on specific points were often stormy, but they agreed on the most basic elements of the peace settlement: the cession of Alsace-Lorraine and the other non-German territories of the Second Reich, and arms limitations so severe that Germany would be no threat to its neighbors in the future. Wilson ultimately compromised most of his Fourteen Points in order to secure French and British support for his League of Nations.

14 The Paris Peace Conference

November 1918	Republics established In Germany, Austria, and Hungary.
January 1919	German "Spartacist Revolt" crushed.
January 18	Peace conference opens.
February–July	German constituent assembly meets at Weimar.
March–August	Hungary as "Soviet republic" under Bela Kun.
April 28	Peace conference approves League of Nations Covenant.
June 21	Germans scuttle warships interned at Scapa Flow.
June 28	Germany signs Treaty of Versailles.
September 10	Austria signs Treaty of St. Germain.
November 27	Bulgaria signs Treaty of Neuilly.
June 4, 1920	Hungary signs Treaty of Trianon.
August 10	Ottoman Empire signs Treaty of Sèvres.

In 1918 Lenin and Wilson presented the world with competing visions of a future peaceful utopia: one of a communism to be created, ultimately, after a global revolution eliminating capitalism and imperialism, the other of a democracy to be spread by example once the elimination of the autocratic Central Powers made the world "safe" for it. Early in the year the first Soviet premier, who would soon establish the first modern totalitarian dictatorship, had engaged in a vigorous debate with the rest of the Bolshevik inner circle before agreeing, against his better judgment, to try Trotsky's "no war, no peace" approach before accepting German terms at Brest-Litovsk, terms that were harsher than Soviet Russia would have gotten if it had concluded an immediate peace, as Lenin had wished. In sharp contrast, the American president, the elected head of the world's largest state with a representative government, who wanted to spread democracy worldwide, took little counsel initially (and even less later) in his single-minded quest to compel everyone else to accept his vision of a peace settlement and the organization of the postwar world. The defeat of Germany in November 1918 enabled Lenin to repudiate the Treaty of Brest-Litovsk, but the bitter experience would deepen the pragmatic instincts of the ostensibly idealistic revolutionary leader, a pragmatism that would serve him well as Soviet Russia, isolated and embattled, made its way in a hostile world. Wilson's vision, and the methods by which he sought to achieve it, had yet to be tested.

Celebrating the Armistice

News of the Armistice set off wild celebrations worldwide, with the largest crowds assembling in the major cities of the victorious Allies. In the French capital the streets filled with revelers, and joyous Parisians mobbed American soldiers (see Box 14.1). The explosion of celebration came after Clemenceau's speech to the Chamber of Deputies at 4:00 p.m., in which the old premier read out the terms of the Armistice, his words punctuated by thunderous applause from the deputies and spectators in the gallery. Then,

the deputies as they rose to adjourn spontaneously began singing the *Marseillaise*. The hymn was taken up by the galleries and by the crowds in the corridors. It spread to the vast throng standing in the twilight outside on the riverbanks and bridges, and soon all Paris was singing its song of victory. All day and everywhere the rejoicing went on, and it continued all night.[1]

In London, 100,000 people turned out to celebrate the news:

The City gave itself up to wholehearted merriment and infectious joyousness. At night all London was brilliantly illuminated and the populace surged to the streets. Spread over three miles from St. Paul's to Oxford Circus and down Whitehall to Victoria, the streets were full from curb to curb with laughing, jostling, happy people, and traffic difficulties were solved in the simplest fashion by turning back nearly all buses.[2]

Box 14.1 *"It was a grand thing to die for"*

Letter from Captain Charles S. Normington, 32nd Division, US Army, to his parents, written in Paris on the day the Armistice was signed:

Paris, November 11, 1918

Dear Folks:

Arrived here last night, and was on the street today when the armistice with Germany was signed. Anyone who was not here can never be told, or imagine the happiness of the people here. They cheered and cried and laughed and then started all over again.

Immediately a parade was started on the Rue de Italiennes (sic) and has been going on ever since. In the parade were hundreds of thousands of soldiers from the US, England, Canada, France, Australia, Italy, and the colonies. Each soldier had his arms full of French girls, some crying, others laughing; each girl had to kiss every soldier before she would let him pass.

The streets are crowded and all traffic held up. There are some things, such as this, that never will be reproduced if the world lives a million years. They have taken movies of the crowds, but you can't get sound nor the expression on the people's faces, by watching the pictures.

There is nowhere on earth I would rather be today than just where I am. Home would be nice, and is next, but Paris and France is Free after four years and three months of war. And oh, such a war! The hearts of these French people have simply bursted with joy. I have had many an old French couple come up to Major Merrill and me and throw their arms about us, cry like children, saying, "You grand Americans; you have done this for us."

Thank God, thank God, the war is over. I can imagine all the world is happy. But nowhere on earth is there a demonstration as here in Paris. I only hope the soldiers who died for this cause are looking down upon the world today. It was a grand thing to die for. The whole world owes this moment of real joy to the heroes who are not here to help enjoy it.

I cannot write any more.

Lovingly, your boy, Chas.

Source: From private collection of Lois Normington Haugner, available at http://www.firstworldwar.com/diaries/normington.htm.

Perhaps the most spectacular scene of all, to the relatively few Britons able to witness it, came on the evening of the 11th off the coast of Scotland, where "on a thirty-mile line, warships of every description were simultaneously illuminated" as the Grand Fleet left Scapa Flow for Wilhelmshaven to meet the High Sea Fleet.[3] Ten days later, the same British warships would escort their German adversaries back to Scapa Flow for internment. Meanwhile, throughout Italy, cheering crowds celebrated what Orlando hailed as "a Roman victory," equating the Armistice with the military triumphs of Ancient Rome.[4] Word of the Armistice reached New York in the predawn hours of November 11, allowing the news to make banner headlines in the morning papers. The ensuing celebration

lasted without interruption for fully twenty-four hours. Whistles, sirens, and bells kept up a constant din the entire day; all business was suspended; the streets were packed and jammed; spontaneous processions formed in every block; effigies of the Kaiser hanging and in coffins were conspicuous; dense snowstorms of bits of paper filled the air and streets, and at night the city was in a state of joyous celebration that almost approached delirium.

The outpouring of emotion was impressive enough, given that the same thing had happened, prematurely, on November 7, when the New York press printed a false report that the Armistice had already been signed.

"That event had let off much surplus steam, and nothing else could quite get up the enthusiasm which was then manifested."[5]

If for no other reason, people rejoiced because the bloodshed had finally ceased. By the time the guns fell silent on November 11, 1918, the total military deaths of World War I had reached 8.5 million. In sheer numbers no one suffered more than Russia which, despite leaving the war eleven months before it ended, registered 2 million dead. Germany followed close behind, with 1.8 million dead, followed by France and its empire with 1.4 million (including more than 1.3 million from France itself), Austria-Hungary with 1.2 million, Britain and its empire with 900,000 (including 700,000 from the United Kingdom), Italy with 460,000, and the Ottoman Empire with 325,000. If measured in terms of size of population, the distribution of deaths and of the overall burden of military service appear quite differently, with the Russians suffering the least of Europe's great powers. For every 1,000 persons, France (minus its empire) mobilized 202 men and lost 34, Germany mobilized 184 and lost 30, Austria-Hungary mobilized 154 and lost 23, Britain (minus its empire) mobilized 141 and lost 16, the Ottoman Empire mobilized 133 and lost 15, Italy mobilized 160 and lost 13, and Russia mobilized 74 and lost 11. For its part, the United States mobilized 41 men per 1,000 persons and lost 1.2, but the 116,000 American military deaths fell almost entirely in the last five and a half months of the fighting, from Cantigny to the Armistice, at a daily rate that, if projected out to the full four years and four months of the war, would have topped 1 million. Estimates of civilian dead range upward from 5 million, depending upon the method used to count them (raw numbers, or numbers of dead exceeding peacetime norms) and when the counting stopped (on November 11, or when the global influenza pandemic ran its course in mid-1919). Even if the lower figures are correct, in human terms World War I generated more deaths than any previous international military conflict. It remains history's third most costly calamity involving armed force, behind only World War II and China's Taiping Rebellion (1850–64).

From the Armistice to the Peace Table

Less than ten weeks passed between the conclusion of the Armistice and the opening of the Paris Peace Conference, but they were, arguably, the ten most eventful weeks in modern world history. Germany and Austria became democratic republics, in each case with women voting for the first time in a general election. Britain likewise held a general election, also the first in which women voted. On the eve of the Armistice the United States elected a Congress dominated by Wilson's Republican opponents, who spent the winter formulating objections to the treaty he had yet to start negotiating. Russia continued to be embroiled in civil war, with Allied contingents around its fringes supporting the White opposition to Lenin's Bolshevik regime. At the same time, from Finland in the Arctic to Georgia in the Caucasus, new countries carved out of Russian territory under German patronage scrambled to secure their borders and make their cases for independence at the peace conference. A similar scramble occurred in the former Dual Monarchy, where successor states Austria, Hungary, and Czechoslovakia contested the spoils along with neighboring Italy, Serbia/Yugoslavia, Romania, and Poland. Beyond Europe, from Africa to the Middle East to east Asia and the Pacific, governments likewise sought to solidify gains or build cases for why the peace conference should overturn existing territorial realities.

The former Central Powers experienced the most profound changes. With the Berlin of November 1918 beginning to look like the Petrograd of March 1917, Ebert moved quickly to prevent the new Soviet-style network of revolutionary councils (*Räte*) from establishing a "dual power" structure independent of his own, or from taking over Germany outright. He established a coalition with Hugo Haase, head of the USPD, which the Workers and Soldiers Council of Berlin accepted on November 10; thereafter, the Ebert "cabinet" doubled as the Council of People's Deputies of the revolution. Ebert covered his other flank by accepting from Groener, acting head of the army, a pledge of troops in case the revolutionaries got out of hand (Figure 14.1). Aside from Eisner's regime in Bavaria, most of the German councils were far more moderate than the Russian soviets of 1917, and many returning soldiers joined right-wing paramilitary *Freikorps* rather than the left-leaning councils. On December 16, the Pan-German Congress of Councils (the German version of the All-Russian Congress of Soviets) convened in Berlin and endorsed Ebert's call for elections to a national assembly, to be held on January 19, 1919, which would write the constitution of the German republic. Such moderation frustrated Liebknecht, Rosa Luxemburg, and other radical Marxists who felt the SPD-USPD coalition had hijacked their revolution. On New Year's Eve they joined other members of the wartime Spartacus League to form the Communist Party of Germany (KPD), then called a general strike that escalated into the "Spartacist Revolt" (January 5–12), in which 1,000 armed Spartacists attempted to emulate the Bolshevik example of November 1917. But army and *Freikorps* units summoned by Ebert to defend the republic easily defeated the Spartacist coup; Liebknecht and Luxemburg were captured and, on January 15, murdered by the *Freikorps*. Four days later, the peace parties of the last Imperial Reichstag triumphed at the polls, with Ebert's SPD winning 38 percent of the seats in the national assembly to 20 percent for the Center Party, 18 percent for the liberal progressives (now known as the German Democratic Party or DDP), and just 8 percent for the USPD. Avoiding the instability of Berlin, the assembly convened on February 6 at Weimar and elected Ebert president of Germany for a seven-year term (after which presidents were to be popularly elected).

Figure 14.1 Ebert inspects a German battalion

Friedrich Ebert (1871–1925) became chairman of the German Social Democratic Party (SPD) in 1913 and orchestrated its support for war credits in the Reichstag. He subsequently supported the peace resolution of July 1917 and joined Prince Max von Baden's coalition government in October 1918. Following the abdication of William II, Ebert served first as chancellor of the German republic, then, from February 1919, as its president. A democratic socialist, Ebert rejected the far Left's appeals for a Soviet-style regime. In January 1919 he turned to the army and far Right *Freikorps* to crush the communist Spartacist Revolt. At that stage the army, though anti-republican, preferred Ebert to the alternative of a Bolshevik Germany; Ebert likewise preferred to tie his fate to the army rather than to the radical Left. Germany's conservative parties rebounded as early as the Reichstag elections of 1920, and following Ebert's death a right-leaning electorate chose former field marshal Paul von Hindenburg as president of the republic.

Scheidemann succeeded him as chancellor, at the head of an SPD-Center-DDP coalition. The election found the German Right still disoriented by the collapse of the Second Reich; the German National People's Party (DNVP) and German People's Party (DVP) – despite their names, mere reincarnations of old conservative parties dominated by landowners and industrialists, respectively – together won just 14 percent of the vote. Even before the new government faced the crisis of having to sign the Treaty of Versailles, the events of the winter of 1918–19 set the political parameters for interwar Germany. The temporary weakness of the Right made the national assembly somewhat more liberal than the public as a whole; as a result, the Weimar constitution and the government it established were never accepted by a significant number of Germans.

In Austria, newly proclaimed chancellor Karl Renner became undisputed head of the ruling Social Democrats after their founder, Viktor Adler, died of influenza on November 11, the day before the republic was proclaimed. The three dominant German Austrian parties of the old Reichsrat remained at loggerheads in the republic owing to the nature of their programs: the Christian Socialists, anti-*Anschluss* and anti-Semitic; the German Nationalists, *pro-Anschluss* and anti-Semitic; and the Social Democrats, pro-*Anschluss* and with Austrians of Jewish heritage playing prominent roles in their leadership. These included, most controversially, Friedrich Adler, son of Viktor and, in October 1916, assassin of the Austrian prime minister, Count Stürgkh. Sentenced to death for murder, he became a free man two years later, as he benefited first from the customary commutation of all death sentences at the onset of a new reign, when Charles became emperor, then from the collapse of the monarchy freeing all "political" prisoners. In contrast to the moderate course of the German SPD, which caused it to lose significant numbers to the German KPD, Renner's Social Democrats were radical enough to leave a smaller percentage of the Left dissatisfied enough to support the Austrian Communist Party. In elections to the national assembly (February 16, 1919) the Social Democrats won 42 percent of the seats, the Christian Socialists 41 percent, and German Nationalists 15 percent. The two largest parties formed an uneasy coalition, with Renner continuing as chancellor. The Social Democrats also dominated the small *Volkswehr*, Austria's only official armed force after the collapse of the Austro-Hungarian Army, but right-wing paramilitary *Heimwehr* units, analogous to Germany's *Freikorps*, were formed throughout the country. Amid widespread hunger and high unemployment, political confusion reigned throughout the winter. German Austrians from the Sudetenland and South Tyrol continued to sit in the assembly in Vienna, and Austria sent representatives to the German national assembly at Weimar. The Austrians had no advocate among the victorious Allies, who dismissed the proposed *Anschluss* (as tantamount to rewarding Germany for having lost the war) and supported whatever claims Czechoslovakia made at Austria's expense. Meanwhile, in Hungary, Count Károlyi proclaimed a republic on November 16, with the support of the local Workers and Soldiers Council. The liberal nobleman won the support of the masses through egalitarian gestures such as giving up his own estate of 50,000 acres (20,000 ha) for redistribution to the peasantry. He attempted to steer a pro-Allied course, to ensure that as much of the Magyar (ethnic Hungarian) population as possible would remain under Hungarian rule. Within days of the Armistice he signed a convention with the Allies that allowed Romania to occupy much of Transylvania, but they did nothing when the Romanians violated its terms, took all of Transylvania, and began to integrate it into their kingdom. Hungary, like Austria and Germany, continued to endure an Allied blockade throughout the winter of 1918–19, although because Hungary could feed itself, a fuel shortage posed the greatest problem for Károlyi, joining his failed foreign policy to leave him discredited in the eyes of the public.

The same months were eventful for the victors, too. In Italy, Orlando called World War I "the greatest political and social revolution recorded by history, surpassing even the French Revolution." His predecessor, Salandra, concurred that "a peaceful return to the past" was impossible.[6] But in both France and Italy, the leading countries that did not enfranchise women, the socialist parties, the prewar catalysts for political and social reform, were hamstrung by the now unpopular anti-war positions they had belatedly adopted (the French SFIO in July 1918, the Italian Socialist Party in September 1918). In Italy the initiative passed to the Right, where Mussolini's Fascist Party appealed to war veterans by combining nationalism with socialism. In January 1919, the Fascists launched their postwar campaign of political violence, attacking Socialist Party targets in Milan. But among the leading Allied powers, Britain had the most eventful winter of all. On December 14, 1918, the country held its first general election since 1910, the 1915 vote having been postponed because of the war. Lloyd George drew criticism for running a "khaki election," capitalizing on the public mood in the moment of victory to gain a fresh mandate, but the strategy worked. His coalition of Conservative, Liberal, and Labour won two-thirds of the seats in the House of Commons, and because the poll came just five weeks after the Armistice, proponents of a harsh peace dominated the new chamber. The most ominous aspect of the election, Sinn Féin's triumph in Ireland, made the Irish republicans the largest single opposition party, holding just over 10 percent of the seats. Rather than take their places in the House of Commons, on January 21, 1919, the Sinn Féin MPs convened in Dublin as the first Irish Parliament (or Dáil Éireann), which reaffirmed the declaration of independence issued in the Easter Rising of 1916 and issued a "Message to the Free Nations of the World" appealing to "every free nation to support the Irish Republic by recognizing Ireland's national status and her right to its vindication at the Peace Congress."[7] The Dáil also recognized the Irish Volunteers as the armed forces of the republic, under the name Irish Republican Army (IRA). On the day the Dáil opened, skirmishing between the IRA and the Royal Irish Constabulary in Tipperary marked the start of a low-intensity conflict in which the armed struggle of the IRA against British authorities punctuated a widespread campaign of Irish passive resistance to British rule.

In the United States, Wilson decided a week after the Armistice to go to the Paris Peace Conference. Aside from Roosevelt, who had toured the Panama Canal construction site in 1906, no American president had ever left the United States while in office. Wilson did so against the advice of Robert Lansing, Bryan's successor as secretary of state, who argued that the president "could practically dictate the terms of the peace if he held aloof," staying in Washington, above the fray of the negotiations.[8] Wilson remained confident despite receiving a stinging rebuke in midterm congressional elections just five days before the Armistice. When the new Congress convened on March 4, 1919, the Republicans would hold majorities in the House of Representatives (240:195) and the Senate (49:47), yet the president took just one Republican with him to Paris, career diplomat Henry White. A wiser politician would have chosen a sympathetic prominent Republican (former president William H. Taft, future chief justice of the Supreme Court, was an obvious choice) to join the delegation rather than the obscure White, and a shrewder one would have invited some of his leading critics in order to reap the benefits of their refusal to go to Paris. But Wilson wanted to put his personal stamp on the peace settlement and rejected all advice regardless of the spirit in which it was offered, including that of W. E. B. DuBois and other African American leaders seeking input on the postwar fate of Africa. On December 4, Wilson's entourage boarded the *George Washington*, the fastest American troopship (ironically, a former North German Lloyd ocean liner), which enabled the president to make each of his four transatlantic crossings of 1918–19 in nine or ten days. His triumphant pre-conference tour of France, Britain, and Italy started in Paris on December 14, where crowds rivaling the size and enthusiasm of those on Armistice Day greeted him. Wilson remained in France through Christmas before visiting Britain on December 26–31, including stops in London and Manchester, public appearances with King George V, and his first meetings with Lloyd George. He spent New Year's Eve in Paris en route from Britain to Italy, where his itinerary included stops in Rome, Genoa, Turin, and Milan, public appearances with King Victor Emmanuel III, discussions with Orlando, and an audience with Pope Benedict XV at the Vatican, before his return to Paris on January 7. Symbolically, the tour served notice of the arrival of the United States on the world stage, as a grateful old world applauded the idealism of the new, personified in Wilson. The adoring crowds and deferential receptions by kings, statesmen, and the pope provided a further boost to the ego of a man not lacking in self-esteem, setting the stage for what was to come.

Germany, the Versailles Treaty, and the League of Nations

The Paris Peace Conference took shape in *ad hoc* decisions made shortly before it convened. When the Supreme War Council met in Paris on January 12, 1919, for the first time each of the "Big Four" – Britain, France, Italy, and the United States – was represented by its head of government and foreign minister. They decided on the spot to limit the direction of the peace conference to themselves and their counterparts from Japan, who would convene as the "Council of Ten." They agreed that the five leading powers would each have five seats in the plenary sessions of the conference, with the remaining Allied and Associated Powers allotted one, two, or three seats based upon their population or contribution to the war effort; thus, Belgium and Serbia/Yugoslavia each received three seats owing to their prominence in the war's opening phase and overall sacrifices. Of the countries at war with the Central Powers at the time of the Armistice, only three were not represented: Montenegro (incorporated into Yugoslavia); Costa

Rica (where a coup had established a dictatorship not recognized by the United States); and microstate Andorra (literally forgotten, and not formally ending hostilities until 1958). The republics of Poland and Czechoslovakia were recognized as belligerents and granted two seats apiece (more than a dozen other countries) even though they did not formally come into existence until the end of the war. At Britain's insistence the four Dominions and India were represented as separate states. Russia was not represented, because no one had granted diplomatic recognition to the Soviet government (or would, until 1924) and, in any event, it had made peace with the Central Powers before the war ended. The other Allied country to leave the war early – Romania, in May 1918 – qualified for a seat by re-entering the war the day before the Armistice. Reflecting the global significance of what had started as a purely European war, the thirty-two delegations included thirteen from the Americas, ten from Europe, five from Asia (China, Siam, and the Hejaz, along with Japan and India), and two from Africa (South Africa and Liberia), plus Australia and New Zealand.

On January 18, 1919, the first plenary session of the Paris Peace Conference convened in the Salle d'Horloge at the French foreign ministry in the Quay d'Orsay. As head of state of the host country, Poincaré delivered a long-winded opening address concluding with the observation that "this very day forty-eight years ago" the German Empire was proclaimed at the Palace of Versailles. "You are assembled in order to repair the evil that it has done and to prevent a recurrence of it."[9] The French president played no further role in the peace conference, as Clemenceau, head of government of the host country, served as "president of the peace conference." But Poincaré's opening remarks pointed the way to the outcome, at least pertaining to Germany, some five months later, for the treaty would be signed in the Hall of Mirrors at Versailles, in the same room where Bismarck had proclaimed the founding of the Second Reich. In the meantime, the proceedings of the peace conference revolved around the Council of Ten: Wilson and the US secretary of state, Lansing; Lloyd George and British foreign secretary Arthur Balfour; Clemenceau and French foreign minister Stéphan Pichon; Orlando and Italian foreign minister Sidney Sonnino; and Japan's representatives, former prime minister Kinmochi Saionji and former foreign minister Nobuaki Makino, sent to Paris as surrogates for the prime minister, Takashi Hara, and foreign minister, Kosai Uchida, who remained in Tokyo.

It took less than a month for the Council of Ten to agree to the main provisions of the settlement with Germany. Reflecting the Fourteen Points, they planned to return Alsace-Lorraine to France (Point VIII) and give Poland an outlet to the sea (Point XIII) via a corridor of German territory and the port of Danzig. The German lands lost to Poland remained to be defined, as did minor adjustments of the German borders with Belgium and Denmark (in the latter case, returning territory Bismarck had taken fifty-five years earlier). The victorious powers kept Germany's colonies but, reflecting Wilson's Point V, the League of Nations would have a role in supervising their eventual transition to independence. In the spirit of Point IV, they envisaged disarmament clauses reducing Germany's army and navy to much smaller forces without the most destructive modern weapons. The Rhineland would continue to be occupied while its long-term fate remained a point of contention. France wanted it detached from Germany to form a buffer state but could never persuade enough Germans to go along with the scheme; on February 1 Cologne mayor Konrad Adenauer, future West German chancellor, called for the creation of a "Rhenish republic" but soon abandoned the cause. Meanwhile, the rest of the council agreed with France and Britain that Germany must accept financial responsibility for the war and pay damages, a commonsense conclusion that gave rise to the treaty's most controversial provision, the demand for reparations. The Council of Ten quickly reached consensus on these points, after which a series of subcommittees worked out the specific details while the heads of government and foreign ministers spent most of their time debating the structure and Covenant of the League of Nations. Wilson could not have guessed that the negotiations were already proceeding on a course that would cause the treaty to be rejected by a majority of Americans and still questioned by historians decades later.

The American plan for the international organization grew out of exchanges between Colonel House and Balfour's predecessor as British foreign secretary, Sir Edward Grey, in February 1915, during House's first peace mission to Europe. Before House's second mission in January 1916, Wilson produced his first sketch of the League, based upon the principle of collective security under a regime of general disarmament. In May 1916, the president gave his first public address advocating the League, and in January 1918, on the eve of Wilson's Fourteen Points speech, Lloyd George endorsed the creation of "some kind of international organization" to facilitate the future preservation of peace.[10] Jan Smuts of South Africa, in London as a member of the Imperial War Cabinet, helped shape the idea during 1918, contributing the structural concept of a council including only the great powers and an assembly including all League members. The French thought less of the project, but their alternative idea of a looser association of states never caught on. Finally, in his address opening the peace conference, Poincaré gave France's endorsement to "a general League of Nations which will be a supreme guarantee against any fresh assaults upon the right of peoples."[11] Thereafter, Clemenceau sought to head off Anglo-American domination of the organization by rejecting Smuts' structure and advocating equality of all members, regardless of their size. Meanwhile, in the United States, Wilson's Republican opponents characterized the League as an instrument of future British global domination, noting Britain's insistence on separate memberships for the Dominions and India, none of which yet controlled its own foreign policy. On February 13, one day before Wilson returned to the United States for the final session of the lame-duck Congress and the inauguration of its successor, Makino raised the issue of racial equality during a discussion concerning a clause in the League Covenant guaranteeing freedom of religion. The segregationist

Wilson, backed by the British and Australians, rejected the Japanese appeal for a statement on race and instead deleted the religious freedom clause that had touched off the debate. The following day, hours before his departure, the League Covenant passed its first reading in a plenary session of the peace conference. Wilson's return to the United States, followed five days later by the wounding of Clemenceau in an assassination attempt, brought a lull in the activity of the peace conference. The Japanese continued to lobby for the Covenant to include an explicit statement of racial equality, while the French expressed doubts that, if the Rhineland remained in German hands, the proposed arms limitations and the collective security offered by the League would suffice to keep France safe. Clemenceau, upon his return to the conference, requested a supplementary treaty of alliance with Britain and the United States to provide France with the security it needed. Even though it violated a fundamental premise of the League of Nations – that alliances would no longer be necessary to ensure anyone's safety – Lloyd George agreed to give Clemenceau what he wanted on the condition that Wilson committed the United States as well. For the sake of saving the treaty and the League from a French veto, Wilson agreed to the alliance on March 14, the day he returned to Paris, knowing that a treaty pledging the United States to come to the aid of France in the event of a future German attack would be less controversial with Senate Republicans than the League itself. To remove a key issue from the upcoming American debate over the treaty, on April 11 Wilson secured Allied approval for a special clause in the Covenant acknowledging the validity of the rights the United States claimed in the Western Hemisphere under the Monroe Doctrine. That same day, the president resolved another controversial issue by dismissing, once and for all, the Japanese claim for a racial equality clause to be inserted in the Covenant. Wilson reasoned that, because the Covenant already acknowledged the equality of all *nations*, an explicit statement on the equality of their *peoples* was unnecessary. In the end, few changes were made to the League Covenant between its first reading in mid-February and final approval, on April 28, in a plenary session of the peace conference.

After March 25, the Council of Ten no longer met and the Japanese ceased to participate in discussions that did not pertain directly to their interests. Clemenceau, Lloyd George, Wilson, and Orlando convened as the Council of Four, accompanied only by secretaries and translators, to finalize the provisions regarding Germany. They agreed to give France not just Alsace-Lorraine but, for fifteen years, the resources of the coal-rich Saar Basin. Poland received a corridor of land consisting of the provinces of Posen (known as the Warthegau during World War II) and West Prussia. Danzig would serve as its outlet to the sea but, at Lloyd George's insistence, as a free city rather than annexed to Poland. A minor adjustment of the German-Belgian frontier gave the border areas of Eupen, Malmedy, and Moresnet to Belgium. Plebiscites were to determine the ultimate fate of the Saar and, more immediately, the German-Polish border in southern East Prussia, where *Freikorps* units had been sparring with the Polish

Army during the winter of 1918–19. On the German-Danish border, another plebiscite would determine the status of Bismarck's 1864 annexation of Schleswig; Denmark also stood to benefit, at least indirectly, from the internationalization of the Kiel Canal. The redistribution of Germany's colonies enriched all interested parties. In German East Africa, Britain received the future Tanzania, while Belgium added Rwanda and Burundi to the Belgian Congo. South Africa received German Southwest Africa, the future Namibia. Most of Cameroon and Togo went to France, but Britain received a strip of land along the western border of each colony, which it attached to its own possessions of Nigeria and Gold Coast (Ghana), respectively. Japan received Tsingtao with Kiaochow Bay and the rest of Germany's possessions on the Shantung Peninsula, along with all German Pacific islands north of the equator, while Australia received the former Kaiser Wilhelmsland (northeast New Guinea) and the adjacent Bismarck Archipelago, and New Zealand the former German Samoa. Except for the mainland Chinese lands inherited by Japan, all former German colonies would have the status of League of Nations mandates, technically under the trusteeship of their new masters until such time as they became self-governing.

The disarmament clauses required Germany to reduce its army to 100,000 men by March 1920, and thereafter to maintain at that strength a long-service professional force with no conscription or military training of the general adult male population. The treaty included specific limits on the numbers of rifles, machine guns, and artillery pieces Germany could maintain, and the numbers of bullets and shells it could have on hand. Forbidden weapons included poison gas, tanks, airplanes, and dirigibles. The Rhineland, defined as all German territory west of a line 30 miles (50 km) east of the Rhine River, became a demilitarized zone but otherwise remained under German authority. The navy had to give up all seventy-four ships then interned at Scapa Flow, sweep all mines it had laid in the Baltic and North Sea, and destroy its coastal fortifications. It was allowed to retain 15,000 naval personnel and a fleet of six antiquated pre-dreadnought battleships, six light cruisers, twelve destroyers, and twelve torpedo boats, a force roughly the size of the Swedish Navy. Future new warships could not exceed 10,000 tons displacement, and the navy could not have submarines. Germany retained the right to produce weapons to meet its own modest needs, but henceforth could neither export nor import arms.

The treaty acknowledged that the territorial losses would leave the Germans unable to "make complete reparation" for the destruction they had caused in the war, yet it obliged them to pay "for all damage done to the civilian population of the Allied and Associated Powers and to their property during the period of the belligerency,"[12] with the total reparations bill ultimately fixed (in 1921) at 132 billion gold marks, or US\$33 billion. The legal justification for reparations was embodied in Article 231: "Germany accepts the responsibility of Germany and her allies for causing all the loss and damage to which the Allied and Associated Governments and their nationals have been subjected as a consequence of the war imposed upon them by the aggression of Germany and her allies."[13] While German outrage at this "war guilt" clause became central to subsequent debates about the fairness of the treaty, the actual text was a statement of financial responsibility for loss and damage, and not a general statement of guilt.[14] Indeed, if the Allies had intended for the treaty to include as its centerpiece a statement of German guilt, it would have been in the first article or close to it, rather than the 231st article of 440.

The German delegates to the Paris Peace Conference finally saw the treaty on May 7. Because individual committees had worked out the details of the various military, territorial, and economic questions, the Allied delegations did not see the whole assembled as a single document until just hours before it was submitted to the Germans, and some British and American delegates had misgivings about it as soon as they saw it in its entirety. Harold Nicolson, who as an MP in the 1930s would join Churchill in opposing Britain's appeasement of Hitler, characterized the reparations demands as "a great crime" and "quite impossible to execute."[15] He joined many of his colleagues in lobbying Lloyd George to soften the terms. After reading the treaty, the foreign minister of the Weimar Republic, Count Ulrich von Brockdorff-Rantzau, condemned the economic provisions as a "death sentence" for the German people (see Box 14.2), rejected most of the territorial clauses, and accepted the disarmament provisions on the condition that the Allies include Germany as a founding member of the League of Nations.

In the wake of the German reaction, and responding to the concerns of his own delegation, Lloyd George called for a revision of the treaty while Clemenceau insisted that the Allies must stand firm. Their differences at this stage reflected the growing divergence of British and French public opinion. British anger against Germany had been focused on German behavior in general, sharpened by the loss of British civilian lives owing to its submarine and aerial bombing campaigns. When the war ended, these ended, and as the months wore on the public mood quickly softened. In contrast, French anger had been focused on German behavior toward France, grounded in the death and destruction wrought by the invasion and occupation of French soil. The end of the war left France liberated but the damage remained unrepaired and thus public anger remained strong. When Clemenceau refused to budge, Wilson agreed with him, conceding only that reparations could be revisited if Germany lacked the capacity to pay. He acknowledged that the terms concerning the Polish corridor and Rhineland were "hard, but the Germans earned that." The schoolmaster in him could not resist commenting that Germany had to learn its lesson, "that a nation should learn once and for all what an unjust war means in itself."[16] Lloyd George ultimately secured only minor revisions to the treaty: the elimination of the clause internationalizing the Kiel Canal and the addition of another plebiscite to determine the German-Polish border in Upper Silesia. In the "final memorandum" of the victors, dated June 16, Clemenceau informed Brockdorff-Rantzau that Germany must first prove itself by fulfilling the terms of the treaty before being considered for League membership. This reflected the

Box 14.2 Germany objects to the terms of the peace treaty

Excerpts from a memorandum of May 13, 1919, by Count Ulrich von Brockdorff-Rantzau (1869–1928), the Weimar Republic's first foreign minister, to France's Georges Clemenceau:

Under the terms of the peace treaty, Germany is to give up her Merchant Marine and vessels now under construction suitable for foreign commerce. Likewise, for five years, German shipyards are to construct primarily a tonnage destined for the Allied and Associated Governments. Moreover, Germany must renounce her Colonies; all her foreign possessions, all her rights and interests in the Allied and Associated countries, in their Colonies, Dominions or Protectorates are to be liquidated and credited to the payment of reparations, and are to be submitted to any other step of economic warfare that the Allied and Associated Powers may see fit to maintain or to take during the years of peace.

Moreover, the intensiveness of our agricultural production would be greatly decreased. On the one hand, the importation of certain raw materials indispensable for the production of fertilizer, such as phosphates, would be hampered; on the other hand, this industry would like all other industries suffer from the shortage of coal. For the Peace Treaty provides for the loss of almost a third of the production of our coal fields; in addition to that loss, enormous deliveries of coal to various Allied countries are imposed on us for ten years. In addition, in conformity to the Treaty, Germany will cede to her neighbors almost three-quarters of her ore production and three-fifths of her production of zinc.

After this privation of her produce, after the economic repression caused by the loss of her Colonies, of her Merchant Fleet and her foreign possession, Germany will no longer be in a position to import raw materials in sufficient quantities from abroad. As a matter of course an enormous part of German industry would thus be condemned to extinction. At the same time the need to import commodities would considerably increase, while the possibility of meeting this need would diminish to the same extent.

The enforcement of the Peace Conditions would therefore logically entail the loss of several million persons in Germany. This catastrophe would not be long in occurring, since the health of the population has been broken during the war by the blockade and during the armistice by the increased vigor of the starvation blockade … The Peace would impose upon Germany many times the number of human lives cost her by this war of four years and a half (1,750,000 killed by the enemy; almost a million as a result of the blockade) … Those who sign this treaty, will sign the death sentence of many millions of German men, women and children.

Source: Norman H. Davis, Box 44, Paris Peace Conference, Versailles Treaty, Manuscript Division, Library of Congress, available at www.ctevans.net/Versailles/Archives/Rantzau_reply.html.

position Wilson had come round to, even though initially he had believed Germany, once it became a democratic republic, should be offered founding membership. After Clemenceau gave the Germans the ultimatum to sign, Wilson left Paris for the first time since his return from the United States three months earlier, visiting Brussels on June 18–19 for a meeting with King Albert and a speech to the Belgian parliament. A side trip took him to the ruins of Louvain. The brief tour of Belgium, the war's most unmistakable victim of German aggression, confirmed in his own mind that he had done the right thing, and that the treaty was not too harsh.

Box 14.3 Clemenceau's moment of triumph

Excerpts from American journalist Harry Hansen's eyewitness account of the signing ceremony in the Hall of Mirrors at the Palace of Versailles, June 28, 1919:

At 2.45 o'clock [Clemenceau] moved up to the middle table and took the seat of the presiding officer ... almost on the exact spot where William I of Prussia stood when he was proclaimed German Emperor in 1871.

President Wilson entered almost immediately after M. Clemenceau and was saluted with discreet applause. The German delegation entered by way of the Hall of Peace and slipped almost unnoticed into its seats at this end of the hall.

It was led by Herr Mueller, a tall man with a scrubby little moustache, wearing black, with a short black tie over his white shirt front. The Germans bowed and seated themselves.

At 3.15 o'clock M. Clemenceau rose and announced briefly that the session was opened – "La séance est ouverte." He then spoke briefly in French as follows:

An agreement has been reached upon the conditions of the treaty of peace between the allied and associated powers and the German empire ... The signatures about to be given constitute an irrevocable engagement to carry out loyally and faithfully in their entirety all the conditions that have been decided upon. I therefore have the honor of asking Messieurs the German plenipotentiaries to approach to affix their signatures to the treaty before me.

Mueller came first, and then Bell, virtually unknown men, performing the final act of abasement and submission for the German people – an act to which they had been condemned by the arrogance and pride of Prussian Junkers, German militarists, imperialists, and industrial barons, not one of whom was present when this great scene was enacted.

The delegation from the United States was the first to be called up after the Germans. President Wilson rose, and as he began his walk to the historic table ... other delegates stretched out their hands to congratulate him. He came forward with a broad smile, and signed his name ...

At 3.50 o'clock all signatures had been completed, and the president of the conference announced:

Messieurs, all the signatures have been given. The signature of the conditions of peace between the Allied and Associated powers and the German Republic is an accomplished fact. The session is adjourned.

Source: Charles F. Horne, ed., *Source Records of the Great War*, vol. 7 (Indianapolis: The American Legion, 1931), 156–58.

Upon its return home from France, the German delegation recommended rejection of the treaty. Brockdorff-Rantzau in particular felt that the Allies were bluffing and would not resume military action, but Erzberger, a member of Scheidemann's cabinet as "minister for armistice affairs," argued that refusal to sign would bring an Allied march on Berlin (for which Foch, indeed, had contingency plans), and result in more suffering for Germany without securing better terms. At the same time, prolonging or worsening the crisis would only fuel radicalism within Germany and increase the likelihood of a civil war. Most of the SPD agreed with his reasoning, and his own Center Party accepted the treaty except for Articles 227 (providing for a trial of William II) and 231 (the "war guilt" clause). Ultimately, the cabinet ministers deadlocked 7:7

over what to do, and on June 19 the government resigned; the "no" votes included Scheidemann and Brockdorff-Rantzau, neither of whom wanted to bear the responsibility for signing the treaty. The SPD's Gustav Bauer and Hermann Mueller succeeded them as chancellor and foreign minister, respectively, in a new government that included the Center Party but not the DDP, whose Weimar representatives for the most part opposed signing. The national assembly ultimately voted 237:138 (48 abstentions) to accept the treaty with the Center Party's reservations on Articles 227 and 231. When the Allies rejected these qualifications, Bauer and Mueller consulted the head of the army, Groener, who advocated signing unconditionally. In the end, neither the SPD-Center coalition nor anyone else in Germany was prepared to follow a path of resistance, although, on the 21st, in far-off Scapa Flow, the skeleton crews manning the German High Sea fleet pulled off a final act of defiance, scuttling most of their interned warships rather than see them become prizes of the victors. On June 23 the Germans informed the Allies of their capitulation, and arrangements were made for the ceremony to take place five days later, the fifth anniversary of the assassination of Archduke Francis Ferdinand at Sarajevo. On the afternoon of the 28th, in the Hall of Mirrors at the Palace of Versailles, Mueller and the Center Party's Johannes Bell signed the treaty (see Box 14.3). While Erzberger did not sign the treaty, afterward he bore the brunt of domestic criticism for it, mostly from conservatives and nationalists who had never forgiven him for the peace resolution of 1917 or for signing the Armistice. Among true believers in the "stab in the back legend," he ranked first among the "November criminals" of 1918. In August 1921 he was assassinated by right-wing extremists.

Austria, Hungary, Bulgaria

The Treaty of Versailles served as a model for the Paris Peace Conference's treaties for Austria, Hungary, and Bulgaria, named for the suburbs of Paris in which they were signed. Each included clauses concerning arms limitations, reparations, and "war guilt," along with the full text of the Covenant of the League of Nations. Like Germany, all three lost territory, usually in blatant contravention of the principle of national self-determination, and in all cases, the losses, proportionally, were much more severe than those imposed upon the Germans. Austria and Hungary suffered, in particular, from Allied acceptance of the utterly inconsistent mixture of historical, ethnic, and strategic-geographic arguments the successor states and expanding neighbors used to justify their claims. Thus, Austria lost the Sudetenland and its 3 million ethnic Germans to Czechoslovakia because it was a part of the historic crownland of Bohemia, and the Sudeten Mountains provided Czechoslovakia with a defendable geographic border against Germany, while Hungary lost "Slovakia" (an entity that had never existed before) on purely ethnic grounds, ceding to Czechoslovakia all lands north of a line drawn to include not only the Slovak homeland but all mixed Slovak-Magyar lands. Similarly, Italy invoked strategic geography in annexing the South Tyrol up to the line of the Brenner Pass (even though this gave them 230,000 German Austrians), cited history to claim predominantly Croatian parts of the former Austrian provinces of Istria and Dalmatia (because they had belonged to the "Italian" Venetian Republic before 1797), and argued ethnicity in claiming the former Hungarian port of Fiume (Rijeka).

The Treaty of St. Germain (September 10, 1919) confirmed Austria's territorial losses to Czechoslovakia and Italy, and with them a population loss equaling nearly 4 million of the 10 million German Austrians. The treaty also limited Austria's army to 30,000 men and, worst of all, prohibited it from joining Germany in an *Anschluss*. Because, at the time, the SPD dominated the Weimar Republic, the Austrian Social Democrats took this news the hardest. Renner, lamenting that "superior forces" had prevented the *Anschluss*, asserted that "no one can ever, ever make us forget that we are Germans."[17] Austrians took some solace in the provision of a plebiscite for the mixed German-Slovenian border area of Carinthia, where fighting between Yugoslav forces and the Austrian *Volkswehr* and *Heimwehr* peaked in May–June 1919; the area eventually (October 1920) voted to join Austria. By then, the peace conference's treaty with Hungary also gave Austria most of the disputed Burgenland region. Renner signed the Treaty of St. Germain under protest. On the day of its ratification (October 17, 1919) the national assembly also passed the "Law Changing the Name of the German-Austrian Republic to That of the Austrian Republic," as required by the treaty. The law's opening words reflected the irony that independence had been forced upon Austria against its will: "The Alpine German lands determined in their frontiers by the Peace of Saint-Germain form a democratic republic under the name Republic of Austria."[18]

Hungary suffered a great deal more than Austria during the months of the peace conference, as the Allies missed their opportunity to lend stability to President Károlyi's Hungarian republic. Nicolson observed at the time that "Károlyi was regarded in Hungary as the proved friend of Western democracy; they imagined that a republic under his guidance would be welcomed almost as an ally. Instead of this he was snubbed and disregarded."[19] In March 1919, when word arrived from Paris that the Allies would allow Romania to keep all of Transylvania, Károlyi pivoted from Wilson to Lenin with a dramatic flourish: "I turn from the Paris Peace Conference to the proletariat of the world for justice and support. I resign, and transfer my authority to the proletariat of the peoples of Hungary."[20] Károlyi's regime gave way to the Hungarian Soviet Republic of Béla Kun. A university instructor of Jewish heritage, Kun had been a reserve officer in a Hungarian unit on the Eastern front, then a POW there; freed by the Bolshevik Revolution, he joined

the Red Army for the opening campaigns of the Russian Civil War before returning home to start a communist revolution in Hungary. The Allies rejected Kun's
regime, as did many Hungarians, who turned to former Austro-Hungarian admiral
Miklós Horthy as their leader. Horthy established an anti-communist resistance at
Szeged, near the Transylvanian frontier, but remained idle as the Allies delegated
the task of overthrowing Kun to neighboring Czechoslovakia and Romania, both
of which were eager to annex more Hungarian territory. A Romanian advance from
the southeast took Budapest in August 1919, toppling the Soviet republic. Horthy
marched on Budapest in November, after the Romanians withdrew. His followers
then launched a "White Terror" against Kun's supporters, which Horthy justified
by remarking that "an iron broom alone could sweep the country clean."[21] Horthy
proclaimed the restoration of the kingdom of Hungary under his regency, but only
to assert Hungary's legal claim to all of what had once been the Hungarian half of
the Dual Monarchy. In the short term the strategy failed, as his government had
little choice but to sign the Treaty of Trianon (June 4, 1920), in which Hungary
lost 72 percent of its former territory and 64 percent of its population, including
3.3 million of the 10.7 million Magyars. The treaty limited the Hungarian Army to
35,000 men.

The most bitter argument over former Austro-Hungarian territory did not involve
the postwar governments of Austria and Hungary. On April 24, 1919, Orlando and
Sonnino walked out of the Paris Peace Conference over the decision of the Allies
to give Yugoslavia the port of Fiume (Rijeka), an Italian city with a Croatian hinterland that had been Hungary's foothold on the Adriatic. Britain and France did
not support Orlando's claim to Fiume because it had not been promised to Italy in
the Treaty of London (1915). The United States rejected it because of the Croatian
hinterland that would have to go with the city, even though Wilson had already
agreed to give Italy almost all of Istria, with its population of Croatians and Slovenes.
The peace conference adopted Wilson's solution of making Fiume a "free city" like
Danzig, but Orlando had staked so much on the issue that his failure to deliver the
city to Italy caused his government to fall on June 23, with the result that he was
not present to sign the Treaty of Versailles five days later. In September 1919, Italian
nationalist Gabriele d'Annunzio's army of volunteers occupied Fiume, attempting
to force the issue. Finally, the following autumn, Italy and Yugoslavia signed the
Treaty of Rapallo (November 12, 1920), confirming Italy's possession of Istria, the
Dalmatian enclave of Zara (Zadar), and most of the Dalmatian islands, but leaving
Fiume a free city.

In contrast to the confusion that reigned in the former territories of Austria-
Hungary, Bulgaria acquiesced in its fate and accepted the terms of the Allies as soon
as they were presented. After inheriting the Bulgarian throne in October 1918, Boris
III formed a government of national reconciliation including popular Agrarian Party

leader Alexander Stamboliyski, who had been imprisoned during the war for his vocal opposition to Bulgaria's decision to join the Central Powers. Stamboliyski became prime minister one month before signing the Treaty of Neuilly (November 27, 1919) on behalf of his government. Bulgaria ceded Western Thrace to Greece and Dobruja to Romania, and thus lost its entire Aegean foothold along with some of its Black Sea coast. It also had to agree to an adjustment with Yugoslavia along their common Macedonian frontier. The treaty limited the Bulgarian armed forces to 33,000 men (including 10,000 gendarmes and 3,000 border police). Despised by Bulgaria's army and social-political elite, Stamboliyski remained popular with the country's rural masses despite his role in signing the treaty. In March 1920, his Agrarian Party won a majority of the seats in parliamentary elections, enabling him to continue as prime minister until his murder in a military coup in June 1923.

The Ottoman Empire and the Middle East

Wilson had little to say about the treaties for Austria, Hungary, and Bulgaria, and took little interest in the terms regarding the Ottoman Empire other than expressing sympathy for an independent Armenia. In February 1919 he also pressed the British and French to agree that the Arab lands taken from the Turks (like Germany's overseas colonies) would be treated as League of Nations mandates rather than outright conquests.

For six months after the Armistice of Mudros (October 30, 1918) the Turks remained oblivious to the growing sentiments among the Allies that the Ottoman Empire should be partitioned entirely. Like the dismemberment of Austria-Hungary, the process evolved piecemeal, out of the notions that Constantinople, the Bosporus, and Dardanelles should be under international control, territories inhabited by Greeks and Armenians annexed to those governments, and the Arab lands added to the British and French empires under the guise of mandates, notions that left little territory for a postwar Turkey. The storm broke in May 1919, when Britain, France, and the United States allowed Greek forces to occupy the predominantly Greek port of Smyrna (Izmir) on the Aegean coast of Asia Minor. The Allies thus forestalled a less justifiable Italian claim to the city, but the action inflamed Turkish opinion in a way that the earlier occupation of more peripheral territories and the Aegean islands had not, providing the impetus for Kemal to form a new government of national resistance.

For the next year Kemal and his followers, based at Samsun on the Black Sea, maintained an ambiguous relationship with the powerless regime of Sultan Mehmed VI at Constantinople. In February 1920 the Ottoman parliament, swayed by Kemal's party, approved the "National Pact," calling for the retention of Asia Minor, Eastern Thrace, and the Kurdish lands of northern Mesopotamia, including Mosul, and for plebiscites to determine the fate of Western Thrace, including Salonika, and the Armenian districts on the eastern fringe of Asia Minor. In March, the British responded by intervening in the name of the sultan and dispersing the parliament, prompting Kemal to convene a new national assembly at Ankara the following month. Thereafter, Kemal's government established the foundations of the modern Turkish state, based on the 1908 nationalist program of the Young Turks. Meanwhile, the sultan's government signed the Treaty of Sèvres (August 10, 1920), conceding to Greece almost all of Eastern Thrace and a large enclave in western Asia Minor, including Smyrna. The new Democratic Republic of Armenia received extensive lands in the northeast. Only the region around Ankara in north central Asia Minor remained under full control of the Turks. Constantinople, with the Bosporus and Dardanelles, became a demilitarized zone under international control, and southern Asia Minor was subdivided into Italian, French, and British spheres of influence. The treaty limited the Ottoman military to 50,700 men, most of whom were dispersed in a gendarmerie that could concentrate its forces only with Allied permission.

In the Arab lands, the peace conference ultimately confirmed the Sykes-Picot agreement of 1916, with minor revisions. Britain received Palestine and Mesopotamia (including Mosul) as mandates, while France received Syria and Lebanon. The French ejected Faisal from his throne in Damascus, but thanks to the British he became "king of Iraq" in Mesopotamia, with his capital at Baghdad. Incensed at his brother's eviction from Syria, Abdullah formed an army in the Hejaz to march on Damascus, but stopped in Amman after the British persuaded him to remain there as "emir of Transjordan," a new mandate carved out of the British-controlled Arab lands across the Jordan River from Palestine. At the same time, in Asia Minor, the humiliating terms of Sèvres made it easier for the Turkish nationalist government at Ankara to gain support; indeed, the treaty never took effect, for the new army Kemal formed was soon fighting the Greeks and others in what the Turks called their "War of Independence," which lasted into 1923.

Conclusion

The Paris Peace Conference officially closed on January 21, 1920, after Germany formally ratified the Treaty of Versailles, but Wilson, Lloyd George, and most of the foreign dignitaries had left the French capital the previous June, as soon as the Germans signed the treaty. After their departure, Clemenceau, the president of the conference, was the only head of government remaining. The visiting foreign ministers left with or shortly after the heads of government. Aside from the host country, most of the Allies designated ambassadors or undersecretaries to represent them in the conclusion of the Austrian, Hungarian, Bulgarian, and Turkish treaties.

Within hours of the signing of the Treaty of Versailles, Wilson boarded the *George Washington* at Brest for his return voyage to the United States. After his arrival in New York on July 8, he hastened to Washington, where he submitted the treaty to the US Senate two days later. He then planned an extensive tour of the country to make his case directly to the American people, urging them to insist that their senators ratify the treaty and accept US membership in the League of Nations. The president was not an old man, having celebrated his 62nd birthday during his visit to London the previous December, but since the age of 39 he had suffered a series of minor strokes and his physical constitution was far from robust. His health declined during the negotiations in Paris, where he had noticeably less stamina than the 77-year-old Clemenceau. When Wilson staked his political career on the ratification of the treaty and the League, he gambled his life and health as well.

As his secretary of state, Lansing, had feared, Wilson's direct involvement at the peace conference reduced him to the level of just another negotiator, albeit a very powerful one. In Paris, Wilson's principles became bargaining chips no less than this or that piece of territory, to be bartered away as needed in exchange for something deemed more valuable. He violated Point I of his own Fourteen Points by agreeing to Clemenceau's demand for an Anglo-Franco-American alliance, clearly a "private international understanding." He did not press the British on Point II and thus did not budge them from their opposition to "absolute freedom of the seas," which they had articulated before the Armistice. His own delegation took advantage of his lack of interest in economic matters to push for American advantages at odds with the goal of Point III, "the establishment of an equality of trade conditions." The arms reduction ideal expressed in Point IV was applied only to Germany and its defeated allies, though after demobilization both the United States and Britain would voluntarily reduce their armies to a size not much greater than Germany's 100,000-man force, and under Wilson's Republican successor, the United States would host the Washington Naval Conference (1921–22) and bring about a dramatic reduction in the size of the leading fleets. Wilson's Point V, concerning the resolution of colonial claims, nowhere took into account the wishes of the inhabitants of the colonies, as he had initially proposed. Point VI, calling for the evacuation of Russian territory occupied by the Central Powers under the Treaty of Brest-Litovsk, was jettisoned by Colonel House in the pre-Armistice talks, in the interest of containing Bolshevism; thereafter, the conference ignored Russian interests entirely, to Europe's future peril. Another source of future conflict stemmed from Wilson's abandonment of the principle of Point IX, calling for the determination of Italy's borders "along clearly recognizable lines of nationality." In the Italian case, and throughout east central Europe, nationality became just one consideration, along with historical claims and geographic-strategic imperatives, used to determine the new borders. Of course, many of those new borders had to be determined because Wilson, prior to the Armistice, had abandoned Point X and Point XII, concerning autonomy for the peoples of Austria-Hungary and the Ottoman Empire, in favor of their outright independence. Point XIII, calling for the restoration of a Poland with an outlet to the sea but also "inhabited by indisputably Polish populations," proved impossible, as the most obvious corridor to the Baltic included predominantly German territory and the German port of Danzig.

Thus, in the end, the only points absolutely honored were those concerning the evacuation of France and return of Alsace-Lorraine, along with the evacuation and restoration of the other Allied countries (Belgium, Serbia, Montenegro, and Romania) that had been occupied by the Central Powers. Wilson compromised or bargained away most of the other points in exchange for Allied agreement to accept Point XIV, and thus revolutionize the conduct of international relations by establishing "a general association of nations ... for the purpose of affording mutual guarantees of political independence and territorial integrity to great and small states alike."[22] The League of Nations was his creation, more so than any other international organization has ever been the creation of one man. It remained to be seen whether his own country would agree to join it.

SUGGESTIONS FOR FURTHER READING

Cooper, John Milton. *Woodrow Wilson: A Biography* (New York: Alfred A. Knopf, 2009).

Dallas, Gregor. *At the Heart of a Tiger: Clemenceau and His World, 1841–1929* (London: Macmillan, 1993).

Fromkin, David. *A Peace to End All Peace: Creating the Modern Middle East, 1914–1922* (New York: Henry Holt, 1989).

MacMillan, Margaret. *Paris 1919: Six Months that Changed the World* (New York: Random House, 2001).

Manela, Erez. *The Wilsonian Moment: Self-determination and the International Origins of Anti-colonial Nationalism* (Oxford: Oxford University Press, 2007).

Marks, Sally. "Mistakes and Myths: The Allies, Germany, and the Versailles Treaty, 1918–21," *Journal of Modern History* 85 (2013): 632–59.

Sharp, Alan. *The Versailles Settlement: Peacemaking after the First World War, 1919–1923* (New York: Palgrave Macmillan, 2008).

Shimazu, Naoko. *Japan, Race, and Equality: The Racial Equality Proposal of 1919* (London: Routledge, 1998).

Wilkinson, Richard. *Lloyd George: Statesman or Scoundrel* (London: I. B. Taurus, 2018).

NOTES

1. *The New York Times Current History: The European War, vol. 17: October–November–December 1918* (New York: The New York Times Publishing Company, 1919), 444.
2. *The New York Times Current History*, 445.
3. *The New York Times Current History: The European War*, vol. 17 (New York: New York Times Company, 1919), 445.
4. Quoted in Christopher Seton-Watson, *Italy from Liberalism to Fascism, 1870–1925* (London: Methuen, 1967), 505.
5. *The New York Times Current History*, 445.
6. Quoted in Seton-Watson, *Italy from Liberalism to Fascism*, 511.
7. Dáil Éireann, Message to the Free Nations of the World, January 21, 1919, available at www.oireachtas.ie/en/debates/debate/dail/1919-01-21/13/.
8. Robert Lansing, *The Peace Negotiations: A Personal Narrative* (Boston, MA: Houghton Mifflin, 1921), 22.
9. Raymond Poincaré's Opening Address, Paris Peace Conference, January 18, 1919, available at firstworldwar.com/source/parispeaceconf_poincare.htm.
10. Quoted in Lloyd E. Ambrosius, *Woodrow Wilson and the American Diplomatic Tradition: The Treaty Fight in Perspective* (Cambridge: Cambridge University Press, 1987), 35.
11. Quoted in Ambrosius, *Woodrow Wilson and the American Diplomatic Tradition*, 65.
12. Treaty of Versailles, Part VIII, Section I, Article 232, available at wwi.lib.byu.edu/index.php/Articles_231_-_247_and_Annexes.
13. Treaty of Versailles, Part VIII, Section I, Article 231, available at wwi.lib.byu.edu/index.php/Articles_231_-_247_and_Annexes.
14. Sally Marks, "Mistakes and Myths: The Allies, Germany, and the Versailles Treaty, 1918–21," *Journal of Modern History* 85 (2013): 642.
15. Nicolson to Vita Sackville-West, May 28, 1919, text in Harold Nicolson, *Peacemaking 1919*, revised edn. (London: Constable, 1945), 287.
16. Quoted in David Stevenson, *The First World War and International Politics* (Oxford University Press, 1988), 278.
17. Statement of Chancellor Renner Relative to the Union of German Austria to Germany, May 8, 1919, text in Malbone W. Graham, Jr., *New Governments of Central Europe* (New York: Henry Holt, 1926), 522.
18. Law Changing the Name of the German-Austrian Republic to That of the Austrian Republic, October 17, 1919, text in Graham, *New Governments of Central Europe*, 533.

19. Diary entry for April 4, 1919, in Nicolson, *Peacemaking 1919*, 244.

20. Károlyi's Resignation Manifesto, March 22, 1919, text in Graham, *New Governments of Central Europe*, 557.

21. Miklós Horthy, *Admiral Nicholas Horthy: Memoirs*, ed. Andrew L. Simon (Safety Harbor, FL: Simon Publishers, 2000), 348.

22. Text in Margaret MacMillan, *Paris 1919: Six Months that Changed the World* (New York: Random House, 2001), 495.

USS *George Washington* enters New York harbor

The USS *George Washington* brings President Wilson home from France, July 8, 1919. Originally a North German Lloyd liner of the same name, the 25,570-ton ship was employed on the Bremen-New York route from its maiden voyage in January 1909 until August 1914, when the British blockade forced the suspension of passenger service between Germany and the United States. Interned in New York harbor, the *George Washington* was recommissioned as an American troopship after the United States entered the war. Its top speed of 19 knots made it Wilson's choice for transportation to and from Europe during the peace conference.

15 Legacy

November 19, 1919	US Senate rejects Versailles Treaty.
November 1920	Assembly of League of Nations convenes in Geneva.
1922	Washington Naval Treaty limits size of largest fleets.
1924	Dawes Plan restructures German reparations payments.
1925	Geneva Protocol outlaws use of chemical and biological weapons.
1926	Germany joins League of Nations.
1929	US stock market crash marks onset of Great Depression.
1931	Japan invades Manchuria, quits League (1933).
1932	Iraq becomes first League mandate granted independence.
1933	Germany quits League, denounces Versailles Treaty.
1939	Onset of World War II in Europe; League suspends operations.
1960–90	Former German colonies granted independence.

For the post-1945 generation throughout much of the world, the sheer scale of the death and destruction in World War II caused World War I to become a forgotten chapter of history. For Germany, Russia, the United States, and Japan, World War II remains a more significant historical experience than World War I, for its role in making or breaking those countries as world powers, in the process generating many more casualties. Yet for a number of the belligerents of World War II, including some of major significance, the death toll of that conflict, especially for men in uniform, did not approach the carnage of World War I. In those countries, most notably Britain, Canada, Australia, and New Zealand, but also France and Italy, the remembrance and commemoration of World War I remains an important part of national life. For people living along the former static fronts, into the twenty-first century the war remains impossible to forget, as tons of shells continue to be collected from their yards and fields on an annual basis, an "iron harvest" that includes the occasional live round and thus still claims at least a victim or two every year.

General Consequences of the War for Europe

World War I featured action in every ocean and on most continents, and yet most of the fighting, dying, and destruction had occurred in Europe, with the vast majority of the dead being not just Europeans but European males in the prime of their lives. Afterward marriage rates did not decline, but the loss of so many men necessitated changes in marriage patterns – for example, British women marrying men below their social class or from outside their region of the country, or French women marrying men the same age or younger – and birth rates fell across the continent, never to rise again. The tens of millions of young men taken from the home front during the war years and the millions who never returned led to Europe as a whole producing several million fewer children. For the majority who survived the war, the experience of it, combined with the turbulent postwar economy, perpetuated the low birth rates and, a generation later, the greater calamity of World War II only confirmed the permanence of the downward trend. From around 1700 until the outbreak of World War I Europe had sustained a remarkable population boom that fueled its rise to world domination; indeed, by 1914 roughly 40 percent of all humans were white Europeans or of white European ancestry. World War I ended that boom, and over the following decades the tremendous growth of the Asian, African, and Latin American populations transformed the world into a place Europeans and their descendants could no longer dominate.

Europe's demographic shock of 1914–19 naturally weakened its workforce and left its economy significantly less productive in the short term. In 1920 Europe's overall manufacturing output stood at just 77 percent of the level for 1913. For the world as a whole, however, the figure for 1920 exceeded 93 percent of the 1913 mark, and by 1922 would nearly equal it, owing to the wartime boom in the United States (and to a lesser extent, Japan) that continued into the postwar era. Peace found most countries awash in debt, as most wartime expenses had been covered with loans rather than by raising taxes, on the assumption that indemnities from the losers would make good their deficits. Only Britain had raised taxes significantly, leading generations of scholars to ignore the fact that it, too, financed most of its war effort with loans.[1] In Germany and Austria-Hungary tens of millions of people had invested their savings in war bonds that were worthless in defeat. On the winning side, both France and Italy were seriously in debt; within the Allied coalition, France and Britain owed the United States, France owed Britain, and everyone else owed France and Britain.

The redrawing of the map of Europe in 1918–19 led to a net increase of six fully independent states, as Montenegro was subordinated to Serbia in the new Yugoslavia, Austria separated from Hungary, and Czechoslovakia, Finland, Poland, and the three Baltic republics were created. The internal revolutions were even more dramatic. The Europe of 1914 included just two republics, and among the six great powers, only France had a republican form of government. In contrast, the Europe of 1919 featured eleven republics, and among the five most significant states just Britain and Italy remained monarchies. The emergence of new countries in central and eastern Europe left the continent with twenty-seven different currencies in 1919, compared with fourteen in 1914, and an additional 12,500 miles (20,000 km) of international borders. Especially in the former Austria-Hungary, many of these new frontiers blocked raw materials from factories, farms from consumers, and agricultural or industrial exports from seaports, all factors that would delay or prevent the recovery of the economy. Within a generation, the same borders would have to be defended militarily, and most could not be, for most of the new or newly expanded countries proved to be too poor or too weak to protect the territories they had claimed in 1918–19.

The Western Democracies

Superficially Britain appeared to have emerged from World War I in a position of unprecedented strength. Its empire and army had never been larger, and its navy remained the world's strongest. But Britain's manufacturing output did not recover to its 1913 level until 1929, later than any other European power, only to have the Great Depression knock it down again, not to surpass the 1913 mark for good until 1934. In addition to supplementing its wartime borrowing with taxation, Britain had helped finance its war effort by liquidating investments overseas and curtailing private lending overseas. Thus, Britain sacrificed a degree of its global economic influence (which it would never regain) in order to ensure that it would not emerge from the war as a net debtor, only to find that being a creditor was a dubious asset in the interwar years, when so many debtors defaulted on their wartime loans.[2] Britain had suffered less of a demographic shock than Germany and especially France, and yet the disproportionately high death toll among educated young men during the first half of the war, before conscription, led many to lament this "lost generation"[3] and wonder if victory had been worth the cost. Reflecting the pervasive gloom and sense of loss, wartime personal notices of this variety continued into the postwar years: "Lady, fiancé killed, will gladly marry officer totally blinded or otherwise incapacitated by the War."[4] The doubts that had plagued the British delegation in the last weeks of the Paris Peace Conference continued after the Treaty of Versailles was signed. The prime minister himself had serious misgivings, remarking prophetically that "we shall have to do the whole thing over again in twenty-five years, at three times the cost."[5] Thanks to Lloyd George, Sir Edward Grey eventually became the whipping-boy of the second-guessers. His criticism of the former foreign secretary set the tone for the conventional wisdom of British foreign policy during the 1930s, that Britain in 1914 had not done as much as it should have to prevent the war from occurring and next time around must do better. Such reasoning provided the underpinning for the appeasement policy of Neville Chamberlain (see Box 15.1).

In the domestic arena, Lloyd George's decision to extend the wartime coalition into the postwar era brought the demise of his own Liberal Party as a leading factor in British politics. After shoring up Lloyd George until 1922, the Conservatives triumphed in the next general election, in which rival Liberal factions headed by Lloyd George and Asquith together won less than 20 percent of the House of Commons. The Labour Party thus became the second strongest party in British politics, and the Liberals have never again ranked in the top two. Before he left office, Lloyd George resolved the Irish question by allowing the six predominantly Protestant counties of Ulster to remain in the United Kingdom, while the remaining twenty-six counties received Home Rule as the Irish Free State. The arrangement, ratified in January 1922, became possible after a truce the previous July ended the low intensity War for Irish Independence, during which the IRA lost 550 dead and the British Army and police more than 700 in thirty months of fighting. As the fifth Dominion, the Irish Free State received control over its own foreign policy under the Statute of Westminster (1931) but, unlike the other four, it broke with Britain and remained neutral during World War II.

Relative to the size of its population, France suffered the greatest demographic shock from World War I, more than twice as severe as that of Britain, to a country that already had Europe's lowest birth rate. Indeed, the sheer number of men lost complicated postwar debates over suffrage for women; proposals to enfranchise widows and mothers of fallen soldiers led nowhere, and ultimately French women did not get the vote until after World War II. Just 6 percent of France's territory had been occupied during the war, but these devastated lands had been home to most of its steel industry and coal

Box 15.1 Versailles, Chamberlain, and appeasement

Excerpts from prime minister Neville Chamberlain's speech at Birmingham, March 17, 1939, two days after Hitler dismembered what remained of Czechoslovakia. He defended the Munich Agreement of the previous autumn by arguing that Czechoslovakia, as constituted under the peace settlement of 1919, could not be preserved even by war:

When I decided to go to Germany I never expected that I was going to escape criticism. Indeed, I did not go there to get popularity. I went there first and foremost because, in what appeared to be an almost desperate situation, that seemed to me to offer the only chance of averting a European war. And I might remind you that, when it was first announced that I was going, not a voice was raised in criticism. Everyone applauded that effort. It was only later, when it appeared that the results of the final settlement fell short of the expectations of some who did not fully appreciate the facts … that the attack began, and even then it was not the visit, it was the terms of settlement that were disapproved.

Well, I have never denied that the terms which I was able to secure at Munich were not those that I myself would have desired. But, as I explained then, I had to deal with no new problem. This was something that had existed ever since the Treaty of Versailles – a problem that ought to have been solved long ago if only the statesmen of the last twenty years had taken broader and more enlightened views of their duty. It had become like a disease which had been long neglected, and a surgical operation was necessary to save the life of the patient.

After all, the first and the most immediate object of my visit was achieved. The peace of Europe was saved; and, if it had not been for those visits, hundreds of thousands of families would today have been in mourning for the flower of Europe's best manhood. I would like once again to express my grateful thanks to all those correspondents who have written me from all over the world to express their gratitude and their appreciation of what I did then and of what I have been trying to do since.

Really I have no need to defend my visits to Germany last autumn, for what was the alternative? Nothing that we could have done, nothing that France could have done, or Russia could have done could possibly have saved Czechoslovakia from invasion and destruction. Even if we had subsequently gone to war to punish Germany for her actions, and if after the frightful losses which would have been inflicted upon all partakers in the war we had been victorious in the end, never could we have reconstructed Czechoslovakia as she was framed by the Treaty of Versailles.

Source: First published in *The British War Blue Book*, Miscellaneous No. 9 (1939), Documents concerning German-Polish Relations and the Outbreak of Hostilities between Great Britain and Germany on September 3, 1939, available at avalon.law.yale.edu/wwii/blbk09.asp.

mines. The resources of Alsace-Lorraine and the Saar helped to compensate for the ruined mines and foundries of the former war zone, enabling France to surpass its 1913 level of manufacturing productivity by 1924, years earlier than Britain or Germany. The financial crisis would be harder to resolve, as France was scheduled to receive the greatest share of German reparations and, without these payments, could not repair the physical damage caused by the invasion and occupation (which the Reparations Commission estimated at US$6.5 billion) and also repay its war debts to Britain (US$3 billion) and the United States (US$4 billion). On the other side of the ledger, France had been the principal creditor for Imperial Russia, which owed it US$3.6 billion as of 1917, a debt the Soviet government had no intention of paying. Thus, the war had left France considerably weaker than it had been in 1914 and more dependent than any other power on the timely execution of the economic and collective security provisions of the 1919 peace settlement.

In postwar French politics, Clemenceau's center-right coalition (running as the *Bloc National*) won a clear majority in legislative elections in 1919. Meanwhile, on the Left, the SFIO declined from 17 percent of the seats in 1914 to just 11 percent, and in 1920 lost fifteen of its sixty-eight deputies to the new French Communist Party. When Poincaré's term as president expired in 1920, Clemenceau fully expected to succeed him, because the indirectly elected executive typically was an elder statesman, and at 79 he fitted that description better than Poincaré had. The outgoing president had been just 52 when elected in 1913 and, during the 1920s, returned to politics to serve four more times as premier. But as was the case with Churchill in Britain a generation later, the respected wartime leader found himself rejected in peacetime. He retired shortly after his failed presidential bid, and France would not have another leader of his fortitude until de Gaulle.

Europe's Revisionist Powers

From the perspective of June 1919, Germany appeared to have little hope of ever securing a revision of the Versailles Treaty, but the conditions that would make revision possible already existed. Relative to Europe as a whole, Germany was stronger in 1919 than it had been in 1914, despite its huge reparations bill, dramatic limits on its armed forces, and the cession of 13 percent of its territory. During World War I the Germans had inflicted far more damage on their enemies than they had sustained. Russia had collapsed in defeat and revolution, while France, in victory, had suffered a demographic shock far greater than Germany's, and Britain had seen its position of global financial and economic leadership pass to the United States. The victorious Allies inadvertently handed Germany another advantage by breaking up Austria-Hungary; before the war 50 percent of the Dual Monarchy's trade had been with Germany, and afterward it would be even easier for the Germans to dominate the economy of a divided east central Europe. Germany enjoyed the small consolation of winning most of the plebiscites held in 1920–21 under the treaty, securing central Schleswig, all of southern East Prussia, and most of Upper Silesia. Only northern Schleswig voted to leave Germany, in favor of Denmark.

In German domestic politics, the Right recovered in time for the 1920 Reichstag elections. Thereafter the SPD was excluded from most governments even though it remained the largest party until 1932. On the Left, the KPD never forgave the SPD for the suppression of the Spartacist Revolt and refused to cooperate with it, even, ultimately, against the rise of Nazism. Meanwhile, widespread belief in the "stab in the back legend" and in the injustice of the treaty did not help Ludendorff, whose premature association with the Nazis during the Munich ("Beer Hall") Putsch of 1923 set him on the road to political obscurity, but two years later it enabled the Right to elect Hindenburg president of the republic. Nevertheless, a politician as conservative as the DVP's Gustav Stresemann (foreign minister 1923–29) concluded that Germany must fulfill its Versailles obligations. Following the reparations crisis and hyperinflation of the early 1920s, Germany adhered to the treaty and, in 1926, Stresemann brought Germany into the League of Nations. Unfortunately, in October 1929 his death, coinciding with the onset of the Great Depression, set Germany on a course to Nazi rule. With economic issues to supplement his patriotic indignation, Adolf Hitler, a product of the unique circumstances of World War I, seized power by making the Nazis the strongest party in the fragmented spectrum of Weimar politics. The final plebiscite authorized by the Treaty of Versailles, determining the fate of the Saar Basin in 1934, gave Nazi Germany its first victory in the international arena, as 91 percent of the Saar's population opted for rule by Hitler.

Under the Nazi dictatorship the vast majority of Germans appear to have accepted Hitler's view that the Left and the Jews were responsible for the lost war, but their rejection of war guilt came much sooner. Recognizing the relevance of the question to a possible future revision of the Versailles settlement, the Weimar Republic published forty volumes of Imperial German diplomatic documents under the title *Die Grosse Politik der Europäischen Kabinette* (1922–27). The other great powers followed suit, but France and Britain took much longer to produce collections that seemed less comprehensive. Thus, the German position won sympathy among academicians abroad, especially in the United States; decades passed before researchers proved that the collection omitted key documents that incriminated Germany. Meanwhile, in 1923 Alfred von Wegerer founded a scholarly journal, *Die Kriegsschuldfrage* (The War Guilt Question), dedicated to rebutting the charge. While Wegerer was an amateur historian, his journal published pieces by some of Germany's leading scholars, who rallied to the national cause in peacetime much as they had during the war. Ironically, the denial of responsibility for World War I took on a greater significance after World War II, when it became key to rebutting the argument that there was a continuity to modern German history, featuring an ever more aggressive foreign policy from Bismarck through to Hitler.

Italy's weakness had kept it from playing a more decisive part in World War I and, afterward, enabled the Allies to break some of the promises they had made to the Italians regarding territorial compensations. They did so not imagining Italy would become a significant voice for treaty revision and, ultimately, an ally of

Germany in the next world war. Aside from being treated as France's equal at the Washington Naval Conference (1921–22), Italy received no more respect immediately after the Paris Peace Conference than during it. Italy's manufacturing output recovered to 1913 levels by 1922, faster than any of the other European powers, but mostly because it had been so low to begin with. As of 1920, Italy's small farmers still accounted for 50 percent of the country's workforce and 40 percent of its gross national product, and because almost all of the new wartime industries had been built in the already industrialized north, the country's traditional north-south divide grew even greater.

The feeling – largely correct – that the Allies had treated Italy with contempt at the peace conference embittered public opinion and accelerated the collapse of its constitutional political system, enabling Mussolini's Fascist Party, another product of the unique circumstances of World War I (see Box 15.2), to bully its way into power in the "March on Rome" of October 1922. During their brief postwar rise to power the Fascists made the redemption of Fiume one of their focal points. After the postwar establishment of the "free city," Italian troops expelled D'Annunzio from Fiume, but a Fascist coup early in 1922 returned the city to Italian control. In 1924, Mussolini officially joined the camp of the revisionists, legitimizing this second occupation by coercing Yugoslavia into an agreement partitioning the free city. The Italians received Fiume and a coastal corridor linking it to Italy, leaving the Yugoslavs with the city's Croatian hinterland. Fiume and Istria would not become part of Yugoslavia until after World War II, when Tito's Partisans seized them.

Box 15.2 **World War I and the emergence of Fascism**

Benito Mussolini (1883–1945) describes the founding of the Italian Fascist Party, March 23, 1919:

Those who came to the meeting for the constitution of the Italian Fascisti of Combat (*Fasci di Combattimento*) used few words. They did not exhaust themselves by laying out dreams. Their aim seemed clear and straight-lined. It was to defend the victory at any price, to maintain intact the sacred memory of the dead, and the admiration not only for those who fell and for the families of those who were dead but for the mutilated, for the invalids, for all those who had fought. The prevalent tone, however, was of anti-socialist character, and as a political aspiration, it was hoped a new Italy would be created that would know how to give value to the victory and to fight with all its strength against treason and corruption, against decay within and intrigue and avarice from without.

The first fighting Fascisti were formed mostly of decided men. They were full of will and courage. In the first years of the anti-socialist, anti-communist struggle, the … war veterans played an important role.

Source: Benito Mussolini, *My Autobiography* (New York: Charles Scribner, 1928), 70–71.

Russia became, arguably, the biggest loser of the Paris Peace Conference, after the Allies denounced the Treaty of Brest-Litovsk, then redistributed the lands Russia had lost to the Central Powers because of it. This action violated the spirit of Point VI of Wilson's Fourteen Points, which ends with a prophetic warning: "The treatment accorded Russia by her sister nations in the months to come will be the acid test of their good will, of their comprehension of her needs as distinguished from their own interests, and of their intelligent and unselfish sympathy."[6] The Allies failed this test miserably, first by landing troops at the White Sea ports and Vladivostok, then (after the Central Powers withdrew) on the Black Sea coast, in each case formally or informally supporting the White armies seeking to overthrow the new Soviet Russian regime. In the Armistice negotiations the Allies, in the interest of fighting Bolshevism, had even agreed to allow Germany to keep troops in the eastern European lands Russia had lost at Brest-Litovsk until such time as Allied forces could be deployed to replace them or to shore up the armies of the newly established states.

The creation of the Red Army by Trotsky, a man with no military experience, ranks among the most remarkable feats of the World War I era. By the end of the Russian Civil War Lenin's regime had crushed internal dissent and managed to reconquer more than half of the ceded territory, and made Ukraine, Belarus, and the Caucasus states republics of the Soviet Union when it was created in 1922, though the Polish-Soviet War (1919–21) left western Ukraine and western Belarus in Polish hands. The Bolsheviks survived by consciously adopting the mentality and the ruthless methods of the Jacobins of 1793–94; while their reign of terror under Lenin paled in comparison with what would come later under Stalin, its targets included key elements of the old regime such as the dynasty and aristocracy, the Orthodox Church, and leaders of the former tsarist army. Prominent generals murdered by the Bolsheviks, or who died fighting against them, included Alekseev, Evert, Ivanov, Kornilov, Ragoza, Rennenkampf, Ruzsky, Yanushkevich, and Zhilinsky.

The Bolshevik takeover in Russia and the establishment of the Soviet Union were direct legacies of World War I. Without Lenin in Russia, the Bolsheviks would never have overthrown the Provisional Government, and without the specific constellation of strategic factors facing Germany in the spring of 1917, he would have remained in Switzerland while the opportunity to seize power passed. In the aftermath of World War II, when Stalin possessed the military might to do so, Russia reasserted its authority over much of the territory Lenin had relinquished during World War I and failed to reconquer in the Civil War. Within the context of the dawning Cold War the Western world characterized Stalin's border adjustments with Finland, Poland, and Romania, and the annexation of the three Baltic states as "spreading communism," yet aside from the northern half of East Prussia (where Königsberg became Kaliningrad) and the Carpatho-Ukraine (the eastern tip of interwar Czechoslovakia) all of his conquests had belonged to Imperial Russia in 1914. Thus, under Soviet rule, Russia was the country most successful in revising the terms of the 1919 peace settlement, although the independence of the non-Russian republics after 1991 left Stalin's gains (except for the Kaliningrad enclave) once again outside Russia's control.

Postwar East Central Europe

In east central Europe, World War I forever changed the relationship among its initial belligerents, Austria-Hungary and Serbia, leaving in its wake the truncated independent states of Austria and Hungary as neighbors of a Serbian-dominated Yugoslavia. In postwar Austria, a German state prohibited from joining Germany, pro-*Anschluss* sentiments persisted. As late as 1921 Salzburg (99 percent) and Tyrol (98 percent) voted overwhelmingly for union with Germany in provincial plebiscites. For the most part, however, the *Anschluss* ban strengthened the hand of the only party that wanted an independent Austria, the Christian Socialists, who held the chancellorship from 1920 until 1938, when Nazi Germany finally annexed Austria. During those years the professional long-service army prescribed by the peace treaty joined the paramilitary *Heimwehr* to become a bastion of Austrian conservatism, while veterans of the disbanded *Volkswehr* migrated to the *Schutzbund*, a socialist paramilitary that had no equivalent in the Weimar Republic. These forces clashed in 1934 in a brief civil war, which crushed the Austrian Left before the advent of Nazi rule, but the socialist Renner, founding chancellor of Austria's First Republic, survived to become founder of the Second Republic in 1945, and served as its first president until his death in 1950.

In Hungary, Admiral Horthy's restoration of the kingdom prompted Charles to make two quixotic postwar attempts to return to power there, both during 1921, both without the support of Horthy, who knew the Allies would never allow a Habsburg to reign in Budapest. After the second attempt the Allies deported the deposed monarch to Madeira, where he died of pneumonia in 1922, at the age of 34. Eventually, Horthy's alliance with Nazi Germany enabled him to recover some of the lands Hungary lost in the Treaty of Trianon, and he remained regent of the kingdom without a king until Hitler overthrew him in 1944 after he attempted to quit the Axis. Meanwhile, Charles became more admired over time, as the only head of state of any of the great powers of World War I to have seriously sought an end to the conflict, thus demonstrating that at least in the long run, the peacemakers are indeed blessed. At his Mass of Beatification in 2004, placing him on the path to recognition as a saint in the Roman Catholic Church, Pope John Paul II called the last Habsburg emperor "an example for all of us, especially for those who have political responsibilities in Europe today."[7]

Among all the belligerents of World War I, Serbia arguably emerged as the biggest winner. The decision of Serbia's leaders to risk a general war rather than accept the Austro-Hungarian ultimatum in its entirety had resulted in the country's complete defeat and occupation by the Central Powers in 1915, but just three years later their boldness was vindicated. Victory brought the fulfillment of national goals beyond the wildest dreams of the most chauvinistic Serbs of 1914, in the incorporation not just of Bosnia but also Croatia and Slovenia into a Yugoslavia under Serbian domination. The belligerents of World War I learned a variety of lessons from the bloody conflict of 1914–18, but thanks to the support of the Entente powers, the Serbs learned that they could set a continent ablaze in pursuit of their own national goals and emerge victorious in the long run. This reckless strain of Serbian nationalism would re-emerge in the early 1990s, following the collapse of Yugoslavia, much to the horror of Europe and the rest of the world.

The United States, the Treaty, and the League

Wilson's quest to get the American people to accept an active, leading role for the United States in the postwar world began in earnest on September 3, 1919, when he left Washington on a national tour to mobilize public opinion behind the Treaty of Versailles and the League of Nations. He made his case not in terms of the national interest or practical realities, but of American ideals and values, identifying the treaty and the League with the common civilization Americans and Europeans shared. As one historian has explained, Wilson deliberately "internationalized the heritage of his country."[8] During and after the war he repeatedly emphasized the roots of the United States in a broader Western civilization, handed down from the ancient Near East via Greece, Rome, and centuries of European history, driven forward by the quest for greater human liberty. It was an academic argument that Wilson, the former professor, felt comfortable making, an argument already piloted in a "War Issues Course" taught at more than 500 US colleges and universities in the autumn term of 1918, for young men enrolled in the Students Army Training Corps (SATC), forerunner of the Reserve Officer Training Corps (ROTC). The course continued after the war, evolving into the survey of Western civilization that became a standard requirement at US colleges and universities during the interwar years.[9]

Unfortunately for Wilson, he was not making his case to the small minority of Americans with access to higher education, but to the public as a whole, including those predisposed to believe that World War I had been someone else's quarrel. The lesson, therefore, had to be tailored to the audience, if necessary with a strong dose of old-time religion that the president, son of a Presbyterian clergyman, had no qualms about mobilizing in the service of his cause. He did not hesitate to invoke the Almighty in presenting the outcome of the war to the Senate on July 10, 1919: the treaty, the League, and the American role in shaping them had "come about by no plan of our conceiving, but by the hand of God … America shall in truth show the way."[10] Thus, Wilson's vision of American exceptionalism was not of a country so unique that it could remain isolated, as if the rest of the world did not matter to it, rather of a country ordained by God to save Western civilization.

In the Senate, most Democrats defended the president's position that the conclusion of peace with Germany could not be separated from the creation of the League of Nations, and that ratification was an all-or-nothing proposition. Henry Cabot Lodge and the Republican majority opposed the treaty as written and, within two months, proposed forty-nine amendments and "reservations" to the text. There is no doubt their goal was to kill the treaty, at least as far as the United States was concerned, for the new order it created could not reasonably accommodate a major power that opted out of so many of its provisions. During the debate, the president's opponents bolstered their case by quoting the vicious criticism of John Maynard Keynes, one of the economists in Lloyd George's entourage at the peace conference, whose newly published *The Economic Consequences of the Peace* predicted that the reparations demanded of Germany would wreck the European economy (see Perspectives 15.1). South Africa's Jan Smuts later remarked that Keynes "strengthened the Americans against the League" and thus "helped to finish Wilson."[11]

Wilson undertook his speaking tour against the advice of his physician, who did not think he could bear the strain. His health held up until September 25, when he collapsed from exhaustion in Pueblo, Colorado, following an emotional speech (see Box 15.3), his fortieth in just twenty-two days, on a tour that had reached nearly 10,000 miles. Back in Washington a week later, Wilson suffered a debilitating stroke; he would spend most of the last seventeen months of his presidency in his bedroom at the White House. The Republicans enjoyed a 49:47 majority in the Senate, but when the treaty and the League came to a vote on November 19, they defeated it by 53:38 with five abstentions. Proponents of the treaty succeeded in bringing it back for a second vote on March 19, 1920, when it again met with defeat. The Anglo-Franco-American alliance, conceded to Clemenceau to buy his approval of the treaty and the League, died in a Senate committee in December 1919, after Wilson refused to proceed with it unless the treaty and the League were approved first. Ironically, because Lodge and other Republican supporters of the war and of an active peacetime foreign policy viewed the alliance as an alternative (rather than a supplement) to the League, it would have passed if brought to a vote.

Reflecting this perspective, at the Republican convention in June 1920, Lodge denounced his party's drift toward isolationism on the grounds that "the world needs us too much."[12] But the same convention nominated an isolationist, Senator Warren Harding of Ohio, as its presidential candidate, and approved a party platform that denounced the League of Nations, while the Democrats nominated Governor James Cox, also of Ohio, who defended the president's record. The November 1920 election signaled a clear rejection of Wilson's foreign policy by the American public. Harding won more than 60 percent of the popular vote, and isolationist candidates also helped put Congress even more firmly in Republican hands (House 302:131, Senate 59:37). In lieu of a peace treaty, in July 1921 a joint resolution of Congress declared an end to the state of war between Germany and the United States. By then, the US contribution to the Allied occupation of the Rhineland had dwindled to fewer than 10,000 men, the last of whom were withdrawn in February 1923. Thereafter, in the Dawes Plan (1924) and Young Plan (1930), the United States involved itself in revising the payment schedule of Germany's reparations to the Allies, but only to facilitate the repayment of war debts owed by the Allies to the United States. The Dawes and Young plans also reflected America's postwar domination of global financial markets. The war transformed the United States from a net debtor to the world's leading creditor, and New York replaced London as the center of the world economy. Capping an industrial boom that contrasted sharply with Europe's postwar malaise, in 1929 the manufacturing output of the United States surpassed its 1913 level by more than 80 percent, enough to account for a staggering 43 percent of global output.

Perspectives 15.1: The reparations controversy

Britain's John Maynard Keynes (1883–1946) ranks with Adam Smith and Karl Marx as one of the most important economists of modern times. He first became internationally known for his criticism of reparations in his book *The Economic Consequences of the Peace* (1919):

It is, in my judgement, as certain as anything can be … that Germany cannot pay anything approaching this sum … There is a great difference between fixing a definite sum, which though large is within Germany's capacity to pay and yet to retain a little for herself, and fixing a sum far beyond her capacity, which is then to be reduced at the discretion of a foreign Commission acting with the object of obtaining each year the maximum which the circumstances of that year will permit. The first still leaves her with some slight incentive for enterprise, energy and hope. The latter skins her alive year by year in perpetuity, and however skillfully and discreetly the operation is performed, with whatever regard for not killing the patient in the process, it would represent a policy which … the judgement of men would soon pronounce to be one of the most outrageous acts of a cruel victor in civilized history.

Source: John Maynard Keynes, *The Economic Consequences of the Peace* (London: Macmillan, 1919), 167–68. (Reproduced with permission of Palgrave Macmillan.)

• • • •

American historian Sally Marks (1931–2018) argued that Germany could have paid its reparations but chose not to, and through a variety of tactics, abetted in particular by the British, succeeded in turning international opinion against the French and against the economic provisions of the Treaty of Versailles:

From start to finish, Germany understandably did not want to pay and was doggedly determined not to pay. This was one of several major reasons from the outset why no wholehearted effort was made to reform Germany's budget and currency; blaming financial chaos on reparations might yield a reduction of the debt. Another consistent German approach was to stress difficulties: if Germany lost territory or if it were impoverished, it could not pay … Throughout the history of reparations, misdirection and propaganda, both designed to conceal reality, remained constant, as did technical sleight of hand … Such technical intricacy … combined with deliberate misdirection, misled not only historians but a great number of people at the time. Journalists, the public, and the intelligentsia, especially in Britain, accepted constantly repeated statements without real reflection … forgetting that Germany's failure to pay said nothing about its capacity to do so.

Source: Sally Marks, "Smoke and Mirrors: In Smoke-Filled Rooms and the Galerie des Glaces," in Manfred Franz Boemeke, Gerald D. Feldman, and Elisabeth Gläser (eds.), *The Treaty of Versailles: A Reassessment after 75 Years* (Cambridge: Cambridge University Press, 1998), 364, 366.

Box 15.3 **Peace and politics: Henry Cabot Lodge versus Woodrow Wilson**

For Senate majority leader Henry Cabot Lodge, the fight against the treaty and the League of Nations was a conservative Republican's fight for US nationalism versus internationalism:

You may call me selfish if you will, conservative or reactionary, or use any other harsh adjective you see fit to apply, but an American I was born, an American I have remained all my life. I can never be anything else but an American, and I must think of the United States first, and when I think of the United States first in an arrangement like this I am thinking of what is best for the world, for if the United States fails, the best hopes of mankind fail with it.

… Internationalism, illustrated by the Bolshevik and by the men to whom all countries are alike provided they can make money out of them, is to me repulsive. National I must remain, and in that way I like all other Americans can render the amplest service to the world. The United States is the world's best hope, but if you fetter her in the interests and quarrels of other nations, if you tangle her in the intrigues of Europe, you will destroy her power for good and endanger her very existence. Leave her to march freely through the centuries to come as in the years that have gone.

After returning from Paris, Wilson ruined his health while touring the country to mobilize public support behind the treaty. In his last, emotional speech prior to suffering a debilitating stroke (in Pueblo, Colorado, September 25, 1919), he referred to his visit to an American cemetery prior to leaving France, and closed with a flourish of the sort of Wilsonian idealism that would become typical of American liberal internationalism:

I wish some men in public life who are now opposing the settlement for which these men died could visit such a spot as that. I wish that the thought that comes out of those graves could penetrate their consciousness. I wish that they could feel the moral obligation that rests upon us not to go back on those boys, but to see the thing through, to see it through to the end and make good their redemption of the world. For nothing less depends upon this decision, nothing less than the liberation and salvation of the world.

… There is one thing that the American people always rise to and extend their hand to, and that is the truth of justice and of liberty and of peace. We have accepted that truth and we are going to be led by it, and it is going to lead us, and through us the world, out into pastures of quietness and peace such as the world never dreamed of before.

Sources: www.firstworldwar.com/source/lodge_leagueofnations.htm; https://www.firstworldwar.com/source/wilsonspeech_league.htm.

Asia and Africa

Among the belligerents of World War I, Japan gained more at less cost than any other country, fueling its growing hubris. In a war that generated 8.5 million military deaths, the Japanese had suffered just 500, while gaining the Shantung Peninsula with the port of Tsingtao and Kaiochow Bay, plus the former German western Pacific islands of the Carolines, Marianas, and Marshalls. Between 1913 and 1929 Japan's manufacturing output more than tripled, yet from such a low baseline that its much smaller industrial base accounted for just 2.5 percent of the world's manufacturing output in 1929. But Japan's continued industrial weakness vis-à-vis the United States did nothing to temper its postwar ambitions. A hawkish faction of Japanese admirals considered it a defeat when the Washington Naval Treaty (1922) conceded Japan a fleet 60 percent as large as the British or American navies, rather than equal status, and looked forward to the day when they would go to war with the United States.

By taking a stand on racial equality at the Paris Peace Conference, Japan further enhanced the popularity of its own "Asia-for-Asians" rhetoric and laid the foundation of its World War II era "Greater East Asia Co-Prosperity Sphere," in which countless Chinese and other East Asians bet their future, and ultimately their lives, on Japanese domination being more benign than Western imperialism. Wellington Koo, the Chinese republic's chief negotiator in Paris, had warned Wilson that his position on the race question would only undermine the faith of east Asian leaders in Western ideals, and push them into the arms of the Japanese, but the Japanese were not the only option. The Allied decision to honor Japan's claim to the Shantung Peninsula sparked the May Fourth Movement, named for the day when the news reached Beijing (May 4, 1919), prompting thousands of Chinese university students to gather in Tiananmen Square to vent their frustration against the Western powers. Many leaders of the May Fourth Movement turned to Soviet Russia as their source of ideas and inspiration, and participated in the founding of the Chinese Communist Party in 1921. Though Shantung was the flashpoint for the May Fourth Movement, in 1922 Japan ceded it back to China, albeit for further concessions elsewhere in the country. Another disillusioned Asian in Paris during the summer of 1919 likewise turned to communism after being disappointed by the West. Vietnamese nationalist Ho Chi Minh addressed a note to Wilson's secretary of state, Lansing, calling for the independence of his country, consistent with the principle of national self-determination (see Box 15.4). It received no response. In 1923 Ho left Paris for Moscow, where he became an agent of Lenin's Communist International (Comintern) and embarked upon his long quest to establish an independent, communist Vietnam.

Except for the mainland Chinese lands added to the Japanese empire, all former German colonies were technically League of Nations mandates, but none received independence until 1960, and the last, Namibia, finally achieved it thirty years later.

Box 15.4 "While waiting for the principle of national self-determination ... "

In a letter to US secretary of state Robert Lansing, June 18, 1919, Ho Chi Minh, in Paris during the Peace Conference with the "Group of Annamite Patriots," anticipates independence for modern-day Vietnam and, in the meantime, appeals to the victors to grant a list of "freedoms":

We take the liberty of submitting to you the accompanying memorandum setting forth the claims of the Annamite people on the occasion of the Allied victory. We count on your kindness to honor our appeal by your support whenever the opportunity arises. We beg your Excellency graciously to accept the expression of our profound respect.

Since the victory of the allies, all subject peoples are frantic with hope at the prospect of an era of right and justice which should begin for them by virtue of the formal and solemn engagements, made before the whole world by the various powers and the entente in the struggle of civilization against barbarism. While waiting for the principle of national self-determination to pass from ideal to reality through the effective recognition of the sacred right of all peoples to decide their own destiny, the inhabitants of the ancient Empire of Annam, at the present time French Indochina, present to the noble Governments of the entente in general and the honorable French Government the following humble claims:

1. General amnesty for all native people who have been condemned for political activity.
2. Reform of the Indochinese justice system by granting to the native population the same judicial guarantees as the Europeans have and the total suppression of the special courts which are the instruments of terrorization and oppression against the most responsible elements of the Annamite people.
3. Freedom of Press.
4. Freedom to associate freely.
5. Freedom to emigrate and to travel abroad.
6. Freedom of education, and creation in every province of technical and professional schools for the native population.
7. Replacement of the regime of arbitrary decrees by a regime of law.
8. A permanent delegation of native people elected to attend the French parliament in order to keep the latter informed of their needs.

For the Group of Annamite Patriots.

Source: http://vietnamwar.lib.umb.edu/origins/docs/Lansing.html.

The delay there stemmed from the mandate of the former German Southwest Africa being administered by South Africa, which after World War II fell under control of an Apartheid regime whose origins also dated from the 1914–18 period. After World War I, several Afrikaner leaders of South Africa's "Maritz rebellion" continued their struggle within the South African political system, using the National Party, founded in 1914, as their vehicle, but their ranks did not include "Manie" Maritz himself, who eventually led a pro-Nazi fringe group. In 1939, as in 1914, Afrikaner leaders failed to stop South Africa from going to war with Germany, but after World War II their party re-emerged to become the majority party of the whites-only electorate, eventually breaking all ties with Britain to establish the Republic of South Africa (1961) and enforcing the Apartheid policy until 1994. South Africa's last white president, F. W. de Klerk, granted independence to Namibia in 1990, the same year he released Nelson Mandela from prison.

The realization that national self-determination, when applied at all, applied only to white people living in Europe also spawned anti-colonial movements in Africa and radicalized the movement for Home Rule in India. Gandhi and Jinnah both were shocked when Britain rewarded India's contributions in World War I not with a transition to self-government, but with the extension of martial law into the postwar era. In February 1919, nearly three years before assuming formal leadership of the Indian National Congress, Gandhi launched his first India-wide campaign of civil disobedience against British authority. Having received nothing in return for encouraging his followers to support the British Empire in World War I, at the onset of World War II he intensified their protests in the "Quit India" movement. The Hindu-Muslim cooperation reflected in the Lucknow Pact of 1916 collapsed by the mid-1920s, but elements of it – especially the acceptance by the Indian National Congress of the Muslim League as the representative of India's Muslims, and of Jinnah's concept of separate Hindu and Muslim constituencies in future elections – laid the foundation for the eventual partition of India in 1947.

The Middle East

After World War I Gandhi condemned the dismemberment of the Ottoman Empire in the Treaty of Sèvres as "a grave offence against God." In June 1920, as soon as the terms were released, he warned the viceroy, Lord Chelmsford, that India's "Muslim soldiers did not fight to inflict punishment on their own Khalifa [caliph, the Ottoman sultan] or to deprive him of his territories."[13] The Treaty of Sèvres became the only product of the Paris Peace Conference never to be ratified or implemented, not because of Muslim outrage over the caliph's loss of his empire, rather because of Turkish outrage skillfully mobilized and led by Mustafa Kemal. His "Turkish War of Independence" registered its first success in November 1920, in the defeat of the Democratic Republic of Armenia, establishing the Caucasus border of modern Turkey; the Red Army invaded what remained of Armenia the following month, and in 1922 it became a republic of the Soviet Union. The end of the Turkish-Armenian conflict allowed Kemal to focus his armies against the Greeks in western Asia Minor, where their reconquest of the Smyrna enclave in September 1922 resulted in a Greco-Turkish armistice and the flight from Constantinople of Mehmed VI, the figurehead sultan. In the Treaty of Lausanne (July 24, 1923) Britain, France, and Italy joined Greece in recognizing the borders of the Republic of Turkey, and the Turks renounced their claims to all other territory that had once belonged to the Ottoman Empire. The Bosporus and Dardanelles were demilitarized under a League of Nations commission but eventually, in 1936, returned to Turkish sovereignty. The most dramatic development came in the exchange of Greek and Turkish populations, eliminating centuries-old Turkish communities in Western Thrace and the Aegean islands, and Greek communities in Asia Minor that dated from ancient times. The exchange marked the first widespread application of a concept the victorious Allies had not considered at the Paris Peace Conference, but which would be a common feature in eastern and central Europe at the end of World War II: given the impossibility of establishing geographic borders "along clearly recognizable lines of nationality," the desired borders were established first, then the people moved.

Thus, Mustafa Kemal, a man made by World War I, deserved to be called Atatürk ("father of the Turks"), which he formally adopted as his surname in 1934, four years before his death. By the end of his dictatorial presidency the Republic of Turkey was already being hailed as an example of how a modern, secular country could be created in the Muslim Middle East, but into the twenty-first century it has remained unique in this regard. Atatürk's legacy had its unsavory side, in Turkey's denial not just of the Armenian genocide but also of the separate national character and culture of its surviving Armenian citizens; ironically he applied the same policy to the Kurds, eager accomplices of the Turks in the wartime persecution of the Armenians, who likewise were given no choice but assimilation in the Turkish national state. Finally, Atatürk achieved his revolutionary vision at a terrible cost in human life. Perhaps 5 million inhabitants of Asia Minor died in the years 1914–22, as a result of World War I, the Armenian genocide, the Turkish war against the Armenians and Greeks, the Greco-Turkish population exchange, and epidemic disease throughout the period. Atatürk's first census, in 1927, recorded a population of less than 14 million.

In world historical terms, the end of the Islamic caliphate ranks as one of the most dramatic consequences of World War I beyond Europe. After Mehmed VI abdicated as sultan and caliph, the Republic of Turkey initially accepted his cousin and heir, Abdülmecid II, as caliph, but Atatürk, in 1924, concluded that the arrangement was incompatible with the new secular state and declared the caliphate abolished. Even though Hussein, sharif of Mecca, had declared the religious as well as political independence of the Arab people from the sultan-caliph in 1916, until the ousting of Abdülmecid II most of the world's Sunni Muslims continued to recognize the Ottoman caliphate as the legitimate successor to the earlier lines of caliphs dating from the death of the Prophet Muhammad in 632. Hussein waited until Atatürk deposed Abdülmecid to proclaim himself caliph, but few Muslims recognized the title outside his own kingdom of the Hejaz and the domains of his sons, Iraq and Transjordan. In any event, his claim lost its validity the following year, 1925, when ibn Saud marched on Mecca, overthrew Hussein, and established his own dynasty as caretaker of the holy city. In the tumultuous post-Ottoman Middle East, Hussein's sons fared somewhat better than their father. In 1932, Faisal's kingdom of Iraq became the first of the League of Nations mandates to achieve independence, and in 1946 Abdullah's emirate of Transjordan became the kingdom of Jordan upon the end of the British mandate there (Figure 15.1). The Hashemite monarchy survived until 1958 in Iraq, and continues to survive in Jordan in the twenty-first century. Over the same decades, on the fringes of the Middle East, other men whose careers were made during World War I reigned long

Figure 15.1 Smiling Faisal

Faisal (1883–1933), photographed in a rare happy moment. The son of Sharif Hussein of Mecca, Faisal served as the primary organizer and commander of the Arab revolt that followed his father's declaration of Arab independence in June 1916. In that capacity he worked closely with T. E. Lawrence, who became the leading champion of his quest to create a unified kingdom from the Arab lands liberated from Ottoman Turkish rule. Disappointed at the Paris Peace Conference, Faisal reigned as king in Damascus for just four months during 1920 before being ousted by the French, who arrived to govern Syria as a League of Nations mandate. He went into exile in Britain, which soon offered him its mandate, Mesopotamia, as a consolation prize; he moved to Baghdad and was crowned King Faisal I of Iraq in 1921. Iraq became the first mandate to achieve independence in 1932, one year before Faisal's death. His Hashemite dynasty was overthrown in 1958, when Iraq became a republic.

into the postwar era. The war established Sayyid Idris as leader of the Sanusi and emir of Cyrenaica; he went on to support Britain against Mussolini's Italy in World War II, then reigned as Idris I, king of Libya, until Colonel Muammar al-Qaddafi overthrew him in 1969. Haile Selassie lasted even longer. De facto ruler of Abyssinia/Ethiopia after the wartime accession of Empress Zewditu, he succeeded her upon her death in 1930 and, aside from a brief exile necessitated by Mussolini's conquest of his empire (1935–40), reigned until deposed in 1974. Meanwhile, given the prevailing divisions in the Muslim world, and in the Arab world within it, the Islamic caliphate remains vacant in the twenty-first century. After the US deposed Saddam Hussein in Iraq (2003) and the regime of Bashar al-Assad in Syria was weakened by the "Arab Spring" revolt (2011), Abu Bakr al-Baghdadi was proclaimed caliph by the Islamic State in Iraq and Syria (ISIS), but neither his government nor his caliphate received formal external recognition during its brief existence (2014–19).

World War I, of course, also gave rise to the modern Arab-Israeli conflict, in the contradictory promises Britain made to both the Arabs and the Zionist movement concerning the disposition of postwar Palestine. Heartened by the promise of the Balfour Declaration, more than 10,000 Jewish settlers entered the mandate in 1919–20 alone. As early as May 1921, the influx caused Arabs to riot in Jaffa, the primary port of entry for the settlers, sparking a cycle of violence that only worsened as the years passed. There were 55,000 Jews in Palestine at the end of World War I; the British allowed another 106,000 to immigrate during the 1920s, followed by 257,000 more during the 1930s. In the interwar period the Arab Palestinian population grew from 668,000 (1922) to 1 million (1937), but its robust birth rate failed to keep pace with the rate of Jewish immigration, and the overall doubling of the population of Palestine in less than two decades only increased the competition for arable land and water resources, the practical issues underlying the post-1945 Israeli-Palestinian conflict. Long before the British withdrawal from Palestine prompted the Zionists to proclaim the state of Israel in 1948, Arab nationalists frustrated by the mandate system viewed the phenomenon of Jewish settlement as a modern-day exercise in European colonialism, and looked forward to the day when circumstances would allow them to eliminate it.

The War and the International System

The system governing international relations after 1919 bore little resemblance to its predecessor before 1914. Gone were the permanent peacetime alliances involving leading powers, not to reappear until the Cold War. In their place, the League of Nations became the focal point of interstate diplomacy, just as Wilson had intended, even without the United States. At least until the 1930s, when crises increasingly involved the revisionist states among the League's leading members, the organization functioned well enough as a venue for conflict resolution. Like its post-1945 successor, the United Nations (UN), the League was only as strong as its members wanted it to be; also like the UN, the League did some of its best work in the lower profile areas of health and human welfare, establishing permanent international agencies to deal with various aspects of misery that had been too often ignored before and during World War I.

The Council of the League of Nations met for the first time in Paris in January 1920, shortly before the peace conference officially adjourned. The Assembly, with forty-one countries represented (all of the former Allied and Associated Powers except the United States, plus ten of the neutral states of World War I), convened for its initial meeting in November 1920 in Geneva, the permanent headquarters of the organization. Critics of the League's ineffectiveness from the start focused on its membership problems, yet the organization at one time or another included six of the seven leading interwar powers and sixty-three countries overall. In its peak years of membership it included five of the seven powers (1926–33) and fifty-eight countries overall (1934–35); counting the colonies and mandates of member states, the only countries in the world never to belong to the League were the United States, Saudi Arabia, Iceland, and the Himalayan states of Nepal and Bhutan. The League Council, like the UN Security Council after World War II, had as its five permanent members the leading powers of the recently victorious Allied coalition, supplemented by non-permanent members serving fixed terms. When the United States did not take its seat, the Council was left with four permanent members until 1926, when Germany joined their ranks for its seven years of membership. The Council fluctuated in size between nine and thirteen members and met, on average, five times per year. The Assembly met annually in September. Unlike the UN, which granted veto power only to the five permanent members of the Security Council (and only in the proceedings of the Council, not in the UN General Assembly), the League Council and Assembly both operated on a principle of unanimity, giving every member a de facto veto over all actions of the organization.

The League Secretariat served as the permanent bureaucracy of the organization, which included a number of entities of lasting significance. The Permanent Court of International Justice, like its successor, the International Court of Justice of the United Nations, was headquartered at the Hague, where it heard sixty-six cases and issued twenty-seven opinions in the years 1923–40. The International Labor Organization (ILO) survived to come under the auspices of the UN after World War II, as did the League's Health Organization, which re-emerged after 1945 as the World Health Organization. The League's International Commission on Intellectual Cooperation was forerunner of the United Nations Educational, Scientific and Cultural Organization (UNESCO). Other League commissions dealt with disarmament, refugees, the administration of mandates, and slavery, the latter broadly defined to include forced prostitution and human trafficking of all kinds. The Permanent Central Opium Board served as forerunner of later efforts against international drug trafficking, and the

League's Committee for the Study of the Legal Status of Women foreshadowed the UN's international promotion of gender equality and women's rights. To deal with the repatriation of POWs still in Russia as of 1920, as well as the large numbers of refugees generated by the territorial changes in eastern Europe and Asia Minor, the League devised the Nansen Passport for stateless persons, named after Norwegian polar explorer Fridtjof Nansen, head of the commission on refugees, whose efforts provided the international legal framework for the UN's efforts on behalf of "displaced persons" after World War II.

The League's greatest success in disarmament, the Geneva Protocol of 1925, outlawed the use (but not the development or possession) of chemical and biological weapons. While all belligerents maintained stockpiles of poison gas during World War II, it was very rarely used as a battlefield weapon after 1918. The Geneva Protocol (which remains in force in the twenty-first century, with more than 130 countries as signatories) had as its forerunner the Washington Treaty on the Use of Submarines and Gases in Wartime, signed in 1922 by the five powers participating in the Washington Naval Conference: Britain, the United States, Japan, France, and Italy. The same five powers subsequently signed the Washington Naval Treaty, limiting their numbers of capital ships (battleships and battle cruisers) and aircraft carriers, with Britain and the United States having equal tonnage, followed by Japan at 60 percent of their total, and France and Italy at 35 percent. Cruisers remained unregulated but new ones could not exceed 10,000 tons displacement, the same limit applied to the largest new German warships under the Treaty of Versailles. The naval reductions and limits devised in Washington and renewed in 1930 in London remained history's most significant arms control regime until the reductions and limits undertaken by the United States and Soviet Union at the end of the Cold War. Other legacies of World War I negotiated beyond the purview of the League of Nations included the Geneva Convention of 1929 (officially the "Convention Relative to the Treatment of Prisoners of War"), approved by an international conference of diplomats convened by the Swiss government at the behest of the International Red Cross, to address specific problems experienced by POWs between 1914 and 1918. The document governed the treatment of POWs during World War II, at least for the countries that ratified it; unfortunately, these did not include the Soviet Union or Japan.

Perhaps the most miserable failure of the international system in the years immediately following World War I came in the area of war crimes trials. In January 1920 the Dutch government formally refused the request to surrender William II to the Allies for trial. The following month, a compromise allowed the Germans to conduct their own trials of other persons the Allies had identified as war criminals. Foreign observers attended the proceedings, held at Leipzig from May 1921, but the few men convicted included no prominent wartime figures, all sentences were lenient, and most countries soon withdrew their observers to protest the sham. Ultimately, France tried and convicted 1,200 German war criminals *in absentia*, Belgium 80, in proceedings that remained purely symbolic as long as none of the condemned men were ever foolish enough to again set foot in those countries. Thus, World War I did nothing to advance the cause of international law in dealing with war-related crimes against humanity, leaving it to the post-1945 war crimes trials at Nuremberg and Tokyo to establish the legal precedents for future action.

Because the Paris Peace Conference had sanctioned the creation of a host of new countries in central and eastern Europe, none of which was strong enough to defend itself, postwar Europe depended more than any other part of the world on the fulfillment of Wilson's vision of a robust League of Nations providing collective security for its members. From the outset France doubted the League could fulfill this promise, even for the leading powers, motivating Clemenceau to seek reassurance in a parallel alliance committing Britain and the United States to come to the aid of France if Germany were to attack again. The Anglo-Franco-American defensive alliance would have been a central feature of the postwar international landscape if it had not died in committee in the US Senate, before ever coming to a vote; Lloyd George, having shrewdly made his commitment to the French contingent on the US commitment, thus left Britain with no bilateral obligation to support France. Britain also made no commitment to Belgium, which placed its hopes in an alliance with France (at least until 1936, when it reverted to its traditional neutrality). Turning eastward, France sought to build a counterweight to a revived Germany via bilateral treaties with Poland, Czechoslovakia, Romania, and Yugoslavia, and also sponsored the "Little Entente" linking the latter three, but (owing to the collapse of the reparations regime) lacked the capital to build up these underdeveloped states as it had Russia before 1914. Fatefully, France responded to the tactical and operational stalemate of 1914–18 by reconfiguring its army for defensive operations tied to the Maginot Line along the Franco-German border, leaving it in no position to help defend its eastern allies even if it had wanted to. The Great Depression further weakened the vulnerable states of eastern and central Europe. By the mid-1930s, between Finland in the north and the Balkans in the south, Czechoslovakia stood as the lone surviving democracy among the thirteen republics and constitutional monarchies established or expanded as a consequence of the war. The rest had become dictatorships.

Remembrance and Commemoration

After the war, the patterns of its commemoration naturally varied from country to country, but the victorious Allies soon developed a series of similar traditions in remembering the conflict and honoring its dead. King George V took the lead in establishing the anniversary of the Armistice, November 11, as a holiday in 1919, ultimately observed as Remembrance Day in Britain, Canada, and Australia, and as Armistice Day in New Zealand. France and the United States likewise commemorated the Armistice from its first anniversary, though the French Remembrance Day (*le jour du Souvenir*) was not formally established until 1922, and the United States did not make Armistice Day an official national holiday until 1938. Italy honored its war dead on November 4, the anniversary of its armistice with Austria-Hungary, also known as the Day of National Unity (*Giorno dell'Unità Nazionale*), in recognition of the incorporation of Trentino and Trieste as a result of the victory in 1918. In the twenty-first century the day of commemoration remains strongest in Canada (where it is a federal statutory holiday) and in France. Britain established Remembrance Sunday in 1946, moving most ceremonies to the second Sunday in November, though a traditional two minutes of silence at 11:00 a.m. remains on November 11. In Australia and New Zealand, ANZAC Day, April 25, the anniversary of the initial landings at Gallipoli, observed since 1916, always overshadowed November 11 and remains the most important national holiday. In 1954 the United States redesignated its Armistice Day as Veterans Day, to honor the service of veterans of all wars of the United States, and eventually its original connection to the end of World War I was no longer known or appreciated by most Americans. November 11 was never marked in the United States with the same solemnity as Remembrance Day celebrations in Britain, the former Dominions, or France, because of the prior existence of Memorial Day in late May (established in 1868 to honor the dead of the American Civil War, subsequently expanded to all American wars). After World War II, Italy's observance of November 4 gradually lapsed and, after 1977, no longer enjoyed the status of a national holiday. By the end of the century it evolved into Armed Forces Day (*Giorno delle Forze Armate*).

Another commonality in the Allied commemoration of the war took the form of tombs of unknown soldiers, holding the unidentified remains of ordinary men killed in World War I who thus represented the sacrifice of all soldiers. On November 11, 1920, France dedicated its Tomb of the Unknown Soldier beneath the Arc de Triomphe, and Britain dedicated the Tomb of the Unknown Warrior in Westminster Abbey. Italy followed their example on its armistice commemoration the following year, November 4, 1921, at the monumental Vittoriano, adjacent to the ruins of the Forum in Rome, and the United States on Armistice Day 1928, at Arlington National Cemetery. In 1922, on the fourth anniversary of the Armistice, Belgium buried five of its unknown war dead at the foot of the Congress Column in Brussels. The former Dominions embraced the "unknown soldier" concept only belatedly, Australia interring one in 1993, Canada in 2000, and New Zealand in 2004, each at the National War Memorial, in each case an unidentified soldier killed on the Western front in World War I. The "unknown soldier" concept has remained limited to representative victims of World War I everywhere except the United States, which eventually accorded similar honors to unidentified dead from World War II and the Korean and Vietnam wars, although in the latter case, the soldier honored was eventually identified thanks to DNA technology, reburied elsewhere, and not replaced. The availability of DNA testing likely has made the concept of "unknown soldiers" an anachronism, thus assuring the uniqueness of the World War I connection to most of those thus honored.

During the interwar years the victors of World War I all erected impressive monuments to their war dead, the construction of which sometimes took several years to complete. These include the Cenotaph in Whitehall, London (1919–20), the India Gate, originally known as the All India War Memorial, in New Delhi (1921–31), and the national war memorials in Wellington, New Zealand (dedicated 1932), Ottawa, Canada (dedicated 1939), and Sydney, Australia (dedicated 1941). France's Douaumont Ossuary (1920–32), housing the unidentified skeletal remains of 130,000 French and German soldiers killed at Verdun, was the most elaborate of several similar structures built during the interwar years by the French government on or near former battlefields. In the years after the war New Zealand erected identical obelisks at Gallipoli, Ypres, the Somme, and Messines Ridge, with the same inscription "From the uttermost ends of the earth." Other notable battlefield monuments include the Menin Gate at Ypres (built 1921–27) and the Thiepval Memorial at the Somme (1928–32). After World War II relatively few new World War I monuments were erected on the Western front. A notable recent exception, the Island of Ireland Peace Tower on Messines Ridge in Belgium, was dedicated on November 11, 1998, on a site chosen because Britain's 16th (Irish) Division and 36th (Ulster) Division fought side-by-side in battle there in June 1917.

From Germany through the former Austria-Hungary and eastern Europe to Russia, remembrance and commemoration of World War I never assumed the proportions or the permanence that it did in the lands of the Western Allies, for in those countries the dead were lost in a losing cause and, a generation later, the entire region suffered a far greater bloodletting in World War II. In Germany, the Reichstag honored the war dead with a *Volkstrauertag*, established in 1926 on the second Sunday of Lent, but the observation lapsed under the Third Reich and was not revived until 1952, in the Federal Republic of Germany, which moved it to the second Sunday prior to the start of Advent. The new time places *Volkstrauertag* close to the Armistice anniversary (November 13–19), but the day no longer has a direct association with World War I for it now honors all casualties of war and political oppression. In the lands of the former Austria-Hungary, veterans gathered for specific postwar occasions (such as the funerals of Habsburg field marshals, most notably that of Conrad von Hötzendorf in 1925), but otherwise did not formally or regularly commemorate the war. In Austria and Hungary, as in Germany, veterans' organizations provided fellowship for the survivors and a catalyst for local rituals of remembrance, but in Habsburg lands awarded to Czechoslovakia or Yugoslavia, remembering World War I proved to be a much more complex exercise (as it was in Ireland, for Irish Catholic veterans of the British

Army). In the Soviet Union the dead of World War I were not honored at all, owing to the revolution's rejection of all that came before it. Their forgotten sacrifice stands in sharp contrast to the official and popular remembrance of the Soviet war dead of World War II. The tradition of honoring these Soviet heroes has been perpetuated in twenty-first-century Russia, where post-Soviet attempts to restore long-neglected cemeteries and rebuild chapels dedicated to the dead of 1914–17 have had mixed results. Turkey remains the only country from the losing side to construct a large memorial to the dead of World War I, the Çanakkale Martyrs' Memorial at Gallipoli (1954–58), which also serves as a monument to the Turkish victory in the 1915 battle.

The remembrance and commemoration of World War I continues to hold a special place in Australia more so than anywhere else, and within it, the sacrifice of Australian lives at Gallipoli remains the focal point. The 8,700 Australians who died there accounted for less than a quarter of the Allied fatalities in the battle, while for Australia the men killed at Gallipoli represented less than 15 percent of the country's 60,000 dead in World War I (of whom 46,000 fell on the Western front). And yet, from the start, Gallipoli has occupied the central place in Australia's memory of the war. Many thousands of Australians have visited Anzac Cove, to see the place where their forefathers fought and died. The annual Dawn Service on the beach, held every April 25, draws the largest crowds and typically features an address by a leading Australian. On the centenary in 2015 the honor went to the prime minister, Tony Abbott, who summed up the significance of the day as follows:

Year after year, from all over our country, from every walk of life, from every background, young and old make this pilgrimage ... We gather in the cold and dark before dawn, wondering what to say and how to honor those whose bones rest in the hills and the valleys before us, and whose spirit has moved our people for a century ... In volunteering to serve, they became more than soldiers; they became the founding heroes of modern Australia ... If they were not still emblematic of the nation we think we are, none of us would be here.[14]

No less than to the average Australian "digger" of World War I, Australians today still consider Gallipoli to have embodied the core values of what it means to be Australian, and thus, as a "baptism of fire" of the Australian nation, it has not mattered so much that the battle was lost. Indeed, the experience of the ANZACs at Gallipoli formed the nucleus of a set of patriotic beliefs that snowballed into a hallowed myth that Australian politicians, even decades later, questioned at their own peril. In 2008, when former prime minister Paul Keating called it "utter and complete nonsense" to "still go on as though the nation was born again or even redeemed" at Gallipoli, then-current prime minister, Kevin Rudd, felt compelled to distance himself at once from those remarks, assuring the Australian public that "Gallipoli ... is absolutely fundamental to the Australian national identity."[15] Australian historians daring to analyze the Gallipoli experience too critically have likewise faced public vilification.[16] Nevertheless, the argument that such forms of remembrance and commemoration have no place in the twenty-first century, because they exclude so much of the population (especially women, but also people from immigrant groups who do not share the same heritage), or because they focus too much on martial heroism in an age in which the majority considers all wars to be folly, has some resonance, more so in Europe and perhaps the United States than in Australia.

Conclusion

In the end, what came of their sacrifice? In the short term, the legacy of World War I, in particular of the peace settlement shaped by Woodrow Wilson, appeared to be overwhelmingly negative. Among the European powers, Britain, helped considerably by its empire, had played the decisive role in the victory, yet afterward would not support a peace that would make the triumph permanent. The settlement left Germany angry enough to seek revenge, France too weak to stop it, and Italy and Russia so unreconciled to the outcome that both would join the Germans in the ranks of the revisionists. The latter ultimately would victimize the host of new and newly enlarged smaller states of central and eastern Europe, states too weak to defend themselves, but at times, like Serbia in 1914, also too reckless or irresponsible in the pursuit of their own national goals to avoid conflicts with more powerful neighbors. More often than not, interwar Europeans blamed Wilson's compromised idealism for this dysfunctional state of affairs. But as Walter Russell Mead has observed, the ideals of Wilson "still guide European politics today: self-determination, democratic government, collective security, international law, and a league of nations," embodied in the European Union. "What was once dismissed as visionary is now accepted as fundamental."[17]

Thus, once one gets past blaming the Paris Peace Conference for starting World War II, the legacy for Europe appears to be one based upon positive principles forged in the heat of 1914–18, revolutionary, in the long term, only in the sense of democratic revolution. The balance sheet for the rest of the world remains far more complex, especially with regard to the Middle East and Asia. The collapse of the Ottoman Empire brought the emergence of the Republic of Turkey, the Middle East's first republic and first secular state, radical enough in its conceptualization to remain, in the twenty-first century, the Muslim world's only secular state. It also brought the frustration of Arab nationalism in the denial of self-determination to the Arab lands freed from Turkish rule, the modern-day seeds of the Arab-Israeli conflict over Palestine, and a host of other problems stemming from the peace conference's capricious redrawing of the map of the Middle East. Finally, the demise of the Ottoman sultanate brought the collapse of the caliphate as well, paving the way for the rise within Arabia of the house of Saud as caretaker in Mecca. In India, the wartime emergence of the Muslim League as the equal of the Indian National Congress foreshadowed the future partition of India and creation of Pakistan. In China, the May Fourth Movement of 1919 – a direct reaction against the Paris Peace Conference – paved the way for the establishment of the Chinese Communist Party under Mao Zedong, while the less direct, more personal reaction of Ho Chi Minh led to the Communist movement in Vietnam. While east Asian communism lost its revolutionary dynamism before the end of the twentieth century, its transformational legacy remains unquestioned. The revolutionary forces spawned or nourished by World War I in the Middle East (Arab nationalism, the Turkish model of secularism, and the Islamic backlash against both) and in south Asia (Indian and Pakistani nationalism) remain vibrant in the twenty-first century.

SUGGESTIONS FOR FURTHER READING

Fischer, Conan, and Alan Sharp (eds.) *After the Versailles Treaty: Enforcement, Compliance, Contested Identities* (London: Routledge, 2008).

Kuhlman, Erika. *Reconstructing Patriarchy after the Great War: Women, Gender, and Postwar Reconciliation between Nations* (New York: Palgrave Macmillan, 2008).

Lamay Licursi, Kimberly J. *Remembering World War I in America* (Lincoln, NE: University of Nebraska Press, 2018).

Lorcin, Patricia M. E., and Daniel Brewer (eds.) *France and its Spaces of War: Experience, Memory, Image* (New York: Palgrave Macmillan, 2009).

Marks, Sally. *The Illusion of Peace: International Relations in Europe, 1918–1933*, 2nd edn. (New York: Palgrave Macmillan, 2003).

Petrone, Karen. *The Great War in Russian Memory* (Bloomington, IN: Indiana University Press, 2011).

Thomas, Gregory M. *Treating the Trauma of the Great War: Soldiers, Civilians, and Psychiatry in France,1914–1940* (Baton Rouge, LA: Louisiana State University Press, 2009).

Winter, Jay. *Remembering War: The Great War between Memory and History in the Twentieth Century* (New Haven, CT: Yale University Press, 2006).

— *War Beyond Words: Languages of Remembrance from the Great War to the Present* (Cambridge: Cambridge University Press, 2017).

NOTES

1. Stephen Broadberry and Peter Howlett, "The United Kingdom during World War I," in Stephen Broadberry and Mark Harrison (eds.), *The Economics of World War I* (Cambridge: Cambridge University Press, 2005), 229.
2. Broadberry and Harrison, *The Economics of World War I*, 229–30.

3. See Reginald Pound, *The Lost Generation* (London: Constable, 1964) and, for statistical corroboration, J. M. Winter, "Britain's 'Lost Generation' of the First World War," *Population Studies* 31 (1977): 449–66.

4. Appeared in *The Times* of London, cited in Vera Brittain to Roland Leighton, Buxton, September 10, 1915, text in *Letters from a Lost Generation: The First World War Letters of Vera Brittain and Four Friends*, eds. Alan Bishop and Mark Bostridge (London: Little, Brown, 1998), 164.

5. Quoted in Hugh Purcell, *Lloyd George* (London: Haus, 2006), 143.

6. Text in Margaret MacMillan, *Paris 1919: Six Months that Changed the World* (New York: Random House, 2001), 495.

7. John Paul II, "Beatification of Five Servants of God," October 3, 2004, available at www.vatican.va/content/john-paul-ii/en/homilies/2004/documents/hf_jp-ii_hom_20041003_beatifications.html.

8. Lloyd E. Ambrosius, *Woodrow Wilson and the American Diplomatic Tradition: The Treaty Fight in Perspective* (Cambridge: Cambridge University Press, 1987), 14.

9. See Carol S. Gruber, *Minerva and Mars: World War I and the Uses of Higher Learning in America* (Baton Rouge, LA: Louisiana State University Press, 1975); Gilbert Allardyce, "The Rise and Fall of the Western Civilization Course," *American Historical Review* 87(3) (June 1982): 695–725.

10. Quoted in Ambrosius, *Woodrow Wilson and the American Diplomatic Tradition*, 137.

11. Quoted in Antony Lentin, *Guilt at Versailles: Lloyd George and the Pre-history of Appeasement* (London: Routledge, 1985), 138, 140.

12. Quoted in Ambrosius, *Woodrow Wilson and the American Diplomatic Tradition*, 264.

13. Quoted in Stanley Wolpert, *Gandhi's Passion: The Life and Legacy of Mahatma Gandhi* (Oxford University Press, 2002), 107.

14. The Hon. Tony Abbott, MP, Speech at Dawn Service, Gallipoli, April 25, 2015, text available at www.businessinsider.com.au/heres-the-touching-speech-prime-minister-tony-abbott-gave-at-the-dawn-service-in-gallipoli-2015-4.

15. Antonette Collins, "Anzac Gallipoli gatherings misguided, Keating says," available at www.abc.net.au/news/stories/2008/10/30/2405820.htm; Leo Shanahan and David Rood, "Keating 'Wrong' on Gallipoli," *Sydney Morning Herald*, November 1, 2008, available at www.smh.com.au/national/keating-wrong-on-gallipoli-20081031-5fkj.html.

16. See Alistair Thomson, *Anzac Memories: Living with the Legend* (Melbourne: Oxford University Press, 1994).

17. Walter Russell Mead, *Special Providence: American Foreign Policy and How it Changed the World* (London: Routledge, 2002), 9.

Conclusion

The first months of World War I set the tone for most of the rest of the conflict, as each of the countries involved endured unprecedented casualties by the spring of 1915, without suffering a serious breach of discipline among the troops or a collapse of will on the home front. The massive bloodletting did not deter the belligerents from carrying on or other countries from joining the war later, starting with Italy in May 1915. As early as August 22, 1914, France suffered 27,000 battle deaths on a single day, almost half again more than the bloodiest day for Britain and its empire, July 1, 1916, when more than 19,000 died on the first day of the Somme; in contrast, total Allied combat deaths in World War II on D-Day, June 6, 1944, numbered just over 4,400. Even after British and Imperial forces, in the summer of 1918, figured out the keys to restoring mobility to the Western front – the combination of an infantry assault under a well-coordinated creeping barrage, supported by tanks, with aircraft disrupting enemy communications, reinforcement efforts, and artillery spotting – they and their Allies continued to resort, more often than not, to brute force in pushing the Germans out of France and western Belgium that autumn. The Germans, likewise, by 1917–18 discovered that their infiltration tactics using storm troopers against enemy strong points effectively cleared the battlefield for general advances by infantry, yet they, too, continued to resort to unimaginative frontal assaults as soon as battles bogged down. In the final analysis, the willingness of most troops to continue to obey their commanders no matter what, and the conviction on the part of most civilians that their leaders should pursue the war to a victorious conclusion, provides the best explanation for the unprecedented carnage.

The war featured extremes of discipline and indiscipline. Examples of discipline could be found in all the leading armies enduring the initial unprecedented casualties of 1914–15, then the bloodshed of the big battles of 1916, without breaking down;

the French Army holding up until the spring of 1917 despite horrific losses; and the German Army maintaining its cohesion in defeat right up to the Armistice. Examples of indiscipline included the mass desertions of certain nationalities from the Austro-Hungarian Army, especially from 1915 onward on the Eastern front; the temporary collapse of the Italian Army after Caporetto; the paralysis of the French Army for a year after the Nivelle offensive; and the complete collapse of the Russian Army after the Kerensky offensive in 1917. The same extremes could be seen on the various home fronts, where the dramatic revolutionary collapses in Russia in 1917 and Germany and Austria-Hungary in 1918 overshadowed the steadfastness of the civilian populations of those countries in holding firm despite their hardships for most of the war, as their counterparts in the Western Allied countries did for the entire conflict.

From its first weeks World War I featured acts of brutality against civilians that fore-shadowed what would happen on a much larger scale a generation later, during World War II: the summary executions of Belgian civilians by German troops and Serbian civilians by Austro-Hungarians; the singling out of Armenians by Turks as a disloyal group to be subjected to persecution and, ultimately, genocide; the aerial bombing of London and other cities by German Zeppelins; the indiscriminate sinking of millions of tons of shipping by German submarines, at a cost of many thousands of lives; the use of civilians as forced labor; and the wanton, often vindictive destruction of property, including targets with cultural as well as economic significance to the enemy. The fact that almost all of these actions were perpetrated by the Central Powers and almost none by the Western Allies enabled the latter to claim the moral high ground in the war, even though the British blockade in the North Sea and the Allied blockade of the mouth of the Adriatic ultimately caused far more civilian deaths on the home fronts of the Central Powers than the Central Powers caused through all of their actions in the various war zones.

Though they bore far less of the responsibility for starting World War I, the Allied and Associated Powers were largely responsible for the global revolution that resulted. The revolutionary nature of their agenda appears in a clearer light when compared with the conservative, restorative agenda of the victorious Allies of World War II. West of the line that, thanks to Winston Churchill, became known during the Cold War as the Iron Curtain, the Allies after 1945 restored the map as it had appeared in 1937, before Nazi Germany annexed Austria. Even east of the Iron Curtain, states seemingly irrevocably broken by the experience of World War II were cobbled together again under communist regimes in Czechoslovakia and Yugoslavia, both of which would endure only as long as did communism. Their post-1945 borders, and those of every other state in eastern Europe, differed at least slightly from the 1937 borders, but even Joseph Stalin did not wipe entire countries off the map (except for the incorporation of the three Baltic states as republics of the Soviet Union). The post-1945 settlement also did not change a single border in Africa or the Middle East, and restored the east Asian borders altered by Japan. In sharp contrast, the peacemakers of 1919 redrew the map of Europe from the western borders of Germany well into Russia, completely reconceptualized the Middle East by breaking up the Ottoman Empire, made significant changes to Africa by redistributing the four German colonies there, and legitimized minor but fateful alterations in east Asia, benefiting Japan at China's expense.

Overall, the most striking legacy of World War I was its role in desensitizing so many people to the brutality, inhumanity, and mass slaughter of modern warfare in the industrial age. This desensitization made possible the even greater carnage of World War II and, indeed, served as a necessary prerequisite to it. As a result, most of our acts of remembrance and commemoration are tinged with regret, if not guilt. Perhaps it is our continuing shame at the ease with which the losses of 1914–18 were accepted that causes World War I to keep its place in our collective memory.

Index